Coll
SPURRELL
WELSH
DICTIONARY
POCKET EDITION

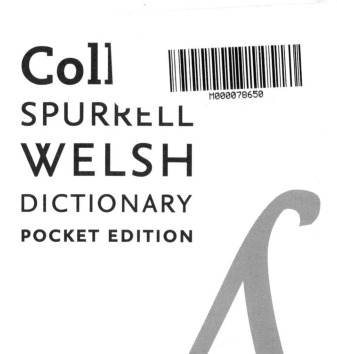

Published by Collins
An imprint of HarperCollins
  Publishers
Westerhill Road
Bishopbriggs
Glasgow G64 2QT

Fifth Edition 2017

10 9 8 7 6 5 4

© William Collins sons & Co. Ltd
1960
© HarperCollins Publishers 1991,
2006, 2009, 2017

ISBN 978-0-00-819482-6

Collins® is a registered
trademark of HarperCollins
Publishers Limited

www.collinsdictionary.com

Typeset by Sharon McTeir

Printed by in Italy by
GRAFICA VENETA S.p.A.

The contents of this publication
are believed correct at the time
of printing. Nevertheless,
the Publisher can accept no
responsibility for errors or
omissions, changes in the detail
given or for any expense or loss
thereby caused.

HarperCollins does not warrant
that any website mentioned
in this title will be provided
uninterrupted, that any website
will be error-free, that defects
will be corrected, or that the
website or the server that makes
it available are free of viruses
or bugs. For full terms and
conditions please refer to the site
terms provided on the website.

A catalogue record for this book
is available from the British
Library.

If you would like to comment on
any aspect of this book, please
contact us at the given address
or online.
E-mail:
dictionaries@harpercollins.co.uk
 facebook.com/collinsdictionary
 @collinsdict

Acknowledgements
We would like to thank those
authors and publishers who
kindly gave permission for
copyright material to be used
in the Collins Corpus. We
would also like to thank Times
Newspapers Ltd for providing
valuable data.

HarperCollins
P U B L I S H E R S
——— 200 ———

CONTENTS

EDITOR/GOLYGYDD
Susie Beattie

CONTRIBUTORS/CYFRANWYR
Eurwen Booth
David Bullock
Harry Campbell
Non Jenkins
Jo Knell
Maggie Seaton

FOR THE PUBLISHER/AR RAN Y CYHOEDDWR
Gerry Breslin
Kerry Ferguson

INTRODUCTION

The first Spurrell Welsh-English dictionary appeared in 1848 published by William Spurrell (1813–89) the Carmarthen printer and publisher. One of his sons, Walter Spurrell (1858–1934), joined his father in the business and the family firm published a series of distinguished Welsh-English, English-Welsh dictionaries and influential Welsh grammars during the latter part of the nineteenth century and the first half of the last century. William Spurrell was advised by and well-acquainted with Daniel Silvan Evans (1818–1903), one of the father figures of Welsh lexicography, sometime lecturer in Welsh at St David's University College, Lampeter and the first professor of Welsh to be appointed by the University of Wales.

The Collins-Spurrell Welsh Dictionary was first published in 1960 and quickly became an essential tool of general reference for Welsh learners as well as those anxious to interpret literature. It was edited by Henry Lewis, Professor of Welsh Language and Literature at University College, Swansea, with valuable contributions from the staff of the Department of Welsh Language and Literature at St David's University College, Lampeter.

D A THORNE

NOTES ON THE PRONUNCIATION OF WELSH

VOWELS

They are sounded, long or short, as the vowels in the English words given below.

A		palm, pat.
E		gate (without dipthongization), get.
I		feet, fit.
O		more, not.
U	(1)	North Wales: like French *u* or German *ü* without rounding lips.
	(2)	South Wales: as I.
W		cool, full.
Y	(1)	In monosyllables generally, and in final syllables, as U (the 'clear' sound).
	(2)	In all but final syllables, and in **y, yr** (the), **fy** (my), **dy** (thy), **yn, yng, ym** (in), the adverbial **yn**, the preverbal and relative particle **y, yr** (**y'm, y'th** etc), **syr** (sir), **nyrs** (nurse), as English f*u*n, (the 'obscure' sound).

DIPHTHONGS

1 Falling diphthongs, in which the second
   sound is consonantal: the two vowels have
   the sound noted above: **ae, oe, ai, oi,** the
   diphthong **ei** as English *by*, **aw, ew, iw, ow,
   uw, ŵy, yw.**
2 Rising diphthongs, in which the first sound
   is consonantal: **ia, ie, io, iw, iy,** ('obscure' y);
   wa, we, wi, wo, wy, ('clear' y), **wy,**
   ('obscure' y).

CONSONANTS

Only those which differ from English need to be noted.

CH   (following C in the alphabet), as Scottish lo*ch*.
DD   (following D in the alphabet), as *th* in
     English *this*, brea*the*.
F   as English *v*.
FF   as English *f*.
G   always as in English *go*.
NG   (following G in the alphabet), as in English
     si*ng*.
     In some words (e.g. **dangos**), however, it is
     sounded *ng-g*, as in English lo*nger*.
     Alphabetically this follows after N.
LL   produced by placing the tongue to pronounce *l*,
     then emitting breath without voice.
PH   (following P in the alphabet), as English *f*.
TH   always as th in English *thin*.

ACCENT

Welsh words are generally accented on the last syllable but one. There are certain exceptions:

1. The reduplicated personal pronouns **myfi, tydi, efe, efô, hyhi, nyni, chwychwi, hwynt-hwy**, accented on the final syllable.

2. Verbs in **-(h)au, -(h)oi, -eu**, accented on the final syllable.

3. A few dissyllabic words beginning **y** + consonant, accented on the final syllable.

4. Certain polysyllabic words with a diphthong resulting in contraction in the final syllable, such as **Cymraeg**.

5. Some borrowed words accented as in the language of origin, generally English.

MUTATIONS

Mutations, or letter changes, can occur at the beginning of Welsh words. Mutations are caused by the preceding word. There are three different mutations:

Llythyren wreiddiol *Original letter*	Treiglad meddal *Soft mutation*	Treiglad trwynol *Nasal mutation*	Treiglad llaes *Aspirate mutation*
	changes to:	*changes to:*	*changes to:*
p	b	mh	ph
t	d	nh	th
c	g	ngh	ch
b	f	m	
d	dd	n	
g	-	ng	
ll	l		
m	f		
rh	r		

COMMON WORDS CAUSING SOFT MUTATION – TREIGLAD MEDDAL

ei	*his*
dy	*your*
dau / dwy	*two (masculine / feminine)*
pa	*which*
neu	*or*
rhy	*too*
yn	*before an adjective*

Adjectives which come before the noun:

Mae'r hen **dd**yn yn byw yn y tŷ.	*The old man lives in the house.*
Dyma fy hoff **g**ân.	*This is my favourite song.*

Some prepositions:

For example:

Mae'r bws yn mynd i **G**aerdydd.	*The bus is going to Cardiff.*
Maen nhw'n chwarae dros **d**îm yr ysgol.	*They play for the school team.*

Certain words which come before a feminine noun:

y and 'r	*the*
un	*one*

Mae castell yn y **d**ref.	*There's a castle in town.*
Mae'r **dd**inas wedi gwella.	*The city has improved.*
Dim ond un **b**roblem sydd ar ôl.	*There's only one problem left.*

Any feminine noun which has an adjective immediately after it:

merch **dd**a	*a good girl*

COMMON WORDS CAUSING NASAL MUTATION
– TREIGLAD TRWYNOL

fy	*my*
yn	*in*

COMMON WORDS CAUSING ASPIRATE MUTATION
– TREIGLAD LLAES

a	*and*
â	*as/to/with*
chwe	*six*
ei	*her*
gyda	*with*
tri	*three*
tua	*approximately*

ABBREVIATIONS

BYRFODDAU

abbreviation	*abbr*	byrfodd
adjective	*adj*	ansoddair
anatomy	*Anat*	anatomeg
automobile	*Aut*	moduro
auxiliary verb	*aux vb*	berf atodol
British English	BRIT	Saesneg Prydain
collective noun	*coll n*	enw torfol
computing	*Comput*	cyfrifiadureg
conjunction	*conj*	cysylltiad
contraction	*contr*	cywasgiad
cookery	*Culin*	coginio
definite article	*def art*	bannod bendant
demonstrative	*dem*	dangosol
emphatic	*emphat*	pwyslais
exclamation	*excl*	ebychiad
formal	*form*	ffurfiol
(phrasal verb) where the particle is inseparable	*fus*	(berf ymadroddol) lle na all y rhangymeriad gael ei wahanu
imperative	*imper*	gorchmynnol
indefinite article	*indef art*	bannod amhendant
indeterminate	*indeter*	amhenderfynadwy
colloquial usage (offensive)	*inf(!)*	defnydd llafar (anweddus)

grammar, linguistics	*Ling*	gramadeg, ieithyddiaeth
masculine	*m*	gwrywaidd
mathematics	*Math*	mathemateg
medical term	*Med*	term meddygol
modal auxiliary verb	*mod aux vb*	berf atodol moddol
music	*Mus*	cerddoriaeth
noun	*n*	enw
noun dual	*nd*	enw deuol
number	*num*	rhif
old-fashioned	*old*	hen ffasiwn
derogatory, pejorative	*pej*	difrïol
plural	*pl*	lluosog
past participle	*pp*	rhangymeriad gorffennol
politics	*Pol*	gwleidyddiaeth
prefix	*pref*	rhagddodiad
preposition	*prep*	arddodiad
pronoun	*pron*	rhagenw
past tense	*pt*	amser gorffennol
relative	*rel*	perthynol
singular	*sing*	unigol
Telecommunications	*Tel*	Telathrebu
American English	*US*	Saesneg America
verb	*vb*	berf
impersonal verb	*vb imper*	berf amhersonol
intransitive verb	*vi*	berf gyflawn
transitive verb	*vt*	berf anghyflawn

WELSH–ENGLISH

a

a¹ *interrogative particle, preverbal particle, rel pron* who, that, which

a², ac *conj* and

a³ *excl* ah, oh

â¹, ag *conj* as

â², ag *prep* with

ab, ap *nm* son *(before name, in place of surname, like 'Mac')*

abad (-au) *nm* abbot

abadaeth (-au) *nf* abbacy, abbotship

abades (-au) *nf* abbess

abatir (-oedd) *nm* abbey-land

abaty (abatai) *nm* abbey

aber (-oedd, ebyr) *nm* confluence; mouth of river, estuary; brook, stream

aberfa (-oedd) *nf* mouth of river, estuary

abergofiant *nm* forgetfulness, oblivion

aberth (-au, ebyrth) *nm* sacrifice

aberthged *nf* oblation; offering of fruits

aberthol *adj* sacrificial

aberthu *vb* to sacrifice

aberthwr (-wyr) *nm* sacrificer

aberu *vb* to flow into

abid *nmf* apparel; dress of religious order

abiéc *nmf* alphabet

abl *adj* able; well-off

abladol *adj* ablative

abledd *nm* ability; plenty

abrwysg *adj* clumsy, drunken

absen *nm* absence; slander

absennol *adj* absent

absennu *vb* to backbite, to slander

absennwr (absenwyr) *nm* backbiter

absenoldeb *nm* absence

absenoli *vb* to absent

absenoliaeth (-au) *nf* absenteeism

abwyd, abwydyn (abwydod) *nm* worm; fishing-bait

ac, a *conj* and

academaidd *adj* academic

academi (-ïau) *nm* academy

acen (-ion) *nf* accent

aceniad *nm* accentuation

acennod *nm* accent mark

acennu *vb* to accent, to stress

acenyddiaeth *nf* accentuation

acer (-i) *nf* acre

aciwbigiad (-au) *nm* acupuncture

acne *nm* acne

acrilig *adj* acrylic

act (-au) *nf* act

actio *vb* to act

actor (-ion) *nm* actor

actores (-au) *nf* actress

acw adv there, yonder
ach¹ excl ugh
ach² (-au, -oedd) nf degree of kinship; (pl) pedigree, ancestry
aches nm tide, flood; eloquence
achfre nmf see **achwre**
achlân adv wholly, entirely
achles (-oedd) nf succour, protection; manure
achlesol adj succouring
achlesu vb to succour, to cherish
achlod nm shame, disgrace
achlust nm rumour
achlysur (-on) nm occasion
achlysurol adj occasional
achos¹ (-ion) nm cause, case
achos² conj because, for
achosi vb to cause
achres (-i, -au) nf genealogical table
achub vb to seize, to snatch; to save, to rescue; **achub y blaen** to forestall; **achub y cyfle** to seize the opportunity
achubiaeth nf salvation
achubol adj saving
achubwr (-wyr), **achubydd** (-ion) nm saviour, rescuer
achul adj thin, emaciated
achwre, achfre nmf under-thatch, protection; covering, garment
achwyn vb to complain ▶ nm (-ion) complaint, plaint
achwyniad (-au) nm complaint, accusation
achwynwr (-wyr) nm complainer; complainant, plaintiff
achwynyddes (-au) nf complainant

achydd (-ion) nm genealogist
achyddiaeth nf genealogy
achyddol adj genealogical
achwyngar adj querulous
ad- prefix very; second; bad, re-
adail nf building, edifice, structure
adain, aden (adenydd) nf wing; fin; spoke
adamant nm adamant, diamond
adamantaidd adj adamantine
adar npl (nm aderyn) birds, fowls; **adar drudwy, adar yr eira** starlings; **adar y to** sparrows
adara vb to catch birds, to fowl
adardy (-dai) nm aviary
adareg nf ornithology
adargi (-gwn) nm retriever, setter, spaniel
adargraffiad (-au) nm reprint
adarwr (-wyr) nm fowler
adarwriaeth nf fowling
adarydd (-ion) nm ornithologist
adarydda n birdwatching ▶ vb to go birdwatching
adaryddiaeth nf ornithology
ad-dalu vb to repay, to requite
ad-drefnu vb to rearrange
adeg (-au) nf time, occasion, opportunity
adeilad (-au) nmf building, edifice
adeiladaeth nf building; edification, construction
adeiladol adj edifying, constructive
adeiladu vb to build, to edify
adeiladwaith nm construction
adeiladwr (-wyr), **adeiladydd** (-ion) nm builder
adeiledd nm structure
adeiniog adj winged

aden (**-ydd, edyn**) *nf* wing; *see also* **adain**

adenedigaeth *nf* regeneration

adeni *vb* to regenerate

adennill *vb* to regain, to recover

aderyn (**adar**) *nm* bird

adfach (**-au**) *nm* barb; liver-fluke

adfail (**-feilion**) *nm* ruin

adfeddiannu *vb* to repossess

adfeiliad *nm* decay, ruin

adfeiliedig *adj* decayed, in ruins

adfeilio *vb* to decay, to moulder

Adfent *nm* Advent

adfer, adferu, adferyd *vb* to restore

adferf (**-au**) *nf* adverb

adferfol *adj* adverbial

adferiad *nm* restoration

adferol *adj* restorative; remedial

adferwr (**-wyr**) *nm* restorer

adflas *nm* after-taste, bad taste

adfyd *nm* adversity

adfydus *adj* adverse, miserable

adfynach *nm* renegade monk

adfyw *adj* half alive, half dead

adfywhau *vb* to revive, to reanimate

adfywiad (**-au**) *nm* revival

adfywio *vb* to revive, to resuscitate

adfywiol *adj* refreshing

adiad *nm* drake

adio *nm* addition ▸ *vb* to add

adiolyn (**adiolion**) *nm* additive

adladd, adlodd *nm* aftermath

adlais (**-leisiau**) *nm* echo

adlam (**-au**) *nm* home; rebound; **cic adlam** drop-kick

adlamu *vb* to rebound

adleisio *vb* to resound

adlewyrch, adlewyrchiad (**adlewyrchiadau**) *nm* reflection

adlewyrchu *vb* to reflect

adlewyrchydd (**-ion**) *nm* reflector

adlog (**-au**) *nm* compound interest

adloniadol *adj* of or for entertainment

adloniant *nm* recreation, entertainment

adlonni *vb* to entertain, to refresh

adlunio *vb* to remodel, to reconstruct

adnabod *vb* to know, to recognize

adnabyddiaeth *nf* knowledge, acquaintance

adnabyddus *adj* known, familiar; well-known

adnabyddwr *nm* knower

adnau (**adneuon**) *nm* deposit, pledge; **ar adnau** on deposit

adneuo *vb* to deposit

adneuol *adj* depositing

adneuwr (**-wyr**) *nm* depositor

adnewyddadwy *adj* renewable

adnewyddiad (**-au**) *nm* renewal, renovation

adnewyddu *vb* to renew, to renovate

adnewyddwr (**-wyr**) *nm* renewer, renovator

adnod (**-au**) *nf* verse

adnoddau *npl* resources

adolygiad (**-au**) *nm* review

adolygu *vb* to review

adolygydd (**-ion**) *nm* reviewer

adran (**-nau**) *nf* division, section, department

adref *adv* homewards, home

Adriatig

Adriatig *nm*: yr Adriatig the Adriatic (Sea)

adrodd *vb* to relate, to recite

adroddgan (-au) *nf* recitative

adroddiad (-au) *nm* report; recitation

adroddwr (-wyr) *nm* narrator, reciter

aduniad *nm* reunion

aduno *vb* to reunite

adwaith (-weithiau) *nm* reaction

adweithio *vb* to react

adweithiol *adj* reactionary

adweithydd (-ion) *nm* reactor

adwerthu *vb* to retail

adwr *nm* coward, churl

adwy (-au, -on) *nf* gap, breach; pass

adwyth (-au) *nm* evil, misfortune, illness

adwythig *adj* cruel; evil, baneful; sore, sick; harmful

adyn (-od) *nm* wretch

adysgrif (-au) *nf* copy, transcript

adysgrifio *vb* to copy, to transcribe

addas *adj* suitable, proper

addasiad (-au) *nm* adjustment, adaptation

addasrwydd *nm* suitableness, fitness

addasu *vb* to suit, to adapt, to fit

addawol *adj* promising

addef *vb* to acknowledge, to own, to admit

addefiad *nm* admission, confession

addewid (-ion) *nf* promise

addfain *adj* slender, shapely

addfed *adj see* aeddfed

addfwyn *adj* gentle, meek, mild

addfwynder *nm* gentleness, meekness

addien *adj* fair, beautiful

addo *vb* to promise

addod *nm*: **wy addod** nest-egg

addoed *nm* death, hurt

addoedi *vb* to delay, to postpone

addoediad *nm* prorogation

addoer *adj* sad, cruel; chilling

addoldy (-dai) *nm* place of worship

addolgar *adj* devout, reverent

addolgarwch *nm* devoutness, reverence

addoli *vb* to worship, to adore

addoliad *nm* worship

addolwr (-wyr) *nm* worshipper

adduned (-au) *nf* vow

addunedu *vb* to vow

addurn (-au, -iadau) *nm* ornament, adornment

addurnedig *adj* decorated

addurniad *nm* ornamentation

addurno *vb* to decorate, to adorn, to ornament

addurnol *adj* ornamental, decorative

addurnwr (-wyr) *nm* decorator

addysg *nf* education, instruction; **addysg gorfforol** PE; **addysg uwch** higher education

addysgiadol *adj* instructive, educational

addysgiaeth *nf* instruction, training

addysgol *adj* educational

addysgu *vb* to educate, to instruct

addysgwr (-wyr), addysgydd (-ion) *nm* educator, instructor, tutor

aeddfed *adj* ripe, mature
aeddfedrwydd *nm* ripeness, maturity
aeddfedu *vb* to ripen; to mature
ael (-iau) *nf* brow
aele *adj* sad, wretched
aelod (-au) *nm* member, limb; **Aelod Seneddol** Member of Parliament
aelodaeth *nf* membership
aelodi *vb* to become a member; to enrol
aelwyd (-ydd) *nf* hearth, fireside
aer¹ (-ion) *nm* heir
aer² *nm* air
aerdymheru *nm* air conditioning
aeres (-au) *nf* heiress
aerfa *nf* slaughter, battle
aerglo *nm* air-lock
aerobeg *nm* aerobics
aeron *npl* fruit, fruits, berries
aerwy (-au, -on) *nm* collar, torque; neck-chain
aes *nf* shield
aestheteg *nf* aesthetics
aesthetig *adj* aesthetic
aeth *nm* pain, grief, fear, shock
aethnen *nf* aspen, poplar
aethus *adj* poignant, grievous, severe
afal (-au) *nm* apple
afallen (-nau) *nf* apple-tree
afan *npl (nf -en)* raspberries
afanc (-od) *nm* beaver
afiach *adj* unwell, unhealthy, morbid
afiachus *adj* sickly; unwholesome
afiaith *nm* zest, mirth, glee
afiechyd (-on) *nm* disease, malady

afieithus *adj* mirthful, gleeful
aflafar *adj* harsh, unmelodious
aflan *adj* unclean, polluted, foul
aflawen *adj* fierce; sad, cheerless, dismal; awful
aflednais *adj* immodest, indelicate
afledneisrwydd *nm* immodesty, indelicacy
aflem *adj* obtuse
aflendid *nm* uncleanness; pollution
aflêr *adj* untidy, slovenly
aflerwch *nm* untidiness, slovenliness
afles *nm* disadvantage, hurt
aflesol *adj* disadvantageous, unprofitable
afliwiog *adj* pale, colourless
aflonydd *adj* unquiet, restless
aflonyddu *vb* to disturb, to molest
aflonyddwch *nm* disturbance, unrest
aflonyddwr (-wyr) *nm* disturber
afloyw *adj* turbid; opaque
afluniaidd *adj* mis-shapen, deformed
aflunio *vb* to disfigure, to deform
aflwydd *nm* misfortune, calamity
aflwyddiannus *adj* unsuccessful
aflwyddiant *nm* failure
aflwyddo *vb* to fail
aflywodraeth *nf* misrule, anarchy
aflywodraethus *adj* ungovernable, uncontrollable
afocado (-s) *nm* avocado
afon (-ydd) *nf* river
afonig *nf* rivulet, streamlet, brook
afradlon *adj* wasteful, prodigal
afradlonedd *nm* prodigality

afradloni, afradu vb to waste, to lavish, to squander

afraid adj unnecessary, needless ▸ nm superfluity

afrasol adj graceless, impious

afrealaidd, afrealistig adj unrealistic

afreidiol adj needless, superfluous

afreol nf misrule, disorder

afreolaidd adj irregular; disorderly

afreoleidd-dra nm irregularity

afreolus adj unruly, disorderly

afreswm nm absurdity

afresymegol adj illogical

afresymol adj unreasonable

afresymoldeb nm unreasonableness

afrifed adj innumerable

afrllad (-au), afrlladen (-nau) nf wafer

afrosgo adj clumsy, unwieldy

afrwydd adj difficult, stiff, awkward

afrwyddineb nm difficulty

afrwyddo vb to obstruct, to hinder

afrywiog adj perverse, cross-grained, improper

afrywiogrwydd nm churlishness, roughness

afu nmf liver; **afu (g)las** gizzard

afwyn (-au) nf rein

affeithiad nm affection (in grammar)

Affganistan nf Afghanistan

afflau nm grip, hug, embrace

affliw nm shred, particle

Affrica nf Africa

Affricanaidd adj African

Affricanwr (-wyr) nm African

affwysol nm abysmal

ag, â conj as ▸ prep with

agen (-nau) nf cleft, chink, fissure

agendor nmf gulf, abyss

agennu vb to split, to crack

ager, agerdd nm steam, vapour

agerfad (-au) nm steamboat

agerlong (-au) nf steamship, steamer

ageru vb to steam, to evaporate

agerw adj bitter, fierce

agor, agoryd vb to open, to expand

agorawd (-au) nf overture

agored adj open; liable

agorfa (-oedd) nf opening, orifice

agoriad (-au) nm opening; key

agoriadol adj opening, inaugural

agorwr (-wyr), agorydd (-ion) nm opener; **agorwr tuniau** can-opener

agos adj near, nigh

agosaol adj approaching

agosatrwydd nm intimacy

agosáu vb to draw near, to approach

agosrwydd nm nearness, proximity

agwedd (-au) nf form; aspect; attitude

agweddi nm dowry, marriage gift

agwrdd adj strong, mighty

angall adj unwise, foolish

angau nmf death

angel (angylion, engyl) nm angel

angen (anghenion) nm need, want; **anghenion arbennig** special needs

angenrheidiol adj necessary, needful

angenrheidrwydd *nm* necessity
angerdd *nm* heat; passion; force
angerddol *adj* ardent, intense, passionate
angerddoldeb *nm* vehemence, intensity
anghaffael *nm* mishap; defect, flaw
anghallineb *nm* unwisdom, imprudence
angharedig *adj* unkind
angharedigrwydd *nm* unkindness
anghelfydd *adj* unskilful, clumsy
anghenfil (angenfilod) *nm* monster
anghenraid (angenrheidiau) *nm* necessity
anghenus *adj* needy, necessitous, indigent
angheuol *adj* deadly, mortal, fatal
anghlod *nm* dispraise, dishonour
anghoelio *vb* to disbelieve
anghofiedig *adj* forgotten
anghofio *vb* to forget
anghofrwydd *nm* forgetfulness
anghofus *adj* forgetful, oblivious
anghred *nf* unbelief, infidelity
anghredadun (anghredinwyr) *nm* unbeliever
anghrediniaeth *nf* unbelief, infidelity
anghrediniol *adj* unbelieving
anghredu *vb* to disbelieve
anghrefyddol *adj* irreligious
anghryno *adj* incompact, prolix
anghwrtais *adj* discourteous
anghwrteisi *nm* discourtesy
anghydbwysedd *nm* imbalance

anghydfod *nm* disagreement, discord
Anghydffurfiaeth *nf* Nonconformity
Anghydffurfiwr (-wyr) *nm* Nonconformist
anghydnaws *adj* uncongenial
anghydsynio *vb* to dissent, to disagree
anghydweddol *adj* incompatible
anghyfaddas *adj* unsuitable, unfit
anghyfaddasu *vb* to disqualify
anghyfamodol *adj* uncovenanted
anghyfanhedd-dra *nm* desolation
anghyfanheddle (-aneddleoedd) *nm* desolate place
anghyfanheddol *adj* desolating; desert
anghyfannedd *adj* uninhabited, desert
anghyfansoddiadol *adj* unconstitutional
anghyfartal *adj* unequal, uneven
anghyfartaledd *nm* disparity
anghyfarwydd *adj* unfamiliar, unskilled
anghyfeillgar *adj* unfriendly
anghyfiaith *adj* foreign, alien
anghyfiawn *adj* unjust, unrighteous
anghyfiawnder *nm* injustice
anghyflawn *adj* incomplete
anghyfleus *adj* inconvenient
anghyfleustra (-terau) *nm* inconvenience
anghyflogaeth *nm* unemployment
anghyfnewidiol *adj* immutable

anghyfraith *nf* transgression, crime

anghyfranogol *adj* incommunicable

anghyfreithlon *adj* unlawful, illegal, illegitimate

anghyfrifol *adj* irresponsible

anghyffredin *adj* uncommon, rare

anghyffwrdd *adj* intangible

anghyffyrddus *adj* uncomfortable

anghymedrol *adj* immoderate

anghymen *adj* rash, coarse, untidy

anghymeradwy *adj* unacceptable

anghymeradwyo *vb* to disapprove

anghymesur *adj* inordinate

anghymharol *adj* incomparable

anghymharus *adj* ill-matched

anghymhendod *nm* foolishness, indelicacy, untidiness

anghymhwyso *vb* to unfit, to disqualify

anghymhwyster *nm* incapacity, disqualification

anghymodlon *adj* implacable

anghymwys *adj* unfit, unsuitable

anghynefin *adj* unfamiliar

anghynefindra *nm* unfamiliarity

anghynhyrchiol *adj* unproductive

anghynnes *adj* odious, loathsome

anghysbell *adj* out-of-the-way; remote

anghyson *adj* inconsistent

anghysondeb (-au), **anghysonder (-au)** *nm* inconsistency

anghysur (-on) *nm* discomfort

anghysuro *vb* to discomfort

anghysurus *adj* uncomfortable

anghytbwys *adj* unbalanced, lopsided

anghytgord (-iau) *nm* discord, dissension

anghytûn *adj* not agreeing, discordant

anghytundeb *nm* disagreement

anghytuno *vb* to disagree

anghywair *adj* ill-equipped; discordant ▸ *nm* disrepair

anghyweithas *adj* uncivil

anghywir *adj* incorrect, inaccurate, false

anghywirdeb (-au) *nm* inaccuracy, falseness

anghywrain *adj* unskilful; slovenly

angladd (-au) *nmf* burial, funeral

angladdol *adj* funereal

angof *nm* forgetfulness, oblivion

angor (-au, -ion) *nm* anchor

angorfa (-oedd, -feydd) *nf* anchorage

angori *vb* to anchor

angylaidd *adj* angelic

angyles (-au) *nf* female angel

ai¹ *adv* is it? what?; **ai e?** is it so?

ai² *conj* or; either; if

AID *nm* AIDS

aidd *nm* zeal, ardour, zest

Aifft *nf*: **yr Aifft** Egypt

aig¹, eigiau *nf* host, shoal

aig² *nf* sea, ocean

ail *adj* second ▸ *adv* a second time, again

ailadrodd *vb* to repeat

ailadroddiad (-au) *nm* repetition

ailarholiad (-au) *nm* resit

ailbriodi *vb* to remarry

aildrydanu *vb* to recharge

ailenedigaeth *nf* rebirth

aileni *vb* to regenerate

Ailfedyddiwr (-wyr) *nm* Anabaptist

ailgylchu *vb* to recycle ▸ *n* recycling

ailgynnig (ailgynigion) *nm* resit

ail-law *adj* second-hand

ail-lenwi *vb* to top up, to refill

ailsefyll *vb* to resit

aillt *nm* vassal, villain, slave

ais *npl* (*nf* **eisen**) laths; ribs

alaeth *nm* wailing, lamentation, grief

alaethu *vb* to lament

alaethus *adj* mournful, lamentable

alarch (-od, elyrch) *nm* swan

alaru *vb* to surfeit; to loathe

alaw (-on) *nf* lily; air, melody, tune

Alban *nf:* **yr Alban** Scotland

Albanwr (-wyr) *nm* Scot

alcali (-ïau) *nm* alkali

alcam *nm* tin

alcohol *nm* alcohol

alch (-au, eilch) *nf* grate, grill

ale (-au, -on) *nf* aisle; gangway; alley

algebra *nm* algebra

Algeraidd *adj* Algerian

Algeria *nf* Algeria

Algeriad (-iaid) *nm* Algerian

Almaen *nf:* **yr Almaen** Germany

Almaeneg *nf* German

Almaenwr (-wyr) *nm* German

almon *nm* almond

aloi (aloeon) *nm* alloy

Alpau *npl:* **yr Alpau** the Alps

Alzheimer *nm:* **clefyd Alzheimer** Alzheimer's (disease)

allan *adv* out

allanfa *nf* exit

allanol *adj* outward, external

allblyg *adj* extrovert

allbrint (-iau) *nm* printout

allforio *vb* to export

allfro *nf* foreigner; foreign land

allfudwr (-wyr) *nm* emigrant

allgarwch *nm* altruism

allgofnodi *vb* to log off, to log out

allor (-au) *nf* altar

allt (elltydd) *nf* hill; cliff; wood

alltud (-ion) *nm* alien; exile

alltudiaeth *nf* banishment, exile

alltudio *vb* to banish, to exile

allwedd (-au, -i) *nf* key, clef (*in music*)

allweddell *nf* keyboard

am¹ *prep* round, about; for; at; on ▸ *conj* for, because; so long as

am² *see* **ym**

amaeth *nm* husbandman; agriculture

amaethdy (-dai) *nm* farm-house

amaethu *vb* to farm, to till

amaethwr (-wyr) *nm* farmer

amaethwraig *nf* farm-wife

amaethyddiaeth *nf* agriculture

amaethyddol *adj* agricultural

amarch *nm* disrespect, dishonour

amau *vb* to doubt, to suspect ▸ *nm* (**-heuon**) doubt

ambell *adj* occasional; **ambell waith** sometimes

amcan (-ion) *nm* purpose, aim; guess; **ar amcan** at random, approximately, at a guess

amcangyfrif *vb* to estimate ▸ *nm* (**-on**) estimate

amcanu *vb* to purpose; to aim; to guess

amdo (-oeau) nm shroud, winding-sheet

amdoi vb to shroud, to enshroud

amdorch (-dyrch) nf chaplet, wreath

amddifad adj destitute, orphan

amddifadrwydd nm destitution, privation

amddifadu vb to bereave, to deprive

amddifaty (-tai) nm orphanage

amddifedi nm destitution, privation

amddiffyn vb to defend, to protect, to shield ▸ nm (**addiffynion**) defence

amddiffynfa (-feydd) nf fortress

amddiffyniad nm protection, defence

amddiffynnwr (-wyr), **amddiffynyddion** nm defender, protector

amddyfrwys adj mighty, rugged; marshy

America Ladin nf Latin America

Amerig nf: yr Amerig America

amfesur (-au) nm perimeter

amgáu vb to enclose, to shut in

amgen adj, adv other, else, otherwise; different; **nid amgen** that is to say, namely

amgenach adj, adv otherwise; better

amgueddfa (-feydd) nf museum

amgyffred vb to comprehend, to comprise ▸ nm (**-ion**) comprehension

amgyffrediad nm comprehension

amgylch (-oedd) nm circuit; environs, surroundings; **o (oddi) amgylch** round about, about

amgylchedd nm circumference; environment

amgylcheddol adj environmental; **yn amgylcheddol** environmentally; **amgylcheddol garedig** environmentally friendly

amgylchfyd nm environment

amgylchiad (-au) nm circumstance; occasion

amgylchiadol adj circumstantial

amgylchu vb to surround

amgylchynol adj surrounding

amgylchynu vb to surround

amharchu vb to dishonour, to disrespect

amharchus adj disrespectful, disreputable

amhariad nm impairment, damage

amharod adj unprepared, unready

amharodrwydd nm unreadiness

amharu vb to impair, to harm, to injure, to damage

amhendant adj indefinite, vague

amhenderfynol adj irresolute

amhenodol adj indefinite

amherchi vb to dishonour, to insult

amherffaith adj imperfect

amherffeithrwydd nm imperfection

amhersonol adj impersonal

amherthnasol, amherthynasol adj irrelevant

amheuaeth nf doubt, scepticism

amheugar adj suspicious; sceptical

amheuol adj doubting, doubtful

amheus *adj* doubting, doubtful, dubious

amheuthun *adj* dainty, savoury ▸ *nm* (**-ion**) dainty, delicacy, treat

amheuwr (**-wyr**) *nm* doubter, sceptic

amhlantadwy *adj* childless, barren

amhleidiol, amhleitgar *adj* impartial

amhoblog *adj* sparsely populated

amhoblogaidd *adj* unpopular

amhosibl *adj* impossible

amhriodol *adj* improper

amhrisiadwy *adj* priceless

amhrofiadol *adj* inexperienced

amhrydlon *adj* unpunctual

amhûr *adj* impure, foul

amhwrpasol *adj* irrelevant

amhwyllo *vb* to lose one's senses, to go mad

aml *adj* frequent, abundant ▸ *adv* often

amlder, amldra *nm* abundance

amldduwiad (**-iaid**) *nm* polytheist

amldduwiaeth *nf* polytheism

amleiriog *adj* wordy, verbose, prolix

amlen (**-ni**) *nf* envelope, wrapper

amlhad *nm* increasing, increase

amlhau *vb* to increase, to multiply

amlinelliad (**-au**) *nm* outline

amlinellu *vb* to outline

aml-lawr *adj* multi-storey

amlochrog *adj* many-sided

amlosgfa *nf* crematorium

amlosgi *vb* to cremate

amlwg *adj* plain, clear, manifest, evident, prominent

amlwreigiaeth *nf* polygamy

amlwreigiwr (**-wyr**) *nm* polygamist

amlygiad (**-au**) *nm* manifestation

amlygrwydd *nm* prominence, limelight

amlygu *vb* to manifest, to reveal, to evince

amnaid (**-neidiau**) *nf* beck, nod

amneidio *vb* to beckon, to nod

amnest (**-au**) *nm* amnesty

amod (**-au**) *nmf* condition

amodi *vb* to covenant, to stipulate

amodol *adj* conditional

amp (**-au**) *nm* amp

amrant (**-au, -rannau**) *nm* eyelid

amrantiad *nm* wink, twinkling, second

amrediad *nm* range

amreiniol *adj* not privileged

amrwd *adj* uncooked, raw, crude

amryddawn *adj* versatile

amryfal *adj* sundry, manifold

amryfus *adj* erroneous, inadvertent

amryfusedd (**-au**) *nm* error, oversight

amryliw *adj* variegated; multicoloured

amryw *adj* several, sundry, various

amrywiad (**-au**) *nm* variant

amrywiaeth *nm* variety, diversity

amrywio *vb* to vary, to differ

amrywiol *adj* sundry

amser (**-oedd, -au**) *nmf* time; **amser sbâr** spare time

amseriad (**-au**) *nm* timing, dating, date

amserlen (**-ni**) *nf* time-table

amserol *adj* timely; temporal

amseru vb to time, to date

amserydd (-ion) nm chronologist

amseryddiaeth nf chronology

amseryddol adj chronological

amwisg (-oedd) nf covering, shroud

amwisgo vb to enwrap, to shroud

amwys adj ambiguous

amwysedd nm ambiguity

amyn conj, prep unless, except, but

amynedd nm patience

amyneddgar adj patient

an- prefix un-, in-, de-, dis-

anabl adj disabled

anabledd nm disability

anad adj: yn anad above all, more than

anadferadwy adj irreparable

anadl (-au, -on) nfm breath

anadliad nm breath, breathing

anadlu vb to breathe

anadlydd (-ion) nm inhaler

anadnabyddus adj unknown

anaddas adj unfit, unsuitable

anaddasu vb to unfit, to disqualify

anaeddfed, anaddfed adj unripe, immature

anaeddfedrwydd nm unripeness, immaturity

anaele adj awful, direful; incurable

anaesthetig adj anaesthetic

anaf (-au) nm blemish, defect; wound

anafu vb to blemish, to maim, to hurt

anafus adj maimed, disabled

anair (-eiriau) nm ill report, slander

anallu nm inability

analluog adj unable

analluogi vb to disable

anaml adj infrequent, rare ▸ adv rarely, seldom

anamlwg adj obscure, inconspicuous

anamserol adj untimely, mistimed

anap (anhapon) nmf mischance, mishap

anarchiaeth nfm anarchy

anarchydd (-ion) nm anarchist

anarferol adj unusual, extraordinary

anarfog adj unarmed

ancr nmf anchorite, anchoress

ancwyn (-ion) nm dinner, supper; delicacy

anchwiliadwy adj unsearchable

andras nm curse; devil, deuce

andwyo vb to spoil, to ruin, to undo

andwyol adj harmful, ruinous

anedifeiriol adj impenitent

aneffeithiol adj ineffectual

aneglur adj indistinct; illegible

aneirif adj innumerable

anelu vb to bend, to aim

anenwog adj unrenowned, ignoble, mean

anerchiad (-au) nm salutation, address

anesboniadwy adj inexplicable

anesgusodol adj inexcusable

anesmwyth adj uneasy, restless

anesmwythder, anesmwythdra nm uneasiness, unrest

anesmwytho vb to be or make uneasy

anesmwythyd nm uneasiness, disquiet

anewyllysgar *adj* unwilling

anfad *adj* wicked, nefarious

anfadrwydd *nm* wickedness, villainy

anfadwaith *nm* villainy; crime

anfadwr (-wyr) *nm* villain, scoundrel

anfaddeugar *adj* unforgiving

anfaddeuol *adj* unpardonable

anfantais (-eision) *nf* disadvantage

anfanteisiol *adj* disadvantageous

anfarwol *adj* undying, immortal

anfarwoldeb *nm* immortality

anfedrus *adj* unskilful

anfedrusrwydd *nm* unskilfulness

anfeidrol *adj* infinite

anfeidroldeb *nm* infinity

anferth *adj* huge, monstrous

anferthedd *nm* hugeness, monstrosity

anfodlon *adj* unwilling

anfodloni *vb* to discontent, to dissatisfy

anfodlonrwydd *nm* discontent

anfodd *nm* unwillingness, displeasure

anfoddhaol *adj* unsatisfactory

anfoddio *vb* to displease, to disoblige

anfoddlon *see* anfodlon

anfoddog *adj* discontented, dissatisfied

anfoddogrwydd *nm* discontentment

anfoesgar *adj* unmannerly, rude

anfoesgarwch *nm* rudeness, incivility

anfoesol *adj* immoral

anfoesoldeb *nm* immorality

anfon *vb* to send, to transmit, to dispatch

anfoneb *nf* invoice

anfoneddigaidd *adj* ungentlemanly

anfonheddig *adj* ignoble, discourteous

anfoniad *nm* sending, transmission

anfri *nm* disrespect, dishonour

anfucheddol *adj* immoral

anfuddiol *adj* unprofitable

anfwriadol *adj* unintentional

anfwyn *adj* unkind, uncivil

anfwytadwy *adj* inedible

anfynych *adj* infrequent, rare
  ▸ *adv* seldom

anffaeledig *adj* infallible

anffaeledigrwydd *nm* infallibility

anffafriol *adj* unfavourable

anffawd (-ffodion) *nf* misfortune

anffodus, anffortunus *adj* unfortunate

anffrwythlon *adj* unfruitful, barren

anffurfio *vb* to disfigure, to deform

anffurfiol *adj* informal

anffyddiaeth *nf* atheism

anffyddiwr (-wyr) *nm* infidel, atheist

anffyddlon *adj* unfaithful

anhaeddiannol *adj* unmerited, undeserved

anhaeddiant *nm* demerit, unworthiness

anhapus *adj* unhappy, unlucky

anhardd *adj* unhandsome, unseemly, ugly

anhawdd adj hard, difficult
anhawddgar adj unamiable, unlovely
anhawster (anawsterau) nm difficulty
anhepgor (-ion) nm essential
anhepgorol adj indispensable
anhoffter nm hatred, dislike
anhraethadwy adj unutterable
anhraethol adj unspeakable, ineffable
anhrefn nm disorder, confusion
anhrefnu vb to disorder, to disarrange
anhrefnus adj disorderly, untidy
anhreiddiol adj impervious, impenetrable
anhreuliedig adj undigested; unspent
anhrugarog adj unmerciful, merciless
anhuddo vb to cover (a fire)
anhunedd nm wakefulness, disquiet
anhwyldeb nm disorder, complaint, illness
anhwylder nm illness
anhwylus adj unwell
anhwylustod nm inconvenience
anhyblyg adj inflexible, stiff, rigid
anhydawdd adj insoluble
anhyder nm distrust, diffidence
anhyderus adj diffident
anhydrin adj unmanageable
anhydyn adj intractable, obstinate
anhyddysg adj unversed, ignorant
anhyfryd adj unpleasant
anhyfrydwch nm unpleasantness
anhygar adj unpleasant, unamiable
anhygoel adj incredible
anhygyrch adj inaccessible
anhylaw adj unhandy, unwieldy
anhynod adj indistinctive; uncertain
anhysbys adj unknown; unversed
anhywaith adj intractable, refractory
anial adj desert, wild ▸ nm wilderness
anialwch nm wilderness
anian (-au) nf nature, instinct, genius
anianawd nm temperament, disposition
anianol adj natural
anianyddol adj physical
anifail (-feiliaid) nm animal, beast
anifeilaidd adj beastly, brutish
anifeileiddio vb to animalize, to brutalize
anlwc nf bad luck, misfortune
anlwcus adj unlucky
anllad adj wanton, lascivious, lewd
anlladrwydd nm wantonness, lewdness
anllygredig adj incorrupt, incorruptible
anllygredigaeth nf incorruption
anllythrennog adj illiterate
anllywodraeth nf misrule, anarchy
annaearol adj unearthly, weird
annatodol adj indissoluble, that cannot be undone
annaturiol adj unnatural
annealladwy adj unintelligible

anneallus adj unintelligent
annedwydd adj unhappy, miserable
annedwyddwch nm unhappiness
annedd (anheddau) nf dwelling
anneddfol adj lawless
annefnyddiol adj useless; immaterial
annel (anelau) nfm trap; purpose, aim
annelwig adj shapeless, unformed; vague
anner (aneirod, -i, -au) nf heifer
annerbyniol adj unacceptable
annerch vb to salute, to greet, to address ▸ nm **(anerchion)** salutation, greeting
annewisol adj ineligible, undesirable, unwelcome
annhebyg adj unlike, dissimilar
annhebygol adj unlikely, improbable
annhebygolrwydd nm improbability
annhebygrwydd nm unlikeness, unlikelihood
annheg adj unfair
annhegwch nm unfairness
annheilwng adj unworthy
annheilyngdod nm unworthiness
annherfynol adj endless; infinitive, infinite
annhirion adj cruel
annhosturiol adj pitiless, ruthless
annhuedd nf disinclination
annhueddol adj disinclined, indisposed
anniben adj untidy, slovenly
annibendod nm untidiness

annibyniaeth nf independence
annibynnol adj independent
Annibynnwr (-wyr) nm Independent
annichellgar adj guileless, simple
annichon, annichonadwy adj impossible
anniddan adj comfortless, miserable
anniddig adj peevish, irritable, fretful
anniddigrwydd nm peevishness
anniddos adj leaky, comfortless
annifeiriol adj innumerable, countless
anniflanedig adj unfading, imperishable
annifyr adj miserable, wretched
annifyrrwch nm misery
anniffoddadwy adj unquenchable
annigonedd nm insufficiency
annigonol adj insufficient, inadequate
annigonolrwydd nm inadequacy
annileadwy adj indelible, ineffaceable
annilys adj unauthentic, spurious, insincere
annillyn adj inelegant, clumsy
annioddefol adj unbearable, intolerable
anniogel adj unsafe, insecure
anniolchgar adj unthankful, ungrateful
anniolchgarwch nm ingratitude
annirnadwy adj incomprehensible
annisgrifiadwy adj indescribable
annisgwyliadwy adj unexpected

anniwair *adj* unchaste, incontinent, lewd
anniwall *adj* insatiable
anniweirdeb *nm* unchastity, incontinence
anniwylliedig *adj* uncultured
annoeth *adj* unwise, imprudent
annoethineb *nm* unwisdom, folly
annog *vb* to incite, to urge; to exhort
annormal *adj* abnormal
annos *vb* to incite, to set (a dog) on
annosbarthus *adj* unruly, disorderly
annuw, annuwiad (annuwiaid) *nm* atheist
annuwiaeth *nf* atheism
annuwiol *adj* ungodly, godless
annuwioldeb *nm* ungodliness
annwn, annwfn *nm* the underworld; hell
annwyd (anwydau, -on) *nm* cold
annwyl *adj* dear, beloved
annyledus *adj* undue, wrongful
annymunol *adj* unpleasant, disagreeable
annynol *adj* inhuman, cruel
annysgedig *adj* unlearned
anobaith *nm* despair
anobeithio *vb* to despair
anobeithiol *adj* hopeless
anochel, anocheladwy *adj* unavoidable, inevitable
anodd *adj* hard, difficult
anoddefgar *adj* impatient, intolerant
anogaeth (-au) *nf* exhortation
anolrheinadwy *adj* untraceable
anolygus *adj* unsightly

anonest *adj* dishonest
anonestrwydd *nm* dishonesty
anorchfygol *adj* irresistible; unconquerable
anorecsig *adj* anorexic
anorfod *adj* insuperable; unavoidable
anorffen *adj* endless, unending
anorffenedig *adj* incomplete, unfinished
anorthrech *adj* invincible
anrasol *adj* graceless
anrhaith (-rheithiau) *nf* prey, spoil, booty
anrheg (-ion) *nf* present, gift
anrhegu *vb* to present, to give
anrheithio *vb* to prey, to spoil, to plunder
anrheithiwr (-wyr) *nm* spoiler, pillager
anrhydedd (-au) *nm* honour
anrhydeddu *vb* to honour
anrhydeddus *adj* honourable
anrhydeddwr (-wyr) *nm* honourer
ansad *adj* unsteady, unstable
ansadrwydd *nm* instability
ansafadwy *adj* unstable; fickle
ansathredig *adj* untrodden, unfrequented
ansawdd (-soddau) *nfm* quality, state
ansefydlog *adj* unsettled, unstable; fickle
ansefydlogi *vb* to unsettle
ansicr *adj* uncertain, doubtful
ansicrwydd *nm* uncertainty, doubt
ansoddair (-eiriau) *nm* adjective
ansoddeiriol *adj* adjectival
ansyber *adj* untidy, slovenly

Antarctig *nf*; **yr Antarctig** the Antarctic

anterliwt (-iau) *nfm* interlude

anterth *nm* meridian, zenith, prime

antur (-iau) *nfm* attempt, venture; adventure; enterprise; **ar antur** at random

anturiaeth (-au) *nf* adventure, enterprise

anturiaethus *adj* adventurous, enterprising

anturiaethwr (-wyr) *nm* adventurer

anturio *vb* to venture, to adventure

anturus *adj* adventurous

anthem (-au) *nf* anthem

anudon (-au) *nm* false oath, perjury

anudoniaeth *nf* perjury

anudonwr (-wyr) *nm* perjurer

anufudd *adj* disobedient

anufudd-dod *nm* disobedience

anufuddhau *vb* to disobey

anundeb *nm* disunion

anunion *adj* crooked; unjust

anuniondeb *nm* injustice, iniquity

anurddo *vb* to spoil, to mar, to disfigure

anwadal *adj* unstable, fickle, changeable

anwadalu *vb* to waver, to vacillate

anwadalwch *nm* fickleness

anwar *adj* wild, barbarous, savage

anwaraidd *adj* uncivilized, barbarous

anwarddyn (-wariaid) *nm* barbarian, savage

anwareidd-dra *nm* barbarity

anwastad *adj* uneven, unstable, fickle

anwe (-oedd) *nf* woof

anwedd *nm* vapour, steam

anweddaidd *adj* unseemly, indecent

anweddus *adj* improper, indecent

anweledig *adj* unseen, invisible

anwes *nm* indulgence; caress

anwesog *adj* pampered, affectionate

anwesu *vb* to fondle, to caress, to pamper, to indulge

anwir *adj* untrue, lying, false; wicked

anwiredd (-au) *nm* untruth; iniquity

anwireddu *vb* to falsify

anwireddus *adj* untruthful, false, lying

anwr (-wyr) *nm* wretch, coward

anwybod *nm* ignorance

anwybodaeth *nf* ignorance

anwybodus *adj* ignorant

anwybyddu *vb* to ignore

anwydog *adj* cold, chilly; having a cold

anwydwst *nf* influenza

anwyldeb *nm* belovedness, dearness

anwyliaid *npl* beloved ones, favourites

anwylo *vb* to cherish, to fondle, to caress

anwylyd (-liaid) *nm* beloved

anwylyn *nm* favourite

anwythiad *nm* induction

anwytho *vb* to induce

anwythol *adj* inductive

anymarferol *adj* impractical, impracticable

anymddiried *vb* to mistrust, to distrust

anymwybodol *adj* unconscious

anymwybyddiaeth *nf* unconsciousness

anynad *adj* peevish, petulant; brawling

anysgrifenedig *adj* unwritten

anysgrythurol *adj* unscriptural

anystwyth *adj* stiff, rigid

anystwytho *vb* to stiffen

anystyriaeth *nf* heedlessness, rashness

anystyriol *adj* heedless, reckless, rash

anystywallt, anystywell *adj* unmanageable

apelio *vb* to appeal

apostol (-ion) *nm* apostle

apostolaidd, apostolig *adj* apostolic

apostoliaeth *nf* apostleship

apwyntiad (-au) *nm* appointment

apwyntio *vb* to appoint

ar *prep* on, upon, over; **ar gau** closed

âr *nm* ploughed land, tilth; ground

Arab (-iaid) *nm* Arab

arab *adj* facetious, merry, pleasant

Arabaidd *adj* Arab

arabedd *nm* facetiousness, wit

Arabeg *nf* Arabic

arabus *adj* witty

aradr (erydr) *nm* plough

araf *adj* slow, soft, gentle, still

arafu *vb* to slow; to quiet; to moderate

arafwch *nm* slowness; moderation

arail *vb* to guard, to care for, to foster ▸ *adj* attending, careful

araith (areithiau) *nf* speech

arall (eraill) *adj, pron* another, other; else

aralleg (-au) *nfm* allegory

aralleiriad (-au) *nm* paraphrase

aralleirio *vb* to paraphrase

araul *adj* sunny, sunlit; serene

arawd *nf* speech, oration

arbed *vb* to spare, to save

arbediad (-au) *nm* save, salvage

arbedol *adj* sparing, saving

arbedwr (-wyr) *nm:* **arbedwr sgrin** screen saver

arbenigaeth *nf* expertise; specialisation

arbenigo *vb* to specialise

arbenigrwydd *nm* speciality, prominence

arbenigwr (-wyr) *nm* specialist

arbennig *adj* special

arbrawf (arbrofion) *nm* experiment

arbrofi *vb* to experiment

arbrofol *adj* experimental

Arctig *nf:* **yr Arctig** the Arctic

arch¹ (eirchion) *nf* request, petition; bidding

arch² (eirch) *nf* ark, coffin; trunk, waist

archaeoleg *nf* archaeology

archangel (-ylion) *nm* archangel

archddiacon (-iaid) *nm* archdeacon

archeb (-ion) *nf* order

archebu *vb* to order

archen *nf* shoe; clothing

archenad *nm* shoe; clothing

Archentaidd adj Argentinian
archesgob (-ion) nm archbishop
archesgobaeth (-au) nf
  archbishopric
archfarchnad (-oedd) nf
  supermarket
archiad nm bidding
archif (-au) nfm archive
archifdy (-dai) nm record office
archifydd (-ion) nm archivist
archoffeiriad (-iaid) nm high priest
archoll (-ion) nf wound
archolli vb to wound
archwaeth nm taste, appetite
archwaethu vb to taste, to savour
archwiliad (-au) nm audit;
  checkup; inspection,
  examination; exploration
archwilio vb to examine, to audit;
  to explore
archwiliwr (-wyr) nm examiner,
  auditor; explorer
ardal (-oedd) nf region, district
ardalydd (-ion) nm marquis
ardreth (-i) nf rent
ardrethu vb to rent
ardystiad (-au) nm pledge,
  attestation
ardystio vb to pledge, to attest
arddangos vb to show, to exhibit,
  to indicate
arddangosfa (-feydd) nf show,
  exhibition
arddegau npl teens
arddegol adj teenage
arddel vb to avow, to own
arddeliad nm claim, avowal;
  unction

a

ardderchog adj excellent, noble,
  splendid
ardderchowgrwydd nm
  excellency
arddodi vb to prefix; to impose
arddodiad (-iaid) nm preposition
arddu vb to plough
arddull (-iau) nf style
arddulleg nf stylistics
ardduniant nm sublimity
arddunol adj sublime
arddwr (-wyr) nm ploughman
arddwrn (-ddyrnau) nm wrist
arddywediad (-au) nm dictation
aredig vb to plough
areitheg nf rhetoric
areithio vb to speak, to make a
  speech
areithiwr (-wyr) nm speaker,
  orator
areithyddiaeth nf oratory;
  elocution
arel nm laurel
aren (-nau) nf kidney; (pl) reins
arestio vb to arrest
arf (-au) nmf weapon; (pl) arms;
  tool
arfaeth (-au) nf purpose; decree
arfaethu vb to purpose, to intend
arfbais (-beisiau) nf coat of arms
arfdy (-dai) nm armoury
arfer vb to use, to accustom ▸ nfm
  (-ion) use, custom, habit
arferiad nmf use, custom, habit
arferol adj usual, customary
arfod nf stroke of a weapon, fight;
  armour; opportunity
arfog adj armed
arfogaeth nf armour

arfogi *vb* to arm
arfoll (-au) *nm* pledge, oath
arfordir (-oedd) *nm* coast
arforol *adj* maritime
arffed (-au) *nf* lap
argae (-au) *nm* dam, embankment; enclosed place
argeisio *vb* to seek
argel *nmf* concealment, refuge ▸ *adj* hidden, occult
arglwydd (-i) *nm* lord
arglwyddaidd *adj* lordly
arglwyddes (-au) *nf* lady
arglwyddiaeth (-au) *nf* lordship, dominion
argoed (-ydd) *nm* enclosure of trees
argoel (-ion) *nf* sign, token, omen
argoeli *vb* to betoken, to portend, to augur
argoelus *adj* ominous
argraff (-ion, -au) *nf* print, impression
argraffdy (-dai) *nm* printer's, printing-house
argraffiad (-au) *nm* impression; edition
argraffu *vb* to print, to impress
argraffwaith *nm* print, typography
argraffwasg *nf* printing-press
argraffwr (-wyr), **argraffydd (-ion)** *nm* printer
argrwm, argrwn *adj* convex
argyfwng (-yngau, -yngoedd) *nm* crisis
argyhoeddi *vb* to reprove; to convince, to convict
argyhoeddiad (-au) *nm* conviction
argyhoeddiadol *adj* convincing

argymell *vb* to urge, to recommend
argymhelliad *nm* recommendation
arholi *vb* to examine
arholiad (-au) *nm* examination; **arholiad mynediad** entrance examination
arholwr (-wyr) *nm* examiner
arhosfa *nf* stop; **arhosfa bws, arhosfa bysiau** bus stop
arhosfan (-nau) *nm* = **arhosfa**
arhosiad *nm* staying, stay
arhosol *adj* abiding, permanent
arial *nm* vigour, mettle
arian *nm* silver ▸ *coll n* money, cash; **arian breiniol** currency; **arian byw** mercury; **arian gleision** silver; **arian parod** cash; **arian pen** exact money; **arian treigl** current money
ariandy (-dai) *nm* bank
ariangar *adj* fond of money, avaricious
ariangarwch *nm* love of money, avarice
ariannaid *adj* silver, silvern
ariannaidd *adj* silvery
arianneg *nmf* finance
Ariannin *nf* Argentina
ariannog *adj* moneyed, wealthy, rich
ariannol *adj* financial, monetary
ariannu *vb* to silver; to finance/fund
ariannydd (arianyddion) *nm* banker, investor, financier
arlais (-leisiau) *nf* temple
arlein, ar-lein *adj, adv* online

arloesi *vb* to clear, to prepare the way, to pioneer

arloesydd (-wyr) *nm* pioneer

arluniaeth *nf* portraiture, painting

arlunio *vb* to draw, to paint, to portray

arlunydd (-wyr) *nm* artist

arlwy (-au, -on) *nmf* provision, feast, menu

arlwyaeth (-au) *nf* catering

arlwyo *vb* to prepare, to provide; to cook

arlywydd (-ion) *nm* president

arlywyddiaeth *nf* presidency

arlywyddol *adj* presidential

arlliw (-iau) *nm* varnish, tint, shade, trace

arlliwio *vb* to colour, to tint, to paint

arllwys *vb* to pour out, to empty

arllwysfa *nf* outfall, outlet, vent

armel *nm* second milk

armes *nf* prophecy; calamity

arnofio *vb* to float

arobryn *adj* worthy, prize-winning

arofun *vb* to intend, to purpose

arogl (-au), aroglau (-euon) *nm* scent, smell

arogldarth *nm* incense

arogldarthu *vb* to burn incense

arogli, arogleuo *vb* to scent; to smell

arogliad *nm* smelling, sense of smell

aroleuadau *npl*: **aroleuadau gwallt** highlights

aroleuydd (-ion) *nm* highlighter (pen)

arolwg *nm* survey

arolygiad (-au) *nm* inspection

arolygiaeth *nf* superintendency

arolygu *vb* to superintend

arolygwr (-wyr), arolygydd (-ion) *nm* superintendent, inspector; supervisor

aros *vb* to wait, to await, to stay, to stop, to tarry, to abide, to remain; **aros ar ôl** stay behind; **aros gartref** stay in

arswyd *nm* dread, terror, horror

arswydo *vb* to dread; to shudder

arswydus *adj* fearful, terrible, dreadful

arsylwi *vb* to observe

arsyllfa (-feydd) *nf* observatory

arsyllu *vb* to observe

artaith (-teithiau) *nf* torture, torment, pang

arteithio *vb* to torture, to rack

arteithiol *adj* racking, excruciating

artisiog (-au) *nm* artichoke

artistig *adj* artistic

arth (eirth) *nfm* bear

arthes (-au) *nf* she-bear

arthio, arthu *vb* to bark, to growl

aruchel *adj* lofty, sublime

arucheledd *nm* loftiness, sublimity

aruthr *adj* marvellous, strange

aruthredd *nm* amazement, horror

aruthrol *adj* huge, prodigious

arwahanrwydd *nm* uniqueness, individuality

arwain *vb* to conduct, to lead, to guide, to carry

arwedd (-au, -ion) *nf* bearing, aspect

arweddu *vb* to bear

arweddwr (-wyr) *nm* bearer

arweiniad *nm* guidance; introduction

arweiniol *adj* leading, introductory

arweinydd (-ion) *nm* guide, leader; conductor

arweinyddiaeth *nf* leadership

arwerthiant (-iannau) *nm* auction

arwerthu *vb* to sell by auction

arwerthwr (-wyr) *nm* auctioneer

arwisgiad *nm* investiture

arwisgo *vb* to enrobe, to array, to invest

arwr (-wyr) *nm* hero

arwraidd *adj* heroic, epic

arwres (-au) *nf* heroine

arwrgerdd (-i) *nf* epic poem

arwriaeth *nf* heroism

arwrol *adj* heroic, gallant

arwybod *nm* awareness

arwydd (-ion) *nmf* sign, signal; ensign; **arwydd ffordd** road sign

arwyddair (-eiriau) *nm* motto

arwyddbost *nm* signpost

arwyddlun (-iau) *nm* emblem, symbol

arwyddluniol *adj* emblematic, symbolic

arwyddnod (-au) *nm* mark, token

arwyddo *vb* to sign; to signify

arwyddocâd *nm* signification, significance

arwyddocaol *adj* significant

arwyddocáu *vb* to signify, to denote

arwyl (-ion) *nf* funeral, funeral rites

arwylo *vb* to mourn over the dead

arwynebedd *nm* surface, superficies

arwynebol *adj* superficial

arwyrain *nmf* praise, panegyric ▸ *vb* to rise, to extol

arwystl *nm* mortgage

arwystlo *vb* to pledge, to mortgage

arysgrif (-au), **arysgrifen (-nau)** *nf* inscription, epigraph

asb (-iaid) *nf* asp

asbri *nm* animation, vivacity, spirits

ased *nm* asset

aseiniad (-au) *nm* assignment

asen¹ (-nau) *nf* rib

asen² (-nod) *nf* she-ass

asesiad *nm*: **asesiad parhaus** continuous assessment

asesu *vb* to assess; **asesu parhaus** continuous assessment

aseth *nf* stake, spar, lath

asgell (esgyll) *nf* wing, fin; **asgell fraith** chaffinch

asgellog *adj* winged

asgellwr (-wyr) *nm* wing, outside-forward

asglod, asglodion *npl* chips

asgre *nf* bosom, heart

asgwrn (esgyrn) *nm* bone

Asia *nf* Asia

Asiad (Asiaid) *nm* Asian

asiad (-au) *nm* joint, weld

Asiaidd *adj* Asian

asiant (-au) *nm* agent

asiantaeth *nf* agency

asid *nm* acid

asidig *adj* acidic

asiedydd *nm* joiner

asio *vb* to join, to weld; to solder; to cement

astell (astyllod, estyll) *nf* plank, shelf

astroleg *nf* astrology
astrus *adj* abstruse, difficult
astud *adj* attentive
astudiaeth (-au) *nf* study;
astudiaethau cyfrifiadurol
computer studies
astudio *vb* to study
astudrwydd *nm* attentiveness
aswy *adj* left
asyn (-nod) *nm* he-ass
asynnaidd *adj* asinine
at *prep* to, towards; for; at; by
atafaeliad *nm* confiscation,
distraint
atafaelu *vb* to confiscate
atal *vb* to stop, to hinder, to
withhold ▶ *nm* (**-ion**) hindrance,
impediment; **atal dweud**
stammering
ataleb (-au) *nf* injunction
atalfa (-feydd) *nf* check; stoppage
ataliad (-au) *nm* stoppage
ataliol *adj* preventive
atalnod (-au) *nf* stop, point
atalnodi *vb* to point, to punctuate
atblygol *adj* reflexive
ateb *vb* to answer, to reply ▶ *nm*
(**-ion**) answer
atebol *adj* answerable, responsible
ateg (-ion) *nf* prop, stay, support
ategiad (-au) *nm* affirmation
ategol *adj* confirming; auxiliary
ategu *vb* to support
atgas *adj* odious, hateful
atgasedd *nm* hatred
atgasrwydd *nm* odiousness,
hatefulness
atgenhedliad *nm* regeneration
atgenhedlu *vb* to regenerate

atgno (-oeau, -oeon) *nm* remorse
atgof (-ion) *nm* remembrance,
reminiscence
atgofio *vb* to recollect, to
remember, to remind
atgofus *adj* reminiscent
atgoffa *vb* to recall, to remind
atgyfnerthion *npl* reinforcements
atgyfnerthu *vb* to reinforce
atgyfodi *vb* to rise, to raise again
atgyfodiad *nm* resurrection
atgynhyrchu *vb* to reproduce
atgyweiriad (-au) *nm* repair
atgyweirio *vb* to repair, to mend
atgyweiriwr (-wyr) *nm* repairer,
mender
atig (-au) *nmf* attic
Atlantaidd *adj* Atlantic
Atlantig *adj* Atlantic
atodi *vb* to add, to append, to affix
atodiad (-au) *nm* addition,
appendix
atodlen (-ni) *nf* supplement;
schedule
atodol *adj* supplementary
atolwg, atolygu *vb* to pray, to
beseech
atom (-au) *nfm* atom
atomfa (-feydd) *nf* nuclear power
station
atomig *adj* atomic
atsain (-seiniau) *nf* echo
atseinio *vb* to resound, to echo
atwf (atyfion) *nm* second growth
atyniad (-au) *nm* attraction
atyniadol *adj* attractive
atynnu *vb* to attract
Athen *nf* Athens
athletau *npl* athletics

athrawes (-au) nf teacher, governess
athrawiaeth (-au) nf doctrine
athrawiaethol adj doctrinal
athrist adj very sad, pensive, sorrowful
athro (athrawon) nm teacher, master
athrod (-ion) nm slander, libel
athrodwr (-wyr) nm slanderer, libeller
athrofa (-feydd) nf college, academy, institute
athrofaol adj academic
athroniaeth nf philosophy
athronydd (-ion, -wyr) nm philosopher
athronyddol adj philosophical
athronyddu vb to philosophize
athrylith (-oedd) nf genius
athrylithgar adj of genius, talented
athrywyn nm mediation, intervention ▸ vb to mediate, to arbitrate
aur nm gold
awch nm edge; ardour, zest; relish, appetite
awchlym adj sharp, keen, acute
awchlymu vb to sharpen, to whet
awchus adj sharp, keen; eager; greedy
awdl (-au, odlau) nf ode
awdur (-on, -iaid) nm author
awdurdod (-au) nmf authority
awdurdodedig adj authorised
awdurdodi vb to authorize
awdurdodol adj authoritative
awdures (-au) nf authoress
awduriaeth nf authorship

awel (-on) nf breeze, wind
awelog adj breezy, windy
awen¹ (-au) nf muse
awen² (-au) nf rein
awenydd (-ion) nm poet
awenyddiaeth nf poetry, poesy
awenyddol adj poetical
awenyddu vb to poetize
awgrym (-au, -iadau) nm hint, suggestion
awgrymiadol adj suggestive
awgrymog adj suggestive
awgrymu vb to hint, to suggest
awr (oriau) nf hour; **oriau hamdden** spare time, leisure; **oriau hyblyg** flexitime; **oriau ychwanegol** overtime
Awst nm August
Awstralia nf Australia
Awstria nf Austria
awtistig adj autistic
awydd (-au) nm desire, eagerness
awyddfryd nm vehement desire, zeal
awyddu vb to desire
awyddus adj desirous, eager, zealous
awyr nf air, sky
awyrdrom (-au) nf aerodrome
awyren (-nau, -ni) nf balloon, aeroplane
awyrendy (-dai) nm hangar
awyrgylch (-au, -oedd) nmf atmosphere
awyriad nm ventilation
awyrlong (-au) nf airship
awyru vb to air, to ventilate

baban (-od) *adj* baby
babanaidd *adj* babyish
babandod *nm* babyhood, infancy
babi *nm* baby
bacas (bacs(i)au) *nf* footless
  stocking; hair on horse's fetlocks
baco *nm* tobacco
bacwn *nm* bacon
bach¹(-au) *nm* hook; **bachau
  petryal** square brackets
bach² *adj* little, small
bachell (-au, -ion) *nf* nook, corner;
  snare
bachgen (bechgyn) *nm* boy
bachgendod *nm* boyhood
bachgennaidd *adj* boyish
bachgennyn (bechgynnos) *nm*
  little boy
bachigyn (bachigion) *nm* little bit,
  diminutive
bachog *adj* hooked
bachu *vb* to hook, to grapple
bachwr (-wyr) *nm* hooker *(in rugby)*

bad (-au) *nm* boat; **bad achub**
  lifeboat
badwr (-wyr) *nm* boatman
badd (-au), baddon (-au) *nm* bath
bae (-au) *nm* bay
baedd (-od) *nm* boar
baeddu *vb* to beat, to buffet; to soil
baetio *vb* to bait, to maltreat
bag (-iau) *nm* bag; **bag aer, bag
  awyr** airbag
bagad (-au) *nm* cluster; troop,
  multitude
bagl (-au) *nf* crook; crutch; leg
baglor (-ion) *nf* bachelor
bagloriaeth *nf* bachelorship
baglu *vb* to entangle, to ensnare,
  to trip
bai (beiau) *nm* fault, vice; defect;
  blame
baich (beichiau) *nm* burden, load
bais *nm* bottom, ford; walking
bala *nm* efflux of river from lake
balch *adj* proud; glad; delighted
balchder *nm* pride
balchdra *nm* joy, gladness
balchïo *vb* to pride
baldordd *nm* babble, balderdash
baldorddi *vb* to babble
bale *nm* ballet
baled (-i) *nf* ballad
baledwr (-wyr) *nm* ballad-monger
balm *nm* balm
balmaidd *adj* balmy
balog (-au, -ion) *nf* fly, cod-piece;
  flap
balleg *nf* hamper, net, purse
ballegrwyd (-au) *nf* drag-net
ban (-nau) *nmf* peak; horn; corner;
  stanza
banadl *npl* (*nf*-**hadlen**) broom

banc¹ (-iau) *nm* bank

banc² (bencydd) *nm* bank, mound, hill

bancaw (-iau) *nm* band, tuft

band (-iau) *nm* band; **band eang, band llydan** broadband

baner (-au, -i) *nf* banner, flag

banerog *adj* with banners, bannered

banerwr (-wyr) *nm* standard-bearer; ensign

banffagl (-au) *nf* bonfire, blaze

bangaw *adj* eloquent, melodious, skilful

Bangladesh *nf* Bangladesh

bangor (-au, bangyr) *nfm* upper row of rods in wattle fence; monastery

baniar (-ieri) *nm* shout; banner

banllawr (-lloriau) *nm* platform

banllef (-au) *nf* loud shout

bannod (banodau) *nf* article

bannog *adj* elevated, conspicuous; horned

bar (-rau) *nm* bar

bâr *nm* fury, greed

bara *nm* bread

barbaraidd *adj* barbarous

barbareidd-dra *nm* barbarity

barbareiddio *vb* to barbarize

barbariad (-iaid) *nm* barbarian

barbariaeth *nm* barbarism

barbwr (-wyr) *nm* barber

barcer (-iaid) *nm* tanner

barclod (-iau) *nm* apron

barcud (-iaid), barcutan (-od) *nm* kite

barcut *nm* kite

barcuta *vb* to hang-glide

bardd (beirdd) *nm* bard, poet

barddas *nfm* bardism

barddol *adj* bardic

barddoni *vb* to compose poetry, to poetize

barddoniaeth *nf* poetry, verse

barddonol *adj* poetic, poetical

barf (-au) *nf* beard, whiskers

barfog *adj* bearded

bargeinio, bargenna *vb* to bargain

bargen (-einion) *nf* bargain

bargod (-ion) *nm* eaves

bargyfreithiwr (-wyr) *nm* barrister

bariaeth *nmf* evil, grief, wrath; greed

baril (-au) *nf* barrel

barilaid (-eidiau) *nf* barrelful

bario *vb* to bar, to bolt

barlad *nm* drake

barlys *nm* barley

barn (-au) *nf* judgment; opinion; sentence

barnais *nf* varnish

barnedigaeth (-au) *nf* judgment

barneisio *vb* to varnish

barnol *adj* judicial, condemnatory, annoying

barnu *vb* to judge

barnwr (-wyr) *nm* judge

baromedr *nm* barometer

barrug *nm* hoar-frost

barugo *vb* to cast hoar-frost

barugog *adj* white with hoar-frost

barus *adj* voracious, greedy

barwn (-iaid) *nm* baron

barwnes (-au) *nf* baroness

barwniaeth (-au) *nf* barony

barwnig (-iaid) *nm* baronet

bas¹ *adj* shallow ▸ *npl* (**bais, beis**) shallows
bas² *adj, nm* bass
basged (**-i, -au**) *nf* basket
basgedaid (**-eidiau**) *nf* basketful
basgedwr (**-wyr**) *nm* basket-maker
basil *nm* basil
basn (**-au, -ys**) *nm* basin
bastard (**-iaid**) *nm* bastard
bastardiaeth *nf* bastardy
batio *vb* to bat
batri *nm* battery
bath (**-au**) *nm* kind, sort; stamp; coin
bathdy (**-dai**) *nm* mint
bathodyn (**-nau**) *nm* medal, badge
bathol *adj* coin, coined
bathu *vb* to coin
baw *nm* dirt, mire, dung, filth
bawaidd *adj* dirty, vile; sordid, mean
bawd (**bodiau**) *nf* thumb, toe
bechan *adj f of* **bychan**
bechgynnos *npl* little boys, youngsters
bedw *npl* (*nf* **-en**) birch
bedydd *nm* baptism
bedyddfa (**-fâu, -feydd**) *nf* baptistry
bedyddfaen (**-feini**) *nm* font
bedyddio *vb* to baptize
bedyddiol *adj* baptismal; baptized
Bedyddiwr (**-wyr**) *nm* Baptist
bedd (**-au**) *nm* grave, tomb, sepulchre
beddargraff (**-iadau**) *nm* epitaph
beddfaen (**-feini**) *nm* tombstone
beddgell (**-oedd**) *nf* vault, catacomb

beddrod (**-au**) *nm* tomb, sepulchre
Beibl (**-au**) *nm* Bible
Beiblaidd *adj* Biblical
beic (**-iau**) *nm* bike; **beic modur** motorbike; **beic mynydd** mountain bike
beicio *vb* to cycle
beiciwr, beicwr (**-wyr**) *nm* cyclist; **beiciwr modur** motorcyclist
beichio *vb* to burden; to low; to sob
beichiog *adj* pregnant
beichiogi *vb* to conceive
beichus *adj* burdensome, oppressive
beiddgar *adj* daring, audacious; outrageous
beiddgarwch *nm* daring, audacity
beiddio *vb* to dare, to presume
beili (**beilïaid**) *nm* bailiff
beio *vb* to blame, to censure
beirniad (**-iaid**) *nm* adjudicator; critic
beirniadaeth (**-au**) *nf* adjudication; criticism
beirniadol *adj* critical
beirniadu *vb* to adjudicate; to criticize
beisgawn (**-au**) *nf* stack, heap of corn sheaves
beiston *nf* sea-shore, beach; surf
beius *adj* faulty; blameworthy
bellach *adv* now, at length
bendigaid, bendigedig *adj* blessed
bendigedigrwydd *nm* blessedness
bendith (**-ion**) *nf* blessing, benediction
bendithio *vb* to bless
bendithiol *adj* conferring blessings

benthyca, benthycio *vb* to borrow, to lend
benthyciad *nm* loan
benthyciwr (-wyr) *nm* borrower, lender
benthyg *nm* loan
benyw *adj* female ▸ *nf* (**-od**) female, woman
benywaidd *adj* feminine; effeminate
benywol *adj* feminine, female
ber *adj* f of **byr**
bêr (berau, -i) *nm* spear; roasting-spit
bera *nfm* rick; pyramid
berdys *npl* (*nm* **-yn,** *nf* **-en**) shrimps
berf (-au) *nf* verb; **berf anghyflawn** transitive verb; **berf gyflawn** intransitive verb
berfa (-fâu, -feydd) *nf* barrow
Berlin *nf* Berlin
berth *adj* beautiful, valuable
berthog *adj* wealthy, fair
berw *nm, adj* boiling, seething, ebullition
berwedig *adj* boiling
berwedydd (-ion) *nm* boiler
berwedd-dy (-dai) *nm* brewery
berweddu *vb* to brew
berwi *vb* to boil, to seethe, to effervesce
berwr *coll n* cress
betgwn *nmf* nightgown
betws *nm* oratory, chapel; birch grove
betys *npl* beetroot
beudy (-dai) *nm* cow-house, byre
beunoeth, beunos *adv* nightly, every night

beunydd *adv* daily, every day, always
beunyddiol *adj* daily, quotidian
bidog (-au) *nf* dagger; bayonet
bing (-oedd) *nm* alley, bin
bil (-iau) *nm* bill
bilidowcar *nm* cormorant
bilwg (-ygau) *nm* billhook
bin (-iau) *nm:* **bin sbwriel** litter bin
biocemeg *nfm* biochemistry
bioleg *nf* biology
bir (-oedd) *nm* beer
bisgeden *nf* biscuit, cracker
biswail *nm* dung
blaen *adj* fore, foremost, first; front ▸ *nm* (**-au, -ion**) point, end, top, tip; front, van, priority, precedence; edge
blaenasgellwr (-wyr) *nm* wing-forward
blaenbrawf (-brofion) *nm* foretaste
blaendal *nm* prepayment, deposit
blaendarddu *vb* to sprout
blaendir *nm* foreground
blaenddalen (-nau) *nf* title page
blaenddodi *vb* to prefix
blaenddodiad (-iaid) *nm* prefix
blaenffrwyth *nm* first-fruits
blaengar *adj* prominent, progressive
blaengroen (-grwyn) *nm* foreskin
blaenllaw *adj* forward, prominent
blaenllym *adj* sharp, keen
blaenllymu *adj* sharpen, whet
blaenor (-iaid) *nm* leader; elder
blaenori *vb* to lead, to precede
blaenoriaeth *nf* preference; precedence

blaenorol _adj_ previous, antecedent
blaenu _vb_ to point; to outrun; to precede
blaenwr (-wyr) _nm_ leader; forward
blagur _coll n_ sprouts, buds, shoots
blaguro _vb_ to sprout, to bud; to flourish
blaguryn _nm_ sprout, bud, shoot
blaidd (bleiddiaid, bleiddiau) _nm_ wolf
blas _nm_ taste, savour, relish
blasio, blasu _vb_ to taste
blasus _adj_ tasty, savoury, delicious
blawd (blodion, -iau) _nm_ flour, meal
blêr _adj_ untidy, slovenly
blerwm _nm_ blabberer
blew _npl (nm -yn)_ hairs; hair; fur
blewog _adj_ hairy, shaggy
blewyn _nm_ straw
bliant _nm_ lawn, fine linen
blif (-iau) _nm_ catapult
blingo _vb_ to skin, to flay
blin _adj_ tired, weary; peevish, irritable
blinder (-au) _nm_ weariness; trouble
blinderog, blinderus _adj_ wearisome
blinfyd _nm_ tribulation
blino _vb_ to tire, to weary; to trouble, to vex
blith (-ion) _nm m_ milk ▸ _adj_ milch
blith draphlith _adv_ helter-skelter
bloc (-iau) _nm_: **bloc swyddfeydd** office block
blodeugerdd (-i) _nf_ anthology
blodeuglwm _nm_ bunch, nosegay
blodeuo _vb_ to flower, to bloom, to flourish

blodeuog _adj_ flowery; flourishing
blodeuyn, blodyn (blodau) _nm_ flower
blodfresychen _nf_ cauliflower
blodiog _adj_ floury, mealy
bloddest _nf_ rejoicing, acclamation
bloedd (-iau, -iadau) _nf_ shout
bloeddio, bloeddian _vb_ to shout, to cry
bloeddiwr (-wyr) _nm_ shouter
bloesg _adj_ lisping, faltering, indistinct
bloesgi _vb_ to lisp, to falter, to speak indistinctly
blog (-iau) _nm_ blog
blogio _vb_ to blog
blogiwr (-wyr) _nm_ blogger
blwch (blychau) _nm_ box; **blwch postio** mailbox
blwng _adj_ angry, sullen, cheerless ▸ _nm_ anger
blwydd (-au, -i) _nf, adj_ year of age; year-old
blwydd-dal _nm_ annuity, pension
blwyddiad (-iaid) _nm_ yearling, annual
blwyddiadur (-on) _nm_ yearbook, annual
blwyddyn (blynyddoedd) _nf_ year; **blwyddyn bwlch** gap year
blychaid (-eidiau) _nm_ boxful
blynedd _npl_ years _(after numerals)_
blynyddol _adj_ annual, yearly
blys (-iau) _nm_ craving, lust
blysig _adj_ greedy, lustful
blysigrwydd _nm_ greediness
blysio _vb_ to crave, to lust
bocs (-ys) _nm_ box
bocsach _nm_ vaunt, boast, brag

bocsio *vb* to box
bocsiwr (-wyr) *nm* boxer
boch (-au) *nf* cheek
bochdew *nf* hamster
bochgoch *adj* rosy-cheeked
bod *vb* to be, to exist ▸ *nm* **(-au)** being, existence; **Y Bod Mawr** God
bod(olaeth) *nm(f)* existence
boda *nmf* buzzard
bodio *vb* to thumb, to finger
bodlon *adj* content, willing
bodloni *vb* to satisfy, to content; to be content
bodlonrwydd *nm* contentment
bodoli *vb* to exist
bodd *nm* pleasure, will, consent
boddfa *nf* flood, drenching
boddhad *nm* pleasure, satisfaction
boddhaol *adj* pleasing, satisfactory
boddhau *vb* to please, to satisfy
boddhaus *adj* pleased
boddi *vb* to drown; to flood
boddio *vb* to please, to satisfy
boddlon *see* bodlon
bogail (-eiliau) *nmf* navel; boss, hub
boglwm (boglymau), boglyn (-nau) *nm* boss, knob, stud, bud, bubble
bol, bola (boliau) *nm* belly
bolaid (-eidiau) *nm* bellyful
bolera *vb* to gorge, to guzzle; to sponge
bolerwr (-wyr) *nm* sponge, parasite
bolgi (-gwn) *nm* gourmand, glutton
bolheulo *vb* to bask in the sun
bolio *vb* to belly, to gorge

boliog *adj* big-bellied, corpulent
boloch *nm* pain, anxiety, destruction
bolrwth *adj* gluttonous, greedy
bolrwym *adj* costive, constipated
bolsothach, bolysothach *nm* hotchpotch; jargon
bolwst *nfm* gripes, colic
bollt (-au, -ydd, byllt) *nf* bolt
bom (-iau) *nmf* bomb
bomio *vb* to bomb
bomiwr (-wyr) *nm* bomber; **bomiwr hunanleiddiol** suicide bomber
bôn (bonau, bonion) *nm* bottom; stump; **yn y bôn** basically
boncath (-od) *nm* buzzard
bonclust (-iau) *nm* box on the ear
boncyff (-ion) *nm* stump, trunk, stock
bondigrybwyll *adv* forsooth ▸ *adj* hardly mentionable
bondo *nm* eaves
bonedd *nm* gentility, nobility
boneddigaidd *adj* noble; gentlemanly
boneddigeiddrwydd *nm* gentlemanliness
boneddiges (-au) *nf* lady
bonesig *nf* lady; Miss
bonet (-i) *nf* bonnet
bonheddig *adj* noble, gentle, gentlemanly
bonheddwr (-wyr) *nm* gentleman
bonllef (-au) *nf* shout
bonllwm *adj* bare-bottomed; bare-backed
Bonn *nf* Bonn
bonyn (bonion) *nm* stump

bord (-ydd, -au) nf table, board
bordhwylio vb to windsurf
bore (-au) nm morning ▸ adj early
boreddydd nm day-break, morning
borefwyd nm breakfast
boreol adj morning
bors nf hernia
bos nf palm of the hand, fist
Bosnia nf Bosnia
bost (-iau) nm boast, brag
bostio vb to boast, to brag
botas, en (-asau) nf boot
botwm (-ymau) nm button
botymog adj buttoned
botymu vb to button
both (-au) nf nave of wheel; boss
bowlio vb to bowl
brac adj free, frank, talkative
bracso vb to wade, to paddle
bracty (-tai) nm malt-house,
brewery
brad (-au) nm treason; plot
bradfwriadu vb to plot, to conspire
bradlofrudd (-ion) nm assassin
bradlofruddiaeth (-au) nf
assassination
bradlofruddio vb to assassinate
bradwr (-wyr) nm traitor
bradwriaeth (-au) nf treason,
treachery
bradwrus adj traitorous,
treacherous
bradychu vb to betray
braen adj rotten, corrupt
braenar (-au) nm fallow
braenaru vb to fallow, to pioneer
braenu vb to rot, to putrify
braf adj fine
brag nm malt

bragad nf army, battle; offspring
bragaldian vb to jabber, to gabble,
to prate
bragio vb to brag, to boast
bragiwr (-wyr) nm bragger,
boaster
bragu vb to malt, to brew
bragwair nm moorland hay, coarse
grass
bragwr (-wyr) nm maltster, brewer
braich (breichiau) nf arm; branch,
handle; headland
braidd adv rather, somewhat
braint (breintiau) nf privilege
braisg adj gross, thick, large;
pregnant
braith adj f of brith
brân (brain) nf crow, rook, raven
bras (breision) adj fat; coarse; rich;
luxuriant
brasáu vb to grow fat or gross
brasbwytho vb to baste, to tack
brasgamu vb to stride
Brasil nf Brazil
braslun (-iau) nm sketch, outline
braslun bywyd nm curriculum
vitae
braslunio vb to sketch, to outline
brasnaddu vb to rough-hew
braster nm fat
brasterog adj fat, greasy
brat (-iau) nm rag, clout; pinafore
bratiaith nf debased language
bratiog adj ragged, tattered
brath (-au) nm stab, wound;
sting; bite
brathog adj that bites; biting
brathu vb to stab, to wound; to
sting; to bite

brau *adj* brittle, frail, fragile; kindly; prompt

braw (-iau) *nm* terror, dread, fright

brawd¹ (brodyr) *nm* brother; friar; **brawd yng nghyfraith** brother-in-law

brawd² (brodiau) *nf* judgment

brawdgarwch *nm* brotherly love

brawdmaeth *nm* foster-brother

brawdol *adj* brotherly, fraternal

brawdoliaeth (-au) *nf* brotherhood, fraternity

brawddeg (-au) *nf* sentence

brawddegu *vb* to construct sentences

brawl *nm* boast, brag; gabble, tattle

brawychu *vb* to frighten, to terrify

brawychus *adj* frightful, terrible

brawychwr *nm* terrorist

bre (-on, -oedd) *nf* hill, highland

brebwl (-yliaid) *nm* blockhead; prattler

brêc *nm* brake

breci *nm* wort; spree

brecio *vb* to brake

brecwast (-au) *nmf* breakfast

brecwasta *vb* to breakfast

brech¹ *nf* eruption, pox; **brech yr ieir** chickenpox

brech² *adj f of* **brych**

brechdan (-au) *nf* slice of bread and butter

brechiad (-au) *nm* inoculation, vaccination

brechu *vb* to vaccinate, to inoculate

bredych (-au, -ion) *nm* betrayal; fear; rascal

bref (-iadau) *nf* lowing; bleat; bray

breferad (-au) *nm* bellowing

brefiad (-au) *nm* lowing; bleating

brefu *vb* to low; to bleat; to bray

breg *nm* guile, blemish, breach
▸ *adj* fragile, faulty

bregliach *vb* to jabber

bregus *adj* frail, brittle, rickety

breichled (-au) *nf* bracelet

breichrwy, breichrwyf (-au) *nmf* bracelet

breindal *nm* royalty

breinio *vb* to privilege, to enfranchise

breiniol *adj* privileged, free

breinlen (-ni) *nf* charter

breintal *nm* bonus; royalty

breintiedig *adj* patented, patent

breintio *vb* to privilege, to favour

brenhinaidd *adj* kingly, regal

brenhindod *nm* royalty

brenhindref (-i) *nf* royal city

brenhindy (-dai) *nm* royal palace

brenhines (breninesau) *nf* queen

brenhinfainc *nf* throne

brenhiniaeth (breniniaethau) *nf* kingdom

brenhinllys *nm* basil

brenhinol *adj* royal, regal

brenin (-hinoedd) *nm* king

brest (-iau) *nf* breast, chest

bresych *npl (nf -en)* cabbages

brethyn (-nau) *nm* cloth

brethynnwr (-ynwyr) *nm* clothier; cloth-worker

breuan (-au) *nf* quern; print of butter

breuder *nm* brittleness, frailty

breuddwyd (-ion) *nmf* dream; **breuddwyd gwrach** wishful thinking

breuddwydio *vb* to dream

breuddwydiol *adj* dreaming, dreamy

breuddwydiwr (-wyr) *nm* dreamer

brëyr, brehyr (brehyrion, -iaid) *nm* nobleman, chief, baron

bri *nm* honour, renown, distinction

briallu *npl* (*nf* **briallen**) primroses

bribys *npl* fragments, scraps

bricsen *nf* brick

bricyllen *nf* apricot

brid *nm* breed

bridio *vb* to breed

brifo *vb* to hurt

brig (-au) *nm* top; (*pl*) twigs

brigâd (-au) *nf* brigade; **brigâd dân** fire-brigade

briger (-au) *nm* hair of head; top

brigo *vb* to top; to branch

brigog *adj* branching; flourishing

brigwyn *adj* white-topped, white-crested

brigyn (brigau) *nm* twig

brith (f braith) *adj* mottled, speckled

britho *vb* to mottle, to speckle; to dazzle

Brithwr (-wyr) *nm* Pict

brithyll (-od, -iaid) *nm* trout

briw *adj* broken, bruised, sore ► *nm* (**-iau**) wound, sore

briwfwyd *nm* crumbs, mince

briwgig *nm* mince

briwlaw *nm* drizzling rain

briwlio *vb* to broil

briwo *vb* to wound, to hurt

briwsion *npl* (*nm* **-yn**) crumbs, fragments

briwsioni *vb* to crumble

briwsionyn *nm* crumb

briwsyn (briwsion) *nm* crumb, morsel

bro (-ydd) *nf* land; region; vale

broch¹ *nm* badger

broch² *nm* froth, anger, tumult

brochi *vb* to chafe, to fume; to bluster

brochus *adj* fuming; blustering

brodio *vb* to embroider; to darn

brodor (-ion) *nm* native; fellow countryman

brodorol *adj* native, indigenous

broga (-od) *nm* frog

brol *nf* boast, brag

broliant *nm* blurb

brolio *vb* to boast, to brag, to vaunt

broliwr (-wyr) *nm* boaster, braggart

bron¹ (-nau, -nydd) *nf* breast; hillside

bron² *adv* almost, nearly, practically; **o'r bron** completely, in succession

bronfraith (-freithod) *nf* thrush

brongoch (-iaid) *nmf* robin redbreast

bronwen *nf* weasel

bru *nm* womb

brud (-iau) *nm* chronicle; divination

brudio *vb* to prognosticate, to divine

brudiwr (-wyr) *nm* wizard, soothsayer

brwd *adj* hot, fervent ► *nm* boil, heat

brwdfrydedd *nm* ardour, enthusiasm

brwdfrydig *adj* ardent, enthusiastic

brwmstan *nm* brimstone, sulphur

brwmstanaidd *adj* sulphury

brwnt (*f* **bront**) *adj* foul, nasty, dirty; harsh

brwyd¹ (**-au**) *nm* embroidering frame; skewer

brwyd² *adj* variegated; bloodstained; shattered

brwydo *vb* to embroider; to tear, to consume

brwydr (**-au**) *nf* battle, combat

brwydro *vb* to battle, to combat

brwydrwr (**-wyr**) *nm* fighter, combatant

brwydwaith *nm* embroidery

brwylio *vb* to broil

brwyn *nm* grief, sadness

brwynen (**brwyn**) *nf* rush

brwynog *adj* rushy

brwysg *adj* drunk; vigorous

brycan, brecan (**-au**) *nfm* blanket, rug

brych (*f* **brech**) *adj* mottled, brindled, freckled ▸ *nm* the after-birth of a cow

brychau *npl* (*nm* **-euyn**) spots, freckles

brycheulyd *adj* spotted, brindled

brycheuyn *nm* spot

brychni *nm* spots, freckles

brychu *vb* to spot, to freckle

bryd *nm* mind, heart, will

brydio *vb* to burn, to inflame, to boil, to throb

brygawthan *vb* to jabber, to prate, to rant

bryn (**-iau**) *nm* hill

bryncyn (**-nau**) *nm* hillock

bryniog *adj* hilly

brynti, bryntni *nm* filthiness, filth

brys *nm* haste, hurry

brysio *vb* to hasten, to hurry

brysiog *adj* hurried, hasty

bryslythyr (**-au**) *nm* dispatch

brysneges (**-au**) *nf* telegram

brytheirio *vb* to belch; to utter oaths, threats *etc*

Brython (**-iaid**) *nm* Briton, Welshman

Brythoneg *nf* British language, Welsh

brythwch *nm* storm, tumult; groan

bryweddu *vb* to brew

brywes *nm* brewis

bual (**buail**) *nm* buffalo, drinking horn

buan *adj* fast, quick, swift, fleet; soon

buander, buandra *nm* swiftness, speed

buandroed *adj* swift-footed

buarth (**-au**) *nm* yard

buchdraeth (**-au**) *nf* biography, memoir

buchedd (**-au**) *nf* life, conduct

bucheddol *adj* right-living, virtuous

bucheddu *vb* to live, to flourish

buches (**-au**) *nf* herd of cows

buchfrechu *vb* to vaccinate

budr *adj* dirty, filthy, foul, vile

budreddi *nm* filthiness, filth

budro vb to dirty, to soil, to foul
budd (-ion) nm benefit, profit, gain
buddai (-eiau) nf churn
buddel (-wydd) nmf cow-house post, pillar
buddiant (-iannau) nm interest
buddio vb to profit, to avail
buddiol adj profitable, beneficial, useful
buddioldeb nm profitableness, expediency
buddran nf dividend
buddsodd (-ion), buddsoddiad (-au) nm investment
buddsoddi vb to invest
buddugol adj winning, victorious
buddugoliaeth (-au) nf victory
buddugoliaethus adj victorious, triumphant
buddugwr (-wyr) nm winner, victor
bugail (-eiliaid) nm shepherd; pastor
bugeiles (-au) nf shepherdess
bugeiliaeth (-au) nf pastorate
bugeilio, bugeilia vb to watch, to shepherd
bugeiliol adj pastoral
bugunad nm bellowing, roar
bun nf maid, maiden
burgyn (-nod, iaid) nm carcass, carrion
burman, burum nm barm, yeast
busnes (-ion) nmf business
busnesa vb to interfere, to meddle
busnesgar, busneslyd adj meddlesome
bustach (-tych) nm bullock, steer

bustachu vb to buffet about, to bungle
bustl nm gall, bile
bustlaidd adj like gall; bitter as gall
buwch (buchod) nf cow; **buwch goch gota** ladybird
bwa (bwâu) nm bow; arch
bwaog adj arched, vaulted
bwbach (-od) nm bugbear, bogey, scarecrow
bwced (-i) nmf bucket
bwci (-ïod) nm bugbear, bogey, ghost
bwcl (byclau) nm buckle
bwcled (-au) nf buckler
bwch (bychod) nm buck; **bwch dihangol** scapegoat; **bwch gafr** he-goat
Bwdhaeth nf Buddhism
Bwdhaidd adj Buddhist
bwgan (-od) nm bogey, ghost, scarecrow
bwgwl (bygylau) nm threat, menace
bwgwth see bygwth, bygythio
bwhwman vb to beat about; to vacillate
bŵl (bylau) nm globe, ball, knob
bwlch (bylchau) nm gap; pass; notch
bwled (-i) nf bullet
Bwlgaria nf Bulgaria
bwn (bynnoedd, byniaid) nm bittern
bwndel (-i) nm bundle
bwngler (-iaid) nm bungler
bwnglera vb to bungle
bwngleraidd adj bungling, clumsy
bwnglerwaith nm bungle, botch

bwnglerwch nm clumsiness
bwr (byr) adj fat, big, strong
bwrdais (-deisiaid) nm burgess
bwrdeistref (-i) nf borough
bwrdd (byrddau) nm table; deck; board; **bwrdd du** black-board
bwrgler nm burglar
bwrglera vb to burgle
bwrgleriaeth nf burglary
bwriad (-au) nm purpose, intention
bwriadol adj intentional
bwriadu vb to purpose, to intend
bwrlwm (byrlymau) nm bubble; gurgling
bwrn (byrnau) nm burden, incubus; bale
bwrw vb to cast, to shed; to strike; to imagine, to suppose; to spend ▸ nm cast, throw; woof
bws (bysiau, bysys) nm bus; **bws mini** minibus
bwtler (-iaid) nm butler
bwtri nm buttery, pantry, dairy
bwth (bythod) nm hut, booth, cot
bwthyn (bythynnod) nm cottage, cabin, hut
bwyall (bwyeill), bwyell (bwyeill) nf axe
bwyd (-ydd) nm food; **bwyd sothach** junk food; **bwyd sydyn** fast food
bwyda, bwydo vb to feed
bwydlen nf menu
bwyd-offrwm (-ymau) nm meat-offering
bwydwr (-wyr) nm feeder
bwygilydd adv (from one) to the other
bwylltid (-au) nm swivel

bwyllwr, bwyllwrw (-yriau) nm provisions for journey
bwysel (-au, -i) nm bushel
bwystfil (-od) nm (wild) beast
bwystfilaidd adj brutal
bwystfiles (-au) nf beast
bwyta vb to eat; to corrode
bwytadwy adj eatable, edible
bwytäwr (-wyr) nm eater
bwyteig adj greedy, voracious
bwyty (-tai, -tyau) nm restaurant
bychan (f bechan) adj little, small
bychander, bychandra nm littleness, smallness
bychanu vb to belittle, to minimize
bychanus adj derogatory
byd (-oedd) nm world; state; life
bydaf (-au) nmf beehive
byd-eang adj worldwide
bydio vb to live, to fare
bydol adj worldly, secular
bydolddyn (-ion) nm worldling
bydolrwydd nm worldliness
bydwraig (-wragedd) nf midwife
bydwreigiaeth nf midwifery
bydysawd nm universe
byddag (-au) nf running knot, noose
byddar adj deaf ▸ nm (-iaid, byddair) deaf person
byddardod nm deafness
byddarol adj deafening
byddaru vb to deafen, to stun
byddin (-oedd) nf army, host
byddino vb to set army in array, to embattle
byddinog adj with armies

bygwth *vb* to threaten, to menace
▸ *nm* (**-ythion, -ythiau**) threat,
menace
bygythiad (**-au**) *nm* threat;
bygythiad bom bomb scare
bygythio *vb* to threaten, to
menace
bygythiol *adj* threatening,
menacing
byl (**-au**) *nfm* edge, brim (of vessel);
hyd y fyl to the brim
bylb (**-au**) *nm* bulb
bylchog *adj* gapped, gappy;
notched
bylchu *vb* to make a gap, to breach;
to notch
byngalo (**-s, -au**) *nm* bungalow
bynnag *pron* -ever, -soever
bynsen *nf* bun
byr (*f* **ber**) *adj* short, brief
byrbryd (**-iau**) *nm* luncheon, snack
byrbwyll *adj* impulsive, rash
byrbwylltra *nm* impulsiveness
byrder, byrdra *nm* shortness,
brevity
byrdwn *nm* burden, refrain, chorus
byrddaid (**-eidiau**) *nm* tableful
byrddio *vb* to board
byrddiwr (**-wyr**) *nm* boarder
byrfodd *nm* abbreviation
byrfyfyr *adj* impromptu
byrgorn *adj* shorthorn
byrgyr *nm* burger
byrhau *vb* to shorten, to abridge
byrhoedlog *adj* short-lived
byrlymu *vb* to bubble, to gurgle
byrllysg (**-au**) *nmf* mace

byrnio (**-u**) *vb* to bale, to bundle
byrnwr (**-wyr**) *nm* baler
byrstio *vb* to burst
bys (**-edd**) *nm* finger; toe; hand of
dial, latch
bysaid (**-eidiau**) *nm* pinch
byseddu *vb* to finger
bysled, bysledr (**-au**) *nm* finger-
stall
byth *adv* ever, for ever ▸ *nm*
eternity
bytheiad (**-aid**) *nm* hound
bytheirio *vb* to belch, to threaten
bythgofiadwy *adj* memorable
bythol *adj* everlasting, eternal,
perpetual
bytholi *vb* to perpetuate
bytholwyrdd (**-ion**) *adj, nm*
evergreen
bythynnwr (**-ynwyr**) *nm* cottager
byw *vb* to live ▸ *adj* alive, living,
quick ▸ *nm* life
bywgraffiad (**-au**) *nm* biography
bywgraffiadol *adj* biographical
bywgraffiadur (**-on**) *nm*
biographical dictionary
bywgraffydd (**-ion**) *nm* biographer
bywgraffyddol *adj* biographical
bywhau, bywiocáu *vb* to animate,
to vivify, to quicken
bywiad *nm see* bywad
bywiog *adj* lively, animated,
vivacious
bywiogi *vb* to enliven, to animate
bywiol *adj* living, animate
bywoliaeth (**-oliaethau**) *nf* living
bywyd (**-au**) *nm* life

bywydeg *nf* biology
bywydegwr (-wyr) *nm* biologist
bywydfad (-au) *nm* lifeboat
bywydol *adj* of life, vital
bywyn (-nau) *nm* pith, core

C

cabaets *npl* (*nf* **cabaetsen**)
  cabbage
caban (-au) *nm* cabin
cabidwl *nm* consistory, chapter
cabl (-au) *nm* blasphemy, reviling
cabledd (-au) *nm* blasphemy
cableddus *adj* blasphemous
cablu *vb* to blaspheme, to revile
cablwr (-wyr), cablydd (-ion) *nm*
  blasphemer
caboli *vb* to polish
cacamwci *nm* burdock
cacen (-nau, -ni) *nf* cake
cacwn *npl* (*nf* **cacynen**) wasps;
  wild bees
cachfa (-feydd) *nf* excretion;
  closet
cachgi (-gwn) *nm* coward; sneak
cachiad *nm* excretion; jiffy; coward
cachlyd *adj* befouled, dirty
cachu *vb* to defecate
cachwr (-wyr) *nm* coward; sneak;
  one who excretes

cad (-au, -oedd) *nf* battle; army, host

cadach (-au) *nm* cloth, kerchief, clout

cadair (-eiriau) *nf* chair, seat; cradle; udder

cadarn (cedyrn) *adj* strong, mighty; firm

cadarnhad *nm* affirmation, confirmation

cadarnhaol *adj* affirmative

cadarnhau *vb* to strengthen, to confirm

cadeirfardd (-feirdd) *nm* chaired bard

cadeirio *vb* to chair

cadeiriog *adj* chaired

cadeiriol *adj* pertaining to a chair, cathedral

cadeirydd (-ion) *nm* chairman

cadernid *nm* strength; stability

cadfarch (-feirch) *nm* war-horse

cadfridog (-ion) *nm* general

cadfwyall (-eill, -yll) *nf* battle-axe

cadlas (-lesydd) *nf* close, enclosure

cadlong (-au) *nf* warship, battleship

cadlys (-oedd) *nf* camp, headquarters

cadno (cadnoid, cadnawon) *nm* fox

cadnöes, cadnawes (-au) *nf* vixen

cadoediad (-au) *nm* armistice, truce

cadofydd (-ion) *nm* tactician, strategist

cadofyddiaeth *nf* tactics, strategy

cadofyddol *adj* tactical, strategic

cadw *vb* to keep, to preserve, to save; to hold; **cadw'n heini** to keep fit

cadwedig *adj* saved

cadwedigaeth *nf* salvation

cadw-mi-gei *nm* money-box

cadwraeth *nf* keeping; observance; conservation

cadwyn (-au, -i) *nf* chain

cadwyno *vb* to chain

cadwynog *adj* chained, in chains

caddug *nm* darkness; mist, fog

caddugo *vb* to darken, to obscure

cae (-au) *nm* field; fence, hedge; brooch

caead (-au) *nm* cover, lid ▸ *adj* shut, closed

caeadle (-oedd) *nm* enclosure

caeedig *adj* closed, fenced

cael *vb* to have; to get; to find

caen (-au) *nf* surface; peel; coating

caenen (-nau) *nf* layer, film, flake

caentach (-au) *nf* wrangle, grumbling ▸ *vb* to wrangle, to grumble

caenu *vb* to coat, to finish

caer (-au, ceyrydd) *nf* wall; castle; city

Caerdydd *nf* Cardiff

Caeredin *nf* Edinburgh

caeriwrch *nm* roebuck

caerog *adj* walled, fortified; brocaded

Caersalem *nf* Jerusalem

caeth *adj* bound, captive, confined ▸ *nm* **(-ion)** bondman, slave; **caeth i gyffuriau** addicted to drugs

caethder *nm* strictness; restraint; asthma

caethfab (-feibion) *nm* slave
caethfasnach *nf* slave-trade
caethferch (-ed) *nf* slave
caethforwyn (-forynion) *nf* slave
caethglud *nf* captivity
caethgludiad (-au) *nm* captivity
caethgludo *vb* to lead captive
caethiwed *nm* slavery, bondage, captivity, detention
caethiwo *vb* to bind, to confine, to enslave
caethiwus *adj* confining; confined, tied
caethlong (-au) *nf* slave-ship
caethwas (-weision) *nm* slave
caethwasanaeth, caethwasiaeth *nm* slavery
cafell (-au) *nf* cell; sanctuary, oracle
cafn (-au) *nm* trough, gutter
cafnedd *nm* concavity
cafnio, cafnu *vb* to hollow out, to scoop, to gouge
cafod *see* cawod
caffael *vb* to get, to obtain
caffaeledd *nm* availability; acquisitiveness
caffaeliad (-au) *nm* acquisition, asset; prey, spoil
caffe (-s), caffi (-s) *nm* café, restaurant; **caffe rhyngrwyd** internet café, cybercafé
caffio *vb* to snatch, to grapple
cafflo *vb* to cheat; to entangle
cagl *nm* clotted dirt
caglu *vb* to befoul, to bedraggle
cangell (-hellau) *nf* chancel
cangelloriaeth *nf* chancellorship
cangen (-hennau) *nf* branch, bough

canghellor (cangellorion) *nm* chancellor
canghennog *adj* branching
canghennu *vb* to branch, to ramify
caib (ceibiau) *nf* pickaxe, mattock
cail (ceiliau) *nf* sheepfold, flock of sheep
caill (ceilliau) *nf* testicle
cain *adj* fair, fine, elegant
cainc (cangau, ceinciau) *nf* branch; strand; strain
cais (ceisiadau) *nm* application; attempt; try
cal, cala (-iau) *nf* penis
calan (-nau) *nm* first day of month; **Dydd Calan** New Year's Day
calcwlws (calcwli) *nm* calculus
calch *nm* lime
calchaidd *adj* calcareous
calchbibonwy *nm* stalactite
calchbost (-byst) *nm* stalagmite
calchen *nf* limestone; lump of lime
calchfaen (-feini) *nm* limestone
calcho, calchu *vb* to lime
caled *adj* hard; severe; harsh; dry
caledfwrdd *nm* hardboard
caledi *nm* hardness; hardship
caledu *vb* to harden, to dry
caledwch *nm* hardness
calen (-nau, -ni) *nf* whetstone; bar
calendr *nm* calendar
calennig *nmf* New Year's gift
calon (-nau) *nf* heart
calondid *nm* encouragement
calon-dyner *adj* tender-hearted
calon-galed *adj* hard-hearted
calon-galedwch *nm* hard-heartedness
calonnog *adj* hearty; high-spirited

calonogi *vb* to hearten, to encourage
calori (**-ïau**) *nm* calorie
calsiwm *nm* calcium
call *adj* wise, sensible, rational
callestr (**cellystr**) *nf* flint
callineb *nm* wisdom, sense
cam¹ (**-au**) *nm* step
cam² *adj* crooked, wry; wrong
  ▸ *nm* (**-au**) injury, wrong
cam- *prefix* wrong, mis-
camarfer *vb* to misuse, to abuse
  ▸ *nmf* (**-ion**) misuse, malpractice
camargraff *nfm* wrong impression
camarwain *vb* to mislead
camarweiniol *adj* misleading
Cambodia *nf* Cambodia
cambren (**-ni**) *nm* swingletree
camchwarae *nm* foul play
camdafliad (**-au**) *nm* foul throw
camdaflu *vb* to foul throw
camder, camdra *nm* crookedness
cam-drefn *nf* disorder
camdreuliad *nm* indigestion
camdreulio *vb* to mis-spend
cam-drin *vb* to ill-treat, to abuse
camdriniaeth (**-au**) *nf* ill-treatment
camdystiolaeth (**-au**) *nf* false witness
camdystiolaethu *vb* to bear false witness
camddeall *vb* to misunderstand
camddealltwriaeth *nm* misunderstanding
camddefnydd *nm* misuse
camddefnyddio *vb* to misuse

camedd *nm* bend, curvature; **camedd y droed** instep; **camedd y gar** knee-joint
cameg (**-au, cemyg**) *nf* felloe
camel (**-od**) *nm* camel
camenw (**-au**) *nm* misnomer
camenwi *vb* to misname
camera (**camerâu**) *nm* camera; **camera digidol** digital camera; **camera fideo** video camera
camfa (**-feydd**) *nf* stile
camfarnu *vb* to misjudge
camgred (**-oau, -au**) *nf* misbelief, heresy
camgredu *vb* to misbelieve
camgredwr (**-wyr**) *nm* heretic
camgwl *nm* penalty, fine; blame
camgyfrif *vb* to miscalculate
camgyhuddiad (**-au**) *nm* false accusation
camgyhuddo *vb* to accuse falsely
camgymeriad (**-au**) *nm* mistake
camgymryd *vb* to mistake, to err
camlas (**-lesi, -lesydd**) *nfm* canal
camliwio *vb* to misrepresent
camochri *vb* to be offside
camog (**-au**) *nf* felloe
camp (**-au**) *nf* feat, exploit; game; prize
campfa (**-feydd**) *nf* gymnasium
campus *adj* excellent, splendid, grand
campwaith (**-weithiau**) *nm* masterpiece, feat
campwr (**-wyr**) *nm* champion
camre *nm* walk, footstep(s)
camsyniad (**-au**) *nm* mistake
camsynied *vb* to mistake
camsyniol *adj* mistaken

camu¹ *vb* to bow, to bend, to stoop
camu² *vb* to step, to stride
camwedd (-au) *nm* iniquity, transgression
camweddu *vb* to transgress
camwri *nm* injury, wrong
camymddwyn *vb* to misbehave
camymddygiad (-au) *nm* misconduct
can *adj* white ▶ *nm* flour
cân (caniadau, caneuon) *nf* song
canabis *nm* cannabis
Canada *nf* Canada
cancr *nm* canker; cancer
cancro *vb* to canker, to corrode
candryll *adj* shattered, wrecked
canfasio *vb* to canvass
canfed *adj* hundredth
canfod *vb* to see, to perceive, to behold
canfyddadwy *adj* perceptible
canfyddiad *nm* perception
canhwyllbren (canwyllbrenni, -au) *nmf* candlestick
canhwyllwr (canhwyllwyr) *nm* chandler
caniad¹ *nm* singing; ringing; crowing
caniad² (-au) *nf* song, poem
caniadaeth *nf* singing, psalmody
caniatâd *nm* leave, permission, consent
caniataol *adj* permissive; granted
caniatáu *vb* to permit, to allow
caniedydd (-ion) *nm* singer, songster; song-book
canlyn *vb* to follow, to pursue
canlyniad (-au) *nm* consequence, result

canlynol *adj* following, consequent
canlynwr (-wyr) *nm* follower
canllaw (-iau) *nfm* hand-rail, parapet, aid
canmlwyddiant *nm* centenary
canmol *vb* to praise, to commend
canmoladwy *adj* praiseworthy
canmoliaeth (-au) *nf* praise, commendation
canmoliaethus *adj* eulogistic, complimentary
cannaid *adj* white, bright, luminous
cannu *vb* to whiten, to bleach
cannwr (canwyr) *nm* bleacher
cannwyll (canhwyllau) *nf* candle
canol *adj, nm* (**-au**) middle, centre, midst; **canol y ddinas** city centre
canolbarth (-au) *nm* middle part, midland
canolbwynt (-iau) *nm* centre, focus
canolbwyntio *vb* to centre, to concentrate
canoldir (-oedd) *nm* inland region
canolddydd *nm* mid-day, noon
canolfan (-nau) *nmf* centre; **canolfan chwaraeon** sports centre; **canolfan galwadau** call centre; **canolfan iechyd** health centre; **canolfan ymwelwyr** visitor centre
canoli *vb* to centre; to arbitrate; to centralize
canolig *adj* middling
canoloesol *adj* mediaeval
canolog *adj* central
canolradd (-ol) *adj* intermediate

canolwr (-wyr) *nm* mediator, referee; centre half, centre; **canolwr blaen** centre forward
canon¹ (-au) *nfm* canon *(music)*
canon² (-iaid) *nm* canon *(priest)*
canonaidd *adj* canonical
canoneiddio *vb* to canonize
canoniaeth (-au) *nf* canonry
canonwr (-wyr) *nm* canon, canonist
canradd (-au) *adj, nf* centigrade, percentile
canran (-nau) *nm* percentage
canrif (-oedd) *nf* century
cansen (-ni) *nf* cane
canser *nm* cancer
canslo *vb* to cancel
cant¹ (-au) *nm* circle, ring, rim; tyre
cant² (cannoedd) *nm* hundred
cantel (-au) *nm* rim, brim
cantîn (cantinoedd) *nf* canteen
cantor (-ion) *nm* singer
cantores (-au) *nf* songstress, singer
cantref (-i, -ydd) *nm* hundred
cantwr (-orion) *nm* singer, songster
cantwraig *nf* songstress, singer
canu *vb* to sing, to chant; to play; to crow; to ring ▶ *nm*, **canu gwlad** country music
canŵ (-od) *nm* canoe
canŵa *vb* to canoe, to go canoeing ▶ *nm* canoeing
canŵo *vb* to canoe
canwr (-wyr) *nm* singer
canwriad (-iaid) *nm* centurion
canwyr (-au, -ion) *nm* plane *(in carpentry)*

canys *conj* because, for
cap (-iau) *nm* cap
capan (-au) *nm* cap; lintel
capel (-i, -ydd, -au) *nm* chapel
capelwr (-wyr) *nm* chapel-goer
caplan (-iaid) *nm* chaplain
caplaniaeth (-au) *nf* chaplaincy
capteiniaeth *nf* captaincy
capten (-einiaid) *nm* captain
car (ceir) *nm* car; **car campau** sports car; **car cefn codi** hatchback; **car llog** hire car
câr (ceraint) *nm* friend; relation
carafán (-nau) *nf* caravan
carbohydrad (-au) *nm* carbohydrate
carbon (-au) *adj, nm* carbon
carbwl *adj* clumsy, awkward
carco *vb* to take care
carcus *adj* solicitous, anxious, careful
carchar (-au) *nm* prison; restraint
carchardy (-dai) *nm* prison-house
carchariad *nm* imprisonment
carcharor (-ion) *nm* prisoner
carcharu *vb* to imprison
carden (cardiau) *nf* card
cardigan (-au) *nf* cardigan
cardod (-au) *nf* charity, alms, dole
cardota *vb* to beg
cardotyn (-wyr) *nm* beggar
cardydwyn, cardodwyn *nm* weakest of brood or litter
caredig *adj* kind
caredigrwydd *nm* kindness
caregog *adj* stony
caregu *vb* to stone; to petrify; to gather stones
carennydd *nm* friendship; kinship

caretsen (**carets**) *nf* carrot
carfaglog *adj* clumsy
carfan (**-au**) *nf* beam; swath; party, faction
cariad¹ (**-au**) *nm* love
cariad² (**-au, -on**) *nm* lover, sweetheart
cariadfab *nm* lover, sweetheart
cariadferch *nf* sweetheart, mistress
cariadlawn *adj* full of love, loving
cariadus *adj* loving, beloved, dear
caridým (**-s**) *nm* ragamuffin
cario *vb* to carry, to bear
carismatig *adj* charismatic
cariwr *nm* carrier; **y Cariwr Dŵr** Aquarius
carlam (**-au**) *nm* prance, gallop
carlamu *vb* to prance, to gallop
carlwm (**-lymod**) *nm* ermine, stoat
carn¹ (**-au**) *nm* hoof; hilt, haft, handle
carn² (**-au**), **carnedd** (**-au**) *nf* cairn
cárnifal *nm* carnival
carniforus *adj* carnivorous
carnog, carnol *adj* hoofed
carol (**-au**) *nmf* carol
carp (**-iau**) *nm* clout, rag
carped (**-au, -i**) *nm* carpet
carpiog *adj* ragged, tattered
carrai (**careiau**) *nf* lace, thong
carreg (**cerrig**) *nf* stone
cart (**ceirt**) *nmf* cart
cartaid, certaid (**-eidiau**) *nm* cartful
cartilag (**-au**) *nm* cartilage
cartref (**-i, -ydd**) *nm* home, abode ▸ *adj* home-made; **cartref henoed**

old people's home; **cartref symudol** mobile home
cartrefle (**-oedd**) *nm* abode
cartreflu *nm* militia
cartrefol *adj* homely, domestic, home; civil
cartrefu *vb* to make one's home, to settle
cartŵn (**cartwnau**) *nm* cartoon
cartwnydd (**-ion**) *nm* cartoonist
carth (**-ion**) *nm* tow, oakum; off-scouring
carthen (**-ni, -nau**) *nf* Welsh blanket, coverlet; **carthen blu** duvet
carthffos (**-ydd**) *nf* sewer
carthffosiaeth *nf* sewerage
carthu *vb* to cleanse, to purge, to scavenge
caru *vb* to love; to like; to court
caruaidd *adj* loving, kind
carw (**ceirw**) *nm* stag, deer
carwden (**-ni**) *nf* back-chain; tall awkward fellow
carwr (**-wyr**) *nm* lover, wooer
carwriaeth (**-au**) *nf* courtship
cas¹ *adj* hateful, odious; nasty, disagreeable ▸ *nm* hatred, aversion
cas² (**caseion**) *nm* hater, foe, enemy
casáu *vb* to hate, to detest, to abhor
casbeth (**-au**) *nm* aversion, nuisance
caseg (**cesig**) *nf* mare
casét (**-iau**) *nm* cassette
casgen (**-ni, casgiau**) *nf* cask
casgl *nfm* collection

casgliad (**-au**) *nm* collection; gathering
casglu *vb* to collect, to gather; to infer
casglwr (**-wyr**), **casglydd** (**-ion**) *nm* collector
casineb *nm* hatred
cast (**-iau**) *nm* vice, knack
castan (**-au**) *nf* chestnut
castanwydd *npl* (*nf*-**en**) chestnut-trees
castell (**cestyll**) *nm* castle
castellog *adj* castled, castellated
castellu *vb* to castle, to encamp
castio *vb* to trick, to cheat; to cast, to calculate
castiog *adj* full of tricks, tricky
casul (**-(i)au**) *nmf* cassock
caswir *nm* unpalatable truth
casyn (**casiau**) *nm* case, casing
cat (**-iau**) *nm* bit, piece, fragment; pipe
catalog (**-au**) *nm* catalogue
catalogio *vb* to catalogue
catalydd (**-ion**) *nm* catalyst
categori (**-ïau**) *nm* category
catel *coll n* chattels; cattle
catgor (**-(i)au**) *nm* ember day(s)
catrawd (**-rodau**) *nf* regiment
cath (**-od, -au**) *nf* cat
cathl (**-au**) *nf* melody, hymn, lay
cathlu *vb* to sing, to hymn
cathod (**-au**) *nf* cathode
catholig *adj* catholic
Catholigiaeth *nf* Catholicism
catholigrwydd *nm* catholicity
cau[1] *adj* hollow, concave
cau[2] *vb* to shut, to close, to enclose

caul (**ceulion**) *nm* maw; rennet; curd
caw (**-(i)au**) *nm* band, swaddling-clothes
cawdel *nm* hotchpotch, mess
cawell (**cewyll**) *nm* hamper, basket, cradle
cawellwr (**-wyr**) *nm* basket-maker
cawg (**-iau**) *nm* basin, bowl, pitcher
cawl *nm* broth, soup; hotchpotch
cawn *npl* (*nf*-**en**) reeds
cawod (**-ydd**) *nf* shower
cawodi *vb* to shower
cawodog *adj* showery
cawr (**cewri**) *nm* giant
cawraidd *adj* gigantic
cawres (**-au**) *nf* giantess
caws *nm* cheese; curd
cawsai, cawsi *nmf* causeway
cawsaidd *adj* cheesy, caseous
cawsellt (**-ydd, -i, -au**) *nm* cheese-vat
cawsio *vb* to curd, to curdle
cawsiog *adj* curdled
CC *adv* BC
CD (**-s, -au**) *nm* CD
cecian *vb* to stammer
cecren (**-nod**) *nf* shrew, scold, cantankerous woman
cecru *vb* to wrangle, to bicker
cecrus *adj* cantankerous, quarrelsome
cecryn (**-nod**) *nm* wrangler, brawler
cedor *nmf* pubic hair
cedrwydd *npl* (*nf*-**en**) cedars
cefn (**-au**) *nm* back; support
cefndedyn *nm* mesentery; diaphragm, pancreas

cefnder (-dyr) *nm* first cousin
cefndir (-oedd) *nm* background
cefnen (-nau) *nf* ridge
cefnfor (-oedd) *nm* main sea, ocean
cefngrwm *adj* hump-backed
cefnog *adj* well-off, well-to-do
cefnogaeth *nf* encouragement, support
cefnogi *vb* to encourage, to support
cefnogol *adj* encouraging
cefnu *vb* to back, to turn the back, to forsake
cefnwlad (-wledydd) *nf* hinterland
cefnwr (-wyr) *nm* back, full-back
ceffyl (-au) *nm* horse
ceg (-au) *nf* mouth
cega *vb* to mouth, to prate
cegaid (-eidiau) *nf* mouthful
cegen (-nau) *nf* gullet, windpipe
cegid, cegiden (cegidau) *nf* green woodpecker, jay
cegin (-au) *nf* kitchen
cegrwth *adj* gaping
cegyr *npl* hemlock
cengl (-au) *nf* band; girth; hank
cenglu *vb* to hank; to girth; to wind
cei (-au) *nm* quay
ceibio *vb* to pick with pickaxe
ceidwad (-aid) *nm* keeper, saviour
ceidwadaeth *nf* conservatism; conservancy
ceidwadol *adj* conservative
Ceidwadwr (-wyr) *nm* Conservative
ceiliagwydd (-au) *nm* gander
ceiliog (-od) *nm* cock; **ceiliog rhedyn** grasshopper

ceinach (-od) *nf* hare
ceincio *vb* to branch out, to ramify
ceinciog *adj* branched, branching
ceinder *nm* elegance, beauty
ceiniog (-au) *nf* penny
ceiniogwerth (-au, -i) *nf* pennyworth
ceinion *npl* beauties, gems
ceintach *vb* to grumble, to croak
ceintachlyd *adj* querulous
ceintachwr (-wyr) *nm* grumbler, croaker
ceirch (nf-en) *coll n* oats
ceirios *npl (nf-en)* cherries
ceisbwl (-byliaid) *nm* catchpole, bailiff
ceisio *vb* to seek; to ask; to try, to attempt, to endeavour; to fetch, to get
cêl *adj* hidden, concealed ▸ *nm* concealment ▸ *npl* kale
celain (celanedd) *nf* dead body
celanedd *coll n* carnage, slaughter
celc *nfm* concealment; hoard
celf (-au) *nf* art, craft
celfi *npl (nm -cyn)* tools, gear; furniture
celfydd *adj* skilled, skilful
celfyddgar *adj* ingenious; artistic
celfyddwr (-wyr) *nm* artificer, artist
celfyddyd (-au) *nf* art, craft; skill; **celfyddydau graffig** graphic arts
celfyddydol *adj* relating to art/ the Arts
celu *vb* to hide, to conceal
celwrn (-yrnau) *nm* tub, bucket, pail

celwydd (-au) *nm* lie, falsehood, untruth

celwyddgi *nm* liar

celwyddog *adj* lying, mendacious; false

celwyddwr (-wyr) *nm* liar

celyn *npl* (*nf*-**nen**) holly

cell (-oedd, -au) *nf* cell, chamber; **celloedd cenhedlu** germ cells; **enyniad y celloedd** cellulitis

celli (celïau, -ïoedd) *nf* grove

cellog *adj* cellular

cellwair *vb* to jest, to trifle ▶ *nm* fun

cellweiriwr (-wyr) *nm* jester, trifler

cellweirus *adj* playful, jocular

cemeg *nm* chemistry

cemegol *adj* chemical

cemegwr (-wyr), cemegydd (-ion) *nm* chemist

cemegyn (cemegau) *nm* chemical

cen *coll n* skin, peel, scales, scurf, film, lichen

cenadwri *nf* message

cenau (cenawon) *nm* cub, whelp; rascal

cenedl (-hedloedd) *nf* nation; gender

cenedlaethol *adj* national

cenedlaetholdeb *nm* nationalism

cenedlaetholi *vb* to nationalize

cenedlaetholwr (-wyr) *nm* nationalist

cenedl-ddyn (-ion) *nm* gentile

cenedligrwydd *nm* nationality

cenfaint (-feiniau) *nf* herd

cenfigen (-nau) *nf* envy, jealousy

cenfigennu *vb* to envy

cenfigennus, cenfigenllyd *adj* envious, jealous

cenhadaeth (cenadaethau) *nf* mission

cenhadol *adj* missionary

cenhadu *vb* to permit; to propagate, to conduct a mission

cenhadwr (-hadon) *nm* missionary

cenhedlaeth (cenedlaethau) *nf* generation

cenhedlig *adj* gentile, pagan

cenhedlu *vb* to beget, to generate

Cenia *nf* Kenya

cenllif *nm* flood, torrent, deluge

cenllysg *coll n* hailstones, hail

cennad (-hadau, -hadon) *nf* leave; messenger

cennin *npl* (*nf*-**hinen**) leeks

cennog *adj* scaly, scurfy

cennu *vb* to scale, to scurf

centimedr (-au) *nm* centimetre

cêr *nf* gear, tools, trappings

cerameg *nmf* ceramics

ceramig *adj* ceramic

cerbyd (-au) *nm* chariot, coach, car

cerbydwr (-wyr) *nm* coachman

cerdyn (cardiau) *nm* card; **cerdyn adnabod** identity card; **cerdyn cof** memory card; **cerdyn crafu** scratch card; **cerdyn credyd** credit card; **cerdyn debyd** debit card; **cerdyn sweip** swipe card

cerdd (-i) *nf* song, poem; music, poetry

cerddbrenni *npl* woodwinds

cerddbresi *npl* brass section (orchestra)

cerdded *vb* to walk; to go; to travel

cerddediad

cerddediad *nm* walking, going; pace
cerddgar *adj* harmonious, musical
cerddin, cerdin *npl* (*nf* **-en**) rowan
cerddor (**-ion**) *nm* singer, musician
cerddorfa (**-feydd**) *nf* orchestra
cerddorfaol *adj* orchestral
cerddoriaeth *nf* music
cerddorol *adj* musical
cerddwr (**-wyr**) *nm* walker
cerfddelw (**-au**) *nf* graven image, statue
cerfio *vb* to carve
cerflun (**-iau**) *nm* statue; engraving
cerfluniaeth *nf* sculpture
cerflunydd (**-lunwyr**) *nm* sculptor
cerfwaith *nm* carving, sculpture
cern (**-au**) *nf* cheek, jaw
cernod (**-iau**) *nf* buffet
cernodio *vb* to buffet, to clout
Cernyw *nm* Cornwall
cerpyn (**carpiau**) *nm* clout, rag
cerrynt *nmf* course, road; current
cert (**-i**) *nf* cart
certiwr (**-wyr**) *nm* carter
certh *adj* right; awful
cerub, ceriwb (**-iaid**) *nm* cherub
cerwyn (**-i**) *nf* tub; vat; winepress
cerydd (**-on**) *nm* correction, chastisement; rebuke, reproof, censure
ceryddol *adj* chastising, chastening
ceryddu *vb* to correct, to chastise; to rebuke
ceryddwr (**-wyr**) *nm* chastiser; rebuker
cesail (**-eiliau**) *nf* arm-pit; bosom
cesair *npl*, *coll n* hailstones, hail

cest (**-au**) *nf* belly, paunch
cestog *adj* corpulent
cetyn (**catiau**) *nm* piece, bit; pipe
cethin *adj* dark, fierce, ugly
ceubren (**-nau**) *nm* hollow tree
ceubwll (**-byllau**) *nm* pit
ceudod *nm* cavity; abdomen; thought, heart
ceudwll *nm* cavern
ceufad *nm* canoe
ceuffordd (**-ffyrdd**) *nf* tunnel
ceuffos (**-ydd**) *nf* drain, ditch
ceugrwm *adj* concave
ceulan (**-nau, -lennydd**) *nf* bank, brink
ceulo *vb* to curdle, to coagulate
ceunant (**-nentydd**) *nm* ravine, gorge
cewyn (**-nau, cawiau**) *nm* napkin
ci (**cŵn**) *nm* dog, hound
ciaidd *adj* dog-like; brutal
cib (**-au**) *nm* pod, husk
cibddall *adj* purblind
cibo *vb* to frown, to scowl
cibog *adj* scowling
cibws, cibwst *nf* kibes, chilblains
cibwts (**-au**) *nm* kibbutz
cibyn (**-nau**) *nm* shell; husk; half a bushel
cic (**-iau**) *nfm* kick; **cic gychwyn** kick-off
cicio *vb* to kick
ciciwr (**-wyr**) *nm* kicker
cidwm (**-ymiaid, -ymod**) *nm* wolf; rascal
cieidd-dra *nm* brutality
cig (**-oedd**) *nm* flesh, meat
cigfran (**-frain**) *nf* raven

cignoeth *adj* touching to the quick, caustic

cigog *adj* fleshy

cigwain (-weiniau) *nf* flesh-hook

cigydd (-ion) *nm* butcher

cigyddiaeth *nf* butchery

cigysol *adj* carnivorous

cigysydd (-ion) *nm* carnivore

cil (-iau, -ion) *nm* back; retreat; corner

cilagor *vb* to open partly

cilagored *adj* ajar

cilbost (cilbyst) *nm* gate-post

cilchwyrn *npl* (*nf* **-en**) glands

cildrem (-iau) *nf* leer

cildremio *vb* to leer

cildroi *vb* to reverse

cildwrn *nm* tip, bribe

cildyn *adj* obstinate, stubborn

cildynnu *vb* to be obstinate

cildynnus *adj* obstinate, stubborn

cildynrwydd *nm* obstinacy

cilddant (-ddannedd) *nm* molar

cilfach (-au) *nf* nook; creek, bay

cilfilyn (-filod) *nm* ruminant

cilgant *nm* crescent

cilgnoi *vb* to chew the cud, to ruminate

cilgwthio *vb* to push, to shove, to jostle

cilgynnyrch (-gynhyrchion) *nm* by-product

cilio *vb* to retreat, to recede, to swerve

cilo *nm* kilo

cilocalori (-ïau) *nm* kilocalorie

cilogram (-au) *nm* kilogram

cilomedr (-au) *nm* kilometre

cilowat *nm* kilowatt

cilwen (-au) *nf* half smile

cilwenu *vb* to simper, to smile, to leer

cilwg (-ygon) *nm* frown, scowl

cilydd (-ion) *nm* fellow, companion

cilyddol *adj* reciprocal

cimwch (-ychiaid) *nm* lobster

ciniawa *vb* to dine

cinio (ciniawau) *nm* dinner; **cinio gwadd** dinner party

cip (-ion) *nm* pluck, snatch; glimpse

cipdrem (-iau) *nfm* glance, glimpse

cipedrych *vb* to glance, to glimpse

cipio *vb* to snatch

cipiwr (-wyr) *nm* snatcher

cipolwg *nmf* glance, glimpse

ciprys *nm* scramble

cis (-iau) *nmf* buffet; slap, touch

cist (-iau) *nf* chest, coffer, box; bin

ciw (-iau) *nm* cue, queue

ciwb *nm* cube

ciwed *coll n* rabble, mob, crew

ciwrad (-iaid) *nm* curate

ciwt *adj* cute, clever, ingenious

claddedigaeth (-au) *nmf* burial

claddfa (-feydd) *nf* burial-ground, cemetery

claddgell *nf* vault

claddu *vb* to bury

claear *adj* lukewarm, tepid; mild; cool

claearineb *nm* lukewarmness

claearu *vb* to make mild *or* tepid; to soothe

claer *adj* clear, bright, shining

claerder *nm* clearness, brightness

claf (cleifion) *adj* sick, ill ▸ *nm* sick person, patient

clafdy (-dai) *nm* hospital, infirmary

clafr *nm* itch, mange
clafrllyd *adj* mangy
clafychu *vb* to sicken, to fall ill
clai (cleiau) *nm* clay
clais (cleisiau) *nm* stripe; bruise
clamp (-iau) *nm* mass, lump; monster
clap (-iau) *nm* lump
clapgi (-gwn) *nm* telltale
clapio *vb* to lump; to strike; to gossip
clapiog *adj* lumpy
clas *nm* monastic community, cloister, college
clasur (-on) *nm* classic
clasurol *adj* classical
clau *adj* quick, swift, soon; true; audible
clawdd (cloddiau) *nm* hedge; dyke, embankment
clawr (cloriau) *nm* face, surface; cover, lid; board
clebar, cleber *nmf* idle talk, gossip, tattle
clebran *vb* to chatter, to gossip, to tattle
clec (-iau, -s) *nf* click; clack; crack; gossip
cleci (-cwn) *nm* telltale
clecian *vb* to click; to clack; to crack, to snap
cledr (-au) *nf* pole; rail; palm (of hand)
cledren (-nau, -ni) *nf* pale, pole, rail
cleddyf, cleddau, cledd (cleddyfau) *nm* sword; brace
cleddyfwr (-wyr) *nm* swordsman
clefyd (-au) *nm* disease; fever; **clefyd melys** diabetes; **clefyd**

y galon heart disease; **clefyd y gwair** hay fever
clegar *vb* to clack, to cluck, to cackle
clegyr, clegr *nm* rock; cairn, stony place
cleiog *adj* clayey
cleiriach *nm* decrepit one
cleisio *vb* to bruise
cleisiog *adj* bruised
clem (-iau) *nf* notion, idea; look, gaze ▸ *pl* grimaces
clep (-iau) *nf* clack, clap; gossip
clepgi (-gwn) *nm* babbler; telltale
clepian *vb* to clap; to slam; to blab
clêr[1] *coll n* itinerant minstrels; bards
clêr[2] *npl* (*nf* **cleren**) flies
clera *vb* to stroll as minstrels
clerc (-od) *nm* clerk
clercio *vb* to serve as clerk
cleren *nf* fly
clerigol *adj* clerical
clerigwr (-wyr) *nm* clergyman
clerwr (-wyr) *nm* itinerant minstrel
clerwriaeth *nf* minstrelsy
clewt (-iau) *nm* clout
clewtian *vb* to clout
clic (cliciau) *nm* clique
clicied (-au) *nf* clicker; trigger
cliciedu *vb* to latch, to fasten
clicio *vb* to click; **clicio dwywaith** double-click
clindarddach *vb* to crackle ▸ *nm* crackling
clinig (-au) *nm* clinic
clir *adj* clear
clirio *vb* to clear
clo (cloeau, cloeon) *nm* lock, conclusion

cloben nf monster
clobyn nm monster
cloc (-iau) nm clock; **cloc larwm** alarm clock
clocian vb to cluck
clocsiau npl (nf **clocsen**) clog
cloch (clych, clychau) nf bell; **o'r/ar gloch** o'clock
clochaidd adj sonorous, noisy
clochdar vb to cluck, to cackle
clochdy (-dai) nm belfry, steeple
clochydd (-ion) nm bell-man; sexton
clod (-ydd) nmf praise, fame, renown
clodfori vb to praise, to extol
clodwiw adj commendable, praiseworthy
cloddfa (-feydd) nf quarry, mine
cloddio vb to dig, to delve; to quarry, to mine
cloddiwr (-wyr) nm digger, navvy
cloëdig adj locked, closed
cloer (-(i)au) nmf locker; niche; pigeon-hole
cloff adj lame
cloffi vb to lame, to halt ▸ nm lameness
cloffni nm lameness
cloffrwym (-au) nm fetter, hobble; **cloffrwym y cythraul, cloffrwym y mwci** great bindweed
clog¹ (-au) nmf cloak
clog² (-au) nf rock, precipice
clogfaen (-feini) nm boulder
clogwyn (-i) nm cliff, crag, precipice
clogwynog adj craggy, precipitous
clogyn (-nau) nm cloak, cape

clogyrnaidd adj rough, rugged, clumsy
cloi vb to lock
clonc nf clank; gossip ▸ adj addled
clopa (-âu) nmf noddle; knob; club
cloren (-nau) nf rump, tail
clorian (-nau) nmf pair of scales
cloriannu vb to weigh, to balance
clorin nm chlorine
clorinio, clorinadu vb to chlorinate
clos¹ (-ydd) nm yard
clos² (closau) nm pair of breeches
clòs adj close
closio vb to close, to near
cludadwy adj portable
cludair (-eiriau) nf heap, load, wood-pile
cludiad nm carriage
cludiant (-nnau) nm transport, haulage
cludo vb to carry, to convey
cludwr (-wyr), cludydd (-ion) nm porter
clul (-iau) nm knell
clun (-iau) nf hip, haunch, thigh, leg; moor
cluro vb to rub, to smear
clust (-iau) nfm ear; handle
clustfeinio vb to prick up the ears; to eavesdrop
clustfys nm little finger
clustffôn (-ffonau) nm earphone
clustlws (-lysau) nm earring
clustnod (-au) nm earmark
clustog (-au) nfm cushion, pillow
clwb (clybiau) nm club
clwc adj addled
clwcian vb to cluck

clwm (clymau) nm knot, tie
clwpa (-od) nm knob, boss; club; dolt
clws (f clos) adj pretty, nice
clwstwr (clystyrau) nm cluster
clwt (clytiau) nm patch, clout, rag
clwyd (-au, -i, -ydd) nf hurdle; gate; roost
clwydo vb to roost
clwyf (-au) nm wound; disease
clwyfo vb to wound
clwyfus adj wounded; sore; sick
clybodeg nf acoustics
clybodig adj acoustic
clyd adj warm, sheltered, snug, cosy
clydwch, clydwr nm warmth, shelter
clyfar adj clever; pleasant, agreeable
clymblaid (-bleidiau) nf clique, cabal
clymog adj knotty, entangled
clymu vb to knot, to tie
clytio vb to patch, to piece
clytiog adj patched; ragged
clytwaith (-weithiau) nm patchwork
clyw nm sense of hearing
clywadwy adj audible
clywed vb to hear; to feel; to taste; to smell
clywedigaeth nf hearing
clywedol adj aural
clywedydd (-ion) nm hearer, auditor
clyweled adj audio-visual
clywelediad nm audition
cnaf (-on, -iaid) nm knave, rascal

cnafaidd adj knavish, rascally
cnaif (cneifion) nm shearing, fleece
cnap (-iau) nm lump, knob, boss
cnapan (-au) nm ball, bowl, kind of ball game
cnapiog adj lumpy
cnau npl (nf cneuen) nuts
cnawd nm flesh
cnawdol adj carnal, fleshly, fleshy
cneifio vb to shear, to fleece
cneifiwr (-wyr) nm shearer
cneua vb to nut
cneuen (cnau) nf nut
cnewyllyn (cnewyll) nm kernel, nucleus
cnith (-iau, -ion) nm slight touch, blow; pluck
cno nm bite, chewing, gnawing
cnoc (-iau) nmf knock
cnocio vb to knock
cnofa (-feydd) nf gnawing, pang
cnofil (-od) nm rodent
cnoi vb to gnaw, to chew, to bite; to ache
cnot (-iau) nm knot, bunch
cnu (-au), cnuf (-iau) nm fleece
cnud (-oedd) nf pack
cnùl, cnul (-iau) nm knell
cnwc nm knob
cnwd (cnydau) nm crop; covering
cnydfawr adj fruitful, productive
cnydio vb to crop, to yield increase
cnydiog adj fruitful, productive
cob (cobau) nf coat, cloak, robe
còb (-iau) nm embankment; miser; wag; cob
coban (-au) nf: **coban nos** nightshirt

coblyn (-nod) nm sprite, goblin, imp

cocos¹ npl cogs; **olwyn gocos** cog-wheel

cocos², cocs npl (nf **cocsen**) cockles

coch adj, nm red

coch-gam nf robin

cochi¹ vb to redden, to blush

cochi², cochder nm redness

cochl (-au) nmf mantle, cloak

cod (-au) nf bag, pouch

codaid (-eidiau) nf bagful

codi vb to rise, to get up; to raise, to lift; to erect

codiad (-au) nm rise, rising; erection

codog adj baggy ▸ nmf (-ion) rich man; miser

codwm (codymau) nm fall, tumble

codwr (-wyr) nm riser; raiser; lifter; **codwr canu** precentor

codymu vb to wrestle

codymwr (-wyr) nm wrestler

codded nm anger; grief

coddi vb to anger, to offend

coed (-ydd) coll n wood, timber, trees

coeden (coed) nf tree

coedio vb to timber

coediog adj wooded, woody

coedwig (-oedd) nf wood, forest

coedwigaeth nf forestry

coedwigo vb to forest

coedwigwr (-wyr) nm woodman, forester

coedd adj public

coeg adj empty, vain; one-eyed; blind

coegddyn (-ion) nm fop, coxcomb, fool

coegedd nm emptiness, silliness

coegen (-nod) nf minx, coquette

coegennaidd adj coquettish

coegfalch adj vain, foppish

coegi vb to jeer at, to mock

coeglyd adj vain, sarcastic

coegni nm vanity; spite; sarcasm

coegwr (-wyr) nm fool

coegwych adj gaudy, garish, tawdry

coegyn (-nod) nm coxcomb

coel (-ion) nf belief, trust, credit

coelbren (-nau, -ni) nm lot

coelcerth (-i) nf bonfire, blaze

coelgrefydd (-au) nf superstition

coelgrefyddol adj superstitious

coelio vb to believe, to credit, to trust

coes (-au) nf leg, shank ▸ nfm handle; stem, stalk

coetgae nm hedge; enclosure

coetmon (-myn) nm lumberjack

coetref nf woodland, homestead

coets nm pushchair

coeth adj fine, refined; elegant

coethder nm refinement, elegance

coethi vb to refine; to chastise; to babble

coethwr (-wyr) nm refiner

cof (-ion) nm memory; remembrance

cofadail (-eiladau) nf monument

cofbin (-nau) nm memory stick, pen drive

cofeb (-ion) nf memorandum; memorial

cof-gerdyn (**cof-gardiau**) *nm* memory card
cofgolofn (**-au**) *nf* monument
cofiadur (**-on, -iaid**) *nm* recorder
cofiadwy *adj* memorable
cofiannydd (**-anyddion**) *nm* biographer
cofiant (**-iannau**) *nm* memoir, biography
cofio *vb* to remember, to recollect
cofl (**-au**) *nf* embrace; bosom
coflaid (**-eidiau**) *nf* armful; bundle
coflech (**-au**) *nf* memorial tablet
cofleidio *vb* to embrace, to hug
coflyfr (**-au**) *nm* record, chronicle
cofnod (**-ion**) *nm* memorandum, minute
cofnodi *vb* to record, to register
cofrestr (**-au**) *nf* register, roll
cofrestrfa *nf* registry
cofrestru *vb* to register
cofrestrydd (**-ion**) *nm* registrar
cofrodd *nf* souvenir
cofus *adj* mindful
cofweini *vb* to prompt
cofweinydd (**-ion**) *nm* prompter
coffa *vb* to remember ▶ *nm* remembrance
coffâd *nm* remembrance
coffadwriaeth *nf* remembrance, memory
coffadwriaethol *adj* memorial
coffáu *vb* to remember; to remind; to commemorate
coffi *nm* coffee
coffr (**-au**) *nm* coffer, trunk, chest
cog¹ (**-au**) *nf* cuckoo
cog² (**-au**) *nm* cook
coginiaeth *nf* cookery

coginio *vb* to cook
cogio *vb* to cog; to sham, to feign, to pretend
cogiwr (**-wyr**) *nm* pretender, swindler
cogor *vb* to chatter, to caw, to croak ▶ *nm* chattering
cogwrn (**-yrnau, cegyrn**) *nm* knob, cone; cock (of corn); shell
cogydd (**-ion**) *nm* cook
cogyddes (**-au**) *nf* cook
cogyddiaeth *nf* cookery
congl (**-au**) *nf* corner
col (**-ion**) *nm* awn, beard
côl *nf* bosom, embrace
coladu *vb* to collate
coledd, coleddu *vb* to cherish, to foster
coleddwr (**-wyr**) *nm* cherisher, fosterer, patron, supporter
coleg (**-au**) *nm* college; **coleg chweched dosbarth** sixth-form college; **coleg technoleg dinasol** city technology college
colegol *adj* collegiate
colegwr (**-wyr**) *nm* collegian
coler (**-i**) *nfm* collar
colfen (**-nau, -ni**) *nf* bough, branch; tree
colofn (**-au**) *nf* column, pillar
colofnydd *nm* columnist
colomen (**-nod**) *nf* dove, pigeon
colomendy (**-dai**) *nm* dove-cot
colomennaidd *adj* dove-like
coluddion *npl* (*nm* **-yn**) bowels
coluddyn *nm* gut
colur (**-au**) *nm* make-up, colour
coluro *vb* to make-up, to paint; to conceal

colwyn (-od) *nm* puppy
colyn (-nau) *nm* pivot; sting; tail
colynnog *adj* stinging; hinged
colynnu *vb* to sting
coll (-iadau) *nm* loss; failing, defect
colladwy *adj* perishable
collddail *adj* deciduous
colled (-ion) *nfm* loss
colledig *adj* lost, damned
colledigaeth *nf* perdition
colledu *vb* to occasion loss
colledus *adj* fraught with loss
colledwr (-wyr) *nm* loser
collen (cyll) *nf* hazel
collfarn (-au) *nf* doom,
  condemnation
collfarnu *vb* to condemn
colli *vb* to lose; to be lost, to perish;
  to spill, to shed
collnod (-au) *nm* apostrophe
collwr (-wyr) *nm* loser
coma (-s) *nm* comma
côma (comâu) *nm* coma
comed (-au) *nf* comet
comedi (-ïau) *nfm* comedy
comig *adj* comic, comical ▸ *nm*
  comic (paper)
comin *nm* common
comisiwn (-iynau) *nm* commission
comisiynu *vb* to commission
comiwnydd (-ion) *nm* communist
comiwnyddiaeth *nf* communism
comiwnyddol *adj* communist
conach *vb* to grumble
conclaf *nm* conclave
concro *vb* to conquer
concwerwr (-wyr) *nm* conqueror
concwest (-au) *nf* conquest,
  victory

condemniad *nm* condemnation
condemnio *vb* to condemn
confensiwn (-iynau) *nm*
  convention
conffederasiwn (-asiynau) *nm*
  confederation
conffirmasiwn *nm* confirmation
conffirmio *vb* to confirm
conifferaidd *adj* coniferous
cono *nm* rascal; wag; old fogey
consesiwn (-iynau) *nm* concession
consol (-au) *nm*: **consol gêmau**
  games console
consuriaeth *nf* conjuring
consurio *vb* to conjure
consuriwr (-wyr) *nm* conjurer
conwydd *npl (nf* **-en)** coniferous
  trees
cop, copyn (-nod, -nau) *nm* spider
copa (-âu) *nf* top, crest; head
copi (-ïau) *nm* copy; copy-book
copïo *vb* to copy, to transcribe
copïwr (-wyr) *nm* copyist,
  transcriber
copr *nm* copper
cor (-rod) *nm* dwarf *(offensive)*;
  spider
côr (corau) *nm* choir; stall, pew;
  côr-feistr choirmaster
corachaidd *adj* dwarfish, stunted
Corân *nm* Koran
corawl *adj* choral
corbwll (-byllau) *nm* whirlpool;
  puddle
corcyn (cyrc) *nm* cork
cord (-iau) *nm* cord; chord
cordeddu *vb* to twist, to twine
corddi *vb* to churn; to turn; to
  agitate

corddiad (-au) *nm* churning
corddwr (-wyr) *nm* churner
Corea *nf* Korea
cored (-au) *nf* weir, dam
coreograffiaeth *nf* choreography
corfan (-nau) *nm* metrical foot
corff (cyrff) *nm* body
corfflu (-oedd) *nm* corps
corffol *adj* corpulent; physical
corffolaeth *nf* bodily form; stature
corfforaeth (-au) *nf* corporation
corffori *vb* to embody, to
  incorporate
corfforiad (-au) *nm* embodiment
corfforol *adj* bodily, corporeal,
  corporal
corgan (-au), **côr-gân** (côr-ganau)
  nf chant
corganu *vb* to chant
corgi (-gwn) *nm* cur, corgi
corgimwch (-ychiaid) *nm* prawn
corhwyad (-aid) *nf* teal; moorhen
corlan (-nau) *nf* fold
corlannu *vb* to fold
corn (cyrn) *nm* horn; pipe, tube;
  roll; corn; stethoscope; **corn
  gwddw(f), corn gwynt** windpipe;
  corn siarad loudspeaker
cornant (-nentydd) *nm* brook, rill
cornboer *nm* phlegm
cornchwiglen (-chwiglod) *nf*
  lapwing
cornel (-i, -au) *nfm* corner
cornelu *vb* to corner
cornicyll (-od) *nm* lapwing, plover,
  peewit
cornio *vb* to horn, to butt; to
  examine with a stethoscope
corniog *adj* horned

cornwyd (-ydd) *nm* boil, abscess,
  sore
coron (-au) *nf* crown
coroni *vb* to crown ▸ *nm*
  coronation
coroniad *nm* coronation
coronog *adj* crowned
corrach (corachod) *nm* dwarf,
  pygmy
corryn (corynnod) *nm* spider
cors (-ydd) *nf* bog, swamp
corsen (-nau, cyrs) *nf* reed; stem,
  stalk; cane
cortyn (-nau) *nm* cord, rope
corun (-au) *nm* crown of the head;
  tonsure
corwg, corwgl (-yg(l)au) *nm*
  coracle
corws *nm* chorus
corwynt (-oedd) *nm* whirlwind
cosb (-au) *nf* punishment,
  penalty; **cosb ddihenydd** capital
  punishment
cosbadwy *adj* punishable
cosbedigaeth *nf* punishment
cosbi *vb* to punish
cosbol *adj* punitive, penal
cosbwr (-wyr) *nm* punisher
cosfa (-feydd) *nf* itch, itching;
  thrashing
cosi *vb* to scratch, to itch ▸ *nm*
  itching
cosmetigau *npl* cosmetics
cosmig *adj* cosmic
Cosofo *nf* Kosovo
cost (-au) *nf* cost, expense
costiad (-au) *nm* costing
costio *vb* to cost
costiwm (-tiymau) *nmf* costume

costog (-ion) nm mastiff; cur ▸ adj surly

costowci (-cwn) nm mastiff, mongrel

costrel (-au, -i) nf bottle

costrelaid (-eidiau) nf bottleful

costrelu vb to bottle

costus adj costly, expensive

cosyn (-nau, -nod) nm a cheese

côt, cot (cotiau) nf coat

cotwm nm cotton

Coweit nf Kuwait

cownter (-au, -i) nm counter

cowntio vb to count, to account, to esteem

crac (-iau) nm crack

cracio vb to crack

craciog adj cracked

crach npl scabs ▸ adj scabby; petty

crachach npl snobs

crachboer nm phlegm

crachen nf scab

crachfardd (-feirdd) nm poetaster

crachfeddyg (-on) nm quack doctor

crachfonheddwr (-wyr) nm snob

crafangio, crafangu vb to claw, to grab

crafanc (-angau) nf claw; talon; clutch

crafellu vb to grate

crafiad (-au) nm scratch

crafog adj cutting, sarcastic

crafu vb to scrape; to scratch ▸ nm itch

crafwr (-wyr) nm scraper

craff adj close; keen; sagacious ▸ nm hold, grip

craffter nm keenness, sagacity

craffu vb to look closely, to observe intently

craffus adj keen, sagacious

cragen (cregyn) nf shell

crai adj new, fresh, raw

craidd (creiddiau) nm middle, centre

craig (creigiau) nf rock

crair (creiriau) nm relic

craith (creithiau) nf scar

cramen (-nau) nf crust, scab

cramwythen nf pancake

cranc (-od) nm crab; **y Cranc** Cancer

crand adj grand

crandrwydd nm grandeur, finery

crap (-iau) nm hold; smattering

crapio vb to grapple; to pick up

cras (creision) adj parched, dry; harsh

crasiad nm baking

craslyd adj harsh, grating

craster nm dryness; harshness

crasu vb to parch, to scorch; to bake

crau¹ (creuau) nm hole, eye, socket

crau² nmf blood, gore

crau³ (creuau) nm sty; stockade

crawcian, crawcio vb to croak, to caw

crawen (-nau) nf crust

crawn nm matter, pus

crawni vb to gather, to suppurate

crawnllyd adj purulent

cread nm creation

creadigaeth (-au) nf creation

creadigol adj creative

creadur (-iaid) nm creature; animal

creadures (-au) nf female creature

creawdwr (-wyr) nm creator

crebach *adj* shrunk, withered
crebachlyd *adj* crabbed, wrinkled
crebachu *vb* to shrink, to shrivel, to wrinkle, to pucker
crebwyll (-ion) *nm* invention, understanding, fancy
crecian *vb* to cluck; to crackle
crechwen *nf* loud laughter, guffaw
crechwenu *vb* to laugh loud, to guffaw
cred (-au) *nf* belief; trust; pledge, troth
credadun (credinwyr) *nm* believer
credadwy *adj* credible
crediniaeth *nf* belief
crediniol *adj* believing
credo (-au) *nmf* creed, belief
credu *vb* to believe
credwr (-wyr) *nm* believer
credyd (-on) *nm* credit
credydu *vb* to credit
cref *adj f of* **cryf**
crefu *vb* to crave, to beg, to implore
crefydd (-au) *nf* religion
crefydda *vb* to profess *or* practise religion
crefyddol *adj* religious, pious
crefyddolder *nm* religiousness, piety
crefyddwr (-wyr) *nm* religionist
crefft (-au) *nf* handicraft, trade; **crefftau'r cartref** DIY, do-it-yourself
crefftus *adj* skilled, workmanlike
crefftwaith *nm* craftwork
crefftwr (-wyr) *nm* craftsman
cregyn *npl* (*nf* **cragen**) shells
creider *nm* freshness
creifion *npl* scrapings

creigiog *adj* rocky
creigiwr (-wyr) *nm* quarryman
creigle (-oedd) *nm* rocky place
creinio *vb* to wallow, to lie *or* fall down; to cringe
creision *npl* flakes, crisps
creithio *vb* to scar
crempog (-au) *nf* pancake
crensio *vb* to grind (the teeth)
crepach *adj* numb ▸ *nf* numbness
crest *nm* crust, scurf
Creta *nf* Crete
creu *vb* to create
creulon *adj* cruel
creulondeb (-derau) *nm* cruelty
crëwr (crewyr) *nm* creator
crëyr (crehyrod) *nm* heron
cri[1] (-au) *nm* cry, clamour
cri[2] *adj* new, fresh, raw; unleavened
criafol, criafolen *nf* mountain ash
crib (-au) *nfm* comb, crest; ridge
cribddeilio *vb* to grab, to extort
cribddeiliwr (-wyr) *nm* extortioner; speculator
cribin (-iau) *nfm* rake; skinflint
cribinio *vb* to rake
cribo *vb* to comb; to card
criced *nm* cricket
cricedwr (-wyr) *nm* cricketer
cricsyn *nm* cricket
crimog (-au) *nf* shin
crimp (-(i)au) *nm* shin
crin *adj* withered, sear, dry
crino *vb* to wither, to dry up
crintach, crintachlyd *adj* niggardly, stingy
crintachrwydd *nm* niggardliness
crintachu *vb* to scrimp, to skimp, to stint

crio vb to cry, to weep
cripio vb to scratch; to climb, to creep
cris-groes nf criss-cross
crisial (-au) nm, adj crystal
crisialu vb to crystallise
Crist nm Christ
Cristion (-ogion), Cristnogion nm Christian
Cristionogaeth nf Christianity
Cristionogol adj Christian
Cristnogaeth nf Christianity
Cristnogol adj Christian
criw (-iau) nm crew
crïwr (-wyr) nm crier
Croatia nf Croatia
crocbont (-ydd) nf suspension bridge
crocbren (-ni) nmf gallows, gibbet
crocbris (-iau) nm exorbitant price
croch adj loud, vehement
crochan (-au) nm pot, cauldron
crochanaid (-eidiau) nm potful
crochenwaith (-weithiau) nm pottery
crochenydd (-ion) nm potter
croen (crwyn) nm skin; hide; peel, rind
croendenau adj thin-skinned
croeni, croenio vb to form skin, to skin over
croes¹ (-au) nf cross ▸ nm transept
croes² (-ion) adj cross, contrary
croesair (-eiriau) nm crossword
croesawgar adj hospitable
croesawiad nm welcome, reception
croesawu vb to welcome
croesawus adj hospitable

croesbren (-nau) nmf cross
croes-ddweud vb to contradict
croesfan (-nau) nf crossing; **croesfan sebra** zebra crossing
croesffordd (-ffyrdd) nf crossroads
croesgad (-au) nf crusade
croesgadwr (-wyr) nm crusader
croeshoeliad nm crucifixion
croeshoelio vb to crucify
croesholi vb to cross-examine
croesholiad (-au) nm cross-examination
croesi vb to cross
croeslinol adj diagonal
croeso nm welcome
croestorri vb to intersect
croesymgroes adj criss-cross; vice-versa
crofen (-nau, -ni) nf rind, crust
crog (-au) nf cross, rood ▸ adj hanging
crogi vb to hang, to suspend
croglath (-au) nf springe, snare, gibbet
Croglith nfm: **Dydd Gwener y Groglith** Good Friday
croglofft (-ydd, -au) nf garret; rood-loft
crogwr (-wyr) nm hangman
cronglwyd (-ydd) nf: **tan fy nghronglwyd** under my roof
crombil (-iau) nf crop; gizzard; bowels
cromen (-ni, -nau) nf dome
cromfach (-au) nf bracket, parenthesis
cromlech (-au, -i) nf cromlech
cromlin nf curve
cromosom (-au) nm chromosome

59

cron *adj f of* **crwn**

cronfa (**-feydd**) *nf* reservoir; fund; **cronfa ddata** database

cronicl (**-au**) *nm* chronicle

croniclo *vb* to chronicle

cronnell (**cronellau**) *nf* sphere, globe

cronni *vb* to collect, to hoard; to dam

cronolegol *adj* chronological

cropian *vb* to creep, to crawl, to grope

crosiet (**-au, -i**) *nm* crotchet

croth (**-au**) *nf* womb; calf (*of leg*)

croyw *adj* clear, plain, distinct; fresh

croywder *nm* clearness; freshness

croywi *vb* to clear; to freshen

crud (**-au**) *nm* cradle

crug (**-iau**) *nm* hillock; tumulus; heap; multitude; abscess; blister

cruglwyth (**-i**) *nm* heap, pile

cruglwytho *vb* to heap, to pile up; to overload

crugo *vb* to fester, to vex, to plague

crwban (**-od**) *nm* tortoise, turtle

crwca *adj* crooked, bowed, bent

crwm (*f* **crom**) *adj* convex, curved, bowed

crwn (*f* **cron**) *adj* round; complete

crwner (**-iaid**) *nm* coroner

crwsâd (**-adau**) *nmf* crusade

crwst (**crystiau**) *nm* crust

crwt (**cryts**) *nm* boy, lad

crwth (**crythau**) *nm* crowd, fiddle; purring; hump

crwybr *nm* honeycomb; mist; hoarfrost

crwydr *nm* wandering; **ar grwydr** astray

crwydro *vb* to wander, to stray, to roam

crwydrol, crwydrus *adj* wandering

crwydrwr (**-wyr**) *nm* rambler; wanderer, rover

crwydryn (**-riaid**) *nm* vagrant, tramp

crwys *nf* cross, crucifix; **dan ei grwys** laid out for burial

crybwyll *vb* to mention ▸ *nm* (**-ion**) mention

crybwylliad *nm* mention, notice

crych *adj* rippling; curly; quavering ▸ *nm* (**-au**) crease, ripple, wrinkle

crychlais (**-leisiau**) *nm* trill, tremolo

crychlyd *adj* wrinkled, puckered

crychnaid (**-neidiau**) *nf* leap, gambol

crychneidio *vb* to skip, to frisk

crychni *nm* curliness; wrinkle

crychu *vb* to wrinkle, to pucker; to ruffle, to ripple

cryd (**-iau**) *nm* shivering; fever; ague

crydd (**-ion**) *nm* cobbler, shoemaker

crydda *vb* to cobble

cryf (*f* **cref**) *adj* strong

cryfder, cryfdwr *nm* strength

cryfhaol *adj* strengthening

cryfhau *vb* to strengthen; to grow strong

cryg (*f* **creg**) *adj* hoarse

cryglyd *adj* hoarse, raucous

crygni *nm* hoarseness

crygu *vb* to hoarsen
cryman (-au) *nm* reaping-hook, sickle
crymanwr (-wyr) *nm* reaper
crymu *vb* to bow, to bend, to stoop
cryn *adj* considerable, much
crŷn, cryn *nm, adj* shivering
crynder *nm* roundness
cryndod *nm* trembling, shivering
crynedig *adj* trembling, tremulous
crynfa (-feydd) *nf* tremble, tremor
crynhoad (-noadau) *nm* collection, digest
crynhoi *vb* to gather together, to collect
cryno *adj* compact; neat, tidy
crynodeb (-au) *nm* summary
crynodi *vb* to concentrate
cryno ddisg (-iau) *nm* CD, compact disc
crynswth *nm* mass, bulk, whole
crynu *vb* to shiver, to tremble, to quake
Crynwr (-wyr) *nm* Quaker
crys (-au) *nm* shirt; **crys chwys** sweatshirt
crysbais (-beisiau) *nf* jacket, jerkin
crystyn (crystiau) *nm* crust
crythor (-ion) *nm* fiddler, violinist
cryw (-iau) *nm* creel; weir
cu *adj* dear, fond, kind
cuchio *vb* to scowl, to frown
cuchiog *adj* scowling, frowning
cudyll (-od) *nm* hawk
cudyn (-nau) *nm* lock (of hair), tuft
cudd *adj* hidden, concealed
cuddfa (-feydd) *nf* hiding-place; hoard

cuddiad *nm* hiding
cuddiedig *adj* hidden, concealed
cuddio *vb* to hide, to conceal
cufydd (-au) *nm* cubit
cul (-ion) *adj* narrow, lean
culfor (-oedd) *nm* strait
culhau *vb* to narrow; to grow lean
culni *nm* narrowness
cun *adj* dear, beloved; lovely
cunnog (cunogau) *nf* pail
cur *nm* throb, ache, pain; care, trouble
curad (-iaid) *nm* curate
curadiaeth (-au) *nf* curacy
curfa (-feydd) *nf* beating, flogging
curiad (-au) *nm* beat, throb, pulse
curio *vb* to pine, to waste
curlaw *nm* pelting rain
curn (-au), curnen (-nau) *nf* mound, core, rick
curnennu *vb* to heap, to stack
curo *vb* to beat, to strike, to knock; to throb; to clap
curwr (-wyr) *nm* beater
curyll (-od) *nm* hawk
cusan (-au) *nmf* kiss
cusanu *vb* to kiss
cut (-iau) *nm* hovel, shed, sty
cuwch (cuchiau) *nm* scowl, frown
CV (-s) *nm* CV
cwafrio *vb* to quaver, to trill
cwar (-rau) *nm* quarry
cwarel *nm* windowpane
cwb (cybiau) *nm* kennel, coop, sty
cwbl *adj, nm* all, whole, total
cwblhad *nm* fulfilment
cwblhau *vb* to fulfil, to complete, to finish
cwcer (-au) *nm* cooker

61

cwcw *nf* cuckoo
cwcwallt (-iaid) *nm* cuckold
cwcwalltu *vb* to cuckold
cwcwll (cycyllau) *nm* hood, cowl
cwch (cychod) *nm* boat; hive; **cwch gwyllt** speed boat
cwd (cydau) *nm* pouch, bag
cweir (-iau) *nm* thrashing, hiding
cweryl (-on) *nm* quarrel
cweryla *vb* to quarrel
cwerylgar *adj* quarrelsome
cwest (-au) *nm* inquest
cwestiwn (-iynau) *nm* question
cwestiynu *vb* to question
cwfaint *nm* convent
cwfl *nm* hood
cwffio *vb* to fight, to box
cwgn (cygnau) *nm* knot; knuckle; joint
cwilt (-iau) *nm* quilt
cwlbren (-ni) *nm* bludgeon
cwlff (cylffiau), cwlffyn (cylffiau) *nm* chunk
cwlwm *see* **clwm**
cwlltwr (cylltyrau) *nm* coulter
cwm (cymau, cymoedd) *nm* valley
cwman *nm* rump; stoop; churn
cwmanu *vb* to stoop
cwmni (-ïau, -ïoedd) *nm* company
cwmnïaeth *nf* companionship
cwmpas (-oedd) *nm* round; **o gwmpas** about
cwmpasog *adj* round about, circuitous
cwmpasu *vb* to round, to wind, to surround
cwmpawd (-odau) *nm* compass
cwmpeini, cwmpni *nm* company
cwmwd (cymydau) *nm* commot

cwmwl (cymylau) *nm* cloud
cŵn *see* **ci**
cwndid (-au) *nm* song, carol
cwningar *nf* warren
cwningen (-ingod) *nf* rabbit
cwnsel (-au, -oedd, -i) *nm* council; counsel, advice, secret
cwnsela *vb* to counsel
cwnsler (-iaid) *nm* counsellor
cwnstabl (-iaid) *nm* constable; **cwnstabl heddlu** PC, police constable; **prif gwnstabl** chief constable
cworwm *nm* quorum
cwota (-âu) *nm* quota
cwpan (-au) *nmf* cup, goblet; chalice
cwpanaid (-eidiau) *nm* cupful
cwpl (cyplau) *nm* couple; tie beam
cwplâd, cwpláu *see* **cwblhad; cwblhau**
cwpled (-i, -au) *nm* couplet
cwplws (cyplysau) *nm* coupling; brace
cwpwrdd (cypyrddau) *nm* cupboard; **cwpwrdd ffeilio** filing cabinet
cwr (cyrrau) *nm* edge, border, skirt
cwrbyn *nm* kerb
cwrcwd *nm* stooping; squatting
cwrdd¹ (cyrddau) *nm* meeting
cwrdd², cwrddyd *vb* to meet, to touch
cwrel *nm* coral
cwricwlwm (cwricwla) *nm* curriculum
cwrlid (-au) *nm* coverlet

cwrs (**cyrsiau**) *nm* course; fit;
  prif gwrs main course; **cwrs
  hyfforddiant** training course
cwrt (**cyrtiau**) *nm* court
cwrtais *adj* courteous
cwrteisi, cwrteisrwydd *nm*
  courtesy
cwrw (**cyrfau**) *nm* ale, beer
cwrwg, cwrwgl *see* corwg
cwsg *nm* sleep
cwsmer (**-iaid**) *nm* customer
cwsmeriaeth *nf* custom
cwstard (**-iau**) *nm* custard
cwstwm (**cystymau**) *nm* custom,
  patronage
cwt¹ (**cytiau**) *nfm* tail, skirt, queue
cwt² (**cytiau**) *nm* hut, sty
cwta *adj* short, curt
cwter (**-i, -ydd**) *nf* gutter, channel
cwtogi *vb* to shorten, to curtail
cwthr (**cythrau**) *nm* anus, rectum
cwthwm (**cythymau**) *nm* puff of
  wind, storm
cwymp (**-au**) *nm* fall, tumble
cwympo *vb* to fall; to fell
cwyn (**-ion**) *nfm* complaint, plaint
cwynfan *vb* to complain, to lament
cwynfanllyd *adj* querulous
cwynfanus *adj* plaintive, mournful
cwyno *vb* to complain, to lament
cwyr *nm* wax
cwyro *vb* to wax
cwys (**-au, -i**) *nf* furrow-slice,
  furrow
cybôl *nm* nonsense, rubbish
cybolfa *nf* hotchpotch, medley
cyboli *vb* to muddle; to talk
  nonsense; to mess, to bother
cybydd (**-ion**) *nm* miser, niggard

cybydda *vb* to stint, to hoard
cybydd-dod, cybydd-dra *nm*
  miserliness
cybyddlyd *adj* miserly
cycyllog *adj* hooded, cowled
cychwr (**-wyr**) *nm* boatman
cychwyn *vb* to rise, to stir, to start;
  to switch on
cychwynfa *nf* start, starting-point
cychwyniad (**-au**) *nm* start,
  beginning
cyd *adj* joint, united, common;
  fellow ▸ *prefix* together
cydadrodd *vb* to recite together
cydaid (**-eidiau**) *nm* bagful
cydbwysedd *nm* balance
cydbwyso *vb* to balance
cyd-destun (**-au**) *nm* context
cyd-drafodaeth *nf* negotiation
cyd-ddigwydd *vb* to coincide
cyd-ddigwyddiad *nm* coincidence
cydfod *nm* agreement, concord
cydfodolaeth *nf* coexistence
cydfyned *vb* to go with, to concur,
  to agree
cyd-fyw *vb* to cohabit
cydffurfio *vb* to conform
cydgordio *vb* to agree, to
  harmonize
cydgwmni (**-ïau**) *nm* consortium
cydiedig *adj* adjoined
cydio *vb* to join; to bite; to take
  hold
cydletywr (**-wyr**) *nm* roommate,
  flatmate, housemate
cydnabod *vb* to acknowledge
  ▸ *nm* acquaintance
cydnabyddiaeth *nf* acquaintance;
  recognition

63

cydnabyddus *adj* acquainted;
familiar
cydnaws *adj* congenial
cydnerth *adj* well set
cydol *nmf, adj* whole
cydradd *adj* equal
cydraddoldeb *nm* equality
cyd-rhwng *prep* between
cydsyniad *nm* consent
cydsynio *vb* to consent
cydwastad *adj* level (with), even
cydweddog *adj* conjugal
cydweddu *vb* to accord, to agree
cydweithfa (-feydd) *nf* co-
operative
cydweithio *vb* to cooperate
cydweithrediad *nm* co-operation
cydweithredol *adj* co-operative
cydweithredu *vb* to co-operate
cydweled *vb* to agree
cydwladol *adj* international
cyd-wladwr (-wyr) *nm* compatriot
cydwybod (-au) *nf* conscience
cydwybodol *adj* conscientious
cydwybodolrwydd *nm*
conscientiousness
cydymaith (cymdeithion) *nm*
companion
cydymdeimlad *nm* sympathy
cydymdeimlo *vb* to sympathize
cydymffurfiad *nm* conformity
cydymffurfio *vb* to conform
cydymgais *nm* competition,
rivalry, joint effort
cydymgeisydd (-wyr) *nm* rival
cyddwysiad (-au) *nm*
condensation
cyddwyso *vb* to condense

cyfadran (-nau) *nf* faculty (in
college), period (in music)
cyfaddas *adj* fit, suitable,
convenient
cyfaddasiad (-au) *nm* adaptation
cyfaddaster *nm* fitness, suitability
cyfaddasu *vb* to fit, to adapt
cyfaddawd (-odau) *nm*
compromise
cyfaddawdu *vb* to compromise
cyfaddef *vb* to confess, to own,
to admit
cyfaddefiad (-au) *nm* confession,
admission
cyfaenad *nm* harmonious song
▸ *adj* harmonious
cyfagos *adj* near, adjacent,
neighbouring
cyfaill (-eillion) *nm* friend
cyfair¹ (-eiriau) *nm* acre
cyfair², cyfer *nm* direction
cyfalaf *nm* capital
cyfalafiaeth *nf* capitalism
cyfalafol *adj* capitalistic
cyfalafwr (-wyr) *nm* capitalist
cyfamod (-au) *nm* covenant
cyfamodi *vb* to covenant
cyfamodol *adj* federal; covenanted
cyfamodwr (-wyr) *nm* covenanter
cyfamser *nm* meantime
cyfamserol *adj* timely;
synchronous
cyfan *adj, nm* whole
cyfandir (-oedd) *nm* continent
cyfandirol *adj* continental
cyfanfor (-oedd) *nm* main sea,
ocean
cyfanfyd *nm* whole world, universe
cyfangorff *nm* whole, bulk, mass

cyfan gwbl *adj*: **yn gyfan gwbl** altogether, completely

cyfanheddol *adj* habitable, inhabited

cyfanheddu *vb* to dwell, to inhabit

cyfannedd *adj* inhabited ▸ *nf* (**-anheddau**) inhabited place, habitation

cyfannol *adj* integrated, integral

cyfannu *vb* to make whole, to complete

cyfanrwydd *nm* wholeness, entirety

cyfansawdd *adj* composite, compound

cyfansoddi *vb* to compose, to constitute

cyfansoddiad (**-au**) *nm* composition; constitution

cyfansoddiadol *adj* constitutional

cyfansoddwr (**-wyr**) *nm* composer

cyfansoddyn (**-ion**) *nm* constituent, compound

cyfanswm (**-symiau**) *nm* total

cyfantoledd (**-au**) *nm* equilibrium

cyfanwaith (**-weithiau**) *nm* complete composition, whole

cyfanwerth *nm* wholesale

cyfarch *vb* to greet, to salute, to address

cyfarchiad (**-au**) *nm* greeting, salutation

cyfaredd (**-ion**) *nf* charm, spell

cyfareddol *adj* enchanting

cyfareddu *vb* to charm, to enchant

cyfarfod *vb* to meet ▸ *nm* (**-ydd**) meeting

cyfarfyddiad (**-au**) *nm* meeting

cyfarpar *nm* provision, equipment; diet; **cyfarpar rhyfel** munitions of war

cyfarparu *vb* to equip

cyfartal *adj* equal, even

cyfartaledd *nm* proportion, average

cyfartalu *vb* to proportion, to equalize

cyfarth *vb, nm* to bark

cyfarwydd *adj* skilled; familiar ▸ *nm* (**-iaid**) storyteller

cyfarwyddo *vb* to direct; to become familiar

cyfarwyddwr (**-wyr**) *nm* director

cyfarwyddyd (**-iadau**) *nm* direction, instruction

cyfatal *adj* unsettled, hindering

cyfateb *vb* to correspond, to agree, to tally

cyfatebiaeth (**-au**) *nf* correspondence, analogy

cyfatebol *adj* corresponding, proportionate

cyfathrach (**-au**) *nf* affinity; intercourse

cyfathrachu *vb* to have intercourse

cyfathrachwr (**-wyr**) *nm* kinsman

cyfathreb (**-au**) *nm* communication

cyfathrebu *vb* to communicate

cyfddydd *nm* day-break, dawn

cyfeb, cyfebr *adj* pregnant (*of mare, ewe*)

cyfebol *adj* in foal

cyfeddach (**-au**) *nf* carousal

cyfeddachwr (**-wyr**) *nm* carouser

cyfeiliant nm musical accompaniment

cyfeilio vb to accompany

cyfeiliorn nm error; wandering, lost (person etc); **ar gyfeiliorn** astray

cyfeiliornad (-au) nm error, heresy

cyfeiliorni vb to err, to stray

cyfeiliornus adj erroneous, mistaken

cyfeilydd (-ion) nm accompanist

cyfeillach (-au) nf fellowship; fellowship-meeting

cyfeillachu vb to associate

cyfeilles (-au) nf female friend

cyfeillgar adj friendly

cyfeillgarwch nm friendship

cyfeiriad (-au) nm direction; reference; (postal) address; **cyfeiriad ebost** email address; **cyfeiriad gwe** web address

cyfeiriannu nm orienteering

cyfeirio vb to point; to direct; to refer; to address (letter)

cyfeirnod (-au) nm mark of reference; aim; direct (in music)

cyfeirydd (-ion) nm indicator, guide

cyfenw (-au) nm surname; namesake

cyfenwi vb to surname

cyfer nm: **ar gyfer** opposite, for

cyferbyn adj opposite

cyferbyniad (-au) nm contrast

cyferbyniol adj opposing, opposite, contrasting

cyferbynnu vb to contrast, to compare

cyfesuryn nm coordinate

cyfethol vb to co-opt

cyfiaith adj of the same language

cyfiawn adj just, righteous

cyfiawnder (-au) nm justice, righteousness

cyfiawnhad nm justification

cyfiawnhau vb to justify

cyfieithiad (-au) nm translation, version

cyfieithu vb to translate, to interpret

cyfieithydd (-wyr) nm translator, interpreter

cyfisol adj of the present month, instant

cyflafan (-au) nf outrage; massacre

cyflafareddiad nm arbitration

cyflafareddu vb to arbitrate

cyflafareddwr (-wyr) nm arbitrator

cyflaith nm toffee

cyflasyn nm flavouring

cyflawn adj full, complete

cyflawnder nm fullness; abundance

cyflawni vb to fulfil, to perform, to commit

cyflawniad (-au) nm fulfilment, performance

cyfle (-oedd) nm place; chance, opportunity

cyfled adj as broad as

cyflegr (-au) nm gun, cannon, battery

cyflegru vb to bombard

cyflenwad (-au) nm supply

cyflenwi vb to supply

cyfleu vb to place, to set; to convey

cyfleus *adj* convenient
cyfleustra (-terau) *nm* opportunity, convenience
cyflin *adj* parallel
cyfliw *adj* of the same colour
cyflo *adj* in calf
cyflog (-au) *nmf* hire, wage, wages
cyflogaeth *nf* employment
cyflogedig (-ion) *nm* employee
cyflogi *vb* to hire; to engage in service
cyflogwr (-wyr) *nm* hirer, employer
cyflwr (-lyrau) *nm* condition; case
cyflwyniad *nm* presentation; dedication
cyflwyno *vb* to present; to dedicate
cyflwynydd (-ion) *nm* compère, presenter
cyflychwr, cyflychwyr *nm* evening twilight, dusk
cyflym *adj* quick, fast, swift
cyflymder, cyflymdra *nm* swiftness, speed
cyflymu *vb* to speed, to accelerate
cyflynu *vb* to stick together
cyflyru *vb* to condition
cyflythreniad (-au) *nm* alliteration
cyfnerthu *vb* to confirm; to aid, to help
cyfnerthydd (-ion, -wyr) *nm* strengthener, booster
cyfnesaf (-iaid, -eifiaid) *nmf* next of kin, kinsman ▸ *adj* next, nearest
cyfnewid *vb* to change, to exchange
cyfnewidfa (-oedd, -feydd) *nf* exchange

cyfnewidiad (-au) *nm* change, alteration
cyfnewidiol *adj* changeable
cyfnewidiwr (-wyr) *nm* changer, trader
cyfnither (-oedd) *nf* female cousin
cyfnod (-au) *nm* period; **cyfnod prawf** trial period
cyfnodol *adj* periodic(al)
cyfnodolyn (-ion) *nm* periodical publication
cyfnos *nm* evening twilight, dusk
cyfochredd *nm* parallelism
cyfochrog *adj* parallel
cyfodi *vb* to rise, to arise; to raise
cyfodiad *nm* rise, rising
cyfoed *adj* contemporary, of the same age ▸ *nm* (-ion) contemporary
cyfoes *adj* contemporary, up-to-date
cyfoesi *vb* to be contemporary
cyfoeswr (-wyr) *nm* contemporary
cyfoeth *nm* power; riches, wealth
cyfoethog *adj* powerful; rich, wealthy
cyfoethogi *vb* to make *or* grow rich
cyfog *nm* sickness
cyfogi *vb* to vomit
cyfor *nm* flood, abundance; rim, brim, edge ▸ *adj* entire, brim-full
cyforiog *adj* brim-full, overflowing
cyfosodiad *nm* apposition
cyfradd (-au) *nf* rate ▸ *adj* of equal rank; **cyfradd llog** rate of interest
cyfraid (-reidiau) *nm* necessity
cyfraith (-reithiau) *nf* law
cyfran (-nau) *nf* part, portion, share

cyfranc (-rangau) *nfm* meeting; combat; incident; story, tale

cyfranddaliad (-au) *nm* share

cyfranddaliwr (-wyr) *nm* shareholder

cyfraniad (-au) *nm* contribution

cyfrannedd *nm* proportion

cyfrannog *adj* participating, partaking

cyfrannol *adj* contributing

cyfrannu *vb* to contribute; to impart

cyfrannwr (-anwyr) *nm* contributor

cyfranogi *vb* to participate, to partake

cyfranogwr (-wyr) *nm* partaker

cyfredol *adj* current, concurrent

cyfreithio *vb* to go to law, to litigate

cyfreithiol *adj* legal

cyfreithiwr (-wyr) *nm* lawyer

cyfreithlon *adj* lawful, legitimate

cyfreithlondeb *nm* lawfulness

cyfreithloni *vb* to legalize; to justify

cyfreithus *adj* legitimate

cyfres (-i) *nf* series

cyfresol *adj* serial

cyfresu *vb* to serialise

cyfresymiad (-au) *nm* syllogism

cyfresymu *vb* to syllogise

cyfrgolli *vb* to lose utterly; to damn

cyfrif *vb* to count, to reckon; to account; to impute ▸ *nm* **(-on)** account, reckoning; **cyfrif banc** bank account

cyfrifeg *nfm* accountancy

cyfrifiad (-au) *nm* counting; census

cyfrifiadur (-on) *nm* computer; **cyfrifiadur personol** PC, personal computer

cyfrifiadureg *nf* computer science

cyfrifiaduro *n* computing

cyfrifiannell *nf* calculator

cyfrifol *adj* of repute; responsible

cyfrifoldeb (-au) *nm* responsibility

cyfrifydd (-ion) *nm* accountant

cyfrin *adj* secret, subtle

cyfrinach (-au) *nf* secret

cyfrinachol *adj* secret, private, confidential

cyfrinair (-eiriau) *nm* password

cyfrinfa *nf* lodge of friendly society or trade union

cyfrin-gyngor (-nghorau) *nm* privy council

cyfriniaeth *nf* mystery; mysticism

cyfriniol *adj* mysterious, mystic

cyfriniwr (-wyr) *nm* mystic

cyfrodedd *adj* twisted, twined

cyfrodeddu *vb* to twist, to twine

cyfrol (-au) *nf* volume

cyfrwng (-ryngau) *nm* medium, means

cyfrwy (-au) *nm* saddle

cyfrwyo *vb* to saddle

cyfrwys *adj* cunning

cyfrwystra *nm* cunning

cyfrwywr (-wyr) *nm* saddler

cyfryngdod *nm* mediation, intercession; mediatorship

cyfryngiad *nm* mediation; intervention

cyfryngol *adj* mediatorial

cyfryngu *vb* to mediate; to intervene

cyfryngwr (-wyr) *nm* mediator

cyfryngwriaeth *nf* mediatorship
cyfryw *adj* like, such
cyfuchlinedd (-au) *nm* contour
cyfuchliniau *npl* contours
cyfundeb (-au) *nm* union;
connexion
cyfundebol *adj* connexional;
denominational
cyfundrefn (-au) *nf* system
cyfundrefnol *adj* systematic
cyfundrefnu *vb* to systematize
cyfuniad (-au) *nm* combination
cyfuno *vb* to unite, to combine
cyfunol *adj* united
cyfunrhywiol *adj* homosexual
cyfuwch *adj* as high
cyfweld *vb* to interview
cyfweliad (-au) *nm* interview
cyfwelydd (-wyr) *nm* interviewer
cyfwerth *adj* equivalent
cyfwng (-yngau) *nm* space;
interval
cyfwrdd *vb* to meet
cyfyng *adj* narrow, confined
cyfyngder (-au) *nm* trouble,
distress
cyfyngdra *nm* narrowness;
distress
cyfyngedig *adj* confined,
restricted, limited
cyfyng-gyngor *nm* perplexity
cyfyngu *vb* to narrow, to confine,
to limit
cyfyl *nm* neighbourhood; **ar ei
gyfyl** near him
cyfyrder (-dyr) *nm* second cousin
cyfystlys *adj* side by side
cyfystyr *adj* synonymous
cyfystyron *npl* synonyms

cyff (-ion) *nm* stock
cyffaith (-ffeithiau) *nm* confection
cyffelyb *adj* like, similar
cyffelybiaeth (-au) *nf* likeness,
similitude
cyffelybiaethol *adj* figurative
cyffelybrwydd *nm* likeness,
similarity
cyffelybu *vb* to liken, to compare
cyffes (-ion) *nf* confession
cyffesgell (-oedd) *nf* confessional
cyffesu *vb* to confess
cyffeswr (-wyr), **cyfesydd** (-ion)
nm confessor
cyffin (-iau, -ydd) *nfm* border,
confine
cyffindir (-oedd) *nm* frontier,
march
cyffio *vb* to stiffen; to fetter, to
shackle; to beat
cyffion *npl* stocks
cyffordd (-ffyrdd) *nf* junction
cyffredin *adj* common; general
cyffredinedd *nm* mediocrity,
banality
cyffredinol *adj* general, universal
cyffredinoli *vb* to universalize, to
generalize
cyffredinolrwydd *nm* universality
cyffredinwch *nm* commonness
cyffro (-adau) *nm* motion, stir;
excitement
cyffroi *vb* to move, to excite; to
provoke
cyffrous *adj* exciting; excited
cyffur (-iau) *nmf* ingredient, drug
cyffuriwr (-wyr) *nm* apothecary,
druggist
cyffwrdd *vb* to meet, to touch

cyffylog (**-od**) *nm* woodcock
cyffyrddiad (**-au**) *nm* touch, contact
cyffyrddus *adj* comfortable
cygnog *adj* knotted, gnarled
cyngaf, cyngaw *nm* burdock; burs
cyngan *adj* suitable, harmonious
cynganeddol *adj* in *cynghanedd*
cynganeddu *vb* to form *cynghanedd*; to harmonize
cynganeddwr (**-wyr**) *nm* writer of *cynghanedd*
cyngaws (**cynghawsau, -ion**) *nm* lawsuit, action; trial; battle
cyngerdd (**-ngherddau**) *nmf* concert
cynghanedd (**cynganeddion**) *nf* music, harmony; Welsh metrical alliteration
cynghori *vb* to counsel, to advise; to exhort
cynghorwr (**-wyr**) *nm* councillor; counsellor; exhorter
cynghrair (**-eiriau**) *nmf* alliance, league
cynghreiriad (**-iaid**) *nm* confederate, ally
cynghreirio *vb* to league, to confederate
cynghreiriwr (**-wyr**) *nm* confederate, ally
cyngor (**-nghorion**) *nm* counsel, advice ▸ *nm* (**-nghorau**) council; **Cyngor Bro** Community Council; **Cyngor Tref** Town Council; **Cyngor Sir** County Council
cyngres (**-au, -i**) *nf* congress
cyngresydd (**-wyr**) *nm* congressman

cyngwystl (**-(i)on**) *nmf* wager, pledge
cyhoedd *adj, nm* public
cyhoeddi *vb* to publish, to announce
cyhoeddiad (**-au**) *nm* publication; announcement; (preaching) engagement
cyhoeddus *adj* public
cyhoeddusrwydd *nm* publicity
cyhoeddwr (**-wyr**) *nm* publisher
cyhuddiad (**-au**) *nm* accusation, charge
cyhuddo *vb* to accuse, to charge
cyhuddwr (**-wyr**) *nm* accuser
cyhwfan *vb* to wave, to heave
cyhyd *adj* as long, so long
cyhydedd *nm* equator
cyhydeddol *adj* equatorial, equinoctial
cyhyr (**-au**) *nm* flesh, muscle
cyhyrog *adj* muscular
cylch (**-au, oedd**) *nm* round, circle, sphere, hoop
cylchdaith (**-deithiau**) *nf* circuit
cylchdro (**-eon, -adau**) *nm* orbit
cylchdroi *vb* to rotate, to revolve
cylched (**-au**) *nm* coverlet, blanket
cylchedd (**-au**) *nmf* compass, circle, circuit
cylchfan *nf* roundabout
cylchgrawn (**-gronau**) *nm* magazine
cylchlythyr (**-au**) *nm* circular
cylchredeg *vb* to circulate
cylchrediad *nm* circulation
cylchres (**-i**) *nf* round, rota
cylchwyl (**-iau**) *nf* anniversary, festival

cylchynol adj surrounding
cylchynu vb to surround, to encompass
cylion npl (nm -**yn**, nf -**en**) flies, gnats
cylymu vb to knot, to tie
cyll npl (nf **collen**) hazel-trees
cylla (-**on**) nm stomach
cyllell (-**yll**) nf knife
cyllid (-**au**) nm revenue, income
cyllideb (-**au**) nf budget
cyllido vb to finance
cyllidol adj financial, fiscal
cyllidwr (-**wyr**), **cyllidydd** (-**ion**) nm tax-gatherer, revenue or excise officer, financier
cymaint adj as big, as much, as many; so big etc
cymal (-**au**) nm joint; clause
cymalwst nf rheumatism
cymanfa (-**oedd**) nf assembly; festival
cymantoledd (-**au**) nm equilibrium
cymanwlad nf commonwealth
cymar (-**heiriaid**) nm fellow, partner
cymathiad nm assimilation
cymathu vb to assimilate
cymdeithas (-**au**) nf society, association; **Cymdeithas yr Iaith Gymraeg** The Welsh Language Society
cymdeithaseg nf sociology
cymdeithasegol adj sociological
cymdeithasgar adj sociable
cymdeithasol adj social
cymdeithasu vb to associate; to socialize

cymdogaeth (-**au**) nf neighbourhood
cymdogol adj neighbourly
cymedr (-**au**) nm mean (in maths), average
cymedrol adj moderate, temperate
cymedroldeb nm moderation, temperance
cymedroli vb to moderate
cymedrolwr (-**wyr**) nm moderator; moderate drinker
cymell vb to urge, to press, to persuade, to induce; to motivate ▸ nm (**cymhellion**) motivation
cymen adj wise, skilful, neat, becoming
cymer (-**au**) nm confluence
cymeradwy adj acceptable, approved, commendable
cymeradwyaeth nf approval; applause; recommendation
cymeradwyo vb to approve; to recommend
cymeradwyol adj commendatory
cymeriad (-**au**) nm character, reputation
cymesur adj proportionate, symmetrical
cymesuredd nm proportion, symmetry
cymesurol adj commensurate, proportionate
cymhareb (**cymarebau**) nf ratio
cymhariaeth (**cymariaethau**) nf comparison
cymharol adj comparative
cymharu vb to pair; to compare

cymhelliad

cymhelliad (**-elliadau**) *nm* motive, inducement

cymhendod *nm* knowledge; proficiency; tidiness; eloquence; affection

cymhennu *vb* to put in order, to trim; to scold, to reprove

cymhercyn *adj* limping, infirm
▸ *nm* valetudinarian

cymhleth (**-au**) *adj* complex, complicated

cymhlethdod (**-au**) *nm* complexity

cymhlethu *vb* to complicate

cymhorthdal (**cymorthdaloedd**) *nm* subsidy, grant

cymhwysiad *nm* application, adjustment

cymhwyso *vb* to apply, to adjust

cymhwyster (**cymwysterau**) *nm* fitness, suitability; (*pl*) qualifications

cymod *nm* reconciliation

cymodi *vb* to reconcile; to be reconciled

cymodol *adj* reconciliatory, propitiatory

cymodwr (**-wyr**) *nm* reconciler

cymon *adj* orderly, tidy; seemly

cymorth *vb* to assist, to aid, to help
▸ *nm* assistance, aid, help

Cymraeg *nfm, adj* Welsh

Cymraes *nf* Welshwoman

cymrawd (**-odyr**) *nm* comrade, fellow

Cymreictod *nm* Welshness

Cymreig *adj* Welsh

Cymreiges (**-au**) *nf* Welshwoman

Cymreigio *vb* to translate into Welsh

Cymreigiwr (**-wyr**) *nm* one versed or skilled in Welsh; Welsh-speaking Welshman

Cymro (**Cymry**) *nm* Welshman

cymrodedd *nm* arbitration; compromise

cymrodeddu *vb* to compromise, to reconcile

cymrodor (**-ion**) *nm* consociate, fellow

cymrodoriaeth *nf* fellowship

Cymru *nf* Wales

cymrwd *nm* mortar, plaster

Cymry *see* **Cymro**

cymryd *vb* to take, to accept; **cymryd ar** pretend

cymudo *vb* to commute

cymun, cymundeb *nm* communion, fellowship

cymuned *nf* community; **y Gymuned Ewropeaidd** the European Community

cymunedol *adj* community

cymuno *vb* to commune

cymunwr (**-wyr**) *nm* communicant

cymwy (**-au**) *nm* affliction

cymwynas (**-au**) *nf* kindness, favour

cymwynasgar *adj* obliging, kind

cymwynasgarwch *nm* obligingness, kindness

cymwynaswr (**-wyr**) *nm* benefactor

cymwys *adj* fit, proper, suitable; exact

cymwysedig *adj* applied

cymwysiadol *adj* applicable

cymydog (**cymdogion**) (*f* **cymdoges**) *nm* neighbour

cymylog *adj* cloudy, clouded
cymylu *vb* to cloud, to dim, to obscure
cymyndod *nm* committal
cymynnu *vb* to bequeath
cymynrodd (-ion) *nf* legacy, bequest
cymynroddi *vb* to bequeath
cymynu *vb* to hew, to fell
cymynwr (-wyr) *nm* hewer, feller
cymysg *adj* mixed
cymysgedd *nmf* mixture
cymysgfa *nf* mixture, medley, hotchpotch
cymysgliw *adj* motley
cymysglyd *adj* muddled, confused
cymysgryw *adj* mongrel; heterogeneous
cymysgu *vb* to mix, to blend; to confuse
cymysgwch *nm* mixture, jumble
cymysgwr (-wyr) *nm* mixer, blender
cyn[1] *prefix* before, previous, first, former, pre-, ex-; **Cyn Crist** Before Christ, B.C.
cyn[2] *adv*: **cyn gynted (â phosib)** as soon (as possible) ; **cyn wynned â** as white as
cŷn (cynion) *nm* wedge, chisel
cynadledda *vb* to meet in conference
cynaeafa, cynhaeafa *vb* to dry in the sun
cynaeafu, cynhaeafu *vb* to harvest
cynaeafwr, cynhaeafwr (-wyr) *nm* harvester

cynamserol *adj* premature, untimely
cynaniad *nm* pronunciation
cynanu *vb* to pronounce
cyndad (-au) *nm* forefather, ancestor
cynderfynol *adj* semi-final
cyndyn *adj* stubborn, obstinate
cyndynnu *vb* to be obstinate
cyndynrwydd *nm* stubbornness, obstinacy
cynddaredd *nf* madness; rabies
cynddeiriog *adj* mad, rabid
cynddeiriogi *vb* to madden, to enrage
cynddeiriogrwydd *nm* rage, fury
cynddrwg *adj* as bad
cynddydd *nm* day-break, dawn
cynefin *adj* acquainted, accustomed, familiar ▸ *nm* haunt, habitat
cynefindra *nm* use, familiarity
cynefino *vb* to get used, to become accustomed
cynefinol *adj* usual, accustomed
cynfas (-au) *nfm* (bed) sheet; canvas
cynfyd *nm* primitive world, antiquity
cynffon (-nau) *nf* tail; tang
cynffonna *vb* to fawn, to toady, to cringe
cynffonnwr (-onwyr) *nm* toady, sycophant; sneak
cyn-geni *adj* antenatal
cynhadledd (cynadleddau) *nf* conference
cynhaeaf (cynaeafau) *nm* harvest
cynhaeafa *vb* see **cynaeafa**

73

cynhaeafu

cynhaeafu *vb see* **cynaeafu**
cynhaeafwr *nm see* **cynaeafwr**
cynhaliaeth *nf* maintenance,
 support
cynhaliol *adj* sustaining
cynhaliwr (-wyr) *nm* supporter,
 sustainer
cynhanesiol *adj* prehistoric
cynhebrwng (-yngau) *nm* funeral
cynhenid *adj* innate
cynhennu *vb* to contend, to
 quarrel
cynhennus *adj* contentious,
 quarrelsome
cynhennwr (-henwyr) *nm*
 wrangler
cynhesol *adj* agreeable, amiable
cynhesrwydd *nm* warmth
cynhesu *vb* to warm, to get
 warm; **cynhesu byd-eang** global
 warming
cynhorthwy (cynorthwyon) *nm*
 help, aid
cynhwynol *adj* natural,
 congenital, innate
cynhwysedd (cynwyseddau) *nm*
 capacity, capacitance
cynhwysfawr *adj* comprehensive
cynhwysiad *nm* contents
cynhwysydd *nm* container
cynhyrchiad (-au) *nm* production
cynhyrchiol *adj* productive
cynhyrchu *vb* to produce
cynhyrchydd (-ion, cynhyrchwyr)
 nm producer, generator
cynhyrfiad (cynyrfiadau) *nm*
 stirring, agitation
cynhyrfiol *adj* stirring, thrilling
cynhyrfu *vb* to stir, to agitate

cynhyrfus *adj* agitated; exciting
cynhyrfwr (-wyr) *nm* agitator,
 disturber
cynhysgaeth *nf* portion, fortune
cyni *nm* anguish, distress,
 adversity
cynifer *adj, nm* as many, so many
cynigiad (-au) *nm* proposal,
 motion
cynigiwr (-wyr), cynigydd (-ion)
 nm proposer, mover
cynildeb *nm* frugality, economy
cynilion *npl* savings
cynilo *vb* to save, to economise
cynio *vb* to chisel, to gouge
cyniwair *vb* to go to and fro, to
 frequent
cyniweirfa (-feydd) *nf* resort,
 haunt
cyniweirydd *nm* wayfarer
cynllun (-iau) *nm* pattern; plan
cynllunio *vb* to plan, to design
cynllunydd (-ion, -wyr) *nm*
 designer
cynllwyn *vb* to plot, to conspire
 ▶ *nm* (-ion) plot
cynllwynio *vb* to conspire, to plot
cynllwynwr (-wyr) *nm* conspirator
cynnal *vb* to hold, to uphold, to
 support, to sustain
cynnar *adj* early
cynnau *vb* to kindle, to light
cynneddf (cyneddfau) *nf* quality,
 faculty
cynnen (cynhennau) *nf*
 contention, strife; **asgwrn y
 gynnen** bone of contention
cynnes *adj* warm

cynnig *vb* to offer; to attempt; to propose, to move; to bid; to apply
  ▸ *nm* (**cynigion**) offer; attempt; motion
cynnil *adj* economical; delicate
cynnor (**cynhorau**) *nf* door-post
cynnud *nm* firewood, fuel
cynnull *vb* to collect, to gather, to assemble
cynnwrf *nm* stir, commotion, agitation
cynnwys *vb* to contain, to include, to comprise, to comprehend
  ▸ *nm* content(s)
cynnydd *nm* increase, growth, progress
cynnyrch (**cynhyrchion**) *nm* produce, product; *(pl)* productions
cynoesol *adj* primeval
cynorthwyo *vb* to help, to assist
cynorthwyol *adj* auxiliary; assistant
cynorthwywr (**-wyr**) *nm* helper, assistant
cynorthwyydd (**-ion**) *nm*: **cynorthwyydd dosbarth** classroom assistant
cynradd *adj* primary
cynrychioladol *adj* representative
cynrychiolaeth *nf* representation
cynrychioli *vb* to represent
cynrychiolwr (**-wyr**), **cynrychiolydd** (**-ion**) *nm* representative, delegate
cynrhon *npl* (*nm* **-yn**) maggots
cynrhoni *vb* to breed maggots
cynrhonllyd *adj* maggoty

cynt *adj* earlier, sooner, quicker
  ▸ *adv see* **gynt**
cyntaf *adj, adv* first
cyntedd (**-au**) *nm* court; porch, foyer
cyntefig *adj* prime, primitive
cyntun *nm* nap
cynulleidfa (**-oedd**) *nf* congregation
cynulleidfaol *adj* congregational
cynulliad (**-au**) *nm* gathering
cynuta *vb* to gather fuel
cynyddol *adj* increasing, growing
cynyddu *vb* to increase
cynysgaeddu *vb* to endow, to endue
cyplad *nm* copula
cypladu *vb* to copulate
cyplu, cyplysu *vb* to couple
cyplysnod *nm* hyphen
cyraeddadwy *adj* attainable
cyraeddiadau *npl* attainments
cyrbibion *npl* atoms, smithereens
cyrcydu *vb* to squat, to cower
cyrch (**-au**) *nm* attack
cyrchfa (**-feydd**) *nf* resort
cyrchfan *nf* destination
cyrchu *vb* to go, to resort, to repair
cyrchwr (**-wyr**) *nm* cursor
cyrens *npl* (*nf* **cyrensen**) currants
cyrhaeddgar *adj* telling, incisive
cyrhaeddiad (**cyraeddiadau**) *nm* reach, attainment
cyrliog *adj* curly
cyrraedd *vb* to reach, to attain; to arrive; to get back
cyrydiad *nm* corrosion
cyrydu *vb* to corrode

75

cysawd (**-odau**) *nm* system; constellation
cysefin *adj* original, primordial
cysegr (**-au, -oedd**) *nm* sanctuary
cysegredig *adj* consecrated, sacred
cysegredigrwydd *nm* sacredness
cysegriad (**-au**) *nm* consecration
cysegr-ladrad *nm* sacrilege
cysegr-lân *adj* holy
cysegru *vb* to consecrate, to dedicate, to devote
cyseinedd *nm* alliteration
cysetlyd *adj* fastidious
cysgadrwydd *nm* sleepiness, drowsiness
cysgadur (**-iaid**) *nm* sleeper
cysglyd *adj* sleepy
cysgod (**-au, -ion**) *nm* shade, shadow; shelter; type
cysgodi *vb* to shadow, to shade; to shelter
cysgodol *adj* shady, sheltered
cysgu *vb* to sleep
cysgwr (**-wyr**) *nm* sleeper
cysidro *vb* to consider
cysodi *vb* to set type, to compose
cysodydd (**-ion, -wyr**) *nm* compositor
cyson *adj* consistent, constant
cysondeb *nm* consistency; regularity
cysoni *vb* to harmonize; to reconcile
cysonwr (**-wyr**), **cysonydd** (**-ion**) *nm* harmonist
cystadleuaeth (**-laethau**) *nf* competition
cystadleuol *adj* competitive

cystadleuwr (**-wyr**), **cystadleuydd** *nm* competitor
cystadlu *vb* to compete; to compare
cystal *adj* as good, so good ▸ *adv* as well, so well
cystrawen (**-nau**) *nf* construction, syntax
cystudd (**-iau**) *nm* affliction; illness
cystuddiedig *adj* afflicted, contrite
cystuddio *vb* to afflict, to trouble
cystuddiol *adj* afflicted
cystuddiwr (**-wyr**) *nm* oppressor
cystwyo *vb* to tell off, to chastise
cysur (**-on**) *nm* comfort, consolation
cysuro *vb* to comfort, to console
cysurus *adj* comfortable
cysurwr (**-wyr**) *nm* comforter
cyswllt (**-ylltiadau**) *nm* joint, junction
cysylltiad (**-au**) *nm* conjunction; joining, connexion; **cysylltiadau cyhoeddus** public relations
cysylltiedig *adj* connected
cysylltiol *adj* connecting; connected
cysylltnod (**-au**) *nm* ligature, hyphen
cysylltu *vb* to join, to connect
cysylltydd (**-ion**) *nm* connector, contact
cysyniad (**-au**) *nm* concept
cytbell *adj* equidistant
cytbwys *adj* of equal weight
cytbwysedd *nm* balance
cytew *nm* batter
cytgan (**-au**) *nmf* chorus
cytgord *nm* concord

cytir (-oedd) *nm* common
cytras *adj* allied, related; cognate
cytsain (-seiniaid) *nf* consonant
cytûn *adj* agreed, of one accord, unanimous
cytundeb (-au) *nm* agreement, consent
cytuno *vb* to agree, to consent
cythlwng *nm* fasting, fast, hunger
cythraul (-euliaid) *nm* devil, demon
cythreuldeb *nm* devilment
cythreulig *adj* devilish, fiendish
cythru *vb* to snatch, to rush
cythruddo *vb* to annoy, to provoke, to irritate
cythrwfl *nm* uproar, tumult
cythryblu *vb* to trouble, to agitate
cythryblus *adj* troubled, agitated
cyw (-ion) *nm* young bird, chick, chicken; baby
cywain *vb* to convey, to carry; to garner
cywair (-eiriau) *nm* order; key; tune
cywaith (-weithiau) *nm* collective work, project
cywarch *nm* hemp
cywasg, cywasgedig *adj* diminished
cywasgiad (-au) *nm* contraction, compression
cywasgu *vb* to contract, to compress
cywasgydd (-ion) *nm* compressor
cyweiriad (-au) *nm* repair
cyweiriadur (-on) *nm* modulator
cyweirio *vb* to set in order; to prepare, to dress

cyweirnod (-au) *nm* key-note
cywen (-nod) *nf* pullet, young hen
cywerth *adj* equivalent
cywilydd *nm* shame; shyness
cywilydd-dra *nm* shamefulness
cywilyddgar *adj* bashful, shy
cywilyddio *vb* to shame; to be ashamed
cywilyddus *adj* shameful, disgraceful; outrageous
cywir *adj* correct, accurate, true, faithful
cywirdeb *nm* correctness; integrity
cywiriad (-au) *nm* correction
cywiro *vb* to correct; to make good; to perform
cywirwr (-wyr) *nm* corrector
cywladu *vb* to naturalize
cywrain *adj* skilful; curious
cywreinbeth (-au, cywreinion) *nm* curiosity
cywreindeb *nm* skill, ingenuity
cywreinrwydd *nm* skill; curiosity
cywydd (-au) *nm* alliterative Welsh poem
cywyddwr (-wyr) *nm* composer of *cywyddau*

ch

Chechnya *nf* Chechnya
Chile *nf* Chile
China *nf* China
chwa (-on) *nf* puff, gust, breeze
chwaer (chwiorydd) *nf* sister
chwaeroliaeth *nf* sisterhood
chwaeth (-au, -oedd) *nf* taste
chwaethu *vb* to taste
chwaethus *adj* tasteful; decent
chwaith *adv* nor either, neither
chwâl *adj* scattered, loose
chwalfa (-feydd) *nf* upset, rout
chwalu *vb* to scatter, to spread
chwalwr (-wyr) *nm* scatterer, demolisher
chwaneg *adj*, *nm* more
chwanegiad (-au) *nm* addition
chwanegol *adj* additional
chwanegu *vb* to add, to augment, to increase
chwannen (chwain) *nf* flea
chwannog *adj* desirous; addicted; prone

chwant (-au) *nm* desire, craving, lust
chwantu *vb* to desire, to lust
chwap *nm* sudden blow; moment ▸ *adv* instantly
chwarae, chware *vb* to play ▸ *nm* play; **chwaraeon y gaeaf** winter sports
chwaraedy (-dai) *nm* playhouse, theatre
chwaraefa (-feydd) *nf* pitch, playground
chwaraegar *adj* playful, sportive
chwaraewr (-wyr) *nm* player, actor, performer; **chwaraewr cryno-ddisgiau** CD player; **chwaraewr DVD** DVD player
chwaraeydd (-ion) *nm* actor
chwarddiad (-au) *nm* laugh
chwarel (-au, -i, -ydd) *nf* quarry
chwarelwr (-wyr) *nm* quarryman
chwareus *adj* playful
chwarren (-arennau) *nf* gland; kernel
chwart (-iau) *nm* quart
chwarter (-i, -au) *nm* quarter
chwarterol *adj* quarterly
chwarterolyn (-olion) *nm* quarterly (magazine)
chwarteru *vb* to quarter
chwe *adj* six (before a noun)
chweban (-nau) *nm* sestet, sextain
chwech (-au) *adj*, *nm* six
chwechawd (-au) *nm* sextet
chweched *adj* sixth; **chweched dosbarth** sixth form
chwedl (-au) *nf* story, tale
chwedleua *vb* to talk, to gossip
chwedleuwr (-wyr) *nm* story-teller
chwedloniaeth *nf* mythology

chwedlonol *adj* mythical, mythological

chwedlonydd (-wyr) *nm* mythologist

chwedyn *adv*: **na chynt na chwedyn** neither before nor after

Chwefror, Chwefrol *nm* February

chwennych, chwenychu *vb* to covet, to desire

chwenychiad (-au) *nm* desire

chweongl (-au) *nm* hexagon

chwephlyg *adj* sixfold

chwerthin *vb* to laugh ▸ *nm* laughter

chwerthiniad (-au) *nm* laugh

chwerthinllyd *adj* laughable, ridiculous

chwerthinog *adj* laughing, merry

chwerw *adj* bitter

chwerwder, chwerwdod *nm* bitterness

chwerwedd *nm* bitterness

chwerwi *vb* to grow bitter, to embitter

chwi *pron* you

chwib (-iau) *nm* whistle

chwiban *vb* to whistle ▸ *nm* whistle

chwibaniad *nm* whistling, whistle

chwibanogl (-au) *nf* whistle, flute

chwibanu *vb* to whistle

chwibon (-iaid) *nm* curlew, stork

chwifio *vb* to wave, to flourish, to brandish

chwiff (-iau) *nf* whiff, puff

chwiffiad *nm* whiff, jiffy

chwil¹ (-od) *nmf* beetle, chafer

chwil² *adj* whirling, reeling

chwilboeth *adj* scorching, piping hot

chwildroi *vb* to whirl, to spin

chwilen (chwilod) *nf* beetle

chwilenna *vb* to rummage; to pry; to pilfer

chwiler (-od) *nm* chrysalis, pupa

chwilfriw *adj* smashed to atoms

chwilfriwio *vb* to smash, to shatter

chwilfrydedd *nm* curiosity

chwilfrydig *adj* curious, inquisitive

chwilgar *adj* curious, inquisitive

chwilgarwch *nm* inquisitiveness

chwiliad (-au) *nm* search, scrutiny

chwiliadur (-on) *nm* search engine

chwilibawa, chwilibawan *vb* to dawdle, to trifle

chwilio *vb* to search; to examine

chwiliwr (-wyr) *nm* searcher

chwil-lys *nm* inquisition

chwilmantan *vb* to pry, to rummage

chwilolau (-oleuadau) *nm* searchlight

chwilota *vb* to rummage, to pry

chwilotwr (-wyr) *nm* searcher, rummager

chwim *adj* nimble, quick, agile

chwimder, chwimdra *nm* nimbleness

chwimio *vb* to move, to stir, to accelerate

chwimwth *adj* nimble, brisk

chwinc *nm* wink

chwinciad *nm* twinkling, trice

chwiorydd *see* chwaer

chwip (-iau) *nf* whip; whipping

chwipiad (-au) *nm* whipping

chwipio *vb* to whip

chwipyn *adv* instantly
chwirligwgan *nf* whirligig
chwisgi *nm* whisky
chwisl (-au) *nm* whistle
chwistrell (-au, -i) *nf* squirt, syringe
chwistrelliad (-au) *nm* injection
chwistrellu *vb* to squirt, to syringe, to inject
chwit-chwat *adj* fickle, inconstant
chwith *adj* left; wrong; sad; strange
chwithau *pron* you (on your part), you also
chwithdod, chwithdra *nm* strangeness
chwithig *adj* strange, wrong, awkward
chwithigrwydd *nm* awkwardness
chwiw (-iau) *nf* fit, attack, malady
chwiwgar *adj* fickle
chwychwi *pron* you yourselves
chwŷd, chwydiad *nm* vomit
chwydu *vb* to vomit, to spew
chwydd, chwyddi *nm* swelling
chwyddiant (-nnau) *nm* inflation; inflammation
chwyddo *vb* to swell, to increase, to magnify
chwyddwydr (-au) *nm* microscope
chwŷl (chwylion) *nmf* turn, rotation
chwyldro (-ion) *nm* rotation; orbit
chwyldroad (-au) *nm* revolution
chwyldroadol *adj* revolutionary
chwyldroadwr (-wyr) *nm* revolutionary
chwyldroi *vb* to whirl, to revolve, to rotate

chwyldrowr *see* chwyldroadwr
chwylolwyn (-ion) *nf* flywheel
chwyn (nm chwynnyn) *coll n, npl* weeds
chwynladdwr *nm* weed-killer
chwynnu *vb* to weed
chwyrligwgan (-od) *nm* spinning top, whirligig
chwyrlïo *vb* to whirl, to spin, to speed
chwyrlwynt (-oedd) *nm* whirlwind
chwyrn *adj* rapid, swift
chwyrnellu *vb* to whirl, to whiz
chwyrnu *vb* to hum; to snore; to snarl
chwyrnwr (-wyr) *nm* snorer; snarler
chwys *nm* sweat, perspiration
chwysfa (-feydd) *nf* sweating
chwysiant *nm* exudation
chwysigen (-igod) *nf* blister, vesicle
chwyslyd *adj* sweaty
chwystyllau *npl* pores
chwysu *vb* to sweat, to perspire; to exude
chwyswr (-wyr) *nm* sweater
chwyth, chwythad *nm* breath
chwythbib (-au) *nf* blowpipe
chwythbrenni *npl* woodwinds
chwythell (-i) *nf* jet
chwythiad (-au) *nm* blow, blast
chwythu *vb* to blow, to blast; to breathe; to hiss
chwythwr (-wyr) *nm* blower

d

da *adj* good, well ▸ *nm* (**-oedd**) good; goods; stock, cattle
dacw *adv* there is, are; behold there
dad-, dat- *prefix* un-, dis-, re-, back
da-da *nm* sweets
dadansoddi *vb* to analyse
dadansoddiad (-au) *nm* analysis
dadansoddol *adj* analytic(al)
dadansoddwr (-wyr) *nm* analyst
dadansoddydd (-wyr) *nm* analyser
dadchwyddiant (-nnau) *nm* deflation
dad-ddyfrio *vb* to dehydrate
dadebriad *nm* resuscitation
dadebru *vb* to resuscitate, to revive
dadelfeniad (-au) *nm* decomposition
dadelfennu *vb* to decompose; to refine
dadeni *vb* to regenerate, to reanimate ▸ *nm* rebirth, renascence, renaissance
dadfachu *vb* to unhook

dadfathiad *nm* dissimulation
dadfeiliad *nm* decay
dadfeilio *vb* to fall to ruin, to decay
dadflino *vb* to rest (after exertion)
dadl (-euon) *nf* debate; doubt; plea
dadlaith *vb* to thaw; to dissolve
dadlau *vb* to argue, to debate; to plead
dadleniad (-au) *nm* disclosure, exposure
dadlennol *adj* revealing, disclosing, exposing
dadlennu *vb* to disclose, to expose
dadleoli *vb* to dislocate
dadleoliad (-au) *nm* dislocation
dadleuaeth *nf* polemics, controversy
dadleugar *adj* argumentative
dadleuol *adj* controversial, polemical
dadleuwr (-wyr), dadleuydd (-ion) *nm* debater, controversialist; advocate
dadluddedu *vb* to rest (after exertion)
dadlwytho *vb* to unload, to unburden; to download
dadlygru *vb* to decontaminate
dadmer *vb* to thaw; to dissolve
dadnitreiddiad *nm* denitrification
dadolwch *nm* propitiation ▸ *vb* to worship, to seek forgiveness
dadorchuddio *vb* to unveil, to uncover
dadreolaeth *nf* decontrol
dadrewlifiant *nm* deglaciation
dadrithiad (-au) *nm* disillusionment
dadrithio *vb* to disillusion
dadsefydlu *vb* to disestablish

dadwaddoli vb to disendow
dadwaddoliad nm disendowment
dadwneuthur, dad-wneud vb to undo, to unmake
dadwrdd nm noise, uproar, hubbub
dadymchwel, dadymchwelyd vb to overturn, to overthrow
daear (-oedd) nf earth, ground, soil
daeardy (-dai) nm dungeon
daeareg nf geology
daearegol adj geological
daearegwr (-wyr), **daearegydd** (-ion) nm geologist
daearen nf the earth; land, country
daearfochyn (-foch) nm badger
daeargell (-oedd) nf dungeon, vault
daeargi (-gwn) nm terrier
daeargryd (-iau) nm earth tremor
daeargryn (-fâu) nmf earthquake
daearol adj terrestrial, earthly, earthy
daearu vb to earth; to inter
daearyddiaeth nf geography
daearyddol adj geographical
daearyddwr (-wyr) nm geographer
dafad (defaid) nf sheep; wart
dafaden (-ennau) nf wart
dafn (-au) nm drop
dafnu vb to trickle
dagr (-au) nm dagger, bayonet, dirk
dagrau npl (nm **deigryn**) tears
dagreuol adj tearful, sad
dail npl (nf **dalen**, nf **deilen**) leaves
daioni nm goodness, good
daionus adj good; beneficial; beneficent

dal, dala vb to hold; to catch; to arrest; to last; **dal ati!** carry on!, don't give up!
dalen (-nau, dail) nf leaf
dalfa (-feydd) nf hold; arrest; custody; prison
dalgylch (-oedd) nm catchment area
daliad (-au) nm holding; tenet; spell
daliwr (-wyr) nm jig, catcher
dall (deillion) adj blind
dallbleidiaeth nf bigotry
dallbleidiol adj bigoted
dallbleidiwr (-wyr) nm bigot
dallineb nm blindness
dallu vb to blind; to dazzle
damcaniaeth (-au) nf theory
damcaniaethol adj theoretical
damcaniaethwr (-wyr) nm theorist
damcanu vb to theorize, to speculate
dameg (-hegion) nf parable
damhegol adj parabolic(al), allegorical
damhegwr (-wyr) nm allegorist
damnedig adj damned, damnable
damnedigaeth nf damnation, condemnation
damnio vb to damn
damniol adj damning, damnatory
damsang vb to tread, to trample
damwain (-weiniau) nf accident, chance, fate
damweinio vb to befall, to happen
damweiniol adj accidental, casual
dan see **tan**
danadl npl (nf **danhadlen**) nettles

danas *coll n* deer; **bwch danas** buck
danfon *vb* to send, to convey; to escort
dangos *vb* to show
dangoseg (-ion) *nf* index; indication
dangosol *adj* indicative, demonstrative
danheddog *adj* jagged, serrated, toothed
dannod *vb* to reproach, to upbraid, to taunt, to twit
dannoedd *nf* toothache
dansoddol *adj* abstract
dant (danedd) *nm* tooth
danteithfwyd (-teithion) *nm* dainty
danteithiol *adj* dainty, delicious
danteithion *npl* delicacies
darbodaeth *nf* thrift
darbodus *adj* provident, thrifty
darbwyllo *vb* to persuade, to convince
darfod *vb* to finish, to end; to perish; to happen
darfodadwy *adj* transitory, perishable
darfodedig *adj* perishable, transient
darfodedigaeth *nm* consumption
darfudiad (-au) *nm* convection
darfudol *adj* convectional
darganfod *vb* to discover, to find out
darganfyddiad (-au) *nm* discovery
darganfyddwr (-wyr) *nm* discoverer
dargludedd *nm* conductivity
dargludo *vb* to conduct

dargludydd (-ion) *nm* conductor
dargyfeiredd *nm* divergence
dargyfeirio *vb* to diverge, to divert
darlith (-iau, -oedd) *nf* lecture
darlithfa (-feydd) *nf* lecture room, lecture theatre
darlithio *vb* to lecture
darlithiwr (-wyr), **darlithydd (-ion)** *nm* lecturer
darlun (-iau) *nm* picture
darluniad (-au) *nm* portrayal, description
darluniadol *adj* pictorial, illustrated
darluniaeth *nf* imagery
darlunio *vb* to portray, to depict, to describe
darluniol *adj* pictorial
darllediad (-au) *nm* broadcast
darlledu *vb* to broadcast
darlledwr (-wyr) *nm* broadcaster
darllen *vb* to read
darllenadwy *adj* readable, legible
darllenfa (-feydd) *nf* reading room; reading-desk; lectern
darllengar *adj* fond of reading, studious
darlleniad (-au) *nm* reading
darllenwr (-wyr), **darllenydd (-ion)** *nm* reader
darn (-au) *nm* piece, fragment, part
darnguddio *vb* to conceal or withhold a part
darniad (-au) *nm* fragmentation
darnio *vb* to cut up, to hack
darn-ladd *vb* to beat mercilessly
darogan *vb* to predict, to foretell, to forebode ▸ *nf* **(-au)** prediction, foreboding

83

daroganu *vb* to predict, to foretell

daroganwr (-wyr) *nm* predictor, prophet, soothsayer, forecaster

darostwng *vb* to lower; to subdue; to subject, to humiliate

darostyngiad *nm* humiliation; subjection

darpar (-ion, -iadau) *nm* preparation, provision ▸ *adj* intended, elect

darpariaeth (-au) *nf* preparation, provision

darparu *vb* to prepare, to provide

darparwr (-wyr) *nm* provider

darwden *nf* ringworm

das (-au, deisi) *nf* rick, stack

dat- *prefix see* **dad-**

data *nm* data

datblygiad (-au) *nm* development, evolution

datblygol *adj* nascent, developing

datblygu *vb* to develop, to evolve

datblygus *adj* developmental

datblygydd (-ion) *nm* developer

datchwyddiant *nm* deflation

datgan *vb* to declare; to recount; to render

datganiad (-au) *nm* declaration; rendering

datganoli *vb* to devolve, to decentralize ▸ *nm* devolution

datganoliad *nm* devolution

datganu *vb* to declare; to sing, to render

datgeliad (-au) *nm* detection; revelation

datgelu *vb* to detect; to reveal

datgloi *vb* to unlock

datglymu *vb* to unhitch, to undo

datgorffori *vb* to dissolve (*parliament*)

datgorfforiad *nm* dissolution

datguddiad (-au) *nm* revelation, disclosure

datguddio *vb* to reveal, to disclose

datgyffesiad *nm* recantation

datgyffesu *vb* to recant

datgymalu *vb* to dislocate, to dismember

datgysylltiad *nm* disestablishment

datgysylltu *vb* to disconnect; to disestablish

datod *vb* to undo, to untie, to dissolve

datrannu *vb* to dissect

datro *vb* to change; to undo

datrys *vb* to solve

datrysiad (-au) *nm* solution, resolution

datseinio *vb* to resound, to reverberate

datsgwar (-au) *nm* square root

datysen (datys) *nf* date

dathliad (-au) *nm* celebration

dathlu *vb* to celebrate

dau (f dwy) *adj, nm* two

dau-, deu- *prefix* two, bi-

dauddyblyg *adj* twofold, double

daufiniog *adj* double-edged

dauwynebog *adj* two-faced

dawn (doniau) *nmf* gift, talent

dawns (-iau) *nf* dance

dawnsio *vb* to dance

dawnsiwr (-wyr) *nm* dancer

dawnus *adj* gifted, talented

de *adj, nf* right ▸ *nm* south

De Affrica *nf* South Africa

deall vb to understand ▸ nm understanding, intellect, intelligence
dealladwy adj intelligible
deallgar adj intelligent
deallol adj intellectual
dealltwriaeth (-au) nf understanding, intelligence
deallus adj understanding, intelligent
deallusion npl intelligentsia
deallusrwydd nm intelligence
deau adj, nf right ▸ nm south
debentur (-on) nm debenture
debyd (-au) nm debit
debydu vb to debit
dec (-iau, -s) nm deck
decilitr (-au) nm decilitre
decimetr (-au) nm decimetre
decstros nm dextrose
dectant nm ten-stringed instrument, psaltery
dechrau vb to begin ▸ nm beginning
dechreuad (-au) nm beginning
dechreunos nf nightfall, dusk
dechreuol adj initial
dechreuwr (-wyr) nm beginner
dedfryd (-au) nf verdict; sentence
dedfrydu vb to sentence
dedlein (-s) nf deadline
dedwydd adj happy, blessed
dedwyddwch, dedwyddyd nm happiness, bliss
deddf (-au) nf law, statute, act
deddfeg nf jurisprudence
deddfegwr (-wyr) nm jurist
deddfol adj legal, lawful
deddfu vb to legislate, to enact

deddfwr (-wyr) nm legislator
deddfwriaeth nf legislation, legislature
deddfwriaethol adj legislative
deddlyfr (-au) nm statute book
de-ddwyrain nm southeast
defni vb to drip, to trickle
defnydd (-iau) nm material, stuff; use
defnyddio vb to use, to utilize, to employ; **defnyddio'r cwbl o**, **defnyddio'r cyfan o** use up
defnyddiol adj useful
defnyddioldeb nm usefulness, utility
defnyddiwr (-wyr) nm user, consumer
defnyn (-nau) nm drop
defnynnu vb to drop, to drip, to dribble, to distil
defod (-au) nf custom; rite, ceremony
defodaeth nf ritualism
defodol adj ritualistic
defosiwn (-ynau) nm devotion
defosiynol adj devotional, devout
deffro, deffroi vb to rouse; to wake
deffroad (-au) nm awakening
deg adj ten ▸ nm (-au) ten
degaidd adj denary
degawd (-au) nm decade
degiad (-au) nm decimal
degol (-ion) nm, adj decimal
degoli vb to decimalise
degoliad nm decimalisation
degolyn (degolion) nm decimal
degwm (-ymau) nm tenth, tithe
degymu vb to tithe
deng adj ten (before certain words)

dehau, deheu *see* deau
deheubarth, deheudir *nm* southern region, south
deheuig *adj* dexterous, skilful
deheulaw *nf* right hand
deheuol *adj* southern
deheurwydd *nm* dexterity, skill
deheuwr (-wyr) *nm* southerner
deheuwynt *nm* south wind
dehongli *vb* to interpret
dehongliad (-au) *nm* interpretation
dehonglwr (-wyr), dehonglydd (-ion) *nm* interpreter
dehydrad (-au) *nm* dehydration
dehydru *vb* to dehydrate
deial (-au) *nm* dial
deialog (-au) *nmf* dialogue
deialu *vb* to dial
deifio *vb* to singe, to scorch; to blast; to dive
deifiol *adj* scorching, scathing
deifiwr (-wyr) *nm* diver
deigryn (dagrau) *nm* tear
deilbridd *nm* humus
deildy (-dai) *nm* bower, arbour
deilen (dail) *nf* leaf
deilgoll *adj* deciduous
deiliad (-on, deiliaid) *nm* tenant; subject
deiliant (-nnau) *nm* foliage
deilio *vb* to leaf
deiliog *adj* leafy
deillio *vb* to proceed, to emanate, to issue
deinameg *nf* dynamics
deinamig *adj* dynamic
deinamo (-s, -au) *nm* dynamo
deincod *nm* teeth on edge

deincryd *nm* chattering or gnashing of teeth
deintio *vb* to nibble
deintrod (-au) *nf* cog
deintydd (-ion) *nm* dentist
deintyddiaeth *nf* dentistry
deintyddol *adj* dental
deiseb (-au) *nf* petition
deisebu *vb* to petition
deisebwr (-wyr), deisebydd (-ion) *nm* petitioner
deisyf, deisyfu *vb* to desire, to wish; to beseech, to entreat
deisyfiad (-au) *nm* request, petition
del *adj* pretty, neat
delfryd (-au) *nm* ideal
delfrydiaeth *nf* idealism
delfrydol *adj* ideal
delfrydu *vb* to idealize
delfrydwr (-wyr) *nm* idealist
delff *nm* churl, oaf, dolt, rascal
delio *vb* to deal
delw (-au) *nf* image; form, mode, manner
delwedd (-au) *nf* image
delweddaeth *nf* imagery
delweddu *vb* to portray
delwi *vb* to pale, to be paralysed with fright
dellni *nm* blindness
dellt *npl* (*nf* -en) laths, lattice, splinters
democratiaeth (-au) *nf* democracy
democratig *adj* democratic
demograffeg *nf* demography
demograffig *adj* demographic
dengar *adj* attractive
dengarwch *nm* attractiveness

deniadau *npl* attractions, allurements
deniadol *adj* attractive
denims *npl* denims
Denmarc *nf* Denmark
denu *vb* to attract, to allure, to entice
deon (-iaid) *nm* dean
deondy (-dai) *nm* deanery
deoniaeth (-au) *nf* deanery
deor *vb* to brood, to hatch, to incubate
deorfa (-fâu, -feydd) *nf* hatchery
de-orllewin *nm* southwest
deorydd (-ion) *nf* incubator
derbyn *vb* to receive; to accept; to admit
derbyniad (-au) *nm* receipt; reception
derbyniadwy *adj* admissible
derbyniol *adj* acceptable
derbyniwr (derbynwyr) *nm* = derbynnydd
derbynneb (-ynebau, -ynebion) *nf* receipt, voucher
derbynnydd (-ynyddion) *nm* receiver
deri *npl* (*nf* **dâr**) oak-trees, oak
dernyn (-nau) *nm* piece, scrap
derwen (derw, deri) *nf* oak-tree, oak
derwydd (-on) *nm* druid
derwyddiaeth *nf* druidism
derwyddol *adj* druidic(al)
desg (-iau) *nf* desk; **desg dalu** checkout
desgant (-au) *nm* descant
desibel (-au) *nm* decibel
destlus *adj* neat

destlusrwydd *nm* neatness
detector (-au) *nm* detector
dethol *vb* to select, to pick, to choose ▸ *adj* select
detholedd *nm* selectivity
detholiad (-au, detholion) *nm* selection, anthology
deu- *see* dau-
deuawd (-au) *nfm* duet
deublyg *adj* double, twofold
deuddeg *adj, nm* twelve
deufin *adj* two-edged
deuffocal *adj* bifocal
deugain *adj, nm* forty
deugraff *nm* digraph
deunaw *adj, nm* eighteen
deunydd (-iau) *nm* stuff, material; **deunydd lapio** packaging
deuocsid *nm* dioxide
deuod (-au) *nm* diode, binary
deuol *adj* dual
deuoliaeth *nf* dualism, duality
deuparth *nd* two-thirds
deuris *adj* two-tier
deurudd *nd* the cheeks
deuryw *adj* bisexual
deurywiol *adj* bisexual
deusain *nd* diphthong
deutu *nd*: **o ddeutu** about
dewin (-iaid) *nm* diviner, magician, wizard
dewines (-au) *nf* witch, sorceress
dewiniaeth *nf* divination, witchcraft
dewinio *vb* to divine
dewiniol, dewinol *adj* prophetic, divinatory
dewis *vb* to choose, to select ▸ *nm* choice

dewisiad

dewisiad *nm* choice, option
dewisol *adj* choice, desirable; optional
dewr *adj* brave ► *nm* (**-ion**) brave man, hero
dewrder *nm* bravery, valour
di- *neg prefix* without, not, un-, non-, -less
diabetig *adj, nm* diabetic
diacon (**-iaid**) *nm* deacon
diacones (**-au**) *nf* deaconess
diaconiaeth *nf* diaconate
diadell (**-au, -oedd**) *nf* flock
diaddurn *adj* unadorned, plain, rude
diaelodi *vb* to dismember; to expel a member
diafael *adj* slippery, careless
diafol (**diefyl, dieifl**) *nm* devil
diaffram (**-au**) *nm* diaphragm
diagnosis *nm* diagnosis
diangen *adj* unnecessary, free from want
dianghenraid *adj* unnecessary, needless
di-ail *adj* unequalled, unrivalled
dial *vb* to avenge, to revenge ► *nm* vengeance, revenge
dialedd (**-au**) *nm* vengeance, nemesis
dialgar *adj* revengeful, vindictive
dialgarwch *nm* vindictiveness
di-alw-amdano *adj* redundant, uncalled for
dialwr (**-wyr**), **dialydd** (**-ion**) *nm* avenger
diamau *adj* doubtless
diamcan *adj* aimless, purposeless
diamedr (**-au**) *nm* diameter

diamedral *adj* diametral
diamheuol *adj* undoubted, indisputable
diamod *adj* unconditional, absolute
diamodol *adj* unconditional, unqualified
diamwys *adj* unambiguous
diamynedd *adj* impatient
dianc *vb* to escape
dianwadal *adj* unwavering, immutable
dianwadalwch *nm* immutability
diarddel *vb* to expel, to excommunicate
diarddeliad *nm* expulsion, excommunication
diarfogi *vb* to disarm
diarfogiad *nm* disarmament
diarffordd *adj* out of the way, inaccessible
diargyhoedd *adj* blameless
diarhebol *adj* proverbial
diaroglydd (**-ion**) *nm* deodorant
diarwybod *adj* unawares
diasbad *nf* cry, scream
diasbedain *vb* to resound, to ring
diatreg *adj* immediate
diau *adj* true, certain; doubtless
diawl (**-iaid**) *nm* devil
diawledig *adj* devilish
di-baid, dibaid *adj* unceasing, ceaseless
di-ball, diball *adj* unfailing, infallible, sure
diben (**-ion**) *nm* end, purpose, aim
di-ben-draw *adj* endless
dibeniad (**-au**) *nm* ending, conclusion; predicate

di-benllanw *adj* off-peak
dibennu *vb* to end, to conclude, to finish
diberfeddu *vb* to disembowel, to eviscerate
dibetrus *adj* unhesitating
dibl (-au) *nm* border, edge
di-blwm *adj* lead-free
diboblogaeth *nf* depopulation
diboblogi *vb* to depopulate
dibrin *adj* abundant, plentiful
dibriod *adj* unmarried, single
dibris *adj* reckless, contemptuous
dibrisio *vb* to depreciate, to despise
dibristod *nm* depreciation, contempt
dibwys *adj* trivial, unimportant
dibwysiant (-nnau) *nm* depression
dibyn (-nau) *nm* steep, precipice
dibynadwy *adj* reliable
dibynadwyedd *nm* reliability
dibyniad *nm* dependence
dibyniant *nm* dependence
dibynnedd *nm* reliability
dibynnol *adj* depending; subjunctive
dibynnu *vb* to depend, to rely
dibynnydd (dibynyddion) *nm* dependant
dicllon *adj* wrathful, angry
dicllonrwydd *nm* wrath, indignation
dicotomi (-ïau) *nm* dichotomy
dicra *adj* squeamish, fastidious, slow
dicter *nm* anger, wrath, displeasure
dichell (-ion) *nf* wile, craft, guile
dichellgar *adj* wily, crafty, cunning

dichlyn *vb* to choose, to pick ► *adj* careful, circumspect, exact
dichon *vb* to be able ► *adv* perhaps, maybe
dichonol *adj* potential
di-dact *adj* tactless
didactig *adj* didactic
didaro *adj* unaffected, unconcerned, cool
di-daw *adj* ceaseless, clamant
diden (-nau) *nf* nipple, teat
diderfyn *adj* unlimited
didoli *vb* to separate, to segregate
didoliad *nm* separation, segregation
didolnod (-au) *nm* diæresis
di-dor, didor *adj* unbroken, uninterrupted
didoreth *adj* shiftless, silly, fickle
didoriad *adj* unbroken, untamed, rough
di-drais, didrais *adj* non-violent, meek
diduedd *adj* impartial, unbiassed
didwyll *adj* guileless, sincere
didwylledd *nm* guilelessness, sincerity
di-ddadl *adj* unquestionable, indisputable
diddan *adj* amusing, diverting, pleasant
diddanion *npl* pleasantries, jokes
diddanu *vb* to amuse, to divert; to comfort
diddanwch *nm* comfort, consolation
diddanwr (-wyr), diddanydd (-ion) *nm* comforter
diddarbod *adj* shiftless

di-dderbyn-wyneb *adj* outspoken

diddig *adj* contented, pleased

diddigrwydd *nm* contentment, placidity

diddim *adj, nm* void

diddordeb *nm* interest

diddori *vb* to interest

diddorol *adj* interesting

diddos *adj* watertight, sheltered; snug

diddosi *vb* to shelter

diddosrwydd *nm* shelter, safety

di-dduw, didduw *adj* ungodly
  ▶ *nm* atheist

di-ddweud *adj* taciturn, stubborn

diddwythiad *nm* deduction

diddwytho *vb* to deduce

diddyfnu *vb* to wean

diddymdra *nm* nothingness, void

diddymiad, diddymiant *nm* annihilation

diddymu *vb* to annihilate, to abolish

dieflig *adj* devilish, diabolical, fiendish

diegwyddor *adj* unprincipled

dieisiau *adj* unnecessary, needless

dieithr *adj* strange, alien, foreign
  ▶ *nm* (**-iaid**) stranger

dieithrio *vb* to estrange, to alienate

dieithrwch *nm* strangeness

diemwnt *nm* diamond

dienaid *adj* soulless, senseless

dienyddiad (**-au**) *nm* execution

dienyddio *vb* to put to death, to execute

dienyddiwr (**-wyr**) *nm* executioner

dieuog *adj* guiltless, innocent

difa *vb* to consume, to destroy, to devour

di-fai, difai *adj* blameless, faultless

difalch *adj* humble

difancoll *nf* total loss, perdition

difaol *adj* consuming, devouring

difater *adj* indifferent, unconcerned

difaterwch *nm* indifference, apathy

difeddiannu *vb* to dispossess, to deprive

di-feind *adj* heedless

difenwad (**-au**) *nm* defamation

difenwi *vb* to revile, to abuse, to belittle

diferlif *nm* stream, issue

diferol *adj* dripping, dropping

diferu *vb* to drip, to drop, to dribble, to distil

diferyn (**-nau, diferion**) *nm* drop

diferynnu *vb* to trickle

difesur *adj* huge, immeasurable, unstinted

di-feth, difeth *adj* infallible, certain

difetha *vb* to destroy, to spoil, to waste

difethwr (**-wyr**) *nm* destroyer

Difiau *nm* Thursday

difidend (**-au**) *nm* dividend

diflanbwynt *nm* vanishing point

diflanedig *adj* evanescent, fleeting

diflaniad *nm* disappearance

diflannu *vb* to vanish, to disappear

di-flas *adj* tasteless

diflas *adj* insipid, dull, wearisome

diflastod *nm* disgust

diflasu *vb* to disgust; to weary, to surfeit

diflin, diflino *adj* untiring, indefatigable

difodi *vb* to annihilate, to exterminate

difodiad, difodiant *nm* annihilation

di-foes, difoes *adj* rude, unmannerly

difreiniad *nm* disfranchisement

difreinio *vb* to disfranchise, to deprive

difrïaeth *nf* abuse, calumny

difrif *nm* seriousness, earnestness

difrifddwys *adj* solemn

difrifol *adj* serious, earnest, solemn, grave

difrifoldeb *see* difrifwch

difrifoli *vb* to sober, to solemnize

difrifwch *nm* seriousness, earnestness, solemnity

difrio *vb* to scold, to abuse, to malign

difrod *nm* waste, havoc, damage

difrodi *vb* to waste, to spoil, to ravage

difrodol *adj* destructive

difrodwr (-wyr) *nm* spoiler, devastator

difrycheulyd *adj* spotless, immaculate

di-fudd, difudd *adj* unprofitable, useless, futile

di-fwlch, difwlch *adj* without a break, continuous

difwyniad (-au) *nm* adulteration, pollution

difwyniant *nm* defilement

difwyno *vb* to mar, to soil, to sully, to defile

difyfyr *adj* impromptu

difynio *vb* to dissect, to vivisect

difyr *adj* pleasant, diverting, amusing

difyrion *npl* diversions, amusements

difyrru *vb* to divert, to amuse, to beguile

difyrrus *adj* diverting, amusing

difyrrwch *nm* diversion, amusement, fun

difyrrwr (-yrwyr) *nm* entertainer

difyrwaith (-weithiau) *nm* hobby

difywyd *adj* inert

diffaith *adj* waste, desert; base, mean ▸ *nm* (**-ffeithydd**) wilderness, desert

diffeithdra *nm* dereliction

diffeithio *vb* to lay waste

diffeithwch (-ychau) *nm* desert, wilderness

diffiniad (-au) *nm* definition

diffinio *vb* to define

diffodd, diffoddi *vb* to put out, to quench, to extinguish; to switch off

diffoddiad *nm* quenching, extinction

diffoddwr (-wyr), diffoddydd (-ion) *nm* quencher

diffrwyth *adj* barren; numb, paralysed

diffrwythder, diffrwythdra *nm* barrenness; numbness

diffrwytho *vb* to make barren; to paralyse

diffuant *adj* unfeigned, sincere, genuine; **yn ddiffuant** sincerely
diffuantrwydd *nm* genuineness
di-ffurf *adj* amorphous
diffwys *adj* wild, waste; high, steep; huge, awful
diffyg (-ion) *nm* defect, want, lack; eclipse
diffygiant *nm* deficiency
diffygio *vb* to fail; to faint, to weary
diffygiol *adj* defective; faint, weary
diffyndoll (-au) *nf* tariff
diffyndollaeth *nf* protectionism
diffynnydd (-ynyddion) *nm* defendant
dig *adj* angry, wrathful ▸ *nm* anger, wrath
digalon *adj* disheartened, depressed, dejected, sad
digalondid *nm* depression, dejection
digalonni *vb* to dishearten, to discourage, to put off
digamsyniol *adj* unmistakable
digasedd *nm* hatred, enmity
digid (-au) *nm* digit
digidiad (-au) *nm* digitation
digidol *adj* digital
digio *vb* to anger, to offend; to take offence
di-glem *adj* inept
digllon *see* **dicllon**
digofaint *nm* anger, wrath, indignation
digofus *adj* angry, indignant
digolledu *vb* to indemnify, to compensate
digon *nm, adj, adv* enough; done (*of cooking*)

digonedd *nm* abundance, plenty
digoni *vb* to suffice; to satisfy; to cook
digonol *adj* satisfying; sufficient, adequate; satisfied
digonolrwydd *nm* sufficiency, abundance
digornio *vb* to dehorn
di-gred *adj* infidel
di-grefft, digrefft *adj* unskilled
digrif, digrifol *adj* mirthful, funny
digriflun (-iau) *nm* caricature, cartoon
digrifwas (-weision) *nm* clown, buffoon
digrifwch *nm* mirth, fun
digroeso *adj* inhospitable
digwydd *vb* to befall, to happen, to occur
digwyddiad (-au) *nm* happening, occurrence, event
digwyddiadol *adj* incidental
digyfnewid *adj* unchangeable
digyffelyb *adj* incomparable
digymysg *adj* unmixed
digyswllt *adj* incoherent
digywilydd *adj* impudent
digywilydd-dra *nm* impudence
dihafal *adj* unequalled, peerless
dihangfa (diangfâu) *nf* escape
dihangol *adj* escaped, safe
dihareb (diarhebion) *nf* proverb
dihatru *vb* to strip, to undress
dihefelydd *adj* unequalled
diheintio *vb* to disinfect
diheintydd (-ion) *nm* disinfectant, sterilizer
di-hid, di-hidio *adj* heedless, indifferent, reckless

dihidlo vb to drop, to distil; to shed
dihidrwydd nm indifference, recklessness
dihiryn (-hirod) nm rascal, scoundrel
dihoeni vb to languish, to pine
dihuno vb to wake, to rouse
di-hwyl adj out of sorts
dihyder adj lacking confidence
dihydradu vb to dehydrate
dihysbydd adj inexhaustible
dihysbyddu vb to empty, to exhaust
dil (-iau) nm: **dil mêl** honeycomb
dilead nm abolition, deletion
dilechdid nm dialectic
diledryw adj pure, genuine
dileu vb to delete, to rub out; to blot out; to abolish
dilewyrch adj dismal; not prosperous
dilorni vb to abuse, to revile
di-lun adj slovenly
diluw see dilyw
dilyffethair adj unencumbered, unfettered
dilyn vb to follow, to pursue; to imitate
dilyniad nm following; imitation
dilyniant (-nnau) nm sequence, progression
dilynol adj following; consequent
dilynwr (-wyr) nm follower; imitator
dilys adj sure, certain; genuine
dilysiant (-nnau) nm validation
dilysnod (-au) nm hallmark
dilysrwydd nm genuineness

dilysu vb to certify, to warrant, to guarantee
dilyw nm flood, deluge
dillad (nm dilledyn) npl clothes, clothing; **dillad isaf** underwear
dilladu vb to clothe
dilledydd nm clothier
dilledyn nm garment
dim adj any (with negative understood); no ▸ nm anything; none, nothing
dimensiwn (-iynau) nm dimension
dimensiynol adj dimensional
di-nam, dinam adj faultless
dinas (-oedd) nf city
dinasol adj municipal
dinasyddiaeth nf citizenship
dincod see deincod
dinesig adj civil, civic
dinesydd (dinasyddion) nm citizen
dinistr nm destruction
dinistrio vb to destroy
dinistriol adj destroying, destructive
dinistriwr (-wyr) nm destroyer
dinistrydd (-ion) nm destroyer
diniwed adj harmless, innocent
diniweidrwydd nm innocence
di-nod, dinod adj insignificant, obscure
dinodedd nm insignificance, obscurity
dinoethi vb to bare, to denude, to expose
diod (-ydd) nf drink, beverage
diodi vb to give drink
dioddef vb to suffer, to bear; to wait ▸ nm (-iadau) suffering
dioddefaint nm suffering, passion

dioddefgar, dioddefus *adj* patient
dioddefgarwch *nm* patience
dioddefwr (-wyr), dioddefydd (-ion) *nm* sufferer, patient
di-oed, dioed *adj* without delay, immediate
diofal *adj* careless
diofalwch *nm* carelessness
diog *adj* slothful, indolent, lazy
diogel *adj* safe, secure; sure, certain
diogelu *vb* to make safe, to secure
diogelwch *nm* safety, security
diogi *vb* to be lazy, to idle ▸ *nm* laziness
dioglyd *adj* lazy, sluggish, indolent
diogyn *nm* lazy one, idler, sluggard
diolch *vb* to thank, to give thanks ▸ *nm* (**-iadau**) thanks, thanksgiving
diolchgar *adj* thankful, grateful
diolchgarwch *nm* thankfulness, gratitude, thanksgiving
diolwg *adj* ugly
diorseddu *vb* to dethrone, to depose
di-os *adj* without doubt
diosg *vb* to undress, to put off, to strip, to divest
diota *vb* to tipple
diotwr (-wyr) *nm* boozer, drunkard
dioty (-tai) *nm* ale-house, public-house
diploma (-âu) *nmf* diploma
diplomateg *nf* diplomacy
diplomydd (-ion) *nm* diplomat
diplomyddol *adj* diplomatic
dipton (-au) *nf* diphthong
dir *adj* certain, necessary

diraddiad (-au) *nm* degradation
diraddio *vb* to degrade
diraddiol *adj* degrading
di-raen *adj* shabby, dull
dirboeni *vb* to torture, to excruciate
dirdyniad (-au) *nm* convulsion
dirdynnol *adj* excruciating
dirdynnu *vb* to rack, to torture
direidi *nm* mischievousness, mischief
direidus *adj* mischievous
direol *adj* unruly, disorderly
direwydd *nm* defroster
direwyn *nm* antifreeze
dirfawr *adj* vast, huge, immense, enormous
dirgel *adj* secret ▸ *nm* (**-ion**) secret
dirgelaidd *adj* mysterious
dirgeledig *adj* hidden, secret; mystical
dirgeledigaeth (-au) *nfm* mystery
dirgelu *vb* to secrete, to conceal, to hide
dirgelwch *nm* secrecy, mystery, secret
dirgryniad (-au) *nm* tremor, vibration
dirgrynol *adj* vibrating
dirgrynu *vb* to tremble, to vibrate
diriaethol *adj* concrete
dirlawn *adj* saturated
dirmyg *nm* contempt, scorn
dirmygu *vb* to despise, to scorn
dirmygus *adj* contemptuous; contemptible
dirnad *vb* to discern, to comprehend

dirnadaeth *nf* discernment, comprehension

dirnadwy *adj* discernible

dirprwy (-on) *nm* deputy; delegate

dirprwyaeth (-au) *nf* commission; deputation

dirprwyo *vb* to deputise, to delegate

dirprwyol *adj* vicarious

dirprwywr (-wyr) *nm* deputy, substitute

dirwasgiad (-au) *nm* depression

dirwest *nm* abstinence, temperance

dirwestol *adj* temperate

dirwestwr (-wyr) *nm* abstainer

dirwy (-on) *nf* fine

dirwyn *vb* to wind, to twist, to twine

dirwynnwr (-wyr) *nm* winder

dirwyo *vb* to fine

di-rym *adj* powerless, void

dirymu *vb* to nullify, to annul, to cancel

diryw *adj* neuter

dirywiad *nm* degeneration, deterioration

dirywiaeth *nf* degeneracy

dirywiedig *adj* degenerate

dirywio *vb* to degenerate, to deteriorate

dirywiol *adj* decadent, retrograde

dis (-iau) *nm* die, dice

di-sail *adj* groundless, baseless

disbaddu *vb* to castrate, to geld, to spay

disbaddwr (-wyr) *nm* castrator

disberod *nm*: **ar ddisberod** wandering, astray

disbyddedig *adj* exhausted

disbyddu *vb* to empty, to exhaust

disbyddwr *nm* exhaust

disel *nm* diesel

diserch *adj* sullen, sulky, loveless

disg (-iau) *nm* disk, record; **disg caled** hard disk

disgen (disgiau) *nf* discus

disglair *adj* bright, brilliant

disgleirdeb, disgleirder *nm* brightness, brilliance

disgleirio *vb* to shine, to glitter

disgloff *adj* free from lameness

disgo (-au) *nm* disco

disgownt (-iau, -s) *nm* discount

disgrifiad (-au) *nm* description

disgrifiadol *adj* descriptive

disgrifio *vb* to describe

disgwyl *vb* to look, to expect, to wait

disgwylfa (-feydd) *nf* watch-tower

disgwylgar *adj* watchful, expectant

disgwyliad (-au) *nm* expectation

disgybl (-ion) *nm* disciple, pupil

disgyblaeth *nf* discipline

disgyblu *vb* to discipline

disgyblwr (-wyr) *nm* disciplinarian

disgyn *vb* to descend, to get off; to fall, to drop; to let down

disgynfa (-feydd) *nf* descent, declivity; landing place

disgyniad (-au) *nm* descent

disgynnol *adj* descending

disgynnydd (-ynyddion) *nm* descendant

disgyrchedd *nm* gravitation

disgyrchiad, disgyrchiant *nm* gravity; **craidd disgyrchiant** centre of gravity

disgyrchu *vb* to gravitate

di-sigl *adj* unshaken, steadfast, firm

disiog *adj* diced

disodli *vb* to trip up, to supplant

dist (-iau) *nm* joist, beam

distadl *adj* insignificant, low, base, mean

distadledd *nm* insignificance, obscurity

distain (-einiaid) *nm* steward

distaw *adj* silent, quiet

distawrwydd *nm* silence, quiet

distewi *vb* to silence; to calm, to quiet

distryw *nm* destruction

distrywgar *adj* destructive, wasteful

distrywio *vb* to destroy

distrywiwr (-wyr) *nm* destroyer

distyll *nm* ebb; distillation

distyllio *vb* to distil

di-sut *adj* unwell; small

diswta *adj* sudden, abrupt

diswyddiad (-au) *nm* dismissal

diswyddo *vb* to dismiss from office, to discharge

disychedu *vb* to quench thirst

di-syfl *adj* immovable, impregnable

disyfyd *adj* sudden, instantaneous

disyml *adj* simple, artless, ingenuous

disymud *adj* immobile

disymwth *adj* sudden, instantaneous

disynnwyr *adj* senseless

ditectif (-s) *nm* detective

diwahân *adj* inseparable, indiscriminate

diwair *adj* chaste; celibate

di-waith, diwaith *adj* unemployed, idle

diwall *adj* satisfied, full, perfect

diwallu *vb* to satisfy, to supply

diwarafun *adj* unforbidden, ungrudging

diwasgedd (-au) *nm* depression (weather)

diwedydd (-iau) *nm* evening, eventide

diwedd *nm* end, conclusion

diweddar *adj* late, modern

diweddaru *vb* to modernize

diweddarwch *nm* lateness

diweddeb *nf* cadence

diweddglo *nm* conclusion

diweddu *vb* to end, to finish, to conclude

diweirdeb *nm* chastity

diweithdra *nm* unemployment

diwelfa (-feydd) *nf* watershed

diwerth *adj* worthless

diwethaf *adj* last

di-wifr *adj* wireless; **rhwydwaith di-wifr** wireless network

diwinydd (-ion) *nm* divine, theologian

diwinyddiaeth *nf* divinity, theology

diwinyddol *adj* theological

diwreiddio *vb* to uproot, to eradicate

diwrnod (-iau) *nm* day

diwrthdro *adj* inexorable

diwyd *adj* diligent, industrious, hard-working
diwydianfa *nf* industrial estate
diwydiannaeth *nf* industrialization, industrialism
diwydiannol *adj* industrial
diwydiannwr (-ianwyr) *nm* industrialist
diwydiant (-iannau) *nm* industry
diwydrwydd *nm* diligence, industry
diwyg *nm* form, dress, garb
diwygiad (-au) *nm* reform, reformation; revival
diwygiadol *adj* reformatory; revivalistic
diwygiedig *adj* reformed; revised
diwygio *vb* to amend, to reform, to revise
diwygiol *adj* reformatory
diwygiwr (-wyr) *nm* reformer; revivalist
diwylliadol *adj* cultural
diwylliannol *adj* cultural
diwylliant (-nnau) *nm* culture
diwylliedig *adj* cultured
diwyllio *vb* to cultivate
diymadferth *adj* helpless
diymadferthedd *nm* helplessness
diymdroi *adj* without delay
diymhongar *adj* unassuming
diymod *adj* steadfast, immovable
diymwad *adj* undeniable, indisputable
diysgog *adj* steadfast, firm, stable
diystyr *adj* contemptuous; contemptible; meaningless
diystyrllyd *adj* contemptuous, disdainful

diystyru *vb* to disregard, to despise
diystyrwch *nm* contempt, disdain, scorn
do *adv* yes *(to questions in preterite tense)*
doc (-iau) *nm* dock
docfa (-feydd) *nf* berth
docio *vb* to shorten; to dock, to berth
doctor (-iaid) *nm* doctor
doctora *vb* to doctor
dod *vb* to come; to become; **dod i mewn** to come in; **dod yn ôl** to come back
dodi *vb* to put, to place; to give; to switch on
dodrefn *npl (nm* **-yn)** furniture
dodrefnu *vb* to furnish
dodrefnwr (-wyr) *nm* furnisher
dodwy *vb* to lay eggs
doe *adv* yesterday
doeth (-ion) *adj* wise
doethineb *nmf* wisdom
doethinebu *vb* to discourse wisely, to pontificate
doethor (-iaid) *nm* doctor *(of university)*
doethur (-iaid) *nm* doctor *(of university)*
doethuriaeth (-au) *nf* doctorate
dof *adj* tame, domesticated; garden
dofednod *npl* fowls, poultry
dofi *vb* to tame, to domesticate; to assuage
dofn *adj f of* **dwfn**
Dofydd *nm* God
dogfen (-ni, -nau) *nf* document
dogfennaeth *nf* documentation

dogfennen (-ennau) *nf* documentary
dogfennol *adj* documentary
dogn (-au) *nm* share, portion; dose
dogni *vb* to ration
doili *nm* doyley
dol (-iau) *nf* doll
dôl¹ *nm* dole
dôl² (dolydd, dolau) *nf* meadow
dolbridd (-oedd) *nm* alluvium, meadow soil
doldir (-oedd) *nm* meadow-land
dolef (-au) *nf* cry
dolefain *vb* to cry out
dolefus *adj* wailing, plaintive
dolen (-nau) *nf* loop, link, ring, bow
dolennog *adj* ringed, looped; winding
dolennu *vb* to loop; to wind, to meander
doler (-i) *nf* dollar
dolffin *nm* dolphin
dolur (-iau) *nm* sore; ailment; grief
dolurio *vb* to hurt, to wound; to grieve
dolurus *adj* sore
dominyddu *vb* to dominate
donio *vb* to endow, to gift
doniol *adj* gifted; witty, humorous
donioldeb, doniolwch *nm* wit, humour
dôr (dorau) *nf* door
dos (-ys, -au) *nf* dose
dosbarth (au, -iadau) *nm* class; district
dosbarthiad *nm* distribution
dosbarthu *vb* to class, to classify; to distribute
dosbarthwr (-wyr) *nm* distributor

dosio *vb* to dose
dosran (-nau) *nf* division, section
dosrannu *vb* to separate, to analyse
dot¹ (-iau) *nmf* dot
**dot² ** *nf* giddiness, vertigo
dotio *vb* to dote
drachefn *adv* again
dracht (-iau) *nm* draught *(of liquor)*
drachtio *vb* to drink deep
draen¹ (draeniau) *nf* drain
draen², draenen (drain) *nf* thorn
draeniad (-au) *nm* drainage
draenio *vb* to drain
draenog (-od) *nm* hedgehog
drafft (-iau) *nm* draft, draught
draffts *npl* draughts
dragio *vb* to drag, to tear, to mangle
draig (dreigiau) *nf* dragon
drain *see* draen
drama (dramâu) *nf* drama
dramateiddio *vb* to dramatize
dramatig *adj* dramatic
dramodiad (-au) *nm* dramatization
dramodwr (-wyr) *nm* dramatist
dramodydd *nm* playwright
drâr *nm* drawer
draw *adv* yonder, away
dreflan *vb* to dribble
dreng *adj* morose, surly, sullen, harsh
dresel (dreseli, dreselydd), dreser *nm* dresser
drewdod *nm* stink, stench
drewi *vb* to stink
drewllyd *adj* stinking
driblo *vb* to dribble

drifft (-iau) *nm* drift
dringad *vb* to climb
dringfa (-feydd) *nf* climb, ascent
dringo *vb* to climb
dringwr (-wyr) *nm* climber
dril (-iau) *nm* drill
drilio *vb* to drill
dripsych *adj* drip-dry
drôr (drors) *nm* drawer
dros *see* **tros**
drud *adj* dear, precious, costly; reckless
drudfawr *adj* costly, expensive
drudwen *nf* starling
drudwy *nm* starling
drwg *adj* evil, bad, naughty, wicked ▸ *nm* (**drygau**) evil, harm, hurt
drwgdybiaeth (-au) *nf* suspicion
drwgdybio *vb* to suspect
drwgdybus *adj* suspicious
drwglosgiad *nm* arson
drwgweithredwr (-wyr) *nm* evildoer
drwm (drymiau) *nm* drum
drws (drysau) *nm* door
drwy *see* **trwy**
drycin (-oedd) *nf* foul weather
drycinog *adj* stormy
drych (-au) *nm* spectacle; mirror; object, pattern
drychfeddwl (-yliau) *nm* idea
drychiolaeth (-au) *nf* apparition, phantom
drygair *nm* ill report; scandal
dryganadl *nm* halitosis
drygfyd *nm* adversity
drygioni *nm* badness, wickedness
drygionus *adj* bad, wicked
drygu *vb* to hurt, to harm, to injure

dryll (-iau) *nm* piece; part ▸ *nmf* gun, rifle
drylliad (-au) *nm* breaking; wreck
drylliedig *adj* broken, shattered
dryllio *vb* to break in pieces, to shatter
drylliog *adj* broken, contrite
drymiwr (-wyr) *nm* drummer
drysi *npl* (*nf*-**ïen**) thorns, briers
dryslwyn (-i) *nm* thicket
dryslyd *adj* perplexing; confused
drysu *vb* to tangle; to perplex; to be confused
dryswch *nm* tangle; perplexity; confusion
dryw (-od) *nmf* wren
DU *nf* UK
du *adj* black
duc, dug (-iaid) *nm* duke
dugiaeth *nf* duchy
Dulyn *nf* Dublin
dull (-iau) *nm* form, manner, mode
dullwedd (-au) *nm* mannerism
duo *vb* to black, to blacken
dur *nm* steel
duw (-iau) *nm* god; **Duw** God
düwch *nm* blackness
duwdod *nm* godhead, divinity, deity
duwies (-au) *nf* goddess
duwiol (-ion) *adj* godly, pious
duwioldeb *nm* godliness, piety
duwiolfrydedd *nm* godliness, piety
duwiolfrydig *adj* god-fearing, pious
DVD (-s) *n* DVD
dwbio *vb* to daub, to plaster
dwbl *adj* double
dweud, dweyd *see* **dywedyd**

dwfn (f **dofn**) adj deep, profound
dwfr, dŵr (**dyfroedd**) nm water
dwl adj dull, stupid, foolish
dwlu vb to dote
dwmbwr-dambar adv helter-skelter
dwndwr nm din, babble, hubbub
dwnsiwn (**-iynau**) nm dungeon
dŵr see **dwfr**
dwrdio vb to scold
dwrn (**dyrnau**) nm fist; knob, handle, hilt
dwsin (**-au**) nm dozen
dwst nm dust, powder
dwster (**-i**) nm duster
dwthwn nm day
dwy see **dau**
dwyfol adj divine
dwyfoldeb nm divinity, deity
dwyfoli vb to deify
dwyfron (**-nau**) nf breast, chest
dwyfronneg nf breastplate
dwyieithedd nm bilingualism
dwyieitheg nf study of bilingualism
dwyieithog adj bilingual
dwyieithrwydd nm bilingualism
dwylaw, dwylo nd, pl two hands, hands
dwyn vb to bear; to bring; to steal
dwyochredd nm bilateralism
dwyochrol adj bilateral
dwyradd adj quadratic, two-tier
dwyrain nm, adj east; **Dwyrain yr Almaen** East Germany
dwyraniad nm dichotomy
dwyrannu vb to bisect
dwyreiniol adj easterly, eastern, oriental

dwyreiniwr (**-wyr**) nm easterner, oriental
dwys adj dense, grave, deep, intense
dwysáu vb to deepen, to intensify
dwysbigo vb to prick, to sting
dwysedd (**-au**) nm density
dwyster nm gravity, solemnity
dwythell (**-au**) nf duct
dwywaith adv twice
dy pron thy, thine
dyblu vb to double; to repeat
dyblyg adj twofold, double
dyblygiad (**-au**) nm duplication, duplicate
dyblygu vb to double, to fold
dyblygydd (**-ion**) nm duplicator
dybryd adj sore, dire; flagrant
dychan (**-au**) nf lampoon, satire
dychangerdd (**-i**) nf satirical poem, satire
dychanol adj satirical
dychanu vb to lampoon, to satirize, to revile
dychanwr (**-wyr**) nm satirist
dychmygadwy adj imaginable
dychmygol adj imaginary
dychmygu vb to imagine
dychmygus adj imaginative, inventive
dychryn (**-iadau**) nm fright, terror ▸ vb to frighten
dychrynllyd adj frightful, terrible
dychrynu vb to frighten, to be frightened
dychweledig adj returned
dychweliad (**-au**) nm return; conversion

dychwelyd *vb* to return, to come back

dychymyg (**dychmygion**) *nm* imagination, fancy; riddle, device

dydd (**-iau**) *nm* day; **dyddiau cŵn** silly season; **Dydd Sant Folant** Valentine's Day

dyddfu *vb* to flag, to pine, to faint

dyddiad (**-au**) *nm* date

dyddiadur (**-on**) *nm* diary, journal

dyddiedig *adj* dated

dyddio *vb* to become day, to dawn; to date

dyddiol *adj* daily

dyddlyfr (**-au**) *nm* diary, journal

dyddodyn (**-odion**) *nm* deposit

dyfais (**-feisiau**) *nf* device, invention

dyfal *adj* diligent

dyfalbarhad *nm* perseverance

dyfalbarhau *vb* to persevere

dyfaliad (**-au**) *nm* guess, conjecture

dyfalu *vb* to guess, to conjecture

dyfalwch *nm* diligence, assiduity

dyfarniad (**-au**) *nm* decision, verdict

dyfarnu *vb* to adjudge; to referee

dyfarnwr (**-wyr**) *nm* judge, umpire, referee

dyfeisio *vb* to make up, to devise, to invent, to imagine; to guess

dyfeisiwr (**-wyr**) *nm* inventor

dyfnant (**-nentydd**) *nf* ravine

dyfnder (**-au, -oedd**) *nm* deep, depth

dyfnhau *vb* to deepen

dyfod *vb* to come; to become

dyfodfa *nf* access, entrance

dyfodiad[1] *nm* coming, arrival, advent

dyfodiad[2] (**-iaid**) *nm* incomer, stranger

dyfodol *adj* coming, future ▸ *nm* future

dyfradwy *adj* watered; watering

dyfredig *adj* irrigated

dyfrffos (**-ydd**) *nm* canal, watercourse

dyfrgi (**-gwn**) *nm* otter

dyfrllyd *adj* watery

dyfrwr *n* waterman, water-carrier; **y Dyfrwr** Aquarius

dyfrhad *nm* irrigation

dyfrhau, dyfrio *vb* to water

dyfyniad (**-au**) *nm* citation, quotation

dyfynnod (**-ynodau**) *nm* quotation mark

dyfynnol *adj* citatory, summoned

dyfynnu *vb* to cite, to quote; to summon

dyffryn (**-noedd**) *nm* valley

dyffryndir (**-oedd**) *nm* low country; vale

dygn *adj* hard, severe, grievous, dire

dygnu *vb* to strive, to persevere

dygnwch *nm* perseverance, assiduity

dygwyl *nm* holiday, feast day

dygymod *vb* to agree (with), to put up (with)

dyhead (**-au**) *nm* aspiration

dyheu *vb* to pant; to long, to yearn, to aspire

dyhiryn *see* **dihiryn**

dyladwy *adj* due

dylanwad

dylanwad (**-au**) *nm* influence
dylanwadol *adj* influential
dylanwadu *vb* to influence
dyled (**-ion**) *nf* debt, obligation
dyledog *adj* in debt, indebted
dyledus *adj* due
dyledwr (**-wyr**) *nm* debtor
dyletswydd (**-au**) *nf* duty, obligation
dylif *nm* flood, deluge ▸ *nf* warp
dylifo *vb* to flow, to stream, to pour
dylni *nm* stupidity, dullness
dyluniad (**-au**) *nm* design, drawing
dylunio *vb* to design
dylunydd (**-ion**) *nm* designer
dylyfu gên *vb* to yawn, to gape
dylluan *see* tylluan
dyma *adv* here is, here are; this is, these are
dymchweliad *nm* overthrow
dymchwelyd *vb* to overthrow, to upset, to subvert
dymuniad (**-au**) *nm* wish, desire
dymuno *vb* to wish, to desire
dymunol *adj* desirable, agreeable, pleasant
dyn (**-ion**) *nm* man, person
dyna *adv* there is, there are; that is, those are
dynad *npl* nettles
dyndod *nm* manhood, humanity
dyneiddiaeth *nf* humanism
dyneiddiol *adj* humanistic
dyneiddiwr (**-wyr**) *nm* humanist
dynes *nf* woman
dynesiad *nm* approach
dynesu *vb* to draw near, to approach
dyngar *adj* humane

dyngarol *adj* philanthropic
dyngarwch *nm* philanthropy
dyngarwr (**-wyr**) *nm* philanthropist
dyniawed (**-iewaid**) *nm* yearling, steer
dynladdiad *nm* manslaughter
dynodi *vb* to denote, to signify
dynodiad (**-au**) *nm* denotation
dynol *adj* human; man-like; manly
dynoliaeth *nf* humanity
dynoliaethau *npl* humanities
dynolryw *coll n* mankind
dynwared *vb* to imitate, to mimic
dynwarededd *nm* mimicry
dynwarediad (**-au**) *nm* imitation, mimicry
dynwaredol *adj* imitative
dynwaredwr (**-wyr**) *nm* imitator, mimic
dyraddiant *nm* degradation
dyraniad (**-au**) *nm* allocation
dyrchafael *vb* to rise, to ascend ▸ *nm* ascension
dyrchafedig *adj* exalted
dyrchafiad *nm* elevation, promotion
dyrchafol *adj* elevating
dyrchafu *vb* to raise, to elevate; to rise, to ascend
dyri (**-ïau**), **dyrif** (**-au**) *nf* ballad, lyric
dyrnaid (**-eidiau**) *nm* handful
dyrnio *vb* to punch
dyrnod (**-iau**) *nmf* blow, stroke
dyrnu *vb* to thump; to thresh
dyrnwr (**-wyr**) *nm* thresher
dyrnwr medi *nm* combine harvester

dyrys *adj* tangled; difficult; perplexing
dyryslyd, dyrysu, dyryswch *see* dryslyd; drysu; dryswch
dysg *nfm* learning
dysgedig (-ion) *adj* learned
dysgeidiaeth *nf* teaching, doctrine
dysgl (-au) *nf* dish; **dysgl loeren** satellite dish
dysglaid (-eidiau) *nf* dishful, dish
dysgu *vb* to learn, to teach
dysgwr (-wyr) *nm* learner, teacher
dyslecsig *adj* dyslexic
dywalgi (-gwn) *nm* tiger
dywediad (-au) *nm* saying
dywedwst *adj* taciturn ► *nm* taciturnity
dywedyd *vb* to say, to speak, to tell
dyweddi (-ïau) *nf* betrothal; fiancé(e)
dyweddïad *nm* betrothal
dyweddïo *vb* to betroth

eang *adj* wide, broad, immense
eangder, eangu *see* ehangder; ehangu
eangfrydedd *nm* magnanimity
eangfrydig *adj* broad-minded, magnanimous
eb, ebe, ebr *vb* said
ebargofiant *nm* oblivion
ebill (-ion) *nm* auger, borer; peg
ebillio *vb* to bore
ebol (-ion) *nm* colt, foal
eboles (-au) *nf* foal, filly
eboni *nm* ebony
ebost (ebyst) *nm* email
ebostio *vb* to email
ebran (-nau) *nm* provender, fodder
Ebrill *nm* April
ebrwydd *adj* quick, swift, soon
ebwch (-ychau) *nm* gasp
ebychiad (-au) *nm* interjection, ejaculation
ebychnod *nm* exclamation

ebychu vb to gasp, to interject, to
ejaculate

eciwmenaidd adj ecumenical

ecliptig adj, nm ecliptic

ecoleg (-au) nf ecology

ecolegol adj ecological

ecolegwr (-wyr) nm ecologist

economaidd adj economic

economeg nf economics

economegol adj economic

economegwr (-wyr) nm
economist

economegydd (-ion) nm
economist

economi (-ïau) nm economy

economydd nm economist

ecsbloetio vb to exploit

ecsbloetiwr (-wyr) nm exploiter

ecseis nm excise

ecseismon (-myn) nm exciseman

ecsema nm eczema

ecsentredd (-au) nm eccentricity

ecsentrig adj eccentric (in maths)

ecstasi nm ecstasy

ecstatig adj ecstatic

echblyg adj explicit, outward

echblygol adj extrovert

echdoe adv day before yesterday

echdoriad (-au) nm eruption

echdorri vb to erupt

echdynnu vb to extract

echel (-au) nf axle, axletree; axis

echelin (-au) nm axis

echnos adv night before last

echrydus adj fearful, frightful,
shocking

echryslon adj dire

echwyn (-ion) nm loan

echwynna vb to borrow, to lend

echwynnwr (-wynwyr) nm lender,
creditor

edau (edafedd) nf thread; (pl)
yarn, wool

edefyn nm thread

edfryd vb to restore

e-diced (-i) nm e-ticket

edifar adj penitent, sorry

edifarus, edifeiriol adj repentant,
penitent

edifarhau, edifaru vb to repent,
to be sorry

edifeirwch nm repentance,
penitence

edliw vb to upbraid, to reproach,
to taunt

edmygedd nm admiration

edmygol adj admiring

edmygu vb to admire

edmygus adj impressed

**edmygwr, edmygydd
(edmygwyr)** nm admirer

edrych vb to look, to examine;
edrych ar to look at

edrychiad nm look

edrychwr (-wyr) nm beholder,
spectator

edwi, edwino vb to fade, to wither,
to decay

eddi npl thrums; fringe, nap

ef, efe pron he, him; it

efallai adv perhaps, peradventure

e-fasnach (-au) nf e-commerce

efengyl (-au) nf gospel

efengylaidd adj evangelical

efengyleiddio vb to evangelize

efengyles (-au) nf female
evangelist

efengylu vb to evangelize

efengylwr, efengylydd
(**efengylwyr**) *nm* evangelist
efelychiad (-au) *nm* imitation
efelychiadol *adj* imitative
efelychu *vb* to imitate
efelychwr (-wyr) *nm* imitator
efelychydd (-ion) *nm* simulator
eferw *adj* effervescent
eferwad (-au) *nm* effervescence
eferwi *vb* to effervesce
efo *prep* with
efô *pron* he, him; it
efrau *npl* tares
Efrog Newydd *nf* New York
efrydiaeth (-au) *nf* study
efrydu *vb* to study
efrydydd (-ion, -wyr) *nm* student
efydd *nm* bronze, copper, brass
effaith (-eithiau) *nf* effect;
   effeithiau arbennig special effects
effeithio *vb* to effect, to affect
effeithiol *adj* effectual, effective
effeithioli *vb* to render effectual
effeithiolrwydd *nm* efficacy
effeithlon *adj* efficient
effeithlonedd *nm* efficiency (of
   machines etc)
effeithlonrwydd *nm* efficiency
effro *adj* awake, vigilant
eger (-au) *nm* bore, eagre
egin *npl* (*nm* -**yn**) germs, sprouts
eginhad, eginiad (-au) *nm*
   germination, sprouting
egino *vb* to germinate, to shoot,
   to sprout
eginol *adj* germinal, shooting
eginyn (egin) *nm* sprout
eglur *adj* clear, plain, evident
eglurdeb, eglurder *nm* clearness

eglureb (-au) *nf* illustration
egluro *vb* to make clear, to explain
eglurhad *nm* explanation,
   demonstration
eglurhaol *adj* explanatory
eglwys (-i, -ydd) *nf* church
eglwysig *adj* church, ecclesiastical
eglwyswr (-wyr) *nm* churchman
eglwyswraig (-wragedd) *nf*
   churchwoman
egni (-ïon) *nm* effort, might, energy
egnïo *vb* to endeavour, to make
   an effort
egnïol *adj* energetic
egnïoli *vb* to energise
ego *nm* ego
egoistiaeth *nm* egoism
egosentrig *adj* egocentric
egöydd *nm* egoist
egr *adj* sharp; sour; severe; savage;
   cheeky
egroes *npl* (*nf* -**en**) hips
egwan *adj* weak, feeble
egwyd (-ydd) *nf* fetlock; fetter
egwyddor (-ion, -au) *nf* rudiment;
   principle; alphabet
egwyddorol *adj* high-principled
egwyl *nf* lull, respite; opportunity
enghraifft (-eifftiau) *nf* example,
   instance
enghreifftiol *adj* exemplary,
   illustrative
englyn (-ion) *nm* Welsh alliterative
   stanza
englyna, englynu *vb* to compose
   englynion
englynwr (-wyr) *nm* composer of
   englynion
engyl *see* angel

ehangder (**eangderau**) *nm* breadth, immensity

ehangu *vb* to enlarge, to extend

ehedeg *vb* to fly; to run to seed

ehedfa (**-feydd**) *nf* flight

ehedfan *vb* to hover, to fly

ehediad¹ (**-au**) *nm* flight

ehediad² (**-iaid**) *nm* fowl, bird

ehedog *adj* flying

ehedydd (**-ion**) *nm* lark

ehofndra *nm* fearlessness, boldness

ei *pron* his, hers; its

eicon (**-au**) *nm* icon

eich *pron* your

Eidal *nf*: **yr Eidal** Italy

eidion (**-nau**) *nm* ox

eiddew *nm* ivy

eiddgar *adj* zealous, ardent

eiddgarwch *nm* zeal, ardour

eiddigedd *nm* jealousy; zeal

eiddigeddu *vb* to be jealous, to envy; to have zeal

eiddigeddus *adj* jealous, envious

eiddigus *adj* jealous; zealous

eiddil *adj* slender, feeble

eiddilwch *nm* slenderness, feebleness

eiddiorwg *nm* ivy

eiddo *nm* property, possessions ▸ *pron* his *etc*

eidduno *vb* to desire, to wish, to pray

Eifftaidd *adj* Egyptian

Eifftiwr (**-wyr**), **Eifftiad** (**-iaid**) *nm* Egyptian

eigion *nm* depth, ocean

eigioneg *nf* oceanography

eigionol *adj* pelagic

eingion (**-au**) *nf* anvil

Eingl *npl* Angles, Englishmen

Eingl-Gymro (**-Gymry**) *nm* Anglo-Welshman

Eingl-Sais (**-Saeson**) *nm* Anglo-Saxon

Eingl-Seisnig *adj* Anglo-Saxon

eil- *prefix* second

eilchwyl *adv* again

eiliad (**-au**) *nfm* second, moment

eiliadur (**-on**) *nm* alternator

eilio *vb* to weave, to plait; to sing; to second

eiliwr (**-wyr**) *nm* seconder

eilradd (**-ol**) *adj* secondary, inferior

eilrif (**-au**) *nm* even number

eilun (**-od**) *nm* image, idol

eilunaddolgar *adj* idolatrous

eilunaddoli *vb* to worship idols

eilunaddolwr (**-wyr**) *nm* idolator

eilwaith *adv* again

eilydd (**-ion**) *nm* seconder, reserve

eillio *vb* to shave

eilliwr (**-wyr**) *nm* shaver, barber

ein *pron* our

einioes *nf* life, lifetime

einion (**-au**) *nf* anvil

eira *nm* snow

eirchion *see* **arch**

eirias *adj* burning, glowing, fiery

eirin *npl* (*nf* **-en**) plums; **eirin gwlanog** peaches; **eirin duon** damsons; **eirin duon bach** sloes; **eirin Mair** gooseberries

eirinen *nf* plum

eiriol *vb* to plead, to pray, to intercede

eiriolaeth *nf* intercession

eiriolwr (-wyr) *nm* intercessor, mediator
eirlaw *nm* sleet
eirlin (-iau) *nm* snow line
eirlithrad (-au) *nm* avalanche
eirlys (-iau) *nm* snowdrop
eironi *nm* irony
eisen (ais) *nf* rib; lath
eisglwyf *nm* pleurisy
eisiau *nm* want, need, lack
eising *nm* icing
eisin *coll n* bran, husk
eisio *vb* to ice
eisoes *adv* already
eistedd *vb* to sit, to seat
eisteddfa (-oedd, -fâu) *nf* seat
eisteddfod (-au) *nf* session; eisteddfod
eisteddfodol *adj* eisteddfodic
eisteddfodwr (-wyr) *nm* frequenter of *eisteddfodau*
eisteddfota *vb* to frequent *eisteddfodau*
eisteddiad (-au) *nm* sitting, session
eisteddle (-oedd) *nm* seat, sitting, pew
eitem (-au) *nf* item
eithaf (-ion) *adj, nm* extreme; superlative ▸ *adv* very, quite
eithafbwynt (-iau) *nm* extremity; apogee
eithafiaeth *nf* extremism
eithafion *npl* extremes, extremities
eithafol *adj* extreme; extremist
eithafwr (-wyr) *nm* extremist
eithin *npl* (*nf*-en) furze, gorse
eithinog *adj* furzy

eithr *prep* except; besides ▸ *conj* but
eithriad (-au) *nm* exception
eithriadol *adj* exceptional
eithrio *vb* to except, to exclude
elastig *adj, nm* elastic
elastigedd *nm* elasticity
electromagneteg *nf* electromagnetism
electromedr (-au) *nm* electrometer
electron (-au) *nm* electron
electroneg *nf* electronics
electronig *adj* electronic
elegeiog *adj* elegiac, mournful
eleni *adv* this year
elfen (-nau) *nf* element
elfennig *adj* elemental
elfennol *adj* elementary
eli (elïoedd) *nm* ointment, salve
elifiant (-nnau) *nm* effluence
elifyn (elifion) *nm* effluent
eliffant (-od, -iaid) *nm* elephant
eliffantaidd *adj* elephantine
elin (-au, -oedd) *nf* elbow; angle, bend
elips (-au) *nm* ellipse
eliptig *adj* elliptical
elor (-au) *nf* bier
elusen (-nau) *nf* alms
elusendy (-dai) *nm* almshouse
elusengar *adj* charitable, benevolent
elusengarwch *nm* charity, benevolence
elusennol *adj* eleemosynary
elusennwr (-enwyr) *nm* almoner
elw *nm* possession, gain, profit
elwa *vb* to gain, to profit

elwlen (-wlod) *nf* kidney

e-lyfr *nm* e-book

ellyll (-on) *nm* fiend; goblin

ellyllaidd *adj* fiendish; elfish

ellylles (-au) *nf* fury, she-goblin

ellyn (-au, -od) *nm* razor

embryo *nm* embryo

embryoleg *nf* embryology

emosiwn (-iynau) *nm* emotion

emosiynol *adj* emotional

empeiraeth *nf* empiricism

empeiraidd *adj* empirical

empirig *adj* empirical

emrallt *nm* emerald

emyn (-au) *nm* hymn

emyn-dôn (-au) *nf* hymn-tune

emyniadur (-on) *nm* hymnal

emynwr (-wyr) *nm* hymnist

emynyddiaeth *nf* hymnody, hymnology

enaid (eneidiau) *nm* life, soul

enamel (-au) *nm* enamel

enamlio *vb* to enamel

enbyd, enbydus *adj* dangerous, perilous

enbydrwydd *nm* peril, danger, jeopardy

encil (-ion) *nm* retreat, flight

encilfa (-feydd) *nf* retreat

enciliad (-au) *nm* retreat; desertion

encilio *vb* to retreat; to desert

enciliwr (-wyr) *nm* retreater; deserter

enclitig *adj* enclitic

encôr *nm* encore

encyd *nm* space; while

enchwythu *vb* to inflate

endemig *adj* endemic

endid *nm* entity, existence

endothermig *adj* endothermic

eneidiog *adj* animate

eneidiol *adj* animate, living

eneiniad (-au) *nm* anointing, unction

eneinio *vb* to anoint

Eneiniog *nm* The Messiah, Christ

eneiniog *adj, nm* anointed

enfawr *adj* enormous, huge, immense

enfys (-au) *nf* rainbow

engiriol *adj* nefarious, cruel, terrible

engrafiad (-au) *nm* engraving

engrafu *vb* to engrave

enhuddo *see* anhuddo

enigma *nm* enigma

enigmatig *adj* enigmatic

enillfawr *adj* lucrative, remunerative

enillgar *adj* gainful; winsome

enillion *npl* profits, earnings

enillwr, enillydd (enillwyr) *nm* gainer, winner

enllib (-ion, -iau) *nm* slander, libel

enllibaidd *adj* slanderous, libellous

enllibio *vb* to slander, to libel

enllibiwr (-wyr) *nm* slanderer, libeller

enllibus *adj* slanderous, libellous

enllyn *nm* relish eaten with bread

ennaint (eneiniau) *nm* ointment

ennill *vb* to gain, to win; to earn
▶ *nm* **(enillion)** gain, profit; *(pl)* earnings; **ennill pwysau** put on weight

ennyd *nmf* while, moment

ennyn *vb* to kindle, to burn, to inflame; to excite

ensyniad (-au) *nm* insinuation
ensynio *vb* to insinuate
entrych (-ion) *nm* firmament, height, zenith
enw (-au) *nm* name; noun; **enw bedydd** first name, Christian name
enwad (-au) *nm* denomination, sect
enwadaeth *nf* sectarianism
enwadol *adj* sectarian; nominative
enwadwr (-wyr) *nm* sectarian, sectary
enwaediad *nm* circumcision
enwaedu *vb* to circumcise
enwebai (-eion) *nm* nominee
enwebiad (-au) *nm* nomination
enwebu *vb* to nominate
enwedig *adj*: **yn enwedig** particularly, especially
enwi *vb* to name
enwog (-ion) *adj* famous, renowned, noted
enwogi *vb* to make famous
enwogrwydd *nm* fame, renown
enwol *adj* nominal, nominative
enwyn *nm*: **llaeth enwyn** buttermilk
enynfa *nf* inflammation; itching
enyniad (-au) *nm* inflammation
enynnol *adj* inflammatory; inflamed
eofn *adj* fearless, bold
eog (-iaid) *nm* salmon
eos (-au) *nf* nightingale
eosaidd *adj* like a nightingale
epa (-od) *nm* ape, monkey
epidemig *adj, nm* epidemic
epig *nf* epic

epiglotis (-au) *nm* epiglottis
epigram (-au) *nm* epigram
epil *nm* offspring, brood
epilepsi *nm* epilepsy
epilgar *adj* prolific, teeming
epiliad (-au) *nm* reproduction
epilio *vb* to bring forth, to teem, to breed
epilog *nm* epilogue
episeicloid (-au) *nm* epicycloid
epistol (-au) *nm* epistle
eples *nm* leaven, ferment
eplesiad *nm* fermentation
eplesu *vb* to leaven, to ferment
er *prep* for, in order to; since ▸ *conj* though
eraill *see* **arall**
erbyn *vb* to receive, to meet ▸ *prep* against, by
erch *adj* speckled; frightful
erchi *vb* to ask, to pray, to command, to demand
erchwyn (-ion) *nm* side, bed-side
erchyll *adj* hideous, horrible
erchyllter (-au) *nm* atrocity
erchylltod, erchylltra *nm* hideousness, horror
eres *adj* wonderful, strange
erestyn *nm* minstrel, buffoon
erfin *npl* (*nf* -**en**) turnips
erfyn *vb* to beg, to pray, to implore, to expect
erfyniad (-au) *nm* prayer, petition
ergyd (-ion) *nmf* blow, stroke; shot; cast
ergydio *vb* to strike; to throw, to cast
ergydiwr (-wyr) *nm* striker
erial (-au) *nm* aerial

erioed *adv* ever
erledigaeth (-au) *nf* persecution
erlid *vb* to persecute ▸ *nm* **(-iau)** persecution
erlidiwr (-wyr) *nm* persecutor
erlyn *vb* to pursue, to prosecute
erlyniad *nm* prosecution
erlynydd (-ion) *nm* prosecutor
ern, ernes (-au) *nf* earnest, pledge, deposit
ers *prep* since
erthwch *nm* grunt, pant
erthygl (-au) *nf* article
erthyl (-od) *nm* abortion
erthylaidd *adj* abortive
erthyliad (-au) *nm* abortion, miscarriage
erthylu *vb* to abort, to miscarry
erw (-au) *nf* acre
erwain *npl* meadow-sweet
erwydd *npl* stave (*in music*)
erydiad (-au) *nm* erosion
erydol *adj* erosive
erydu *vb* to erode
erydydd (-ion) *nm* erosive agent
eryr (-od) *nm* eagle; shingles
eryraidd *adj* eagle-like, aquiline
esblygiad (-au) *nm* evolution
esblygiadaeth *nf* evolutionism
esblygu *vb* to evolve
esboniad (-au) *nm* explanation; commentary
esboniadaeth *nf* exposition, exegesis
esboniadol *adj* expository, explanatory
esbonio *vb* to explain, to expound
esboniwr (-wyr) *nm* expositor, commentator

esbonydd (-ion) *nm* exponent
esbonyddol *adj* exponential
escaladur (-on) *nm* escalator
esgair (-eiriau) *nf* shank, leg; ridge
esgeirlwm *adj* exposed, wind-swept
esgeulus *adj* neglectful, negligent
esgeuluso *vb* to neglect
esgeulustod, esgeulustra *nm* negligence
esgid (-iau) *nf* boot, shoe; **esgidiau ymarfer** trainers
esgob (-ion) *nm* bishop
esgobaeth (-au) *nf* bishopric, see, diocese
esgobyddiaeth *nf* episcopalianism
esgoli *vb* to escalate
esgor *vb* to bring forth, to bear
esgud *adj* quick, swift, active
esgus (-ion, -odion) *nm* excuse, pretext
esgusodi *vb* to excuse
esgusodol *adj* excusable, excused
esgymun *adj* execrable, excommunicate
esgymuno *vb* to excommunicate
esgyn *vb* to ascend, to rise; to take off
esgynbren (-nau) *nm* perch
esgynfa (-feydd) *nf* ascent, rise
esgynfaen *nm* horse-block
esgyniad *nm* ascension
esgynneb (esgynebau) *nf* climax
esgynnol *adj* ascending
esgyrn *see* **asgwrn**
esgyrnog *adj* bony
esiampl (-au) *nf* example
esmwyth *adj* soft, smooth; easy
esmwythâd *nm* ease, relief

esmwytháu *vb* to soothe, to ease
esmwythder, esmwythdra *nm* ease
esmwytho, esmwytháu *vb* to ease, to soothe, to soften
esmwythyd *nm* ease, luxury
estron¹ (-iaid) *nm* foreigner, alien
estron² *adj* foreign, strange, alien
estrones (-au) *nf* alien woman
estronol *adj* strange, foreign, alien
estrys (-od) *nfm* ostrich
estyll *npl (nf-en)* planks, boards
estyn *vb* to extend, to reach; to stretch, to prolong
estynadwy *adj* extensible
estyniad *nm* extension, prolongation
estheteg *nf* aesthetics
esthetig *adj* aesthetic
etifedd (-ion) *nm* heir, inheritor
etifeddeg *nf* heredity
etifeddes (-au) *nf* heiress
etifeddiaeth (-au) *nf* inheritance
etifeddol *adj* hereditary
etifeddu *vb* to inherit
eto *conj* yet, still ▶ *adv* again; yet, still
ether *nm* ether
ethnig *nm* ethnic
ethnoleg *nf* ethnology
ethol *vb* to elect
etholaeth (-au) *nf* constituency
etholedig (-ion) *adj* elect
etholedigaeth *nf* election (*theology*)
etholfraint *nf* franchise
etholiad (-au) *nm* election
etholiadol *adj* electoral, elective
etholwr (-wyr) *nm* elector, voter
ethos *nm* ethos

eu *pron* their
euog *adj* guilty
euogfarn *nf* conviction
euogfarnu *vb* to convict
euogrwydd *nm* guiltiness, guilt
euraid, euraidd *adj* golden, (of) gold
euro *vb* to apply *or* bestow gold; to gild
eurych (-od) *nm* goldsmith
ewig (-od) *nf* hind
ewin (-edd) *nmf* nail, talon, claw; hoof
ewino *vb* to claw
ewinog *adj* having nails or claws
ewinrhew *nf* frost-bite
ewro (-aid, -s) *nm* euro
Ewrop *nf* Europe
Ewropead (-aid) *nm* European
Ewropeaidd *adj* European
ewyllys (-iau) *nf* will
ewyllysio *vb* to will, to wish
ewyn *nm* foam, froth, surf
ewynnog *adj* foaming, foamy, frothy
ewynnu *vb* to foam, to froth
ewythr (-edd) *nm* uncle

e

f

figanaidd *adj* vegan
fila *nf* villa
finegr *nm* vinegar
fiola (-s) *nf* viola
firws (-au, fira) *nm* virus
fitamin (-au) *nm* vitamin
fo *pron* him
folt (-iau) *nf* volt
foltamedr (-au) *nm* voltameter
foltedd (-au) *nm* voltage
foltmedr (-au) *nm* voltmeter
fortais (-eisiau) *nm* vortex
fory (yfory) *adv* tomorrow
fry *adv* above, aloft
fwltur (-iaid) *nm* vulture
fy *pron* my
fyny *adv* up, upwards

fagddu *nf*: **y fagddu** gross darkness
falf (-iau) *nf* valve
fan (-iau) *nf* van
fandal (-iaid) *nm* vandal
fandaleiddio *vb* to vandalize
fandaliaeth *nf* vandalism
farnais (-eisiau) *nm* varnish
farneisio *vb* to varnish
fe *pron* he, him
feallai *adv* perhaps, peradventure
fegan (-iaid) *nm* vegan
feganaidd *adj* vegan
fel *adv, conj, prep* so, as, that, thus,
    like; how; **fel arall** otherwise; **fel
    arfer, fel rheol** usually
felly *adv* so, thus
festri (-ïoedd) *nf* vestry
fi *pron* me
ficer (-iaid) *nm* vicar
ficerdy (-dai) *nm* vicarage
fideo (-s) *nm* video; **gêm fideo**
    video game
figan (-iaid) *nm* vegan

ff

ffa *npl* (*nf* **ffäen,** *nf* **ffeuen**) beans; ffa'r gors buckbeans; **ffa pob** baked beans
ffabrigo *vb* to fabricate
ffacbys *npl* fitches, vetches
ffacbysen (ffacbys) *nf* chickpea
ffactor (-au) *nmf* factor; **fffactor cyffredin mwyaf** highest common factor; **fffactor cysefin** prime factor
ffactori, -o *vb* to factorize
ffactri (-ïoedd) *nf* factory, mill
ffaeledig *adj* fallible, ailing
ffaeledigrwydd *nm* fallibility
ffaeledd (-au) *nm* failing, defect
ffaelu *vb* to fail
ffafr (-au) *nf* favour
ffafraeth *nf* favouritism
ffafrio *vb* to favour
ffafriol *adj* favourable
ffagl (-au) *nf* blaze, flame; torch
ffair (ffeiriau) *nf* fair, exchange; **ffair sborion** jumble sale

ffaith (ffeithiau) *nf* fact
ffald (-au) *nf* fold; pound
ffals (ffeilsion) *adj* false, deceitful
ffalsedd *nm* falsehood, deceit
ffalster *nm* deceitfulness, cunning
ffalwm *nm* whitlow
ffan (-nau) *nf* fan
ffanatig *nm* fanatic
ffanatigiaeth *nf* fanaticism
ffansi *nf* fancy
ffansïo *vb* to fancy
ffansïol *adj* fanciful
ffantasi, ffantasia (-ïau) *nf* fantasy
ffarm (ffermydd) *nf* farm
ffarmio *vb* to farm
ffarmwr (ffermwyr) *nm* farmer
ffarmwraig (-wragedd) *nf* farmer
ffârs (-iau) *nf* farce
ffarwél *nf* farewell
ffarwelio *vb* to bid farewell
ffas (-ys, -au) *nf* face, coal-face
ffasâd (ffasadau) *nm* facade
ffasgaeth *nf* fascism
ffasiwn (-iynau) *nm* fashion
ffasiynol *adj* fashionable
ffasner (-i) *nm* fastener
ffasnin (-au) *nm* fastening
ffasno *vb* to fasten
ffasnydd (-ion) *nm* fastener
ffatri (-ïoedd) *nf* factory, mill
ffatrïaeth *nf* manufacturing
ffau (ffeuau) *nf* den
ffawd (ffodion) *nf* fortune, fate
ffawdheglu *vb* to hitch-hike
ffawdheglwr (-wyr) *nm* hitch-hiker
ffawna *nf* fauna
ffawydd *npl* (*nf* **-en**) beech trees
ffederal *adj* federal

ffederaliaeth

ffederaliaeth *nf* federalism
ffederasiwn (-iynau) *nm* federation
ffedereiddio, ffedreiddio *vb* to federate
ffefryn (-nau) *nm* favourite
ffeil *nf* file; **ffeil sip** zip file
ffeilio *vb* to file
ffein, ffeind *adj* fine
ffeirio *vb* to barter, to exchange
ffeithiol *adj* factual
ffelt *nm* felt
ffelwm *nm* whitlow
ffemwr (ffemora) *nm* femur
ffendir *nm* fenland
ffenestr (-i) *nf* window; **ffenestri dwbl** double glazing
ffenigl *nm* fennel
ffenomen (-au) *nf* phenomenon
ffens (-ys) *nf* fence
ffensio *vb* to fence
ffêr (fferau) *nf* ankle
fferdod *nm* numbness
fferi (-ïau) *nf* ferry
fferins *npl* sweets
fferm (-ydd) *nf* farm
ffermdy (-dai) *nm* farm-house
ffermio *vb* to farm
ffermwr (-wyr) *nm* farmer
fferru *vb* to congeal, to freeze; to perish with cold
fferyllfa (-feydd) *nf* dispensary
fferylliaeth *nf* pharmacy
fferyllol *adj* chemical, pharmaceutical
fferyllydd (-wyr) *nm* chemist, pharmacist
ffesant (-s, -au) *nm* pheasant
ffest¹ *adj* fast

ffest² *nf* feast
ffetan (-au) *nf* sack, bag
ffeuen *nf* bean
ffi (-oedd) *nf* fee
ffiaidd *adj* loathsome, abominable
ffibr (-au) *nm* fibre
ffibrog, -us *adj* fibrous
Ffichtiad (-iaid) *nm* Pict
ffidil (ffidlau) *nf* fiddle
ffidlan *vb* to fiddle, to dawdle
ffidler (-iaid) *nm* fiddler
ffidlo *vb* to fiddle
ffieiddbeth (-au) *nm* abomination
ffieidd-dra *nm* abomination
ffieiddio *vb* to loathe, to abominate, to abhor
ffigur (-au) *nf* figure, type
ffigurol *adj* figurative
ffigys *npl* (*nf*-**en**) figs
ffigysbren (-nau) *nm* fig-tree
ffigysen *nf* fig
ffiled (-au, -i) *nf* fillet
ffilharmonig *adj* philharmonic
ffilm (-iau) *nf* film
ffilmio *vb* to film
ffiloreg *nf* rigmarole, nonsense
ffilter (-au, -i) *nm* filter
ffin (-iau) *nf* boundary, limit
Ffindir *nf*: **y Ffindir** Finland
ffindir (-oedd) *nm* borderland
ffinio *vb* to border (upon), to abut
ffiniol *adj* bordering
ffiol (-au) *nf* vial; cup
ffiseg *nf* physics
ffisegol *adj* physical
ffisegwr (-wyr) *nm* physicist
ffisig *nm* physic, medicine
ffisigwr (-wyr) *nm* physician
ffisigwriaeth *nm* physic, medicine

ffisioleg *nfm* physiology
ffisiotherapi *nm* physiotherapy
ffit *adj* fit ▸ *nf* (**-iau**) fit, paroxysm
ffit-ffatio *vb* to flip-flop
ffitrwydd *nm* fitness
ffiwdal *adj* feudal
ffiwg (**-iau**) *nf* fugue
ffiws (**-iau**) *nm* fuse
ffiwsio *vb* to fuse
fflach (**-iau**) *nf* flash
fflachiad (**-au**) *nm* flash
fflachio *vb* to flash
fflachiog *adj* flashing
fflag (**-iau**) *nf* flag
fflagen (**-ni**) *nf* flagon, flag-stone
fflangell (**-au**) *nf* scourge
fflangelliad (**-au**) *nm* flagellation
fflangellu *vb* to scourge, to whip, to flog
fflam (**-au**) *nf* flame
fflamadwy *adj* (in)flammable
fflamio *vb* to flame, to blaze
fflamllyd *adj* flaming, blazing
fflan (**-iau**) *nm* flan
fflap (**-iau**) *nm* flap
fflasg (**-iau**) *nf* flask, basket
fflat *adj* flat ▸ *nm* (**-iau**) flat-iron
 ▸ *nf* (**-au, -iau**) a flat
fflatio *vb* to flat, to flatten
fflatwadn *adj* flatfooted
fflaw *nm* splinter
fflecs (**-ys**) *nm* flex
fflêm, fflem *nf* phlegm
fflint *nm* flint
ffliwt (**-iau**) *nf* flute
ffloch (**-au**) *nm* floe; **ffloch iâ** ice floe
fflodiad, -iart *nf* floodgate
ffo *nm* flight

ffoadur (**-iaid**) *nm* fugitive, refugee
ffodus *adj* fortunate, lucky
fföedigaeth *nf* flight
ffoi *vb* to flee, to run away
ffôl *adj* foolish, silly ▸ *nf* (**ffols**) fall (in a slate quarry)
ffoledd *nm* foolishness, folly, fatuity
ffolen (**-nau**) *nf* buttock
ffoli *vb* to infatuate, to dote; to fool
ffolineb *nm* foolishness, folly
ffon (**ffyn**) *nf* stick, staff
ffôn (**ffonau**) *nm* phone; **ffonau clust** headphones; **ffôn camera** camera phone; **ffôn symudol** mobile phone
ffonnod (**ffonodiau**) *nf* stroke, blow, stripe
ffonodio *vb* to cudgel, to beat
fforc (**ffyrc**) *nf* (table) fork
fforch (**-au, ffyrch**) *nf* fork
fforchi *vb* to fork
fforchio *vb* to fork
fforchog *adj* forked, cleft, cloven
ffordd (**ffyrdd**) *nf* way, road; distance
fforddio *vb* to afford
fforddol (**-ion**) *nm* wayfarer, passer-by
fforest (**-ydd, -au**) *nf* forest; **fforest law** rainforest
fforffedu *vb* to forfeit
fforio *vb* to explore
ffortiwn (**-iynau**), **-un** (**-au**) *nf* fortune
fforwm (**-ymau**) *nm* forum
ffos (**-ydd**) *nf* ditch, trench
ffosffad (**-au**) *nm* phosphate
ffosil (**-au**) *nm* fossil

ffracsiwn (-iynau) *nm* fraction
ffrae (-au) *nf* quarrel
ffraeo *vb* to quarrel
ffraeth *adj* fluent; witty, facetious
ffraetheb (-ion) *nf* joke, witticism
ffraethineb *nm* wit, facetiousness
Ffrangeg *nf* French (language)
Ffrainc *nf* France
ffrâm (fframiau) *nf* frame
fframio *vb* to frame
fframwaith *nm* framework
Ffrances (-au) *nf* Frenchwoman
Ffrancwr (-wyr, Ffrancod) *nm*
Frenchman
Ffrengig *adj* French; **llygod
fffrengig** rats
ffres *adj* fresh
ffresgo (-au) *nm* fresco
ffresni *nm* freshness
ffretwaith *nm* fretwork
ffreutur *nf* refectory
ffrewyll (-au) *nf* whip, scourge
ffridd (-oedd) *nf* mountain pasture
ffrimpan (-au) *nf* frying pan
ffrind (-iau) *nm* friend
ffrio *vb* to fry; to hiss
ffrîs (-iau) *nf* frieze
ffrit (-iau) *nm* frit, flop ▸ *adj*
worthless, unsubstantial
ffrith (-oedd) *nf* mountain pasture
ffrithiant (-nnau) *nm* friction
ffroch, ffrochwyllt *adj* furious
ffroen (-au) *nf* nostril; muzzle
(of gun)
ffroenell (-au) *nf* nozzle
ffroeni *vb* to snort, to snuff, to sniff
ffroenuchel *adj* haughty,
disdainful
ffroes *npl* (*nf*-**en**) pancakes

ffrog (-iau) *nf* frock
ffrom *adj* angry, irascible, testy,
touchy
ffromi *vb* to fume, to chafe, to rage
ffrostgar *adj* boastful
ffrwd (ffrydiau) *nf* stream, torrent
ffrwgwd (ffrygydau) *nm* squabble
ffrwst *nm* hurry, haste, bustle
ffrwtian *vb* to splutter
ffrwydriad (-au) *nm* explosion
ffrwydro *vb* to explode
ffrwydrol *adj* explosive
ffrwydryn (-nau, ffrwydron) *nm*
mine, explosive
ffrwyn (-au) *nf* bridle
ffrwyno *vb* to bridle, to curb
ffrwyth (-au, -ydd) *nm* fruit;
vigour, use
ffrwythlon *adj* fruitful, fertile
ffrwythlondeb, -der *nm*
fruitfulness, fertility
ffrwythloni *vb* to become fruitful;
to fertilize
ffrwytho *vb* to bear fruit
ffrydio *vb* to stream, to gush
ffrydlif *nmf* stream, flood, torrent
ffrynt *nm* front
ffuantus *adj* insincere
ffug *adj* fictitious, false, sham
▸ *nm* (-**ion**) fiction, sham
ffug-bas (-ys) *nf* dummy (pass)
ffugbasio *vb* to dummy
ffugenw (-au) *nm* pseudonym
ffugiad (-au) *nm* forgery
ffugio *vb* to feign; to forge
ffugiwr (-wyr) *nm* impostor; forger
ffuglen *nf* fiction; **ffuglen
wyddonol** science fiction
ffugliw (-iau) *nm* camouflage

ffugliwio *vb* to camouflage
ffunud *nm* form, manner; **yr un ffunud â** exactly like
ffured (-au) *nf* ferret
ffureta *vb* to ferret
ffurf (-iau) *nf* form, shape
ffurfafen *nf* firmament, sky
ffurfdro (-eon) *nm* inflection
ffurfeb (-au) *nf* formula
ffurfiad (-au) *nm* formation
ffurfiant (-nnau) *nm* accidence; formation
ffurfio *vb* to form
ffurfiol *adj* formal
ffurfiolaeth *nf* formalism
ffurfioldeb *nm* formality, formalism
ffurflen (-ni) *nf* form (to fill); **ffurflen gais** application form
ffurfwasanaeth (-au) *nm* liturgy
ffurfwedd (-au) *nf* configuration
ffust (-iau) *nf* flail
ffustio, -o *vb* to beat
ffwdan *nf* fuss, bustle, flurry
ffwdanllyd *adj* fussy, bustling
ffwdanu *vb* to fuss, to bustle
ffwdanus *adj* fussy, fidgety, flurried
ffwng (ffyngoedd, ffyngau) *nm* fungus
ffwngleiddiad (-au) *nm* fungicide
ffŵl (ffyliaid) *nm* fool
ffwlbart (-iaid) *nm* polecat
ffwlbri *nm* fudge, nonsense, tomfoolery
ffwlcyn *nm* fool, nincompoop
ffwndro *vb* to founder, to become confused
ffwndrus *adj* confused, bewildered
ffwndwr *nm* confusion, hurly-burly
ffwr *nm* fur

ffwrdd *nm* way; **i ffwrdd** away
ffwrn (ffyrnau) *nf* furnace, oven
ffwrnais (-eisiau) *nf* furnace
ffwrwm (ffyrymau) *nf* form, bench
ffwythiannol *adj* functional
ffydd *nf* faith
ffyddiog *adj* strong in faith, trustful
ffyddlon *adj* faithful
ffyddlondeb *nm* faithfulness, fidelity
ffyddloniaid *npl* faithful ones
ffynhonnell (ffynonellau) *nf* fount, source
ffyniannus *adj* prosperous
ffyniant *nm* prosperity
ffynidwydd *npl* (*nf* **-en**) fir-trees, pine-trees
ffynnon (ffynhonnau) *nf* fountain, well, spring
ffynnu *vb* to prosper, to thrive
ffyrf (*f* **fferf**) *adj* thick, stout
ffyrfder *nm* thickness, stoutness
ffyrling (-au, -od) *nf* farthing
ffyrm *nf* firm
ffyrnig *adj* fierce, savage, ferocious
ffyrnigo *vb* to grow fierce; to enrage
ffyrnigrwydd *nm* fierceness, ferocity

ff

g

gadael, gadu *vb* to leave, to forsake; to let, to allow
gaeaf (-au, -oedd) *nm* winter
gaeafaidd, gaeafol *adj* wintry
gaeafu *vb* to winter, to hibernate
Gaeleg *nf* Gaelic
gafael, gafaelyd *vb* to hold, to grasp ▸ *nf* (**gafaelion**) hold, grasp
gafaelgar *adj* gripping, tenacious
gafl (-au, geifl) *nf* fork, groin
gafr (geifr) *nf* goat; **yr Afr** Capricorn
gafrewig (-od) *nf* gazelle, antelope
gagendor *see* agendor
gaing (geingau) *nf* chisel; **gaing gau** gouge
gair (geiriau) *nm* word
galanas (-au) *nf* murder, massacre
galanastra *nm* slaughter; mess
galar *nm* mourning, grief, sorrow
galarnad (-au) *nf* lamentation
galarnadu *vb* to lament
galaru *vb* to mourn, to grieve, to lament
galarus *adj* mournful, lamentable, sad
galarwr (-wyr) *nm* mourner
galw *vb* to call ▸ *nm* call, demand
galwad (-au) *nmf* call, demand
galwedigaeth (-au) *nf* occupation, vocation, calling
galwedigaethol *adj* vocational
galwyn (-i) *nm* gallon
gallt (gelltydd) *nf* wooded slope; hill, rise
gallu *vb* to be able ▸ *nm* (**-oedd**) power, ability
galluog *adj* able, powerful, mighty
galluogi *vb* to enable, to empower
gan *prep* with, by; of, from
gar (-rau) *nfm* thigh, shank
garan (-od) *nf* heron, crane
Garawys *nm* Lent
gardas, gardys (gardysau) *nfm* garter
gardd (gerddi) *nf* garden; garth, yard
garddio *vb* to garden ▸ *nm* gardening
garddwr (-wyr) *nm* gardener
garddwriaeth *nf* horticulture
gargam *adj* knock-kneed
garlant (-au) *nm* garland
garlleg *npl* (*nf*-**en**) garlic
gartref *adv* at home
garth *nm* hill; enclosure
garw (geirwon) *adj* coarse, rough, harsh
garwedd *nm* roughness
garwhau *vb* to roughen; to ruffle
gast (geist) *nf* bitch (*offensive*)
gau *adj* false; hollow

gefail (-eiliau) nf smithy
gefeilldref (-i) nf twinned town
gefel (-eiliau) nf tongs, pincers
gefell (-eilliaid) n twin; **yr Efeilliaid** Gemini
gefyn (-nau) nm fetter, shackle
gefynnu vb to fetter, to shackle
geingio vb to chisel, to gouge
geilwad (-waid) nm caller
geirbrosesu n word processing
geirda nm reference
geirfa (-oedd) nf vocabulary, glossary
geiriad nm wording, phraseology
geiriadur (-on) nm dictionary, lexicon
geiriadurol adj lexicographical
geiriadurwr (-wyr) nm lexicographer
geirio vb to word, to phrase
geiriol adj verbal
geirlyfr (-au) nm word-book, dictionary
geirwir adj truthful, truth-speaking
geirwiredd nm truthfulness
gel (-iau) nmf gel; **gel cawod** shower gel
gelau, gelen (gelod) nf leech
gelyn (-ion) nm foe, enemy
gelyniaeth nf enmity, hostility
gelyniaethus adj hostile, inimical
gelynol adj hostile, adverse
gellyg npl (nf -en) pears
gem (-au) nf gem, jewel
gêm (gêmau, gemau) nf game; **gêm cyfrifiadur** computer game; **gêm fideo** video game
gemog adj gemmed, jewelled

gemwaith nm jewellery
gemydd (-ion) nm jeweller
gên nf jaw, chin
genau (-euau) nm mouth, orifice
genau-goeg, geneugoeg (-ion) nf lizard; newt
genedigaeth (-au) nf birth
genedigol adj native
Genefa nf Geneva
geneth (-od) nf girl
genethaidd adj girlish
genethig nf little girl, maiden
geneufor nm gulf
geni vb to be born
genni vb to be contained
genwair (-eiriau) nf fishing-rod
genweirio vb to angle, to fish
genweiriwr (-wyr) nm angler
genyn (-nau) nm gene
ger prep by, near
gêr coll n gear, tackle
gerbron prep before (place); in the presence of
gerfydd prep by
geri nm bile, gall; **geri marwol** cholera
geriach coll n gear, odds and ends
gerllaw prep near ▸ adv at hand
gerwin adj rough, severe, harsh
gerwindeb, gerwinder nm roughness, severity
gerwino vb to roughen
gewyn (-nau, gïau) nm sinew, tendon
gewynnog adj sinewy
Ghana nf Ghana
gïach (-od) nm snipe
Gibraltar n Gibraltar
gieuwst nf neuralgia

g

119

gig (**-iau**) *nm* gig (concert)
gildio *vb* to yield; to gild
gilydd *nm*: **ei gilydd** each other; **gyda'i gilydd** together
gimbill *nf* gimlet
gitarydd (**-ion**) *nm* guitarist
glafoerio *vb* to drivel, to slobber
glafoerion *npl* drivel, slobber
glaif, gleifiau *nm* lance, sword, glaive
glain (**gleiniau**) *nm* gem, jewel; bead
glan (**-nau, glennydd**) *nf* bank, shore
glân *adj* clean; holy; fair, beautiful
glanfa *nf* landing
glanhad *nm* cleansing, purification
glanhaol *adj* cleansing, purging
glanhau *vb* to cleanse, to purify
glanhäwr *nm* cleanser
glaniad *nm* landing, disembarkation
glanio *vb* to land, to disembark
glanwaith *adj* clean, tidy
glanweithdra *nm* cleanliness
glas (**gleision**) *adj* blue, green, grey, silver ▸ *nm* blue
glasgoch *adj, nm* purple
glaslanc (**-iau**) *nm* youth, stripling
glasog (**-au**) *nf* crop, gizzard
glastwr *nm* milk and water
glastwraidd *adj* watered down, feeble; muddled
glasu *vb* to become blue, green or grey; to turn pale
glaswellt *coll n* grass
glaswelltyn *nm* blade of grass; tigridia
glaw (**-ogydd**) *nm* rain

glawiad (**-au**) *nm* rainfall
glawio *vb* to rain
glawlen (**-ni**) *nf* umbrella
glawog *adj* rainy
gleisiad (**-iaid**) *nm* sewin
gleision *npl* whey
glendid *nm* cleanness; fairness, beauty
glesni *nm* blueness, verdure
glew (**-ion**) *adj* brave, daring; astute
glewdra, glewder *nm* courage, resource
glin (**-iau**) *nm* knee
gliniadur (**-on**) *nm* laptop, laptop computer
glo *nm* coal
globaleiddio *nm* globalization
gloddest (**-au**) *nm* carousal, revelling
gloddesta *vb* to carouse, to revel
gloddestwr (**-wyr**) *nm* reveller
gloes (**-au, -ion**) *nf* pang; qualm
glofa (**-feydd**) *nf* colliery
glöwr (**glowyr**) *nm* collier
glowty (**-tai**) *nm* cow-house, shippon
glöyn *nm* coal; **glöyn byw** butterfly
gloyw (**-on**) *adj* bright, clear; shiny, glossy
gloywder *nm* brightness, clearness
gloywi *vb* to brighten, to polish
glud (**-ion**) *nm* glue; bird-lime
gludio *vb* to glue
gludiog *adj* sticky
glwth[1] (**glythau**) *nm* couch
glwth[2] (**glythion**) *adj* gluttonous ▸ *nm* glutton
glwys *adj* fair; holy

glyn (-noedd) nm glen, valley
glynu vb to stick, to adhere, to cleave
glythineb, glythni nm gluttony
glythinebu, glythu vb to glut
go adv rather, somewhat
goachul adj lean; puny; sickly, poorly
gobaith (-eithion) nm hope
gobeithio vb to hope
gobeithiol adj hopeful
gobeithlu (-oedd) nm Band of Hope
gobennydd (-enyddiau) nm bolster, pillow
goblygiad nm implication
goblygu vb to fold, to wrap
gochel see gochelyd
gocheladwy adj avoidable
gochelgar adj wary, cautious
gocheliad nm avoidance; **ar ei ocheliad** on his guard
gochelyd vb to avoid, to shun
godidog adj excellent, splendid
godidowgrwydd nm excellence
godineb nm adultery
godinebu vb to commit adultery
godinebus adj adulterous
godinebwr (-wyr) nm adulterer
godre (-on) nm skirt, border, edge
godriad (-au) nm milking
godro vb to milk
goddaith (-eithiau) nf fire, bonfire
goddef vb to bear, to suffer, to allow, to permit
goddefgar adj forbearing, tolerant
goddefgarwch nm forbearance, tolerance

goddefiad (-au) nm licence; toleration
goddefol adj tolerable; passive
goddiweddyd, goddiwes vb to overtake
goddrych nm subject (in grammar)
goddrychol adj subjective
gof (-aint) nm smith
gofal (-on) nm care, charge
gofalaeth nf maintenance
gofalu vb to care, to mind, to take care; **gofalu (am)** to look after
gofalus adj careful; **yn ofalus** carefully
gofalwr nm caretaker
gofaniaeth nf smith's craft
gofer (-oedd, -ydd) nm overflow of well; rill
gofid (-iau) nm grief, sorrow, trouble
gofidio vb to afflict, to grieve, to vex
gofidus adj grievous, sad
gofod nm space; **llong ofod** spaceship
gofodwr (-wyr) nm astronaut
gofyn vb to ask, to demand, to require ▸ nm **(-ion)** demand, requirement
gofyniad (-au) nm question, query
gofynnod (-ynodau) nm note of interrogation, question-mark
gofynnol adj necessary, requisite; interrogative (pronoun etc)
gogan nf defamation, satire
goganu vb to defame, to satirize, to lampoon
goganwr (-wyr) nm satirist
gogledd nm, adj north

121

gogledd-ddwyrain

gogledd-ddwyrain *nm* northeast
Gogledd Iwerddon *nf* Northern Ireland
gogleddol *adj* northern
gogledd-orllewin *nm* northwest
gogleddwr (-wyr) *nm* northerner; North Walian
gogleddwynt *nm* north wind
gogleisio *vb* to tickle
gogleisiol *adj* tickling, titillating, amusing
gogoneddu *vb* to glorify
gogoneddus *adj* glorious
gogoniant *nm* glory
gogor (-ion) *nf* fodder, provender
gogr (-au) *nm* sieve, riddle
gogri, gogrwn, gogryn *vb* to sift, to riddle
gogwydd *nm* slant, inclination, bent
gogwyddiad (-au) *nm* inclination
gogwyddo *vb* to incline, to slope, to lean
gogyfer *adj* opposite; for, by
gogyfuwch *adj, prep* of equal height
gogyhyd *adj* of equal length
gogymaint *adj* equal in size
gohebiaeth (-au) *nf* correspondence
gohebol *adj* corresponding
gohebu *vb* to correspond (*by letter etc*); to reply
gohebydd (-wyr) *nm* correspondent, reporter
gohiriad (-au) *nm* postponement
gohirio *vb* to delay, to postpone, to defer; to put off
golau *adj, nm* light ▸ *vb* to light

golau-leuad *nm* moonlight
golch (-ion) *nm* wash; coating; lye
golchdy (-dai) *nm* wash-house, laundry
golchfa *nf* wash; lathering
golchi *vb* to wash; to coat
golchiad (-au) *nm* washing; plating, coating
golchion *npl* slops; suds
golchwr (-wyr), golchydd (-ion) *nm* washer
golchwraig (-wragedd) *nf* washerwoman
golchyddes (-au) *nf* laundress
goledd, goleddf *nm* slant, slope
goleddu, goleddfu *vb* to slant, to slope
goleuad (-au) *nm* light, luminary
goleudy (-dai) *nm* lighthouse
goleuni *nm* light
goleuo *vb* to light, to enlighten, to illuminate
gôl-geidwad *nm* goalkeeper
golosg *nm* coke, charcoal
golud (-oedd) *nm* wealth, riches
goludog *adj* wealthy, rich
golwg (-ygon) *nfm* sight, look; (*pl*) eyes
golwr (-wyr) *nm* goalkeeper
golwyth (-ion) *nm* chop, slice, cut
golygfa (-feydd) *nf* scene, view; (*pl*) scenery
golygiad (-au) *nm* view
golygu *vb* to view; to mean; to edit
golygus *adj* comely, handsome
golygwedd (-au) *nf* feature, aspect
golygydd (-ion, -wyr) *nm* editor
golygyddiaeth *nf* editorship
golygyddol *adj* editorial

gollwng vb to drop, to release, to let go; to discharge; to dismiss; to leak; to let down

gollyngdod nm release; absolution

gollyngiadau npl emissions

gomedd vb to refuse

gomeddiad nm refusal, omission

gonest, onest adj honest

gonestrwydd nm honesty

gor- prefix over-, super-

gôr nm pus

goramser nm overtime

gorau (-euon) adj best; **o'r gorau** very well

gorawen nf joy, ecstasy

gorblu npl immature feathers

gorboblogi vb to overpopulate

gorbwyso vb to outweigh, to overweigh

gorchest (-ion) nf feat, exploit

gorchestol adj excellent, masterly

gorchfygu vb to overcome, to conquer

gorchfygwr (-wyr) nm victor; conqueror

gorchmynnol adj imperative

gorchudd (-ion) nm cover, covering, veil

gorchuddio vb to cover

gorchwyl (-ion) nm task, undertaking

gorchymyn vb to command ▸ nm **(gorchmynion)** command, commandment

gor-dewdra nm obesity

gordoi vb to overspread, to cover

gordyfu vb to overgrow

gordd (gyrdd) nf sledge-hammer, mallet

gordderch (-adon) nf concubine; lover; bastard

gorddogn (-au) nm overdose

gorddrafft nm overdraft

goresgyn vb to overrun, to invade; to conquer

goresgyniad nm invasion; conquest

goresgynnydd nm invader; conqueror

goreuro vb to gild

gorfod vb to be obliged ▸ nm obligation, necessity

gorfodaeth nf obligation, compulsion

gorfodi vb to oblige, to compel

gorfodol adj obligatory, compulsory

gorfoledd nm joy, rejoicing, triumph

gorfoleddu vb to rejoice, to triumph

gorfoleddus adj jubilant, triumphant

gorffen vb to finish, to complete, to conclude

gorffeniad nm finishing, finish

Gorffennaf nm July

gorffennol adj, nm past

gorffwyll adj mad, frenzied

gorffwyllo vb to rave

gorffwyllog adj mad, insane

gorffwylltra nm madness, insanity

gorffwys, gorffwyso vb to rest, to repose ▸ nm rest, repose

gorffwysfa (-oedd) nf resting-place, rest

gorffwysfan nm lay-by

gorffwysiad (-au) nm rest, pause

gorffwystra nm rest, repose

gorhendaid nm great-great-grandfather

gorhennain nf great-great-grandmother

gori vb to hatch

gorifyny nm ascent, hill, steep climb

goris prep below, beneath, under

goriwaered nm descent, declivity

gorlawn adj superabundant; packed

gorlenwi vb to overfill

gorlifo vb to swamp

gorliwio vb to colour too highly, to exaggerate

gorllewin nm west; **Gorllewin yr Almaen** West Germany

gorllewinol adj westerly, western

gorllewinwr (-wyr) nm westerner

gormes nm oppression, tyranny

gormesol adj oppressive, tyrannical

gormesu vb to oppress, to tyrannize

gormeswr (-wyr), **gormesydd (-ion)** nm oppressor, tyrant

gormod (-ion) nm too much, excess

gormodedd nm excess, superfluity

gormodiaith nf hyperbole, exaggeration

gormodol adj excessive

gormwyth nm catarrh

gornest, ornest (-au) nf contest, match

goroesi vb to outlive, to survive

goroesiad (-au) nm survival

goroeswr (-wyr) nm survivor

goror (-au) nm border, coast, frontier

gorsaf (-oedd) nf station; **gorsaf dân** fire station; **gorsaf fysiau** bus station

gorsedd (-au), gorseddfa (-oedd), gorseddfainc (-feinciau) nf throne

gorseddu vb to throne, to enthrone, to install

gorsin, gorsing (-au) nf door-post

gorthrech nm oppression; coercion

gorthrechu vb to oppress; to coerce

gorthrwm nm oppression

gorthrymder nm oppression, tribulation

gorthrymedig adj oppressed

gorthrymu vb to oppress

gorthrymus adj oppressive

gorthrymwr (-wyr), **gorthrymydd** nm oppressor

goruchaf adj most high, supreme

goruchafiaeth nf supremacy; triumph

goruchel adj high, exalted

goruchwyliaeth (-au) nf oversight, supervision; dispensation

goruchwylio vb to oversee, to supervise

goruchwyliwr (-wyr) nm supervisor, steward

goruwch prep above, over

goruwchnaturiol adj supernatural

goruwchreoli vb to overrule

gorwedd vb to lie; **gorwedd i lawr** lie down

gorweddfa (-oedd), gorweddfan (-au) nf bed, couch

gorweddian vb to lounge, to loll
gorweiddiog adj bedridden
gorwel (-ion) nm horizon
gorwych adj gorgeous
gorwyr (-ion) nm great-grandson
gorwyres (-au) nf great-granddaughter
gorymdaith (-deithiau) nf procession
gorymdeithio vb to walk in procession
gorynys (-oedd) nf peninsula
goryrru vb to drive too fast ▸ n speeding
gosber (-au) nm vespers
gosgedd (-au) nm form, figure
gosgeiddig adj comely, graceful
gosgordd (-ion) nf retinue, train, escort
gosgorddlu (-oedd) nm bodyguard
goslef (-au) nf tone, intonation
gosod vb to put, to place, to set; to let ▸ adj false, artificial
gosodiad (-au) nm proposition, statement
gosteg (-ion) nf silence; (pl) banns
gostegu vb to silence, to still, to quell
gostwng vb to lower, to reduce; to bow; to put down, to humble
gostyngedig adj humble
gostyngeiddrwydd nm humility
gostyngiad nm reduction; humiliation
gostyngol adj reduced
gowt nm gout
gradell (gredyll) nf griddle
gradd (-au) nfm grade, degree, stage
graddedig adj postgraduate

graddedigion npl graduates
graddfa (-feydd) nf scale
graddiant nm gradient
graddio vb to graduate
graddol adj gradual
graddoli vb to grade, to graduate
graean coll n gravel
graeanu vb to granulate
graeanwst nf gravel (complaint)
graen nm grain, gloss, lustre
graenus adj of good grain, glossy, sleek
graff (-iau) nm graph
gramadeg (-au) nm grammar
gramadegol adj grammatical
gramadegwr (-wyr), **gramadegydd** nm grammarian
gran (-nau) nm cheek
gras (-au, -usau) nm grace
graslawn, graslon adj full of grace, gracious
graslonrwydd nm graciousness, grace
grasol, grasusol adj gracious
grât (gratiau) nm grate
grawn npl (nm gronyn) grain; grapes; roe
grawnfwyd (-ydd) coll n cereal
grawnffrwyth nm grapefruit
grawnwin npl grapes
Grawys nm Lent
gre (-oedd) nf stud, flock
greddf (-au) nf instinct, intuition
greddfol adj instinctive, intuitive, rooted
greddfu vb to become ingrained
grefi nm gravy
gresyn nm pity
gresyni, gresyndod nm misery, wretchedness

gresynu vb to commiserate, to pity
gresynus adj miserable, wretched
greyenyn nm grain, granule
gridyll (-au) nmf griddle
griddfan vb to groan, to moan
▶ nm (**-nau**) groan
grillian, grillio vb to squeak, to creak; to chirp; to crunch
gris (-iau) nm step, stair
grisial nm crystal
grisialaidd adj crystal, crystalline
gro coll n (nm **gröyn**) gravel, pebbles
Groeg nf Greek language; Greece
▶ adj Greek
Groegaidd adj Grecian, Greek
Groeges (-au) nf Greek woman
Groegwr (-wyr, -iaid) nm Greek
gronell (-au) nf roe
Grønland nf Greenland
gronyn (-nau) nm grain, particle; while
grot (-iau) nm groat, fourpence
grual nm gruel
grud nm grit
grudd (-iau) nf cheek
gruddfan see griddfan
grug nm heather
grugiar (-ieir) nf moor-hen, grouse
grugog adj heathery
grwgnach vb to grumble, to murmur
grwgnachlyd adj given to grumbling
grwgnachwr (-wyr) nm grumbler
grwn (grynnau) nm ridge (in ploughing)
grŵn, grwndi nm purr
grwnan vb to croon, to purr
grwndwal (-au) nm foundation

grydian vb to murmur; to grunt
grym (-oedd) nm force, power, might
grymial vb to mutter, to murmur, to grumble
grymus adj strong, powerful, mighty
grymuso vb to strengthen
grymuster, grymustra nm power, might
gwacáu vb to empty
gwacsaw adj trivial, frivolous
gwacsawrwydd nm levity, vanity
gwacter nm emptiness, vacuity
gwachul see goachul
gwad, gwadiad nm denial, disavowal
gwadn (-au) nm sole
gwadnu vb to sole; to foot it
gwadu vb to deny, to disown; to renounce, to forsake
gwadwr (-wyr) nm denier
gwadd¹ (-od) nf mole
gwadd² see gwahodd
gwaddod (-ion) nm sediment, lees, dregs
gwaddodi vb to deposit sediment
gwaddol (-ion, -iadau) nm endowment; dowry
gwaddoli vb to endow
gwae (-au) nmf woe
gwaed nm blood
gwaedlif, gwaedlyn nm hæmorrhage, dysentery
gwaedlyd adj bloody, sanguinary
gwaedoliaeth nf blood, consanguinity
gwaedu vb to bleed
gwaedd (-au) nf cry, shout
gwaeddi see gweiddi**

gwaeg (gwaegau) nf buckle, clasp
gwael adj poor, vile; poorly, ill
gwaelder, gwaeldra nm poorness, vileness
gwaeledd nm illness
gwaelod (-ion) nm bottom; (pl) sediment
gwaelodi vb to settle, to deposit sediment
gwaelodol adj basic
gwaelu vb to sicken
gwaell (gwëyll, gweill) nf knitting-needle
gwaered nm descent; **i waered** down
gwaeth adj worse
gwaethwaeth adj worse and worse
gwaethygu vb to worsen
gwaew see gwayw
gwag (gweigion) adj empty, vacant, vain
gwagedd nm vanity
gwagelog adj wary, circumspect
gwagen (-i) nf waggon
gwagenwr (-wyr) nm waggoner
gwagfa (-feydd) nf vacuum
gwagle (-oedd) nm space, void
gwagu vb to empty
gwahadden (gwahaddod) nf mole
gwahan, gwahân nm: **ar wahân** apart, separately
gwahangleifion npl lepers
gwahanglwyf nm leprosy
gwahanglwyfus adj leprous ▶ nm leper
gwahaniaeth (-au) nm difference
gwahaniaethol adj distinguishing
gwahaniaethu vb to differ; to distinguish

gwahanol adj different
gwahanredol adj distinctive
gwahanu vb to divide, to part, to separate
gwahardd vb to forbid, to prohibit
gwaharddedig adj forbidden
gwaharddiad (-au) nm prohibition, veto
gwahodd vb to invite
gwahoddedigion npl guests
gwahoddiad (-au) nm invitation
gwahoddwr (-wyr) nm inviter, host
gwain (gweiniau) nf sheath, scabbard
gwair (gweiriau) nm hay
gwaith¹ (gweithiau) nm work
gwaith² (gweithiau) nf time, turn
gwal (-iau, gwelydd) nf wall
gwâl (gwalau) nf couch, bed; lair
gwala nf enough, plenty
gwalch (gweilch) nm hawk; rogue, rascal
gwaled (-au) nf wallet
gwalio vb to wall, to fence
gwall (-au) nm defect, want; mistake, error
gwallgof adj mad, insane
gwallgofdy (-dai) nm madhouse, lunatic asylum
gwallgofddyn (-gofiaid) nm madman
gwallgofi vb to go mad, to rave
gwallgofrwydd nm madness, insanity
gwallt (-iau) nm, coll n hair of the head
gwalltog adj hairy
gwallus adj faulty, incorrect, inaccurate

127

gwamal adj fickle, frivolous

gwamalio, gwamalu vb to waver; to behave frivolously

gwamalrwydd nm frivolity, levity

gwan (gweiniaid, gweinion) adj weak, feeble

gwanaf (-au) nf layer; row, swath

gwanc nm greed, voracity

gwancus adj greedy, voracious

gwaneg (-au, gwenyg) nf wave, billow

gwangalon adj faint-hearted

gwangalonni vb to lose heart

gwanhau vb to weaken, to enfeeble

gwanllyd, gwannaidd adj weakly, delicate

gwant nm caesura; division

gwantan adj unsteady, fickle; feeble, poor

gwanu vb to pierce, to stab

gwanwyn (-au) nm spring

gwanwynol adj vernal, spring-like

gwanychu vb to weaken, to enfeeble

gwar (-rau) nfm (nape of) neck

gwâr adj civilised, tame, gentle

gwaradwydd (-iadau) nm shame, disgrace

gwaradwyddo vb to shame, to disgrace

gwaradwyddus adj shameful, disgraceful

gwarafun vb to forbid, to refuse, to grudge

gwaraidd adj gentle, civilized

gwarant (-au) nf warrant

gwarantu vb to warrant, to guarantee

gwarchae vb to besiege ▶ nm siege

gwarcheidiol adj guardian, tutelary

gwarcheidwad (-waid) nm guardian

gwarchod vb to watch, to look after, to ward, to mind; **gwarchod plant** to baby-sit, to do baby-sitting

gwarchodaeth nf ward, custody

gwarchodfa (-feydd) nf: **gwarchodfa natur** nature reserve

gwarchodlu (-oedd) nm garrison, guards

gwarchodwr (-wyr) nm custodian; security guard; babysitter, childminder

gward (-iau) nmf ward

gwarden (-deiniaid) nm warden

gwared vb to rid; to deliver, to redeem

gwaredigaeth (-au) nf deliverance

gwaredigion npl redeemed, ransomed

gwaredu vb to save, to deliver, to redeem; to rid

gwaredwr (-wyr), gwaredydd (-ion) nm saviour

gwaredd nm mildness, gentleness

gwareiddiad nm civilization

gwareiddiedig adj civilized

gwareiddio vb to civilize

gwargaled adj stiff-necked, stubborn

gwargaledwch nm stubbornness

gwargam adj stooping

gwargamu vb to stoop

gwarged nm remains

gwargrwm adj round-shouldered

gwargrymu *vb* to stoop
gwariant *nm* expenditure
gwario *vb* to spend
gwarogaeth *see* gwrogaeth
gwarth *nm* shame, disgrace
gwarthaf *nm* top, summit; **ar warthaf** on top of, upon
gwarthafl (-au) *nf* stirrup
gwartheg *npl* cows, cattle
gwarthnod (-au) *nm* stigma
gwarthnodi *vb* to stigmatize
gwarthol (-ion) *nf* stirrup
gwarthrudd *nm* shame, disgrace
gwarthruddo *vb* to shame, to disgrace
gwarthus *adj* shameful, disgraceful, outrageous
gwas (gweision) *nm* lad; servant
gwasaidd *adj* servile, slavish
gwasanaeth (-au) *nm* service
gwasanaethferch (-ed) *nf* handmaid
gwasanaethgar *adj* serviceable; obliging
gwasanaethu *vb* to serve, to minister
gwasanaethwr (-wyr) *nm* manservant, servant
gwasanaethwraig (-wragedd) *nf* maidservant
gwasanaethydd (-ion) *nm* servant
gwasanaethyddes (-au) *nf* handmaid
gwasarn *nm* litter
gwaseidd-dra *nm* servility
gwasg (-au, -oedd, gweisg) *nf* press ▶ *nm* waist; bodice
gwasgar *nm* dispersion; **ar wasgar** scattered, dispersed
gwasgaredig (-ion) *adj* scattered

gwasgarog *adj* scattered; divided
gwasgaru *vb* to scatter, to disperse; to spread
gwasgarwr (-wyr) *nm* scatterer; spreader
gwasgfa (-feydd, -feuon) *nf* squeeze; fit
gwasgod (-au) *nf* waistcoat
gwasgu *vb* to press, to squeeze, to crush, to wring
gwasod *adj* in heat (*of a cow*)
gwastad *adj* level, flat; even; constant, continual
gwastadedd (-au) *nm* plain
gwastadol *adj* continual, perpetual
gwastadrwydd *nm* evenness
gwastatáu *vb* to make even, to level; to settle
gwastatir (-oedd) *nm* level ground, plain
gwastraff *nm* waste, extravagance
gwastraffu *vb* to waste, to squander
gwastraffus *adj* wasteful, extravagant
gwastrawd (-odion) *nm* groom, ostler
gwastrodaeth¹ *nf* grooming; discipline
gwastrodaeth², gwastrodi *vb* to discipline
gwatwar *vb* to mock; to mimic ▶ *nm* mockery
gwatwareg *nf* sarcasm, satire, irony
gwatwarus *adj* mocking, scoffing
gwatwarwr (-wyr) *nm* mocker, scoffer
gwau *vb* to knit, to weave

gwaun (gweunydd) *nf* moor, meadow

gwawch (-iau) *nf* scream, yell

gwawchio *vb* to scream, to yell

gwawd *nm* scoff, scorn, ridicule

gwawdiaeth *nf* ridicule

gwawdio *vb* to mock, to scoff, to jeer, to ridicule

gwawdiwr (-wyr) *nm* mocker, scoffer

gwawdlyd *adj* mocking, jeering, sneering

gwawl *nm* light

gwawn *nm* gossamer

gwawr *nf* dawn, day-break; hue, nuance

gwawrio *vb* to dawn

gwayw (gwewyr) *nm* pang, pain, stitch

gwaywffon (-ffyn) *nf* spear

gwden (-ni, gwdyn) *nf* withe

gwdihŵ *nm* owl

gwddf (gyddfau) *nm* neck, throat

gwe (-oedd) *nf* web; texture; y We (Fyd-Eang) the (World-Wide) Web

gwead *nm* weaving, knitting; texture

gwedd¹ (-au) *nf* aspect, form; appearance

gwedd² (-oedd) *nf* yoke; team

gweddaidd *adj* seemly, decent

gweddeidd-dra *nm* seemliness, decency

gwedder (gweddrod) *nm* wether; cig gwedder mutton

gweddgar *adj* plump, sleek

gweddi (-ïau) *nm* prayer

gweddigar *adj* prayerful

gweddill (-ion) *nm* remnant, remainder, rest; *(pl)* remains

gweddillio *vb* to leave spare, to leave a remnant

gweddïo *vb* to pray

gweddïwr (-ïwyr) *nm* one who prays

gweddol *adj* fair, fairly

gweddu *vb* to suit, to become, to befit

gweddus *adj* seemly, decent, proper

gweddustra *nm* decency, propriety

gweddw *adj* single; widow, widowed ► *nf* (-on) widow; gŵr gweddw widower

gweddwdod *nm* widowhood

gweddwi *vb* to widow

gwefan (-nau) *nfm* website

gwefl (-au) *nf* lip (usu. of animal)

gwefr *nmf* thrill, excitement; charge

gwefreiddio *vb* to electrify, to thrill

gwefreiddiol *adj* thrilling

gwefus (-au) *nf* (human) lip

gwefusol *adj* of the lip, labial

gwe-gamera (gwe-gamerâu) *nm* webcam

gwegi *nm* vanity, levity

gwegian *vb* to sway, to totter

gwegil *nm* back of head

gwehelyth *nmf* lineage, pedigree

gwehilion *npl* refuse, trash, riffraff

gwehydd (-ion) *nm* weaver

gwehyddu *vb* to weave

gwehynnu *vb* to draw, to pour, to empty

gweiddi *vb* to cry, to shout

gweilgi *nf* sea, torrent

gweili *adj* empty, idle

gweini *vb* to serve, to minister; to be in service

gweinidog (-ion) *nm* minister, servant

gweinidogaeth (-au) *nf* ministry, service

gweinidogaethol *adj* ministerial

gweinidogaethu *vb* to minister

gweinio *vb* to sheathe

gweinydd (-ion) *nm* waiter; server

gweinyddes (-au) *nf* attendant, nurse; waitress

gweinyddiaeth (-au) *nf* administration

gweinyddol *adj* administrative

gweinyddu *vb* to administer, to officiate

gweinyddwr (-wyr) *nm* administrator

gweirglodd (iau) *nf* meadow

gweitied, gweitio *vb* to wait

gweithdy (-dai) *nm* workshop

gweithfa (-oedd, -feydd) *nf* works

gweithfaol *adj* industrial

gweithgar *adj* hard-working, industrious

gweithgaredd (-au), **gweithgarwch** *nm* activity

gweithio *vb* to work; to ferment; to purge

gweithiol *adj* executive

gweithiwr (-wyr) *nm* workman, worker; **gweithiwr cymdeithasol** social worker

gweithle *nm* workspace

gweithred (-oedd) *nf* act, deed, work

gweithrediad (-au) *nm* action, operation

gweithredol *adj* active, actual, virtual

gweithredu *vb* to act, to work, to operate

gweithredwr (-wyr) *nm* doer

gweithredydd (-ion) *nm* doer, factor, agent

gweladwy *adj* perceptible, visible

gweled, gweld *vb* to see, to perceive

gwelediad *nm* sight, appearance

gweledig *adj* seen, visible

gweledigaeth (-au) *nf* vision

gweledol *adj* visual

gweledydd (-ion) *nm* seer

gwelw *adj* pale

gwelwi *vb* to pale

gwely (-au, gwelâu) *nm* bed; river basin; sea bed; stratum; flat surface; **gwely haul** sunbed

gwell *adj* better, superior

gwella *vb* to better, to mend, to improve, to recover

gwellau, gwellaif (-eifiau) *nm* shears

gwellen (gweill) *nf* knitting-needle

gwellhad *nm* recovery, improvement

gwellhau *vb* to better, to improve

gwelliant (-iannau) *nm* amendment, improvement

gwellt *coll n* grass; sward; straw

gwelltglas *nm* grass, greensward

gwelltog *adj* grassy, green

gwelltyn *nm* blade of grass; a straw

gwellwell *adv* better and better

gwen *adj f of* **gwyn**

gwên (gwenau) *nf* smile

gwenci (-iod) *nf* stoat, weasel

gwendid (-au) *nm* weakness, frailty

Gwener *nf* Venus; **dydd Gwener** Friday

g

gwenerol

gwenerol *adj* venereal
gwenfflam *adj* blazing, ablaze
gweniaith *nf* flattery
gwenieithio *vb* to flatter
gwenieithiwr (-wyr) *nm* flatterer
gwenieithus *adj* flattering
gwenith *npl* (*nf-en*) wheat
gwenithfaen *nm* granite
gwennol (gwenoliaid) *nf* swallow, martin; shuttle
gwenu *vb* to smile
gwenwisg (-oedd) *nf* surplice
gwenwyn *nm* poison, venom; jealousy
gwenwynig, gwenwynol *adj* poisonous, venomous
gwenwynllyd *adj* peevish; jealous
gwenwyno *vb* to poison; to fret; to be jealous
gwenyn *npl* (*nf-en*) bees
gwep *nf* visage, grimace
gwêr *nm* tallow, suet *etc*
gŵer *nm* shade
gwerchyr *nm* cover, lid, valve
gwerdd *adj f of* gwyrdd
gwerin *coll n* men, people; democracy; crew
gweriniaeth (-au) *nf* democracy; republic; **Gweriniaeth Tsiec** Czech Republic; **Gweriniaeth Iwerddon** Irish Republic
gwerinlywodraeth (-au) *nf* republic
gwerinol *adj* plebeian, vulgar
gwerinos *coll n* rabble, mob
gwerinwr (-wyr) *nm* democrat
gwern¹ (-i, -ydd) *nf* swamp, meadow; alder-grove
gwern² *npl* (*nf-en*) alder-trees

gwerog *adj* tallowy, suety
gwers (-i) *nf* verse; lesson; **gwers yrru** driving lesson
gwerslyfr *nm* textbook
gwersyll (-oedd) *nm* camp, encampment
gwersylla, gwersyllu *vb* to camp; to encamp
gwerth *nm* worth, value; **ar werth** for sale
gwerthfawr *adj* valuable, precious
gwerthfawredd *nm* preciousness
gwerthfawrogi *vb* to appreciate
gwerthfawrogiad *nm* appreciation
gwerthfawrogol *adj* appreciative
gwerthiant *nm* sale
gwerthu *vb* to sell
gwerthwr (-wyr) *nm* seller; **gwerthwr cyffuriau** drug dealer; **gwerthwr eiddo** estate agent
gwerthyd (-au) *nf* spindle, axle
gweryd (-au) *nm* earth, soil; sward ▸ *nf* groin
gweryriad *nm* neighing
gweryru *vb* to neigh
gwestai (-eion) *nm* guest
gwesty (-au, -tai) *nm* inn, hotel
gweu *vb* to weave, to knit
gwewyr *nm* anguish
gwg *nm* frown, scowl; disapproval
gwglo *vb* to google
gwgu *vb* to frown, to scowl, to lower
gwialen (gwiail) *nf* rod, switch
gwialennod (-enodiau) *nf* stroke, stripe
gwialenodio *vb* to beat with a rod
gwib *nf* wandering, jaunt ▸ *adj* wandering

gwibdaith (-deithiau) *nf* excursion
gwiber (-od) *nf* viper
gwibio *vb* to flash, to flit, to dart, to wander
gwibiog *adj* flitting, darting, wandering
gwiblong (-au) *nf* cruiser
gwich *nf* squeak; creak; wheeze, wheezing
gwichiad (-iaid) *nm* periwinkle
gwichian *vb* to squeak, to squeal; to creak; to wheeze
gwichlyd *adj* creaking; wheezy
gwiddon¹ (-od) *nf* witch
gwiddon² *npl* mites
gwif (-iau) *nm* lever, crowbar
gwifren *nf* wire
gwig (-oedd) *nf* wood
gwingo *vb* to wriggle, to fidget; to writhe; to kick, to struggle
gwin (-oedd) *nm* wine
gwinau *adj* bay, brown, auburn
gwinc (-od) *nf* chaffinch
gwinegr *nm* vinegar
gwinllan (-noedd, -nau) *nf* vine-yard
gwinllannwr, gwinllanydd *nm* vine-dresser
gwinwryf (-oedd) *nm* wine-press
gwinwydd *npl* (*nf*-en) vines
gwir *adj* true ► *nm* truth
gwireb (-au, -ion) *nf* truism, axiom
gwireddu *vb* to verify, to substantiate
gwirfodd *nm* goodwill; own accord
gwirfoddol *adj* voluntary, spontaneous
gwirfoddoli *vb* to volunteer
gwirfoddolwr (-wyr) *nm* volunteer
gwirio *vb* to verify

gwirion (-iaid) *adj* innocent; silly
gwiriondeb *nm* innocence; silliness
gwirionedd (-au) *nm* truth, verity, reality
gwirioneddol *adj* true, real, genuine
gwirioni *vb* to infatuate, to dote
gwirionyn *nm* simpleton
gwiriwr (-wyr) *nm* verifier; **gwiriwr sillafu** spellchecker
gwirod (-ydd) *nm* liquor, spirits
gwisg (-oedd) *nf* dress, garment, robe
gwisgi *adj* brisk, lively, nimble; ripe
gwisgo *vb* to dress; to wear; to put on
gwisgwr (-wyr) *nm* wearer
gwiw *adj* fit, meet; worthy
gwiwer (-od) *nf* squirrel
gwlad (gwledydd) *nf* country, land
gwladaidd *adj* countrified, rustic
Gwlad Belg *nf* Belgium
gwladfa (-oedd) *nf* colony, settlement
gwladgar *see* gwlatgar
gwladgarol *adj* patriotic
gwladgarwch *nm* patriotism
gwladgarwr (-wyr) *nm* patriot
gwladol *adj* of a country, civil, state
gwladoli *vb* to nationalize
Gwlad Thai *nf* Thailand
gwladweiniaeth *nf* statesmanship
gwladweinydd (-ion, -wyr) *nm* statesman
gwladwr (-wyr) *nm* countryman, peasant
gwladwriaeth (-au) *nf* state
gwladwriaethol *adj* state, political
gwladychfa (-oedd) *nf* settlement, colony

gwladychu *vb* to inhabit, to settle, to colonize; to rule
gwladychwr (-wyr) *nm* settler, colonist
Gwlad yr Iâ *nf* Iceland
gwlân (gwlanoedd) *nm* wool
gwlana *vb* to gather wool
gwlanen (-ni) *nf* flannel
gwlanog *adj* woolly
gwlatgar *adj* patriotic
gwlaw *see* glaw
gwledig *adj* countrified, country, rural
gwledd (-oedd) *nf* feast, banquet
gwledda *vb* to feast
gwleddwr (-wyr) *nm* feaster
gwleidydd (-ion) *nm* politician, statesman
gwleidyddiaeth *nf* politics
gwleidyddol *adj* political
gwleidyddol-gywir *adj* politically correct
gwleidyddwr (-wyr) *nm* politician
gwlith (-oedd) *nm* dew
gwlithen *nf* slug
gwlitho *vb* to dew, to bedew
gwlithog *adj* dewy; inspiring
gwlithyn *nm* dewdrop
gwlyb (-ion) *adj* wet, fluid, liquid ▸ *nm* fluid, liquid
gwlybaniaeth *nm* wet, moisture
gwlybwr *nm* wet, moisture, liquid, fluid
gwlybyrog *adj* wet, damp, rainy
gwlych *nm* wet; **rhoi yng ngwlych** steep
gwlychu *vb* to wet, to moisten; to get wet; to dip
gwlydd *npl, coll n (nm* -**yn)** haulm
gwn (gynnau) *nm* gun

gŵn (gynau) *nm* gown
gwndwn *see* gwyndwn
gwneud, gwneuthur *vb* to do, to make; to make up
gwneuthuriad *nm* make, making
gwneuthurwr (-wyr) *nm* maker, doer, manufacturer
gwnïad *nm* sewing, stitching, seam
gwniadur (-iau, on) *nmf* thimble
gwniadwraig *nf* stitcher, seamstress
gwniadyddes (-au) *nf* seamstress
gwnïo *vb* to sew, to stitch
gwniyddes (-au) *nf* seamstress
gwobr (-au) *nfm* reward, prize
gwobrwy (-au, -on) *nfm* reward, prize
gwobrwyo *vb* to reward
gwobrwywr (-wyr) *nm* rewarder
gŵr (gwŷr) *nm* man; husband
gwrach (-ïod, -od) *nf* hag, witch; **breuddwyd gwrach** wishful thinking
gwrachïaidd *adj* old-womanish
gwraidd (gwreiddiau) *coll n* roots
gwraig (gwragedd) *nf* woman; wife
gwrandaw *see* gwrando
gwrandawiad *nm* listening, hearing
gwrandäwr (gwrandawyr) *nm* listener, hearer
gwrando *vb* to listen, to hearken
gwrcath (-od) *nm* tom-cat
gwregys (-au) *nm* girdle, belt, truss; zone
gwregysu *vb* to girdle, to gird
gwrêng *nm, coll n* (one of the) common people

gwreichion *npl* (*nf* **-en**) sparks
gwreichioni *vb* to emit sparks, to sparkle
gwreiddio *vb* to root
gwreiddiol *adj* radical, rooted; original
gwreiddioldeb *nm* originality
gwreiddyn (**gwreiddiau**) *nm* root
gwres *nm* heat, warmth
gwresfesurydd (**-ion**) *nm* thermometer
gwresog *adj* warm, hot; fervent
gwresogi *vb* to warm, to heat
gwresogydd *nm* heater
gwrhyd (**-oedd**), **gwryd** *nm* fathom
gwrhydri *nm* exploit; valour
gwrid *nm* blush, flush
gwrido *vb* to blush, to flush
gwridog, gwritgoch *adj* rosy-cheeked, ruddy
gwrogaeth *nf* homage
gwrogi *vb* to do homage
gwrol *adj* brave, courageous
gwroldeb *nm* bravery, courage
gwroli *vb* to hearten
gwron (**-iaid**) *nm* hero
gwroniaeth *nf* heroism
gwrtaith (**-teithiau**) *nm* manure, fertiliser
gwrteithiad *nm* cultivation, culture
gwrteithio *vb* to manure; to cultivate, to culture
gwrth- *prefix* counter-, contra-, anti-
gwrthban (**-au**) *nm* blanket
gwrthblaid *nf* (party in) opposition
gwrthbrofi *vb* to disprove, to refute

gwrthbwynt *nm* counterpoint
gwrthdaro *vb* to clash, to collide
gwrthdrawiad (**-au**) *nm* collision
gwrth-droi *vb* to reverse
gwrthdystiad (**-au**) *nm* protest
gwrthdystio *vb* to protest
gwrthddadl (**-euon**) *nf* objection
gwrthddadlau *vb* to object, to controvert
gwrth-ddweud *vb* to contradict
gwrthddywediad (**-au**) *nm* contradiction
gwrthddywedyd *vb* to contradict
gwrthfiotig *nm* antibiotic
gwrthgiliad (**-au**) *nm* backsliding
gwrthgilio *vb* to backslide, to secede
gwrthgiliwr (**-wr**) *nm* backslider, seceder
gwrthglawdd (**-gloddiau**) *nm* rampart
gwrthglocwedd *adj* anticlockwise
gwrthgyferbyniad (**-au**) *nm* contrast, antithesis
gwrthgyferbynnu *vb* to contrast
gwrthnaws *nm* antipathy ▸ *adj* repugnant
gwrthnysig *adj* obstinate, stubborn
gwrthod *vb* to refuse, to reject
gwrthodedig *adj* rejected, reprobate
gwrthodiad *nm* refusal, rejection
gwrthodwr (**-wyr**) *nm* refuser, rejecter
gwrthol *nm, adv* back; **ôl a gwrthol** to and fro
gwrthrych (**-au**) *nm* object; subject (*of biography*)
gwrthrychol *adj* objective

135

gwrthryfel

gwrthryfel (**-oedd**) *nm* rebellion, mutiny
gwrthryfela *vb* to rebel
gwrthryfelgar *adj* rebellious, mutinous
gwrthryfelwr (**-wyr**) *nm* rebel, mutineer
gwrthsafiad *nm* resistance
gwrthsefyll *vb* to withstand, to resist
gwrthun *adj* repugnant, odious, absurd
gwrthuni *nm* odiousness, absurdity
gwrthuno *vb* to mar, to deform, to disfigure
gwrthweithio *vb* to counteract
gwrthwenwyn *nm* antidote
gwrthwyneb *nm* opposite, contrary
gwrthwynebiad (**-au**) *nm* objection
gwrthwynebol *adj* opposed
gwrthwynebu *vb* to resist, to oppose
gwrthwynebus *adj* repugnant; antagonistic
gwrthwynebwr (**-wyr**), **gwrthwynebydd** *nm* opponent, adversary
gwrych¹ (**-oedd**) *nm* hedge
gwrych² *npl*, *coll n* (*nm* **-yn**) bristles
gwryd *see* gwrhyd
gwryf (**-oedd**) *nm* press
gwrym (**-iau**) *nm* seam; wale
gwrysg *npl* (*nf* **-en**) stalks, haulm
gwryw *adj* male ▸ *nm* (**-od**) male
gwrywaidd, gwrywol *adj* masculine
gwth *nm* push, thrust, shove; gust

gwthio *vb* to push, to thrust, to shove
gwthiwr (**-wyr**) *nm* pusher
gwyar *nm* gore, blood
gwybed *npl* (*nm* **-yn**) flies
gwybedyn *nm* midge
gwybod *vb* to know ▸ *nm* (**-au**) knowledge; **gwybodau** studies
gwybodaeth (**-au**) *nf* knowledge
gwybodeg *nm* epistemology
gwybodus *adj* knowing, well-informed
gwybyddus *adj* known, aware of
gwych *adj* fine, splendid, brilliant
gwychder *nm* splendour, pomp
gwŷd (**gwydiau**) *nm* vice
gwydn *adj* tough
gwydnwch *nm* toughness
gwydr (**-au**) *nm* glass
gwydraid (**-eidiau**) *nm* glassful, glass
gwydro *vb* to glaze; **gwydro dwbl** double glazing
gwydrwr (**-wyr**) *nm* glazier
gwydryn (**gwydrau**) *nm* drinking-glass
gwŷdd¹ (**gwehyddion, gwyddion**) *nm* loom; plough
gwŷdd² *npl* (*nf* **gwydden**) trees
gŵydd¹ *nm* presence
gŵydd² (**gwyddau**) *nm* goose
gwyddbwyll *nf* chess
Gwyddel (**-od, Gwyddyl**) *nm* Irishman
Gwyddeleg *nf* Irish language
Gwyddeles (**-au**) *nf* Irishwoman
Gwyddelig *adj* Irish
gwyddfa *nf* tumulus, grave
gwyddfid *nm* honeysuckle
gwyddfod *nm* presence

gwyddoniadur (-on) *nm* encyclopædia
gwyddoniaeth *nf* science
gwyddonol *adj* scientific
gwyddonydd (-wyr) *nm* scientist
gwyddor (-ion) *nf* rudiment; science; **yr wyddor** the alphabet
gwyddori *vb* to instruct, to ground
gwyfyn (-od) *nm* moth
gwŷg *coll n* vetch
gwygbysen (gwygbys) *nf* chickpea
gŵyl¹ *adj* bashful, modest
gŵyl² (gwyliau) *nf* holiday, feast, festival
gwylaidd *adj* bashful, modest
gwylan (-od) *nf* sea-gull
gwylder *nm* bashfulness, modesty
gwyleidd-dra *nm* bashfulness, modesty
gwylfa (-fâu, -feydd) *nf* watch; lookout
gwyliadwriaeth *nfm* watchfulness, caution; watch, guard
gwyliadwrus *adj* watchful, cautious
gwyliedydd (-ion) *nm* watchman, sentinel
gwylio *vb* to watch, to mind, to beware
gwyliwr (-wyr) *nm* watchman, sentinel
gwylmabsant (-au) *nf* wake
gwylnos (-au) *nf* watch-night, wake, vigil
gwyll *nm* darkness, gloom
gwylliad (-iaid) *nm* robber, bandit
gwyllt *adj* wild, savage, mad; rapid; **bywyd gwyllt** wildlife
gwylltineb *nm* wildness; rage, fury

gwylltio, gwylltu *vb* to frighten; to fly into a passion
gwymon *nm* seaweed
gwyn (f gwen) *adj* white; blessed
gwŷn (gwyniau) *nmf* ache, smart; lust
gwynder, gwyndra *nm* whiteness
gwyndwn *nm* unploughed land
gwyneb *see* **wyneb**
gwynegon *nm* rheumatism
gwynegu *vb* to throb, to ache
gwynfa *nf* paradise
gwynfyd (-au) *nm* blessedness, bliss; *(pl)* beatitudes
gwynfydedig *adj* blessed, happy, beatific
gwyngalch *nm* whitewash
gwyngalchog *adj* whitewashed
gwyngalchu *vb* to whitewash
gwyniad (-iaid) *nm* whiting
gwynias *adj* white-hot
gwyniedyn *nm* sewin
gwynio *vb* to throb, to ache
gwynnu *vb* to whiten, to bleach
gwynnwy *nm* white of egg
gwynt (-oedd) *nm* wind; breath; smell
gwyntell (-i) *nf* round basket without handle
gwyntio *vb* to smell
gwyntog *adj* windy
gwyntyll (-au) *nf* fan
gwyntylliad *nm* ventilation
gwyntyllio, gwyntyllu *vb* to ventilate, to winnow
gwŷr *see* **gŵr**
gŵyr *adj* crooked, oblique, sloping
gwyrdraws *adj* perverse
gwyrdro (-ion) *nm* perversion
gwyrdroi *vb* to pervert, to distort

137

gwyrdd (-ion) *adj, nm* green
gwyrddlas *adj* green, verdant
gwyrddlesni *nm* verdure
gwyrddni *nm* greenness
gwyrgam *adj* crooked
gwyriad *nm* vowel mutation
gwyrni *nm* crookedness, perverseness
gwyro *vb* to swerve; to slope; to stoop; to tilt; to deviate
gwyrth (-iau) *nf* miracle
gwyrthiol *adj* miraculous
gwyry, gwyryf (gwyryfon) *nf* virgin; **y Wyryf** Virgo
gwyryfdod *nm* virginity
gwyryfol *adj* virgin
gwŷs (gwysion) *nf* summons
gwysio *vb* to summon
gwystl (-on) *nm* pledge; hostage
gwystlo *vb* to pledge, to pawn
gwystno *vb* to dry, to wither, to flag
gwythïen (gwythi, gwythiennau) *nf* vein, blood vessel, artery; **cwlwm gwythi** cramp
gwyw *adj* withered, faded, sere
gwywo *vb* to wither, to fade
gyda, gydag *prep* with
gyddfol *adj* guttural
gyferbyn *prep* over against, opposite
gylfin (-od) *nm* bill, beak
gylfinir *nm* curlew
gynfad (-au) *nm* gunboat
gynnau *adv* a little while ago, just now
gynt *adv* formerly, of yore
gyr (-roedd) *nm* drove
gyrfa (-oedd, -feydd) *nf* race; course; career

gyrfaol *adj* vocational
gyriant (gyriannau) *nm* drive; **gyriant disg** disk drive
gyriedydd (-ion) *nm* driver
gyrru *vb* to drive; to send; to work, to forge; **gyrru tra'n feddw** drink-driving
gyrrwr (gyrwyr) *nm* driver; sender
gyrwynt (-oedd) *nm* hurricane, tornado

h

ha *excl* ha
hac (-iau) *nf* cut, notch, hack
hacio *vb* to hack
haciwr (-wyr) *nm* hacker
had (-au) *nm, coll n (nm* **hedyn)** seed
hadlif *nm* seminal fluid
hadog *nm* haddock
hadu *vb* to seed
hadyd *coll n* seed-corn
haearn (heyrn) *nm* iron; **haearn bwrw** cast iron; **haearn gyr** wrought iron
haearnaidd *adj* like iron
haeddiannol *adj* meritorious; merited
haeddiant (-iannau) *nm* merit, desert
haeddu *vb* to deserve, to merit
hael *adj* generous, liberal
haelfrydedd *nm* liberality
haelfrydig *adj* generous, free
haelioni *nm* generosity

haelionus *adj* generous, liberal
haen (-au) *nf* layer, stratum; seam; **haen osôn** ozone layer
haenen (-nau) *nf* layer, film
haenu *vb* to stratify
haeriad (-au) *nm* assertion
haerllug *adj* importunate; impudent
haerllugrwydd *nm* importunity; impudence
haeru *vb* to affirm, to assert
haf (-au) *nm* summer
hafaidd *adj* summer-like, summery
hafal *adj* like, equal
hafaliad *nm* equation
hafan *nf* haven
hafn (-au) *nf* hollow, gorge, ravine
hafod (-ydd) *nf* summer dwelling, upland farm
hafog *nm* havoc
hafoty (-tai) *nm* summer residence
hagr *adj* ugly
hagru *vb* to mar, to disfigure
hagrwch *nm* ugliness
haid (heidiau) *nf* swarm, drove, horde
haidd (heiddiau) *nm, coll n (nf* **heidden)** barley
haig (heigiau) *nf* shoal
haint (heintiau) *nmf* pestilence; faint
hala *vb* to send, to spend
halen *nm* salt, brine
halog, halogedig *adj* defiled, polluted
halogi *vb* to defile, to profane, to pollute
halogrwydd *nm* defilement, pollution
halogwr (-wyr) *nm* defiler, profaner

hallt *adj* salt, salty; severe
halltedd, halltrwydd *nm* saltness, saltiness
halltu *vb* to salt
halltwr (-wyr) *nm* salter
hambwrdd (-byrddau) *nm* tray
hamdden *nf* leisure, respite
hamddenol *adj* leisurely
hanerob (-au) *nf* flitch of bacon
haneru *vb* to halve
hanes (-ion) *nm* history, story, account
hanesydd (-wyr) *nm* historian
hanesyddol *adj* historical
hanesyn (-nau) *nm* anecdote
hanfod *vb* to descend from, to issue ▸ *nm* essence
hanfodion *npl* essentials
hanfodol *adj* essential
haniad *nm* derivation, descent
haniaeth *nf* abstraction
haniaethol *adj* abstract
hanner (hanerau, haneri) *nm, adj, adv* half; **hanner ffordd (i)** halfway (to); **hanner pris** half fare; **hanner tymor** half term
hanner-sgim *adj* semi-skimmed
hanu *vb* to proceed, to be derived, to be descended
hap *nf* luck
hapchwarae *nm* lottery
hapus *adj* happy
hapusrwydd *nm* happiness
hardd *adj* beautiful, handsome
harddu *vb* to beautify, to embellish, to adorn
harddwch *nm* beauty
harnais (-eisiau) *nm* harness
harneisio *vb* to harness

hatling (-au, -od) *nf* mite, half a farthing
hau *vb* to sow, to disseminate
haul (heuliau) *nm* sun
hawdd *adj* easy; **hawdd ei drin** user-friendly
hawddamor *nm, excl* good luck, welcome
hawddfyd *nm* ease, prosperity
hawddgar *adj* amiable; comely
hawddgarwch *nm* amiability
hawl (-iau) *nf* claim; right; **hawl ac ateb** question and answer
hawlfraint *nf* title; copyright
hawlio *vb* to claim, to demand
hawlydd (-ion) *nm* claimant, plaintiff
haws *adj* easier
heb *prep* without; **heb afael** hands-free
heblaw *prep* beside(s)
hebog (-au) *nm* hawk, falcon
Hebraeg *nf, adj* Hebrew (*language*)
Hebreaidd, Hebreig *adj* Hebrew, Hebraic
Hebrees (-au) *nf* Hebrew woman
Hebreigydd (-ion) *nm* Hebraist
Hebrëwr (-wyr) *nm* a Hebrew
hebrwng *vb* to accompany, to conduct, to convey, to escort
hebryngydd (-ion) *nm* conductor, guide
hedeg *vb* to fly; to run to seed
hedegog *adj* flying; high-flown
hedfa (-feydd) *nf* flight
hedfan *vb* to fly, to hover
hedydd (-ion) *nm* lark
hedyn (hadau) *nm* seed, germ
hedd *nm* peace, tranquillity

heddgeidwad (-waid) *nm* police officer

heddiw *adv* today

heddlu *nm* police force

heddwas (-weision) *nm* police officer

heddwch *nm* peace, quiet, tranquillity

heddychiaeth *nf* pacifism

heddychlon *adj* peaceful, peaceable

heddychol *adj* peaceable, pacific

heddychu *vb* to pacify, to appease

heddychwr (-wyr) *nm* pacifist, peace-maker

heddyw *see* **heddiw**

hefelydd *adj* similar

hefyd *adv* also, besides

heffer (heffrod) *nf* heifer

hegl (-au) *nf* leg, shank

heglog *adj* leggy, long-legged

heglu *vb* to foot it

heibio *adv* past

heidio *vb* to swarm, to throng, to flock

heidden *nf* grain of barley

heigio *vb* to shoal, to teem

heini *adj* active, lively, nimble, brisk

heintio *vb* to infect

heintus *adj* infectious, contagious

heislan (-od) *nf* hackle

heislanu *vb* to hackle flax

hel *vb* to gather, to collect; to drive, to chase

hela *vb* to hunt, to spend *(money, time)*; **cŵn hela** hounds

helaeth *adj* ample, abundant, extensive

helaethrwydd *nm* abundance

helaethu *vb* to enlarge, to extend, to amplify

helaethwych *adj* sumptuous

helbul (-on) *nm* trouble

helbulus *adj* troubled, troublous

helcyd *vb* to hunt ▸ *nm* worry, trouble

helfa (-fâu, -feydd) *nf* hunt, catch

helfarch (-feirch) *nm* hunter *(horse)*

helgi (-gwn) *nm* hound

heli *nm* salt water, brine

heliwr (-wyr) *nm* hunter, huntsman

helm (-au) *nf* helm, helmet, stack

help *nm* help, aid, assistance

helpio, helpu *vb* to help, to aid, to assist

helwriaeth *nf* game, hunting; chase

helyg *npl* (*nf* -**en**) willows

helynt (-ion) *nf* trouble, fuss, bother, hassle

helltni *nm* saltiness, saltness

hem¹ *nm* rivet

hem² (-iau) *nf* hem, border

hen *adj* old, aged, ancient, of old

henadur (-iaid) *nm* alderman

henaduriad (-iaid) *nm* Presbyterian, elder

henaduriaeth (-au) *nf* presbytery

henaint *nm* old age

hendaid (-deidiau) *nm* great-grandfather

hender *nm* oldness

hendref (-i, -ydd) *nf* winter dwelling, lowland farm

heneb (-ion) *nf* ancient monument

heneiddio *vb* to grow old, to age

henfam *nf* grandmother

henffasiwn *adj* old-fashioned

hennain (**heneiniau**) *nf* great-grandmother
heno *adv* tonight
henoed *coll n* elderly people
henuriad (**-iaid**) *nm* elder, presbyter
heol (**-ydd**) *nf* road
hepgor *vb* to spare, to dispense with ▸ *nm* (**-ion**) what may be dispensed with
hepian *vb* to slumber, to doze
her (**-iau**) *nf* challenge
herc (**-iau**) *nf* hop; limp
hercian *vb* to hop, to hobble, to limp
heresi (**-ïau**) *nf* heresy
heretic (**-iaid**) *nm* heretic
hereticaidd *adj* heretical
herfeiddio *vb* to dare, to brave, to defy
herfeiddiol *adj* daring, defiant
hergwd *nm* push, thrust, shove
hergydio *vb* to bump
herio *vb* to challenge, to dare, to brave, to defy
heroin *nm* heroin
herw *nm* raid; outlawry
herwa *vb* to scout, to prowl, to raid
herwgipio *vb* to kidnap
herwgipiwr (**-wyr**) *nm* kidnapper; hijacker
herwhela *vb* to poach (*game*)
herwr (**-wyr**) *nm* scout, raider; outlaw
herwydd *see* oherwydd
hesb *adj* f of hysb
hesben (**-nau**) *nf* hasp
hesbin (**-od**) *nf* yearling ewe
hesbio *vb* to dry up
hesbwrn (**-yrniaid**) *nm* young ram

hesg *npl* (*nf* **-en**) sedge, rushes
het (**-iau**) *nf* hat
heulo *vb* to shine (*as the sun*); to sun
heulog *adj* sunny
heulwen *nf* sunshine
heuwr (**-wyr**) *nm* sower
hi *pron* she, her; it
hidio *vb* to heed
hidl¹ *adj*: wylo yn hidl weep abundantly
hidl² (**-au**) *nf* strainer, sieve
hidlen (**-ni**) *nf* strainer, sieve
hidlo *vb* to distil, to run; to strain, to filter
hidlydd *nm* filter
hil *nf* race, lineage, posterity
hiliaeth *nf* racism
hilio *vb* to bring forth, to teem, to breed
hiliogaeth *nf* offspring, issue, posterity
hiliol *adj* racist
hiliwr (**-wyr**) *nm* racist
hilydd (**-ion**) *nm* racist
hilyddiaeth *nf* racism
hin *nf* weather
Hindŵ (**-iaid**) *nm* Hindu
hinfynegydd (**-ion**) *nm* barometer
hiniog (**-au**) *nf* threshold, door-frame
hinon *nf* fair weather
hinsawdd (**-soddau**) *nf* climate
hinsoddol *adj* climatic
hir (**hirion**) *adj, prefix* long
hiraeth *nm* longing, nostalgia, grief; homesickness
hiraethu *vb* to long, to yearn, to sorrow
hiraethus *adj* longing; homesick

hirbell *adj*: **o hirbell** from afar
hirben *adj* long-headed, shrewd
hirymaros *nm* long-suffering
hirymarhous *adj* long-suffering
hirhoedledd *nm* longevity
hirhoedlog *adj* long-lived
hithau *pron* she (on her part), she also
HIV *n* HIV; **HIV negyddol/positif** HIV negative/positive
hobaid (-eidiau) *nf* peck
hobi (hobïau) *nm* hobby
hoced (-ion) *nf* deceit, fraud
hocedu *vb* to cheat, to deceive, to defraud
hocedwr (-wyr) *nm* cheat, fraud
hoci *nm* hockey
hocys *npl* mallows
hodi *vb* to shoot, to ear, to run to seed
hoe *nf* spell, rest
hoeden (-nau) *nf* hoyden
hoedl (-au) *nf* lifetime, life
hoel, hoelen (heolion) *nf* nail
hoelio *vb* to nail
hoeliwr (-wyr) *nm* nailer
hoen *nf* joy, gladness; vigour
hoenus *adj* joyous, blithesome, gay
hoenusrwydd *nm* liveliness, sprightliness
hoenyn (-nau) *nm* snare
hoew *see* **hoyw**
hofran *vb* to hover
hofrennydd *nm* helicopter
hoff *adj* dear, fond; favourite
hoffi *vb* to like, to love
hoffter *nm* fondness; delight
hoffus *adj* lovable, amiable, affectionate
hogen (-nod) *nf* girl

hogennaidd *adj* girlish
hogfaen (-feini) *nm* whetstone, hone
hogi *vb* to sharpen, to whet
hogyn (hogiau) *nm* boy, lad
hongiad (-au) *nm* suspension
hongian *vb* to hang, to dangle
holgar *adj* inquisitive, curious
holi *vb* to ask, to question, to inquire
holiad (-au) *nm* interrogation, question
holiadur (-on) *nm* questionnaire
holwr (-wyr) *nm* questioner, interrogator; catechist, question-master
holwyddoreg (-au) *nf* catechism
holwyddori *vb* to catechize
holl *adj* all, whole
hollalluog *adj* almighty, omnipotent
hollalluowgrwydd *nm* omnipotence
hollbresennol *adj* omnipresent
hollbresenoldeb *nm* omnipresence
hollfyd *nm* universe
hollgyfoethog *adj* almighty
holliach *adj* whole, sound
hollol *adj* quite
hollt (-au) *nf* split, slit, cleft
hollti *vb* to split, to cleave, to slit
hollwybodaeth *nf* omniscience
hollwybodol *adj* omniscient
homeopatheg *nf* homeopathy
homili (-ïau) *nf* homily
hon *pron f of* **hwn**
honcian *vb* to waggle; to jolt; to limp
honedig *adj* alleged

h

honiad

honiad (-au) *nm* claim, assertion, allegation

honni *vb* to assert, to allege, to profess, to pretend

honno *pron f of* hwnnw

hopran (-au) *nf* mill-hopper; mouth

hosan (-au) *nf* stocking

hoyw *adj* alert, sprightly, lively, gay

hoywdeb, hoywder *nm* sprightliness

hoywi *vb* to brighten, to smarten

hual (-au) *nm* fetter, shackle

hualu *vb* to fetter, to shackle

huan *nf* the sun

huawdl *adj* eloquent

hud *nm* magic, illusion, charm, enchantment

hudlath (-au) *nf* magic wand

hudo *vb* to charm, to allure, to beguile

hudol *adj* enchanting ▸ *nm* (**-ion**) enchanter

hudoles (-au) *nf* enchantress, sorceress

hudoliaeth (-au) *nf* enchantment, allurement

hudolus *adj* enchanting, alluring

hudwr (-wyr) *nm* enticer, allurer

huddygl *nm* soot

hufen *nm* cream; **hufen iâ** ice cream

hufennog *adj* creamy

hugan (-au) *nf* cloak, covering; rug

hulio *vb* to cover, to spread

hun¹ (-au) *nf* sleep, slumber

hun² *pron* self; **ei dŷ ei hun** his own house

hunan (-ain) *pron* self ▸ *prefix* self-

hunan-dyb *nm* self-conceit

hunangar *adj* selfish

hunanhyderus *adj* self-confident

hunaniaeth *nf* identity

hunanladdiad *nm* self-murder, suicide

hunanol *adj* selfish, conceited

hunanoldeb *nm* selfishness; conceit

hunanymwadiad *nm* self-denial

hunanymwadu *vb* to deny oneself

hunanysgogol *adj* automatic

hunell (-au) *nf* wink (of sleep)

hunllef (-au) *nf* nightmare

huno *vb* to sleep

huodledd *nm* eloquence

hur (-iau) *nm* hire, wage

hurbwrcas *nm* hire purchase

hurio *vb* to hire

huriwr (-wyr) *nm* hirer; hireling

hurt *adj* stunned, stupid

hurtio *vb* to stun, to stupefy

hurtrwydd *nm* stupidity

hurtyn (-nod) *nm* stupid, blockhead

hwb (hybiau) *nm* push; effort; lift

hwde (hwdiwch) *vb imper* take, accept

hwdi (-s) *nm* hoodie

Hwngari *nf* Hungary

hwiangerdd *nf* lullaby

hwn (f hon) *adj, pron* this (one)

hwnnw (f honno) *adj, pron* that one (absent)

hwnt *adv* beyond, away, aside; **tu hwnt** beyond

hwp *nm* push

hwpio, hwpo *vb* to push

hwrdd¹ (hyrddod) *nm* ram; **yr Hwrdd** Aries

hwrdd² (**hyrddiau**) *nm* impulse, stroke
hwre *vb see* **hwde**
hwsmon (**-myn**) *nm* farm-bailiff
hwtio *vb* to hoot, to hiss
hwy *pron* they, them
hwyad, hwyaden (**hwyaid**) *nf* duck
hwyhau *vb* to lengthen, to elongate
hwyl! *excl* bye!
hwyl (**-iau**) *nf* sail; humour; religious fervour
hwylbren (**-nau, -ni**) *nm* mast
hwylio *vb* to sail; to prepare, to order
hwyliog *adj* fervent, eloquent
hwylus *adj* easy, convenient, comfortable
hwyluso *vb* to facilitate
hwylustod *nm* ease, facility, convenience
hwynt *pron* them, they
hwynt-hwy *pron* they, they themselves
hwyr *adj* late ▸ *nm* evening
hwyrach *adv* perhaps ▸ *adj* later
hwyrdrwm *adj* sluggish, drowsy, dull
hwyrfrydig *adj* slow, tardy, reluctant
hwyrfrydigrwydd *nm* tardiness, reluctance
hwyrol *adj* evening
hwyrhau *vb* to get late
hwythau *pron* they (on their part), they also
hy *adj* bold
hybarch *adj* venerable
hyblyg *adj* flexible, pliant, pliable

hyblygrwydd *nm* flexibility, pliancy
hybu *vb* to improve in health; to promote
hyd (**-au, -oedd**) *nm* length ▸ *prep* to, till, as far as
hydawdd *adj* soluble
hydeiml *adj* sensitive
hyder *nm* confidence, trust
hyderu *vb* to confide, to rely, to trust
hyderus *adj* confident
hydred (**-ion**) *nm* longitude
hydredol *adj* longitudinal
hydref (**-au**) *nm* autumn; **Hydref** October
hydrefol *adj* autumnal
hydrin *adj* tractable, docile
hydwyll *adj* gullible
hydwylledd *nm* gullibility
hydwyth *adj* supple, elastic
hydwythedd *nm* elasticity
hydyn *adj* tractable, docile
hydd (**-od**) *nm* stag
hyddysg *adj* well versed, learned
hyf *see* **hy**
hyfder, hyfdra *nm* boldness
hyfedr *adj* expert, skilful, clever
hyfryd *adj* pleasant, delightful, agreeable
hyfrydu *vb* to delight
hyfrydwch *nm* delight, pleasure
hyfwyn *adj* kindly, genial
hyfforddedig *adj* trainee
hyfforddi *vb* to direct, to instruct, to train
hyfforddiadol *adj* training
hyfforddiant *nm* instruction, training; **cwrs hyfforddiant** training course

hyfforddwr (-wyr) nm guide, instructor; **hyfforddwr gyrru** driving instructor
hygar adj amiable
hygarwch nm amiability
hyglod adj celebrated, renowned, famous
hyglwyf adj vulnerable
hyglyw adj audible
hygoel adj credible
hygoeledd nm credibility; credulity
hygoelus adj credulous, gullible
hygyrch adj accessible
hyhi pron she, her; herself
hylaw adj handy, convenient; dexterous
hylif (-au) nm, adj fluid, liquid
hylifydd nm liquidizer
hylithr adj slippery, fluent
hylosg adj combustible, inflammable
hylwydd adj prosperous
hyll adj ugly, hideous
hylltra nm ugliness
hyllu vb to mar, to disfigure
hyn adj, pron this; these; that
hynafgwr (-gwyr) nm old man, elder
hynafiad (-iaid) nm ancestor
hynafiaeth (-au) nf antiquity
hynafiaethol adj antiquarian
hynafiaethwr (-wyr), **hynafiaethydd** nm antiquary
hynafol adj ancient
hynaws adj kind, genial
hynawsedd nm kindness, geniality
hynny adj, pron that; those
hynod adj noted, notable, remarkable
hynodi vb to distinguish, to characterize
hynodion npl peculiarities
hynodrwydd nm peculiarity
hynt (-iau, -oedd) nf way, course
hyrddio, hyrddu vb to hurl, to impel
hyrddwynt (-oedd) nm hurricane
hyrwyddiad nm promotion
hyrwyddo vb to facilitate, to promote
hyrwyddwr (-wyr) nm sponsor, promoter
hysb (f hesb) adj dry, barren
hysbio vb to dry
hysbyddu vb to exhaust, to drain
hysbys adj known, evident; **dyn hysbys** wise man, sorcerer; **tra hysbys** well-known
hysbyseb (-ion) nf advertisement
hysbysebu vb to advertise
hysbysebwr (-wyr) nm advertiser
hysbysfwrdd nm noticeboard
hysbysiad (-au) nm announcement, advertisement
hysbyslen nf prospectus
hysbysrwydd nm information
hysbysu vb to inform, to announce
hysbyswr (-wyr) nm informant, informer
hysian, hysio vb to hiss; to set on, to incite
hytrach adv rather
hywaith adj industrious, dexterous
hywedd adj trained, tractable

i¹ *prep* to, into

i² *pron* I, me

iâ *nm* ice

iach *adj* healthy, well

iachâd *nm* healing

iachaol *adj* therapeutic

iacháu *vb* to heal; to save

iachawdwr (-wyr) *nm* saviour

iachawdwriaeth *nf* salvation

iachäwr (iachawyr) *nm* healer

iachus, iachol *adj* healthy, healthful, wholesome

iachusol *adj* wholesome

iad (-au) *nf* pate, cranium

iaith (ieithoedd) *nf* language; **yr iaith fain** English

iâr (ieir) *nf* hen

iard (ierdydd) *nf* yard

iarll (ieirll) *nm* earl

iarllaeth (-au) *nf* earldom

iarlles (-au) *nf* countess

ias (-au) *nf* shiver; thrill

iasol *adj* weird

Iau *nm* Jupiter; **dydd Iau** Thursday

iau¹ (ieuau) *nm* liver

iau² (ieuau, ieuoedd) *nf* yoke

iawn *adj* right ▸ *nm* right; atonement ▸ *adv* very; **yn iawn** all right

iawndal *nm* compensation

iawnder (-au) *nm* right, equity

iawnol *adj* atoning, expiatory

idealaeth *nf* idealism

ideoleg (-au) *nf* ideology

idiom (-au) *nm* idiom

Iddew (-on) *nm* Jew

Iddewes (-au) *nf* Jewish woman

Iddewiaeth *nf* Judaism

Iddewig *adj* Jewish

iddwf *nm*: **tân iddwf** erysipelas

ie *adv* yes, yea

iechyd *nm* health

iechydaeth *nf* hygiene, sanitation

iechydol *adj* hygienic, sanitary

iechydwriaeth *nf* salvation

ieitheg *nf* philology

ieithegydd (-ion, -wyr) *nm* philologist

ieithwedd (-au, -ion) *nf* diction, (literary) style

ieithydd (-ion) *nm* linguist

ieithyddiaeth *nf* linguistics, philology

ieithyddol *adj* linguistic, philological

Iesu *nm* Jesus

iet (-au, -iau) *nf* gate

ieuanc (-ainc) *adj* young

ieuenctid *nm* youth

ieuo *vb* to yoke

ifanc (-ainc) *adj* young

ifori *nm* ivory

ig (-ion) *nm* hiccup

igam-ogam *adj* zigzag
igian *vb* to hiccup
ing (**-oedd**) *nm* agony, anguish
ingol *adj* agonizing, agonized
ildio *vb* to give in, to give way
ill *pron* they; **ill dau** they both
impio *vb* to sprout, to shoot; to bud, to graft
impyn *nm* graft; scion
inc *nm* ink
incil (**-iau**) *nm* tape
incio *vb* to ink
incwm *nm* income
India *nf* India
India'r Gorllewin *npl* West Indies
Indonesia *nf* Indonesia
iod *nm* iota, jot
ioga *nmf* yoga
Iôn *nm* the Lord
Ionawr *nm* January
Iôr *nm* the Lord
Iorddonen *nf* Jordan
iorwg *nm* ivy
ir *adj* fresh, green, raw
irai *nm* ox-goad
iraid (**ireidiau**) *nm* grease
iraidd *adj* fresh, succulent, luxuriant
Iran *nf* Iran
Iraq *nf* Iraq
irder *nm* freshness, greenness
ireidd-dra *nm* freshness, vigour
ireiddio *vb* to freshen
iriad (**-au**) *nm* lubrication, greasing
iro *vb* to grease, to smear, to rub, to anoint
irwr (**-wyr**) *nm* greaser
is *adj* inferior, lower ▸ *prep* below, under ▸ *prefix* under-, sub-, vice-
isadran (**-nau**) *nf* subsection

Isalmaen *nf* Holland
is-deitl (**-au**) *nm* subtitle
isel *adj* low; base; humble; depressed
iselder (**-au**) *nm* lowness, depth; depression
iseldir (**-oedd**) *nm* lowland
Iseldiroedd *npl*: **yr Iseldiroedd** the Netherlands
iselfryd *adj* humble-minded
iselfrydedd *nm* humility, condescension
iselhau *vb* to lower, to abase, to degrade
isel-ysbryd *adj* despondent
isetholiad (**-au**) *nm* by-election
isffordd *nf* subway
is-gadeirydd *nm* vice-chairman
is-ganghellor *nm* vice-chancellor
is-gapten (**-iaid, -einiaid**) *nm* lieutenant
isgell *nm* broth, stock
isiarll (**-ieirll**) *nm* viscount
islais *nm* undertone
Islâm *nf* Islam
Islamaidd *adj* Islamic
islaw *prep* below, beneath
islawr *nm* basement
isod *adv* below, beneath
isop *nm* hyssop
isosod *vb* to sublet
isradd (**-iaid**) *nm* inferior, subordinate
israddol *adj* inferior
israddoldeb *nm* inferiority
Israel *nf* Israel
iswasanaethgar *adj* subservient
isymwybod *nm* subconscious
isymwybyddiaeth *nf* subconsciousness

ithfaen *nm* granite
Iwerddon *nf* Ireland
Iwerddon Rydd *nf* Eire
Iwerydd *nm*: **yr Iwerydd** the
 Atlantic (Ocean)
Iwganda *nf* Uganda
Iwgoslavia *nf* Yugoslavia
iwrch (iyrchod) *nm* roebuck

j

jac codi baw *nm* JCB
jac-y-do *nm* jackdaw
jam *nm* jam
Jamaica *nf* Jamaica
jamio *vb* to preserve
jar (-iau) *nf* jar, hot water bottle
jel *n* gel
jersi (-s) *nf* jersey
jest *adv* just, almost
jeti (-iau) *nm* jetty
jetlif *nm* jet stream
jet-sgi (-sgïau) *nf* jet-ski
jet-sgïo *vb* to jet-ski
ji-binc (-od) *nf* chaffinch
jîns *npl* jeans
job (-sys) *nf* job
jobyn *nm* job
jôc *nf* joke
jocan *vb* to joke
joci (-s) *nm* jockey
jwg (jygiau) *nf* jug
jyngl (-oedd) *nm* jungle

l

label (-i) *nf* label
labelu *vb* to label
labordy (-dai) *nm* laboratory
labro *vb* to labour
labrwr (-wyr) *nm* labourer
lafant *nm* lavender
lamp (-au) *nf* lamp
lamplen (-ni) *nf* lampshade
lansio *vb* to launch
lapio *vb* to lap, to wrap
larwm *nmf* alarm; **larwm lladron** burglar alarm; **larwm mwg, larwm fwg** smoke alarm
laser (-au, -i) *nm* laser
lawnt (-iau) *nf* lawn
lawrlwytho *vb* to download
lefain *nm* leaven
lefeinio *vb* to leaven
lefeinllyd *adj* leavened
lefel (-au) *nf* level; **Lefel A** A level
leicio *vb* to like
lein (-iau) *nf* clothes line; line-out (*rugby*)

lesbiad (-iaid) *nf* lesbian
lesbiaidd *adj* lesbian
letys *npl (nf -en)* lettuce
Libanus *nf* Lebanon
libart *nm* back-yard
Libya *nf* Libya
lifrai *nmf* livery
lifft (-iau) *nm* lift
lili *nf* lily
limwsîn (-s, -au) *nm* limousine
lindys *npl (nm -yn)* caterpillars
locust (-iaid) *nm* locust
lodes *nf* girl, lass
loetran *vb* to loiter
lol *nf* nonsense
lolfa (-feydd) *nf* lounge, sitting room; **lolfa ymadael** departure lounge
lolian *vb* to talk nonsense
lôn (lonydd) *nf* lane
loncian *vb* to jog
lonciwr (-wyr) *nm* jogger
lori (-ïau) *nf* lorry
losin *npl (nf -en)* sweets
lot (-iau) *nf* lot
Luxembourg *nf* Luxembourg
lŵans, lwfans *nm* allowance
lwc *nf* luck
lwcus *adj* lucky
lwmp (lympiau) *nm* lump

llabed (-au) *nf* lappet, lapel, flap
llabwst (-ystiau) *nm* lubber, lout
llabyddio *vb* to stone
llac *adj* slack, loose, lax
llacio *vb* to slacken, to loosen, to relax
llacrwydd *nm* slackness, laxity
llacs *nm* mud, dirt
llacsog *adj* muddy, dirty
llach (-iau) *nf* lash, slash
llachar *adj* bright, brilliant, flashing
llachio *vb* to lash, to slash
Lladin *nf* Latin
lladmerydd (-ion) *nm* interpreter
lladrad (-au) *nm* theft, robbery
lladradaidd *adj* stealthy, furtive
lladrata *vb* to thieve, to steal
lladron *see* lleidr
lladrones (-au) *nf* female thief
lladronllyd *adj* thievish, pilfering
lladd *vb* to cut; to kill, to slay, to slaughter
lladd-dy (-dai) *nm* slaughter-house

lladdedig (-ion) *adj* killed, slain
lladdwr (-wyr) *nm* killer, slayer
llaes *adj* long, loose; **treiglad llaes** spirant mutation
llaesod, llaesodr *nf* litter (for animals)
llaesu *vb* to slacken, to loosen, to relax, to droop, to flag
llaeth *nm* milk
llaetha *vb* to yield milk
llaethdy (-dai) *nm* milk-house, dairy
llaethog *adj* rich in milk; milky
llafar *nm* utterance, speech ► *adj* vocal; loud
llafariad (-iaid) *nf* vowel
llafn (-au) *nm* blade
llafrwyn *npl* (*nf* -en) bulrushes
llafur (-iau) *nm* labour; corn
llafurfawr *adj* elaborate; laborious
llafurio *vb* to labour, to toil; to till
llafurlu (-oedd) *nm* manpower, labour force, workforce
llafurus *adj* laborious, toilsome, painstaking
llafurwr (-wyr) *nm* labourer, husbandman
llai *adj* smaller
llaid *nm* mud, mire
llain (lleiniau) *nf* patch, piece, narrow strip
llais (lleisiau) *nm* voice, vote
llaith *adj* damp, moist
llall (lleill) *pron* other, another
llam (-au) *nm* stride, leap, jump, bound
llamhidydd (llamidyddion) *nm* porpoise
llamsachus *adj* prancing, frisky
llamu *vb* to stride, to leap, to bound

llan (-nau) nf church; village

llanast, llanastr nm confusion, mess

llanc (-iau) nm young man, youth, lad

llances (-au, -i) nf young woman, lass

llannerch (llennyrch), llanerchau (-i, -ydd) nf spot, patch, glade

llanw nm flow (of tide) ▸ vb to flow, to fill

llaprwth nm lout

llariaidd adj mild, meek, gentle

llarieidd-dra nm meekness, gentleness

llarieiddio vb to soothe, to mollify

llarp (-iau) nm shred, clout

llarpio vb to rend, to tear, to mangle, to maul

llarpiog adj tattered, ragged

llaswyr (-au) nm psalter

llath (-au) nf yard; wand

llathen (-ni) nf yard

llathr adj bright, glossy, smooth

llathraidd adj smooth; of fine growth

llathru vb to polish

llau npl (nf lleuen) lice

llaw (dwylaw, dwylo) nf hand

llawcio vb to gulp, to gorge, to gobble

llawchwith adj left-handed

llawdde adj dexterous

llawddryll (-iau) nm pistol, revolver

llawen adj merry, joyful, glad, cheerful

llawenhau vb to rejoice, to gladden

llawenychu vb to rejoice

llawenydd nm joy, gladness, mirth

llawer (-oedd) nm, adj, adv many, much

llawes (llewys) nf sleeve

llawfaeth adj reared by hand

llawfeddyg (-on) nm surgeon

llawfeddygaeth nf surgery

llawfeddygol adj surgical

llaw-fer nf shorthand

llawfom (-iau) nf grenade

llawforwyn (-forynion) nf handmaid

llawlyfr nm manual

llawn adj full ▸ adv quite

llawnder, llawndra nm fullness, abundance

llawr (lloriau) nm floor, ground, earth

llawrydd adj freelance

llawryf (-oedd) nm laurel, bay

llawryfog, llawryfol adj laureate

llawysgrif (-au) nf manuscript

llawysgrifen nf handwriting

lle (-oedd, llefydd) nm place

llecyn (-nau) nm place, spot

llech (-au, -i) nf slab, flag, slate

llechen nf tablet

llechgi (-gwn) nm sneak

llechres (-i) nf table, catalogue, list

llechu vb to hide, to shelter; to lurk, to skulk

llechwedd (-au, -i) nf slope, hillside

llechwraidd adj stealthy, underhand, insidious

lled¹ (-au) nm breadth, width

lled² adv partly, rather

lledaenu vb to spread, to disseminate, to circulate

lleden (lledod) nf flat-fish

llediaith nf foreign accent

llednais adj modest, delicate; meek

llednant (-nentydd) *nf* tributary
lledneisrwydd *nm* modesty, delicacy
lled-orwedd *vb* to recline, to lounge, to loll
lledr (-au) *nm* leather; **lledr y gwefusau** gums
lledred (-ion) *nm* latitude
lledrith *nm* magic, illusion, phantasm
lledrithio *vb* to appear, to haunt
lledrithiol *adj* illusory, illusive
lledrwr (-wyr) *nm* leather-merchant
lledryw *adj* degenerate
lledu *vb* to widen, to broaden, to expand, to spread
lleddf *adj* slanting; flat, minor; plaintive
lleddfol *adj* sedative
lleddfolyn (-olion) *nm* sedative
lleddfu *vb* to flatten; to soften, to soothe, to allay
llef (-au) *nf* voice, cry
llefain *vb* to cry
llefareg *nf* speech training
llefaru *vb* to speak, to utter
llefarwr (llefarwyr), llefarydd (-ion) *nm* speaker
lleferydd *nmf* utterance, voice, speech
llefn *adj* of **llyfn**
llefrith *nm* sweet milk, new milk, milk
llegach *adj* weak, feeble, infirm, decrepit
lleng (-oedd) *nf* legion
lleiaf *adj* least, smallest
lleiafrif (-au) *nm* minority
lleiafswm *nm* minimum

lleian (-od) *nf* nun
lleiandy (-dai) *nm* nunnery, convent
lleibio *vb* to lap, to lick
lleidiog *adj* miry
lleidr (lladron) *nm* thief, robber
lleiddiad (-iaid) *nm* assassin
lleihad *nm* diminution, decrease
lleihau *vb* to lessen, to diminish, to decrease
lleill *see* **llall**
lleisio *vb* to sound, to utter, to voice
lleisiol *adj* vocal
lleisiwr (-wyr) *nm* vocalist
lleithder, lleithdra *nm* damp, moisture
lleithig *nf* couch; footstool
lleitho *vb* to damp, to moisten
llem *adj* of **llym**
llen (-ni) *nf* sheet; veil, curtain
llên *nf* literature, lore, learning
llencyn *nm* stripling, lad
llencyndod *nm* adolescence
llengar *adj* literary, learned
llengig *nf* diaphragm, midriff; **tor llengig** rupture
llên-ladrad (-au) *nm* plagiarism
llenor (-ion) *nm* literary man
llenwi *vb* to fill; to fill in; to flow in
llenydda *vb* to practise literature
llenyddiaeth (-au) *nf* literature
llenyddol *adj* literary
lleol *adj* local
lleoli *vb* to locate; to localize
lleoliad *nm* location; localization
llercian *vb* to lurk, to loiter
lles *nm* benefit, profit, good, advantage; **y wladwriaeth les** the welfare state

153

llesâd *nm* advantage, profit, benefit
llesáu *vb* to benefit, to advantage
llesg *adj* feeble, faint; languid, sluggish
llesgáu *vb* to weaken, to languish, to faint
llesgedd *nm* weakness, languor, debility
llesmair (-meiriau) *nm* faint, swoon
llesmeirio *vb* to faint, to swoon
llesmeiriol *adj* faint
llesol *adj* advantageous, profitable, beneficial
llestair, llesteirio *vb* to hinder, to impede, to baulk
llestr (-i) *nm* vessel
llesyddiaeth *nf* utilitarianism
lletbai *adj* askew, awry; oblique
lletchwith *adj* awkward, clumsy
lletem (-au) *nf* wedge, stud, rivet
lletraws *adj* diagonal
lletwad (-au) *nf* ladle
llety (-au) *nm* lodging(s)
lletya *vb* to lodge
lletygar *adj* hospitable
lletygarwch *nm* hospitality
lletywr (-wyr) *nm* lodger; host
lletywraig (-wragedd) *nf* landlady
llethol *adj* oppressive, overpowering
llethr (-au) *nf* slope, declivity
llethrog *adj* sloping, steep, declining
llethu *vb* to overlie; to smother; to oppress, to overpower, to overwhelm
lleuad (-au) *nf* moon
lleuog *adj* lousy

llew (-od) *nm* lion; **dant y llew** dandelion; **y Llew** Leo
llewaidd *adj* lionlike, leonine
llewes (-au) *nf* lioness
llewpart (-pardiaid) *nm* leopard
llewych *nm* light, brightness
llewyg (-on) *nm* faint, swoon
llewygu *vb* to faint, to swoon
llewyrch *nm* brightness, radiance, gleam
llewyrchu *vb* to shine
llewyrchus *adj* flourishing, prosperous
lleyg (-ion) *adj* lay
lleygwr (-wyr) *nm* layman
lliain (-einiau) *nm* linen; cloth; towel
lliaws *nm* host, multitude
llibin *adj* limp, feeble; awkward, clumsy
llid *nm* wrath; irritation, inflammation
llidiart (-ardau) *nm* gate
llidio *vb* to be angry, to chafe, to inflame
llidiog *adj* angry, wrathful; inflamed
llidiowgrwydd *nm* wrath, indignation
llidus *adj* inflamed
llieiniwr (-wyr) *nm* linen-draper
llif¹ (-iau) *nf* saw
llif² (-ogydd) *nm* stream, flood, current
llifbridd *nm* alluvium
llifddor (-au) *nf* floodgate
llifddwfr (-ddyfroedd) *nm* flood, torrent
llifeiriant (-iaint) *nm* flood
llifeirio *vb* to flow, to stream

llifeiriol *adj* streaming, overflowing
llifio *vb* to saw
llifiwr (-wyr) *nm* sawyer
llifo¹ *vb* to flow, to stream
llifo² *vb* to grind (tool)
llifo³ *vb* to dye
llifogydd *npl* flooding
llifolau (-euadau) *nm* floodlight
llifoleuo *vb* to floodlight
llifwr (-wyr) *nm* dyer
llifyn (-nau, -ion) *nm* dye
llilinio *vb* to streamline
llin *nm* flax; **had llin** linseed
llinach (-au) *nf* lineage, pedigree
llindagu *vb* to strangle, to throttle, to choke
llinell (-au) *nf* line; **llinell gais** try line; **llinell gymorth** helpline
llinelliad (-au) *nm* lineation, drawing
llinellog *adj* lined, ruled
llinellol *adj* lineal
llinellu *vb* to rule
llinglwm *nm*: **cwlwm llinglwm** tight knot
lliniaru *vb* to ease, to soothe, to allay
llinol *adj* linear
llinorog *adj* eruptive; purulent, suppurating
llinos (-od) *nf* linnet
llinyn (-nau) *nm* line, string, twine
llinynnu *vb* to string
llipa *adj* limp, weak
llipryn (-nod) *nm* hobbledehoy, weakling
lliprynnaidd *adj* limp, flabby
llith (-iau, -oedd) *nf* lesson, lecture; bait, mash

llithio *vb* to entice, to allure, to seduce; to feed
llithren (-nau) *nf* chute
llithriad (-au) *nm* slip, glide
llithrig *adj* slippery, glib, fluent
llithrigrwydd *nm* slipperiness, glibness
llithro *vb* to slip, to glide, to slide
lliw (-iau) *nm* colour, hue, dye
lliwgar *adj* colourful
lliwio *vb* to colour, to dye
lliwiog *adj* coloured
lliwur *nm* dye
llo (lloi) *nm* calf
lloc (-iau) *nm* fold, pen
lloches (-au) *nf* refuge, shelter, den
llochesu *vb* to harbour, to shelter
llochi *vb* to stroke, to caress, to fondle
llodig *adj* in heat (of a sow)
llodrau *npl* trousers, breeches
Lloegr *nf* England
lloer (-au) *nf* moon
lloeren (-ni, -nau) *nf* satellite
lloerig *adj, nm* lunatic
llofnod (-au), llofnodiad *nm* signature
llofnodi *vb* to sign
llofrudd (-ion) *nm* murderer; **llofrudd cyfresol** serial killer
llofruddiaeth (-au) *nf* murder
llofruddio *vb* to murder
llofruddiog *adj* guilty of murder
lloffa *vb* to glean
lloffion *npl* gleanings
llofft (-ydd) *nf* loft, bedroom, gallery
lloffwr (-wyr) *nm* gleaner
lloffyn *nm* bundle of gleanings
llog (-au) *nm* interest

ll

llogi

llogi *vb* to hire
llogwr (-wyr) *nm* hirer
llong (-au) *nf* ship; **llong ofod** spaceship
llongddrylliad (-au) *nm* shipwreck
llongddryllio *vb* to wreck
llongwr (-wyr) *nm* sailor
llongwriaeth *nf* seamanship
llom *adj f of* llwm
llon *adj* glad, merry
llonaid, llond *nm* full
llonder *nm* gladness, joy
llongyfarch *vb* to congratulate
llongyfarchiad (-au, -archion) *nm* congratulation
lloniant *nm* joy, cheer
llonni *vb* to cheer, to gladden
llonydd *adj* quiet, still ▸ *nm* quiet, calm
llonyddu *vb* to quiet, to still, to calm
llonyddwch *nm* quietness, quiet
llorgynllun (-iau) *nm* ground plan
llorio *vb* to floor; to ground *(rugby)*
llorwedd *adj* horizontal
llosg *nm, adj* burning
llosgach *nm* incest
llosgadwy *adj* combustible
llosgfa (-fâu, -feydd) *nf* burning, inflammation
llosgfynydd (-oedd) *nm* volcano
llosgi *vb* to burn, to scorch; to smart
llosgwrn (-yrnau) *nm* tail
llosgydd (-ion) *nm* incinerator
llu (-oedd) *nm* host
lluched *npl (nf -en)* lightning
lluchfa (-feydd) *nf* snowdrift
lluchio *vb* to throw, to fling, to pelt; to throw away

lluchiwr (-wyr) *nm* thrower
lludlyd *adj* ashy
lludu, lludw *nm* ashes, ash
lludded *nm* weariness, fatigue
lluddedig *adj* wearied, tired, fatigued
lluddedu *vb* to tire, to weary
lluddias, lluddio *vb* to hinder; to forbid
lluest (-au) *nm* tent, booth
lluestfa (-feydd) *nf* encampment
lluestu *vb* to encamp
lluesty (-tai) *nm* tent, booth
llugoer *adj* lukewarm
lluman (-au) *nm* banner, standard, ensign
llumanwr (-wyr) *nm* linesman
llumon *nm* chimney stack, peak
Llun, dydd Llun *nm* Monday
llun (-iau) *nm* form, image, picture
Llundain *nf* London
llungopïo *vb* to photocopy
lluniad (-au) *nm* drawing
lluniadaeth (-au) *nf* draughtsmanship
lluniadu *vb* to draw
lluniaeth *nm* food, nourishment
lluniaethu *vb* to order, to ordain, to decree
lluniaidd *adj* shapely
lluniedydd *nm* draughtsman
llunio *vb* to form, to shape, to fashion
lluniwr (-wyr) *nm* former, maker
llun-recordydd (-ion) *nm* video-tape recorder
lluosflwydd *adj* perennial
lluosi *vb* to multiply
lluosiad *nm* multiplication

lluosill, lluosillafog *adj* polysyllabic
lluosog *adj* numerous; plural
lluosogi *vb* to multiply
lluosogiad *nm* multiplication
lluoswm *nm* product *(in maths)*
lluosydd *nm* multiplier
llurgunio *vb* to mangle, to mutilate
llurguniwr (-wyr) *nm* mangler, mutilator
llurig (-au) *nf* coat of mail, cuirass
llurigog *adj* mail-clad
llus *npl (nf* **-en)** bilberries, whinberries
llusern (-au) *nf* lantern, lamp
llusg (-ion) *nm* draught; drag
llusgfad (-au) *nm* tugboat
llusgo *vb* to drag; to trail; to crawl; to drawl
llusgwr (-wyr) *nm* dragger, slowcoach
llutrod *nm* mire, ashes, debris
lluwch *nm* dust; spray; snowdrift
lluwchio *vb* to drift
lluydd *nm* host, army
lluyddu *vb* to mobilise
llw (-on) *nm* oath
llwch *nm* dust, powder
llwdn (llydnod) *nm* young of animals
llwfr *adj* timid, cowardly
llwfrdra *nm* cowardice
llwfrddyn, llwfrgi *nm* coward
llwfrhau *vb* to faint
llwglyd *adj* hungry, famished
llwgr *nm* corruption ▸ *adj* corrupt
llwgrwobrwy (-on) *nm* bribe
llwgrwobrwyo *vb* to bribe
llwgu *vb* to starve, to famish

llwm (f llom) *adj* bare; destitute, poor
llwnc *nm* gulp, swallow; gullet
llwncdestun *nm* toast *(health)*
llwr, llwrw *nm* track; **llwr ei ben** headlong; **llwr ei gefn** backwards
llwy (-au) *nf* spoon, ladle
llwyaid (-eidiau) *nf* spoonful
llwybr (-au) *nm* path, track
llwybreiddio *vb* to direct, to forward
llwybro *vb* to walk
llwyd *adj* brown; grey; pale; hoary
llwydaidd *adj* greyish, palish
llwydi, llwydni *nm* greyness; mould, mildew
llwydnos *nf* dusk, twilight
llwydo *vb* to turn grey; to become mouldy
llwydrew *nm* hoar-frost
llwydrewi *vb* to cast hoar-frost
llwydd *nm* welfare
llwyddiannus *adj* successful, prosperous
llwydd, -iant *nm* success, prosperity
llwyddo *vb* to succeed, to prosper
llwyfan (-nau) *nfm* platform, stage
llwyfandir (-oedd) *nm* plateau
llwyfannu *vb* to stage
llwyfen (llwyf) *nf* elm
llwyn¹ (-i) *nm* grove; bush
llwyn² (-au) *nf* loin
llwynog (-od) *nm* fox
llwynoges (-au) *nf* vixen
llwynwst *nf* lumbago
llwyo *vb* to use a spoon; to ladle
llwyr *adj* entire, complete, total ▸ *adv* entirely, altogether ▸ *prefix* total

157

llwyredd *nm* entireness, completeness

llwyrymatal, llwyrymwrthod *vb* to abstain totally

llwyrymwrthodwr (-wyr) *nm* teetotaller

llwyth¹ (-au) *nm* tribe, clan

llwyth² (-i) *nm* load, burden

llwytho *vb* to load, to burden

llwythog *adj* laden, burdened

llychlyd *adj* dusty

Llychlyn *nf* Scandinavia

llychwino *vb* to spot, to tarnish, to soil, to sully

llychyn *nm* particle of dust, mote

llydan *adj* broad, wide

Llydaw *nf* Brittany

llydnu *vb* to bring forth, to foal

llyfn (*f* llefn) *adj* smooth, sleek

llyfnder, -dra *nm* smoothness, sleekness

llyfndew *adj* plump, sleek

llyfnhau *vb* to smooth, to level

llyfnu *vb* to smooth, to level; to harrow

llyfr (-au) *nm* book; **llyfr nodiadau** notebook

llyfrbryf (-ed) *nm* bookworm

llyfrfa *nf* (-feydd) library; book room; official publishing house of religious denomination, government etc

llyfrgell (-oedd) *nf* library

llyfrgellydd (-ion) *nm* librarian

llyfrifeg *nmf* book-keeping

llyfrnod (-au) *nm* bookmark

llyfrwerthwr (-wyr) *nm* bookseller

llyfrydd (-ion) *nm* bibliographer, transcriber of books

llyfryddiaeth *nf* bibliography

llyfryn (-nau) *nm* booklet, pamphlet

llyfu *vb* to lick

llyffant (-od, llyffaint) *nm* frog, toad

llyffethair (-eiriau) *nf* fetter, shackle

llyffetheirio *vb* to fetter, to shackle

llyg (-od) *nmf* shrew(-mouse)

llygad (llygaid) *nm* eye; **llygad y dydd** daisy

llygad-dynnu *vb* to bewitch

llygad-dyst *nm* eyewitness

llygadog *adj* eyed, sharp-eyed

llygadrwth *adj* wide-eyed, staring

llygadrythu *vb* to stare

llygadu *vb* to eye

llygatgraff *adj* keen-eyed, sharp-sighted

llygedyn *nm* ray of light

llygeidiog *adj* eyed

llygoden (llygod) *nf* mouse; **llygoden fawr, llygoden ffrengig** rat

llygota *vb* to catch mice

llygotwr (-wyr) (*f* llygotwraig) *nm* mouser, ratter

llygradwy *adj* corruptible

llygredig *adj* corrupt, depraved, degraded

llygredigaeth (-au) *nf* corruption

llygredd *nm* corruptness, depravity

llygriad (-au) *nm* corruption, adulteration

llygru *vb* to corrupt, to adulterate

llygrwr (-wyr) *nm* corrupter, adulterator

llynges (-au) *nf* fleet, navy

llyngeswr (-wyr) *nm* navy-man
llyngesydd (-ion) *nm* admiral
llyngyr *npl* (*nf* **-en**) (intestinal) worms
llym (*f* **llem**) *adj* sharp, keen, severe
llymaid (-eidiau) *nm* sip, drink
llymarch (llymeirch) *nm* oyster
llymder¹ *nm* sharpness, keenness, severity
llymder², llymdra *nm* bareness, poverty
llymeitian, llymeitio *vb* to sip, to tipple
llymeitiwr (-wyr) *nm* tippler, sot
llymhau¹ *vb* to make bare
llymhau² *vb* to sharpen
llymrïaid *npl* (*nf* **-ïen**) sand-eels
llymru *nm* flummery
llymsur *adj* acrid
llymu *vb* to sharpen, to whet
llyn (-noedd) *nm* lake, pond, pool
llynciad (-au) *nm* draught, gulp
llyncu *vb* to swallow, to gulp, to absorb
llyncwr (-wyr) *nm* swallower, guzzler
llynedd *nf* last year
llyo *vb* to lick
llys (-oedd) *nm* court, hall, palace
llysaidd *adj* courtly, polite
llysblant *npl* step-children
llyschwaer *nf* step-sister
llysenw (-au) *nm* nickname
llysenwi *vb* to nickname
llysfab *nm* step-son
llysfam *nf* step-mother
llysferch *nf* step-daughter
llysfrawd *nm* step-brother

llysgenhadaeth *nf* embassy, legation
llysgenhadol *adj* ambassadorial
llysgennad (-genhadon) *nm* ambassador
llysiau *npl* (*nm* **-ieuyn**) herbs, vegetables
llysieueg *nm* botany
llysieuol *adj* herbal, vegetable
llysieuwr *nm* vegetarian
llysieuydd (-ion, llysieuwyr) *nm* botanist; vegetarian
llysieuyn *nm* plant
llysnafedd *nm* snivel, slime
llystad *nm* step-father
llystyfiant *nm* vegetation
llyswenwyn *nm* herbicide
llysysol *adj* herbivorous
llyswen (llysywod) *nf* eel
llysywenna *vb* to catch eels
llythrennedd *nm* literacy
llythrennol *adj* literal
llythyr (-au) *nm* letter, epistle
llythyrdy (-dai) *nm* post-office
llythyren (llythrennau) *nf* letter, type
llythyrwr (-wyr) *nm* letter-writer
llyw (-iau) *nm* ruler; rudder, helm
llywaeth *adj* hand-fed, tame, pet
llywiawdwr (-wyr) *nm* ruler, governor
llywio *vb* to rule, to govern, to direct, to steer
llywiwr (llywyr) *nm* steersman, helmsman
llywodraeth (-au) *nf* government
llywodraethol *adj* governing, dominant
llywodraethu *vb* to govern, to rule

159

llywodraethwr (-wyr) *nm*
  governor, ruler
llywydd (-ion) *nm* president
llywyddiaeth (-au) *nf* presidency
llywyddol *adj* presidential
llywyddu *vb* to preside

mab (meibion) *nm* boy, son; man,
  male
mabaidd *adj* filial
maban (-od) *nm* babe, baby
mabandod *nm* childhood, infancy
mabinogi *nm* tale, story
mablygad *nm* eyeball
mabmaeth (-au, -od) *nm* foster-
  son
maboed *nm* childhood, infancy,
  youth
mabolaeth *nf* sonship; boyhood,
  youth
mabolaidd *adj* youthful, boyish
mabolgamp (-au) *nf* game, sport,
  feat
mabsant *nm* patron saint
mabwysiad *nm* adoption
mabwysiadol *adj* adoptive;
  adopted
mabwysiadu *vb* to adopt
macrell (mecryll) *nfm* mackerel
macsu *vb* to brew

macwy (-aid) *nm* youth, page

machlud, machludo *vb* to set, to go down; **machlud haul** sunset

machludiad *nm* setting, going down

machnïydd *nm* mediator

madarch *npl* (*nf* **-en**) mushrooms

madfall (-od) *nm* lizard

madrondod *nm* giddiness, stupefaction

madroni *vb* to make *or* become giddy

madru *vb* to putrefy, to fester, to rot

madruddyn *nm* cartilage; **madruddyn y cefn** spinal cord

maddau *vb* to pardon, to forgive, to remit

maddeuant *nm* pardon, forgiveness

maddeugar *adj* of a forgiving disposition

maddeuol *adj* pardoning, forgiving

maddeuwr (-wyr) *nm* pardoner

mae *vb* tis, are; there is, there are

maeden *nf* slut, jade

maeddu *see* baeddu

maen (meini) *nm* stone

maenol, maenor (-au) *nf* manor

maentumio *vb* to maintain

maer (-od, meiri) *nm* mayor

maeres (-au) *nf* mayoress

maerol *adj* mayoral

maeryddiaeth *nf* mayoralty

maes (meysydd) *nm* field ▸ *adj* free-range; **i maes** out; **maes glanio** airport

maesglaf (-gleifion) *nm* outpatient

maeslywydd (-ion) *nm* field-marshal

maestir (-oedd) *nm* open country, plain

maestref (-i, -ydd) *nf* suburb

maesu *vb* to field

maeth *nm* nourishment, nutriment

maethiad *nm* nutrition

maethlon *adj* nourishing, nutritious

maethu *vb* to nourish, to nurture

maethydd (-ion) *nm* nourisher

maethyn (-nau) *nm* nutrient; suckling

mafon *npl* (*nf* **-en**) raspberries

magl (-au) *nf* snare; mesh

maglu *vb* to snare, to mesh, to trip

magnel (-au) *nf* gun, cannon

magnelaeth *nf* artillery

magnelwr (-wyr) *nm* gunner

magnesiwm *nm* magnesium

magnetedd *nm* magnetism

magneteiddio *vb* to magnetise

magu *vb* to breed, to rear, to nurse; to gain, to acquire

magwraeth *nf* nourishment, nurture

magwrfa *nf* nursery

magwyr (-ydd) *nf* wall

maharen (meheryn) *nm* ram; wether

Mai *nm* May

mai *conj* that it is

maidd *nm* whey

main (meinion) *adj* fine, slender, thin; **main y cefn** small of the back

mainc (meinciau) *nf* bench, form, seat

maint *nm* size, quantity, number

maintioli *nm* size, stature

Maiorca *nf* Majorca

m

maip *npl* (*nf* **meipen**) turnips
maith (**meithion**) *adj* long, tedious
mâl *adj* ground
malais *nm* malice
maldod *nm* dalliance, affection
maldodi *vb* to pet, to pamper, to indulge
Maleisia *nf* Malaysia
maleisus *adj* malicious
maleithiau *npl* chilblains
malio *vb* to care, to mind, to heed
Malta *nf* Malta
malu *vb* to grind, to mince, to chop, to smash
malurio *vb* to pound; to crumble, to moulder
malurion *npl* fragments, debris
malwen *nf* snail
malwod *npl* (*nf*-**en**, *nf* **malwen**) snails
malwr (-**wyr**) *nm* grinder
mall *nf* blight; **y fall** Belial, perdition
malltod *nm* rot, blight, blast
mallu *vb* to rot, to blast
mam (-**au**) *nf* mother, mum; **mam-gu** grandmother
mamaeth (-**od**) *nf* nurse
mamal (-**iaid**) *nm* mammal
mam-gu *nf* granny
mamiaith (-**ieithoedd**) *nf* mother-tongue
mamog (-**iaid**) *nf* dam, sheep with young
mamol *adj* maternal
mamolaeth (-**au**) *nf* maternity
mamwlad (-**wledydd**) *nf* motherland
man¹ *nmf* place, spot, location
man² *nm* speck, blemish
mân *adj* small, fine, petty

mandyllog *adj* porous
maneg (**menig**) *nf* glove, gauntlet
mangre *nf* place, spot
manion *npl* scraps, trifles, minutiæ
mantais (-**eision**) *nf* advantage
manteisio *vb* to take advantage, to profit
manteisiol *adj* advantageous; profitable
mantell (-**oedd, mentyll**) *nf* mantle
mantellog *adj* mantled
mantol (-**ion**) *nf* balance; **y Fantol** Libra
mantolen (-**ni**) *nf* balance-sheet
mantoli *vb* to turn scale, to balance, to weigh
manŵaidd *adj* delicate, fine
manwerthu *vb* to retail
mân-werthu *vb* to retail
mân-werthwr *nm* retailer
manwl *adj* exact, precise, strict, particular
manwl-gywir *adj* precise
manylion *npl* particulars, details
manylrwydd *nm* exactness, precision
manylu *vb* to go into detail, to particularize
manylwch *nm* exactness, precision
map (-**iau**) *nm* map
mapio *vb* to map
mapiwr (-**wyr**) *nm* cartographer
marathon (-**au**) *nf* marathon
marblen (**marblys**) *nf* marble
marc (-**iau**) *nm* mark
marcio *vb* to mark
Marcsiaeth *nf* Marxism
march (**meirch**) *nm* horse, stallion
marchlu (-**oedd**) *nm* cavalry
marchnad (-**oedd**) *nf* market

marchnadfa (-oedd) *nf*
marketplace
marchnata *vb* to market, to trade
marchnatwr (-wyr) *nm* merchant
marchnerth (-oedd) *nm*
horsepower
marchocáu *vb* to ride a horse
marchog (-ion) *nm* horseman,
rider; knight
marchogaeth *vb* to ride
marchogwr (-wyr) *nm* rider,
horseman
marchredyn *npl* (*nf*-**en**) polypody
fern
marchwellt *nm* tall, coarse grass
marian *nm* holm, strand, moraine
marlad *nm* drake
marmalêd (-ledau) *nm* marmalade
marmor *nm* marble
marsialydd (-ion) *nm* marshal
marsiandïaeth *nf* merchandise
marsiandïwr (-wyr) *nm* merchant
marsipan *nm* marzipan
marw¹ *vb* to die
marw²(meirw, meirwon) *nm*,
adj dead
marwaidd *adj* lifeless, sluggish,
moribund
marwdon *nf* dandruff
marweidd-dra *nm* deadness,
sluggishness
marweiddio *vb* to deaden, to
mortify
marwhad *nm* mortification
marwhau *vb* to deaden, to mortify
marwnad (-au) *nf* lament, elegy
marwol *adj* deadly, mortal, fatal
marwolaeth (-au) *nf* death
marwoldeb *nm* mortality
marwolion *npl* mortals

marwor *npl* (*nm* -**yn**) embers;
charcoal
marwydos *npl* embers
masarnen (masarn) *nf* sycamore
masgl (-au) *nf* shell, pod
masglo, masglu *vb* to shell; to
interlace
masnach (-au) *nf* trade, traffic,
commerce; **masnach deg** fair
trade
masnachol *adj* commercial,
business
masnachu *vb* to do business, to
trade, to traffic
masnachwr (-wyr) *nm* dealer,
merchant
masw *adj* wanton
maswedd *nm* wantonness,
ribaldry
masweddol *adj* wanton, ribald
maswr (-wyr) *nm* outside half
mat (-iau) *nm* mat
mater (-ion) *nm* matter
materol *adj* material; materialistic
materoliaeth *nf* materialism
matog (-au) *nf* mattock
matras (-resi) *nm* mattress
matrics (-au) *nm* matrix
matsien (matsys) *nf* match
math (-au) *nm* sort, kind
mathemateg *nm* mathematics,
maths
mathru *vb* to trample, to tread
mathrwr (-wyr) *nm* trampler
mawl *nm* praise
mawn *coll n* (*nf*-**en**) peat
mawnog *adj* peaty ▶ *nf* peat-bog
mawr (-ion) *adj* big, great, large
mawredd *nm* greatness, grandeur,
majesty

mawreddog adj grand, majestic; grandiose

mawrfrydig adj magnanimous

mawrfrydigrwydd nm magnanimity

Mawrth nm Mars; March; **dydd Mawrth** Tuesday

mawrygu vb to magnify, to extol

mawrhau vb to magnify, to enlarge

mawrhydi nm majesty

mebyd nm childhood, infancy, youth

mecaneg nf mechanics

mecanwaith (-weithiau) nm mechanism

mecanyddol adj mechanical

Mecsico nf Mexico

mechnïaeth nf surety, bail

mechnïo vb to go bail, to become surety

mechnïol adj vicarious

mechnïydd (-ion) nm surety, bail

medel (-au) nf reaping; reaping party

medelwr (-wyr) nm reaper

Medi nm September

medi vb to reap

medr nm skill, ability

medru vb to know, to be able

medrus adj clever, skilful

medrusrwydd nm cleverness, skilfulness, skill

medrydd (-ion) nm gauge

medd¹ nm mead

medd² vb says

meddal adj soft, tender

meddalhau, meddalu vb to soften

meddalwch nm softness

meddalwedd nm software

meddiannol adj possessing, possessive

meddiannu vb to possess, to occupy

meddiant (-iannau) nm possession

meddu vb to possess, to own

meddw (-on) adj drunk, intoxicated

meddwdod nm drunkenness, intoxication

meddwi vb to get drunk, to intoxicate, to inebriate

meddwl vb to think; to mean ▶ nm (**meddyliau**) thought; meaning; opinion

meddwol adj intoxicating

meddwyn (-won) nm drunkard, inebriate

meddyg (-on) nm physician, doctor; **meddyg teulu** GP, general practitioner

meddygaeth nf medicine

meddygfa (-feydd) nf surgery

meddyginiaeth (-au) nf medicine, remedy, medication

meddyginiaethol adj medicinal, remedial

meddyginiaethu vb to cure, to remedy, to heal

meddygol adj medicinal; medical

meddylfryd nm mind, affection, bent

meddylgar adj thoughtful

meddylgarwch nm thoughtfulness

meddyliol adj mental, intellectual

meddyliwr (-wyr) nm thinker

mefus npl (nf-en) strawberries

megin (-au) nf bellows

megino vb to work bellows, to blow

megis *conj, prep* as, so as, like a
Mehefin *nm* June
meicrobioleg *nm* microbiology
meicro-brosesydd *nm* microprocessor
meicroffon (-au) *nm* microphone
meicrosglodyn (-ion) *nm* microchip
meicrosgop (-au) *nm* microscope
meichiad (-iaid) *nm* swineherd
meichiau (-iafon) *nm* surety, bail
meidrol *adj* finite
meidroldeb *nm* finiteness
meiddio *vb* to dare, to venture
meiddion *npl* curds and whey
meiddlyd *adj* wheyey, curdled
meigryn *nm* migraine
meilart *nm* drake
meillion *npl (nf-en)* clover
meim (-iau) *nmf* mime
meimio *vb* to mime
meinder *nm* fineness, slenderness
meindio *vb* to mind, to care
meindwr *nm* spire
meinedd *nm* slender part, small
meingefn *nm* small of the back
meinhau *vb* to grow slender, to taper
meini *see* **maen**
meinllais *nm* shrill voice, treble
meintoli *vb* to quantify
meintoliad *nm* quantification
meinwe (-oedd) *nf* tissue
meipen (maip) *nf* turnip
meirch *see* **march**
meirioli *vb* to thaw
meirw *see* **marw**
meistr (-iaid, -i, -adoedd) *nm* master
meistres (-i) *nf* mistress

meistrolaeth *nf* mastery
meistrolgar *adj* masterful, masterly
meistroli *vb* to master
meitin *nm*: **ers meitin** some time since
meitr (-au) *nm* mitre
meithder *nm* length
meithrin *vb* to nurture, to rear, to foster
meithrinfa (-oedd) *nf* nursery
mêl *nm* honey
mela *vb* to gather honey
melan *nf* melancholy
melen *adj f of* **melyn**
melfaréd *nm* corduroy
melfed *nm* velvet
melin (-au) *nf* mill
melinydd (-ion) *nm* miller
melodaidd *adj* melodious
melodi *nm* melody
melyn (f melen) *adj* yellow ▸ *nm* yellow; **melyn wy** yolk of egg; **y clefyd melyn** jaundice
melynaidd *adj* yellowish, tawny
melynder, melyndra *nm* yellowness
melynddu *adj* tawny, swarthy
melyngoch *adj* yellowish red, orange
melyni *nm* yellowness; jaundice
melynu *vb* to yellow
melynwy *nm* yolk
melynwyn *adj* yellowish white, cream
melys *adj* sweet ▸ *npl* **(-ion)** sweets
melysfwyd *nm* dessert
melyster, melystra *nm* sweetness
melysu *vb* to sweeten

m

mellt *npl (nf-***en**) lightning
melltennu *vb* to flash lightning
melltigaid, melltigedig *adj*
accursed, cursed
melltith (-ion) *nf* curse
melltithio *vb* to curse
memorandwm (-anda) *nm*
memorandum
memrwn (-rynau) *nm* parchment,
vellum
men (-ni) *nf* wain, waggon, cart
mên *adj* mean
mendio *vb* to mend, to heal, to
recover
menestr *nm* cup-bearer
menig *see* maneg
mentr *nf* venture, hazard
mentro *vb* to venture, to hazard
mentrus *adj* adventurous
mentrwr (-wyr) *nm* entrepreneur
menyw (-od) *nf* woman
mêr (merion) *nm* marrow
mercwri *nm* mercury
merch (-ed) *nf* daughter, woman
Mercher *nm* Mercury; **dydd**
Mercher Wednesday
mercheta *vb* to womanise
merchetaidd *adj* effeminate
merch-yng-nghyfraith *nf*
daughter-in-law
merddwr (-ddyfroedd) *nm*
stagnant water
merf, merfaidd *adj* insipid,
tasteless, flat
merfdra, merfeidd-dra *nm*
insipidity
merlen *nf* pony
merlota *vb* to pony-trek
merlyn (-nod, merlod) (*f* merlen)
nm pony

merllyd *adj* insipid
merllys *nm* asparagus
merthyr (-on, -i) *nm* martyr
merthyrdod *nm* martyrdom
merthyru *vb* to martyr
merwindod *nm* numbness,
tingling
merwino *vb* to benumb, to tingle,
to smart
meryw *npl (nf-***en**) juniper trees
mes *npl (nf-***en**) acorns
mesa *vb* to gather acorns
mesur¹ (-au) *nm* measure; metre;
tune; bill
mesur², mesuro *vb* to measure,
to mete
mesureg *nf* mensuration
mesuriad (-au) *nm* measurement
mesurwr (-wyr) *nm* measurer;
surveyor
mesurydd (-ion) *nm* measurer,
meter
metamorffedd *nm*
metamorphism
metel (-oedd) *nm* metal; mettle
metelaidd *adj* metallic
metelydd (-ion) *nm* metallurgist
metelyddiaeth *nf* metallurgy
metr (-au) *nm* metre
metrig *adj* metric
metrigeiddio *vb* to metricate
meth (-ion) *nm* miss, failure
methdaliad (-au) *nm* bankruptcy
methdalwr (-wyr) *nm* bankrupt
methedig (-ion) *adj* decrepit,
infirm, disabled
methiannus *adj* failing, decayed
methiant *nm* failure
methodoleg *nf* methodology
methu *vb* to fail, to miss

meudwy (-aid, -od) nm hermit, recluse

meudwyaidd adj hermit-like, retiring

meudwyol adj eremitic

mewian vb to mew

mewn prep in, within

mewnanadlu vb to inhale

mewnblyg adj introvert

mewnbwn nm input

mewnforio vb to import ▸ npl (-ion) imports

mewnfudwr (-wyr) nm immigrant

mewngofnodi vb to log in, to log on

mewnol adj inward, internal; subjective

mewnosod vb to insert

mewnrwyd (-i, -au) nf intranet

mewnwr (-wyr) nm scrum-half

mewnyn (mewnion) nm filling

mi pron I, me

mieri npl (nf miaren) brambles

mig nf: **chwarae mig** to play bo-beep

mign, mignen nf bog, quagmire

migwrn (-yrnau) nm knuckle; ankle

mil¹ (-od) nm animal

mil² (-oedd) nf thousand

milain adj angry, fierce, savage, cruel

mileindra nm savageness, ferocity

mileinig adj savage, ferocious, malignant

milfed adj thousandth

milfeddyg (-on) nm veterinary surgeon

milfil nf million, an indefinite number

milflwyddiant nm millennium

milgi (-gwn) nm greyhound

miliast (-ieist) nf greyhound bitch

milimedr nm millimetre

militariaeth nf militarism

militarydd nm militarist

miliwn (-iynau) nf million

miliynydd (-ion) nm millionaire

milodfa (-oedd, -feydd) nf menagerie

milwr (-wyr) nm soldier

milwraidd adj soldierly

milwriad (-iaid) nm colonel

milwriaeth nf warfare

milwriaethus adj militant

milwrio vb to militate

milwrol adj military

milltir (-oedd) nf mile

min (-ion) nm edge; brink; lip

mindlws adj simpering, affected, precious

mingamu vb to grimace

minibws (-bysiau, -bysys) nm minibus

minio vb to edge, to sharpen; to make impression

miniog adj sharp, keen, cutting

minlliw (-iau) nm lipstick

minnau pron I (on my part), I also

mintai (-eioedd) nf band, troop

mintys nm mint

mirain adj fair, beautiful, comely

mireinder nm beauty, comeliness

miri nm merriment, fun, festivity

mis (-oedd) nm month

misglwyf nm period

misio vb to miss, to fail

misol (-ion) adj monthly

misolyn (-olion) nm monthly (magazine)

m

mitsio *vb* to mitch, to play truant

miwsig *nm* music

mo *contr. of* **dim o**; **nid oes mo'i debyg** there is none like him

moch *npl* (*nm* **-yn**) swine, pigs, hogs

mocha *vb* to pig, to litter

mochaidd *adj* swinish, hoggish

mochynnaidd *adj* piggish, swinish

modfedd (**-i**) *nf* inch

modiwl (**-au**) *nm* module

modrwy (**-au**) *nf* ring

modrwyo *vb* to ring

modrwyog *adj* ringed

modryb (**-edd**) *nf* aunt

modur (**-on**) *nm* motor

modurdy (**-dai**) *nm* garage

modurwr (**-wyr**) *nm* motorist

modylu *vb* to modulate

modylydd (**-ion**) *nm* modulator

modd (**-ion, -au**) *nm* mode, manner; means; mood

moddion *npl* means; medicine

moddol *adj* modal

moel¹ (**-ion**) *adj* bare, bald; hornless, polled

moel² (**-ydd**) *nf* hill

moeli *vb* to make or become bald; to hang (*ears*)

moelni *nm* bareness, baldness

moelyn *nm* bald-head

moes¹ *vb imper* give, bring hither

moes² (**-au**) *nf* morality; (*pl*) manners, morals

moeseg *nf* ethics

moesegol *adj* ethical

Moesenaidd *adj* Mosaic

moesgar *adj* mannerly, polite

moesgarwch *nm* politeness

moesol *adj* moral, ethical

moesoldeb *nm* morality

moesoli *vb* to moralize

moesolwr (**-wyr**) *nm* moralist

moeswers (**-i**) *nf* moral

moesymgrymu *vb* to bow

moeth (**-au**) *nm* luxury, indulgence

moethi *vb* to pamper, to indulge

moethlyd *adj* pampered, spoilt

moethus *adj* luxurious, pampered

moethusrwydd *nm* luxuriousness, luxury

molawd *nm* eulogy

molecwl (**-cylau**) *nm* molecule

molecwlar *adj* molecular

moled (**-au**) *nf* kerchief; muffler

moli, moliannu *vb* to praise, to laud

moliannus *adj* praised, praiseworthy

moliant (**-iannau**) *nm* praise

mollt (**myllt**) *nm* wether

molltgig *nm* mutton

moment (**-au**) *nf* moment

momentwm (**momenta**) *nm* momentum

monarchiaeth *nf* monarchy

monarchydd (**-ion**) *nm* monarchist

monni *vb* to sulk, to pout

monocsid (**-au**) *nm* monoxide

monopoli (**-ïau**) *nm* monopoly

mor *adv* how, so, as

môr (**moroedd**) *nm* sea, ocean; **Môr Adria** the Adriatic; **y Môr Canoldir, Môr y Canoldir** the Mediterranean; **Môr Hafren** the Bristol Channel; **Môr y Gogledd** the North Sea; **Môr Iwerddon** the Irish Sea; **y Môr Coch** the Red Sea; **y Môr Iwerydd** the Atlantic; **y Môr**

Tawel the Pacific; **y Môr Udd** the English Channel
moratoriwm (-atoria) *nm* moratorium
mordaith (-deithiau) *nf* voyage
mordeithiwr (-wyr) *nm* voyager
mordwyaeth *nf* navigation
mordwyo *vb* to go by sea, to voyage, to sail
mordwyol *adj* nautical
mordwywr (-wyr) *nm* mariner, sailor
morddwyd (-ydd) *nfm* thigh
morfa (-feydd) *nm* moor, fen, marsh
morfil (-od) *nm* whale
môr-filwr *nm* marine
môr-forwyn (-forynion) *nf* mermaid
morfran (-frain) *nf* cormorant
morffoleg *nf* morphology
morffolegol *adj* morphological
morgainc (-geinciau) *nf* gulf
morgais (-geisiau) *nm* mortgage
morgeisî *nm* mortgagee
morgeisio *vb* to mortgage
môr-gerwyn *nf* whirlpool, vortex, abyss
morgi *nm* shark
morglawdd (-gloddiau) *nm* embankment, mole
morgrug *npl* (*nm* **-yn**) ants
morio *vb* to voyage, to sail
môr-ladrad (-au) *nm* piracy
môr-leidr (-ladron) *nm* pirate
morlen (-ni) *nm* chart
morlo (-loi) *nm* sea-calf, seal
morllyn (-noedd) *nmf* lagoon
Moroco *nf* Morocco
morol *adj* maritime

moron *npl* (*nf* **-en**) carrots
mortais (-eisiau) *nf* mortise
morteisio *vb* to mortise
morter (-au) *nm* mortar
morthwyl (-ion) *nm* hammer
morthwylio *vb* to hammer
morthwyliwr (-wyr) *nm* hammerer
morwr (-wyr) *nm* seaman, sailor, mariner
morwriaeth *nf* seamanship, navigation
morwydd *npl* (*nf* **-en**) mulberry-trees
morwyn (-ynion) *nf* maid, virgin; **y Forwyn** Virgo
morwyndod *nm* virginity
morwynol *adj* virgin, maiden
moryd (-iau) *nf* estuary
moryn (-nau) *nm* billow, breaker
mosaig (-au) *nm, adj* mosaic
Moscow *nf* Moscow
Moslem *nmf* Muslim
Moslemaidd *adj* Muslim
motif (-au) *nm* motive
motiff (-au) *nm* motif
MP3 *n* MP3; **peiriant MP3** MP3 player
muchudd *nm* jet
mud *adj* unable to speak; dull
mudan (-od) *nm* man who is unable to speak
mudandod *nm* speech disorder
mudanes (-au) *nf* woman who is unable to speak
mudferwi *vb* to simmer
mudiad (-au) *nm* removal; movement
mudo *vb* to move, to remove

169

mudol *adj* mobile, moving, migratory
mudwr (-wyr) *nm* remover
mul (-od) *nm* mule; donkey
mulaidd *adj* mulish, asinine
mules (-au) *nf* she-mule, she-ass
mulfran (-frain) *nf* cormorant
mun *see* bun
munud¹ (-au) *nfm* minute, moment
munud² (-iau) *nm* sign, gesture; nod
munudio *vb* to make gestures, to gesticulate
mur (-iau) *nm* wall
murddun (-od) *nm* ruin, ruins
murio *vb* to wall
murlun (-iau) *nm* mural
murmur *vb* to murmur ▸ *nm* (-on) murmur
mursen (-nod) *nf* coquette; prude
mursendod *nm* prudery, affectation
mursennaidd *adj* prudish, affected
mursennu *vb* to coquette, to mince
musgrell *adj* feeble, decrepit
musgrellni *nm* feebleness, debility
mwclis *npl* necklace
mwd *nm* mud
mwdlyd *adj* muddy
mwdwl (mydylau) *nm* cock (of hay)
mwg *nm* smoke
mwgwd (mygydau) *nm* blind mask
mwng (myngau) *nm* mane
mwngial *vb* to mumble
mwlsyn *nm* nincompoop; mule
mwlwg *nm* refuse, sweepings, chaff
mwll *adj* close, warm, sultry
mwmian *vb* to hum, to mumble

mŵn *see* mwyn
mwnci (-ïod) *nm* monkey
mwncïaidd *adj* monkeyish, apish
mwnglawdd *see* mwynglawdd
mwnwgl (mynyglau) *nm* neck
mwnws *coll n* small particles, dust, debris
mwrdro *vb* to murder
mwrllwch *nm* fog, mist, vapour
mwrn *adj* sultry, close, warm
mwrndra *nm* sultriness
mwrthwl (myrthylau) *nm* hammer
mws *adj* stale, rank, stinking
mwsg *nm* musk
mwsged (-i) *nmf* musket
Mwslim *nm* = Moslem
Mwslimaidd *adj* = Moslemaidd
mwsogl, mwswgl *nm* moss
mwstard, mwstart *nm* mustard
mwstro *vb* to fidget, to hurry
mwstwr *nm* muster; bustle, commotion
mwy *adj* more, bigger ▸ *adv* more, again
mwyach *adv* any more, henceforth
mwyafrif (-au) *nm* majority
mwyalch, mwyalchen (mwyalchod) *nf* blackbird
mwyar *npl* (*nf* -en) blackberries
mwyara *vb* to gather blackberries
mwydion *npl* crumb; pith, pulp
mwydo *vb* to moisten, to soak, to steep
mwydro *vb* to moider, to bewilder
mwydyn (mwydod) *nm* worm
mwyfwy *adv* more and more
mwynglawdd (-gloddiau) *nm* mine

mwyhau *vb* to increase, to enlarge, to magnify

mwyn[1] *nm* sake

mwyn[2], **mŵn** (**-au**) *nm* ore, mineral

mwyn[3] *adj* kind, gentle, mild; dear

mwynder (**-au**) *nm* gentleness; (*pl*) delights

mwyndoddi *vb* to refine

mwyneidd-dra *nm* kindness, gentleness

mwyngloddio *vb* to mine

mwynhad *nm* enjoyment, pleasure

mwynhau *vb* to enjoy

mwyniant (**-iannau**) *nm* pleasure

mwynofydd (**-ion**) *nm* mineralogist

mwynol *adj* mineral

mwynoleg *nf* mineralogy

mwynwr (**-wyr**) *nm* miner

mwys *adj* ambiguous, equivocal

mwythau *npl* indulgence, caresses

mwytho *vb* to pet, to fondle, to pamper

mwythus *adj* pampered

myctod *nm* asphyxia

mydr (**-au**) *nm* metre, verse

mydryddiaeth *nf* versification

mydryddol *adj* metrical

mydryddu, mydru *vb* to versify

mydylu *vb* to cock

myfi *pron* I, me, myself

myfiaeth *nf* egotism

myfiol *adj* egotistic

myfyrdod (**-au**) *nm* meditation

myfyrgar *adj* studious, contemplative

myfyrgell (**-oedd**) *nf* study

myfyrio *vb* to meditate, to study

myfyriol *adj* meditative

myfyriwr (**-wyr**) *nm* student; **myfyriwr hŷn** mature student

mygedol *adj* honorary

mygfa (**-feydd**) *nf* suffocation

myglyd *adj* smoky; close; asthmatic

myglys *nm* tobacco

mygu *vb* to smoke; to suffocate, to stifle, to smother

mygydu *vb* to blindfold

mygyn *nm* a smoke

myngial *vb* to mumble, to mutter

myngog *adj* maned

myngus *adj* indistinct, mumbling

myllni *nm* sultriness

mympwy (**-on**) *nm* whim, caprice, fad

mympwyol *adj* arbitrary, capricious

mymryn (**-nau**) *nm* particle, bit, mite

myn[1] *prep* by (*in swearing*)

myn[2] (**-nod**) *nm* kid

mynach (**-od, mynaich**) *nm* monk

mynachaeth *nf* monasticism

mynachdy (**-dai**) *nm* monastery, convent

mynachlog (**-ydd**) *nf* monastery, abbey

mynawyd (**-au**) *nm* awl

mynci (**-ïau**) *nm* hame(s)

myned, mynd *vb* to go, to proceed

mynedfa (**-oedd, -feydd**) *nf* entrance, passage

mynediad *nm* going; access, admission

mynegai (**-eion**) *nm* index, exponent

mynegair (**-eiriau**) *nm* concordance

mynegbost *nm* signpost
mynegfys (-edd) *nm* forefinger, index
mynegi *vb* to tell, to express, to relate, to declare
mynegiad (-au) *nm* statement, declaration
mynegiant *nm* expression
mynegol *adj* indicative
mynnu *vb* to will, to wish; to insist; to get, to obtain
mynor (-ion) *nm* marble
mynwent (-au, -ydd) *nf* churchyard, graveyard
mynwes (-au) *nf* breast, bosom
mynwesol *adj* bosom
mynwesu *vb* to cherish
mynych *adj* frequent, often
mynychder *nm* frequency
mynychiad *nm* frequenting; repetition
mynychu *vb* to frequent, to attend; to repeat
mynydd (-oedd) *nm* mountain
mynydda *n* mountaineering ▸ *vb* to go mountaineering
mynydd-dir *nm* hill-country
mynyddig *adj* mountainous, hilly
mynyddwr (-wyr) *nm* mountaineer
myrdd, myrddiwn (myrddiynau) *nm* myriad
myrndra *nm* sultriness
myrr *nm* myrrh
myrtwydd *npl (nf* **-en)** myrtles
mysg *nm* middle, midst; **ymysg** among
mysgu *vb* to loose, to undo
myswynog (-ydd) *nf* barren cow
mysyglog *adj* mossy

mytholeg *nf* mythology
mytholegol *adj* mythological

n

na *conj* nor, neither; than ▸ *adv* no, not

nac *adv* no, not ▸ *conj* nor, neither

nacâd *nm* refusal, denial

nacaol *adj* negative

nacáu *vb* to refuse, to deny

nad *adv* not

nâd (nadau) *nf* cry, howl; clamour

Nadolig *nm* Christmas

Nadoligaidd *adj* Christmassy

nadu¹ *vb* to cry (out), to howl

nadu² *vb* to stop, to hinder

nadd *adj* hewn, wrought

naddion *npl* chips; shreds; lint

naddo *adv* no *(to questions in preterite tense)*

naddu *vb* to hew, to chip, to whittle

Naf *nm* Lord

nag *conj* than

nage *adv* not so, no

nai (neiaint) *nm* nephew

naid (neidiau) *nf* jump, leap, bound

naïf *adj* naïve

naïfder *nm* naïveté

naill *dem pron* the one ▸ *conj* either

nain (neiniau) *nf* grandmother

nam (-au) *nm* mark, blemish, flaw

namyn *pron* except, but, save

nant (nentydd) *nf* brook; gorge, ravine

napcyn (-au) *nm* napkin

narcotig *nm, adj* narcotic

natur *nf* nature; temper

naturiaeth (-au) *nf* nature

naturiaethwr (-wyr) *nm* naturalist

naturiol *adj* natural

naturioldeb *nm* naturalness

naturus *adj* angry, quick-tempered

naw *adj, nm* nine

nawdd *nm* protection; patronage

nawddogaeth *nf* patronage, protection

nawfed *adj* ninth

nawn *nm* noon

naws *nf* nature, disposition; essence, tincture

nawseiddio *vb* to temper, to soften

neb *nm* any one *(with negative understood)*; no one

nedd *npl (nf-en)* nits

neddau, neddyf (neddyfau) *nf* adze

nef (-oedd) *nf* heaven

nefi-blw *n, adj* navy blue

nefol, nefolaidd *adj* heavenly, celestial

nefoli *vb* to make *or* become heavenly

nefrosis *nm* neurosis

neges (-au, -euau) *nf* errand, message; **neges destun** text message; **neges lais** voicemail

negesa, negeseua vb to run errands; to trade

negeseuwr (-wyr) nm messenger

negodi vb to negotiate

negyddiaeth nf negativism

negyddol adj negative

neidio vb to leap, to jump; to throb

neidiwr (-wyr) nm leaper, jumper

neidr (nadroedd, nadredd) nf snake

neiedd nm nepotism

neillog (-ion) nm alternative

neilltu nm one side; **o'r neilltu** aside, apart

neilltuad nm separation

neilltuaeth nf separation, privacy, seclusion

neilltuedig adj separated, secluded

neilltuo vb to set apart, to separate

neilltuol adj particular, peculiar, special

neilltuolion npl peculiarities

neilltuolrwydd nm peculiarity, distinction

neis adj nice

neisied (-i) nf kerchief

neithdar nm nectar

neithior (-au) nf marriage feast

neithiwr adv last night

nemor adj few; **nid nemor** hardly any

nen (-nau, -noedd) nf ceiling; heaven; **nen tŷ** house-top

nenbren nm roof-tree

nendwr nm skyscraper

nenfwd (-fydau) nm ceiling

nenlofft nf attic

nepell adv far; **nid nepell** not far

nerf (-au) nf nerve

nerfus adj nervous

nerfwst nm neurasthenia

nerth (-oedd) nm might, power, strength

nerthol adj strong, powerful, mighty

nerthu vb to strengthen

nes¹ adj nearer; **yn nes ymlaen** further on

nes² adv till, until

nesaf adj nearest, next

nesáu vb to draw near, to approach

nesnes adv nearer and nearer

nesu vb to draw near; **nesu draw** move away

neu conj or

neuadd (-au) nf hall

newid vb to change, to alter ▶ nm change; **newid hinsawdd** climate change

newidiant nm variability

newidiol adj changeable, variable

newidydd (-ion) nm transformer

newidyn (-nau) nm variable

newydd adj new, novel; fresh ▶ nm (-ion) news

newyddbeth (-au) nm novelty

newydd-deb, newydd-der nm newness, novelty

newyddiadur (-on) nm newspaper

newyddiaduraeth nf journalism

newyddiaduriaeth nf journalism

newyddiadurwr (-wyr) nm journalist

newyddian (-od) coll n novice, neophyte

newyn nm hunger, famine

newynog adj hungry, starving

newynu vb to starve, to famish

ni¹ pron we, us

ni², nid adv not

nifer (-oedd, -i) nmf number
nifwl nm mist, fog; nebula
Nigeria nf Nigeria
Nihon nf Japan
ninnau pron we (on our part), we also
nionyn (nionod) nm onion
nis adv not … it; **nis cafodd** he did not find it
nitrad (-au) nm nitrate
nith (-oedd) nf niece
nithio vb to sift, to winnow
nithiwr (-wyr) nm sifter, winnower
nithlen (-ni) nf winnowing-sheet
niwclear adj nuclear
niwed (-eidiau) nm harm, injury
niweidio vb to harm, to hurt, to injure, to damage
niweidiol adj harmful, injurious
niwl (-oedd) nm mist, fog, haze
niwlen nf mist, fog, haze
niwliog, niwlog adj misty, foggy, hazy
niwmatig adj pneumatic
niwmonia nm pneumonia
niwtral adj neutral
niwtraleiddio vb to neutralise
niwtraliaeth nf neutrality
nobyn (nobiau) nm knob
nod (-au) nmf note; mark, token
nodachfa (-feydd) nf bazaar
nodedig adj appointed, set; remarkable
nodi vb to mark, to note, to appoint, to state
nodiad (-au) nm note
nodiadur (-on) nm notebook
nodiant nm notation
nodlyfr (-au) nm notebook

nodwedd (-ion) nf character, characteristic, feature
nodweddiadol adj characteristic
nodweddu vb to characterize
nodwydd (-au) nf needle
nodwyddiad nm acupuncture
nodyn (-nau, nodau, nodion) nm note
nodd (-ion) nm moisture; juice, sap
nodded nm refuge, protection
noddfa (-fâu, -feydd) nf refuge
noddi vb to protect
noddlyd adj juicy, sappy
noddwr (-wyr) nm protector; patron
noe (-au) nf dish; kneading-trough
noeth adj naked, bare, exposed, raw
noethder nm bareness, nakedness
noethi vb to bare, to denude
noethlymun adj nude
noethlymunwr (-wyr) nm streaker
noethlymunwraig nf stripper
noethni nm nakedness, nudity
noethwr (-wyr) nm nudist
nofel (-au) nf novel
nofelwr (-wyr), nofelydd nm novelist
nofiadwy adj swimmable
nofiedydd (-ion) nm swimmer
nofio vb to swim; to float
nofiwr (-wyr) nm swimmer
nogio vb to jib
noglyd adj jibbing
nôl vb to fetch, to bring
Norwy nf Norway
nos (-au, nosweithiau) nf night; **Nos Galan** New Year's Eve
nosi vb to become night

noson, noswaith (nosweithiau) *nf* night, an evening; **noson stag** stag night

noswyl (-iau) *nf* eve of festival, vigil; **Noswyl Nadolig** Christmas Eve

noswylio *vb* to cease work at eve

nudden *nf* fog, mist, haze

nwy (-on) *nm* gas; **nwy tŷ gwydr** greenhouse gas

nwyd (-au) *nm* passion; emotion

nwydwyllt *adj* passionate

nwydd (-au) *nm* substance, article; (*pl*) goods

nwyf *nm* vivacity, energy, vigour

nwyfiant *nm* vivacity, vigour

nwyfus *adj* sprightly, spirited, lively

nwyol *adj* gaseous

nychdod *nm* feebleness, infirmity

nychlyd *adj* sickly, feeble

nychu *vb* to sicken, to pine, to languish

nydd-dro (-droeau, -droeon) *nm* twist

nydd-droi *vb* to twist, to screw

nyddu *vb* to spin, to twist

nyddwr (-wyr) *nm* spinner

nyf *nm* snow

nyni *pron* we, us

nyrs (-ys) *nfm* nurse

nyrsio *adj* nurse

nytmeg *nm* nutmeg

nyth (-od) *nmf* nest

nythu *vb* to nest, to nestle

o¹ *prep* from; of, out of; by

o² *excl* oh!, O!

oblegid *conj, prep* because, for

obry *adv* beneath, below

obstetreg *nm* obstetrics

obstetregydd (-wyr) *nm* obstetrician

ocsid (-iau) *nm* oxide

ocsidiad *nm* oxidisation

ocsidio *vb* to oxidise

ocsidydd (-ion) *nm* oxidising agent

ocsigen *nm* oxygen

ocsiwn *nm* auction

och *excl* oh, alas, woe

ochain *vb* to moan

ochenaid (-eidiau) *nf* sigh

ocheneidio, ochneidio *vb* to sigh

ochr (-au) *nf* side

ochrgamu *vb* to sidestep

ochri *vb* to side

od *adj* odd, remarkable

ôd *nm* snow

odiaeth *adj* excellent, exquisite
▸ *adv* very, most, extremely
odid *adv* perchance, peradventure
odl (-au) *nf* rhyme; ode, song
odli *vb* to rhyme
odrif (-au) *nm* odd number
odrwydd *nm* oddity
odyn (-au) *nf* kiln
oddeutu *prep* about
oddi *prep* out of, from
oddieithr, oddigerth *prep* except, unless
oed (-au) *nm* age; time
oed-dâl (-iadau) *nm* superannuation
oedfa (-on, -feuon) *nf* meeting, service
oedi *vb* to delay; to postpone, to defer
oediad (-au) *nm* delay
oedolyn (-ion) *nm* grown-up
oedran *nm* age, full age
oedrannus *adj* aged
oedd *vb* was, were
oel *nm* oil
oen (ŵyn) *nm* lamb
oena *vb* to lamb, to yean
oenig *nf* ewe-lamb
oer *adj* cold, chill, frigid; sad
oeraidd *adj* cool, chilly
oerddrws (-ddrysau) *nm* wind gap
oerfel *nm* cold
oergell (-oedd) *nf* refrigerator
oeri *vb* to cool, to chill
oerllyd *adj* chilly, frigid; cool
oernad (-au) *nf* howl, wail, lamentation
oernadu *vb* to howl, to wail, to lament
oerni *nm* cold, coldness, chillness

oes¹ (-oedd, -au) *nf* age, lifetime; **yn oes oesoedd** for ever and ever
oes² *vb* there is, there are; is there?
oesoffagws *nm* oesophagus
oesol *adj* age-long, perpetual
ofer *adj* vain, idle; prodigal, dissipated; waste
ofera *vb* to waste, to squander, to idle
oferedd *nm* vanity, dissipation
ofergoel (-ion) *nf* superstition
ofergoeledd, ofergoeliaeth *nm* superstition
ofergoelus *adj* superstitious
oferwr (-wyr) *nm* idler, waster
ofn (-au) *nm* fear, dread
ofnadwy *adj* awful, terrible, dreadful
ofnadwyaeth *nf* awe, terror, dread
ofni *vb* to fear, to dread
ofnog *adj* fearful, timorous
ofnus *adj* timid, nervous, frightened
ofnusrwydd *nm* timidity, nervousness
ofwl (-au) *nm* ovule
ofydd (-ion) *nm* ovate
offeiriad (-iaid) *nm* priest, clergyman
offeiriadaeth *nf* priesthood
offeiriades (-au) *nf* priestess
offeiriadol *adj* priestly, sacerdotal
offeiriadu *vb* to officiate, to minister
offer *npl* implements, tools, gear
offeren (-nau) *nf* mass
offeryn (-nau, offer) *nm* instrument, tool; **offeryn cerdd** musical instrument
offerynnol *adj* instrumental

offerynoliaeth *nf* instrumentality

offrwm (-ymau) *nm* offering, oblation

offrymu *vb* to offer, to sacrifice

offrymwr (-wyr) *nm* offerer, sacrificer

offthalmia *nm* ophthalmia

offthalmosgop (-au) *nm* ophthalmoscope

og (-au), oged (-au, -i) *nf* harrow

ogof (-au, -fâu, -feydd) *nf* cave, cavern; den

ogylch *prep* about

ongl (-au) *nf* angle, corner

onglog *adj* angled, angular

oherwydd *conj, prep* because, for, owing to

ôl *adj* back, hind, hindmost ▸ *nm* (**olion**) mark, print, trace, track; **yn ôl** ago; according to

ôl-dâl (-oedd) *nm* back-pay

ôl-ddodiad (-iaid) *nm* suffix

ôl-ddyddio *vb* to post-date

ôl-ddyled (-ion) *nf* arrears

olew (-au) *nm* oil

olewydd *npl* (*nf* **-en**) olive-trees

olifaid *npl* olive-berries

olrhain *vb* to trace

ôl-troed (olion traed) *nm* footprint; **ôl-troed carbon** carbon footprint

olwr (-wyr) *nm* back (*in rugby*)

olwyn (-ion) *nf* wheel

olwyno *vb* to wheel, to cycle

olwynog *adj* wheeled

Olympaidd *adj* Olympic

olyniaeth *nf* succession, sequence

olynol *adj* successive, consecutive

olynu *vb* to succeed (to)

olynwr (-wyr), olynydd (-ion) *nm* successor

ôl-ysgrif (-au) *nf* postscript

oll *adv* all, wholly; ever, at all

ombwdsman (-myn) *nm* ombudsman

omlet (-i) *nm* omelette

ond *conj* but, only ▸ *prep* except, save, but

onest *adj* honest

onestrwydd *nm* honesty

oni, onid *adv* not?, is it not? ▸ *conj* if not, unless ▸ *prep* except, save, but

onid e *adv* otherwise, else; is it not?

onis *conj* if it is not; **onis caiff** if he does not get it

onnen (onn, ynn) *nf* ash

opiniwn (-ynau) *nm* opinion

opiniynllyd, opiniynus *adj* opinionated

optimistaeth *nf* optimism

optimistaidd *adj* optimistic

optimwm (-tima) *nm* optimum

oracl (-au) *nm* oracle

oraclaidd *adj* oracular

oraens *nm* orange

ordeiniad (-au) *nm* ordination, ordinance

ordeinio *vb* to ordain

ordinhad (-au) *nf* ordinance, sacrament

oren (-nau) *nfm* orange

organ (-au) *nfm* organ

organaidd *adj* organic

organeb (-au) *nf* organism

organig *adj* organic

organydd (-ion) *nm* organist

orgraff (-au) *nf* orthography

orgraffyddol *adj* orthographical

oriawr (oriorau) *nf* watch
oriel (-au) *nf* gallery
orig *nf* little while
oriog *adj* fickle, changeable, inconstant
os *conj* if
osgo *nm* slant, slope, inclination
osgoi *vb* to swerve, to avoid, to evade, to shirk
oslef *nmf* tone, voice
osôn *nm* ozone
ow *excl* oh!, alas!

pa *adj* what, which
pab (-au) *nm* pope
pabell (pebyll) *nf* tent, tabernacle
pabellu *vb* to tent, to tabernacle, to encamp
pabi *nm* poppy
pabwyr¹ *npl* (*nf* **-en**, *nm* **-yn**) rushes
pabwyr² *nm* wick, candle-wick
pac (-iau) *nm* pack, bundle
pacio *vb* to pack
Pacistan *nf* Pakistan
padell (-au, -i, pedyll) *nf* pan, bowl
padellaid (-eidiau) *nf* panful
pader (-au) *nm* paternoster, Lord's Prayer
pae *nm* pay, wage
paediatreg *nm* paediatrics
paediatregydd *nm* paediatrician
paent *nm* paint
paentiad (-au) *nm* painting
pafiliwn *nm* pavilion
paffio *vb* to box, to fight
paffiwr (-wyr) *nm* boxer

pagan (**-iaid**) *nm* pagan, heathen
paganaidd *adj* pagan, heathen
paganiaeth *nf* paganism, heathenism
paham *adv* why, wherefore
paill *nm* flour; pollen
pair (**peiriau**) *nm* cauldron, furnace
pais (**peisiau**) *nf* coat, petticoat
paith (**peithiau**) *nm* prairie
pâl (**palau**) *nf* spade
paladr (**pelydr**) *nm* ray, beam; staff; stem
palaeolithig *adj* palaeolithic
palas (**-au**) *nm* palace
Palestina *nf* Palestine
palf (**-au**) *nf* palm, hand; paw
palfais (**-eisiau**) *nf* shoulder
palfalu *vb* to feel, to grope
palfod (**-au**) *nf* smack, slap, buffet
palff *nm* fine, well-built man
pali *nm* silk brocade
palis (**-au**) *nm* pale, partition, wainscot
palmant (**-mentydd**) *nm* pavement
palmantu *vb* to pave
palmwydd *npl* (*nf* **-en**) palm-trees
palu *vb* to dig, to delve
palwr (**-wyr**) *nm* digger
pall¹ (**-au**) *nm* mantle; tent
pall² *nm* fail, failing; lack; lapse
pallu *vb* to fail, to cease; to neglect; to refuse
pam *adv* why, wherefore
pamffled, pamffledyn (**pamffledi, pamffledau**) *nm* pamphlet
pan *conj* when
pannas *npl* (*nf* **panasen**) parsnips
pannwl (**panylau**) *nm* dimple, hollow
pant (**-iau**) *nm* hollow, valley

pantio *vb* to depress, to dent, to sink
pantiog *adj* hollow, sunken; dimpled
papur (**-au**) *nm* paper
papuro *vb* to paper
papurwr (**-wyr**) *nm* paperer, paperhanger
papuryn *nm* scrap of paper
pâr¹ (**parau**) *nm* pair; suit
pâr² (**peri**) *nm* spear, lance
para *vb* to last, to endure, to continue
parabl (**-au**) *nm* speech, discourse
parablu *vb* to speak
paradeim (**-au**) *nm* paradigm
paradwys *nf* paradise
parafeddyg (**-on**) *nm* paramedic
paragraff (**-au**) *nm* paragraph
paratoad (**-au**) *nm* preparation
paratoawl *adj* preparatory
paratoi *vb* to prepare, to get ready
parc (**-iau**) *nm* park, field; **parc cenedlaethol** national park
parch *nm* respect, reverence
parchedig (**-ion**) *adj* reverend; reverent
parchedigaeth *nf* reverence
parchu *vb* to respect, to revere, to reverence
parchus *adj* respectful; respectable
parchusrwydd *nm* respectability
pardwn (**-ynau**) *nm* pardon
pardynu *vb* to pardon
parddu *nm* fire-black, smut; soot
pardduo *vb* to blacken, to vilify, to defame
pared (**parwydydd**) *nm* partition wall, wall
paredd *nm* parity

parhad *nm* continuance, continuation
parhaol *adj* lasting, perpetual
parhau *vb* to last, to continue; to persevere
parhaus *adj* lasting; continual, perpetual
Paris *nf* Paris
parlwr (-yrau) *nm* sitting room; parlour
parlys *nm* paralysis, palsy
parlysu *vb* to paralyse
parod *adj* ready, prepared; prompt
parodrwydd *nm* readiness, willingness
parôl (-ion) *nm* parole
parsel (-i, -ydd) *nm* parcel
parti (-ïon) *nm* party
partïaeth *nf* partisanship
partïol *adj* partial, biased, partisan
parth (-au) *nm* part, region; floor
parthed *prep* about, concerning
parthu *vb* to part, to divide
parwyden (-nau) *nf* wall, side; breast
pas *nm* whooping-cough
Pasg *nm* Passover, Easter
pasgedig (-ion) *adj* fatted, fattened, fat
pasiant (-iannau) *nm* pageant
pasio *vb* to pass
past *nm* paste
pastai (-eiod) *nf* pasty, pie
pastio *vb* to paste
pasturedig *adj* pasteurised
pasturo *vb* to pasteurise
pastwn (-ynau) *nm* baton, club, cudgel
pastynu *vb* to club, to cudgel, to bludgeon

patriarch (-iaid, patrieirch) *nm* patriarch
patriarchaeth (-au) *nf* patriarchate
patriarchaidd *adj* patriarchal
patrwm (-ymau) *nm* pattern
patrymlun (-iau) *nm* template
pathew (-od) *nm* dormouse
patholeg *nf* pathology
patholegol *adj* pathological
patholegydd (-egwyr) *nm* pathologist
pau *nf* country
paun (peunod) *nm* peacock
pawb *pron* everybody, all
pawen (-nau) *nf* paw
pawl (polion) *nm* pole, stake
pe *conj* if
pebyll *nf see* pabell
pecyn (-nau) *nm* packet, package
pechadur (-iaid) *nm* sinner, offender
pechadures (-au) *nf* woman sinner
pechadurus *adj* sinful, wicked
pechod (-au) *nm* sin, offence
pechu *vb* to sin, to offend
ped *conj* if
pedair *adj f of* pedwar
pedeirongl *adj* foursquare
pedi *vb* to worry, to grieve
pedoffeil (-s), pedoffilydd (-ion) *nm* paedophile
pedol (-au) *nf* horseshoe
pedoli *vb* to shoe
pedrain *nf* haunches, crupper
pedrongl *adj* square ▸ *nf* (-au) square
pedronglog *adj* quadrangular
pedryfwrdd (-fyrddau) *nm* quarter-deck

pedwar (*f* **pedair**) *adj* four
pedwarawd *nm* quartette
pedwarcarnol (**-ion**) *adj* four-footed, quadruped
pedwaredd *adj f of* **pedwerydd**
pedwarplyg *adj* fourfold, quarto
pedwerydd (*f* **pedwaredd**) *adj* fourth
peddestr *nm* pedestrian
peddestrig *nm* walking; pedestrian
pefr *adj* radiant, bright, beautiful
pefrio *vb* to radiate, to sparkle
peg (**-iau**) *nm* peg
pegio *vb* to peg
pegor (**-au**) *nm* manikin; imp
pegwn (**-ynau**) *nm* pivot, pole, axis
Pegwn y Gogledd *nm* North Pole
pegynol *adj* axial, polar
peidio *vb* to cease, to stop, to desist
peilon (**-au**) *nm* pylon
peilot (**-iaid**) *nm* pilot
peillio *vb* to bolt, to sift
peint (**-iau**) *nm* pint
peintiad (**-au**) *nm* painting
peintio *vb* to paint
peintiwr (**-wyr**) *nm* painter
peipen (**peipiau**) *nf* pipe
peirianneg *nm* engineering
peiriannol *adj* mechanical
peiriannydd (**-ianyddion**) *nm* engineer
peiriant (**-iannau**) *nm* machine, engine; **peiriant arian** ATM, cash machine; **peiriant chwilio** search engine; **peiriant golchi** washing machine; **peiriant MP3/DVD** MP3/DVD player
peirianwaith *nm* mechanism
peirianyddol *adj* mechanical

peiswyn *nm* chaff
peithyn (**-au**) *nm* ridge-tile
pêl (**pelau, peli**) *nf* ball
pelawd (**-au**) *nf* (cricket) over
pêl-droed *nf* football
peldroediwr *nm* footballer
pelen *nf* pill
pel-fâs *nf* baseball
pêl-fasged *nf* basketball
pelferyn (**-nau**) *nm* ball-bearing
pêl-foli *nf* volleyball
pêl-rwyd *nf* netball
pelten (**pelts**) *nf* blow
pelydr (**-au**) *nm* ray, beam
pelydru *vb* to beam, to gleam, to radiate
pelydryn *nm* ray, beam
pell *adj* far, distant, remote, long
pellen (**-nau, -ni**) *nf* ball (of yarn)
pellennig *adj* far, distant, remote
pellhau *vb* to put *or* remove far away
pellter (**-au, -oedd**) *nm* distance
pen¹ (**-nau**) *nm* head; chief; end; top
pen² *adj* head, chief, supreme
penadur (**-iaid**) *nm* sovereign
penaduriaeth *nf* sovereignty
penagored *adj* open, indefinite, undecided
penarglwyddiaeth *nf* sovereignty
penbaladr *adj* general, universal
penben *adv* at loggerheads
penbleth *nf* perplexity, quandary
pen-blwydd (**-i**) *nm* birthday
penboeth *adj* hot-headed, fanatical
penboethni *nm* fanaticism
penboethyn (**-boethiaid**) *nm* fanatic

penbwl (-byliaid) *nm* blockhead; tadpole
pencadlys *nm* head-quarters
pencampwr (-wyr) *nm* champion
pencampwriaeth (-au) *nf* championship
pencerdd (-ceirddiaid) *nm* chief musician
penchwiban *adj* giddy, flighty
pendant *adj* positive, emphatic
pendantrwydd *nm* positiveness
pendefig (-ion) *nm* prince, peer, noble
pendefigaeth *nf* aristocracy, peerage
pendefigaidd *adj* noble, aristocratic
pendefiges (-au) *nf* peeress
penderfyniad (-au) *nm* determination, resolution
penderfynol *adj* determined, resolute
penderfynu *vb* to determine, to resolve
pendew *adj* thick-headed, stupid
pendifaddau *adj*: **yn bendifaddau** especially
pendil (-iau) *nm* pendulum
pendramwnwgl *adj* topsy-turvy; headlong
pendraphen *adj* helter-skelter, confused
pendro *nf* giddiness, vertigo; staggers
pendroni *vb* to perplex oneself, to worry over
pendrwm *adj* top-heavy; drowsy
pendrymu *vb* to drowse, to droop
pendwmpian *vb* to nod, to doze, to slumber

penddaredd *nm* giddiness
penddaru *vb* to make *or* become giddy
penddelw *nm* bust
pendduyn (-nod) *nm* botch, boil
penelin (-oedd) *nmf* elbow
penelino *vb* to elbow
penflingo *vb* to scalp
penffest (-au) *nm* headgear
penffol *adj* silly, idiotic
penffrwyn (-au) *nfm* head-stall, halter
pengaled *adj* headstrong ► *nf* knapweed
pengaledwch *nm* stubbornness
pengam *adj* wrong-headed, perverse
pen-glin (-iau) *nf* knee
penglog (-au) *nf* skull
pengryf *adj* headstrong, stubborn
pengryniad (-iaid) *nm* roundhead
peniad (-au) *nm* header
penigamp *adj* excellent, splendid
penio *vb* to head
peniog *adj* brainy
penisel *adj* downcast, crestfallen
penlinio *vb* to kneel
penllanw *nm* tide
penllwyd *adj* grey-headed
penllwydni *nm* grey hair, white hair
penllywydd (-ion) *nm* sovereign
penllywyddiaeth *nf* sovereignty
pennaeth (penaethiaid) *nm* chief
pennaf *adj* chief, principal
pennawd (pennawdau) *nm* heading; headline
pennill (penillion) *nm* verse, stanza
pennod (penodau) *nf* chapter
pennoeth *adj* bare-headed

P

pennog (penwaig) nm herring
pennu vb to specify, to appoint, to determine
penodi vb to appoint
penodiad (-au) nm appointment
penodol adj particular, specific
penrhydd adj unbridled, loose
penrhyddid nm licence, licentiousness
penrhyn (-noedd, -nau) nm cape, foreland
pensaer (-seiri) nm architect
pensaernïaeth nf architecture
pensil (-iau) nm pencil
pensiwn (-iynau) nm pension
pensiynwr nm pensioner
pen-swyddog (-ion) nm chief officer
pensyfrdan adj stunned, dazed
pensyfrdandod nm giddiness, dizziness
pensyfrdanu vb to stun, to daze
pensyth adj perpendicular
pentan (-au) nm hob
penteulu (pennau teuluoedd) nm head of family
pentewyn (-ion) nm firebrand
pentir (-oedd) nm headland
pentis nm penthouse
pentref (-i, -ydd) nm village; homestead
pentrefan (-nau) nm hamlet
pentrefol adj village
pentrefwr (-wyr) nm villager
pentwr (-tyrrau) nm heap, pile
penty (-tai) nm cottage, shed
pentyrru vb to heap, to pile, to accumulate
penuchel adj proud, haughty
penwan adj weak-minded

penwyn adj white-headed
penwynni nm white hair, grey hair
penwythnos nm weekend
penyd (-iau) nm penance, punishment
penyd-wasanaeth nm penal servitude
penysgafn adj light-headed, giddy, dizzy
penysgafnder nm giddiness, dizziness
pêr adj sweet, delicious, luscious
peraidd adj sweet, mellow
perarogl (-au) nm perfume, fragrance
perarogli vb to perfume; to embalm
peraroglus adj fragrant, scented
percoladur (-on) nm percolator
perchen, perchennog (perchenogion) nm owner
perchenogaeth nf ownership
perchenogi vb to possess, to own
perchentywr (-wyr) nm householder
pereidd-dra nm sweetness
pereiddio vb to sweeten
pererin (-ion) nm pilgrim
pererindod (-au) nmf pilgrimage
pererinol adj pilgrim
perfedd (-ion) nm guts, bowels
perfeddwlad (-wledydd) nf interior, heartland
perffaith adj perfect
perffeithio vb to perfect
perffeithrwydd nm perfection
perffeithydd (-ion) nm perfecter
perfformiad (-au) nm performance
perfformio vb to perform
perfformiwr (-wyr) nm performer

peri vb to cause, to bid
perl (-au) nm pearl
perlewyg (-on) nm ecstasy, trance
perlysiau npl aromatic herbs;
spices
perllan (-nau) nf orchard
perocsid (-au) nm peroxide
peroriaeth nf melody, music
persawr (-au) nm fragrance;
persawr eillio aftershave (lotion)
persawrus adj aromatic
perseiniol adj melodious
persli nm parsley
person¹ (-au) nm person
person² (-iaid) nm parson,
clergyman
personadu vb to impersonate
personadwr (-wyr) nm
impersonator
persondy (-dai) nm parsonage
personol adj personal
personoli vb to personify
personoliad (-au) nm
personification
personoliaeth (-au) nf personality
perswâd nm persuasion
perswadio vb to persuade
pert adj quaint, pretty; pert
perth (-i) nf bush, hedge
perthnasedd (-au) nm relativity,
relevance
perthnasiad (-au) nm affiliation
perthnasol adj relevant
perthyn vb to belong, to pertain,
to be related
perthynas (-au) nf relation;
relationship
perthynol adj relative
perwyl nm purpose, effect
perygl (-on) nm danger, peril, risk

peryglu vb to endanger, to imperil
peryglus adj dangerous, perilous
pesgi vb to feed, to fatten
pesimist (-iaid) nm pessimist
pesimistaidd adj pessimistic
pesimistiaeth nf pessimism
pestl (-au) nm pestle
peswch nm cough
pesychiad (-au) nm cough
pesychu vb to cough
petris npl (nf -en) partridges
petrocemegolau (nm -yn) npl
petrochemicals
petrol (-au) nm petrol
petroleg nmf petrology
petrus adj hesitating; doubtful
petruso vb to hesitate, to doubt
petruster nm hesitation, doubt
petryal nm, adj square
peth (-au) nm thing; part, some
petheuach npl odds and ends,
trifles
peunes (-od) nf peahen
pianydd (-ion) nm pianist
piau vb owns, possesses
pib (-au) nf pipe, tube; diarrhœa
pibell (-au, -i) nf pipe, tube
pibgod nf bagpipe
pibgorn (-gyrn) nm recorder
(music)
pibo vb to pipe; to squirt
pibonwy (nf -en) npl icicles
pibydd (-ion) nm piper
picell (-au) nf dart, javelin, spear
picellu vb to spear, to stab
picfforch (-ffyrch) nf pitchfork
picil nm pickle, trouble
picio vb to dart, to hie
piclo vb to pickle
pictiwr (-tiyrau) nm picture

P

picwns

picwns (*nf* **picwnen**) *npl* wasps
piff (**-iau**) *nm* puff, sudden blast
piffian *vb* to snigger, to giggle
pig (**-au**) *nf* point, spike; beak; spout
pigan *vb* to drizzle
pigdwr (**-dyrau**) *nm* spire, steeple
pigiad (**-au**) *nm* prick, sting; injection
pigion *npl* pickings, selections
pigo *vb* to pick; to peck; to prick; to sting
pigog *adj* prickly
pigoglys *nm* spinach
pigyn *nm* thorn, prickle
pilcod *npl* (*nm* **-yn**) minnows
pilen (**-nau**) *nf* membrane, film; cataract
piler (**-au, -i**) *nm* pillar
pilio *vb* to peel, to pare
pili-pala *nm* butterfly
Pilipinas *npl* the Philippines
pilsen (**pils**) *nf* pill
pilyn *nm* garment, rag, clout
pin (**-nau**) *nmf* pin ▸ *nm* pen; **pin blaen ffelt** felt-tip pen
pîn *nm* pine, fir
pinacl (**-au**) *nm* pinnacle
pinaclog *adj* pinnacled
pinafal (**-au**) *nf* pineapple
pinbwyntio *vb* to pinpoint
pinc (**-od**) *nm* finch, chaffinch
pincio *vb* to pink; **parlwr pincio** beauty parlour
pincws (**-cysau**) *nm* pincushion
pindwll (**-dyllau**) *nm* pinhole
pinsiad (**-au**) *nm* pinch
pinsio *vb* to pinch
pinwydden *nf* pine
pioden (**pïod**) *nf* magpie

piser (**-au, -i**) *nm* pitcher, jug, can
pistyll (**-oedd**) *nm* spout; cataract
pistyllio *vb* to spout, to gush
pisyn (**-nau, pisiau**) *nm* piece
piti *nm* pity
pitw *adj* petty, puny, paltry
piw (**-od**) *nm* dug, udder
Piwritan (**-iaid**) *nm* Puritan
piwritanaidd *adj* puritan, puritanical
piwritaniaeth *nf* puritanism
pla (**plâu**) *nmf* plague; nuisance
pladur (**-iau**) *nf* scythe
pladurwr (**-wyr**) *nm* mower
plaen[1] *adj* plain, clear
plaen[2] (**-au**) *nm* plane
plaenio *vb* to plane
plagio *vb* to plague, to tease, to torment
plagus *adj* annoying, troublesome
plaid (**pleidiau**) *nf* side, party; **Plaid Cymru** the Welsh Nationalist Party, the Party of Wales
planced (**-i**) *nf* blanket
planed (**-au**) *nf* planet
planhigfa (**-feydd**) *nf* plantation
planhigyn (**-higion**) *nm* plant; **planhigyn wy** aubergine
plannu *vb* to plant; to dive
plannwr (**planwyr**) *nm* planter
plant *npl* (*nm* **plentyn**) children
planta *vb* to bear children
plantos *npl* (little) children
plas (**-au**) *nm* hall, mansion, palace
plasaidd *adj* palatial
plastr (**-au**) *nm* plaster
plastro *vb* to plaster
plastrwr (**-wyr**) *nm* plasterer
plât, plat (**-iau**) *nm* plate
platŵn (**-tynau**) *nm* platoon

platwydr *nm* plate-glass
ple *nm* plea
pledio *vb* to plead, to argue
pledren (-nau, -ni) *nf* bladder
pleidgarwch *nm* partisanship
pleidio *vb* to side with, to support
pleidiol *adj* favourable, partial
pleidiwr (-wyr) *nm* partisan, supporter
pleidlais (-leisiau) *nf* vote, suffrage
pleidleisio *vb* to vote
pleidleisiwr (-wyr) *nm* voter
plencyn (planciau) *nm* plank
plentyn (plant) *nm* child, infant
plentyndod *nm* childhood, infancy
plentyneiddiwch *nm* childishness
plentynnaidd *adj* childish, puerile
plentynrwydd *nm* childishness
pleser (-au) *nm* pleasure
pleserdaith (-deithiau) *nf* trip, excursion
pleserus *adj* pleasurable, pleasant
plesio *vb* to please
plet, pleten (pletiau) *nf* pleat
pletio *vb* to pleat
pletiog *adj* pleated
pleth (-au) *nf* plait
plethdorch (-au) *nf* wreath
plethu *vb* to plait, to weave, to fold
plewra (-e) *nf* pleura
plicio *vb* to pluck, to peel, to strip
plisg *npl* (*nm* **-yn**) shells, husks, pods
plisgo *vb* to shell, to husk
plisman, plismon (plismyn) *nm* police officer
plismones (-au) *nf* police officer
plith *nm* midst
pliwrisi *nm* pleurisy
plocyn (plociau) *nm* block

plod *adj, nm* plaid, tartan
ploryn (-nod) *nm* pimple
plorynnod *npl* acne
pluen (plu) *nf* feather; **plu eira** snow-flakes
plufyn (pluf) *nm* = **pluen**
pluo, plufio *vb* to pluck, to deplume; to plume
pluog *adj* feathered, fledged
plwc (plyciau) *nm* pluck; space, while
plwg (plygiau) *nm* plug
plwm *nm* lead
plws *nm* plus
plwtonium *nm* plutonium
plwyf (-i, -ydd) *nm* parish
plwyfol *adj* parochial
plwyfolion *npl* parishioners
plycio *vb* to pluck
plyg (-ion) *nm* fold, double; hollow
plygadwy *adj* collapsible
plygain *nm* cock-crow, dawn; matins
plygeiniol *adj* dawning; very early
plygell (-au) *nf* folder
plygiad (-au) *nm* folding, fold
plygu *vb* to fold; to bend, to stoop; to bow
plymio *vb* to plumb, to sound
plymwr (-wyr) *nm* plumber
po *particle*: **gorau po gyntaf** the sooner the better
pob *adj* each, every; all
pobi *vb* to bake; to roast; to toast
pobiad (-au) *nm* baking, batch
pobl (-oedd) *nf* people
poblog *adj* populous
poblogaeth (-au) *nf* population
poblogaidd *adj* popular
poblogeiddio *vb* to popularize**P**

poblogi *vb* to people, to populate
poblogrwydd *nm* popularity
pobwr (-wyr), pobydd (-ion) *nm* baker
poced (-i) *nf* pocket
pocedu *vb* to pocket
pocer (-i, -au) *nm* poker
podlediad *nm* podcast
poen (-au) *nmf* pain, torment
poenedigaeth *nf* torment
poeni *vb* to pain, to torment; to worry, to grieve
poenus *adj* painful
poenwr (-wyr) *nm* tormentor, torturer
poenydio *vb* to torment, to torture; to fret, to vex
poenydiwr (-wyr) *nm* tormentor
poer (-ion) *nm* spittle, saliva
poeri *vb* to spit, to expectorate
poeryn *nm* spittle
poeth *adj* hot; burning; **dŵr poeth** heart-burn
poethder, poethni *nm* hotness, heat
poethdon (-nau) *nf* heat wave
poethi *vb* to heat
pôl (polau) *nm* poll
polaredd *nm* polarity
polareiddiad *nm* polarisation
polareiddio *vb* to polarise
polymorff *nm* polymorph
polymorffedd *nm* polymorphism
polyn (polion) *nm* pole
pomgranad (-au) *nm* pomegranate
pompiwn (-iynau) *nm* pumpkin, gourd
pompren *nf* plank bridge, footbridge

ponc, poncen (ponciau) *nf* hillock; bank
poncyn *nm* hillock; bank
pont (-ydd) *nf* bridge, arch
pontffordd (-ffyrdd) *nf* fly-over, viaduct
pontio *vb* to bridge
popeth *nm* everything
poplys *npl* (*nf* -**en**) poplar-trees
popty (-tai) *nm* bakehouse; oven; **popty ping** microwave (oven)
porc *nm* pork
porchell (perchyll) *nm* piglet
porfa (-feydd) *nf* pasture, grass
porfelu *vb* to pasture
porffor *adj, nm* purple
pori *vb* to graze, to browse; to eat
pornograffi *nm* pornography
pornograffiaeth *nf* pornography
Portiwgal *nf* Portugal
portread (-au) *nm* portrayal, pattern
portreadu *vb* to portray
porth¹ *nm* aid, help, succour
porth² (pyrth) *nm* gate, gateway; porch door; **porth awyr** airport
porthfa (-feydd) *nf* port, harbour; ferry
porthi *vb* to feed
porthiannus *adj* well-fed, high-spirited
porthiant *nm* food, sustenance, support
porthladd (-oedd) *nm* port, harbour, haven
porthmon (-myn) *nm* cattle-dealer
porthor (-ion) *nm* porter, door-keeper, commissionaire
pos (-au) *nm* riddle, conundrum, puzzle

posib, posibl adj possible
posibilrwydd nm possibility
positif adj positive
positifiaeth nf positivism
post (pyst) nm post; pillar; **post sothach** junk mail
poster (-i) nm poster
postfarc (-iau) nm postmark
postio vb to post
postman, postmon (postmyn) nm postman
postyn (pyst) nm post
pot (-iau) nm pot
potel (-i) nf bottle
potelaid (-eidiau) nf bottleful
potelu vb to bottle
poten (-ni) nf paunch; pudding
potensial (-au) nm, adj potential
potes nm pottage, broth, soup
potio vb to pot; to tipple
potsiar (-s) nm poacher
potsio vb to poach
pothell (-au, -i) nf blister
pothellu vb to blister
powdr (-au) nm powder
powl, powlen (powliau) nf bowl, basin
powlio vb to roll; to wheel, to trundle
powltis (-au) nm poultice
practis nm practice
praff adj thick, stout
praffter nm thickness, stoutness, girth
pragmatiaeth nf pragmatism
praidd (preiddiau) nm flock
pranc (-iau) nm frolic, prank
prancio vb to caper, to prance
pratio vb to pat, to stroke, to caress

praw, prawf (profion) nm test, trial, proof; **prawf gyrru** driving test
preblan vb to chatter, to babble
pregeth (-au) nf sermon, discourse
pregethu vb to preach
pregethwr (-wyr) nm preacher
pregethwrol adj preacher-like
pregowtha vb to jabber, to rant
preifat adj private
preifatrwydd nm privacy
preimin nm ploughing match
prelad (-iaid) nm prelate
preladiaeth nf prelacy
preliwd (-au) nm prelude
premiwm (-iymau) nm premium
pren (-nau) nm tree, timber; wood
prentis (-iaid) nm apprentice
prentisiaeth nf apprenticeship
prentisio vb to apprentice
prepian vb to babble, to blab
pres nm brass; bronze; copper; money
preseb (-au) nm crib, stall
presennol adj, nm present
presenoldeb nm presence; attendance
presenoli vb to be present (reflexive)
presgripsiwn (-iynau) nm prescription
preswyl nm abode, dwelling
preswylfa (preswylfeydd) nf abode, dwelling
preswylio vb to dwell, to reside, to inhabit
preswylydd (-ion, -wyr) nm dweller, inhabitant
pric (-iau) nm stick, chip

prid *adj* dear, costly ▸ *nm* price, value

pridwerth *nm* ransom

pridd *nm* mould, earth, soil, ground

priddell (-au, -i) *nf* clod

priddglai *nm* loam

priddio, priddo *vb* to earth

priddlech (-au, -i) *nf* tile

priddlestr (-i) *nm* earthenware vessel

priddlyd *adj* earthy

priddo *vb see* **priddio**

priddyn *nm* earth, soil, mould

prif *adj* prime, principal, chief; **prif gwrs** main course

prifardd (-feirdd) *nm* chief bard

prifathro (-athrawon) *nm* headmaster, principal

prifddinas (-oedd) *nf* metropolis, capital

prifiant *nm* growth

prifio *vb* to grow

priflythyren *nf* capital

prifodl (-au) *nf* chief rhyme

prifysgol (-ion) *nf* university

priffordd (-ffyrdd) *nf* highway

prin *adj* scarce, rare ▸ *adv* scarcely

prinder, prindra *nm* scarceness, scarcity

prinhau *vb* to make or grow scarce, to diminish

print (-iau) *nm* print

printiedig *adj* printed

printio *vb* to print

printiwr (-wyr) *nm* printer

priod *adj* own; proper; married ▸ *n* husband or wife, spouse

priodas (-au) *nf* marriage, wedding

priodasfab (-feibion) *nm* bridegroom

priodasferch (-ed) *nf* bride

priodasol *adj* matrimonial

priod-ddull (-iau) *nm* idiom

priodfab (-feibion) *nm* bridegroom

priodferch (-ed) *nf* bride

priodi *vb* to marry

priodol *adj* proper, appropriate

priodoldeb (-au) *nm* propriety

priodoledd (-au) *nf* attribute

priodoli *vb* to attribute

prior (-iaid) *nm* prior

priordy (-dai) *nm* priory

pris (-iau) *nm* price, value

prisiad, prisiant *nm* valuation

prisio *vb* to price, to value; to prize

prisiwr (-wyr) *nm* valuer

problem (-au) *nf* problem

proc (-iau) *nm* poke

procer (-au, -i) *nm* poker

procio *vb* to poke; to throb

procsi *nm* proxy

prodin (-au) *nm* protein

profedig *adj* approved, tried

profedigaeth (-au) *nf* trouble, tribulation

profedigaethus *adj* beset with trials

profi *vb* to prove; to taste; to try; to experience

profiad (-au) *nm* experience; **profiad gwaith** work experience

profiadol *adj* experienced

profiannaeth (-au) *nf* probation

proflen (-ni) *nf* proof-sheet

profocio *vb* to provoke, to tease

profoclyd *adj* provoking, provocative

profwr (-wyr) *nm* taster, tester

proffes (-au) *nf* profession

proffesiwn (-iynau) *nm* profession

proffesu *vb* to profess
proffid *nf* profit
proffidio *vb* to profit, to benefit
proffidiol *adj* profitable
proffwyd (-i) *nm* prophet
proffwydes (-au) *nf* prophetess
proffwydo *vb* to prophesy
proffwydol *adj* prophetic
proffwydoliaeth (-au) *nf* prophecy
project (-au) *nm* project
proses (-au) *nmf* process
prosesu *vb* to process
prosesydd *nm* processor;
  prosesydd geiriau word processor
protest (-au) *nf* protest
Protestannaidd *adj* Protestant
Protestant (-aniaid) *nm*
  Protestant
protestio *vb* to protest
protestiwr (-wyr) *nm* protestor
prudd *adj* grave, serious, sad; wise
pruddaidd *adj* sad, gloomy,
  mournful
prudd-der *nm* sadness, gloom
pruddglwyf *nm* depression,
  melancholy
pruddglwyfus *adj* depressed,
  melancholy
pruddhau *vb* to sadden, to depress
Prwsia *nf* Prussia
pryd¹ (-iau) *nm* time; season ▸ *nm*
  (-au) meal
pryd² *adv* while, when, since
pryd³ *nm* form, aspect; complexion
Prydain *nf* Britain; **Prydain Fawr**
  Great Britain
Prydeindod *nm* Britishness
Prydeinig *adj* British
Prydeiniwr (-wyr) *nm* Brit (*inf*),
  British person

pryder (-on) *nm* anxiety, solicitude
pryderu *vb* to be anxious
pryderus *adj* anxious, solicitous
prydferth *adj* beautiful, handsome
prydferthu *vb* to beautify
prydferthwch *nm* beauty
prydles (-au, -i) *nf* lease
prydlesu *vb* to lease
prydlon *adj* timely, punctual
prydlondeb *nm* punctuality
prydydd (-ion) *nm* poet
prydyddu *vb* to compose poetry,
  to poetize
pryf (-ed) *nm* insect; worm; vermin
pryfedog *adj* verminous
pryfleiddiad (-au) *nm* insecticide
pryfoclyd *adj* irritating
pryfyn *nm* worm
prŷn *adj* bought, purchased
prynedigaeth *nmf* redemption
prynhawn (-au) *nm* afternoon
prynhawnol *adj* afternoon,
  evening
pryniad *nm* purchase
pryniant *nm* purchase
prynu *vb* to buy, to purchase; to
  redeem
prynwr (-wyr) *nm* buyer; redeemer
prysg *nm* bush, wood
prysgwydd *npl* brushwood
prysur *adj* busy, hasty; diligent;
  serious
prysurdeb *nm* haste, hurry;
  busyness
prysuro *vb* to hurry, to hasten
pulpud (-au) *nm* pulpit
pum, pump *adj* five
pumawd (-au) *nm* quintet
pumed *adj* fifth
pumongl (-au) *nm* pentagon

punt (**punnoedd, punnau**) *nf* pound (*money*)

pupur *nm* pepper

pur *adj* pure, sincere ▸ *adv* very, fairly

purdan *nm* purgatory

purdeb *nm* purity, sincerity

puredigaeth *nf* purification

puredd *nm* purity, innocence

purfa (**-feydd**) *nf* refinery

purion *adj* very well; right enough

puro *vb* to purify, to cleanse

puror *nm* harpist

purydd (**-ion**) *nm* purist

putain (**-einiaid**) *nf* prostitute

puteindra *nm* prostitution

pwdin *nm* pudding, dessert

pwdlyd *adj* sulking

pwdr *adj* rotten, corrupt, putrid

pwdu *vb* to pout, to sulk

pŵer (**-au**) *nm* power

pwerdy *nm* power station

pwerus *adj* powerful

pwff (**pyffiau**) *nm* puff, blast

pwffian *vb* to puff

pwl (**pyliau**) *nm* fit, attack, paroxysm

pŵl *adj* blunt, obtuse; dull, dim

pwll (**pyllau**) *nm* pit, pool, pond; **pwll glo** coal pit; **pwll tro** whirlpool

pwmp (**pympiau**) *nm* pump

pwn (**pynnau**) *nm* pack, burden

pwnc (**pynciau**) *nm* point, subject, question

pwniad (**-au**) *nm* nudge, dig

pwnio *vb* to nudge; to beat, to thump, to wallop

pwrcas (**-au**) *nm* purchase

pwrcasu *vb* to purchase

pwrffil *nm* train

pwrpas (**-au**) *nm* purpose

pwrpasol *adj* suitable

pwrpasu *vb* to purpose, to intend

pwrs (**pyrsau**) *nm* purse, bag; udder; scrotum

pwt¹ (**pytiau**) *nm* stump, bit

pwt², pwtian *vb* to prod, to poke

pwti *nm* putty

pwy *pron* who

Pwyl *nf* Poland

Pwylaidd *adj* Polish

Pwyleg *nf* Polish

pwyll *nm* sense, discretion

pwyllgor (**-au**) *nm* committee

pwyllgorwr (**-wyr**) *nm* committee-man

pwyllo *vb* to pause, to consider, to reflect

pwyllog *adj* discreet, prudent, deliberate

pwynt (**-iau**) *nm* point

pwyntil *nm* tab, tag; pencil

pwyntio *vb* to point; to fatten

pwyo *vb* to beat, to batter, to pound

pwys (**-au, -i**) *nm* weight, burden, pressure; pound (lb.); importance

pwysau *nm* weight

pwysedd *nm* pressure

pwysi (**-ïau**) *nm* posy

pwysig *adj* important

pwysigrwydd *nm* importance

pwyslais (**-leisiau**) *nm* emphasis

pwysleisio *vb* to emphasize, to highlight

pwyso *vb* to weigh, to press; to lean, to rest; to rely

pwyswr (**-wyr**) *nm* weigher

pwyth (**-au**) *nm* stitch

pwytho vb to stitch
pwythwr (-wyr) nm stitcher
pybyr adj strong, stout, staunch, valiant
pybyrwch nm stoutness, vigour, valour
pydew (-au) nm well, pit
pydredig adj rotten, putrid
pydredd nm rottenness, putridity, rot
pydru vb to rot, to putrefy
pyg nm pitch, bitumen
pygddu adj pitch-black
pygu vb to pitch
pyngad, pyngu vb to cluster
pylni nm bluntness, dullness
pylor nm dust, powder
pylu vb to blunt, to dull
pyllog adj full of pits
pyllu vb to pit
pymtheg adj, nm fifteen
pymthegfed adj fifteenth
pyncio vb to sing, to play, to make melody
pynio vb to burden, to load
pys npl (nf-en) peas
pysgod npl (nm **pysgodyn**) fish, fishes; **sglodion pysgod** fish fingers; **pysgod a sglodion** fish and chips; **y Pysgod** Pisces
pysgodfa (-feydd) nf fishery
pysgota vb to fish
pysgotwr (-wyr) nm fisherman
pystylad vb to stamp with the feet
pytaten (-tws) nf potato
pythefnos (-au) nmf fortnight

r

rabi (-niaid) nm rabbi
rabinaidd adj rabbinical
radio nm radio
radioleg nf radiology
radiws nm radius
ras (-ys) nf race
rasal, raser (-elydd, -erydd) nf razor
realaidd adj realistic
realistig adj realistic
record (-iau) nf record
recordiad (-au) nm recording
reiat nf row, riot
reis nm rice
reit adv right, very, quite
ridens nf fringe, nap
riwl nf ruler
robin goch nm robin
robin y gyrrwr nm gadfly
roced (-i) nf rocket
Romania nf Romania
ruban (-au) nm ribbon
rŵan adv now

rwbel *nm* rubble, rubbish
rwber *nm* rubber
rwdins *npl* (*nf* **rwden**) swedes
Rwmania *nf* Rumania
Rwsia *nf* Russia
Rwsiad (**Rwsiaid**) *nm* Russian
  (citizen)
Rwsieg *nm* Russian (language)
rysáit *nf* recipe

rhaca (**-nau**) *nf* rake
rhacanu *vb* to rake
rhacs (*nm* **rhecsyn**) *npl* rags
rhad¹ *adj* free; cheap
rhad² (**-au**) *nm* grace, favour,
  blessing
rhadlon *adj* gracious, kind; genial
rhadlondeb, rhadlonrwydd *nm*
  graciousness, cheapness
rhadus *adj* economical
rhaeadr (**-au**) *nf* cataract, waterfall
rhaeadru *vb* to pour, to gush
rhaff (**-au**) *nf* rope, cord
rhaffo, rhaffu *vb* to rope
rhag *prep* before, against; from;
  lest ▸ *prefix* pre-, fore-, ante-
rhagafon (**-ydd**) *nf* tributary
rhagair (**-au**) *nm* preface
rhagarfaethiad *nm* predestination
rhagarfaethu *vb* to predestine
rhagarweiniad *nm* introduction
rhagarweiniol *adj* introductory,
  preliminary

rhagarwyddo *vb* to foretoken, to portend

rhagbaratoawl *adj* preparatory

rhagbrawf (-brofion) *nm* foretaste; preliminary test

rhagdraeth (-au) *nm* preface, introduction

rhag-dyb (-ion) *nm* presupposition

rhagdybied, rhagdybio *vb* to presuppose

rhagddodiad (-iaid) *nm* prefix

rhagddywedyd, rhag-ddweud *vb* to foretell

rhagenw (-au) *nm* pronoun

rhagenwol *adj* pronominal

rhagfarn (-au) *nf* prejudice

rhagfarnllyd *adj* prejudiced

rhagfarnu *vb* to prejudice

rhagferf (-au) *nf* adverb

rhagflaenor (-iaid) *nm* forerunner

rhagflaenu *vb* to precede, to anticipate, to forestall

rhagflaenydd (-ion, -wyr) *nm* predecessor, precursor

rhagflas *nm* foretaste

rhagfur (-iau) *nm* bulwark

rhagfyfyrio *vb* to premeditate

rhagfynegi *vb* to foretell

Rhagfyr *nm* December

rhaglaw (-iaid, -lofiaid) *nm* prefect, viceroy, governor

rhaglawiaeth *nf* prefecture, governorship

rhaglen (-ni) *nf* program(me); **rhaglen gyfrifiadur** computer program

rhaglennu *vb* to program(me)

rhaglennydd (rhaglenwyr) *nm* programmer

rhagluniaeth (-au) *nf* providence

rhagluniaethol *adj* providential

rhaglunio *vb* to predestine, to predestinate

rhagod *vb* to ambush, to hinder, to waylay

rhagofal *nm* precaution

rhagofnau *npl* forebodings

rhagolwg (-ygon) *nm* prospect, outlook; **rhagolygon y tywydd** weather forecast

rhagolygon *npl* forecast

rhagor (-au, -ion) *nm* difference; more

rhagorfraint (-freintiau) *nf* privilege

rhagori *vb* to exceed, to excel, to surpass

rhagoriaeth (-au) *nf* superiority; excellence

rhagorol *adj* excellent, splendid

rhagoroldeb *nm* excellence

rhagorsaf (-oedd) *nf* out-station; outpost

rhagredegydd (-ion) *nm* forerunner

rhagrith (-ion) *nm* hypocrisy

rhagrithio *vb* to practise hypocrisy

rhagrithiol *adj* hypocritical

rhagrithiwr (-wyr) *nm* hypocrite

rhagrybuddio *vb* to forewarn

rhag-weld *vb* to foresee

rhagwelediad *nm* foresight, prescience

rhagwybod *vb* to foreknow

rhagwybodaeth *nf* foreknowledge

rhagymadrodd (-ion) *nm* introduction

rhai *pron* ones ▸ *adj* some

rhaib *nm* rapacity, greed; spell

rhaid (rheidiau) *nm* need, necessity

rh

rhaidd (rheiddiau) *nf* antler
rhain *pron* these
rhamant (-au) *nf* romance
rhamantu *vb* to romance
rhamantus *adj* romantic
rhan (-nau) *nf* part, portion; fate
rhanbarth (-au) *nm* division, district
rhanbarthol *adj* regional
rhandir (-oedd) *nfm* division, district
rhangymeriad (-iaid) *nm* participle
rhaniad (-au) *nm* division
rhannu *vb* to divide, to share, to distribute
rhannwr (rhanwyr) *nm* divider, sharer
rhanrif *nm* fraction
rhathell (-au) *nf* rasp
rhathiad *nm* friction, chafing
rhathu *vb* to rub, to rasp, to file
rhaw (-iau, rhofiau) *nf* spade, shovel
rhawd *nf* course, career
rhawg *adv* for a long time (to come)
rhawio, rhofio *vb* to shovel
rhawn *coll n* coarse long hair, horse-hair
rhech *nf* fart
rhechain *vb* to fart
rhedeg *vb* to run; to flow; **rhedeg allan (o)** run out (of); **rhedeg i ffwrdd, rhedeg ymaeth** run away
rhedegfa (-feydd) *nf* racecourse, race
rhedegog *adj* running, flowing
rhedegydd (-ion, -wyr) *nm* runner
rhedfa *nf* running, course, race
rhediad *nm* running, trend; slope

rhedweli (-ïau) *nf* artery
rhedyn *npl* (*nf-***en**) fern
rheffyn (-nau) *nm* cord; string, rigmarole
rheg (-au, -feydd) *nf* curse; swearword
rhegen yr ŷd, rhegen ryg *nf* corncrake
rhegi *vb* to curse
rheglyd *adj* given to cursing, profane
rheng (-au, -oedd) *nf* row, rank
rheibio *vb* to raven, to ravage, to ravish
rheibus *adj* rapacious, of prey
rheidiol *adj* necessary, needful
rheidrwydd *nm* necessity, need
rheidus *adj* necessitous, needy
rheiddiadur *nm* radiator
rheilen *nf* rail
rheilffordd (-ffyrdd) *nf* railway
rheini *pron* those
rheitheg *nf* rhetoric
rheithfarn (-au) *nf* verdict
rheithgor (-au) *nm* jury
rheithiwr (-wyr) *nm* juryman, juror
rheithor (-ion, -iad) *nm* rector
rhelyw *nm* residue, rest, remainder
rhemp *nf* excess; defect
rhent (-i) *nm* rent
rhentu *vb* to rent
rheol (-au) *nf* rule, regulation
rheolaeth *nf* rule, management, control; **rheolaeth bell** remote control
rheolaidd *adj* regular; **yn rheolaidd** regularly
rheoleiddio *vb* to regulate; to regularize

rheoli vb to rule, to govern, to control

rheoliadur (-on) nm: rheoliadur calon, rheoliadur y galon pacemaker

rheolwr (-wyr) nm ruler, controller

rhes (-i) nf line, stripe; row, rank

rhesen (rhesi) nf line, parting, streak, stripe

rhesin (-au, -ingau) nm raisin

rhesog adj striped; ribbed

rhestl (-au) nf rack

rhestr (-au, -i) nf list; row

rhestru vb to list

rheswm (-ymau) nm reason

rhesymeg nf logic

rhesymegol adj logical

rhesymol adj reasonable, rational

rhesymoldeb nm reasonableness

rhesymolwr (-wyr) nm rationalist

rhesymu vb to reason

rhetoreg, rhethreg nf rhetoric

rhew (-oedd, -ogydd) nm frost, ice

rhewfryn (-iau) nm iceberg

rhewgell (-oedd) nf freezer

rhewgist nf freezer

rhewi vb to freeze

rhewlif nm glacier

rhewllyd adj icy, frosty, frigid

rhewyn (-au) nm ditch, stream

rhewynt (-oedd) nm freezing wind

rhi nm king, lord

rhiain (rhianedd) nf maiden

rhialtwch nm pomp; festivity, jollity

rhiant (rhieni) nm parent; **rhiant sengl** single parent

rhibidirês nf rigmarole

rhibin nm streak

rhic (-iau) nm notch, nick; groove

rhicio vb to score

rhiciog adj notched; grooved; ribbed

rhidyll (-iau) nm riddle, sieve

rhidyllio, rhidyllu vb to riddle, to sift

rhieingerdd (-i) nf love-poem

rhieni npl parents

rhif (-au) nm number

rhifo vb to number, to count, to reckon

rhifol (-ion) nm numeral

rhifyddeg, rhifyddiaeth nf arithmetic

rhifyddwr (-wyr) nm arithmetician

rhifyn (-nau) nm number

rhigol (-au, -ydd) nf rut, groove

rhigwm (-ymau) nm rigmarole; rhyme

rhigymu vb to rhyme, to versify

rhigymwr (-wyr) nm rhymester

rhingyll (-iaid) nm sergeant, bailiff

rhimyn (-nau) nm strip, string

rhin (-iau) nf virtue, essence

rhincian vb to creak; to gnash

rhiniog (-au) nm threshold

rhinwedd (-au) nfm virtue

rhinweddol adj virtuous

rhip nm strickle

rhisgl nm bark

rhith (-iau) nm form, guise, appearance, image; foetus

rhithio vb to appear

rhithyn nm atom, particle, scintilla

rhiw (-iau) nf hill, acclivity

rhoch nf grunt, groan; death rattle

rhochain, rhochian vb to grunt

rhod (-au) nf wheel, orb; ecliptic

rhodfa (-feydd) nf walk, promenade, avenue

rh

rhodiad

rhodiad *nm* walk
rhodianna *vb* to stroll
rhodio *vb* to walk, to stroll
rhodres *nm* ostentation, affectation
rhodresa *vb* to behave ostentatiously
rhodresgar *adj* ostentatious, affected
rhodreswr (-wyr) *nm* swaggerer
rhodd (-ion) *nf* gift, present
rhoddi *vb* to give, to bestow, to yield; to put
rhoddwr (-wyr) *nm* giver, donor
rhoi *vb* to give, to bestow, to yield; to put; **rhoi yn ôl, rhoi nôl** put back
rhol, rhôl (-iau) *nf* roll
rholbren (-ni) *nm* rolling-pin
rholen (rholiau) *nf* roll; roller
rholio *vb* to roll
rholyn (rholion) *nm* roll; roller; **rholyn bara, rholyn o fara** bread roll; **rholyn tŷ bach, rholyn toiled** toilet roll
rhombws (rhombi) *nm* rhombus
rhonc *adj* rank, stark, out-and-out
rhos¹ (-ydd) *nf* moor, heath; plain
rhos² *npl* (*nm* **-yn**) roses
rhost *adj* roast, roasted
rhostio *vb* to roast
rhosyn (-nau) *nm* rose
rhu *nm* roar
rhuad (-au) *nm* roaring, roar
rhuadwy *adj* roaring
rhuchen (rhuchion) *nf* husk; film, pellicle
rhudd *adj* red, crimson
rhuddell *nf* rubric
rhuddem (-au) *nf* ruby
rhuddin *nm* heart of timber

rhuddion *npl* bran
rhuddygl *nm* radish
Rhufain *nf* Rome
Rhufeinaidd *adj* Roman
Rhufeiniad (-iaid), Rhufeiniwr (-wyr) *nm* Roman
Rhufeinig *adj* Roman
rhugl *adj* free, fluent, glib
rhuglen (-ni) *nf* rattle
rhuglo *vb* to rattle
rhuo *vb* to roar, to bellow, to bluster
rhusio *vb* to start, to scare, to take fright
rhuthr (-au) *nm* rush; attack; sally
rhuthro *vb* to rush; to attack, to assault
rhwbio *vb* to rub, to chafe; **rhwbio allan** rub out
rhwd *nm* rust
rhwng *prep* between, among
rhwnc *nm* snort, snore; death-rattle
rhwth *adj* gaping, distended
rhwyd (-au, -i) *nf* net, snare
rhwydo *vb* to net, to ensnare
rhwydog *adj* reticulated, netted
rhwydwaith (-weithiau) *nm* network
rhwydweithio *vb* to network ▸ *nm* networking; **rhwydweithio cymdeithasol** social networking
rhwydd *adj* easy, expeditious, prosperous
rhwyddhau *vb* to facilitate
rhwyddineb *nm* ease, facility
rhwyf (-au) *nf* oar
rhwyflong (-au) *nf* galley
rhwyfo *vb* to row; to sway; to toss about

rhwyfus *adj* restless
rhwyfwr (**-wyr**) *nm* rower, oarsman
rhwyg (**-iadau**) *nf* rent, rupture; schism
rhwygo *vb* to rend, to tear
rhwyllwaith *nm* fretwork, lattice-work
rhwym *adj* bound ▸ *nm* (**-au**) bond, tie; obligation
rhwymedig *adj* bound, obliged
rhwymedigaeth (**-au**) *nf* bond, obligation
rhwymedd *nm* constipation
rhwymiad (**-au**) *nm* binding
rhwymo *vb* to bind, to tie; to constipate
rhwymwr (**-wyr**) *nm* binder
rhwymyn (**-nau**) *nm* band, bond, bandage
rhwysg (**-au**) *nm* sway; pomp
rhwysgfawr *adj* pompous, ostentatious
rhwystr (**-au**) *nm* hindrance, obstacle
rhwystro *vb* to hinder, to prevent, to obstruct
rhwystrus *adj* embarrassed, confused
rhy *adv* too
rhybedio *vb* to rivet
rhybudd (**-ion**) *nm* notice, warning
rhybuddio *vb* to warn, to admonish, to caution
rhybuddiwr (**-wyr**) *nm* warner
rhych (**-au**) *nmf* furrow, rut, groove
rhychog *adj* furrowed, seamed
rhychwant (**-au**) *nm* span
rhychwantu *vb* to span
rhyd (**-au, -iau**) *nf* ford

rhydio *vb* to ford
rhydlyd *adj* rusty
rhydu *vb* to rust
rhydwytho *vb* to reduce
rhydd *adj* free; loose; liberal
rhyddfraint *nf* freedom
Rhyddfrydiaeth *nf* Liberalism
rhyddfrydig *adj* liberal, generous
Rhyddfrydol *adj* Liberal (in politics)
Rhyddfrydwr (**-wyr**) *nm* Liberal, Radical
rhyddhad *nm* liberation, emancipation
rhyddhau *vb* to free, to release, to liberate
rhyddhäwr (**rhyddhawyr**) *nm* liberator
rhyddiaith *nf* prose
rhyddid *nm* freedom, liberty
rhyddieithol *adj* prose, prosaic
rhyddni *nm* looseness, diarrhœa
rhyfedd *adj* strange, queer, wonderful
rhyfeddnod (**-au**) *nm* note of exclamation
rhyfeddod (**-au**) *nmf* wonder, marvel
rhyfeddol *adj* wonderful, marvellous
rhyfeddu *vb* to wonder, to marvel
rhyfel (**-oedd**) *nmf* war, warfare
rhyfela *vb* to wage war, to war
rhyfelgar *adj* warlike, bellicose
rhyfelgri *nm* war-cry, battle-cry
rhyfelgyrch (**-oedd**) *nm* campaign
rhyfelwr (**-wyr**) *nm* warrior
rhyferthwy *nm* torrent, inundation
rhyfon *npl* currants

rh

199

rhyfyg *nm* presumption, foolhardiness

rhyfygu *vb* to presume, to dare

rhyfygus *adj* presumptuous; foolhardy

rhyg *nm* rye

rhyglyddu *vb* to deserve, to merit

rhygnu *vb* to rub, to grate, to jar; to harp

rhygyngu *vb* to amble; to caper, to mince

rhyngrwyd *nf* internet

rhyngu *vb*: **rhyngu bodd** to please

rhyngweithiol *adj* interactive

rhyngwladol *adj* international

rhyndod *nm* shivering, chill

rhynion *npl* grits, groats

rhynllyd *adj* shivering, chilly

rhysedd *nm* abundance, excess

rhython *npl* cockles

rhythu *vb* to gape; to stare

rhyw *adj* some, certain ▸ *nmf* (**-iau**) sort; sex

rhywbeth *nm* something

rhywfaint *nm* some amount

rhywfodd, rhywsut *adv* somehow

rhywiaeth *nf* sexism

rhywiaethol *adj* sexist

rhywiog *adj* kindly, genial; fine; tender

rhywiol *adj* sexual

rhywioldeb *nm* sexuality

rhywle *adv* somewhere, anywhere

rhywogaeth (-au) *nf* species, sort, kind

rhywun (rhywrai) *nm* someone, anyone

S

Sabath, Saboth (-au) *nm* Sabbath

Sabothol *adj* Sabbath, sabbatic(al)

sacrament (-au) *nmf* sacrament

sacramentaidd *adj* sacramental

sach (-au) *nfm* sack

sachaid (-eidiau) *nf* sackful

sachu *vb* to sack, to bag

sad *adj* firm, steady, solid; sober

sadio *vb* to firm, to steady

sadistiaeth *nf* sadism

sadrwydd *nm* firmness, steadiness

Sadwrn (-yrnau) *nm* Saturn; **dydd Sadwrn** Saturday

saer (seiri) *nm* wright, mason, carpenter

saernïaeth *nf* workmanship, construction

saernïo *vb* to fashion, to construct

Saesneg *nf, adj* English

Saesnes (-au) *nf* Englishwoman

saets *nm* sage

saeth (-au) *nf* arrow, dart

saethiad (-au) *nm* shooting

saethu *vb* to shoot, to dart; to blast
saethwr (-wyr) *nm* shooter, shot
saethydd (-ion) *nm* shooter, archer; **y Saethydd** Sagittarius
saethyddiaeth *nf* archery
saethyn (-nau) *nm* projectile
safadwy *adj* stable
safanna *nm* savannah
safbwynt (-iau) *nm* standpoint
safiad *nm* standing; stature; stand
safio *vb* to save
safle (-oedd) *nm* position, station, situation; **safle gwe** website
safn (-au) *nf* mouth, jaws
safnrhwth *adj* open-mouthed, gaping
safnrhythu *vb* to gape, to stare
safon (-au) *nf* standard, criterion; **safon byw** standard of living
safoni *vb* to standardise
safonol *adj* standard
saff *adj* safe
saffir *nm* sapphire
saffrwm, saffron *nm* crocus
sagrafen (-nau) *nf* sacrament
sang (-au) *nf* pressure, tread
sangu, sengi *vb* to tread, to trample
saib (seibiau) *nm* leisure; pause, rest
saig (seigiau) *nf* meal, dish
sail (seiliau) *nf* base, foundation
saim (seimiau) *nm* grease
sain (seiniau) *nf* sound, tone
Sais (Saeson) *nm* Saxon, Englishman
saith *adj, nm* seven
sâl *adj* poor; poorly, ill; **sâl môr** seasick
salad (-au) *nm* salad

saldra *nm* poorness; illness
salm (-au) *nf* psalm
salmydd (-ion) *nm* psalmist
salw *adj* poor, mean, vile; ugly
salwch *nm* illness
Sallwyr *nm* Psalter
sampl (-au) *nf* sample
samplu *vb* to sample
Sanct *nm* the Holy One
sanctaidd *adj* holy
sancteiddio *vb* to sanctify, to hallow
sancteiddrwydd *nm* holiness, sanctity
sandal (-au) *nm* sandal
sant (saint, seintiau) *nm* saint
santes (-au) *nf* female saint
sarff (seirff) *nf* serpent
sarhad (-au) *nm* insult, disgrace, injury
sarhau *vb* to insult, to affront, to injure
sarhaus *adj* insulting, offensive, insolent
sarn (-au) *nf* causeway ▸ *nm* litter, ruin, destruction
sarnu *vb* to trample; to litter; to spoil, to ruin
sarrug *adj* gruff, surly, morose
sarugrwydd *nm* gruffness, surliness
sasiwn (-iynau) *nm* C.M. Association
satan (-iaid) *nm* satan
sathredig *adj* common, vulgar
sathru *vb* to tread, to trample
Saudi Arabia, Sawdi Arabia *nf* Saudi Arabia
sawdl (sodlau) *nmf* heel

S

sawl *pron* whoso, he that; **pa sawl** how many

sawr, sawyr *nm* savour

sawrio, sawru *vb* to savour

sawrus *adj* savoury

saws *nm* sauce

sba (-on) *nm* spa

Sbaen *nf* Spain

sbageti *nm* spaghetti

sbam *nm* spam

sbamio *vb* to spam

sbamiwr (-wyr) *nm* spammer

sbaner (-i) *nm* spanner

sbâr (sbarion) *nm* spare; *(pl)* leavings

sbario *vb* to spare, to save

sbectol *nf* spectacle(s)

sbeit *nf* spite

sbeitio *vb* to spite

sbeitlyd *adj* spiteful

sbel (-iau) *nf* spell

sbon *adv*: **newydd sbon** brand-new

sbonc (-iau) *nm* leap, jerk

sboncen *nf* squash

sbort *nf* sport, fun, game

sbri *nm* spree, fun

sbring *nm* spring

sbwylio *vb* to spoil

sebon (-au) *nm* soap

seboni *vb* to soap, to lather; to soft-soap, to flatter

sebonwr (-wyr) *nm* flatterer

secsist *adj* sexist

sect (-au) *nf* sect

sectyddiaeth *nf* sectarianism

sectyddol *adj* sectarian

sech *adj f of* **sych**

sedd (-au) *nf* seat, pew

sef *conj* that is to say, namely, to wit

sefnig *nm* pharynx

sefydledig *adj* established

sefydliad (-au) *nm* establishment, institution

sefydlog *adj* fixed, settled, stationary, stable

sefydlogrwydd, sefydlowgrwydd *nm* stability

sefydlu *vb* to establish, to found, to settle

sefyll *vb* to stand; to stop; to stay

sefyllfa (-oedd) *nf* situation, position

sefyllian *vb* to stand about, to loiter

sefyllwyr *npl* bystanders

segur *adj* idle

segura *vb* to idle

segurdod *nm* idleness

segurwr (-wyr) *nm* idler

seguryd *nm* idleness

seguryn, segurwr (-wyr) *nm* idler

sengi *vb* to tread, to trample

sengl *adj* single

seiat (-adau) *nf* fellowship meeting, 'society'

seiber-fwlio *vb* to cyberbully

seibiant *nm* leisure, respite; **seibiant salwch** sick leave

seibio *vb* to pause

seiciatreg *nf* psychiatry

seiciatrydd *nm* psychiatrist

seicoleg *nf* psychology

seicolegydd (-wyr) *nm* psychologist

seidin *nm* sidings

seilio *vb* to ground, to found

seilwaith *nm* infrastructure

seimio *vb* to grease

seimllyd *adj* greasy

seinber *adj* melodious, euphonious

seindorf (-dyrf) nf band
seineg nf phonetics
seinfawr adj loud
seinfforch (-ffyrch) nf tuning-fork
seinio vb to sound, to resound; to pronounce
seintio vb to saint, to canonize
seintwar nf sanctuary
seinyddol adj phonetic
Seisnig adj English
Seisnigaidd adj English, Anglicized
Seisnigeiddio, Seisnigo vb to Anglicize
seithblyg adj sevenfold
seithfed adj seventh
seithongl (-au) nf heptagon
seithug adj futile, fruitless, bootless
sêl¹ nf zeal
sêl² (seliau) nf seal
sêl³ (-s) nf sale; **sêl cist car** car boot sale
Seland Newydd nf New Zealand
seld (-au) nf dresser, sideboard, bookcase
seler (-au, -i, -ydd) nf cellar
selio vb to seal
selni nm illness
selog adj zealous, ardent
selsig (-od) nf black-pudding, sausage
semanteg nf semantics
seminar (-au) nf seminar
seml adj f of **syml**
sen (-nau) nf reproof, rebuke, censure, snub
senedd (-au) nf senate; parliament
seneddol adj senatorial, parliamentary
seneddwr (-wyr) nm senator

sennu vb to rebuke, to censure
sentimentaleiddiwch nm sentimentality
sêr see **seren**
seraff (-iaid) nm seraph
Serbia nf Serbia
serch¹ conj, prep although, notwithstanding
serch² (-iadau) nm affection, love
serchog adj affectionate, loving
serchowgrwydd nm affection, love
serchu vb to love
serchus adj loving, affectionate, pleasant
sêr-ddewin (-iaid) nm astrologer
sêr-ddewiniaeth nf astrology
seremoni (-ïau) nf ceremony
seremonïol adj ceremonial
seren (sêr) nf star; asterisk; **seren ffilmiau** film star
serennog adj starry
serennu vb to sparkle, to scintillate
serfyll adj unsteady
seri nm causeway, pavement
serio vb to sear
sero (-au) nm zero
serth adj steep, precipitous; obscene
serthedd nm ribaldry, obscenity
serwm nm serum
seryddiaeth nf astronomy
seryddol adj astronomical
seryddwr (-wyr) nm astronomer
sesbin nm shoehorn
sesiwn (sesiynau) nm session; **sesiwn ymarfer** workout
set (-iau) nf set
sêt (seti) nf seat, pew; **sêt fawr** deacons' pew

S

setl (**-au**) *nf* settle
setlo *vb* to settle
sethrydd (**-ion**) *nm* treader, trampler
sew (**-ion**) *nm* juice; pottage; delicacy
sffêr *nf* sphere
sg- *see also* **ysg-**
sgaldan(u) *vb* to scald
sgâm (**sgamiau**) *nf* scheme, dodge, scam
sgamio *vb* to scheme, to dodge
sgamiwr (**-wyr**) *nm* scammer
sganiwr (**-wyr**) *nm* scanner; **sganiwr feirws** virus scanner
sgaprwth *adj* uncouth, rough
sgarff (**-iau**) *nf* scarf
sgêri *adj* scary
sgil *nm* pillion; **sgil effaith** side effect
sgil-effaith *nf* side effect
sgïo *vb* to ski
sgipio *vb* to skip
sgiw *nf* settle; **ar y sgiw** askew
sglefren *nf* slide
sglefrio *vb* to skate, to slide
sglefrolio *vb* to roller-skate
sgolor (**-ion**) *nm* scholar
sgon *nf* scone
sgôr *nfm* score
sgori(o) *vb* to score
sgorpion (**-au**) *nm* scorpion **y Sgorpion** Scorpio
sgrafell (**-i**) *nf* scraper
sgrechian *vb* to shriek
sgrech y coed *nf* jay
sgrin (**-au**) *nf* screen
sgriw (**-iau**) *nf* screw
sgwâr (**-iau**) *nm* square

sgwd (**sgydiau**) *nf* cataract, waterfall
sgwrs (**sgyrsiau**) *nf* talk, chat, conversation
sgwrsio *vb* to talk, to chat
sgwter (**-i**) *nm* scooter
si *nm* whiz, buzz; rumour, murmur
siaced (**-i**) *nf* jacket, coat
siâd (**siadau**) *nf* pate
sialc *nm* chalk
sialens *nf* challenge
sialensio *vb* to challenge
siambr *nf* chamber
sianel (**-i, -ydd**) *nf* channel
siant (**-au**) *nf* chant
siâp *nm* shape
siapio *vb* to shape
siâr *nf* share
siarad *vb* to talk, to speak ▸ *nm* talk
siaradus *adj* talkative, garrulous
siaradwr (**-wyr**) *nm* talker, speaker
siario *vb* to share
siars *nf* charge, command
siarsio *vb* to charge, to enjoin, to warn
siart (**-iau**) *nm* chart
siartr (**-au**) *nf* charter
siasbi *nm* shoehorn
siawns *nf* chance
siawnsio *vb* to chance
sibrwd *vb* to whisper, to murmur ▸ *nm* (**-ydion**) whisper, murmur
sicr *adj* sure, certain; secure
sicrwydd *nm* certainty, assurance
sicrhau *vb* to assure, to affirm, to confirm; to secure
sidan (**-au**) *nm* silk
sidanaidd *adj* silky
sidanbryf (**-ed**) *nm* silkworm

sidydd *nm* zodiac
sied (**-au**) *nf* shed
siêd *nm* escheat, forfeit
siesbin *nm* shoehorn
siew *nf* show
siffrwd *vb* to rustle, to shuffle
sigâr *nf* cigar
sigarét (**sigaretau**) *nf* cigarette
sigledig *adj* shaky, rickety, unstable
siglen (**-nydd**) *nf* swing; bog, swamp
siglo *vb* to shake, to quake, to rock, to swing, to wag
sil (**-od**) *nm* spawn, fry
silff (**-oedd**) *nf* shelf
silwair *nm* silage
sill (**-iau**), **sillaf** (**-au**) *nf* syllable
sillafiad *nm* spelling
sillafiaeth *nf* spelling
sillafu *vb* to spell
sillgoll (**-au**) *nf* apostrophe
simnai (**-neiau**) *nf* chimney
simsan *adj* unsteady, tottering, rickety
simsanu *vb* to totter
sinach (**-od**) *nf* balk, waste ground; skinflint
sinc *nm* zinc
sinema (**sinemâu**) *nf* cinema
sinig *nm* cynic
sinigaidd *adj* cynical
sinsir *nm* ginger
sïo *vb* to hiss, to whiz; to murmur, to purl
sioe (**-au**) *nf* show; **sioe gêm, sioe gêmau** game show; **sioe sgwrsio** chat show
siofinydd *nm* chauvinist
siol (**-au**) *nf* skull, pate
siôl (**siolau**) *nf* shawl

siom (**-au**) *nm* disappointment
siomedig *adj* disappointed, disappointing
siomedigaeth (**-au**) *nf* disappointment
siomi *vb* to disappoint, to let down; to balk, to thwart; to deceive
siomiant *nm* disappointment
sionc *adj* brisk, nimble, agile, active
sioncio *vb* to brisk
Siôn Corn *nm* Father Christmas
sioncrwydd *nm* briskness, agility
sioncyn y gwair *nm* grasshopper
siop (**-au**) *nf* shop; **dyn siop** shop assistant; **merch siop** shop assistant
siopa *vb* to shop
siopladrad (**-au**) *nm* shoplifting
siopwr (**-wyr**) *nm* shopkeeper
sipian *vb* to sip, to sup, to suck
sipio *vb* to zip
siprys *nm* mixed corn (oats and barley)
sipsiwn *npl* gypsies
sir (**-oedd**) *nf* shire, county
siriol *adj* cheerful, bright, pleasant
sirioldeb *nm* cheerfulness
sirioli *vb* to cheer, to brighten
sirydd (**-ion**), **siryf** (**-ion**) *nm* sheriff
siryddiaeth *nf* shrievalty
sisial *vb* to whisper
siswrn (**-yrnau**) *nm* scissors
siwgr *nm* sugar
siwgro *vb* to sugar
siwmper (**-i**) *nf* jumper
siwr, siŵr *adj* sure, certain
siwrnai (**-eiau**) *nf* journey ▸ *adv* once
siwt (**-iau**) *nf* suit
siwtio *vb* to suit

S

slaf (slafiaid) *nm* slave, drudge
slei *adj* sly
sleifio *vb* to slink
sleisen *nf* slice
slic *adj* slick
Slofacia *nf* Slovakia
Slofenia *nf* Slovenia
slotian *vb* to paddle, to dabble; to tipple
slumyn *see* **ystlum**
slwt *nf* slut *(offensive)*
smala *adj* droll
smalio *vb* to joke
sment *nm* cement
smocio *vb* to smoke (tobacco)
smociwr (-wyr) *nm* smoker
smotiog *adj* spotty
smotyn (smotiau) *nm* spot
smwddio *vb* to iron
smwt *adj* snub
smyglo *vb* to smuggle
smygu *see* **smocio**
snisin *nm* snuff
snwffian *vb* to snuff, to sniff; to snuffle; to whimper
sobr *adj* sober, serious
sobreiddio, sobri *vb* to sober
sobrwydd *nm* sobriety, soberness
socas (-au) *nf* gaiter, legging
sodli *vb* to heel
sodomiaeth *nf* sodomy
sodr *nm* solder
soddi *vb* to submerge
soeg *nm* brewers' grains, draff
sofl *npl* (*nm* **-yn**) stubble
sofliar (-ieir) *nf* quail
sofraniaeth *nf* sovereignty
sofren (sofrod) *nf* sovereign (coin)
solas *nm* solace, joy
sol-ffa *nm* sol-fa

solffaeo *vb* to sol-fa
sôn *vb* to talk, to mention ▸ *nm* report, mention, word
soned (-au) *nf* sonnet
sonedwr (-wyr) *nm* composer of sonnets
soniarus *adj* melodious, tuneful; loud
soriant *nm* indignation, displeasure
sorod *npl* dross, dregs, refuse
sorri *vb* to chafe, to sulk, to be displeased
sosban (-nau, -benni) *nf* saucepan
sosej (-ys) *nf* sausage
soser (-i) *nf* saucer; **soser lloeren** satellite dish
sosialaeth *nf* socialism
sosialydd *nm* socialist
sothach *nfm* refuse, rubbish, trash
sownd *adj* fast
st- *see also* **yst-**
stac (-iau) *nf* stack
stad (-au) *nf* estate; state; **stad ddiwydiannol** industrial estate
staen (-au) *nm* stain
staenio *vb* to stain
staer *nm* stair
stafell (-oedd) *nf* room; **stafell sgwrsio** chat room
stâl (-au) *nf* stall
stamp (-iau) *nmf* stamp
stampio *vb* to stamp
starts *nm* starch
steil (-iau) *nf* style; surname; **steil gwallt** hairdo
stên (stenau) *nf* pitcher
stesion (-au) *nf* station
sticil, sticill *nf* stile
stilio *vb* to question

stiward (-iaid) *nm* steward
stiwdio *nf* studio
stoc (-au) *nf* stock
stomp *nf* bungle, mess, muddle
stompio *vb* to beat, to pound; to bungle, to mess
stompiwr (-wyr) *nm* bungler
stôr *nf* storage
stori (-ïau, -iâu, straeon) *nf* story, tale
storm, storom (stormydd) *nf* storm
stormus *adj* stormy
storom *nf* see **storm**
straegar *adj* gossiping, gossipy
strancio *vb* to play tricks
strategaeth *nf* strategy
strategol *adj* strategic
strategydd (-ion) *nm* strategist
streic (-iau) *nf* strike
stremp *nf* streak
striplun *nm* strip
strwythur *nm* structure
stryd (-oedd) *nf* street; **stryd fawr** high street
stumog *nf* stomach
stwc (stycau) *nm* pail, bucket
stwff (styffiau) *nm* stuff
stwffio *vb* to stuff, to thrust
stwffwl (styffylau) *nm* post; staple
stŵr *nm* stir
styffylwr *nm* stapler
styffylydd (-ion) *nm* stapler
styntiwr *nm* stuntman
su *nm* buzz, murmur, hum
suad *nm* buzzing, lulling; hum
sucan *nm* gruel
sudd (-ion) *nm* juice, sap
suddgloch (-glychau) *nf* diving-bell

suddlong (-au) *nf* submarine
suddo *vb* to sink, to dive; to invest (money)
sug (-ion) *nm* juice, sap
sugn *nm* suck; suction; sap
sugno *vb* to suck, to imbibe, to absorb
Sul (-iau) *nm*: **dydd Sul** Sunday
Sulgwyn *nm* Whitsunday
suo *vb* to buzz, to hum; to lull, to hush
sur (-ion) *adj* sour, acid
surbwch *nm* spoilsport
surdoes *nm* leaven
surni *nm* sourness, staleness, tartness
suro *vb* to sour
suryn *nm* acid
sut *nm* manner; plight; **(pa) sut?** how? what sort of?
sw *nf* zoo
swalpio *vb* to flounder, to jump, to bounce
swci *adj* tame, pet
swcro *vb* to succour
swcwr *nm* succour
swch (sychau) *nf* ploughshare; tip; lips
Sweden *nf* Sweden
swil *adj* shy, bashful
swilder *nm* shyness, bashfulness
Swistir *nf*: **y Swistir** Switzerland
switsfwrdd (switsfyrddau) *nm* switchboard
swllt (sylltau) *nm* shilling
swm (symiau) *nm* sum, bulk
swmbwl (symbylau) *nm* goad
swmer (-au) *nm* beam; pack
swmp *nm* bulk
swmpus *adj* bulky

S

sŵn *nm* noise, sound

swnian *vb* to murmur, to grumble, to nag

swnio *vb* to sound, to pronounce

swnllyd *adj* peevish, querulous

swnt *nm* sound, strait

sŵoleg *nf* zoology

swp (sypiau) *nm* mass, heap; cluster

swper (-au) *nmf* supper

swrn (syrnau) *nf* fetlock, ankle
▸ *nm* good number

swrth *adj* heavy, sluggish; sullen

sws (-ys) *nf* kiss

swta *adj* abrupt, curt

swydd (-au, -i) *nf* office; county

swyddfa (-feydd) *nf* office

swyddog (-ion) *nm* officer, official

swyddogaeth *nf* office, function

swyddogol *adj* official

swyngyfaredd (-ion) *nf* sorcery, witchcraft

swyngyfareddwr (-wyr) *nm* sorcerer

swyn (-ion) *nm* charm, fascination, spell, magic

swyno *vb* to charm, to enchant, to bewitch

swynol *adj* charming, fascinating

swynwr (-wyr) *nm* magician, wizard

swynwraig (-wragedd) *nf* sorceress

sy *see* sydd

syber *adj* sober, decent; clean, tidy

sych (f sech) *adj* dry

sychder *nm* dryness, drought

sychdir (-oedd) *nm* dry land

sychdwr *nm* drought

syched *nm* thirst

sychedig *adj* thirsty, parched, dry

sychedu *vb* to thirst

sychin *nf* drought

sychlyd *adj* dry

sychu *vb* to dry, to dry up; to wipe dry, to wipe

sychwr *nm* dryer

sychydd *nm* dryer

sydyn *adj* sudden, abrupt

sydynrwydd *nm* suddenness

sydd *vb* is, are

syfi *npl* (*nf* syfien) strawberries

syflyd *vb* to stir, to move, to budge

syfrdan *adj* giddy, dazed, stunned

syfrdandod *nm* giddiness, stupor

syfrdanol *adj* stunning

syfrdanu *vb* to daze, to bewilder, to stupefy, to stun

sylfaen (-feini) *nf* foundation

sylfaenol *adj* basic

sylfaenu *vb* to found

sylfaenwr (-wyr), sylfaenydd (-ion) *nm* founder

sylw (-adau) *nm* notice, attention, remark

sylwadaeth *nf* observation

sylwebaeth *nf* commentary

sylwebydd *nm* commentator

sylwedydd (-ion) *nm* observer

sylwedd (-au) *nm* substance, reality

sylweddol *adj* substantial, real

sylweddoli *vb* to realize

sylweddoliad *nm* realization

sylwi *vb* to observe, to regard, to notice

syllu *vb* to gaze

symbal (-au) *nm* cymbal

symbol *nm* symbol

symboliaeth *nf* symbolism

symbyliad *nm* stimulus, encouragement
symbylu *vb* to goad, to spur, to stimulate
symbylydd (-ion) *nm* stimulant
symio *vb* to sum
syml (*f* **seml**) *adj* simple
symledd *nm* simplicity
symleiddiad *nm* simplification
symleiddio *vb* to simplify
symlrwydd *nm* simplicity
symol *adj* middling, fair
symud *vb* to move, to remove
symudiad (-au) *nm* movement, removal
symudol *adj* moving, movable, mobile
syn *adj* amazed; astonishing, surprising
synagog (-au) *nm* synagogue
synamon *nm* cinnamon
syndod *nm* marvel, amazement, surprise
syndrom (-au) *nm* syndrome
syndrom Down Down's syndrome
synfyfyrdod *nm* reverie
synfyfyrio *vb* to muse
synfyfyriol *adj* vacant
synhwyro *vb* to sense
synhwyrol *adj* sensible
synhwyrus *adj* sensuous
syniad (-au) *nm* notion, idea, view
syniadaeth *nf* conception
synied, synio *vb* to think, to believe, to feel
synnu *vb* to marvel, to be amazed, to surprise, to be surprised
synnwyr (synhwyrau) *nm* sense; **synnwyr digrifwch** sense of humour

synwyroldeb *nm* sensibleness
synwyrusrwydd *nm* sensuousness
sypio *vb* to pack, to heap, to bundle
sypyn (-nau) *nm* package, packet
syr *nm* sir
syrcas *nf* circus
syrffed *nm* surfeit
syrffedu *vb* to surfeit
syrffio *vb* to surf
Syria *nf* Syria
syrthiedig *adj* fallen
syrthio *vb* to fall, to tumble
syrthni *nm* listlessness, sloth; inertia
system *nmf* system
systematig *adj* systematic
syth *adj* stiff; straight
sythu *vb* to stiffen, to straighten
sythwelediad *nm* intuition

S

209

t

tabernacl (-au) *nm* tabernacle
tabl (-au) *nm* table
tablen *nf* ale, beer
tabŵ *nm* taboo
tabwrdd (-yrddau) *nm* drum
tabyrddu *vb* to drum, to thrum
taclau *npl* (*nm* **teclyn**) tackle, gear
taclo *vb* to tackle
taclu *vb* to put in order, to trim
taclus *adj* neat, trim, tidy
tacluso *vb* to trim, to tidy
taclusrwydd *nm* tidiness
tacsi (-s) *nm* taxi; **gyrrwr tacsi**
taxi driver
tacteg (-au) *nf* tactic
Tachwedd *nm* November
tad (-au) *nm* father
tad-cu *nm* grandpa, grandfather
tadmaeth (-au, -od) *nm* foster
father
tadogaeth *nf* paternity; derivation
tadogi *vb* to father
tadol *adj* fatherly, paternal

tad-yng-nghyfraith *nm* father-
in-law
taenelliad *nm* sprinkling, affusion
taenellu *vb* to sprinkle
taenellwr (-wyr) *nm* sprinkler
taenlen (-ni) *nf* spreadsheet
taenu *vb* to spread, to expand, to
stretch
taenwr (-wyr) *nm* spreader,
disseminator
taeog *adj* churlish, blunt ▸ *nm*
(**-au, -ion**) churl
taeogaidd *adj* churlish, rude
taer *adj* earnest, importunate,
urgent
taerineb, taerni *nm* earnestness,
importunity
taeru *vb* to insist, to maintain; to
contend, to wrangle
tafarn (-au) *nfm* tavern, inn,
public-house
tafarndy (-dai) *nm* public-house
tafarnwr (-wyr) *nm* inn-keeper,
publican
tafell (-au, -i, tefyll) *nf* slice
tafellu *vb* to slice
tafl (-au) *nf* cast; scale; **ffon dafl**
sling
tafladwy *adj* disposable
tafledigion *npl* projectiles
taflegryn (taflegrau) *nm* missile
tafleisiaeth *nf* ventriloquism
tafleisydd (-ion, -wyr) *nm*
ventriloquist
taflen (-nau, -ni) *nf* table, list,
leaflet; **taflen waith** worksheet
taflennu *vb* to tabulate
tafliad (-au) *nm* throw; set-back
taflod (-ydd) *nf* loft; **taflod y genau**
palate

taflodol *adj* palatal
taflu *vb* to throw, to fling, to cast, to hurl; to throw away
tafluniad *nm* projection
taflunio *vb* to project
taflunydd *nm* projector
tafod (-au) *nm* tongue
tafodi *vb* to berate, to scold
tafodiaith (-ieithoedd) *nf* speech, language, dialect
tafod-leferydd *nm* speech, utterance; **ar dafod-leferydd** by rote
tafol¹ *nf* scales, balance
tafol² *npl* dock
tafoli *vb* to weigh up, to assess
tafotrwg *adj* foul-mouthed, abusive
tafotrydd *adj* garrulous, flippant
Tafwys *nf* Thames
taffi *nm* toffee
tagell (-au, tegyll) *nf* gill; wattle; dewlap; double chin
tagellog *adj* wattled; double-chinned
tagfa (-feydd) *nf* choking, strangling
tagu *vb* to choke, to stifle; to strangle
tangnefedd *nmf* peace
tangnefeddu *vb* to make peace; to appease
tangnefeddus *adj* peaceable, peaceful
tangnefeddwr (-wyr) *nm* peacemaker
tai *see* **tŷ**
taid (teidiau) *nm* grandfather
tail *nm* dung, manure
tair *adj f of* **tri**

taith (teithiau) *nf* journey, voyage, progress
tal *adj* tall, high, lofty
tâl¹ (talau, taloedd) *nm* end, forehead
tâl² (taliadau) *nm* pay, payment; **taloedd** rates
talaith (-eithiau) *nf* diadem; province, state
talar (-au) *nf* headland in field
talcen (-nau, -ni) *nm* forehead; gable
taldra *nm* tallness, loftiness, stature
taleb (-au, -ion) *nf* receipt, voucher
taledigaeth *nf* payment, recompense
taleithiol *adj* provincial
talent (-au) *nf* talent
talentog *adj* talented
talfyriad (-au) *nm* abbreviation, abridgement
talfyrru *vb* to abbreviate, to abridge
talgryf *adj* sturdy, robust; impudent
taliad (-au) *nm* payment
talm *nm* space, while; quantity, number; **er ys talm** long ago
talog *adj* jaunty
talp (-au, -iau) *nm* mass, lump
talpiog *adj* lumpy
talu *vb* to pay, to render; to answer, to suit; to be worth
talu-wrth-ddefnyddio *adj* pay-as-you-go
talwr (-wyr) *nm* payer
talwrn *nm* threshing floor; poetic contest

t

tamaid (-eidiau) nm morsel, bit, bite

tan prep to, till, until, as far; under

tân (tanau) nm fire

tanbaid adj fiery, hot, fervent; brilliant

tanbeidrwydd nm fierce heat, ardour

tanchwa (-oedd) nf fire-damp; explosion

tanddaearol adj underground, subterranean

tanddwr adj underwater

tanforol adj submarine

tanffordd nf underpass

taniad nm ignition, firing

tanio vb to fire, to stoke

taniwr (-wyr) nm firer, firefighter, stoker

tanlinellu vb to underline

tanlwybr nm subway

tanlli adj: **newydd sbon danlli** brand new

tanllwyth (-i) nm blazing fire

tanllyd adj fiery

tannu vb to adjust, to spread, to make (bed)

tanodd adv below, beneath

tanosodiad (-au) nm understatement

Tansanïa nf Tanzania

tant (tannau) nm chord, string

tanwent nm fuel

tanwydd coll n firewood, fuel

tanysgrifiad (-au) nm subscription

tanysgrifio vb to subscribe

tanysgrifiwr (-wyr) nm subscriber

taradr (terydr) nm auger; **taradr y coed** woodpecker

taran (-au) nf (peal of) thunder

taranfollt (-au) nf thunderbolt

taranu vb to thunder

tarddell nf source, spring

tarddiad (-au) nm source, derivation

tarddle (-oedd) nm source

tarddu vb to sprout, to spring; to derive, to be derived

tarfu vb to scare, to scatter

targed (-au) nm target

tarian (-au) nf shield

tario vb to tarry

taro vb to strike, to smite, to hit, to knock; to tap; to stick; to hot; to suit

tarren (tarenni, -ydd) nf knoll, rock

tarth (-oedd) nm mist, vapour

tarw (teirw) nm bull; **y Tarw** Taurus

tarwden nf ringworm

tas (teisi) nf rick, stack

tasel nm tassel

tasg (-au) nf task

tasgu vb to task; to start, to jump; to splash, to spirt

tato, tatws npl (nf **taten,** nf **tatysen**) potatoes

taw¹ nm silence; **rhoi taw ar** silence

taw² conj that

tawch nm vapour, haze, mist, fog

tawdd adj melted, molten, dissolved

tawedog adj silent, taciturn

tawedogrwydd nm taciturnity

tawel adj calm, quiet, still, tranquil

tawelu vb to calm; to grow calm

tawelwch nm calm, quiet, tranquillity

tawelydd nm silencer

tawelyn nm tranquillizer

tawlbwrdd nm draughtboard, backgammon
tawtologiaeth nf tautology
te nm tea; **te llysieuol** herbal tea
tebot (-au) nm teapot
tebyg adj similar, like, likely
tebygol adj likely, probable
tebygolrwydd nm likelihood, probability
tebygrwydd nm likeness, resemblance
tebygu vb to liken, to resemble; to suppose
tecáu vb to beautify, to adorn, to embellish
teclyn (taclau) nm tool, instrument; **teclyn heb afael** hands-free kit
tecstio vb to text
techneg nf technique
technegol adj technical
technegydd nm technician
technoleg (-au) nf technology; **technoleg gwybodaeth** information technology, IT
technolegol adj technological
teg adj fair, beautiful, fine
tegan (-au) nm plaything, toy, bauble
tegell (-au, -i) nm kettle, teakettle
tegwch nm fairness, beauty
tei nmf tie
teiar nm tyre
teigr (-od) nm tiger
teilchion npl fragments, atoms, shivers
teiliwr (-eilwriaid) nm tailor
teilo vb to dung, to manure
teilsen nf tile
teilwng adj worthy; deserved

teilwra vb to tailor
teilwres (-au) nf tailoress
teilwriaeth nf tailoring
teilyngdod nm worthiness, merit
teilyngu vb to deserve, to merit; to deign
teim nm thyme
teimlad (-au) nm feel, feeling, sensation, emotion
teimladol adj emotional
teimladrwydd nm feelingness, sensibility
teimladwy adj feeling; sensitive
teimlo vb to feel, to touch, to handle, to manipulate
teimlydd (-ion) nm feeler, antenna, tentacle
teios npl cottages
teip (-iau) nm type
teipiadur (-ion) nm typewriter
teipio vb to type
teipydd (-ion) nm typist
teisen (-nau) nf cake
teitl (-au) nm title
teithi npl traits, characteristics, qualities
teithio vb to travel, to journey
teithiol adj travelling, itinerant
teithiwr (-wyr) nm traveller, passenger
telathrebiaeth nf telecommunication
teledu nm television ▸ vb to televise; **teledu cylch cyfyng** CCTV
teleffon (-au) nm telephone
teler (-au) nm term, condition
teligraff nm telegraph
telm (-au) nf snare
telori vb to warble; to quaver
telyn (-au) nf harp

telyneg (-ion) *nf* lyric
telynegol *adj* lyrical
telynegwr *nm* lyric poet
telynor (-ion) *nm* harpist
telynores *nf* female harpist
teml (-au) *nf* temple
tempro *vb* to temper
temtasiwn (-iynau) *nfm* temptation
temtio *vb* to tempt
temtiwr (-wyr) *nm* tempter
tenant (-iaid) *nm* tenant
tenantiaeth *nf* tenancy
tenau *adj* thin, lean; slender; rarified; sensitive
tendio *vb* to tend, to mind
teneuad *nm* dilution
teneuo *vb* to thin, to become thin, to dilute
teneuwch *nm* thinness, leanness; tenuity
tenewyn (-nau) *nm* flank
tenlli, tenllif *nm* lining
tennis *nm* tennis
tennyn (tenynnau) *nm* cord, rope, halter
têr *adj* clear, refined, pure, fine
teras (-au) *nm* terrace
terfyn (-au) *nm* end, extremity, bound
terfyniad (-au) *nm* ending, termination
terfynol *adj* final; conclusive
terfynu *vb* to end, to terminate, to determine
terfysg (-oedd) *nm* tumult, riot
terfysgaeth *nf* terrorism
terfysgaidd, terfysglyd *adj* riotous, turbulent

terfysgu *vb* to riot, to rage, to surge
terfysgwr (-wyr) *nm* rioter, insurgent
term (-au) *nm* term
terminoleg *nf* terminology
tes *nm* sunshine, warmth, heat; haze
tesog *adj* sunny, hot, close, sultry
testament (-au) *nm* testament
testamentwr (-wyr) *nm* testator
testun (-au) *nm* text, theme, subject
testunio *vb* to taunt, to deride
tetanws *nm* tetanus
teth (-au) *nf* teat
teulu (-oedd) *nm* family; **teulu-yng-nghyfraith** in-laws
teuluaidd *adj* family, domestic
tew *adj* thick, fat, plump
tewdra, tewdwr *nm* thickness, fatness
tewhau *vb* to thicken, to fatten
tewi *vb* to keep silence, to be silent
tewychu *vb* to thicken, to fatten; to condense
tewychydd *nm* condenser
tewyn (-ion) *nm* ember, brand
teyrn (-edd, -oedd) *nm* monarch, sovereign
teyrnas (-oedd) *nf* kingdom, realm; **y Deyrnas Gyfunol, y Deyrnas Unedig** the United Kingdom
teyrnasiad (-au) *nm* reign
teyrnasu *vb* to reign
teyrnfradwr (-wyr) *nm* traitor
teyrnfradwriaeth *nf* (high) treason
teyrngar *adj* loyal
teyrngarwch *nm* loyalty

teyrnged (-au) *nf* tribute
teyrnwialen (-wiail) *nf* sceptre
TG *n* IT
ti *pron* you
ticed (-i) *nmf* ticket
tician *vb* to tick
tid (-au) *nf* chain
tila *adj* feeble, puny, insignificant
tîm (timau) *nm* team
tin (-au) *nf* bottom; rump; tail
tinc (-iadau) *nm* clang, tinkle
tincian *vb* to tinkle, to chink, to
  clink, to clank
tip (-iadau) *nm* tick (of clock)
tipian *vb* to tick
tipyn (-nau, tipiau) *nm* bit
tir (-oedd) *nm* land, ground,
  territory
tirio *vb* to land, to ground
tiriog *adj* landed
tiriogaeth (-au) *nf* territory
tiriogaethol *adj* territorial
tirion *adj* kind, tender, gentle,
  gracious
tiriondeb *nm* kindness, tenderness
tirlun (-iau) *nm* landscape
tirol *adj* relating to land
tirwedd *nf* relief (*geographic*)
tisian *vb* to sneeze
tithau *pron* thou (on thy part),
  thou also
tiwmor *nm* tumour
tiwn (-iau) *nf* tune
tiwnio *vb* to tune
tlawd (tlodion) *adj* poor
tlodaidd *adj* poorish, mean, dowdy
tlodi *vb* to impoverish ▸ *nm*
  poverty
tlos *adj f of* **tlws**

tloty (-ai) *nm* poorhouse,
  workhouse
tlotyn (tlodion) *nm* pauper
tlws¹ (f tlos) *adj* pretty
tlws² (tlysau) *nm* jewel, gem;
  medal
tlysni *nm* prettiness
to (toeau) *nm* roof; generation
toc *adv* shortly, presently, soon
tocio *vb* to clip, to dock, to prune
tocyn¹ (tociau) *nm* pack, heap,
  hillock; slice of bread
tocyn² (-nau) *nm* ticket
tocynnwr (-ynwyr) *nm* bus
  conductor
toddadwy *adj* soluble
toddedig *adj* molten; melting
toddi *vb* to melt, to dissolve, to
  thaw
toddiant (-nnau) *nm* solution
toddion *npl* dripping
toddwr (-wyr), toddydd (-ion)
  nm melter
toes *nm* dough
toesen *nf* doughnut
toi *vb* to cover; to roof; to thatch
toili *nm* spectral funeral
tolach *vb* to fondle
tolc (-iau) *nm* dent, dinge
tolcio *vb* to dent, to dinge
tolciog *adj* dented, dinged
tolchen (-au) *nf* clot
tolchennu *vb* to clot
toll (-au) *nf* toll, custom
tolli *vb* to take toll
tom *nf* dirt, mire, dung
tomen (-nydd) *nf* heap; dunghill
tomlyd *adj* dirty, miry
ton¹ (-nau) *nf* wave, billow, breaker
ton² (-nau) *nm* lay-land

t

215

tôn (tonau) *nf* tone; tune; **tôn ffôn** ring tone

tonc (-iau) *nf* tinkle, ring, clash

toncio, -ian *vb* to tinkle, to ring

tonfedd (-i) *nf* wavelength

tonig (-iau) *adj* tonic

tonnen (tonennydd, -au) *nf* skin; sward; bog

tonni *vb* to wave, to undulate

tonnog *adj* wavy, billowy

tonyddiaeth *nf* tone, intonation

topio *vb* to plug, to stop up

topyn *nm* plug, stopper

tor¹(-ion) *nm* break, interruption

tor²(-rau) *nf* belly; palm (of hand)

torcalonnus *adj* heartbreaking

torch (-au) *nf* wreath; coil

torchi *vb* to wreathe; to coil; to roll, to tuck

torchog *adj* wreathed; coiled

tordyn *adj* tight-bellied; hectoring

toredig *adj* broken

toreithiog *adj* abundant, teeming

toreth *nf* abundance

torf (-eydd) *nf* crowd, multitude

torfynyglu *vb* to break neck of; to behead

torgoch (-ion) *nm* roach

torgwmwl *nm* cloudburst

torheulo *vb* to bask, to sunbathe

Tori (-ïaid) *nm* Tory

toriad (-au) *nm* cut, break; fraction

Torïaeth *nf* Toryism

Torïaidd *adj* Tory, Conservative

torlan (-nau, -lennydd) *nf* river bank

torllengig *nm* rupture

torllwyth (-i), torraid *nf* litter

torogen (-ogod) *nf* tick (in cattle)

torri *vb* to break, to cut; to dig; to write, to trace; **torri i lawr** break down

torrwr (torwyr) *nm* breaker, cutter

tors *nmf* torch

torsyth *adj* swaggering

torsythu *vb* to strut, to swagger

torth (-au) *nf* loaf

tost¹ *adj* severe, sharp, sore; ill

tost² *nm* toast

tosturi (-aethau) *nm* compassion, pity

tosturio *vb* to be compassionate, to pity

tosturiol *adj* compassionate

tosyn (tosau) *nm* pimple

töwr (towyr) *nm* roofer, tiler

tra *adv* over; very ▶ *conj* while, whilst

tra-arglwyddiaeth (-au) *nf* tyranny

tra-arglwyddiaethu *vb* to tyrannize

tra-awdurdodi *vb* to lord it over, to domineer

trabludd *nm* trouble, tumult, turmoil

trac (-iau) *nm* track

tractor (-s, -au) *nm* tractor

tracwisg *nf* tracksuit

trachefn *adv* again

trachwant (-au) *nm* lust, covetousness

trachwanta, trachwantu *vb* to lust, to covet

trachwantus *adj* covetous

tradwy *adv* three days hence

traddodi *vb* to deliver; to commit

traddodiad (-au) *nm* tradition; delivery

traddodiadol *adj* traditional

traddodwr (-wyr) *nm* deliverer

traean *nm* one third, the third part

traed *see* **troed**

traeth (-au) *nm* strand, shore, beach

traethawd (-odau) *nm* treatise, essay; tract

traethell (-au) *nf* strand, sandbank

traethiad (-au) *nm* predicate

traethodydd (-ion) *nm* essayist

traethu *vb* to utter, to declare; to treat

trafael (-ion) *nf* travail, trouble

trafaelio *vb* to travel

trafaeliwr (-wyr) *nm* traveller

trafaelu *vb* to travel; to travail

traflyncu *vb* to guzzle, to gulp, to devour

trafnidiaeth *nf* traffic

trafod *vb* to handle; to discuss; to transact

trafodaeth (-au) *nf* discussion, transaction

trafodion *npl* transactions

trafferth (-ion) *nmf* trouble

trafferthu *vb* to trouble

trafferthus *adj* troublesome; troubled

traffordd *nf* motorway

tragwyddol *adj* everlasting, eternal

tragwyddoldeb *nm* eternity

tragywydd *adj* everlasting, eternal

traha *nm* arrogance, presumption

trahaus *adj* arrogant, haughty

trahauster *nm* arrogance, presumption

trai *nm* ebb

trais *nm* oppression, force, violence

trallod (-ion, -au) *nm* trouble, tribulation

trallodi *vb* to afflict, to vex, to trouble

trallodus *adj* troubled; troublous

trallodwr (-wyr) *nm* troubler

tramgwydd (-iadau) *nm* stumbling; offence

tramgwyddo *vb* to stumble; to offend; to take offence

tramgwyddus *adj* scandalous; offensive

tramor *adj* foreign

tramorwr (-wyr) *nm* foreigner

trampolîn (trampolinau) *nm* trampoline

tramwy, tramwyo *vb* to pass, to traverse

tramwyfa (-feydd) *nf* passage, thoroughfare

tranc *nm* end, dissolution, death

trancedig *adj* deceased

trancedigaeth *nf* death, decease

trannoeth *adv* next day ▸ *nm* the morrow

trapio *vb* to trap

traphlith *adv*: **blith draphlith** higgledy-piggledy

tras *nf* kindred, affinity

traserch *nm* great love, infatuation

trasiedi (trasiedïau) *nf* tragedy

traul (treuliau) *nf* wear; cost, expense; digestion

traw *nm* pitch

trawiad (-au) *nm* stroke, beat, flash

trawiadol *adj* striking, spectacular

traws *adj* cross; froward, perverse

trawsblannu *vb* to transplant

trawsenwad *nm* metonymy

trawsfeddiannu *vb* to usurp

t

217

trawsfudo

trawsfudo *vb* to transmigrate
trawsffurfio *vb* to transform
trawsgludo *vb* to transport, to conduct
trawsgyweiriad *nm* transposition, modulation
trawsgyweirio *vb* to transpose, to change key
trawslif *nm* cross-saw
trawslythrennu *vb* to transliterate
traws-sylweddiad *nm* transubstantiation
trawst (-iau) *nm* beam
trawstoriad *nm* cross-section
trebl *nm, adj* treble
treblu *vb* to treble
trech *adj* superior, stronger, mightier
trechu *vb* to overpower, to overcome, to conquer
tref (-i, -ydd) *nf* home; town
trefedigaeth (-au) *nf* settlement, colony
trefgordd (-au) *nf* township
treflan (-nau) *nf* small town, townlet
trefn (-au) *nf* order, method, system
trefniad (-au) *nm* arrangement, ordering
trefniadaeth *nf* organization
trefniant *nm* arrangement, organization
trefnlen (-ni) *nf* schedule
trefnu *vb* to order, to arrange, to dispose
trefnus *adj* orderly, methodical
trefnusrwydd *nm* orderliness
trefnydd (-ion) *nm* arranger; Methodist

trefol *adj* town, urban
treftadaeth *nf* patrimony, inheritance
trengi *vb* to die, to perish, to expire
treial (-on) *nm* trial
treiddgar *adj* penetrating, keen
treiddgarwch *nm* penetration, acumen
treiddio *vb* to pass, to penetrate
treiddiol *adj* penetrating
treigl (-au) *nm* turn, revolution, course
treiglad, treigliad (-au) *nm* mutation; inflection
treiglo *vb* to roll; to mutate; to inflect; to decline
treio¹ *vb* to ebb
treio² *vb* to try
treisiad (-iedi) *nf* heifer
treisio *vb* to force, to ravish, to violate, to oppress, to rape
treisiwr (-wyr) *nm* violator, oppressor; rapist
trem (-iau) *nf* sight, look, aspect
tremio *vb* to look, to gaze
trên (trenau) *nm* train
trenars, treners *npl* trainers
trennydd *adv* day after tomorrow
tres (-i) *nf* trace, chain; tress
tresbasu, tresmasu *vb* to trespass
tresglen *nf* thrush
treth (-i) *nf* rate; tax; **treth ffordd** road tax; **treth y pen** poll tax
trethadwy *adj* rateable, taxable
trethdalwr (-wyr) *nm* ratepayer
trethu *vb* to tax, to rate, to assess
trethwr (-wyr) *nm* taxer
treuliad *nm* digestion
treulio *vb* to wear, to consume; to spend; to digest

tri (*f* **tair**) *adj, nm* three
triagl *nm* treacle, balsam, balm
triawd (-au) *nm* trio
triban (-nau) *nm* triplet *(metre)*
tribiwnlys (-oedd) *nm* tribunal
tric (-iau) *nm* trick
tridiau *npl* three days
trigain *adj, nm* sixty
trigfa (trigfeydd), trigfan (-nau) *nf* dwelling-place, abode
trigiannol *adj* residentiary
trigiannu *vb* to reside, to dwell
trigiannydd (-ianwyr) *nm* resident
trigo *vb* to stay, to abide; to dwell; to die *(animals)*
trigolion *npl* inhabitants, dwellers
trimio *vb* to trim
trin¹ (-oedd) *nf* battle
trin² *vb* to handle; to treat; to dress; to till; to transact
trindod (-au) *nf* trinity
tringar *adj* skilful, tender
triniaeth (-au) *nf* treatment
trioedd *npl* triads
triongl (-au) *nm* triangle
trionglog *adj* triangular
triphlyg *adj* triple
trist *adj* sad, sorrowful
tristáu *vb* to sadden, to grieve
tristwch *nm* sadness, sorrow
triw *adj* loyal, faithful
tro (troeau, troeon) *nm* turn, twist; conversion
troad (-au) *nm* bend, turning; figure of speech
trobwll (-byllau) *nm* whirlpool
trobwynt (-iau) *nm* turning-point
trochfa (-feydd) *nf* plunge, immersion

trochi *vb* to dip, to plunge, to immerse; to soil
trochion *npl* lather, suds, foam
trochioni *vb* to lather, to foam
trochwr (-wyr) *nm* immerser, immersionist
troed (traed) *nmf* foot, base; leg; handle
troedfainc (-feinciau) *nf* footstool
troedfedd (-i) *nf* foot (=12 inches)
troedfeddyg *nm* chiropodist
troëdig *adj* turned, converted, perverse
tröedigaeth (-au) *nf* turning, conversion
troedio *vb* to foot, to tread, to trudge
troednodyn *nm* footnote
troednoeth *adj* barefoot, barefooted
troedwisg *nf* footwear
troedwst *nf* gout
troell (-au) *nf* wheel, spinning-wheel
troelli *vb* to spin; to twist, to wind
troellog *adj* winding, tortuous
troellwr (-wyr) *nm* disc-jockey
troetffordd (-ffyrdd) *nf* footway, footpath
troeth *nm* urine
trofa (-feydd) *nf* turn; bend, turning
trofan (-nau) *nf* tropic
trofannol *adj* tropical
trofaus *adj* perverse
trofwrdd (-fyrddau) *nm* turntable
trogen *see* **torogen**
trogylch (-au) *nm* orbit

219

troi

troi *vb* to turn, to revolve; to convert; to plough; **troi ymlaen** switch on

trol (-iau) *nf* cart

trolian, trolio *vb* to roll

troliwr (-wyr) *nm* carter

trom *adj f of* **trwm**

trôns *nm* underpants; trunks; **trôns bocsiwr** boxer shorts

tros *prep* over, for, instead of, on behalf of

trosadwy *adj* convertible

trosedd (-au) *nm* transgression, offence, crime

troseddol *adj* criminal

troseddu *vb* to transgress, to trespass, to offend

troseddwr (-wyr) *nm* transgressor, trespasser, offender; criminal

trosgais (trosgeisiau) *nm* converted try *(in rugby)*

trosglwyddiad *nm* transference, transfer

trosglwyddo *vb* to hand over, to transfer

trosgynnol *adj* transcendental

trosi *vb* to turn; to translate; to convert (a try)

trosiad (-au) *nm* translation; metaphor; conversion *(in rugby)*

trosodd *adv* over, beyond

trosol (-ion) *nm* lever, crow-bar, bar; staff

trostan (-au) *nf* pole

trotian *vb* to trot

trothwy (-au) *nm* threshold

trowr (-wyr) *nm* ploughman

trowsus (-au) *nm* trousers; **trowsus nofio** swimming trunks

trowynt (-oedd) *nm* whirlwind, tornado

truan (truain) (*f* **truanes**) *adj* poor, wretched, miserable ▸ *nm* (**trueiniaid**) wretch

trueni *nm* wretchedness; misery; pity

truenus *adj* wretched, miserable

trugaredd (-au) *nmf* mercy, compassion

trugarhau *vb* to have mercy, to take pity

trugarog *adj* merciful, compassionate

trugarowgrwydd *nm* mercifulness

trulliad (-iaid) *nm* butler, cupbearer

trum (-au, -iau) *nm* ridge

truth *nm* flattery; rigmarole

trwbl *nm* trouble

trwblo *vb* to trouble

trwch¹ *nm* thickness; **trwch y blewyn** hair's breadth

trwch² *adj* broken; unfortunate; wicked

trwchus *adj* thick

trwm (trymion) (*f* **trom**) *adj* heavy

trwnc (trynciau) *nm* trunk

trwodd *adv* through

trwsgl *adj* awkward, clumsy, bungling

trwsiad *nm* dress, attire

trwsiadus *adj* well-dressed, smart

trwsio *vb* to dress, to trim; to mend, to repair

trwsiwr (-wyr) *nm* mender, repairer

trwst *nm* noise, din, tumult

trwstan *adj* awkward, clumsy, untoward

trwstaneiddiwch *nm* awkwardness

trwy *prep* through, by, by means of

trwyadl *adj* thorough

trwydded (-au) *nf* leave, licence

trwyddedig *adj* licensed

trwyddedu *vb* to license

trwyn (-au) *nm* nose, snout; point, cape

trwyno *vb* to nose, to nuzzle, to sniff

trwynol *adj* nasal

trwynsur *adj* sour, morose

trwyth (-i) *nm* decoction, infusion, urine

trwytho *vb* to steep, to saturate, to imbue

trybedd, trybed *nf* tripod, trivet

trybelid *adj* bright, brilliant

trybestod *nm* commotion, bustle, fuss

trybini *nm* trouble, misfortune, misery

tryblith *nm* muddle, chaos

trychfil (-od) *nm* insect, animalcule

trychiad (-au) *nm* cutting, fracture, section

trychineb (-au) *nmf* disaster, calamity

trychinebus *adj* disastrous, calamitous

trychu *vb* to cut, to hew, to pierce, to lop

trydan *nm* electric fluid, electricity

trydaneg *nmf* electrical engineering

trydaniaeth *nf* electricity; thrill

trydanol *adj* electric, electrical

trydanu *vb* to electrify

trydar *vb* to chirp, to chatter ▶ *nm* chirping, twittering

trydydd (f trydedd) *adj* third

tryfer (-i) *nf* harpoon, trident

tryferu *vb* to spear, to harpoon

tryfesur *nm* diameter

tryfrith *adj* speckled; swarming, teeming

trylediad (-au) *nm* diffusion

tryledu *vb* to diffuse

tryloyw *adj* pellucid, transparent

tryloywder *nm* transparency

trylwyr *adj* thorough

trylwyredd *nm* thoroughness

trymaidd *adj* heavy, close, oppressive

trymder *nm* heaviness, drowsiness

trymfryd *nm* sadness, sorrow

trymhau *vb* to make or grow heavy

trymllyd *adj* heavy, close, oppressive

tryryw *adj* thoroughbred

trysor (-au) *nm* treasure

trysordy (-dai) *nm* treasure house

trysorfa (-feydd) *nf* treasury, fund

trysori *vb* to treasure

trysorlys *nm* treasury, exchequer

trysorydd (-ion) *nm* treasurer

trystio *vb* to make a noise; to trust

trystiog *adj* noisy, rowdy

trythyll *adj* wanton, lascivious

trythyllwch *nm* lasciviousness

trywanu *vb* to transfix, to stab, to pierce

trywel *nm* trowel

trywydd *nm* scent, trail

Tsiecaidd *adj* Czech

Tsieceg *nf* Czech

Tsieciad *nm* Czech

Tsiecoslofacia *nf* Czechoslovakia

t

Tsieina

Tsieina *nf* China
Tsieinead (-eaid) *nmf* Chinese person
Tsieineaidd *adj* Chinese
tsili *nm* chilli
tu *nm* side, part, direction
tua, tuag *prep* towards; about
tuchan *vb* to grumble, to groan, to murmur
tudalen (-nau) *nmf* page; **tudalen cartref, tudalen gartref, tudalen hafan** home page; **tudalen we** web page
tudded (-i) *nf* covering; pillowcase
tuedd¹ (-iadau) *nf* tendency, inclination
tuedd² (-au) *nm* district, region
tueddfryd *nm* inclination, bent
tueddol *adj* inclined, apt
tueddu *vb* to incline, to tend, to trend
tufewnol *adj* inward, internal
tulath (-au) *nf* beam, rafter
tun *nm* tinned
Tunisia *nf* Tunisia
tunnell (tunelli) *nf* ton; tun
turio *vb* to root up, to burrow, to delve
turn *nm* lathe
turniwr (-wyr) *nm* turner
turtur (-od) *nf* turtle-dove
tusw (-au) *nm* wisp, bunch
tuth (-iau) *nm* trot
tuthio *vb* to trot
twb (tybiau) *nm* tub
twca *nm* tuck-knife
twf *nm* growth
twffyn (twffiau) *nm* tuft
twlc (tylciau) *nm* sty
twlcio *vb* to horn, to butt, to gore

twlciog *adj* given to horning
twll (tyllau) *nm* hole
twmpath (-au) *nm* tump, hillock; bush; folk-dance
twndis (-au) *nm* funnel
twndra (-âu) *nm* tundra
twnffed (-i) *nm* funnel
twnnel (twnelau, twneli) *nm* tunnel; **Twnnel y Sianel** the Channel Tunnel
twp *adj* stupid, dull, obtuse
twpdra *nm* stupidity
twpsyn *nm* stupid person
twr (tyrrau) *nm* heap; group, crowd
twˆr (tyrau) *nm* tower
Twrc (Tyrciaid) *nm* Turk
Twrci *nf* Turkey
twrci (-ïod) *nm* turkey
twrch (tyrchod) *nm* hog; **twrch daear** mole
twrf (tyrfau) *nm* noise; *(pl)* thunder
twrist *nm* tourist
twrnai (-eiod) *nm* attorney, lawyer
twrw *nm* noise
twt¹ *excl* tut!
twt² *adj* tidy, neat, smart
twtio *vb* to tidy
twyll *nm* deceit, deception, fraud
twyllo *vb* to deceive, to cheat, to swindle
twyllodrus *adj* deceitful, false
twyllresymeg *nf* sophism
twyllresymiad (-au) *nm* sophistry
twyllwr (-wyr) *nm* deceiver
twym *adj* warm, hot, sultry
twymder, twymdra *nm* warmness, warmth
twymgalon *adj* warm-hearted

twymo, twymno vb to warm, to heat

twymyn (-au) nf fever; **y dwymyn goch** scarlet fever; **y dwymyn doben** mumps

twyn (-i) nm hill, hillock, knoll; bush

twysged nf lot, quantity

tŷ (tai, teiau) nm house; **tŷ pâr** semidetached (house)

tyaid (-eidiau) nm houseful

tyb (-iau) nmf opinion, notion, surmise

tybaco nm tobacco

tybed adv I wonder; is that so?

tybiaeth (-au) nf supposition

tybied, tybio vb to suppose, to think, to imagine

tybiedig adj supposed, putative

tycio vb to prosper, to succeed, to avail

tydi pron thou, thyself

tyddyn (-nod) nm (small) farm, holding

tyddynnwr (-ynwyr) nm smallholder

tyfadwy adj growing

tyfiant nm growth

tyfu vb to grow; **tyfu i fyny, tyfu lan** grow up

tyfwr (-wyr) nm grower

tynged nf destiny, fate

tyngedfennol adj fateful, fatal

tynghedu vb to destine, to fate; to adjure

tyngu vb to swear, to vow

tyngwr (-wyr) nm swearer

tylath see tulath

tyle nm slope, hill

tylino vb to knead; **tylino y corff** massage

tylinwr (-wyr) nm kneader, masseur

tylwyth (-au) nm household, family; **tylwyth teg** fairies

tyllog adj holey

tyllu vb to hole, to bore, to perforate, to pierce

tylluan (-od) nf owl

tyllwr (-wyr) nm borer

tymer (-herau) nf temper

tymestl (-hestloedd) nf tempest, storm

tymheredd nm temperature

tymherus adj temperate

tymhestlog adj tempestuous, stormy

tymhoraidd adj seasonable

tymhorol adj temporal

tymor (-horau) nm season; **tymor y gaeaf** wintertime

tymp nm (appointed) time, season

tympan (-au) nf drum; timbrel

tyn adj tight

tynder, tyndra nm tightness, tension

tyndro (tyndroeon) nm wrench

tyner adj tender, gentle

tyneru vb to make tender, to soften

tynerwch nm tenderness, gentleness

tynfa (-feydd) nf draw, attraction

tynfaen (-feini) nm loadstone, magnet

tynhau vb to tighten, to strain

tynnu vb to draw, to pull; to take off, to remove

tyno nm hollow; tenon

tyrchu vb to root up, to burrow

tyrchwr (-wyr) nm mole-catcher

223

tyrfa

tyrfa (-oedd) *nf* multitude, host, crowd
tyrfau *npl* thunder
tyrfedd (-au) *nm* turbulence, thunder
tyrfo, tyrfu *vb* to make a noise *or* commotion
tyrpant *nm* turpentine
tyrpeg *nm* turnpike
tyrru *vb* to heap, to amass; to crowd together
tyst (-ion) *nm* witness
tysteb (-au) *nf* testimonial
tystio *vb* to testify, to witness
tystiolaeth (-au) *nf* testimony, evidence
tystiolaethu *vb* to bear witness, to testify
tystlythyr (-au) *nm* testimonial
tystysgrif (-au) *nf* certificate
tywallt *vb* to pour, to shed, to spill
tywalltiad (-au) *nm* outpouring
tywarchen (tywyrch) *nf* sod, turf
tywel (-ion) *nm* towel
tywod *nm* sand
tywodfaen *nm* sandstone
tywodlyd, tywodog *adj* sandy
tywodyn *nm* grain of sand
tywydd *nm* weather
tywyll *adj* dark, obscure; blind
tywyllu *vb* to darken, to obscure
tywyllwch *nm* darkness
tywyn (-au) *nm* sea-shore, strand
tywynnu *vb* to shine
tywys *vb* to lead, to guide
tywysen (-nau, tywys) *nf* ear of corn
tywysog (-ion) *nm* prince
tywysogaeth (-au) *nf* principality
tywysogaidd *adj* princely
tywysoges (-au) *nf* princess
tywysydd (-ion) *nm* leader, guide

th u

theatr (**-au**) *nf* theatre
thema (**themâu**) *nf* theme
theorem (**-au**) *nf* theorem
theori (**-ïau**) *nf* theory
thermomedr *nm* thermometer
thesis (**-au**) *nm* thesis
thus *nm* frankincense

ubain *vb* to howl, to wail, to moan;
  to sob
uchaf *adj* uppermost, highest
uchafbwynt (**-iau**) *nm* climax;
  zenith
uchafiaeth *nf* supremacy;
  ascendancy
uchafion *npl* heights
uchafrif (**-au**) *nm* maximum
uchafswm *nm* maximum
uchder *nm* height; top
uchdwr *nm* storey
uchel *adj* high, lofty; uppish; loud
uchelbwynt (**-iau**) *nm* highlight
uchelder (**-au**) *nm* highness,
  height
ucheldir (**-oedd**) *nm* highland
uchelfryd *adj* high-minded
uchelgais *nf* ambition
uchelgeisiol *adj* ambitious
uchelion *npl* heights
uchelradd *adj* of high degree,
  superior

uchelseinydd (-ion) *nm* loudspeaker

uchelwr (-wyr) *nm* gentleman, nobleman

uchelwydd *nm* mistletoe

uchgapten (-teiniaid) *nm* major

uchod *adv* above

UDA *n* US, USA

udo *vb* to howl

udd *nm* lord

UE *nf* EU, European Union

ufudd *adj* obedient, humble

ufudd-dod *nm* obedience, humility

ufuddhau *vb* to obey

uffern *nf* hell

uffernol *adj* infernal, hellish

ugain (ugeiniau) *adj, nm* twenty, score

Uganda *nf* Uganda

Ulster *nf* Ulster

ulw *coll n* ashes, powder ▸ *adv* utterly

un *adj* one, only; same ▸ *coll n* (**-au**) one, unit

unawd (-au) *nm* solo

unawdydd (-wyr) *nm* soloist

unben (-iaid, unbyn) *nm* sovereign lord, despot

unbenaethol *adj* despotic

unbennaeth *nf* sovereignty, despotism

undeb (-au) *nm* unity; union; **yr Undeb Ewropeaidd** the European Union; **yr Undeb Sofietaidd** the Soviet Union

undebaeth *nf* unionism

undebol *adj* united, union

undebwr (-wyr) *nm* unionist

undod (-au) *nm* unity; unit

Undodaidd *adj* Unitarian

Undodiaeth *nf* Unitarianism

Undodwr (-wyr, -iaid) *nm* Unitarian

undonedd *nm* monotony

undonog *adj* monotonous

uned (-au) *nf* unit

unedig *adj* united

unfan *nm* same place

unfarn *adj* unanimous

unfryd, unfrydol *adj* unanimous

unfrydedd *nm* unanimity

unffurf *adj* uniform

unffurfiaeth *nf* uniformity

uniad *nm* union

uniaethu *vb* to identify

uniaith *adj* monoglot

uniawn *adj* straight; right, upright; just

unig *adj* sole, only; alone, lonely

unigedd *nm* loneliness, solitude

unigol *adj* singular; individual ▸ *nm* (**-ion**) individual

unigoliaeth *nf* individuality

unigolrwydd *nm* individuality

unigolyn *nm* individual

unigrwydd *nm* loneliness, solitude

union *adj* straight, direct; just, exact

uniondeb *nm* straightness; rectitude

uniongred *adj* orthodox

uniongrededd *nmf* orthodoxy

uniongyrch, uniongyrchol *adj* immediate, direct

unioni *vb* to straighten; to rectify; to make for

unionsgwar *adj* perpendicular

unionsyth *adj* straight, direct; erect

unllygeidiog *adj* one-eyed

unman *adv* anywhere
unnos *adj* of one night
uno *vb* to join, to unit, to amalgamate
unochrog *adj* unilateral, biased
unodl *adj* of the same rhyme
unol *adj* united; **yr Unol Daleithiau** the United States
unoli *vb* to unify
unoliaeth *nf* unity, oneness, identity
unplyg *adj* of one fold; folio; simple, ingenuous
unplygrwydd *nm* sincerity
unrhyw *adj* same; any
unrhywiol *adj* unisexual
unsain *adj* unison; **yn unsain** in unison
unsill *adj* monosyllabic
unswydd *adj* of one purpose
unwaith *adv* once
unwedd *adj* like ▸ *adv* likewise
urdd (-au) *nf* order; rank
urddas (-au) *nm* dignity, honour
urddasol *adj* dignified, noble
urddo *vb* to ordain, to confer degree *or* rank
us *nm* chaff
ust *excl*, *nm* hush
ustus (-iaid) *nm* justice, magistrate
usuriaeth *nf* usury
utganu *vb* to sound a trumpet
utganwr (-wyr) *nm* trumpeter
utgorn (-gyrn) *nm* trumpet
uwch *adj* higher ▸ *prep* above, over
uwchbridd (-oedd) *nm* topsoil
uwchgapten (-iaid) *nm* major
uwchradd *nm*, *adj* superior

uwchsonig *adj* ultrasonic, supersonic
uwd *nm* porridge

u

W

wadi (-iau) *nm* wadi
wado *vb* to beat, to thrash
wagen (-ni) *nf* truck, waggon
waldio *vb* to wallop, to beat
warws (warysau) *nm* warehouse
wats (-iau) *nm* watch
wedi *prep* after ▸ *adv* afterwards
wedyn *adv* afterwards, then
weiren *nf* wire
weirio, weiro *vb* to wire
weithian, weithion *adv* now, now at length
weithiau *adv* sometimes
wel *excl* well
wele *excl* behold, lo
wermod *nf* wormwood
wfft *excl* fie, for shame
wfftio *vb* to cry fie, to flout, to scout
wiced (-i) *nf* wicket
wicedwr (-wyr) *nm* wicket-keeper
widw *nf* widow
wlser (-au) *nm* ulcer
wmbredd *nm* abundance

wraniwm *nm* uranium
wrth *prep* by; with; to; because, since
wy (-au) *nm* egg
wybr (-au), wybren (-nau, -nydd) *nf* sky; cloud
wybrol *adj* ethereal
wyf *vb* I am
wygell (-oedd) *nf* ovary
wylo *vb* to weep, to cry
wylofain *vb* to wail, to weep ▸ *nm* wailing
wylofus *adj* wailing, doleful, tearful
ŵyn *see* oen
wyna *vb* to lamb
wyneb (-au) *nm* face, surface; front
wyneb-ddalen *nf* title-page
wynebgaled *adj* barefaced, impudent
wyneblun (-iau) *nm* frontispiece
wynebu *vb* to face, to front
wynepryd *nm* countenance
wynwyn *npl* onions
ŵyr (wyrion) *nm* grandchild, grandson
wyres *nf* granddaughter
wysg *nm* track; **yn wysg ei gefn** backwards
wystrys *npl* oysters
wyth (-au) *adj, nm* eight
wythawd (-au, -odau) *nf* octave
wythblyg *adj* octavo
wythfed *adj* eighth
wythnos (-au) *nf* week
wythnosol (-ion) *adj* weekly
wythnosolyn (-olion) *nm* weekly paper
wythongl (-au) *nf* octagon
wythwr (-wyr) *nm* number eight (in rugby)

y

y¹, yr, 'r *adj* the

y², yr *conj* that

ych (-en) *nm* ox

ychwaith *adv* (nor) either, neither

ychwaneg *nm* more

ychwanegiad (-au) *nm* addition

ychwanegol *adj* additional

ychwanegu *vb* to add, to augment, to increase

ychydig *adj, adv, nm* little, few

ŷd (ydau) *nm* corn

ydfran *nf* rook

ydwyf *vb* I am

ydys *vb*: **yr ydys yn disgwyl** it is expected

ydyw *vb* is, are

yfed *vb* to drink; to absorb

yfory *adv* tomorrow

yfwr (-wyr) *nm* drinker

yfflon *npl* (*nm* **yfflyn**) shivers, pieces, bits ▶ *adj* highly annoyed

yng *prep* in **yn**

yngan, ynganu *vb* to utter, to speak

ynghyd *adv* together

ynghylch *prep* about, concerning

ynglŷn â *prep* in connection with

ym *prep* in **yn**

ym- *prefix usu. reflexive or reciprocal*

yma *adv* here, in this place; this

ymadael, ymadaw *vb* to depart

ymadawedig *adj* departed, deceased

ymadawiad *nm* departure; decease

ymadawol *adj* farewell, valedictory

ymado *vb* to depart

ymadrodd (-ion) *nm* speech, saying, expression

ymadroddus *adj* eloquent

ymaddasu *vb* to adjust, to adapt

ymaelodi *vb* to become a member, to join

ymaelyd, ymafael, ymaflyd *vb* to take hold

ymageru *vb* to evaporate

ymagor *vb* to open, to unfold, to expand

ymagweddiad (-au) *nm* demeanour, attitude

ymaith *adv* away, hence

ymarfer *vb* to practise, to exercise ▶ *nf* (**-ion**) practice, exercise

ymarferiad (-au) *nm* exercise

ymarhous *adj* dilatory; long-suffering, patient

ymaros *vb* to bear with, to endure ▶ *nm* long-suffering, patience

ymarweddiad *nm* conduct, behaviour

ymatal *vb* to forbear, to refrain, to abstain

ymateb *vb* to answer, to respond, to correspond

ymbalfalu *vb* to grope

ymbaratoi *vb* to get oneself ready

ymbarél *nm* umbrella

ymbelydredd *nm* radiation

ymbelydrol *adj* radioactive

ymbellhau *vb* to go further away

ymbil¹ (-iau) *nm* supplication, entreaty

ymbil², ymbilio *vb* to implore, to beseech, to entreat

ymboeni *vb* to take pains

ymborth *nm* food, sustenance

ymbortheg *nf* dietetics

ymborthi *vb* to feed

ymbriodi *vb* to marry; to intermarry

ymbwyllo *vb* to pause, to reflect

ymchwelyd *vb* to turn, to return; to overturn

ymchwil *nf* search, research, quest

ymchwiliad (-au) *nm* investigation

ymchwilio *vb* to research

ymchwydd (-iadau) *nm* swelling, surge

ymchwyddo *vb* to swell; to surge

ymdaith *vb* to journey, to march ▸ *nf* (**-deithiau**) journey, march

ymdebygu *vb* to grow like; to resemble

ymdeimlad *nm* feeling, sense

ymdeimlo *vb* to feel; to be conscious of

ymdeithio *vb* to travel, to journey; to sojourn

ymdoddi *vb* to melt, to become dissolved

ymdopi *vb* to manage

ymdrech (-ion) *nfm* effort, endeavour, struggle

ymdrechgar *adj* striving, energetic

ymdrechu *vb* to wrestle; to strive, to endeavour

ymdrin *vb* to treat, to deal with

ymdriniaeth *nf* treatment; discussion

ymdrochi *vb* to bathe

ymdrochwr (-wyr) *nm* bather

ymdroi *vb* to linger, to loiter, to dawdle

ymdrybaeddu *vb* to wallow

ymdynghedu *vb* to vow

ymddangos *vb* to appear, to seem

ymddangosiad (-au) *nm* appearance

ymddangosiadol *adj* seeming, apparent

ymddarostwng *vb* to submit

ymddarostyngiad *nm* humiliation, submission

ymddatod *vb* to dissolve

ymddeol *vb* to resign, to retire

ymddeoliad (-au) *nm* retirement; **ymddeoliad cynnar** early retirement

ymddiddan *vb* to talk, to converse ▸ *nm* (**-ion**) talk, conversation

ymddihatru *vb* to divest, to undress

ymddiheuriad (-au) *nm* apology

ymddiheuro *vb* to apologize

ymddiosg *vb* to strip, to undress

ymddiried *vb* to trust ▸ *nm* trust, confidence

ymddiriedaeth *nf* trust, confidence

ymddiriedolwr (-wyr) *nm* trustee

ymddiswyddo *vb* to resign

ymddwyn *vb* to behave, to act

ymddygiad (-au) *nm* behaviour, conduct; *(pl)* actions

ymddyrchafu *vb* to exalt oneself; to rise, to ascend

ymegnïo *vb* to exert oneself

ymehangu *vb* to become enlarged, to expand

ymennydd (ymenyddiau) *nm* brain

ymenyn *nm* butter

ymerawdwr (-wyr) *nm* emperor

ymerodraeth (-au) *nf* empire

ymerodres (-au) *nf* empress

ymerodrol *adj* imperial

ymesgusodi *vb* to excuse oneself, to apologize

ymestyn *vb* to stretch, to extend, to reach

ymestyniad (-au) *nm* extension

ymestynnol *adj* extensive

ymfalchïo *vb* to pride oneself

ymfodloni *vb* to acquiesce

ymfudo *vb* to emigrate

ymfudwr (-wyr) *nm* emigrant

ymffrost *nm* boast

ymffrostio *vb* to boast, to vaunt

ymffrostiwr (-wyr) *nm* boaster

ymgadw *vb* to keep oneself (from), to forbear

ymgais *nmf* effort, attempt

ymgasglu *vb* to gather together

ymgecru *vb* to quarrel, to wrangle

ymgeisio *vb* to try, to apply; to aim at

ymgeisydd (-wyr) *nm* applicant, candidate

ymgeledd *nm* succour, care

ymgeleddu *vb* to cherish, to succour

ymgeleddwr (-wyr) *nm* succourer; tutor, guardian

ymgilio *vb* to retreat, to recede

ymgiprys *vb, nm* to scramble

ymglymu *vb* to involve, to bind together

ymglywed *vb* to feel (oneself), to be inclined

ymgnawdoliad *nm* incarnation

ymgodymu *vb* to wrestle, to fight

ymgofleidio *vb* to mutually embrace

ymgom (-ion) *nf* chat, conversation

ymgomio *vb* to chat, to converse

ymgorffori *vb* to incorporate

ymgorfforiad *nm* embodiment

ymgreinio *vb* to prostrate oneself; to grovel

ymgroesi *vb* to cross oneself; to beware

ymgryfhau *vb* to strengthen oneself, to be strong

ymgrymu *vb* to bow down, to stoop

ymguddfa *nf* shelter, hiding-place

ymguddio *vb* to hide (oneself)

ymgydio *vb* to copulate

ymgydnabod *vb* to acquaint oneself

ymgyfathrachu *vb* to have dealings with

ymgyfeillachu *vb* to associate

ymgyfoethogi *vb* to get rich

ymgynghori *vb* to consult, to confer

ymgynghoriad *nm* consultation

y

231

ymgymeriad (-au) *nm* undertaking

ymgymryd *vb* to undertake

ymgynefino *vb* to become familiar, to get used to

ymgynnal *vb* to bear up; to support oneself; to control oneself

ymgynnull *vb* to assemble, to congregate

ymgyrch (-oedd) *nmf* campaign, expedition

ymgyrraedd *vb* to stretch, to strive after

ymgysegriad *nm* devotion, consecration

ymgysegru *vb* to devote oneself

ymhél *vb* to meddle

ymhelaethu *vb* to abound; to enlarge

ymhell *adv* far, afar

ymhellach *adv* further, furthermore

ymherodr *see* **ymerawdwr**

ymhlith *prep* among

ymhlyg *adj* implicit

ymhoelyd *vb* to overturn, to topple

ymhoffi *vb* to take delight; to boast

ymholi *vb* to inquire

ymholiad (-au) *nm* inquiry

ymhonni *vb* to lay claim to, to pretend

ymhonnwr (-honwyr) *nm* pretender

ymhŵedd *vb* to beseech, to implore, to crave

ymhyfrydu *vb* to delight (oneself)

ymiacháu *vb* to become healed, to get well

ymlacio *vb* to relax

ymladd *vb* to fight ▸ *nm* (**-au**) fighting

ymlâdd *vb* to kill oneself (with exertion), to tire oneself out; **wedi ymlâdd** dead beat

ymladdfa (-feydd) *nf* fight

ymladdgar *adj* pugnacious, warlike

ymladdwr (-wyr) *nm* fighter, combatant

ymlaen *adv* on, onward

ymlafnio *vb* to toil, to strive, to struggle

ymlawenhau *vb* to rejoice

ymledu *vb* to spread, to expand

ymlenwi *vb* to fill oneself

ymlid *vb* to pursue, to chase

ymlidiwr (-wyr) *nm* pursuer

ymlonyddu *vb* to grow calm *or* still

ymlosgiad *nm* combustion

ymlusgiad (-iaid) *nm* reptile

ymlusgo *vb* to creep, to crawl

ymlwybro *vb* to make one's way

ymlyniad *nm* attachment

ymlynu *vb* to attach, to adhere, to cleave (to)

ymlynwr (-wyr) *nm* adherent

Ymneilltuaeth *nf* Nonconformity

ymneilltuo *vb* to retire

Ymneilltuol *adj* Nonconformist

Ymneilltuwr (-wyr) *nm* Nonconformist

ymnesáu *vb* to approach, to draw near

ymochel, ymochelyd *vb* to shelter; to beware

ymod, ymodi *vb* to move, to stir

ymofyn *vb* to ask, to inquire, to seek ▸ *nm* (**-ion**) inquiry

ymofynnydd (**-ofynwyr**) *nm* inquirer

ymolchfa (**-feydd**) *nf* wash; lavatory

ymolchi *vb* to wash oneself, to bathe

ymollwng *vb* to sink, to drop, to give way, to collapse

ymorchestu *vb* to strive, to labour

ymorffwys *vb* to rest, to repose

ymorol *vb* to seek; to take care, to attend to, to see to it

ymosod *vb* to attack, to assail, to assault

ymosodiad (**-au**) *nm* attack, assault

ymosodol *adj* aggressive, offensive, forward

ymosodwr (**-wyr**) *nm* attacker, assailant

ymostwng *vb* to stoop; to humble oneself; to submit

ymostyngar *adj* submissive

ymostyngiad *nm* submission

ympryd (**-ion**) *nm* fast

ymprydio *vb* to fast

ymprydiwr (**-wyr**) *nm* faster

ymrafael (**-ion**) *nm* quarrel, contention

ymrafaelgar *adj* quarrelsome, contentious

ymraniad (**-au**) *nm* division, schism

ymrannu *vb* to part, to divide, to separate

ymrannwr (**-ranwyr**) *nm* separatist

ymreolaeth *nf* self-government, Home Rule

ymrestru *vb* to enlist

ymresymiad (**-au**) *nm* reasoning, argument

ymresymu *vb* to reason, to argue

ymresymwr (**-wyr**) *nm* reasoner

ymrithio *vb* to appear

ymroad *nm* application, devotion

ymroddedig *adj* devoted

ymroddgar *adj* of great application

ymroddi, ymroi *vb* to apply *or* devote oneself; to yield *or* resign oneself, to surrender, to do one's best

ymroddiad *nm* application, devotion

ymron *adv* nearly, almost

ymrous *adj* assiduous

ymrwyfo *vb* to struggle, to toss about

ymrwygo *vb* to tear, to burst

ymrwymiad (**-au**) *nm* engagement

ymrwymo *vb* to commit *or* bind oneself

ymrysongar *adj* contentious

ymryson *vb* to contend, to strive ▶ *nm* (**-au**) contention, strife, rivalry

ymsefydlu *vb* to establish oneself, to settle

ymsefydlwr (**-wyr**) *nm* settler

ymserchu *vb* to cherish, to dote

ymson *vb* to soliloquize ▶ *nm* (**-au**) soliloquy

ymsuddiant *nm* subsidence

ymswyno *vb* to cross oneself; to beware

ymsymud *vb* to move

ymuno *vb* to join, to unite

ymwacâd *nm* kenosis

ymwacáu *vb* to empty oneself

ymwadiad *nm* denial, abnegation

ymwadu *vb* to deny (oneself); to renounce

ymwahanu *vb* to part, to divide, to separate

ymwahanwr (-wyr) *nm* separatist

ymwared *nm* deliverance

ymwasgu *vb* to embrace, to hug

ymweithydd (-ion) *nm* reactor

ymweld *vb* to visit

ymweliad (-au) *nm* visit, visitation

ymwelwr, ymwelydd (ymwelwyr) *nm* visitor, visitant; **canolfan ymwelwyr** visitor centre

ymwneud *vb* to involve

ymwrando *vb* to hearken

ymwroli *vb* to take heart, to be of good courage

ymwrthod *vb* to abstain; to renounce

ymwrthodiad *nm* abstinence

ymwthgar *adj* pushing, obtrusive

ymwthio *vb* to push oneself, to obtrude

ymwthiol *adj* obtrusive, intrusive

ymwybodol *adj* conscious

ymwybyddiaeth *nf* consciousness

ymwylltio *vb* to fly into a passion

ymyl (-au, -on) *nmf* edge, border, margin

ymylu *vb* to border

ymylwe *nf* selvedge

ymyrgar *adj* meddlesome, officious

ymyrraeth¹, ymyrru, ymrryd *vb* to meddle, to interfere

ymyrraeth² *nf* interference

ymyrrwr (-yrwyr) *nm* meddler

ymyrryd *vb* to meddle

ymysg *prep* among, amid

ymysgaroedd *npl* bowels

ymysgwyd *vb* to bestir oneself

yn¹ *prep* in, at, into; for *(also introduces verb-nouns)*

yn²

yna *adv* there; then; thereupon; that

ynad (-on) *nm* judge, justice, magistrate

yn awr *adv* now, at present

yndeintiad (-au) *nm* indentation

ynfyd (-ion) *adj* foolish, rash

ynfydrwydd *nm* foolishness, folly

ynfydu *vb* to rave, to be mad

ynfytyn (-fydion) *nm* fool, madman

ynni *nm* energy, vigour; **ynni haul, ynni'r haul** solar power

yno *adv* there

yntau *pron* he (on his part), he also

ynteu, ynte *conj* or, or else, otherwise; then

Ynyd *nm* Shrovetide

ynys (-oedd) *nf* island, river meadow; **Ynys Cyprus** Cyprus; **yr Ynysoedd Dedwydd** the Canary Islands

ynysfor (-oedd) *nm* archipelago

ynysol *adj* island, insular

ynysu *vb* to insulate

ynyswr (-wyr) *nm* islander

ynysydd (-ion) *nm* insulator

yr *see* y

yrŵan *adv* now

yrhawg *adv* for a long time (to come)

ys *vb* it is ▶ *conj* as

ysbaddu *vb* to castrate

ysbaid (-beidiau) *nfm* space (of time)

ysbail (-beiliau) *nf* spoil, plunder

ysbardun *nmf* spur
ysbarduno *vb* to spur
ysbeidiol *adj* occasional, intermittent
ysbeilio *vb* to spoil, to plunder
ysbeiliwr (-wyr) *nm* spoiler, robber
ysbienddrych (-au) *nm* spying-glass
ysbïo *vb* to spy, to look
ysbïwr (ysbïwyr) *nm* spy
ysblander *nm* splendour
ysblennydd *adj* splendid
ysbonc (-iau) *nf* jump, bound; spurt
ysboncio *vb* to jump, to bounce; to spurt, to splash
ysborion *npl* cast-offs
ysbrigyn *nm* sprig, twig
ysbryd (-ion, -oedd) *nm* spirit, ghost
ysbrydegaeth *nf* spiritualism
ysbrydegol *adj* spiritualistic
ysbrydegydd (-ion) *nm* spiritualist
ysbrydiaeth *nf* encouragement, inspiration
ysbrydol *adj* spiritual; high-spirited
ysbrydoli *vb* to spiritualize; to inspire; to inspirit
ysbrydoliaeth *nf* inspiration
ysbwng *nm* sponge
ysbwrial, ysbwriel *nm* rubbish, refuse
ysbwylio *vb* to spoil
ysbyty (-tai) *nm* hospital; hospice; **ysbyty'r meddwl** psychiatric hospital
ysfa (-feydd) *nf* itching; hankering
ysg- *see* **sg-**
ysgadan *npl (nm* **-enyn)** herrings
ysgafala *adj* secure, careless, free

ysgafn *adj* light ▶ *nm* stack
ysgafnder *nm* lightness, levity
ysgafnhau, ysgafnu *vb* to lighten
ysgafnu *vb* to heap, to pile
ysgall *npl (nf* **-en)** thistles
ysgar(u) *vb* to divorce
ysgariad *nm* separation, divorce
ysgariadiaeth *nf* separation, divorce
ysgarlad *nm* scarlet
ysgarmes (-oedd, -au) *nf* skirmish; punch-up
ysgaru *vb* to part, to separate, to divorce
ysgatfydd *adv* perhaps, peradventure
ysgathru *vb* to spread, to scatter
ysgaw *npl (nf* **-en)** elder (tree)
ysgeintio *vb* to sprinkle
ysgeler *adj* wicked, villainous, infamous
ysgerbwd (-bydau) *nm* skeleton, carcase
ysgithr (-edd) *nm* tusk, fang
ysgithrog *adj* fanged, tusked; craggy, rugged
ysgiw (-ion) *nf* settle
ysglefrio *vb* to slide (on ice); to skate
ysglyfaeth (-au) *nf* prey, spoil; carrion, filth
ysglyfaethus *adj* of prey; rapacious
ysgogi *vb* to move, to stir; to motivate
ysgogiad (-au) *nm* movement, motion
ysgogol *adj* motive
ysgol¹ (-ion) *nf* school; schooling; **ysgol breswyl** boarding school;

235

ysgol fach infant school; **ysgol feithrin** nursery school; **ysgol fonedd** public school; **ysgol ganolraddol** middle school
ysgol² (**-ion**) *nf* ladder
ysgoldy (**-dai**) *nm* schoolhouse, schoolroom
ysgolfeistr (**-i, -iaid**) *nm* schoolmaster
ysgolfeistres (**-i**) *nf* schoolmistress
ysgolhaig (**-heigion**) *nm* scholar
ysgolheictod *nm* scholarship
ysgolheigaidd *adj* scholarly
ysgolor (**-ion**) *nm* scholar
ysgoloriaeth (**-au**) *nf* scholarship
ysgorpion (**-au**) *nm* scorpion
Ysgotyn (**-gotiaid**) *nm* Scot, Scotsman
ysgrafell (**-od, -i**) *nf* scraper; curry-comb
ysgrafellu *vb* to scrape, to curry
ysgraff (**-au**) *nf* boat, barge, ferry-boat
ysgraffinio *vb* to scarify, to graze, to abrade
ysgrech (**-feydd**) *nf* scream, shriek
ysgrechian, ysgrechin *vb* to scream, to shriek
ysgrepan (**-au**) *nf* wallet, scrip
ysgrif (**-au**) *nf* writing, article, essay
ysgrifbin (**-nau**) *nm* pen
ysgrifell (**au**) *nf* pen
ysgrifen, ysgrifeniad (**ysgrifeniadau**) *nf* writing
ysgrifennu *vb* to write
ysgrifennwyr (**-enwyr**) *nm* writer
ysgrifennydd (**-enyddion**) *nm* scribe, secretary
ysgrifenyddiaeth *nf* secretaryship

ysgriw (**-iau**) *nf* screw
ysgriwio *vb* to screw
ysgrwbio *vb* to scrub
ysgryd *nm* shiver
ysgrythur (**-au**) *nf* scripture
ysgrythurol *adj* scriptural
ysgrythurwr (**-wyr**) *nm* scripturist
ysgub (**-au**) *nf* sheaf; broom
ysgubo *vb* to sweep
ysgubol *adj* sweeping
ysgubor (**-iau**) *nf* barn, granary
ysgubwr (**-wyr**) *nm* sweeper, sweep
ysgutor (**-ion**) *nm* executor
ysguthan (**-od**) *nf* wood-pigeon; jade
ysgwâr *adj, nf* square
ysgwario *vb* to square
ysgŵd *nm* jerk, toss, fling, shove
ysgwïer (**ysgwieriaid**) *nm* squire
ysgwrfa *nf* scouring, lathering
ysgwrio *vb* to scour, to scrub; to lather
ysgwyd *vb* to shake; to flutter; to wag
ysgwydd (**-au**) *nf* shoulder
ysgwyddo *vb* to shoulder, to jostle
ysgydwad *nm* shaking, shake
ysgyfaint *npl* lungs, lights
ysgyfarnog (**-od**) *nf* hare
ysgymun *adj* excommunicate, accursed
ysgymundod *nm* excommunication, ban
ysgymuno *vb* to excommunicate
ysgyrion *npl* staves, splinters, shivers
ysgyrnygu *vb* to grind the teeth, to snarl
ysgytiad (**-au**) *nm* shock

ysgytio *vb* to shake violently, to shock

ysgytiol *adj* shocking

ysgythru *vb* to cut, to carve; to prune

ysictod *nm* contusion; sprain

ysig *adj* bruised, sore, sprained

ysigo *vb* to bruise, to crush; to sprain

yslotian *vb* to dabble, to tipple

ysmala *adj* droll, funny, amusing

ysmaldod *nm* fun, drollery

ysmalio *vb* to joke, to jest

ysmaliwr (-wyr) *nm* joker, wit

ysmotyn (ysmotiau) *nm* spot

ysmwddio *vb* to iron

ysmygu *vb* to smoke (tobacco)

ysmygwr (-wyr) *nm* smoker

ysol *adj* consuming, devouring; corrosive

yst- *see also* **st-**

ystabl (-au) *nf* stable

ystad (-au) *nf* state; estate; furlong

ystadegau *npl* statistics

ystadegol *adj* statistical

ystadegydd (-ion) *nm* statistician

ystafell (-oedd) *nf* chamber, room; **ystafell fyw** living room; **ystafell molchi** bathroom

ystalwyn (-i) *nm* stallion

ystanc (-iau) *nm* stake, bracket

ystarn (-au) *nf* stern

ystelcian *vb* to skulk, to loaf, to loiter

ystelciwr (-wyr) *nm* loafer, loiterer

ystên (-enau) *nf* pitcher, ewer, milk-can

ystinos *nm* asbestos

ystiwart (-wardiaid) *nm* steward

ystlum (-od) *nm* bat

ystlys (-au) *nf* side, flank

ystlyswr (-wyr) *nm* linesman

ystod (-ion) *nf* course; swath; **yn ystod** during

ystof *nmf* warp

ystofi *vb* to warp; to weave, to plan

ystôl (-olion) *nf* stool, chair

ystôr (-orau) *nm* store, abundance

ystordy (-dai) *nm* storehouse, warehouse

ystorfa (-feydd) *nf* store, storehouse

ystorio *vb* to store

ystoriwr (-iwyr) *nm* storyteller

ystorm (-ydd) *nf* storm

ystormus *adj* stormy

ystrad (-au) *nfm* vale, flat

ystranc (-iau) *nf* trick

ystrancio *vb* to play tricks; to jib

ystrodur (-iau) *nf* cart-saddle

ystryd (ystrydoedd) *nf* street

ystrydebol *adj* stereotyped

ystryw (-iau) *nf* wile, craft, ruse

ystrywgar *adj* wily, crafty

ystum (-iau) *nmf* bend; form; posture; *(pl)* grimaces

ystumio *vb* to bend, to distort; to pose

ystumog (-au) *nf* stomach

ystŵr *nm* stir, noise, bustle, fuss

Ystwyll *nm* Epiphany

ystwyrian *vb* to stretch and yawn, to stir

ystwyth *adj* flexible, pliant, supple

ystwythder *nm* flexibility, pliancy

ystwytho *vb* to make flexible; to bend, to soften

ystyfnig *adj* obstinate, stubborn

ystyfnigo *vb* to behave obstinately

ystyfnigrwydd *nm* obstinacy

ystyr (-on) *nmf* sense, meaning
ystyrgar *adj* thoughtful,
meditative
ystyriaeth (-au) *nf* consideration,
heed
ystyried *vb* to consider, to regard,
to heed
ystyriol *adj* mindful, heedful
ysu *vb* to eat, to consume; to
hanker; to itch
yswain (-weiniaid) *nm* esquire
yswil *adj* shy, bashful, timid
yswildod *nm* shyness, bashfulness
yswiriant *nm* insurance
yswirio *vb* to insure
ysywaeth *adv* more's the pity
yw¹ *vb* is, are
yw² *npl* (*nf*-**en**) yew

GRAMADEG Y GYMRAEG
WELSH GRAMMAR

Contents

Cynnwys

NUMBERS/RHIFAU

There are two systems of counting in Welsh: the traditional method (based on units of 20) and the modern method (based on units of 10). It is useful to be familiar with the traditional method for telling the time and for giving dates. Schools use the modern method for mathematics.

Traditional forms		Modern forms
dim	0	dim
un	1	un
dau	2	dau
tri	3	tri
pedwar	4	pedwar
pump	5	pump
chwech	6	chwech
saith	7	saith
wyth	8	wyth
naw	9	naw
deg	10	deg
un ar ddeg	11	un deg un
deuddeg	12	un deg dau
tri ar ddeg	13	un deg tri
pedwar ar ddeg	14	un deg pedwar
pymtheg	15	un deg pump
un ar bymtheg	16	un deg chwech
dau ar bymtheg	17	un deg saith
deunaw	18	un deg wyth
pedwar ar bymtheg	19	un deg naw
ugain	20	dau ddeg
un ar hugain	21	dau ddeg un
dau ar hugain	22	dau ddeg dau
tri ar hugain	23	dau ddeg tri
pedwar ar hugain	24	dau ddeg pedwar
pump ar hugain	25	dau ddeg pump

chwech ar hugain	26	dau ddeg chwech
saith ar hugain	27	dau ddeg saith
wyth ar hugain	28	dau ddeg wyth
naw ar hugain	29	dau ddeg naw
deg ar hugain	30	tri deg
un ar ddeg ar hugain	31	tri deg un
deuddeg ar hugain	32	tri deg dau
tri ar ddeg ar hugain	33	tri deg tri
pedwar ar ddeg ar hugain	34	tri deg pedwar
pymtheg ar hugain	35	tri deg pump
un ar bymtheg ar hugain	36	tri deg chwech
dau ar bymtheg ar hugain	37	tri deg saith
deunaw ar hugain	38	tri deg wyth
pedwar ar bymtheg ar hugain	39	tri deg naw
deugain	40	pedwar deg
hanner cant	50	pum deg
cant	100	cant
mil	1000	mil
miliwn	1 000 000	miliwn

DATES/DYDDIADAU

1st	1af	y cyntaf
2nd	2il	yr ail
3rd	3ydd	y trydydd
4th	4ydd	y pedwerydd
5th	5ed	y pumed
6th	6ed	y chweched
7th	7fed	y seithfed
8th	8fed	yr wythfed
9th	9fed	y nawfed
10th	10fed	y degfed
11th	11eg	yr unfed ar ddeg
12th	12fed	y deuddegfed
13th	13eg	y trydydd ar ddeg
14th	14eg	y pedwerydd ar ddeg
15th	15fed	y pymthegfed
16th	16eg	yr unfed ar bymtheg
17th	17eg	yr ail ar bymtheg
18th	18fed	y deunawfed
19th	19eg	y pedwerydd ar bymtheg
20th	20fed	yr ugeinfed
21st	21ain	yr unfed ar hugain
22nd	22ain	yr ail ar hugain
23rd	23ain	y trydydd ar hugain
24th	24ain	y pedwerydd ar hugain
25th	25ain	y pumed ar hugain
26th	26ain	y chweched ar hugain
27th	27ain	y seithfed ar hugain
28th	28ain	yr wythfed ar hugain
29th	29ain	y nawfed ar hugain
30th	30ain	y degfed ar hugain
31st	31ain	yr unfed ar ddeg ar hugain

DAYS OF THE WEEK

Monday
Tuesday
Wednesday
Thursday
Friday
Saturday
Sunday

DYDDIAU'R WYTHNOS

Dydd Llun
Dydd Mawrth
Dydd Mercher
Dydd Iau
Dydd Gwener
Dydd Sadwrn
Dydd Sul

MONTHS OF THE YEAR

January
February
March
April
May
June
July
August
September
October
November
December

MISOEDD Y FLWYDDYN

Ionawr
Chwefror
Mawrth
Ebrill
Mai
Mehefin
Gorffennaf
Awst
Medi
Hydref
Tachwedd
Rhagfyr

TIME

What time is it?

It's ...

one o'clock
two o'clock
three o'clock
four o'clock
five o'clock
six o'clock
seven o'clock
eight o'clock
nine o'clock
ten o'clock
eleven o'clock
twelve o'clock
quarter past one (1:15)
half past one (1:30)
quarter to two (1:45)
five past one (1:05)
ten past one (1:10)
twenty past one (1:20)
twenty-five past one (1:25)
twenty-five to two (1:35)
twenty to two (1:40)
ten to two (1:50)
five to two (1:55)
midday (12:00)
midnight (0:00)

AMSER

Faint o'r gloch ydy hi?

Mae hi'n ...

un o'r gloch
ddau o'r gloch
dri o'r gloch
bedwar o'r gloch
bump o'r gloch
chwech o'r gloch
saith o'r gloch
wyth o'r gloch
naw o'r gloch
ddeg o'r gloch
un ar ddeg o'r gloch
ddeuddeg o'r gloch
chwarter wedi un
hanner awr wedi un
chwarter i ddau
bum munud wedi un
ddeg munud wedi un
ugain munud wedi un
bum munud ar hugain wedi un
bum munud ar hugain i ddau
ugain munud i ddau
ddeg munud i ddau
bum munud i ddau
ganol dydd
ganol nos

TIME VOCABULARY   GEIRFA AMSER

day	diwrnod / dydd
week	wythnos
fortnight	pythefnos
month	mis
year	blwyddyn
today	heddiw
tonight	heno
this morning	y bore 'ma
this afternoon	y prynhawn 'ma
yesterday	ddoe
last night	neithiwr
the day before yesterday	echdoe
the night before last	echnos
tomorrow	yfory
tomorrow afternoon	prynhawn yfory
tomorrow night	nos yfory
the day after tomorrow	trennydd
every day	pob dydd
last Tuesday	dydd Mawrth diwethaf
a week on Saturday	wythnos i ddydd Sadwrn
a fortnight tomorrow	pythefnos i yfory
a month on Thursday	mis i ddydd Iau
in September	ym mis Medi

QUESTION WORDS

GEIRIAU CWESTIWN

Who?	Pwy?
Who is the best player?	**Pwy** ydy'r chwaraewr gorau?
How?	Sut?
How do you know James?	**Sut** rwyt ti'n nabod James?
Where?	Ble?
Where is Haverfordwest?	**Ble** mae Hwlffordd?
What?	Beth?
What do you want to do tomorrow?	**Beth** rwyt ti eisiau gwneud yfory?
Why?	Pam?
Why do you like vegetarian food?	**Pam** rwyt ti'n hoffi bwyd llysieuol?
Which?	Pa?
Which boy plays ice hockey?	**Pa** fachgen sy'n chwarae hoci iâ?
What kind of ...?	Pa fath o ...?
What kind of music do you like?	**Pa fath** o gerddoriaeth rwyt ti'n hoffi?
When?	Pryd?
When is half term?	**Pryd** mae hanner tymor?
How much? / How many?	Faint?
How much do the tickets cost?	**Faint** mae'r tocynnau yn costio?
What time?	Faint o'r gloch?
What time do you go to bed?	**Faint o'r gloch** rwyt ti'n mynd i'r gwely?

How many ...?

In Welsh there are two ways to ask 'How many ...?'
Both forms translate in the same way in English.

(i) **Sawl** ...? (+ singular noun)

How many cats?	**Sawl** <u>cath</u>?
How many children are in the class?	**Sawl** <u>plentyn</u> sydd yn y dosbarth?

(ii) **Faint o** ...? (+ plural noun)

How many cats?	**Faint o** <u>gathod</u>?
How many children are in the class?	**Faint o** <u>blant</u> sydd yn y dosbarth?

SENTENCE ORDER/TREFN Y FRAWDDEG

Simple sentences/Brawddegau syml

In a simple Welsh sentence the order of words is:

verb → subject → rest of the sentence

This is shown in these examples in the past tense:

Verb	subject	rest of the sentence	English meaning
Prynais	i	siaced newydd.	*I bought a new jacket.*
Darllenodd	hi	ddau lyfr.	*She read two books.*
Chwaraeon	nhw	yn y parc.	*They played in the park.*

In the present tense it can seem more difficult to recognise this because the verb at the beginning of the sentence is often a form of the verb **bod** (*to be*):

Verb	subject	rest of the sentence	English meaning
Dw	i	'n hoffi bwyta reis.	*I like eating rice.*
Mae	Sioned	yn hapus iawn.	*Sioned is very happy.*
Rydyn	ni	'n mynd i'r sinema.	*We are going to the cinema.*

Emphatic sentences/Brawddegau pwyslais

In an emphatic sentence in Welsh what is being emphasised will come first:

Emphasis	rest of the sentence	English meaning
Mefus	dw i'n tyfu.	*I grow <u>strawberries</u>.*
Meddyg	ydy Mari.	*Mari is <u>a doctor</u>.*
Yn Abertawe	maen nhw'n byw.	*They live <u>in Swansea</u>.*

THE PRESENT TENSE

To be:
Positive

I / I am
You / You are
He / He is It / It is
She / She is It / It is
John / John is
We / We are
You / You are
They / They are

Negative

I do not / I am not
You do not / You are not
He/It does not / He/It is not
She/It does not / She/It is not
John does not / John is not
We do not / We are not
You do not / You are not

They do not / They are not

Examples of sentences

I like playing rugby.
You are tall.
He lives in Swansea.
She is very funny.
John is driving to the party.
We are winning the game.
You are polite.
They work hard.

YR AMSER PRESENNOL

Bod:
Cadarnhaol

Dw i
Rwyt ti *(singular informal)*
Mae e
Mae hi
Mae John
Rydyn ni
Rydych chi *(plural, or singular formal)*
Maen nhw

Negyddol

Dw i ddim
Dwyt ti ddim *(singular informal)*
Dydy e ddim
Dydy hi ddim
Dydy John ddim
Dydyn ni ddim
Dydych chi ddim *(plural, or singular formal)*
Dydyn nhw ddim

Enghreifftiau o frawddegau

Dw i'n hoffi chwarae rygbi.
Rwyt ti'n dal.
Mae e'n byw yn Abertawe.
Mae hi'n ddoniol iawn.
Mae John yn gyrru i'r parti.
Rydyn ni'n ennill y gêm.
Rydych chi'n gwrtais.
Maen nhw'n gweithio'n galed.

13

THE PAST TENSE/
YR AMSER GORFFENNOL

Regular verbs/Berfau rheolaidd

In the past tense regular verbs follow the same pattern formed from the verb stem and the appropriate ending for the person involved:

I walked	Cerdd**ais** i
You walked	Cerdd**aist** ti
He/It walked	Cerdd**odd** e
She/It walked	Cerdd**odd** hi
Nia walked	Cerdd**odd** Nia
We walked	Cerdd**on** ni
You walked	Cerdd**och** chi
They walked	Cerdd**on** nhw

Irregular verbs/Berfau afreolaidd

There are four irregular verbs:

- mynd   *to go*
- dod   *to come*
- gwneud   *to do/to make*
- cael   *to get*

These four verbs do not follow the usual pattern:

mynd

I	Es i	*I went*
You	Est ti	*You went*
He	Aeth e	*He went*
She	Aeth hi	*She went*
Dafydd	Aeth Dafydd	*Dafydd went*
We	Aethon ni	*We went*
You	Aethoch chi	*You went*
They	Aethon nhw	*They went*

dod

I	Des i	I came
You	Dest ti	You came
He	daeth e	He came
She	Daeth hi	She came
Dafydd	Daeth Dafydd	Dafydd came
We	Daethon ni	We came
You	Daethoch chi	You came
They	Daethon nhw	They came

gwneud

I	Gwnes i	I did/made
You	Gwnest ti	You did/made
He	Gwnaeth e	He did/made
She	Gwnaeth hi	She did/made
Dafydd	Gwnaeth Dafydd	Dafydd did/made
We	Gwnaethon ni	We did/made
You	Gwnaethoch chi	You did/made
They	Gwnaethon nhw	They did/made

cael

I	Ces i	I got
You	Cest ti	You got
He	Cafodd e	He got
She	Cafodd hi	She got
Dafydd	Cafodd Dafydd	Dafydd got
We	Cawson ni	We got
You	Cawsoch chi	You got
They	Cawson nhw	They got

ADJECTIVES/ANSODDEIRIAU

Almost all adjectives in Welsh come after the noun that they describe, for example: **llyfr diddorol** – an interesting book.

Here is a selection:

bad / naughty	drwg	late	hwyr
big	mawr	lively	bywiog
boring	diflas	local	lleol
busy	prysur	mad	gwallgof
clean	glân	nasty	cas
close	agos	neat	twt
cold	oer	new	newydd
comfortable	cyffyrddus	next	nesaf
complicated	cymhleth	nice	neis
confident	hyderus	noisy	swnllyd
constructive	adeiladol	odd	od
correct	cywir	ok	iawn
critical	beirniadol	organised	trefnus
dangerous	peryglus	outstanding	rhagorol
difficult	anodd	quiet	tawel
dirty	brwnt	sad	trist
early	cynnar	safe	diogel
easy	hawdd	shy	swil
empty	gwag	similar	tebyg
excellent	ardderchog	simple	syml
exciting	cyffrous	short	byr
fair	teg	small	bach
famous	enwog	special	arbennig
far	pell	strange	rhyfedd
fat	tew	strict	llym
full	llawn	strong	cryf
generous	hael	stupid	twp
good	da	talkative	siaradus
great	gwych	tall	tal
happy	hapus	thin	tenau
hot	poeth	tidy	taclus

huge	enfawr	uncomfortable	anghyffyrddus
ideal	delfrydol	unfair	annheg
important	pwysig	untidy	anniben
incorrect	anghywir	useful	defnyddiol
incredible	anhygoel	warm	cynnes
interesting	diddorol	weak	gwan
kind	caredig	wonderful	bendigedig
last	olaf	young	ifanc

The following adjectives usually come *before* the noun that they describe, for example:

hen ddyn – an old man

dear	**annwyl**	main/head	**prif**
every	**pob**	old	**hen**
favourite	**hoff**		

PREPOSITIONS/ARDDODIAID

Many verbs in Welsh are followed by a specific preposition.

- Verbs followed by a preposition which translates as expected into English:

to call **on**	galw **ar**
to defend **from**	amddiffyn **rhag**
to look **after**	gofalu **am**
to send **to** (a place)	anfon **i**
to think **about**	meddwl **am**

- Verbs followed by a preposition which does not translate as expected into English:

to beware **of**	gwylio **rhag**
to listen **to**	gwrando **ar**
to look **at**	edrych **ar**
to send **to** (a person)	anfon **at**
to shout **at**	gweiddi **ar**
to smile **at**	gwenu **ar**
to speak **to**	siarad **â**
to write **to**	ysgrifennu **at**

- Verbs followed by a preposition in Welsh but not in English:

to ask	gofyn **i**
to bring	dod **â**
to meet	cwrdd **â** / cyfarfod **â**
to hold	cydio **yn**
to stop	peidio **â**
to take	mynd **â**
to tell	dweud **wrth**
to visit	ymweld **â**

- The following prepositions cause a soft mutation to the first letter of the next word:

am	*about/at*	ar	*on*	at	*to*	gan	*by*
heb	*without*	i	*to*	o	*from/of*	dan	*under*
dros	*over/for*	drwy	*through/by*	wrth	*by/at*	hyd	*until*

For example:

Mae'r cyfarfod am **dd**au o'r gloch.   *The meeting is at two o'clock.*
Dw i'n dod o **F**angor.   *I come from Bangor.*

For more information on mutations in Welsh see page ix of the introduction.

- Some prepositions change according to the pronoun used. For example:

o	*of*	am	*about*
ohono i	*of me*	amdana i	*about me*
ohonot ti	*of you*	amdanat ti	*about you*
ohono fe	*of him*	amdano fe	*about him*
ohoni hi	*of her*	amdani hi	*about her*
ohonon ni	*of us*	amdanon ni	*about us*
ohonoch chi	*of you*	amdanoch chi	*about you*
ohonyn nhw	*of them*	amdanyn nhw	*about them*

CONNECTIVES/CYSYLLTEIRIAU

and   a / ac   **a** is used before a consonant
                                     ac is used before a vowel

- afal **a** banana   apple and banana
- afal **ac** oren   apple and orange

with   gyda
without   heb

- Dw i'n gwisgo'r trowsus   I wear the trousers
  gyda gwregys.   with a belt.
- Dw i'n gwisgo'r sgert   I wear the skirt without
  heb wregys.   a belt.

in   yn
in a   mewn

- Dw i'n byw **yn** Abertawe.   I live in Swansea.
- Dw i'n byw **mewn** fflat.   I live in a flat.

here   yma
there   yna

- Mae e'n byw **yma** gyda fi.   He lives here with me.
- Mae hi'n byw **yna** gyda Ben.   She lives there with Ben.

at/about   am
approximately   tua

- Dw i'n darllen llyfr **am**   I'm reading a book
  bysgota.   about fishing.
- Dw i'n dal trên mewn   I'm catching a train in
  tua deg munud.   about ten minutes.

| such as/like | fel |
| unlike | yn wahanol i |

- **Fel** Sara dw i'n siarad Sbaeneg. — Like Sara I speak Spanish.
- **Yn wahanol i** Sara dw i ddim yn siarad Ffrangeg. — Unlike Sara I don't speak French.

DYWEDIADAU

IDIOMATIC EXPRESSIONS

a dweud y gwir	to be honest
am byth	forever
ar fy mhen fy hun	on my own
ar hyn o bryd	at the moment
ar y cyfan	on the whole
ar y llaw arall	on the other hand
beth bynnag	whatever
byth eto	never again
cadw sŵn	make a noise
cyn bo hir	before long
chwarae teg	fair play
dal ati	keep at it
dim ond	only
diolch byth	thank goodness
does dim ots	it doesn't matter
dros ben	extremely
dros ben llestri	over the top
erbyn hyn	by now
fel arfer	usually
gorau glas	very best
gwaetha'r modd	worse luck
gwell hwyr na hwyrach	better late than never
gwneud hwyl ar ben	to make fun of
gyda llaw	by the way
heb os nac onibai	without a doubt
hen bryd	high time
llond bol	a bellyful
mynd o ddrwg i waeth	to go from bad to worse
newydd sbon	brand new
rhag ofn	in case

rhoi'r gorau i	to give up
siarad trwy ei het	talk nonsense
trwy'r amser	all the time
tu chwith	inside out
unwaith ac am byth	once and for all
wedi blino'n lân	exhausted
wrth gwrs	of course
wyneb i waered	upside down
yn awr ac yn y man	now and again

ENGLISH–WELSH

a

abduct *vt* dwyn ymaith drwy drais, cipio
abhor *vt* ffieiddio, casáu
abide *vb* aros, trigo; goddef
ability *n* gallu, medr
able *adj* abl, galluog
abnormal *adj* anghyffredin, annormal
aboard *adv* ar fwrdd (llong)
abolish *vt* diddymu, dileu
abominable *adj* ffiaidd
abomination *n* ffiedd-dra
abort *vb* erthylu, atal
abortion *n* erthyliad

KEYWORD

about *adv* **1** (*approximately*) tua, oddeutu, o gwmpas, rhyw; **about a hundred/thousand** tua chant/ mil; **it takes about 10 hours** mae'n cymryd tua/oddeutu/o gwmpas/ rhyw 10 awr; **at about 2 o'clock** tua 2 o'r gloch; **I've just about finished** rwyf bron â gorffen
2 (*referring to place*) o gwmpas/ yma ac acw; **to run about** rhedeg o gwmpas/rhedeg yma ac acw; **to walk about** cerdded o gwmpas; **they left all their things lying about** gadawsant eu pethau ar hyd y lle
3: **to be about to do sth** bod ar wneud rhth/bod ar fin gwneud rhth
▸ *prep* **1** (*relating to*) am, ynghylch, ynglŷn â; **a book about Cardiff** llyfr am Gaerdydd/llyfr ynghylch Caerdydd/llyfr ynglŷn â Chaerdydd; **what is it about?** beth sydd dan sylw?; **we talked about**

KEYWORD

a (*before vowel and silent h* **an**) *indef art* **1** (*no equivalent word in Welsh*): **a book** llyfr; **an apple** afal; **she's a doctor** meddyg yw hi
2 (*in expressing ratios, prices etc*): **three a day/week** tri y diwrnod/yr wythnos; **10 km an hour** 10 km yr awr; **£5 a person** £5 yr un/£5 y pen; **30p a kilo** 30c y cilo

aback *adv* yn ôl; **taken aback** wedi synnu
abandon *vt* rhoi'r gorau i, gadael
abandoned *adj* wedi ei adael
abate *vb* gostwng, lleihau; gostegu
abattoir *n* lladd-dy
abbey *n* abaty, mynachlog
abbreviate *vt* byrhau, talfyrru
abbreviation *n* byrfodd
abdomen *n* bol
abdominal *adj* perthynol i'r bol

it buom yn siarad am y peth; **what
or how about doing this?** beth
amdani?
2 (referring to place) o amgylch/o
gwmpas; **to walk about the town**
cerdded o amgylch y dref/cerdded
o gwmpas y dref

above prep uwch, uwchlaw ▸ adv
fry
abroad adv allan, ar led, dros y dŵr
abrupt adj disymwth; serth
abscess n cornwyd, crynhofa
absence n absenoldeb
absent adj absennol ▸ vt absenoli
absenteeism n absenoliaeth
absent-minded adj anghofus
absolute adj cwbl, hollol; diamodol
▸ n diamod, absolwt
absolutely adv yn hollol
absorb vt yfed, llyncu, sugno, sychu
absorbent adj amsugnol ▸ n
amsugnydd
abstain vb ymatal, ymgadw
abstract adj haniaethol ▸ n
crynodeb
absurd adj gwrthun, afresymol
abundance n digonedd,
helaethrwydd
abundant adj aml, helaeth, digonol
abuse¹ vt camddefnyddio, cam-
drin; difrio
abuse² n camddefnydd,
camdriniaeth; difrïaeth
abusive adj sarhaus, gwatwarus
abysmal adj diwaelod, dwys; enbyd
academic adj athrofaol, academig
academy n ysgol, athrofa, academi
accelerate vt cyflymu, chwimio

accelerator n ysbardun,
chwimiadur
accent n acen; llediaith ▸ vt
acennu
accept vt derbyn (yn gymeradwy)
acceptable adj derbyniol,
cymeradwy
acceptance n derbyniad
access n mynedfa, mynediad
accessary n cynorthwywr,
cefnogydd
accessible adj hygyrch; hawdd
dod ato
accessory adj cynorthwyol,
cyfranogol; atodol
accident n damwain, anap
accidental adj damweiniol
accidentally adv yn ddamweiniol
acclaim vt datgan cymeradwyaeth
accommodate vt cymhwyso;
lletya
accommodating adj cyfaddasol
accommodation n lle, llety
accompaniment n cyfeiliant
accompany vb hebrwng; cyfeilio
accomplice n cynorthwywr mewn
trosedd
accomplish vt cyflawni, cwblhau
accomplishment n medr, dawn,
camp
accord vb cytuno; cyflwyno ▸ n
cydfod
accordance n: **in accordance with**
yn unol â
according adv: **according to** yn ôl
accordingly adv felly, gan hynny
according to prep yn ôl
account vb cyfrif ▸ n cyfrif; hanes
accountable adj cyfrifol, atebol
accountant n cyfrifydd

account number n rhif cyfrif

accumulate vb casglu, pentyrru, cronni

accuracy n cywirdeb

accurate adj cywir

accurately adv yn gywir

accusation n cyhuddiad

accuse vt cyhuddo

accustomed adj cyfarwydd, cyffredin

ace n as; mymryn

ache vi poeni, gwynio ▸ n poen, cur

achieve vt cyflawni, gorffen, cwblhau

achievement n cyflawniad, camp

acid adj siarp, sur ▸ n suryn, asid

acid rain n glaw asid

acknowledge vt cydnabod, cyfaddef

acknowledgment n cydnabyddiaeth

acne n acne, plorynnod

acorn n mesen

acoustic adj clybodig

acquaintance n cydnabod

acquire vt cael, ennill

acquisition n caffaeliad

acquit vt rhyddhau

acre n erw, cyfair, acer

across adv, prep yn groes, ar draws; trosodd

acrylic adj acrylig

act vb gweithredu; actio ▸ n act, gweithred; deddf

action n gweithred, gweithrediad

activate vb gweithredoli

active adj bywiog; gweithredol

activity n gweithgarwch, gweithgaredd

actor n actor, actiwr

actress n actores

actual adj gwir, gwironeddol

actually adv mewn gwirionedd

acupuncture n nodwyddiad, aciwbigiad

acute adj llym, tost; craff

ad n hysbys

A.D. abbr (= Anno Domini) O.C., A.D.

adamant adj pendant, sicr

adapt vt cyfaddasu

adapter n adaptydd

add vb chwanegu, atodi; adio; **add up** vt adio; **to add up to** gwneud

addict vt ymroddi, gorddibynnu

addicted adj: **addicted (to sth)** caeth (i rywbeth), dibynnol (ar rywbeth)

addiction n ymroddiad, gorddibyniaeth, tueddiad

addition n ychwanegiad

additional adj ychwanegol

additive n adiolyn

address vb annerch; cyfeirio ▸ n anerchiad; cyfeiriad

adequate adj digonol

adhere vi ymlynu, glynu wrth

adhesive adj glynol, ymlynol ▸ n adlyn, glud

adjacent adj cyfagos, gerllaw

adjective n ansoddair

adjourn vt gohirio, oedi

adjust vt cymhwyso, addasu

administer vt gweinyddu

administration n gweinyddiaeth

administrative adj gweinyddol

administrator n gweinyddwr

admirable adj rhagorol, campus

admiral n llyngesydd

admiration n edmygedd

admire *vt* edmygu
admission *n* derbyniad; addefiad
admit *vt* derbyn; addef, cyfaddef
admittance *n* derbyniad;
trwydded
adolescence *n* llencyndod,
adolesens
adolescent *n* adolesent, llencyn,
llances
adopt *vb* mabwysiadu
adopted *adj* mabwysiedig; **he's
adopted** mae e wedi'i fabwysiadu
adoption *n* mabwysiad
adore *vt* addoli
adorn *vt* addurno
Adriatic *n*: **the Adriatic (Sea)** Môr
Adria, yr Adriatig
adrift *adv* yn rhydd, diangor
adult *n* (un) mewn oed, oedolyn
adultery *n* godineb
advance *vb* symud ymlaen; rhoi
benthyg ▸ *n* benthyg, echwyn
advanced *adj* ar y blaen
advantage *n* mantais
advantageous *adj* manteisiol
advent *n* dyfodiad; yr Adfent
adventure *n* antur, anturiaeth
adverb *n* adferf
adversary *n* gwrthwynebydd
adverse *adj* adfydus,
gwrthwynebus, croes
advert *n* hysbyseb
advertise *vt* hysbysu, hysbysebu
advertisement *n* hysbysiad,
hysbyseb
advertiser *n* hysbysydd
advertising *adj* hysbysebol
advice *n* cyngor, cyfarwyddyd
advisable *adj* doeth, buddiol
advise *vt* cynghori; hysbysu

advisory *adj* ymgynghorol
advocate *n* eiriolwr, bargyfreithiwr
▸ *vt* eiriol, cefnogi, pleidio
aerial *adj* awyrol, wybrol
aerobics *n* aerobeg
aeroplane *n* awyren
aerosol *n* erosol
affair *n* achos, mater; helynt
affect *vt* effeithio; cymryd arno,
ffugio
affection *n* serch, cariad; clefyd
affectionate *adj* serchog, caruaidd
afflict *vt* cystuddio
affluence *n* cyfoeth, digonedd
affluent *adj* goludog, cyfoethog,
cefnog
afford *vt* rhoddi; fforddio
Afghanistan *n* Affganistan,
Afghanistan
afraid *adj* ag ofn arno, ofnus
Africa *n* Affrica
African *adj* Affricanaidd ▸ *n*
Affricanwr
after *prep, conj* wedi, ar ôl, yn ôl
▸ *adv* wedyn
aftercare *n* gofal wedyn, ôl-ofal
after-effects *n* ôl-effeithiau
aftermath *n* adladd, adlodd
afternoon *n* prynhawn
afters *n* (*Brit, inf: dessert*) y cwrs
terfynol
aftershave, aftershave lotion *n*
persawr eillio
**aftersun, aftersun cream,
aftersun lotion** *n* hufen i drin
llosg haul, hylif ar ôl haul
afterthought *n* syniad diweddar
afterwards *adv* wedi hynny, wedyn
again *adv* eilwaith, drachefn, eto
against *prep* erbyn, yn erbyn

age n oed, oedran; oes; henaint
▸ vb heneiddio
aged adj hen, oedrannus
agency n cyfrwng, asiantaeth
agenda n agenda
agent n asiant, gweithredydd, cynrychiolydd
aggravate vt gwneuthur yn waeth
aggression n ymosodiad, gormes
aggressive adj ymosodol
agile adj heini, sionc, gwisgi
ago adv yn ôl; **long ago** ers talm
agony n ing, poen
agree vi cytuno; dygymod; cyfateb
agreeable adj clên, dymunol
agreement n cytundeb
agricultural adj amaethyddol
agriculture n amaethyddiaeth
ahead adv ymlaen, o flaen
aid vt cynorthwyo, helpu ▸ n cymorth, cynhorthwy
AIDS n abbr AID, afiechyd imiwnedd diffygiol
ailment n dolur, afiechyd, anhwyldeb
aim vb anelu, amcanu ▸ n amcan, nod
air n awyr; osgo; cainc, alaw ▸ vt awyru
airbag n bag awyr, bag aer
air-conditioned n gyda system dymheru
air conditioning n aerdymheru
aircraft n awyren
airforce n llu awyr
airline n cwmni hedfan
air mail n post awyr
airport n maes glanio
airtight adj aerglos, aerdyn
aisle n ystlys eglwys; llwybr; eil

ajar adv cilagored
à la carte adv à la carte
alarm vt dychrynu ▸ n braw, dychryn; rhybudd; larwm
alarm clock n cloc larwm
albeit conj er, er hynny, eto
album n albwm
alcohol n alcohol
alcoholic adj, n alcoholig
alcove n cilfach, alcof
ale n cwrw
alert adj effro, gwyliadwrus
A level n Lefel A
algebra n algebra
Algeria n Algeria
Algerian adj Algeraidd ▸ n Algeriad
alias adv mewn modd, dan enw arall
alibi n alibi
alien adj estronol ▸ n estron
alight vi disgyn
align vb cyfunioni
alike adj yr un fath ▸ adv yn gyffelyb
alive adv, adj yn fyw, byw
alkali n alcali

[KEYWORD]

all adj (the whole of) cyfan, oll, i gyd; **all Wales** Cymru gyfan; **all day** trwy gydol y dydd; **all night** trwy gydol y nos; **all men** y dynion i gyd; **all five** pob un o'r pump; **all the books** pob un o'r llyfrau; **all his life** trwy gydol ei oes
▸ pron **1** (everyone) pawb/pob un **2** (everything) y cyfan/y cwbl/pob dim/popeth; **I ate it all, I ate all of it** bwyteais y cyfan; **all of us went**

aethom bawb; **all of the boys
went** aeth pob un o'r bechgyn; **is
that all?** ai dyna'r cyfan?
3 (in phrases): **above all** uwchlaw
pob dim/yn anad dim/yn bennaf
oll; **after all** wedi'r cyfan; **at all**, **not
at all** (in answer to question) dim o
gwbl (in answer to thanks) croeso!
I'm not at all tired nid wyf wedi
blino o gwbl **anything at all will
do** bydd unrhyw beth o gwbl yn
gwneud y tro; **all in all** at ei gilydd,
rhwng popeth
▸ adv: **all alone** ar eich pen eich
hun bach; **it's not as hard as all
that** nid yw mor anodd â hynny i
gyd; **all the better** gorau oll, gorau
i gyd; **all but** popeth ond; **the score
is 2 all** 2 yr un yw'r sgôr

allegedly adv yn honedig
allegiance n teyrngarwch,
gwrogaeth
allergic adj alergig
allergy n alergedd
alleviate vt ysgafnhau, esmwytho
alley n llwybr, ale
alliance n cyfathrach, cynghrair
allied adj cynghreiriol
all-night adv drwy'r nos
allocate vt rhannu, dosbarthu
allot vb gosod, penodi
all-out adv yn llwyr, a'i holl egni
allow vt caniatáu, goddef
allowance n dogn; lwfans
all right adv yn iawn
ally vt cynghreirio ▸ n cynghreiriad
almighty adj hollalluog,
hollgyfoethog
almond n almon

almost adv bron
alone adv, adj unig, ar ei ben ei hun
along adv ymlaen; ar hyd; **all along**
o'r cychwyn
aloof adv, adj yn cadw draw; pell
aloud adv yn uchel, yn groch
alphabet n egwyddor, abiéc
alphabetical adj yn nhrefn yr
wyddor
Alps npl: **the Alps** yr Alpau
already adv eisoes, yn barod
also adv hefyd
altar n allor
alter vb newid, altro
alteration n newid, cyfnewidiad
alternate adj bob yn ail ▸ vb
digwydd bob yn ail
alternative n dewis arall
alternatively adv o ddewis arall
although conj er
altitude n uchder
altogether adv oll, i gyd, yn gyfan
gwbl
aluminium n alwminiwm
always adv yn wastad(ol), bob
amser
Alzheimer's, Alzheimer's disease
n clefyd Alzheimer
a.m. abbr (= anti meridiem) a.m.
amalgamate vb cymysgu, cyfuno,
uno
amass vt casglu, cronni, pentyrru
amateur n amatur
amaze vt synnu, rhyfeddu
amazement n syndod
amazing adj rhyfeddol
ambassador n llysgennad
amber n ambr
ambiguous adj amwys
ambition n uchelgais

ambitious *adj* uchelgeisiol
ambulance *n* ambiwlans
ambush *n, vb* cynllwyn, rhagod
amend *vb* gwella, diwygio
amendment *n* gwelliant
amenities *n* mwynderau
America *n* yr Amerig
American *adj* Americanaidd ▸ *n* Americanwr
amiable *adj* hawddgar, serchus
amicable *adj* cyfeillgar
amid, amidst *prep* ynghanol, ymhlith, ymysg
ammunition *n* pylor
amnesty *n* maddeuant
amok *adv* yn wyllt, yn ddilywodraeth
among, amongst *prep* ymhlith; among you/them yn eich/eu plith
amount *vi* cyrraedd; codi ▸ *n* swm
amp *n* amp
ample *adj* helaeth, eang, digon
amputate *vt* torri aelod, trychu
amuse *vt* difyrru, diddanu
amusement *n* difyrrwch, digrifwch
amusement arcade *n* arcêd difyrion
an *see* a
anaemia *n* diffyg gwaed
anaemic *adj* di-waed, diwryg
anaesthetic *adj, n* anesthetig
analogy *n* cyfatebiaeth, cydweddiad
analyse *vt* dadansoddi, dadelfennu
analysis *n* dadansoddiad
analyst *n* dadansoddwr
analytical *adj* dadansoddol
anarchic, anarchical *adj* anarchol
anarchy *n* anhrefn, anarchaeth
anatomy *n* anatomeg

ancestor *n* cyndad, hynafiad
anchor *n* angor ▸ *vb* angori
ancient *adj* hen, hynafol; oesol
and *conj* a, ac
angel *n* angel
anger *n* dicter, llid ▸ *vt* digio, llidio
angle *n* ongl ▸ *vi* genweirio, pysgota
Anglican *adj* perthynol i Eglwys Loegr, Anglicanaidd
angling *n* pysgota
angry *adj* dig, llidiog
anguish *n* ing
animal *n* anifail, mil ▸ *adj* anifeilaidd
animation *n* (of person) bywiogrwydd; (Cinema) animeiddiad
ankle *n* migwrn, ffêr
annex *vt* cysylltu, cydio; meddiannu
annihilate *vt* diddymu, difodi
annihilation *n* diddymiant, difodiant
anniversary *n* pen blwydd
annotate *vb* gwneud nodiadau
announce *vt* datgan, cyhoeddi
announcement *n* cyhoeddiad, hysbysiad
announcer *n* cyhoeddwr
annoy *vt* poeni, blino, cythruddo
annoying *adj* trafferthus, blinderus
annual *adj* blynyddol
anonymous *adj* dienw, anhysbys
anorak *n* anorac
anorexic *adj* anorecsig
another *pron, n* arall
answer *vb* ateb ▸ *n* ateb, atebiad
answerable *adj* atebol, cyfrifol**

answering machine n peiriant ateb

ant n morgrugyn

Antarctic n: the Antarctic yr Antarctig

antarctic adj o gylch y pegwn deheuol

antelope n gafrewig, antelop

antenatal adj cyn-geni

anthem n anthem

anthology n blodeugerdd

anthropology n anthropoleg

anti- prefix gwrth-, yn erbyn

antibiotic n, adj gwrthfiotig

anticipate vt achub y blaen, disgwyl

anticlimax n disgynneb

anticlockwise adj o chwith, gwrthglocwedd ▶ adv yn wrthglocwedd

antics npl ystumiau, stranciau

antidote n gwrthwenwyn

antifreeze n, adj gwrthrew, direwyn

antique¹ adj hen, hynafol

antique² n hen beth

antique shop n siop hen bethau

anti-Semitism n gwrth-Iddewiaeth

antiseptic adj, n antiseptig

antisocial adj gwrthgymdeithasol

anxiety n pryder

anxious adj pryderus, awyddus

⸢KEYWORD⸣

any adj 1 (in questions etc; often no equivalent word in Welsh): **do you have any butter/children/ink?** a oes gennych fenyn/blant/inc? 2 (with negative): **I don't have any**

money/books nid oes gennyf arian/lyfrau 3 (no matter which) unrhyw; **choose any book you like** dewiswch unrhyw lyfr a ddymunwch; **any teacher you ask will tell you** bydd unrhyw athro a holwch yn dweud wrthych 4 (in phrases): **in any case** beth bynnag; **any day now** unrhyw ddiwrnod nawr; **at any moment** unrhyw eiliad; **at any rate** beth bynnag; **any time** unrhyw bryd; **he might come (at) any time** gallai ddod unrhyw bryd; **come (at) any time** dewch unrhyw bryd

▶ pron 1 (in questions etc; often no equivalent word in Welsh): **have you got any milk?** a oes gennych laeth?; **can any of you sing?** a all unrhyw rai ohonoch ganu? 2 (with negative) ddim; **they aren't any better** nid ydynt ddim gwell 3 (no matter which) unrhyw; **take any of those books (you like)** cymerwch unrhyw rai o'r llyfrau hynny (a ddymunwch)

▶ adv 1 (in questions etc): **do you want any more soup/sandwiches?** gymerwch chi ragor o gawl/frechdanau?; **are you feeling any better?** a ydych yn teimlo rywfaint yn well? 2 (with negative): **I can't hear him any more** ni allaf ei glywed bellach, ni allaf ei glywed mwyach; **don't wait any longer** peidiwch ag aros bellach

anybody pron unrhyw un, rhywun

anyhow *adv* (*anyway*) beth bynnag; (*haphazardly*) unrhyw sut
anyone *pron* rhywun
anything *pron* dim, rhywbeth, rhywfaint
anyway *adv* beth bynnag
anywhere *adv* rhywle
apart *adv* o'r neilltu, ar wahân
apartment *n* rhandy, llety
apathetic *adj* difater, didaro
apathy *n* difrawder, difaterwch
ape *n* epa ▸ *vt* dynwared
aperture *n* bwlch, twll, agorfa
apex *n* blaen, brig
apocalypse *n* datguddiad
apologize *vi* ymddiheuro, ymesgusodi
apology *n* ymddiheuriad, esgusawd
apostrophe *n* sillgoll, collnod (')
app *n* (*inf, Comput*) (*application*) ap
appal *vt* brawychu, digalonni
appalling *adj* arswydus, gwarthus
apparatus *n* offer, aparatws
apparent *adj* amlwg, eglur
apparently *adv* mae'n debyg
appeal *vi* apelio, erfyn ▸ *n* apêl
appear *vi* ymddangos, ymrithio
appearance *n* ymddangosiad
appease *vt* llonyddu, tawelu, dofi
appendicitis *n* enyniad y coluddyn crog, apendiseitis
appendix *n* atodiad, ychwanegiad
appetite *n* archwaeth, chwant, awydd
appetizer *n* lluniaeth i greu blas, blasyn
applaud *vt* cymeradwyo, curo dwylo
applause *n* cymeradwyaeth

apple *n* afal; **apple of the eye** cannwyll llygad
appliance *n* offeryn, dyfais
applicant *n* ymgeisydd
application *n* cymhwysiad; cais; ymroddiad
application form *n* ffurflen gais
apply *vb* cymhwyso; ymroi; ymgeisio
appoint *vb* gosod, penodi, pennu
appointment *n* cyhoeddiad; penodiad
appreciate *vt* prisio, gwerthfawrogi
appreciation *n* gwerthfawrogiad
appreciative *adj* gwerthfawrogol
apprehend *vt* ymaflyd mewn; dirnad; ofni
apprehension *n* dirnadaeth; ofn
apprehensive *adj* ofnus, pryderus
apprentice *n* prentis, dysgwr ▸ *vt* prentisio
approach *vb* nesáu, dynesu ▸ *n* dyfodfa
approachable *adj* hawdd mynd ato
appropriate *vt* meddiannu ▸ *adj* priodol, addas
approval *n* cymeradwyaeth
approve *vt* cymeradwyo; profi
approximate *vi* agosáu ▸ *adj* agos
approximately *adv* oddeutu, tua, yn agos i
apricot *n* bricyllen
April *n* Ebrill
apron *n* (ar)ffedog, barclod
apt *adj* tueddol; cymwys
aquarium *n* pysgodlyn, pysgoty
Aquarius *n* y Cariwr Dŵr
Arab *n* Arab ▸ *adj* Arabaidd

Arabic n Arabeg
arbitrary adj gormesol, mympwyol
arc n bwa, arc
arcade n arcêd
arch n bwa, pont ▸ vt pontio
archaeologist n archaeolegwr
archaeology n archaeoleg
archbishop n archesgob
architect n pensaer
architecture n pensaernïaeth
archive n archif
Arctic n: **the Arctic** yr Arctig
arctic adj gogleddol
area n arwynebedd; wyneb
Argentina n Ariannin
Argentinian adj Archentaidd;
  o'r Ariannin ▸ n Archentwr
  (Archentwraig)
argue vb dadlau, ymresymu
argument n dadl, ymresymiad
Aries n yr Hwrdd
arise (pt **arose**, pp **arisen**) vi
  cyfodi, codi
aristocracy n pendefigaeth
aristocratic adj pendefigaidd,
  bonheddig
arithmetic n rhifyddeg
arm¹ n braich; cainc
arm² n (weapon) arf ▸ vb arfogi
armchair n cadair freichiau
armed adj arfog
armour n arfogaeth, arfwisg
armpit n cesail
armrest n man i orffwys braich
army n byddin
aroma n perarogl(au)
around adv, prep am, o amgylch
arouse vt deffro(i), dihuno; cyffroi
arrange vb trefnu

arrangement n trefn, trefniad,
  trefniant
array vt trefnu; gwisgo ▸ n trefn;
  gwisg
arrears npl ôl-ddyled
arrest vt atal; dal, restio
arrival n dyfodiad, cyrhaeddiad
arrive vi cyrraedd, dyfod
arrogance n balchder, traha
arrogant adj balch, trahaus
arrow n saeth
arson n llosgiad, llosg
art n celfyddyd; ystryw
artery n rhedweli
art gallery n oriel gelf
arthritis n gwynegon,
  crydcymalau
artichoke n artisiog
article n erthygl; nwydd; bannod
articulate vb cymalu; cynanu
  ▸ adj â meddwl clir, trefnus
artificial adj gosod, ffug
artillery n offer rhyfel, magnelau
artist n celfyddydwr, arlunydd,
  artist
artistic adj celfydd, celfyddgar,
  artistig

(KEYWORD)

as conj **1** (time, moment) fel y, pan,
  wrth, tra; **he came in as I was
  leaving** daeth i mewn wrth imi
  ymadael; **as the years went by**
  wrth i'r blynyddoedd fynd heibio;
  as from tomorrow o yfory ymlaen
  2 (because) gan; **he left early as he
  had to be home by 10** ymadawodd
  yn gynnar gan fod rhaid iddo fod
  gartref erbyn 10
  3 (referring to manner, way) fel; **do as**

a

you wish gwnewch fel y mynnoch;
as she said fel y dywedodd
▸ adv 1 (in comparisons): as big
as cymaint â, mor fawr â; twice
as big as dwywaith mor fawr â;
as much as cymaint â; as many
as cynifer â; as much money as
cymaint o arian â; as many books
as cynifer o lyfrau â; as soon as cyn
gynted â
2 (concerning): as for or to that o
ran hynny, gyda golwg ar hynny
3: as if or though fel pe; he looked
as if he was ill edrychai fel petai'n
sâl see also long, such, well
▸ prep (in the capacity of) fel; he
works as a driver mae'n gweithio
fel gyrrwr; as chairman of the
company, he ... yn rhinwedd ei
swydd fel cadeirydd y cwmni,
...; he gave me it as a present fe'i
rhoddodd imi yn anrheg

a.s.a.p. abbr (= as soon as possible)
cyn gynted, cyn gynted â phosib
asbestos n ystinos, asbestos
ascent n esgynfa, rhiw, gorifyny
ash¹ n onnen, onn
ash² n (powder) lludw, ulw
ashamed adj ag arno gywilydd
ashore adv i'r lan, ar y lan
ashtray n plat lludw
Asia n Asia
Asian n Asiad ▸ adj Asiaidd
aside adv o'r neilltu
ask vb gofyn, holi; ceisio
asleep adv yng nghwsg, yn cysgu
asparagus n merllys, asbaragws
aspect n golwg, wyneb, agwedd
aspire vi dyheu

aspirin n asbrin
ass n asyn
assailant n ymosodwr
assassin n bradlofrudd, llofrudd
assassinate vt bradlofruddio
assault n ymosodiad ▸ vt ymosod
assemble vb cynnull, ymgynnull
assembly n cynulliad, cymanfa
assert vt haeru, honni, mynnu
assess vt asesu
assessment n asesiad
asset n ased
assets npl eiddo, meddiannau
assign vt gosod, penodi;
trosglwyddo
assignment n aseiniad
assimilate vb cymathu; tebygu
assist vb cynorthwyo, helpu
assistance n cymorth
assistant n cynorthwyydd
associate vb cymdeithasu,
cyfeillachu, cysylltu ▸ n
cydymaith
association n cymdeithas,
cymdeithasfa
assorted adj amryfath
assortment n dosbarthiad, pigion
assume vt cymryd ar; tybied;
honni
assumption n tyb(iaeth), honiad;
dyrchafiad (Mair i'r nefoedd)
assurance n sicrwydd; hyder
assure vt sicrhau; yswirio
asterisk n serennig
asthma n y fogfa
asthmatic adj asthmatig
astonish vt synnu
astonished adj syn
astonishing adj syfrdanol
astound vt synnu, syfrdanu

astray *adv* ar gyfeiliorn, ar grwydr
astrologer *n* sêr-ddewin
astrology *n* sêr-ddewiniaeth
astronaut *n* gofodwr
astronomer *n* serydd, seryddwr
astronomy *n* seryddiaeth
astute *adj* craff, cyfrwys, call
asylum *n* noddfa; **lunatic asylum** gwallgofdy

[KEYWORD]

at *prep* **1** (*referring to position, direction*) ar, yn; **at the top** ar y brig; **at home** gartref; **at school** yn yr ysgol; **at the baker's** yn siop y pobydd; **to look at sth** edrych ar rth
2 (*referring to time*): **at 4 o'clock** am 4 o'r gloch; **at Christmas** adeg y Nadolig; **at night** gyda'r nos, yn ystod y nos; **at times** ar adegau
3 (*referring to rates, speed etc*): **at £1 a kilo** am £1 y cilo; **two at a time** dau ar y tro; **at 50 km/h** am 50km/a
4 (*referring to manner*): **at a stroke** ar amrantiad; **at peace** mewn heddwch
5 (*referring to activity*): **to be at work** (*in the office etc*) bod yn y gwaith (*working*) gweithio; **to play at cowboys** chwarae cowbois; **to be good at sth** bod yn dda am wneud rhth
6 (*referring to cause*): **shocked/surprised at sth** synnu/rhyfeddu at rhth; **I went at his suggestion** euthum ar ei awgrym ef

atheist *n* anffyddiwr
Athens *n* Athen

athlete *n* mabolgampwr
athletic *adj* athletaidd
athletics *npl* mabolgampau
Atlantic *adj* Atlantaidd, Atlantig
  ▶ *n*: **the Atlantic (Ocean)** yr Iwerydd, Môr Iwerydd
atlas *n* llyfr mapiau, atlas
ATM *n abbr* peiriant arian
atmosphere *n* awyrgylch
atom *n* atom
atomic *adj* atomig
atrocious *adj* erchyll, anfad, ysgeler
attach *vb* gosod, glynu; atafaelu
attached *adj*: **attached to** (*fond of*) hoff iawn o
attachment *n* ymlyniad, serch
attack *vt* ymosod ar ▶ *n* ymosodiad
attain *vt* ennill; cyrraedd; cael gafael
attempt *vt* ceisio, cynnig ▶ *n* cynnig, ymgais
attend *vb* gweini; ystyried; dilyn, mynychu
attendance *n* gwasanaeth; presenoldeb
attendant *n* gweinydd ▶ *adj* yn dilyn, ynghlwm wrth
attention *n* sylw, ystyriaeth
attic *n* nenlofft, nenlawr
attitude *n* ystum, agwedd, osgo
attorney *n* twrnai
attract *vt* tynnu, denu, hudo
attraction *n* atyniad
attractive *adj* atyniadol
attribute[1] *n* priodoledd
attribute[2] *vt* priodoli, cyfrif i
aubergine *n* planhigyn wy
auburn *adj* gwinau, browngoch

auction *n* arwerthiant, ocsiwn
audible *adj* hyglyw, clywadwy
audience *n* gwrandawyr, cynulleidfa
audit *vt* archwilio cyfrifon ► *n* archwiliad
audition *n* clywelediad
auditor *n* archwilydd
August *n* Awst
august *adj* urddasol, mawreddog
aunt *n* modryb
au pair *n* au pair
aura *n* naws, awyrgylch
austerity *n* gerwindeb, llymder
Australia *n* Awstralia
Australian *n* Awstraliad ► *adj* Awstralaidd
Austria *n* Awstria
Austrian *n* Awstriad ► *adj* Awstriaidd
authentic *adj* dilys, gwir
author *n* awdur, awdwr
authority *n* awdurdod
authorize *vt* awdurdodi
autobiography *n* hunangofiant
autograph *n* llofnod
automatic *adj* hunanysgogol, awtomatig
automatically *adv* yn awtomatig
automobile *n* cerbyd, modur
autonomy *n* ymreolaeth
autumn *n* hydref
auxiliary *adj* cynorthwyol, ategol ► *n* cynorthwywr
avail *vb* llesáu, tycio ► *n* lles, budd
available *adj* ar gael
avalanche *n* syrthfa, cwymp (eira *etc*)
avenge *vt* dial cam
avenue *n* mynedfa, rhodfa

average *n* canolbris; cyfartaledd; cyffredin
aversion *n* gwrthwynebiad; casbeth
avert *vt* troi heibio, gochel, osgoi
avocado *n* afocado
avoid *vt* osgoi
await *vt* disgwyl, aros
awake (*pt* **awoke**, *pp* **awoken**) *vb* deffro, dihuno ► *adj* effro
award *vt* dyfarnu ► *n* dyfarniad
aware *adj* hysbys, ymwybodol
awareness *n* arwybod, ymwybyddiaeth
away *adv* ymaith, i ffwrdd
awe *n* (parchedig) ofn ► *vt* rhoi arswyd
awful *adj* ofnadwy, arswydus
awkward *adj* trwsgl, lletchwith, anghyfleus
axe *n* bwyall, bwyell
axle *n* echel
ay *adv* ie
aye *adv* yn wastad(ol), byth

b

baby n baban, babi
babysit vi gwarchod plant ▸ vt gwarchod
babysitter n gwarchodwr plant
babysitting n gwarchod plant
bachelor n dyn dibriod, hen lanc; baglor
back n cefn ▸ vb cefnogi; bacio ▸ adv yn ôl; **back out** vi bacio allan; **back up** vt cefnogi
backache n poen cefn
backbone n asgwrn cefn
backfire vi bacffeirio
background n cefndir
backing n (support) cefnogaeth
backpack n cefnbwn
backpacker n bacpacwr
backside n (inf) pen-ôl
backup n (support) cefnogaeth
backward adv yn ôl, ar ôl
bacon n cig moch, bacwn
bad adj drwg, drygionus; gwael, sâl
badge n bathodyn

badger n mochyn daear, broch ▸ vt profocio, poeni
badly adv (poorly) yn wael; (seriously) yn ddifrifol
badminton n badminton
bad-tempered adj â thymer ddrwg
bag n cwd, cod, bag
baggage n celfi, pac
bagpipe n pibgod
bail n meichiau, gwystl ▸ vt mechnïo
bait vt abwydo ▸ n abwyd
bake vb pobi, crasu
baked adj pob; wedi'i bobi; **baked beans** ffa pob
baked potato n taten bob
baker n pobydd
bakery n popty
balance n clorian, mantol; gweddill ▸ vt mantoli; cydbwyso
balanced adj cytbwys, cymesur
balcony n oriel, balcon
bald adj moel, penfoel
baleful adj alaethus
ball¹ n pêl, pellen
ball² n (dance) dawns, dawnsfa
ballerina n balerina
ballet n bale
ballet dancer n dawnsiwr bale
ballet shoes n esgidiau bale
balloon n balŵn
ballot n balot, tugel
ballpoint pen n beiro
ban vt gwahardd, ysgymuno
banana n banana
band n band, rhwymyn; mintai; seindorf
bandage n rhwymyn ▸ vb rhwymo, rhwymynnu
Band-Aid n plastr glynu

bandit n herwr, ysbeiliwr
bang vb (inf) curo ▸ n ergyd, twrf
Bangladesh n Bangladesh
bangle n breichled
banish vt alltudio, deol
bank¹ n (shore) glan, torlan; traethell
bank² n (building) banc ▸ vb bancio
bank account n cyfrif banc
banker n bancwr
bank holiday n gŵyl banc
banknote n papur banc
bankrupt n methdalwr
bankruptcy n methdaliad
bank statement n datganiad banc, adroddiad banc
banner n baner, lluman
banquet n gwledd ▸ vb gwledda
banter n ysmaldod, cellwair ▸ vb cellwair, profocio
baptism n bedydd
baptize vt bedyddio
bar n bar, bollt; rhwystr; traethell ▸ vt bario; eithrio
barbaric adj barbaraidd
barbecue n rhostfa
barbed wire n weiar bigog
barber n barbwr
bare adj noeth, llwm, moel, prin ▸ vt dinoethi
barefoot adj troednoeth
barefooted adj troednoeth
barely adv prin, o'r braidd
bargain n bargen ▸ vb bargeinio
barge n bad mawr
bark¹ vi cyfarth, coethi ▸ n cyfarthiad
bark² n rhisgl ▸ vt dirisglo, digroeni
barley n haidd, barlys

barmaid n barferch
barman n barmon
barn n ysgubor
barometer n hinfynegydd, baromedr
baron n barwn, arglwydd
barrage n argae, clawdd
barrel n baril, casgen
barren adj diffrwyth
barricade n atalglawdd ▸ vt cau
barrier n atalfa, rhwystr
barrister n bargyfreithiwr
barrow n berfa, whilber; crug
base¹ adj isel, gwael
base² n sylfaen, sail; bôn ▸ vt sylfaenu, seilio
baseball n pel-fâs
based adj (based on) wedi'i seilio ar
basement n islawr
bash (inf) n: to have a bash (at sth) rhoi cynnig (ar rth) ▸ vt pwnio
basic adj gwaelodol, sylfaenol
basically adv yn y bôn
basics npl: the basics yr hanfodion
basil n brenhinllys, basil
basin n basn, cawg, dysgl
basis n sail, sylfaen
basket n basged, cawell
basketball n pêl-fasged
bass n bas; bàs, draenogiad y môr
bass drum n drwm bas
bastard n (inf) bastard, plentyn gordderch
bat¹ n (mammal) ystlum
bat² n bat ▸ vi batio
batch n pobiad, ffyrnaid; swp, sypyn
bath n baddon; bàth
bathe vb ymdrochi, ymolchi, golchi
bathroom n ystafell ymolchi

bath towel n tywel bàth
baton n baton
batter vt curo, pwyo ▸ n defnydd crempog, cytew
battery n magnelfa; batri
battle n brwydr, cad ▸ vi brwydro
battlefield n maes y gad
bay¹ n bae
bay² vb, n cyfarth; **to hold at bay** rhoi cyfarth
bay³ n (tree) llawryf
bay⁴ adj gwinau, gwineugoch
bazaar n basâr
B.C. abbr (= before Christ) CC, Cyn Crist

[KEYWORD]

be (pt **was, were**, pp **been**) aux vb
1 (with present participle; forming continuous tenses): **what are you doing?** beth rydych yn ei wneud?; **they're coming tomorrow** maent yn dod yfory; **I've been waiting for you for 2 hours** rwyf yn aros amdanoch ers 2 awr
2 (with pp; forming passives): **to be killed** cael eich lladd; **the box had been opened** roedd y blwch wedi [cael] ei agor; **he was nowhere to be seen** nid oedd i'w weld yn unman
3 (in tag questions): **it was fun, wasn't it?** roedd yn hwyl onid oedd?; **he's good-looking, isn't he?** mae'n olygus, on'd yw e?; **she's back, is she?** mae yn ôl, ydy hi?
4 (+to +infinitive): **the house is to be sold** (necessity) rhaid i'r tŷ gael ei werthu (future) mae'r tŷ i'w werthu; **he's not to open it** rhaid

iddo beidio â'i agor
▸ vb + complement 1 (gen) bod; **I'm Welsh** Cymro/Cymraes ydw i; **I'm tired** rwyf wedi blino; **I'm hot/cold** rwy'n boeth/oer; **he's a doctor** meddyg yw e; **be careful/good/quiet!** byddwch yn ofalus/yn dda/yn dawel!; **2 and 2 are 4** 2 a 2 yw 4; **2** (of health) bod; **how are you?** sut rydych chi?; **I'm better now** rwy'n well bellach; **he's very ill** mae'n sâl iawn
▸ vi 1 (exist, occur etc) bod, bodoli; **the prettiest girl that ever was** y ferch bertaf a fu erioed; **is there a God?** a oes yna Dduw?; **be that as it may** bid a fo am hynny; **so be it** boed/bydded felly, felly y bo
2 (referring to place) bod; **I won't be here tomorrow** ni fyddaf yma yfory
▸ vb imper 1 (referring to time) bod; **it's 5 o'clock** mae'n 5 o'r gloch; **it's the 28th of April** yr 28ain o Ebrill yw hi
2 (referring to distance): **it's 10 km to the village** mae'n 10 km i'r pentref
3 (referring to the weather): **it's too hot/cold** mae'n rhy boeth/oer; **it's windy today** mae'n wyntog heddiw
4 (emphatic: to emphasize a word or words they are placed first in Welsh); **it's me/the postman** fi sydd yma/y postmon sydd yna; **it was Maria who paid the bill** Maria a dalodd y bil

beach n traeth, traethell ▸ vt gyrru ar y traeth

beacon n coelcerth
bead n glain; **beads** npl paderau
beak n pig, gylfin
beam n trawst; pelydryn ▸ vi pelydru
bean n ffäen, ffeuen
bear¹ n arth; arthes
bear² (pt **bore**, pp **borne**) vt dwyn, cludo; geni; goddef
▸ **bear up** vi: bear up! daliwch ati!
beard n barf; col ŷd
bearded adj barfog, â barf
bearing n ymddygiad; traul
beast n bwystfil, anifail
beat (pt **beat**, pp **beaten**) vt curo ▸ n cur, curiad
beautiful adj prydferth, hardd, teg
beautifully adv yn hardd
beauty n prydferthwch, harddwch, tegwch
beaver n afanc, llostlydan
because adv, conj oherwydd, oblegid, o achos, gan, am
beckon vb amneidio
become vb dyfod; gweddu
bed n gwely; cefn, pâm
bed and breakfast n gwely a brecwast
bedclothes n dillad gwely
bedding n dillad gwely
bedraggled adj wedi caglo; aflêr
bedroom n ystafell wely, llofft
bedsit n fflat un ystafell
bedspread n cwrlid
bedtime n amser gwely
bee n gwenynen
beech n ffawydden
beef n eidion; cig eidion
beer n cwrw
beet n betys

beetle n chwilen
beetroot n betys
before prep o flaen, gerbron, cyn ▸ adv o'r blaen
beforehand adv ymlaen llaw
befriend vt ymgeleddu, bod yn gefn
beg vb erfyn, deisyf, ymbil; cardota
beggar n cardotyn ▸ vt tlodi, llymhau
begin (pt **began**, pp **begun**) vb dechrau
beginner n dechreuwr
beginning n dechreuad
behalf n plaid, rhan, achos, tu
behave vb ymddwyn
behaviour n ymddygiad
behind adv, prep ar ôl, yn ôl, tu ôl, tu cefn
beige adj beis
being n bod
belated adj diweddar, hwyr
belch vb bytheirio
Belgian adj Belgaidd; o Wlad Belg ▸ n Belgiad
Belgium n Gwlad Belg
belief n cred, crediniaeth, coel
believe vb credu, coelio
believer n credwr, credadun
belittle vt bychanu
bell n cloch
belligerent adj rhyfelog ▸ n rhyfelblaid
bellow vb rhuo, bugunad
belly n bol, cest, tor ▸ vb bolio
belong vi perthyn
belongings n meddiannau, eiddo
beloved adj annwyl, cu ▸ n anwylyd
below adv, prep is, islaw, isod

belt *n* gwregys
bemused *adj* syfrdan
bench *n* mainc
bend (*pt, pp* **bent**) *vb* plygu, camu
▸ *n* tro, camedd; **bend down** *vi*
plygu drosodd; **bend over** *vi*
plygu drosodd
beneath *adv, prep* is, tan, oddi
tanodd
beneficial *adj* buddiol, llesol
benefit *n* budd, lles, elw ▸ *vb*
llesáu, elwa
benign *adj* tirion, mwyn
bent *n* tuedd, gogwydd
beret *n* bere
Berlin *n* Berlin
berry *n* aeronen, mwyaren
berth *n* lle llong; gwely llongwr;
swydd
beside *prep* gerllaw, wrth, yn ymyl;
to be beside oneself o'i bwyll
besides *adv, prep* heblaw, gyda
best *adj, adv* gorau
best man *n* gwas priodas
bet (*pt, pp* **bet, betted**) *vb* betio,
dal am ▸ *n* bet, cyngwystl
betray *vt* bradychu
betrayal *n* brad
better *adj* gwell, rhagorach ▸ *adv*
yn well ▸ *vt* gwella
between *prep* rhwng, cydrhwng
beverage *n* diod
beware *vi* gochel, ymogelyd
beyond *adv, prep* tu hwnt
bias *n* tuedd, gogwydd, rhagfarn
▸ *vt* tueddu
Bible *n* Beibl
bicker *vi* ffraeo, ymgecru
bicycle *n* beic

bid *vt* (*pt* **bade**, *pp* **bidden**) erchi
▸ *vi* (*pt, pp* **bid**) gwahodd; cynnig
big *adj* mawr
bigheaded *adj* bras, mawreddog
bike *n* beic
bikini *n* bicini
bilingual *adj* dwyieithog
bilingualism *n* dwyieithedd,
dwyieithrwydd; dwyieitheg
bill¹ *n* bil; mesur; rhaglen
bill² *n* (*beak*) pig, gylfin
billiards *n* biliards
billion *n* biliwn
bin *n* cist
bind (*pt, pp* **bound**) *vt* rhwymo,
caethiwo
binge *n* (*inf*) gloddest, sbri
bingo *n* bingo
binoculars *n* deulygadur
biochemistry *n* biocemeg
biography *n* bywgraffiad, cofiant
biological *adj* biolegol
biology *n* bywydeg, bioleg
birch *n* bedwen; gwialen fedw
bird *n* aderyn
birdwatching *n* adarydda, gwylio
adar
Biro® *n* Biro
birth *n* genedigaeth
birth certificate *n* tystysgrif geni
birth control *n* atal cenhedlu
birthday *n* pen-blwydd
birthday card *n* carden pen-
blwydd
birthmark *n* man geni
biscuit *n* bisgeden
bisexual *adj* deurywiol
bishop *n* esgob
bit *n* tamaid; tipyn; genfa
bitch *n* (*dog*) gast

bite (*pt* **bit**, *pp* **bitten**) *vb* cnoi, brathu ▸ *n* cnoad, brath; tamaid
bitter *adj* chwerw, bustlaidd, tost
bitterness *n* chwerwedd, chwerwder
bizarre *adj* rhyfedd, od, chwithig
black *adj* du
blackberry *n* mwyraen, mwyaren ddu
blackbird *n* aderyn du, mwyalchen
blackboard *n* bwrdd du
blackcurrant *n* cyrensen ddu ▸ *adj* cwrens du
black ice *n* iâ du
blackmail *n* arian bygwth, blacmel
black pudding *n* pwdin gwaed
bladder *n* pledren, chwysigen
blade *n* llafn; eginyn, blewyn
blame *vt* beio ▸ *n* bai
bland *adj* mwyn, tyner, tirion
blank *adj* gwag, syn; **blank verse** mesur di-odl
blank cheque *n* siec wag
blanket *n* blanced, gwrthban
blast *n* chwa, chwythiad, deifiad ▸ *vt* deifio; saethu
blatant *adj* digywilydd, haerllug
blaze *n* fflam, ffagl ▸ *vi* fflamio, ffaglu
blazer *n* blaser
bleach *vb* cannu, gwynnu
bleak *adj* oer, digysgod, noeth, noethlwm
bleed (*pt*, *pp* **bled**) *vb* gwaedu
blemish *vt* anafu, anurddo ▸ *n* anaf, bai, mefl
blend *vb* cymysgu ▸ *n* cymysgedd
blender *n* hylifydd
bless (*pt*, *pp* **blessed**, **blest**) *vt* bendithio

blessing *n* bendith
blight *n* malltod ▸ *vt* mallu, deifio
blind *adj* dall, tywyll ▸ *vt* dallu ▸ *n* llen, bleind
blindness *n* dallineb
blink *vb* cau'r llygaid, ysmicio, amrantu
bliss *n* gwynfyd, dedwyddyd
blister *n* chwysigen, pothell ▸ *vb* pothellu
blizzard *n* ystorm erwin o wynt ac eira
blob *n* ysmotyn, bwrlwm
block *n* plocyn, cyff ▸ *vt* cau, rhwystro
blockade *n* gwarchae ▸ *vb* gwarchae ar
blog *n* blog
blogger *n* blogiwr
blonde *adj* o bryd golau
blood *n* gwaed; gwaedoliaeth
blood pressure *n* pwysedd gwaed
blood test *n* prawf gwaed
bloody *adj* gwaedlyd
bloom *n* blodeuyn; gwawr, gwrid ▸ *vi* blodeuo
blossom *n* blodeuyn ▸ *vi* blodeuo
blot *n* ysmotyn du, blot, mefl ▸ *vb* blotio
blouse *n* blows
blow[1] *n* dyrnod, ergyd
blow[2] (*pt* **blew**, *pp* **blown**) *vb* chwythu
 ▸ **blow up** *vi* (*explode*) ffrwydro
 ▸ *vt* (*inflate*) llenwi
blow-dry *vb* chwythu'n sych
blue *adj*, *n* glas ▸ *vt* glasu
bluff *adj* garw, brochus
blunder *n* amryfusedd ▸ *vb* amryfuso

blunt adj pŵl, di-fin; plaen ▸ vt pylu

blur n ysmotyn, ystaen

blush vi cochi, gwrido ▸ n gwrid

board n bwrdd, bord; ymborth ▸ vb byrddio

board game n gêm fwrdd

boarding card n cerdyn byrddio

boarding school n ysgol breswyl

boast n ymffrost ▸ vb ymffrostio

boat n bad, cwch

body n corff

bog n cors, mignen

bogus adj ffug, gau, ffuantus

boil¹ n cornwyd, casgliad

boil² vb berwi
▸ **boil over** vi berwi drosodd

boiled adj berw; wedi'i ferwi

boiler n pair, crochan

boiling n berwedig

bold adj hy, eofn; eglur

bollard n bolard

bolt n bollt ▸ vb bolltio; dianc; traflyncu

bomb n bom

bomber n (person) bomiwr bomwraig); (plane) bomiwr

bombing n bomio

bomb scare n bygythiad bom

bond n rhwymyn; ysgrifrwym ▸ adj caeth

bone n asgwrn

bonfire n coelcerth, banffagl

bonnet n bonet

bonus n bonws, ychwanegiad

book n llyfr

bookcase n cwpwrdd llyfrau

book cover n clawr llyfr

booklet n llyfryn

bookshelf n silff lyfrau

bookshop n siop lyfrau

boom¹ n (on boat) bŵm

boom² vb trystio, utganu ▸ n trwst, swae

boost vb gwthio, hybu

boot n botasen, esgid

booth n bwth, lluest

booze (inf) vi diota, meddwi ▸ n diod feddwol

border n ffin, goror, ymyl ▸ vb ymylu

bore¹ vb (drill) tyllu, ebillio

bore² n rhywun diflas ▸ vt blino, diflasu

bored adj wedi syrffedu ar beth, wedi alaru

boring adj diflas, annifyr

born adj wedi ei eni

borough n bwrdeistref

borrow vt benthyca

bosom n mynwes, côl

boss n meistr

bossy adj tra-awdurdodus

both adj, pron, adv y ddau, ill dau

bother vb blino, trafferthu ▸ n helynt, trafferth

bottle n potel, costrel ▸ vt potelu, costrelu

bottle bank n banc poteli

bottle opener n agorwr poteli

bottom n gwaelod, godre; pen ôl, tin

boulder n carreg fawr, clogfaen

bounce vb neidio, adlamu

bouncer n (inf) bownsyr

bound¹ vt ffinio

bound² vi llamu, neidio

boundary n ffin, terfyn

bouquet n blodeuglwm, pwysi

bout n sbel; ornest, ffrwgwd

bow¹ n bwa; dolen
bow² vb plygu, crymu, ymgrymu ► n moesymgrymiad
bow³ n (of ship) pen blaen llong, bow
bowels npl ymysgaroedd, perfedd
bowl n cawg, basn
bowler n het galed; bowliwr
bowling n bowlio
box¹ n bocs, pren bocs
box² n bocs, blwch; sedd, côr
box³ vb taro bonclust; paffio
boxer n paffiwr, bocsiwr
boxer shorts npl trôns bocsiwr
boxing n (Boxing) paffio, bocsio
Boxing Day n Gŵyl San Steffan
box office n swyddfa docynnau
boy n bachgen, hogyn
boycott n boicot ► vb boicotio
boyfriend n cariadfab, anwylyd
bra n bra
brace n rhwymyn; pâr ► vt tynhau, cryfhau
bracelet n breichled
bracket n braced, cromfach
brag n brol, ymffrost, bocsach ► vb brolio, ymffrostio
braid n pleth, brwyd ► vt plethu, brwydo
brain n ymennydd
brainy adj peniog
brake n brêc ► vt brecio
bran n eisin, bran
branch n cangen, cainc ► vi canghennu
brand n pentewyn; nod ► vt gwarthnodi
brand-new adj newydd sbon
brandy n brandi
brash adj byrbwyll, ehud

brass n pres, efydd
brat n (inf!) cnaf bach, cenau bach
brave adj dewr, gwrol, glew ► vt herio
brawl vi ffraeo, terfysgu ► n ffrae, ffrwgwd
bray vi brefu (megis asyn), nadu
Brazil n Brasil
breach n adwy, rhwyg, tor; trosedd
bread n bara
breadth n lled
break (pt **broke**, pp **broken**) vb torri ► n toriad, tor; **break down** vi (car) torri i lawr; **break in** vi torri i mewn; **break off** vt torri; **break open** vt: to break sth open torri rhywbeth i'w agor; **break out** vi torri allan; **break up** vb chwalu
breakfast n brecwast ► vb brecwasta
break-in n lladrad
breast n bron, dwyfron, mynwes ► vt wynebu, ymladd â
breath n anadl, gwynt
Breathalyser® n Breathalyser
breathe vb anadlu, chwythu; **breathe in** vi mewnanadlu; **breathe out** vi allanadlu
breathing n anadliad
breed (pt, pp **bred**) vb magu; epilio; bridio ► n brid
breeze n awel, awelan, chwa
brew vt darllaw, bragu
brewery n bragdy
bribe n llwgrwobrwy ► vt llwgrwobrwyo
brick n bricsen, priddfaen ► vt bricio
bride n priodferch, priodasferch
bridegroom n priodfab

259

bridesmaid *n* morwyn briodas
bridge *n* pont ▸ *vt* pontio
bridle *n* ffrwyn ▸ *vt* ffrwyno
brief *adj* byr
briefcase *n* briffces
briefly *adv* am ychydig; *(in a few words)* mewn ychydig eiriau
briefs *n* briffs
bright *adj* disglair, claer, gloyw
brilliant *adj* disglair, llachar ▸ *n* gem
brim *n* ymyl, min; cantel
brine *n* heli
bring *(pt, pp* **brought)** *vt* dwyn, dod â; **bring back** *vt:* **to bring sth back** dod â rhywbeth yn ôl; **bring forward** *vt:* **to bring sth forward** dod â rhywbeth ymlaen; **bring up** *vt (child)* magu
brink *n* min, ymyl, glan
brisk *adj* bywiog, heini, sionc
bristle *n* gwrychyn, gwrych ▸ *vi* codi gwrychyn
Britain *n* Prydain
British *adj* Prydeinig, Brytanaidd
Briton *n* Brython, Prydeiniwr
Brittany *n* Llydaw
brittle *adj* brau, bregus
broad *adj* llydan, eang, bras
broadband *n* band llydan, band eang
broadcast *(pt, pp* **broadcast)** *n* darllediad ▸ *vb* darlledu
broaden *vb* lledu, ehangu
broccoli *n* brocoli, math o fresych
brochure *n* llyfryn
broke *adj (inf)* heb arian
broken *adj* toredig, briw, drylliedig
broker *n* brocer, dyn canol
bronchitis *n* bronceitis

bronze *n* pres, efydd
brooch *n* tlws
brood *n* nythaid; hil, epil ▸ *vi* deor; synfyfyrio
broom *n* banadl; ysgub
broth *n* potes, cawl
brothel *n* puteindy
brother *n* brawd
brother-in-law *n* brawd yng nghyfraith
brow *n* talcen; crib
brown *adj* brown, llwyd, gwinau
brown paper *n* papur llwyd
brown sugar *n* siwgr coch
browse *vi* pori
bruise *vb* cleisio, ysigo ▸ *n* clais
brunette *n* gwineuferch
brush *n* brws ▸ *vt* brwsio, ysgubo
Brussels *n* Brwsel
Brussels sprouts *npl* ysgewyll Brwsel
brutal *adj* creulon, bwystfilaidd
bubble *n* bwrlwm ▸ *vb* byrlymu
bubble gum *n* gwm chwythu
buck *n* bwch; coegyn ▸ *vb* llamsachu
bucket *n* bwced, ystwc
buckle *n* bwcl, gwäeg ▸ *vb* byclu, gwaegu
bud *n* blaguryn, eginyn ▸ *vb* blaguro, egino
Buddhism *n* Bwdhaeth
Buddhist *n* Bwdhaidd
budge *vb* syflyd, chwimio
budget *n* cyllideb
buff *adj* llwydfelyn
buffalo *n* bual
buffet *n* cernod ▸ *vt* cernodio, baeddu
buffet car *n* cerbyd bwffe

bug n drewbryf, bwg
build (pt, pp **built**) vt adeiladu ▸ n corffolaeth; **build up** vt cynyddu
builder n adeiladwr
building n adeilad
bulb n bwlb
Bulgaria n Bwlgaria
bulge n chwydd ▸ vt chwyddo
bulk n swm, crynswth
bull n tarw
bulldozer n peiriant clirio ffordd, tarw dur
bullet n bwled, bwleden
bulletin n bwletin
bullfight n ymladdfa deirw
bully n gormeswr, bwli ▸ vt gormesu, erlid
bum n (inf) tin
bumble-bee n cacynen
bump vb bwmpio, hergydio ▸ n bwmp, hergwd; **bump into** vt taro ar
bumper adj llawn, helaeth
bumpy adj anwadal, garw
bun n bynsen
bunch n swp; pwysi ▸ vb sypio
bundle n bwndel, coflaid ▸ vt bwndelu
bungalow n tŷ unllawr, byngalo
bunion n corn ar fys troed
bunk n bync
bunker n bwncer
buoy n bwi ▸ vt cynnal, cadw rhag suddo
buoyant adj hynawf; calonnog
burden n baich ▸ vt beichio, llwytho
bureau n ysgrifgist; swyddfa
bureaucracy n biwrocratiaeth

burger n byrgyr
burglar n bwrgler, lleidr
burglar alarm n larwm lladron
burglary n bwrgleriaeth
burgle vt bwrglera
burial n claddedigaeth
burn (pt, pp **burned**, **burnt**) vb llosgi, ysu ▸ n llosg, llosgiad; **burn down** vt llosgi i lawr
burrow n twll cwningen ▸ vb tyllu, tyrchu
burst (pt, pp **burst**) vb byrstio, torri ▸ n rhwyg
bury vt claddu
bus n bws
bush n perth, llwyn, prysgwydd, drysi
business n busnes
businessman n gŵr busnes
business trip n taith fusnes
businesswoman n gwraig fusnes
bus station n gorsaf fysiau, gorsaf bws
bus stop n arhosfan bysiau, arhosfan bws
bust n penddelw; mynwes
busy adj prysur

[KEYWORD]

but conj ond; **I'd love to come, but I'm busy** fe hoffwn ddod, ond rwy'n brysur; **he's not Welsh but English** nid Cymro mohono ond Sais; **but that's far too expensive!** ond mae hynny'n llawer rhy ddrud! ▸ prep (apart from, except) ond, ac eithrio, heblaw; **nothing but** dim [byd] ond; **we've had nothing but trouble** dim ond trafferth a

261

gawsom; **no-one but him can do it** dim ond ef a all ei wneud; **who but a lunatic would do such a thing?** pwy ond gwallgofddyn a wnâi sut beth?; **but for you/your help** heblaw amdant ti/heblaw am dy gymorth di; **anything but that** unrhyw beth ond hynny, unrhyw beth heblaw hynny

▸ *adv (just, only)* dim ond; **she's but a child** dim ond plentyn yw hi; **had I but known** petawn i ond yn gwybod; **I can but try** ni allaf ond rhoi cynnig arni; **all but finished** bron iawn â gorffen

butcher *n* cigydd ▸ *vt* cigyddio, lladd
butcher's (shop) *n* siop gig
butler *n* trulliad, bwtler
butt *vt* cornio, hyrddu, twlcio
butter *n* ymenyn ▸ *vt* rhoi ymenyn ar
buttercup *n* blodyn yr ymenyn
butterfly *n* glöyn byw, iâr fach yr haf, pili-pala
button *n* botwm ▸ *vt* botymu
buy (*pt, pp* **bought**) *vt* prynu
buzz *vb* suo, sisial, mwmian ▸ *n* su, sŵn gwenyn

〔KEYWORD〕

by *prep* **1** *(referring to cause, agent)* gan; **killed by lightning** wedi'i ladd gan fellt; **surrounded by a fence** wedi'i amgylchynu gan ffens; **a painting by Picasso** darlun gan Picasso
2 *(referring to method; manner; means):* **by bus/car** mewn bws/

car; **by train** mewn trên; **to pay by cheque** talu â siec; **by moonlight/ candlelight** yng ngolau'r lleuad/ gannwyll; **by saving hard** drwy gynilo'n ddiwyd
3 *(via, through)* trwy; **we came by Holyhead** daethom trwy Gaergybi
4 *(close to, past)* yn ymyl, ger, heibio; **the house by the school** y tŷ yn ymyl yr ysgol; **a holiday by the sea** gwyliau ger y môr; **she went by me** aeth heibio yn fy ymyl; **I go by the post office every day** rwy'n mynd heibio swyddfa'r post bob dydd
5 *(with time, not later than)* erbyn; *(during)* **by daylight** yn ystod golau dydd **by night** yn ystod y nos, liw nos; **by 4 o'clock** erbyn 4 o'r gloch; **by this time tomorrow** erbyn yr amser hwn yfory; **by the time I got here it was too late** erbyn imi gyrraedd roedd yn rhy hwyr
6 *(amount)* fesul; **by the kilo/metre** fesul kilo/metr; **paid by the hour** talu fesul awr
7 *(Math): (measure):* **to divide/ multiply by 3** rhannu/lluosi â 3; **a room 3 metres by 4** ystafell 3 metr wrth 4; **it's broader by a metre** mae fetr yn lletach
8 *(according to)* yn ôl, gan; **it's 3 o'clock by my watch** mae'n 3 o'r gloch yn ôl fy oriawr i; **it's all right by me** mae'n iawn gennyf i
9: (all) by oneself ar fy mhen fy hun

▸ *adv* **1** *see* **go, pass**
2: by and by maes o law, ymhen

amser; **by and large** ar y cyfan, at
ei gilydd

bye *excl* hwyl!
by-election *n* isetholiad
bypass *n* ffordd osgoi
bystander *n* un yn sefyll gerllaw

cab *n* cab
cabaret *n* cabare
cabbage *n* bresychen
cabin *n* caban ▸ *vt* cabanu,
caethiwo
cabinet *n* cabinet
cable *n* cebl
cable car *n* car codi
cable television *n* teledu cebl
cactus *n* cactws
café *n* tŷ bwyta, caffe
cage *n* cawell, caets ▸ *vt* cau,
carcharu
cake *n* teisen, cacen ▸ *vb* torthi;
caglu
calculate *vb* cyfrif, bwrw cyfrif
calculation *n* cyfrif
calculator *n* cyfrifiannell
calendar *n* calendr, almanac
calf[1] *n* llo
calf[2] *n* (*of the leg*) croth (coes)
calibre *n* calibr
call *vb* galw ▸ *n* galwad;
ymweliad; **call back** *vb* (*telephone*)

galw yn ôl; **call for** vt galw am;
call off vt canslo
call box n blwch ffôn
call centre n canolfan galwadau
callous adj croendew, dideimlad,
caled
calm adj tawel ▶ n tawelwch ▶ vb
tawelu; **calm down** vb tawelu
calorie n calori, uned gwres
Cambodia n Cambodia
Cambrian adj Cymreig
camel n camel
camera n ystafell; camera
camera phone n ffôn camera
camouflage n cuddliw, dull o
ddieithrio ▶ vb dieithrio, cuddio
camp n gwersyll ▶ vi gwersyllu
campaign n ymgyrch, rhyfelgyrch
camp bed n gwely plyg
camper n (person) gwersyllwr
gwersyllwraig); (van) cerbyd
gwersylla
camping n gwersylla; **to go
camping** gwersyllu
campsite n maes gwersylla
campus n campws
can¹ n tyn, piser, stên

KEYWORD

can² (negative **cannot, can't**,
conditional, pt **could**) aux vb **1** (be
able to) gallu, medru; **you can
do it if you try** gallwch ei wneud
os rhowch gynnig arno; **I can't
hear you** ni allaf eich clywed,
rwy'n methu'ch clywed; **can you
speak Welsh?** allwch chi siarad
Cymraeg?, ydych chi'n medru
Cymraeg?
2 (may) cael; **can I use your phone?**

a ga i ddefnyddio'ch ffôn?
3 (expressing disbelief, puzzlement
etc): **it can't be true!** does bosibl!;
what can he want? beth all fod
arno ei eisiau?
4 (expressing possibility, suggestion
etc): **he could be in the library** fe
allai fod yn y llyfrgell; **she could
have been delayed** fe allai fod
wedi'i dal yn ôl

Canada n Canada
Canadian adj Canadaidd ▶ n
Canadiad
canal n camlas; pibell
Canaries n: **the Canaries** yr
Ynysoedd Dedwydd
canary n caneri
cancel vt dileu, dirymu, diddymu
cancer n cancr; **Cancer** y Cranc
candidate n ymgeisydd
candle n cannwyll
candlestick n canhwyllbren
candy n candi
cane n corsen, cansen ▶ vt curo
â chansen
canister n tun cadw te, bocs (te)
cannabis n canabis
canned adj ar gadw mewn can, tun
cannon n magnel
canoe n ceufad, canŵ
canoeing n canŵa
canon n canon, rheol
can-opener n agorwr tuniau
canteen n cantîn
canter vi rhygyngu ▶ n rhygyng
canvas n cynfas, lliain bras
canvass vb trafod; canfasio
canyon n ceunant, canion
cap n cap, capan ▶ vt capio

capable *adj* galluog, cymwys
capacity *n* gallu, cymhwyster; cynnwys
cape¹ *n (headland)* penrhyn, pentir, trwyn
cape² *n (cloak)* mantell, cêp
caper *n* pranc ▸ *vi* prancio
capital *adj* prif, pen ▸ *n* priflythyren; prifddinas; cyfalaf
capitalism *n* cyfalafiaeth
capital punishment *n* y gosb eithaf
Capricorn *n* yr Afr
capsize *vb* dymchwelyd, troi
capsule *n* capswl
captain *n* capten
caption *n* pennawd, teitl
captivity *n* caethiwed
capture *n* daliad ▸ *vt* dal
car *n* car, cerbyd; **car wash** golchfa geir
caramel *n* caramel
caravan *n* carafán
caravan site *n* maes carafannau
carbohydrate *n* carbohydrad
carbohydrates *npl* carbohydradau
carbon *n* carbon
carbon footprint *n* ôl troed carbon
car boot sale *n* sêl cist car
carburettor *n* carburadur
carcass *n* celain, ysgerbwd
card¹ *n* cerdyn, carden
card² *vt* cribo gwlân
cardboard *n* cardbord
Cardiff *n* Caerdydd
cardigan *n* cardigan
cardinal *adj* prif, arbennig ▸ *n* cardinal
care *n* gofal, pryder ▸ *vi* gofalu, malio

career *n* gyrfa, hynt ▸ *vi* carlamu
careful *adj* gofalus, gwyliadwrus
carefully *adv* yn ofalus
careless *adj* diofal, esgeulus
caretaker *n* gofalwr
car-ferry *n* fferi geir
cargo *n* llwyth (llong), cargo
car hire (company) *n* cwmni llogi ceir
Caribbean *adj*: the Caribbean (Sea) y Caribî
caring *adj* gofalus
carnation *n* blodyn cigliw
carnival *n* carnifal
carol *n* carol ▸ *vi* caroli, canu
car park *n* maes parcio
carpenter *n* saer coed
carpentry *n* saernïaeth
carpet *n* carped ▸ *vt* carpedu
carriage *n* cerbyd; cludiad
carrier *n* cariwr, cludydd
carrier bag *n* cludfag
carrot *n* moronen
carry *vb* cario, cludo; **carry on** *vi* mynd ymlaen, dal ati; **carry out** *vt* gweithredu
carrycot *n* cot cario
cart *n* trol, cert, cart
carton *n* carton
cartoon *n* digriflun, cartŵn
cartridge *n* cetrisen
carve *vt* cerfio, naddu; torri cig
case¹ *n* achos; cyflwr; dadl
case² *n (holder)* cas, gwain
cash *n* arian parod
cash desk *n* safle talu
cashier *n* ariannwr, trysorydd
cashmere *n* cashmir
cash point *n* peiriant arian
casino *n* casino

casket n cistan, blwch
casserole n llestr coginio a dal bwyd
cassette n casét
cast vb bwrw, taflu ▸ n tafliad; **cast iron** haearn bwrw
castle n castell ▸ vi castellu
casual adj damweiniol, achlysurol
casualty n un wedi ei anafu
cat n cath
catalogue n catalog
cataract n rhaeadr; pilen
catarrh n llif annwyd, gormwyth
catastrophe n trychineb
catch (pt, pp **caught**) vt dal ▸ n bach, clicied; dalfa; **catch up** vi: **to catch up with sb** dal rhywun
catching adj heintus
category n trefn, dosbarth
cater vi arlwyo, darparu
caterpillar n lindysyn
cathedral n eglwys gadeiriol
catholic adj catholig ▸ n catholigydd
cattle npl gwartheg, da
cauliflower n blodfresychen
cause n achos ▸ vt achosi, peri
caution n pwyll; rhybudd ▸ vt rhybuddio
cautious adj gwyliadwrus
cave n ogof
caviar, caviare n grawn pysgod, cafiâr
cavity n ceudod, gwagle
CCTV n abbr teledu cylch cyfyng
CD n abbr CD, crynoddisg
CD player n chwaraewr cryno-ddisgiau
CD-ROM n CD-ROM
cease vb peidio, darfod

cedar n cedrwydden
ceiling n nen, nenfwd
celebrate vt dathlu; gweinyddu
celebrity n bri, enwogrwydd; person o fri
celery n seleri
cell n cell
cellar n seler
cello n sielo
cement n sment ▸ vt smentio; cadarnhau
cemetery n mynwent, claddfa
censor n sensor
census n cyfrifiad
cent n sent
centenary n canmlwyddiant
centigrade adj canradd, sentigred
centimetre n sentimedr
central adj canol, canolog
central heating n gwres canolog
centre n canol, canolfan ▸ vb canolbwyntio
centre forward n canolwr blaen
century n canrif
ceramic adj perthynol i grefft y crochenydd, ceramig
cereal n grawn, ŷd
ceremony n seremoni, defod
certain adj sicr; neilltuol; rhyw, rhai
certainly adv yn sicr, yn siwr
certainty n sicrwydd
certificate n tystysgrif
certify vt hysbysu, tystio
chain n cadwyn ▸ vt cadwyno
chair n cadair ▸ vt cadeirio
chairlift n cadair godi
chairman n cadeirydd
chalet n bwthyn (haf)
chalk n sialc ▸ vt sialcio

challenge n her, sialens ▸ vt herio, sialensio

chamber n ystafell, siambr

champagne n gwin Champagne

champion n pencampwr; pleidiwr ▸ vt cymryd plaid

championship n pencampwriaeth

chance n damwain, siawns ▸ vt digwydd

chancellor n canghellor

chandelier n canhwyllyr

change vb newid, cyfnewid ▸ n newid

changing-room n ystafell newid

channel n sianel, gwely; rhigol

Channel Tunnel n: the Channel Tunnel Twnel y Sianel

chant vt corganu ▸ n corgan, salmdon

chaos n tryblith, anhrefn

chap vt agennu, torri (am ddwylo)

chapel n capel

chapter n pennod; cabidwl

character n cymeriad; nod, arwydd

characteristic adj nodweddiadol ▸ n nodwedd

charcoal n marwor, golosg, sercol

charge vb cyhuddo; rhuthro; codi; llwytho ▸ n cyhuddiad; rhuthr; pris; ergyd

charger n (old) march rhyfel, cadfarch

charity n cariad; elusen

charity shop n siop elusennol

charm n swyn, cyfaredd ▸ vt swyno

charming adj cyfareddol, swynol, cwrtais

chart n siart

charter n siarter, breinlen ▸ vt breinio; llogi

charter flight n hediad siartr

chase vt ymlid, erlid, hel ▸ n helwriaeth

chat vi sgwrsio, ymgomio ▸ n sgwrs, ymgom

chat room n (Internet) stafell sgwrsio

chat show n sioe sgwrsio

chatter vi trydar; clebran; rhincian

chauffeur n gyrrwr

chauvinist n siofinydd

cheap adj rhad, salw

cheat n twyll; twyllwr ▸ vt twyllo

Chechnya n Chechnya

check n rhwystr, atalfa ▸ vt atal, ffrwyno; **check in** vi cofrestru

checkout n (in supermarket) desg dalu

checkup n (Med) archwiliad

cheek n grudd, boch; digywilydd-dra

cheeky adj digywilydd, haerllug, eg(e)r

cheer n calondid; arlwy ▸ vb llonni, sirioli

cheerful adj llon, siriol

cheese n caws

chef n prif gogydd

chemical adj cemegol ▸ n cyffur

chemist n fferyllydd; cemegydd

chemistry n cemeg

cheque n archeb (ar fanc), siec

cheque book n llyfr siec

cheque card n carden siec

cherry n ceiriosen

chess n gwyddbwyll

chessboard n bwrdd gwyddbwyll

chest n cist, coffr; brest

chestnut n castan
chew vb cnoi; **to chew the cud** cnoi cil
chewing gum n gwm cnoi
chick n cyw
chicken n cyw iâr
chickenpox n brech yr ieir
chickpea n gwygbysen, ffacbysen
chickpeas n gwygbys
chief adj pen, pennaf, prif ▸ n pennaeth
child n plentyn
childhood n plentyndod, mebyd
childish adj plentynnaidd
child minder n gwarchodwr
Chile n Chile
chill n oerni; annwyd ▸ adj oer; anwydog ▸ vb oeri, fferru, rhynnu
chilli n tsili
chilly adj (weather) oer; (manner) oeraidd
chimney n corn mwg, simnai
chin n gên
China n China, Tseina
china n llestri te (tsieni)
Chinese adj Tsieineaidd ▸ n Tsieinead
chip vb hacio, naddu ▸ n asglodyn, pric
chips npl sglodion
chiropodist n troedfeddyg
chisel n cŷn, gaing
chives n cennin sifi
chocolate n siocled
choice n dewis, dewisiad ▸ adj dewisol, dethol
choir n côr
choke vb tagu; mygu; cau
choose (pt **chose**, pp **chosen**) vb dewis, dethol, ethol

chop vt torri ▸ n golwyth
chopsticks n gweill bwyta
chord n tant; cord
chore n y dwt
chorus n côr, cytgan, corws
Christ n Crist
christen vt bedyddio, enwi
christening n bedydd
Christian adj Cristnogol ▸ n Cristion
Christianity n Cristnogaeth
Christian name n enw bedydd
Christmas n Nadolig
Christmas Eve n Noswyl Nadolig
chrome n crôm
chronic adj parhaol (am anhwyldeb)
chrysanthemum n ffarwel haf
chubby adj wynepgrwn, tew
chuck vt (inf) taflu, lluchio
chuckle vi chwerthin yn nwrn dyn
chum n cyfaill mebyd ▸ vi cyfrinachu
chunk n tafell dew, toc
church n eglwys, llan ▸ vt eglwysa
churchyard n mynwent
churn n buddai ▸ vb corddi
chutney n picl cymysg
cider n seidr
cigar n sigâr
cigarette n sigarét
cigarette lighter n taniwr sigaréts
cinema n sinema
cinnamon n sinamon
circle n cylch ▸ vb cylchu
circuit n cylch; cylchdaith
circular adj crwn ▸ n cylchlythyr
circulate vb cylchredeg, lledaenu
circumstances npl amgylchiadau
circus n syrcas

cite *vt* gwysio; dyfynnu
citizen *n* dinesydd
citizenship *n* dinasyddiaeth
city *n* dinas
city centre *n* canol y ddinas
city technology college *n* coleg
technoleg dinasol
civic *adj* dinesig
civil *adj* dinesig, gwladol; moesgar
civilian *n* dinesydd (anfilwrol)
civilization *n* gwareiddiad
civil servant *n* gwas sifil
civil service *n* gwasanaeth sifil,
gwasanaeth gwladol
civil war *n* rhyfel cartref
claim *vt* hawlio ► *n* hawl
clamp *n* ystyffwl, craff
clan *n* tylwyth, llwyth
clap *n* twrf, trwst ► *vb* curo; taro
claret *n* claret
clarify *vt* gloywi, puro; egluro
clarinet *n* clarinet
clash *vb* taro, gwrthdaro ► *n*
gwrthdrawiad
clasp *n* bach, clesbyn ► *vt* cofleidio
class *n* dosbarth ► *vt* dosbarthu
classic *n* clasur, campwaith ► *adj*
clasurol
classical *adj* clasurol
classify *vb* dosbarthu
classmate *n* cyd-ddisgybl
classroom *n* ystafell ddosbarth
classroom assistant *n*
cynorthwyydd dosbarth
clatter *vb* clewtian, clepian, trystio
► *n* trwst
clause *n* adran, cymal
claw *n* crafanc, ewin ► *vt*
crafangu, cripio
clay *n* clai

clean *adj* glân, glanwaith ► *vt*
glanhau
cleaner *n* glanhäwr, glanhëydd
cleaner's *n* siop glanhau dillad
cleaning *n* glanhad, glanheuad
cleanser *n* glanhäwr
cleansing lotion *n* hufen glanhau
clear *adj* clir, eglur, gloyw; croyw
► *vt* clirio; **clear off** *vi* (*inf*) **clear
off!** hel dy bac!; **clear up** *vi*
(*weather*) codi'n braf
clearly *adv* yn glir
clench *vt* cau yn dynn, clensio
clergy *n* offeiriaid
clerk *n* clerc
clever *adj* medrus, clyfar
cleverness *n* medr, clyfrwch
click *vi* clician, clepian ► *n* clic
client *n* cyflogydd cyfreithiwr,
cwsmer
cliff *n* clogwyn, allt
climate *n* hinsawdd
climate change *n* newid hinsawdd
climax *n* uchafbwynt
climb *vb* dringo
climber *n* dringwr
climbing *adj* dringol
clinch *vt* clensio; cau, cloi
cling (*pt, pp* clung) *vi* glynu, cydio
clingfilm *n* clingffilm
clinic *n* meddygfa, clinig
clip *vt* tocio, clipio
cloak *n* mantell, clogyn ► *vt*
cuddio, celu
cloakroom *n* ystafell ddillad
clock *n* cloc
clog *n* clocsen ► *vt* llesteirio; tagu;
clocsio
close¹ *vb* cau; terfynu ► *n* diwedd,
diweddglo

269

close² adj agos, clòs; tyn
close³ n (courtyard) clas, clos, buarth
closed adj ar gau
closely adv yn agos
closet n cell, ystafell; geudy
close-up n llun agos
closure n cau, gorffen, darfod
clot n tolchen ▸ vb tolchi, ceulo
cloth n brethyn, lliain
clothes npl dillad, gwisgoedd
clothes peg n bachyn dillad
clothing n dillad
cloud n cwmwl ▸ vt cymylu
cloudy adj cymylog
clown n lleban; clown
club n pastwn; clwb ▸ vb pastynu; clybio; **club together** vi casglu arian
clubbing n clybio
clue n pen llinyn, arwydd
clump n clwmp, clamp, cyff
clumsy adj trwsgl, lletchwith
cluster n clwstwr, swp ▸ vb casglu, tyrru
clutch n crafanc; gafael; hafflau ▸ vb crafangu
coach n coets, bws; hyfforddwr ▸ vb hyfforddi
coal n glöyn, glo
coalition n cyfuniad; cynghrair, clymblaid
coarse adj garw, bras; aflednais
coast n arfordir, glan ▸ vi hwylio gyda'r lan
coastal adj arfordirol
coastguard n gwyliwr y glannau
coastline n morlin
coat n cot
coat hanger n cambren (dillad)

coating n caen, golchiad
coax vb hudo, denu, perswadio
cobweb n gwe pryf cop, gwe'r cor
cock n ceiliog; mwdwl; clicied (dryll) ▸ vb mydylu; codi clicied
cockerel n cyw ceiliog, ceiliogyn
cockpit n sedd peilot; ymladdfan ceiliogod
cockroach n chwilen ddu
cocktail n coctêl
cocoa n coco
coconut n cneuen goco, coconyt
cod n penfras; còd
code n cod
coffee n coffi
coffee table n bwrdd coffi
coffin n arch, ysgrîn
cog n dant olwyn, còg
coil vb torchi ▸ n torch
coin n arian bath ▸ vb bathu
coincide vi cyd-ddigwydd, cyd-daro
coincidence n cyd-ddigwyddiad
coke n golosg
colander n hidl
cold adj oer ▸ n oerfel, oerni; annwyd; **to catch a cold** dal annwyd
coleslaw n colslo
colic n bolwst, colig
collapse vb disgyn, cwympo ▸ n cwymp, methiant
collar n coler ▸ vb coleru
collarbone n pont yr ysgwydd
colleague n cydweithiwr
collect n colect ▸ vb crynhoi, hel, casglu; ymgynnull
collection n casgliad
collector n casglwr
college n coleg

collide vb gwrthdaro
collision n gwrthdrawiad
colon n colon (:); coluddyn mawr
colonel n cyrnol
colonial adj trefedigaethol
colony n trefedigaeth, gwladfa
colour n lliw, baner ▸ vb lliwio;
  cochi; **colour blind** lliwddall
colourful adj lliwgar
colouring n lliwiad
column n colofn
coma n hunglwyf, côma
comb n crib ▸ vb cribo
combat n brwydr, gornest ▸ vb
  brwydro
combination n cyfuniad
combine vb cyfuno; **combine
  harvester** cynaeafydd,
  combein

[KEYWORD]

come (pt **came**, pp **come**) vi **1**
(movement towards) dod; **to come
running** dod dan redeg; **he's come
here to work** mae wedi dod yma
i weithio; **come with me** dewch
gyda mi
2 (arrive) cyrraedd; **to come home**
dod adref; **we've just come from
Cardiff** rydym newydd gyrraedd
o Gaerdydd
3 (reach): **to come to** (decision etc)
dod i; **the bill came to £40** £40
oedd y bil
4 (occur): **an idea came to me**
daeth syniad imi, cododd syniad
yn fy mhen
5 (be, become): **to come loose/
undone** dod yn rhydd, mynd yn
rhydd; **I've come to like him** rwyf

wedi dod i'w hoffi
  ▸ **come across** vt fus dod ar
draws
  ▸ **come along** vi (pupil, work) dod
ymlaen
  ▸ **come back** vi dod yn ôl,
dychwelyd
  ▸ **come down** vi dod i lawr;
(prices) disgyn, syrthio; (buildings)
disgyn, syrthio; (be demolished)
cael ei ddymchwel
  ▸ **come from** vt fus (source) dod o,
tarddu o; (place) dod o, hanu o
  ▸ **come in** vi dod i mewn;
(fashion) dod i mewn i ffasiwn; (on
deal etc) ymuno â, cymryd rhan
mewn
  ▸ **come off** vi (button) dod yn
rhydd, datod; (attempt) llwyddo
  ▸ **come on** vi (lights, electricity)
dod ymlaen; (pupil, work, project)
dod ymlaen, gwneud cynnydd;
come on! (singular) dere!, tyrd!
(plural) dewch!
  ▸ **come out** vi dod allan
  ▸ **come round** vi (after faint,
operation) dod at ei hun, dadebru
  ▸ **come to** vi dadebru
  ▸ **come up** vi codi; (sun) codi;
(problem) codi; (event) codi; (in
conversation) codi
  ▸ **come up with** vt fus (money)
darparu; **he came up with an idea**
cafodd syniad, cynigiodd syniad

comedian n comedïwr
comedy n comedi
comfort n cysur, diddanwch ▸ vt
  cysuro, diddanu

comfortable *adj* cysurus, cyffyrddus
comic *adj* comic, digrif, ysmala
comma *n* atalnod, coma
command *vb* gorchymyn ▸ *n* gorchymyn, awdurdod
commander *n* cadlywydd, comander
commemorate *vt* coffáu, dathlu
commence *vb* dechrau
commend *vt* cymeradwyo, canmol
comment *vi* sylwi, esbonio ▸ *n* sylw
commentary *n* sylwebaeth
commentator *n* esboniwr, sylwebydd
commerce *n* masnach
commercial *adj* masnachol
commission *n* comisiwn, dirprwyaeth ▸ *vb* comisiynu
commissioner *n* comisiynydd
commit *vt* cyflawni; traddodi; cyflwyno
commitment *n* ymrwymiad; traddodiad
committee *n* pwyllgor
commodity *n* nwydd (masnachol)
common *adj* cyffredin ▸ *n* tir cyffredin, comin
commonplace *adj* dibwys, cyffredin
commons *npl* y cyffredin; **House of Commons** Tŷ'r Cyffredin
common sense *n* synnwyr cyffredin
commonwealth *n* cymanwlad
communal *adj* cymunol, cymunedol
commune *vi* ymddiddan; cymuno ▸ *n* cymundod

communicate *vb* cyfathrebu; cymuno
communication *n* cyfathrebiad, cysylltiad, neges
communion *n* cymun, cymundeb
communism *n* comiwnyddiaeth
communist *n* comiwnydd
community *n* cymdeithas, cymuned; **community centre** canolfan gymuned
commute *vt* cymudo, pendilio
commuter *n* cymudwr, pendiliwr
compact *n* cytundeb, cyfamod; compact ▸ *adj* cryno ▸ *vt* crynhoi
compact disc *n* cryno-ddisg, CD
companion *n* cydymaith
company *n* cymdeithas, cwmni; **to keep company with** cadw cwmni â
comparative *adj* cymharol
comparatively *adv* yn gymharol
compare *vt* cymharu, cyffelybu
comparison *n* cymhariaeth
compartment *n* adran, cerbydran
compass *n* cwmpawd; cwmpas ▸ *vt* amgylchu
compassion *n* tosturi
compatible *adj* cydweddol, cyson
compel *vt* cymell, gorfodi
compensate *vt* talu iawn, digolledu
compensation *n* iawndal
compete *vi* cystadlu
competent *adj* cymwys, digonol
competition *n* cystadleuaeth
competitive *adj* cystadleuol
competitor *n* cystadleuydd
complacent *adj* hunan-foddhaus, digonol

complain vi cwyno, achwyn, grwgnach

complaint n cwyn, achwyniad; anhwyldeb

complement n cyflawnder, cyflenwad

complementary adj cyflenwol

complete adj cyflawn ▶ vt cyflawni

completely adv yn llwyr

completion n cwblhad

complex adj cymhleth, dyrys

complexion n gwedd, pryd, gwawr

compliance n cydsyniad

complicate vt cymhlethu; drysu

complicated adj cymhleth, dyrys

complication n cymhlethdod

compliment n cyfarchiad; canmoliaeth

comply vi cydsynio, ufuddhau

component n cydran, cyfansoddyn

compose vt cyfansoddi; cysodi; tawelu

composer n cyfansoddwr

composition n cyfansoddiad, traethawd

composure n tawelwch, hunan-feddiant

compound adj cyfansawdd ▶ n cymysg ▶ vb cymysgu

comprehension n amgyffred, dirnadaeth

comprehensive adj cynhwysfawr

comprehensive school n ysgol gyfun

compress vt gwasgu, crynhoi ▶ n plastr

comprise vt amgyffred, cynnwys

compromise n cymrodedd, cyfaddawd ▶ vb cymrodeddu, cyfaddawdu

compulsive adj trwy orfod, o anfodd

compulsory adj gorfodol

computer n cyfrifiadur

computer game n gêm gyfrifiadur

computer programmer n rhaglennydd cyfrifiaduron

computer science n cyfrifiadureg

computer studies npl astudiaethau cyfrifiadurol

computing n cyfrifiaduro

conceal vb cuddio, celu, dirgelu

concede vt caniatáu, addef

conceited adj hunandybus, hunanol, balch

conceive vb dirnad; tybied; beichiogi

concentrate vt crynodi, canolbwyntio

concentration n crynodiad, ymroddiad

concept n cysyniad

concern vt ymwneud (â), pryderu, bod a wnelo â ▶ n busnes, diddordeb; gofal, pryder

concerned adj pryderus, gofalus

concerning prep ynglŷn â, ynghylch

concert n cyngerdd ▶ vt cyd-drefnu

conclude vb diweddu; casglu, barnu

conclusion n diwedd; casgliad

concrete adj diriaethol ▶ n concrit

concussion n cyd-drawiad, ysgytiad

condemn vb condemnio, collfarnu

condensation *n* cywasgiad, cyddwysedd

condense *vb* cywasgu, cyddwyso, cwtogi

condition *n* cyflwr, ansawdd; amod ► *vb* cyflyru; amodi

conditional *adj* amodol

conditioner *n* cyflyrydd

condom *n* condom

condominium *n* cydlywodraeth, condominiwm

condone *vt* maddau, esgusodi

conduct[1] *n* ymddygiad, ymarweddiad

conduct[2] *vt* arwain

conductor *n* arweinydd; tocynnwr

cone *n* pigwrn, côn

confer *vb* ymgynghori, cyflwyno

conference *n* cynhadledd

confess *vb* cyffesu, cyfaddef

confession *n* cyffesiad, cyffes

confide *vb* ymddiried

confidence *n* ymddiried, hyder; **self-confidence** hunanhyder

confident *adj* hyderus

confidential *adj* cyfrinachol

confine *vt* cyfyngu, carcharu, caethiwo

confined *adj* caeth, cyfyng

confirm *vt* cadarnhau; conffirmio

confirmation *n* cadarnhad; bedydd esgob, conffirmasiwn

confiscate *vt* atafaelu

conflict[1] *n* gwrthdrawiad, ymryson

conflict[2] *vi* anghytuno, gwrthdaro

conform *vb* cydymffurfio

confront *vt* wynebu

confrontation *n* gwrthdaro

confuse *vt* cymysgu, drysu

confused *adj* cymysg; didrefn; dyrys

confusing *adj* dryslyd

confusion *n* anhrefn

congestion *n* gorlenwad, tagfa, crynhoad

congratulate *vt* llongyfarch

congratulations *n* llongyfarchiadau

congregation *n* cynulleidfa

congress *n* cyngres, cymanfa

conjunction *n* cysylltiad

conjure *vb* consurio

connect *vb* cysylltu, cydio

connection *n* cysylltiad, perthynas; **in connection with** ynglŷn â

conquer *vt* gorchfygu, trechu

conquest *n* buddugoliaeth, concwest

conscience *n* cydwybod

conscientious *adj* cydwybodol

conscious *adj* ymwybodol

consciousness *n* ymwybyddiaeth

consecutive *adj* olynol

consent *vi* cydsynio ► *n* cydsyniad, caniatâd

consequence *n* canlyniad

consequently *adv* o ganlyniad

conservation *n* cadwraeth, gwarchodaeth

conservative *adj* ceidwadol ► *n* ceidwadwr

conservatory *n* tŷ gwydr

consider *vb* ystyried

considerable *adj* cryn

considerate *adj* ystyriol, tosturiol

consideration *n* ystyriaeth

considering *prep* ac ystyried

consist *vt* cynnwys

consistency n cysondeb
consistent n cyson
consolation n cysur, diddanwch
console vt cysuro, diddanu
consonant adj cysain; cyson ▸ n cytsain
conspicuous adj amlwg
conspiracy n cynllwyn
constable n cwnstabl, heddgeidwad
constant adj cyson
constantly adv yn gyson
constipated adj rhwym
constipation n rhwymedd
constituency n etholaeth
constitution n cyfansoddiad
constraint n cyfyngydd, cyfyngiad
construct vt llunio, adeiladu, saernïo
construction n adeiladwaith, lluniad; cystrawen
constructive adj ymarferol, adeiladol
consul n ynad, conswl
consulate n consuliaeth
consult vb ymgynghori
consultant n ymgynghorwr
consume vb treulio, difa, ysu; nychu
consumer n prynwr, treuliwr, defnyddiwr
consumption n traul; darfodedigaeth
contact n cyffyrddiad, cyswllt
contact lenses npl lensys cyffwrdd
contagious adj heintus
contain vt cynnwys, dal
container n cynhwysydd
contaminate vt halogi, llygru

contemplate vb ystyried, myfyrio; bwriadu
contemporary adj cyfoes(ol) ▸ n cyfoeswr
contempt n dirmyg, diystyrwch; **contempt of court** dirmyg llys
contend vb ymryson, cystadlu
content¹ adj bodlon ▸ vt bodloni
content² n cynnwys
contented adj bodlon
contest¹ n cystadleuaeth, ymryson
contest² vb amau, ymryson, ymladd
contestant n cystadleuydd
context n cyd-destun
continent n cyfandir
continental adj cyfandirol
continental breakfast n brecwast cyfandirol
continual adj parhaus, gwastadol
continue vb parhau, para, dal (i)
continuous adj parhaol, di-fwlch, di-dor
continuous assessment n asesiad parhaus, asesu parhaus
contour n amlinell, cyfuchlinedd
contraceptive n cyfarpar gwrth-genhedlu
contract¹ n cytundeb, cyfamod, contract
contract² vb byrhau; cytuno, cyfamodi
contractor n contractwr, adeiladydd
contradict vt gwrth-ddweud
contrary adj gwrthwyneb, croes; **on the contrary** i'r gwrthwyneb
contrast n gwrthgyferbyniad ▸ vb gwrthgyferbynnu
contribute vb cyfrannu

contribution n cyfraniad
contributor n cyfrannwr
control vt llywodraethu, rheoli ▸ n rheolaeth, awdurdod; **self control** hunanreolaeth
controversial adj dadleuol
controversy n dadl
convenience n cyfleustra, hwylustod
convenient adj cyfleus, hwylus
convent n cwfaint, lleiandy
convention n confensiwn, cynhadledd
conventional adj confensiynol
conversation n ymddiddan, sgwrs
conversion n trõedigaeth, tro
convert vt troi, newid, trosi; **converted try** trosgais
convertible adj trosadwy
convey vt cludo; trosglwyddo; cyfleu
conveyor belt n cludfelt
convict¹ vt barnu'n euog, euogfarnu; argyhoeddi
convict² n troseddwr
conviction n euogfarn; argyhoeddiad
convince vt argyhoeddi
convincing adj argyhoeddiadol
cook n cogydd, cogyddes ▸ vb coginio, gwneud bwyd
cooker n cwcer; **pressure cooker** gwascogydd, sosban wyllt
cookery n coginiaeth
cookie n (biscuit) bisgeden; (Comput) cwci
cooking n coginiaeth

cool adj oer, oeraidd; hunanfeddiannol ▸ vb oeri, claearu
cooperate vi cydweithio, cydweithredu
cooperation n cydweithrediad
cop (inf) n plismon ▸ vt dal
cope vi ymdaro â, ymdopi â
copper n copr, copor
copy n copi ▸ vt copïo
copyright n hawlfraint
coral n cwrel
cord n cortyn, rheffyn ▸ vt rheffynnu
corduroy n melfaréd, rib
core n calon, perfedd, craidd
cork n corc, corcyn ▸ vt corcio
corkscrew n corcsgriw
corn¹ n ŷd, llafur
corn² n (on foot) corn (ar droed)
corned beef n corn-bîff
corner n congl, cornel, cil ▸ vt cornelu; **corner kick** cic gornel
cornflakes npl creision ŷd
cornflour n blawd corn
Cornwall n Cernyw
coronation n coroniad
coroner n crwner
corporal adj corfforol
corporate adj yn un corff, corfforedig
corporation n corfforaeth
corps n corfflu
corpse n corff (marw), celain
correct adj cywir ▸ vt cywiro; ceryddu
correction n cywiriad; cerydd
correctly adv yn gywir
correspond vi cyfateb; gohebu

correspondence n cyfatebiaeth; gohebiaeth
correspondent n gohebydd
corridor n coridor
corrode vb cyrydu, ysu, rhydu, treulio
corrupt adj llygredig, pwdr ▸ vb llygru
corruption n llygredigaeth
cosmetic n cosmetig
cosmetics npl cosmetigau
cosmetic surgery n llawfeddygaeth gosmetig
cost (pt, pp **cost**) vi costio ▸ n cost, traul
costly adj drudfawr, drud
costume n gwisg, costiwm
cosy adj cysurus, clyd
cot n gwely bychan, cot
cottage n bwthyn
cotton n cotwm; edau; **cotton wool** gwlân cotwm
couch n glwth, soffa ▸ vb gorwedd
cough n peswch ▸ vb pesychu
council n cyngor; **council house** tŷ cyngor
councillor n cynghorwr
counsel n cyngor ▸ vt cynghori
counsellor n cynghorwr, cyfarwyddwr
count¹ n cyfrif ▸ vb rhifo, cyfrif; **count the cost** bwrw'r draul ▸ **count on** vt dibynnu ar
count² n (title) iarll
counter n cownter
counter- adj croes ▸ adv yn erbyn, yn groes
counterfeit n ffug, twyll ▸ adj gau, ffug ▸ vt ffugio

counterpart n rhan gyfatebol, cymar
countess n iarlles
countless adj aneirif, di-rif
country n gwlad, bro ▸ adj gwladaidd, gwledig; **country music** canu gwlad
countryside n cefn gwlad
county n sir, swydd
coup n ergyd, trawiad; llwyddiant
couple n cwpl ▸ vt cyplu, cyplysu
coupon n cwpon
courage n gwroldeb, dewrder
courgette n corbwmpen
courier n cennad; tywyswr
course n cwrs, hynt ▸ vt hela, ymlid; **of course** wrth gwrs; **in the course of** yn ystod; **in due course** yn ei bryd; **crash course** cwrs carlam
court n llys; cwrt; cyntedd ▸ vt caru
courtesy n cwrteisrwydd, cwrteisi
courtyard n cwrt, clos, iard
cousin n cefnder; cyfnither
cover vt gorchuddio, toi; amddiffyn ▸ n gorchudd, clawr; **to take cover** cuddio, cysgodi
cover charge n tâl am wasanaeth
covert adj cêl, cudd, dirgel
cow n buwch; **barren cow** myswynog; **milking cow** buwch odro; **cow in calf** buwch gyflo
coward n llwfrgi
cowardly adj llwfr
cowboy n cowboi
crab n cranc

crack

crack vb cracio, hollti ▶ n crac;
  crack down on vi syrthio'n
  drwm ar
cracked adj wedi cracio
cracker n cracer; bisgeden
crackle vi clindarddach
cradle n crud, cawell; cadair fagu
craft n crefft; cyfrwystra, dichell;
  llong, bad
craftsman n crefftwr
craftsmanship n crefftwriaeth
cram vb gorlenwi, stwffio, saco
cramp n cwlwm gwythi, cramp
  ▶ vt caethiwo, gwasgu
cramped adj clòs
crane n garan, crëyr, crychydd;
  craen ▶ vt estyn (gwddf)
crash vb gwrthdaro, cwympo ▶ n
  gwrthdrawiad, cwymp
crash helmet n helmed
  ddiogelwch
crate n cawell
crave vb deisyf, dyheu
crawl vi ymlusgo, cropian; crafu
crayon n creon
craze n ysfa
crazy adj penwan, gorffwyll, o'i gof
creak vi gwichian
cream n hufen
creamy adj hufennog
crease n ôl plygiad, plyg ▶ vt
  crychu
creased adj crychlyd
create vt creu
creation n cread, creadigaeth
creative adj creadigol
creator n crëwr, creawdwr
creature n creadur
credentials npl credlythyrau

credible adj credadwy
credit n coel, cred; clod, credyd
  ▶ vt coelio
credit card n cerdyn credyd
creek n cilfach
creep (pt, pp **crept**) vi ymlusgo,
  cropian; **creep** vi ymlusgo,
  cropian
cremate vt amlosgi
crematorium n amlosgfa
crescent n hanner lleuad; cilgant
  ▶ adj cynyddol
cress n berwr
crest n crib; arwydd ar arfbais
crew n criw; haid
crib n preseb; gwely plentyn ▶ vt
  (inf) copïo
cricket n criced; cricsyn
crime n trosedd
criminal adj troseddol ▶ n
  troseddwr
crimson adj, n rhuddgoch
cringe vi cynffonna, ymgreinio
cripple n (offensive) cloff, efrydd
  ▶ vt cloffi, efryddu
crisis n argyfwng
crisp adj cras, crych
crisps npl creision tatws
criterion n maen prawf, safon
critic n beirniad
critical adj beirniadol; pryderus;
  peryglus
criticism n beirniadaeth
criticize vt beirniadu
Croatia n Croatia
crockery n llestri
crocodile n crocodil
crocus n saffrwn, crocus

crook n crwca, ffon fugail; (inf) troseddwr

crooked adj crwca, cam

crop n cnwd, cynnyrch; crombil ▸ vt tocio, torri

cross n, adj croes ▸ vb croesi; **cross out** vt croesi allan; **cross over** vi croesi

cross-country n, adj traws gwlad

crossing n croesfan

crossroads n croesffordd

crossword n croesair

crouch vi cyrcydu ▸ n cwrcwd; **crouch down** vi cyrcydu

crow¹ n brân

crow² vi canu fel ceiliog; ymffrostio

crowd n torf, tyrfa ▸ vb tyrru, heidio

crowded adj llawn o bobl

crown n coron; corun ▸ vt coroni

crucial adj hanfodol, terfynol

crucifix n croeslun

crude adj cri, crai; llymrig, amrwd

cruel adj creulon

cruelty n creulondeb

cruise vi morio ▸ n mordaith

crumb n briwsionyn

crumble vb briwsioni, malurio ▸ n briwsiongrwst

crumpet n crymped

crumple vb crychu, gwasgu

crunch vb creinsio

crush vb gwasgu, llethu ▸ n gwasgiad, torf

crust n crawen, crofen, crystyn

crutch n bagl, ffon fagl

cry vb llefain, wylo, crio ▸ n llef, sgrech, cri

crystal n grisial ▸ adj grisialaidd

cub n cenau

cube n ciwb ▸ vb ciwbio

cubicle n cuddygl

cuckoo n cog, cwcw; gwirionyn

cucumber n cucumer

cuddle vb anwylo, anwesu

cue n awgrym; ciw

cuff n torch llawes

cul-de-sac n pen ffordd, heol hosan

cull vt dewis, pigo

culminate vi cyrraedd ei anterth, diweddu

culprit n troseddwr, drwgweithredwr

cult n addoliad, cwlt

cultivate vt diwyllio, trin, meithrin

cultural adj diwylliannol

culture n diwylliant; gwrtaith

cunning adj dichellgar, cyfrwys ▸ n cyfrwystra

cup n cwpan

cupboard n cwpwrdd

curator n curadur

curb n atalfa; cwrbyn ▸ vt ffrwyno

curdle vb ceulo, cawsio

cure n iachâd, gwellhad; meddyginiaeth ▸ vb iacháu, gwella; halltu

curfew n hwyrgloch

curiosity n cywreinrwydd, chwilfrydedd

curious adj cywrain; chwilfrydig; hynod

curl n cwrl, cudyn ▸ vb cyrlio

curly adj cyrliog, crych

currency n arian breiniol

current adj cyfredol, cyfoes ▸ n ffrwd, llif; **current account** cyfrif

cyfredol; **current affairs** materion
cyfoes
currently *adv* ar hyn o bryd
curriculum *n* cwricwlwm;
National Curriculum Cwricwlwm
Cenedlaethol
curriculum vitae *n* braslun bywyd,
manylion personol
curry *vt* trin lledr ▸ *n* cyrri; **to curry
favour** cynffonna, ceisio ffafr
curse *n* melltith, rheg ▸ *vb*
melltithio, rhegi
cursor *n* (*Comput*) cyrchwr
curt *adj* cwta, byr
curtain *n* llen
curve *vb* camu, gwyro, troi ▸ *n*
tro; cromlin
cushion *n* clustog
custard *n* cwstard
custody *n* dalfa, cadwraeth
custom *n* defod; cwsmeriaeth; toll
customer *n* cwsmer
customs *npl* y tollau
customs officer *n* swyddog tollau
cut (*pt, pp* **cut**) *vb* torri ▸ *n* toriad,
archoll, briw; **cut back** torri yn ôl;
cut in torri ar draws; **cut out** torri
allan; **cut through** torri trwodd;
cut down *vt* (*tree*) torri; **cut off** *vt*
torri; **cut up** *vt* torri
cute *adj* ciwt, cyfrwys
cutlery *n* cwtleri
cutlet *n* golwyth, cydled
CV *n abbr* (= *curriculum vitae*) CV,
braslun bywyd
cyberbullying *n* seiber-fwlio
cybercafé *n* caffi rhyngrwyd, caffe
rhyngrwyd

cycle *n* cylch; cyfres; beic ▸ *vb*
beicio, seiclo
cycling *n* beicio, seiclo
cyclist *n* beiciwr
cyclone *n* trowynt
cylinder *n* rhol; silindr
cynical *adj* gwawdlyd, dirmygus
Cyprus *n* Ynys Cyprus
cyst *n* coden
cystitis *n* llid y bledren
Czech *n* (*person*) Tsieciad;
(*language*) Tsieceg ▸ *adj* Tsiecaidd;
(*in language*) Tsieceg
Czech Republic *n*: **the Czech
Republic** y Weriniaeth Tsiec

d

dab vt dabio ► n dab
dad, daddy n tad, tada, dada
daffodil n cenhinen Bedr
daft adj (inf) hurt, gwirion
dagger n dagr, bidog
daily adj dyddiol, beunyddiol ► adv beunydd, bob dydd
dairy n llaethdy; **dairy products** cynhyrchion llaeth
daisy n llygad y dydd
dam n argae, cronfa ► vt argáu, cronni
damage n niwed, difrod ► vt niweidio, difrodi; **damages** npl iawn
damn vb damnio
damp adj llaith ► n lleithder ► vb lleithio
dance vb dawnsio ► n dawns; **folk dance** dawns werin; **public folk dance** twmpath dawns
dancer n dawnsiwr

dandelion n dant y llew
dandruff n marwdon, cen
Dane n brodor o Ddenmarc, Daniad
danger n perygl, enbydrwydd
dangerous adj peryglus, enbyd
dangle vb hongian; siglo
Danish n (language) Daneg ► adj Danaidd; (in language) Daneg
dare vb beiddio, mentro
daring adj beiddgar, mentrus ► n beiddgarwch
dark adj tywyll ► n tywyllwch, nos
darken vb tywyllu
darkness n tywyllwch
darling n anwylyd, cariad ► adj annwyl
dart n dart ► vb dartio, rhuthro
dash vb rhuthro; chwalu, chwilfriwio ► n rhuthr; llinell (-)
dashboard n dashfwrdd
data npl data
database n cronfa ddata
date n dyddiad, amseriad; datysen ► vb dyddio; **out of date** henffasiwn, wedi dyddio; **up to date** hyd yn hyn, cyfoes
dated adj dyddiedig
daughter n merch; **daughter-in-law** merch yng nghyfraith
dawn vi gwawrio, dyddio ► n gwawr
day n diwrnod, dydd; **by day** liw dydd; **today** heddiw; **next day** trannoeth; **the day before yesterday** echdoe
day-dream vb pensynnu, synfyfyrio
daylight n golau dydd
day-time n y dydd
dazzle vb disgleirio; dallu

dazzling adj disglair, llachar
dead adj marw ▶ adv hollol; **the dead** y meirw; **dead centre** yn ei ganol; **dead tired** wedi blino'n lân; **dead heat** cwbl gyfartal
deadline n dedlein
deadly adj marwol, angheuol
Dead Sea n: the Dead Sea y Môr Marw
deaf adj byddar
deafen vb byddaru
deafening adj byddarol
deal (pt, pp **dealt**) vb delio; trin ▶ n trafodaeth, dêl; **a great deal** llawer iawn; **to deal with** ymwneud â
dealer n masnachwr
dean n deon
dear adj annwyl, hoff; drud ▶ n anwylyd, cariad; **dear me** o'r annwyl!
death n angau, marwolaeth, tranc; **Black Death** y Pla Du
debate vb dadlau, ymryson ▶ n dadl
debit n debyd
debit card n cerdyn debyd
debt n dyled
decade n degawd
decaffeinated adj digaffein
decay vi dadfeilio, pydru ▶ n dadfeiliad
deceased n ymadawedig, trancedig
deceit n twyll, dichell, hoced
deceive vt twyllo, hocedu, siomi
December n Rhagfyr
decent adj gweddus, gweddaidd
deception n twyll, ffug, dichell

deceptive adj twyllodrus, dichellgar
decide vb penderfynu
decimal adj degol ▶ n degolyn; **decimal system** system ddegol; **decimal point** pwynt degol; **recurring decimal** degolyn cylchol
decision n penderfyniad
decisive adj penderfynol, pendant
deck n bwrdd llong, dec
deck chair n cadair haul
declaration n datganiad; cau batiad
declare vb mynegi, datgan, cyhoeddi
decline vb dadfeilio, dirywio; gwrthod ▶ n dadfeiliad; darfodedigaeth
decorate vt addurno, arwisgo
decoration n addurn, tlws
decorator n addurnwr, peintiwr tai
decrease vb lleihau, gostwng ▶ n lleihad
decree n gorchymyn, dyfarniad ▶ vb gorchymyn, dyfarnu
dedicate vt cysegru, cyflwyno
dedication n cysegriad, cyflwyniad
deduce vt tynnu, casglu
deduct vt tynnu ymaith, didynnu
deduction n diddwythiad, didyniad
deed n gweithred
deem vt (form) ystyried, barnu
deep adj dwfn; dwys ▶ n dwfn, dyfnder
deep freeze n rhewgell
deeply adv yn ddwys
deer n carw, hydd
default n diffyg ▶ vb methu, torri

defeat vt gorchfygu, trechu ► n gorchfygiad

defect n diffyg, nam

defective adj diffygiol

defence n amddiffyn, amddiffyniad

defend vt amddiffyn

defendant n diffynnydd

defender n amddiffynnwr

defer vb oedi, gohirio

defiance n her, herfeiddiad

defiant adj herfeiddiol

deficient adj diffygiol, prin, yn eisiau

deficit n diffyg

defile vt halogi, difwyno

define vt diffinio

definite adj penodol, pendant

definitely adv yn bendant, heb os

definition n diffiniad

deflate vb dadchwythu

deflect vb gwyro, osgoi

defraud vt twyllo, hocedu

defrost vt (fridge) dadrewi

defy vt beiddio, herfeiddio, herio

degree n gradd

delay vb oedi, gohirio ► n oediad

delegate vt dirprwyo ► n dirprwy, cynrychiolydd

delete vt dileu

deliberate vb ystyried yn bwyllog ► adj pwyllog, bwriadol

deliberately adv yn fwriadol

delicacy n amheuthun, danteithfwyd; **delicacies** danteithion

delicate adj tyner; cain; gwanllyd

delicatessen n delicatesen

delicious adj danteithiol, blasus

delight vb difyrru; ymhyfrydu ► n hyfrydwch

delighted adj balch; **I'd be delighted to ...** Mi fyddai'n bleser gen i ...

delightful adj hyfryd, braf

delinquent n troseddwr, tramgwyddwr ► adj troseddol, tramgwyddus

deliver vt traddodi; gwaredu; danfon; cludo

delivery n traddodiad; danfoniad

delusion n twyll, cyfeiliornad; lledrith

delve vb cloddio, palu, ymchwilio

demand vt gofyn, hawlio, mynnu ► n gofyn, hawl

demise n marwolaeth

democracy n democratiaeth

democrat n gwerinydd, gweriniaethwr

democratic adj gwerinol, democratig

demolish vt dymchwelyd, distrywio

demonstrate vb arddangos, profi; gwrthdystio

demonstration n arddangosiad; gwrthdystiad

demonstrator n arddangoswr; gwrthdystiwr

demote vb darostwng

den n ffau, gwâl, lloches

denial n gwadiad; nacâd, gwrthodiad; **self-denial** hunanymwadiad

denim n denim

Denmark n Denmarc

denomination n enw, enwad

denounce vt lladd ar, cyhuddo, condemnio

dense

dense *adj* tew, dwys; *(inf)* pendew, hurt
density *n* dwysedd, trwch
dent *n* tolc ▸ *vt* tolcio
dental *adj* deintiol
dentist *n* deintydd
dentures *npl* dannedd gosod
deny *vt* gwadu
deodorant *n* diaroglydd
depart *vi* ymadael; cychwyn
department *n* adran, dosbarth
department store *n* siop adrannol
departure *n* ymadawiad; cychwyniad
departure lounge *n* lolfa ymadael
depend *vi* dibynnu
dependant *n* dibynnydd
dependent *adj* dibynnol
depict *vt* darlunio
deport *vt* alltudio
deposit *vt* dodi i lawr; adneuo; gwaddodi ▸ *n* adnau, blaendal; gwaddod; **deposit account** cyfrif cadw
depot *n* storfa; gorsaf
depreciate *vb* dibrisio
depress *vt* gostwng, iselu; digalonni
depressed *adj* digalon, iselfryd
depressing *adj* trist
depression *n* iselder (ysbryd); dibwysiant (tywydd); pant; dirwasgiad (diwydiant)
deprive *vt* amddifadu
deprived *adj* amddifadus
depth *n* dyfnder
deputy *n* dirprwy
deputy head *n* dirprwy brifathro
derail *vb* taflu oddi ar gledrau

derelict *adj* wedi ei adael, diberchen, diffaith
derive *vb* derbyn, cael; tarddu, deillio
descend *vi* disgyn
descent *n* disgyniad, disgynfa; hil, ach
describe *vt* disgrifio, darlunio
description *n* disgrifiad, darluniad
desert[1] *adj* diffaith, anial ▸ *n* diffeithwch
desert[2] *vb* gadael, cefnu ar; encilio
deserve *vb* haeddu, teilyngu
design *n* arfaeth; cynllun ▸ *vb* arfaethu; cynllunio
designer *n* cynllunydd, dylunydd
desirable *adj* dymunol, dewisol
desire *vb* dymuno ▸ *n* dymuniad, chwant
desk *n* desg
desktop *n* *(Comput)* cyfrifiadur desg
despair *n* anobaith ▸ *vi* anobeithio
desperate *adj* diobaith, anobeithiol
desperately *adv (try, fight)* yn enbyd; *(ill, worried, poor)* ofnadwy
desperation *n* anobaith
despise *vt* dirmygu, diystyru
despite *prep* er, er gwaethaf
dessert *n* pwdin, melysfwyd
destination *n* cyrchfan, pen y daith
destiny *n* tynged, tynghedfen
destroy *vt* distrywio, dinistrio
destruction *n* distryw, dinistr
detach *vt* datod, gwahanu, datgysylltu
detached *adj* ar wahân
detached house *n* tŷ ar wahân

detail n manylyn ▸ vb manylu, neilltuo; **details** npl manylion; **in detail** yn fanwl

detailed adj manwl

detain vt cadw, caethiwo

detect vt canfod, darganfod

detection n darganfyddiad, datgeliad

detective n cuddswyddog, ditectif; **detective story** stori dditectif

detention n carchariad, ataliad

deter vt cadw rhag, atal, rhwystro

detergent n golchydd

deteriorate vb dirywio, gwaethygu

determination n penderfyniad

determine vb penderfynu, pennu

determined adj penderfynol

deterrent n atalrym, ataliad

detest vt ffieiddio, casáu

detour n cylch

detract vt tynnu oddi wrth, bychanu

detrimental adj niweidiol

devastated adj difrodedig

devastating adj difrodus

develop vb datblygu

development n datblygiad

device n dyfais

devil n diafol, diawl, cythraul

devious adj diarffordd, troellog; cyfeiliornus

devise vt dyfeisio

devolution n datganoli

devote vt cysegru, cyflwyno, ymroddi

devoted adj ffyddlon, ymroddgar

devotion n defosiwn, ymroddiad

devour vt ysu, difa, traflyncu

devout adj duwiol, crefyddol, defosiynol

dew n gwlith ▸ vb gwlitho

diabetes n clefyd melys

diabetic adj, n diabetig

diagnosis n diagnosis

diagonal n croeslin ▸ adj croeslinol

diagram n darlun eglurhaol, diagram

dial n deial ▸ vb deialu

dialect n tafodiaith

dialling tone n tôn deialu

dialogue n ymddiddan, deialog

diameter n tryfesur, diamedr

diamond n diemwnt

diarrhoea n rhyddni, dolur rhydd

diary n dyddiadur, dyddlyfr

dice n dîs

dictate vb arddywedyd; gorchymyn

dictation n arddywediad

dictionary n geiriadur

die vi marw, trengi, trigo, darfod

diesel n disel

diet n deiet

differ vi gwahaniaethu

difference n gwahaniaeth

different adj gwahanol

differentiate vb gwahaniaethu

difficult adj anodd, caled

difficulty n anhawster

dig (pt, pp **dug**) vb palu, cloddio, ceibio

digest vb treulio, toddi; cymathu

digestion n treuliad, traul

digit n digid, bys

digital adj digidol

digital camera n camera digidol

digital radio n radio digidol

digital television *n* teledu digidol
digital watch *n* oriawr ddigidol
dignified *adj* urddasol
dignity *n* urddas, teilyngdod
dilemma *n* dilema
dilute *vt* cymysgu â dwfr, gwanhau
dim *adj* pŵl, aneglur ▸ *vb* tywyllu, cymylu
dimension *n* dimensiwn
diminish *vb* lleihau, prinhau
din *n* twrf, dadwrdd, mwstwr
dine *vi* ciniawa
diner *n* ciniawr
dinghy *n* dingi
dingy *adj* tywyll, dilewyrch; tlodaidd
dining room *n* ystafell fwyta
dinner *n* cinio
dinner jacket *n* cot ginio, cot giniawa
dinner party *n* cinio gwadd
dinner time *n* amser cinio
dinosaur *n* deinosor
dip *vb* trochi, gwlychu; gostwng ▸ *n* trochfa
diploma *n* tystysgrif, diploma
diplomacy *n* diplomyddiaeth
diplomat *n* diplomydd
diplomatic *adj* diplomyddol
dire *adj* dygn, arswydus, echryslon
direct *adj* union, uniongyrchol ▸ *vt* cyfarwyddo, cyfeirio
direction *n* cyfarwyddyd; cyfeiriad
directly *adv* yn union, yn ddi-oed
director *n* cyfarwyddwr
directory *n* cyfarwyddiadur
dirt *n* baw, llaid, llaca
dirty *adj* budr, brwnt ▸ *vt* budro, difwyno, maeddu
disability *n* anabledd

disabled *adj* anabl
disadvantage *n* anfantais
disagree *vi* anghytuno
disagreeable *adj* annymunol, cas
disagreement *n* anghytundeb
disappear *vi* diflannu
disappearance *n* diflaniad
disappoint *vt* siomi
disappointed *adj* siomedig
disappointing *adj* siomedig
disappointment *n* siomedigaeth
disapprove *vb* anghymeradwyo
disarm *vb* diarfogi
disarmament *n* diarfogiad
disaster *n* trychineb, aflwydd
disastrous *adj* trychinebus
disbelief *n* anghrediniaeth, angoel
disc *n* disg(en)
discard *vt* rhoi heibio, gwrthod
discharge *vb* dadlwytho, rhyddhau ▸ *n* gollyngdod, rhyddhad
discipline *n* disgyblaeth ▸ *vt* disgyblu
disc jockey *n* troellwr disgiau
disclose *vt* dadlennu, datguddio
disco *n* disgo
discomfort *vt* anghysuro ▸ *n* anghysur
disconnect *vb* datgysylltu
discontent *n* anfodlonrwydd
discontinue *vb* torri, atal
discount *n* disgownt
discourage *vt* digalonni
discover *vt* darganfod, canfod
discovery *n* darganfyddiad
discredit *n* anfri, anghlod, amarch ▸ *vt* anghoelio; amau, difrio
discreet *adj* call, pwyllog
discrepancy *n* anghysondeb
discretion *n* barn, pwyll**

discriminate vb gwahaniaethu

discrimination n gwahaniaethu, anffafriaeth

discuss vt trin, trafod

discussion n trafodaeth, sgwrs

disease n afiechyd, clefyd, clwyf

disembark vb glanio

disgrace vt gwaradwyddo ► n gwaradwydd, gwarth

disgraceful adj gwaradwyddus, gwarthus

disguise vt dieithrio, ffugio, lledrithio ► n rhith, dieithrwch

disgust n diflastod, ffieidd-dod ► vt diflasu, ffieiddio

disgusted adj wedi ffieiddio

disgusting adj ffiaidd, gwrthun

dish n dysgl; dysglaid

dishcloth n cadach llestri

dishonest adj anonest

dishwasher n peiriant golchi llestri

disillusion vb dadrithio

disinfectant n diheintydd

disintegrate vb datod, chwalu

disk n disg(en)

disk drive n gyriant disg

dislike vt casáu ► n casineb

dislocate vt rhoi o'i le, datgymalu

dismal adj tywyll, dilewyrch, digalon

dismay vt siomi, digalonni ► n siom, chwithdod

dismiss vt gollwng; diswyddo

disobedient adj anufudd

disobey vb anufuddhau

disorder n anhrefn; anhwyldeb ► vt anhrefnu

disown vt gwadu, diarddel

dispatch vb anfon; diweddu ► n neges

dispel vt chwalu, gwasgaru

dispense vb rhannu; gweinyddu; hepgor

disperse vb gwasgaru, chwalu, taenu

display vt arddangos ► n arddangosiad

displease vt anfodloni, digio

disposable adj tafladwy

dispose vt hepgor, gwaredu

disposition n anianawd

dispute vb dadlau, ymryson ► n dadl

disqualify vb difreinio, atal

disregard vt diystyru, esgeuluso ► n diystyrwch, esgeulustra

disrupt vb rhwygo, amharu ar

dissatisfaction n anfodlonrwydd

dissect vb difynio, trychu; dadansoddi

dissent vi anghytuno ► n anghytundeb; ymneilltuaeth

dissertation n traethawd

dissolve vb toddi; datod, diddymu

distance n pellter

distant adj pell, pellennig; oeraidd

distil vb distyllu, dihidlo

distillery n distyllty

distinct adj gwahanol; eglur

distinction n rhagoriaeth, gwahaniaeth

distinctive adj gwahanredol, arbennig

distinguish vb gwahaniaethu; hynodi

distinguished adj enwog, amlwg

distort vt ystumio, anffurfio, gwyrdroi

distract vb tynnu ymaith, drysu, mwydro

distraction n dryswch, diffyg sylw

distress n ing, trallod

distressing adj trallodus, blin, poenus

distribute vt rhannu, dosbarthu

distribution n dosbarthiad, rhaniad

distributor n dosbarthydd, dosbarthwr

district n dosbarth, ardal; **district council** cyngor dosbarth

distrust n drwgdybiaeth ▸ vb drwgdybio

disturb vt aflonyddu, cyffroi

disturbance n aflonyddwch, cyffro

disturbed adj blinderus, cynhyrfus

ditch n ffos

ditto adv eto, yr un, yr un peth

dive vi ymsuddo, deifio

diver n deifiwr

diverse adj gwahanol; annhebyg

diversion n difyrrwch, adloniant; dargyfeiriad, gwyriad

divert vt dargyfeirio, difyrru

divide vb rhannu, gwahanu ▸ n gwahanfa

divine adj dwyfol ▸ n diwinydd ▸ vb dewinio, dyfalu

diving n deifio

division n rhan, rhaniad, adran; cyfraniaeth; **long division** rhannu hir

divorce vt ysgar(u) ▸ n ysgariad

divorced adj wedi ysgaru

DIY n abbr (= do-it-yourself) crefftau'r cartref, DIY

dizzy adj penysgafn, pensyfrdan

DJ n troellwr

[KEYWORD]

do (pt **did**, pp **done**) n (inf) (party etc) achlysur m, parti m
▸ aux vb 1 (in negative constructions) no equivalent; **I don't understand** nid wyf yn deall
2 (to form questions) no equivalent; **didn't you know?** oni wyddech?, wyddech chi ddim?; **what do you think?** beth yw'ch barn chi?
3 (for emphasis; in polite expressions): **people do make mistakes sometimes** fe fydd pobl yn cymryd cam gwag weithiau, fe fydd pobl yn gwneud camgymeriad weithiau; **she does seem rather late** mae hi braidd yn hwyr yn fy marn i; **do sit down/help yourself** eisteddwch/helpwch eich hunain da chi; **do take care!** cymerwch ofal da chi!
4 (used to avoid repeating vb): **she swims better than I do** mae'n nofio'n well na mi; **do you agree? — yes, I do/no I don't** a ydych yn cytuno? ydw/nac ydw; **she lives in Swansea — so do I** mae'n byw yn Abertawe — a minnau hefyd; **he didn't like it and neither did we** nid oedd yn hoffi'r peth, na ninnau ychwaith; **who broke it? — I did** pwy a'i torrodd? — minnau; **he asked me to help him and I did** gofynnodd imi ei helpu, ac fe wnes
5 (in question tags): **you like him, don't you?** rydych yn ei hoffi, on'd ydych?; **I don't know him, do I?** dwy ddim yn ei adnabod, ydw i?
▸ vt 1 (gen, carry out, perform etc) gwneud; **what are you doing**

tonight? beth wnewch chi heno?,
beth fyddwch chi'n ei wneud
heno; **what do you do?** (*job*) beth
yw'ch gwaith chi?; **what can I do
for you?** a gaf i'ch helpu?; **to do
the cooking** gwneud y [gwaith]
coginio; **to do one's teeth/hair/
nails** brwsio'ch dannedd/gwneud
eich gwallt/gwneud eich ewinedd
2 (*Aut, etc, distance*): gwneud,
teithio; (*speed*) gwneud, mynd;
we've done 200 km already rydym
wedi teithio 200 km yn barod;
the car was doing 100 roedd y
car yn mynd 100 (milltir yr awr);
he can do 100 in that car mae'n
gallu gwneud 100 (milltir yr awr)
yn y car yna
▸ *vi* **1** (*act, behave*) gwneud; **do as I
do** gwnewch yr un fath â minnau
2 (*get on, fare*) dod ymlaen; **the
firm is doing well** mae'r ffyrm yn
gwneud yn dda; **he's doing well/
badly at school** mae'n gwneud yn
dda/wael yn yr ysgol; **how do you
do?** sut [r]wyt ti?, sut [r]ydych chi?
(*in reply*) iawn diolch
3 (*suit*) gwneud; **will it do?** a wnaiff
y tro?
4 (*be sufficient*) bod yn ddigon;
will £10 do? a fydd £10 yn ddigon?;
that'll do bydd hynny'n ddigon,
bydd hynny'n gwneud y tro; **that'll
do!** (*in annoyance*) dyna ddigon!; **to
make do (with)** bodloni (ar)
▸ **do up** *vt* (*laces, dress*) cau,
clymu; (*buttons*) botymu, cau;
(*zip*) cau; (*renovate: room*) ail-
wneud, atgyweirio, cyweirio
▸ **do with** *vt fus* (*need*) **I could do**

with a drink/some help mae arnaf
angen diod/cymorth; **it could do
with a wash** byddai golchi'r peth
yn gwneud lles; (*be connected with*)
that has nothing to do with you
does a wneloch chi ddim â'r peth; **I
won't have anything to do with it**
rwy'n gwrthod ymwneud â'r peth
▸ **do without** *vi* gwneud y tro
heb; **if you're late for tea then
you'll do without** os byddwch yn
hwyr i de yna rhaid ichi wneud y
tro hebddo
▸ *vt fus* ymdopi; **I can do without a
car** gallaf ymdopi heb gar

dock¹ *n* (dail) tafol
dock² *vt* tocio, cwtogi
dock³ *n* doc ▸ *vt* docio; cwtogi
doctor *n* doctor, meddyg; doethur
document *n* dogfen
documentary *adj* dogfennol
dodge *vb* osgoi, twyllo ▸ *n* cast,
ystryw
dog *n* ci ▸ *vb* dal i ddilyn
do-it-yourself *n* crefftau'r cartref,
DIY
dole *n* dôl, dogn ▸ *vt* dogni,
rhannu; **on the dole** yn ddi-waith,
ar y clwt
doll *n* dol, doli
dollar *n* doler
dolphin *n* dolffin
dome *n* cromen, cryndo
domestic *adj* teuluaidd, cartrefol;
gwâr, dof
dominant *adj* trech
dominate *vb* dominyddu
dominoes *npl* dominos
donate *vb* rhoddi

289

donation

donation n rhodd
donkey n asyn, mul
donor n rhoddwr
doodle vb dwdlan
doom n dedfryd, tynged ▸ vt dedfrydu, tynghedu
door n drws, dôr, porth
doorbell n cloch drws
door-step n rhiniog, trothwy
doorway n porth, drws
dope (inf) n cyffur ▸ vb rhoi cyffur
dormitory n ystafell gysgu, hundy
dose n dogn ▸ vt dogni
dot n dot ▸ vb dotio
double adj, n dwbl ▸ vb dyblu, plygu; **double flat** meddalnod dwbl
double-bass n bas dwbl
double-click vi clicio dwywaith
double glazing n gwydro dwbl, ffenestri dwbl
doubles n parau
doubt vb amau, petruso ▸ n amheuaeth
doubtful adj amheus, petrus
doubtless adv yn ddiamau, diau
dough n toes
doughnut n toesen
dove n colomen
down¹ n manblu
down² adv i lawr, i waered; **down and out** digalon, truenus
downcast adj digalon, prudd
downfall n cwymp, codwm
download vt lawrlwytho, dadlwytho
downright adj diamheuol
Down's syndrome n syndrom Down

downstairs n y llawr ▸ adv ar y llawr
downwards adv i lawr, i waered
doze vi hepian ▸ n cyntun; **doze off** vi pendwmpian
dozen n deuddeg, dwsin
drab adj llwydaidd, salw
draft n drafft, braslun ▸ vb drafftio, braslunio
drag vb llusgo ▸ n car llusg
dragon n draig
dragon-fly n gwas y neidr
drain¹ n draen
drain² vb draenio, diferu, yfed; **draining board** bwrdd diferu
drainage n draeniad; **drainage basin** dalgylch afon
drama n drama
dramatic adj dramatig
drape vt gwisgo, gorchuddio
drastic adj cryf, llym
draught n dracht, llymaid; drafft(en); tynfa (llong)
draughts npl drafftiau
draw n atyniad, tynfa ▸ vb tynnu; lluniadu, darlunio; **draw to scale** graddluniadu; **drawn game** gêm gyfartal
drawback n anfantais
drawer n drâr, drôr
drawing n lluniad, llun
drawing pin n pin bawd
drawing room n ystafell groeso
dread vb ofni, arswydo ▸ n ofn, arswyd
dreadful adj ofnadwy
dream (pt, pp **dreamed**, **dreamt**) vb breuddwydio ▸ n breuddwyd
dreary adj llwm, diflas
drench vt gwlychu; drensio

dress vb gwisgo, dilladu ► n
gwisg; **dress up** vi gwisgo'n ffansi
dresser n dreser, gwisgwr
dressing n dresin; **salad dressing**
dresin salad; **dressing gown** gŵn
gwisgo
dressing table n bwrdd gwisgo
dressmaker n gwniadwraig
dribble n dribl(ad), drefl ► vb
driblo, dreflu, glafoerio
drier n peiriant sychu
drift n drifft, lluwch; tuedd ► vb
drifftio, lluwchio
drill vb drilio ► n dril
drink (pt **drank**, pp **drunk**) vb yfed
► n diod, llymaid
drink-driving n gyrru tra'n feddw
drinker n yfwr, diotwr
drinking water n dŵr yfed
drip vb diferu, defnynnu ► n
diferiad
drive (pt **drove**, pp **driven**) n dreif,
gyriant, cymhelliad ► vb dreifio,
gyrru
driver n gyrrwr
driving adj grymus ► n gyrru
driving instructor n hyfforddwr
gyrru
driving lesson n gwers gyrru
driving licence n trwydded gyrru
driving test n prawf gyrru
drizzle vb briwlan ► n glaw mân
droop vi llaesu, ymollwng; nychu
drop n diferyn, dafn; cwympiad
► vb diferu, cwympo, gollwng;
drop goal gôl adlam
drought n sychder, sychdwr
drown vb boddi
drowsy adj cysglyd
drug n cyffur

drug addict n caeth i gyffuriau
drug dealer n gwerthwr cyffuriau
drum n tabwrdd, drwm ► vb
tabyrddu
drummer n drymiwr
drunk adj meddw, brwysg
dry adj sych, cras ► vb sychu
dry cleaner's n sychlanhawyr
dryer n sychwr
dual adj deuol; **dual carriageway**
ffordd ddeuol
dubious adj amheus, petrus
duck¹ n hwyaden
duck² vb trochi; gostwng pen
due adj dyledus, dyladwy ► n
dyled, haeddiant
duel n gornest
duet n deuawd
duke n dug
dull adj hurt; marwaidd; diflas;
cymylog; pŵl ► vb pylu, lleddfu
dumb adj (inf!) mud
dummy n dymi; delw; ffug-bas
(rygbi) ► vb ffug-basio
dump n dymp, storfa ► vb dympio
dumpling n tymplen, poten
dune n twyn
dungarees npl dyngarîs
dungeon n dwnsiwn
duplex adj dwplecs
duplicate adj dyblyg ► n copi ► vt
dyblygu
durable adj parhaol, parhaus, cryf
duration n parhad
during prep yn ystod
dusk n cyfnos, gwyll
dust n llwch ► vt taenu neu sychu
llwch, dwstio
dustbin n bin sbwriel
duster n cadach, dwster

dustman n dyn lludw
dusty adj llychlyd
Dutch n (language) Iseldireg
Dutchman n Iseldirwr
Dutchwoman n Iseldirwraig
duty n dyletswydd; toll; **customs duty** tolldal; **import duty** toll fewnforio; **export duty** toll allforio
duty-free adj di-doll
duvet n carthen blu
DVD n abbr DVD
DVD player n chwaraewr DVD
dwarf n (infl) cor, corrach ▸ adj corachaidd
dwell (pt, pp **dwelt**) vi trigo, preswylio
dwindle vi darfod, lleihau, dirywio
dye vb lliwio, llifo ▸ n lliw, lliwur
dynamic adj dynamig
dyslexia n dyslecsia
dyslexic adj dyslecsig

e

each adj, pron pob, pob un; **each other** ei gilydd
eager adj awyddus, awchus
eagle n eryr
ear n clust, dolen; tywysen
earache n pigyn clust, clust dost
earl n iarll
earlier adv gynt
early adj cynnar, bore ▸ adv yn fore
early retirement n ymddeoliad cynnar
earmark n clustnod, nod clust ▸ vb clustnodi, neilltuo
earn vt ennill, elwa
earnest adj difrif, difrifol, taer
earnings npl enillion
earphone n ffôn clust
earring n clustdlws
earth n daear, pridd ▸ vt priddo
earthquake n daeargryn
ease n esmwythdra; rhwyddineb ▸ vb esmwytho
easily adv yn hawdd

east n dwyrain ► adj dwyreiniol
Easter n y Pasg
Easter egg n wy Pasg
eastern adj dwyreiniol
easy adj hawdd, rhwydd
easy-going adj didaro, di-hid
eat (pt **ate**, pp **eaten**) vt bwyta, ysu
eavesdrop vb clustfeinio
e-book n e-lyfr
eccentric adj od, hynod; echreiddig
echo n atsain, carreg ateb ► vb atseinio
eclipse n eclips, diffyg, clip ► vb tywyllu
eco-friendly adj amgylcheddol-gyfeillgar
ecological adj ecolegol
ecology n ecoleg
e-commerce n e-fasnach
economic adj economaidd
economical adj cynnil, darbodus
economics n economeg
economist n economegydd
economize vb cynilo
economy n darbodaeth, economi
ecstasy n gorfoledd, gorawen
eczema n ecsema
edge n min, ymyl ► vb minio, hogi; **to be on edge** bod ar bigau'r drain
edible adj bwytadwy
Edinburgh n Caeredin
edit vt golygu, paratoi i'r wasg
edition n argraffiad
editor n golygydd
editorial adj golygyddol
educate vt addysgu
education n addysg
educational adj addysgol
eel n llysywen
eerie adj iasol, annaearol

effect n effaith ► vb peri; **after-effects** sgil-effeithiau
effective adj effeithiol
effectively adv (in an effective way) yn effeithiol; (in effect) mewn gwirionedd
efficiency n effeithlonrwydd
efficient adj effeithiol, cymwys
effort n ymdrech, ymgais
e.g. abbr (= exempli gratia) er enghraifft, e.e.
egg n wy; **scrambled egg** cymysgwy
egg cup n cwpan wy
egg shell n masgl/plisgyn wy
ego n ego, yr hunan
Egypt n yr Aifft
eight adj, n wyth
eighteen adj, n deunaw, un deg wyth
eighteenth adj deunawfed
eighth adj wythfed
eighty adj, n pedwar ugain, wyth deg
Eire n Iwerddon Rydd, Gweriniaeth Iwerddon
either adj un o'r ddau ► conj naill ai ► adv, conj na, nac, ychwaith
eject vt bwrw allan; diarddel
elaborate¹ adj llafurfawr, manwl
elaborate² vb manylu
elastic adj hydwyth, ystwyth
elastic band n cylch lastig
elbow n elin, penelin
elder n henuriad, hynafgwr ► adj hŷn
elderly adj oedrannus
eldest adj hynaf
elect vt ethol, dewis ► adj etholedig

e

election *n* etholiad
electorate *n* etholaeth
electric *adj* trydanol, electrig
electrical *adj* trydanol
electric blanket *n* blanced drydan
electric fire *n* tân trydan
electrician *n* trydanwr
electricity *n* trydan
electrify *vt* gwefreiddio, trydanu
electronic *adj* electronig
electronics *n* electroneg
elegant *adj* cain, lluniaidd
element *n* elfen
elementary *adj* elfennol
elephant *n* cawrfil, eliffant
elevate *vt* dyrchafu, codi
eleven *adj, n* un ar ddeg
eleventh *adj* unfed ar ddeg
eligible *adj* cymwys
eliminate *vt* dileu, deol
elm *n* llwyf, llwyfen
eloquent *adj* huawdl
else *adv* arall, amgen
elsewhere *adv* mewn lle arall
elusive *adj* di-ddal, gwibiog
email *n* ebost ▸ *vt* ebostio
email address *n* cyfeiriad ebost
embankment *n* clawdd, cob
embargo *n* gwaharddiad
embark *vb* mynd/gosod ar long;
 hwylio; **to embark on** ymgymryd
 â, dechrau
embarrass *vt* rhwystro, drysu
embarrassed *adj* mewn penbleth,
 trafferthus
embarrassing *adj* dyrys, anffodus
embarrassment *n* chwithedd,
 embaras
embassy *n* llysgenhadaeth

embrace *vt* cofleidio; cynnwys ▸ *n*
 cofleidiad
embroider *vt* brodio
embroidery *n* brodwaith
embryo *n* cynelwad, embryo
emerald *n* emrallt
emerge *vi* dyfod allan, dyfod i'r
 golwg
emergency *n* argyfwng
emigrate *vi* allfudo, ymfudo
eminent *adj* enwog, amlwg, o fri
emissions *npl* gollyngiadau
emit *vt* rhoddi neu fwrw allan
emotion *n* emosiwn
emotional *adj* emosiynol
emperor *n* ymerawdwr, ymherodr
emphasis *n* pwys, pwyslais
emphasize *vt* pwysleisio
empire *n* ymerodraeth
employ *vt* cyflogi; arfer, defnyddio
 ▸ *n* gwasanaeth
employee *n* gŵr cyflog
employer *n* cyflogwr
employment *n* cyflogaeth, gwaith
empower *vt* awdurdodi, galluogi
empress *n* ymerodres
empty *adj* gwag ▸ *vb* gwacáu
empty-handed *adj* gwaglaw
emulsion *n* emwlsiwn
enable *vt* galluogi
enclose *vt* amgáu
enclosure *n* lle caeëdig, lloc
encore *n* encôr ▸ *adv* eto
encounter *vt* cyfarfod, taro ar ▸ *n*
 ymgyfarfod, brwydr
encourage *vt* calonogi, annog
encyclopaedia *n* gwyddoniadur
encyclopedia *n* gwyddoniadur

end n diwedd ▸ vb diweddu, terfynu; **end point** pwynt terfyn; **from end to end** o ben bwy gilydd

endanger vt peryglu

endeavour vi ymdrechu ▸ n ymdrech

ending n diwedd; terfyniad

endless adj diddiwedd

endorse vt cefnogi, arnodi

endorsement n arnodiad, ardystiad

endurance n dycnwch

endure vb parhau; dioddef, goddef

enemy n gelyn

energetic adj grymus, egnïol

energy n ynni, egni

enforce vt gorfodi

engaged adj wedi dyweddïo; prysur

engagement n dyweddïad; brwydr

engaging adj deniadol

engine n peiriant, injan

engineer n peiriannydd

engineering n peirianneg

England n Lloegr

English adj Saesneg, Seisnig ▸ n (language) Saesneg; **English Channel** Môr Udd

Englishman n Sais

Englishwoman n Saesnes

engrave vt ysgythru

engraving n ysgythrad

enhance vb mwyhau, chwyddo, gwella

enjoy vt mwynhau; meddu

enjoyable adj pleserus

enjoyment n mwynhad

enlarge vt ehangu, helaethu

enlist vb ymrestru, listio

enormous adj anferth, enfawr

enough adj, n, adv digon

enquire vb ymholi, gofyn, holi

enquiry n ymholiad

enrage vt ffyrnigo, cynddeiriogi

enrich vt cyfoethogi

enrol vt cofrestru

enrolment n cofrestrad

ensure vt diogelu, sicrhau

entail vt gorfodi, gofyn

enter vb mynd i mewn, treiddio; cofnodi

enterprise n anturiaeth, menter

enterprising adj anturiaethus, mentrus

entertain vt difyrru; croesawu

entertainer n difyrrwr, diddanwr

entertaining adj difyrrus, diddan

entertainment n difyrrwch, adloniant

enthusiasm n brwdfrydedd

enthusiast n: **she's a real enthusiast** mae hi'n frwdfrydig iawn

enthusiastic adj brwdfrydig, eiddgar

entire adj cyfan, hollol, llwyr

entirely adv yn gyfan gwbl, yn llwyr

entrance¹ n mynediad, mynedfa; **entrance examination** arholiad mynediad; **entrance fee** tâl mynediad

entrance² vt swyno

entrust vt ymddiried

entry n mynediad, mynedfa; cofnodiad

entry phone n intercom

envelope n amlen

envious adj cenfigennus

environment n amgylchedd, amgylchfyd

environmental

environmental *adj* amgylcheddol
environmentally *adv* yn
  amgylcheddol; **environmentally**
  friendly yn amgylcheddol garedig
environment-friendly *adj*
  amgylcheddol-gyfeillgar
envisage *vb* rhagweld
envoy *n* cennad, negesydd
envy *n* cenfigen, eiddigedd ▸ *vt*
  cenfigennu, eiddigeddu
epic *adj* arwrol, arwraidd ▸ *n*
  arwrgerdd, epig
epidemic *adj* heintus ▸ *n* haint
epilepsy *n* epilepsi
epileptic *adj* epileptig
episode *n* digwyddiad, episôd
equal *adj* cyfartal ▸ *n* cydradd
  ▸ *vt* bod yn gyfartal; **without**
  equal heb ei ail
equality *n* cydraddoldeb,
  cyfartaledd
equalize *vb* cydraddoli, cyfartalu
equally *adv* yn ogystal â, yn llawn,
  yn gyfartal
equate *vt* cyfartalu, cymharu
equation *n* hafaliad; **simple**
  equation hafaliad syml; **quadratic**
  equation hafaliad dwyradd;
  simultaneous equation hafaliad
  cydamserol
equator *n* y cyhydedd
equip *vt* taclu, paratoi, cymhwyso,
  cyfarparu
equipment *n* cyfarpar, offer
equivalent *adj* cyfwerth, cyfartal
era *n* cyfnod
erase *vt* dileu, rhwbio allan
eraser *n* dilëydd, rwber
erect *adj* syth, unionsyth ▸ *vt* codi,
  adeiladu

erode *vb* ysu, treulio, erydu
erosion *n* erydiad
errand *n* neges, cenadwri
erratic *adj* ansefydlog, crwydraidd
error *n* cyfeiliornad, camgymeriad;
  gwall; **in error** ar gam
erupt *vb* echdorri, torri allan
eruption *n* echdoriad, tarddiad
escalator *n* escaladur
escape *vb* dianc, osgoi ▸ *n*
  dihangfa
escort *vt* hebrwng ▸ *n* gosgordd
especially *adv* yn arbennig, yn
  enwedig
espionage *n* ysbïaeth
essay *n* ymgais; traethawd, ysgrif
essence *n* hanfod; rhinflas
essential *adj* hanfodol, anhepgor
  ▸ *n* hanfod, anghenraid
essentially *adv* yn hanfodol
essentials *npl* hanfodion,
  anhepgorion
establish *vt* sefydlu
establishment *n* sefydliad
estate *n* stad, ystad, eiddo;
  industrial estate stad
  ddiwydiannol
estate agent *n* gwerthwr eiddo
estate car *n* car ystad
estimate *vt, n* amcangyfrif
etc *abbr* (= *et cetera*) ayyb
eternal *adj* tragwyddol, bythol
eternity *n* tragwyddoldeb
ethical *adj* moesegol
ethics *npl* moeseg
Ethiopia *n* Ethiopia
ethnic *adj* ethnig, cenhedlig
e-ticket *n* e-docyn, e-diced
etiquette *n* moesau, arfer
EU *n abbr* (= *European Union*) UE

euro *n* ewro
Europe *n* Ewrob, Ewrop
European *adj* Ewropeaidd ▸ *n* Ewropead
European Union *n* Undeb Ewropeaidd
evacuate *vt* ymgilio, ymadael (â)
evade *vt* gochelyd, osgoi
evaporate *vb* ymageru, anweddu
eve *n* min nos, noswyl
even *adj* gwastad, llyfn; cyfartal ▸ *adv* hyd yn oed; **even number** eilrif
evening *n* noswaith, yr hwyr, min nos
evening class *n* dosbarth nos
event *n* digwyddiad; **in the event of** os bydd
eventful *adj* llawn digwyddiadau
eventually *adv* o'r diwedd
ever *adv* bob amser, erioed, byth; **ever and anon** byth a hefyd
evergreen *n, adj* bythwyrdd, anwyw

KEYWORD

every *adj* 1 *(each)* pob; **every one of them** pob un ohonynt; **every shop in town was closed** roedd pob siop yn y dref ynghau
2 *(all possible)* pob, yr holl; **I gave you every assistance** rhoddais bob cymorth ichi; **I have every confidence in him** mae gennyf bob ffydd ynddo; **we wish you every success** dymunwn bob llwyddiant ichi
3 *(showing recurrence)* pob; **every day** bob dydd/diwrnod; **every other car** bob yn ail gar; **every other/third day** bob yn dridiau; **every now and then** bob hyn a hyn

everybody *pron* pawb, pob un
everyday *adj* bob dydd, beunyddiol
everyone *pron* pawb, pob un
everything *pron* popeth
everywhere *adv* ym mhobman
evict *vt* troi allan, dadfeddiannu
evidence *n* tystiolaeth, prawf
evident *adj* amlwg, eglur
evil *adj* drwg, drygionus ▸ *n* drwg, drygioni
evoke *vt* galw allan, tynnu allan; gwysio
evolution *n* esblygiad
evolve *vb* datblygu; esblygu
ewe *n* dafad, mamog
ex *n (inf)* ex; **my ex** fy ex
ex- *prefix* allan o; cyn-
exact[1] *adj* manwl, cywir, union
exact[2] *vt* hawlio, mynnu
exactly *adv* yn union, i'r dim
exaggerate *vt* chwyddo, gorliwio
exaggeration *n* gormodiaith, gorliwiad
exam *n* arholiad
examination *n* arholiad, archwiliad
examine *vt* arholi, archwilio
examiner *n* arholwr, archwiliwr
example *n* esiampl, enghraifft
excavate *vt* cloddio
exceed *vt* rhagori ar, bod yn fwy na
exceedingly *adv* tros ben, tra
excel *vb* rhagori
excellent *adj* rhagorol, ardderchog, godidog, campus
except *prep* ac eithrio, eithr, namyn, heblaw

exception

exception *n* eithriad
exceptional *adj* eithriadol
excerpt *n* dyfyniad, detholiad
excess *n* gormod, gormodedd
excessive *adj* gormodol, eithafol
exchange *vt* cyfnewid, ffeirio ▸ *n*
cyfnewid, cyfnewidfa; **exchange
rate** cyfradd cyfnewid
excite *vt* cynhyrfu, cyffroi
excited *adj* cynhyrfus
excitement *n* cynnwrf
exciting *adj* cyffrous
exclaim *vt* ebychu
exclamation *n* ebychiad;
exclamation mark ebychnod
exclude *vt* cau allan, bwrw allan
exclusion *n* gwaharddiad,
gwrthodiad
exclusive *adj* cyfyngedig
excruciating *adj* dirdynnol
excursion *n* gwibdaith, pleserdaith
excuse *vt* esgusodi ▸ *n* esgus
execute *vt* cyflawni, gweithredu;
dienyddio
execution *n* cyflawniad;
dienyddiad
executive *adj* gweithiol,
gweithredol ▸ *n* gweithredwr;
executive committee pwyllgor
gwaith
exempt *adj* rhydd, esgusodol ▸ *vt*
rhyddhau, esgusodi
exercise *n* ymarfer, ymarferiad
▸ *vb* ymarfer; **exercise book** llyfr
ysgrifennu, ymarfer
exert *vt* ymegnïo, ymdrechu
exertion *n* ymdrech, ymroddiad
exhale *vb* anadlu allan
exhaust *vt* disbyddu, diffygio,
gwacáu ▸ *n* disbyddwr, gwacäwr

exhausted *adj* lluddedig, wedi
ymlâdd
exhaust fumes *n* nwy gwacáu
exhaustion *n* gorludded
exhibit *vt* dangos, arddangos
exhibition *n* arddangosfa
exile *n* alltud; alltudiaeth ▸ *vt*
alltudio
exist *vi* bod, bodoli
existence *n* bod(olaeth), hanfod; **in
existence** mewn bod, ar glawr
exit *n* allanfa ▸ *vb* mynd allan,
ymadael
exotic *adj* estron, egsotig
expand *vb* lledu, ehangu
expansion *n* ehangiad, ymlediad
expect *vb* disgwyl
expectation *n* disgwyliad
expedition *n* ymgyrch, alldaith
expel *vt* bwrw allan, diarddel
expenditure *n* gwariant
expense *n* traul, cost
expenses *npl* treuliau
expensive *adj* drud, costus
experience *n* profiad ▸ *vt* profi
experienced *adj* profiadol
experiment *n* arbrawf ▸ *vi* arbrofi
expert *n* arbenigwr ▸ *adj* medrus,
deheuig
expertise *n* arbenigaeth
expire *vb* anadlu allan; darfod,
marw
expiry *n* diwedd, terfyn
explain *vt* egluro, esbonio
explanation *n* eglurhad, esboniad
explicit *adj* eglur, manwl, echblyg
explode *vb* ffrwydro, chwalu
exploit *n* camp, gorchest ▸ *vt*
gweithio, gwneud elw o, ymelwa
ar

exploitation n ymelwad
explore vt fforio, chwilio
explorer n fforiwr
explosion n ffrwydriad; tanchwa
explosive n ffrwydrydd, ffrwydryn
▸ adj ffrwydrol
export vt allforio ▸ n allforyn
exporter n allforiwr
expose vt amlygu, dinoethi
express vt mynegi, datgan ▸ adj
cyflym, clir ▸ n trên cyflym
expression n mynegiant
expressway n traffordd
exquisite adj odiaeth, rhagorol,
coeth
extend vb estyn, ymestyn; ehangu
extension n helaethiad, ehangiad,
(ym)estyniad
extensive adj ymestynnol, helaeth
extent n ehangder, maint, hyd,
mesur; **to some extent** i raddau
exterior adj allanol ▸ n tu allan
external adj allanol
extinct adj wedi darfod, diflanedig
extinguish vt diffodd; diddymu,
dileu
extra adj ychwanegol ▸ adv tu
hwnt, dros ben ▸ n peth dros ben,
ychwanegiad
extract vt echdynnu, tynnu;
dyfynnu, rhinio ▸ n echdyniad;
dyfyniad; rhin, darn
extraordinary adj hynod,
anghyffredin
extravagant adj gwastraffus,
afradlon
extreme adj i'r eithaf, eithafol ▸ n
eithaf
extremely adv dros ben, gor-

extremist adj eithafol ▸ n
eithafwr
extrovert adj allblyg, alltro ▸ n
alltröedydd, person allblyg
eye n llygad; crau; dolen ▸ vt
llygadu
eyeball n cannwyll y llygad
eyebrow n ael
eyelid n amrant
eyeliner n pensel llinellu
eye shadow n colur llygaid
eyesight n golwg
eyewitness n llygad-dyst

e

f

fabric n ffabrig, defnydd
fabulous adj chwedlonol, diarhebol
face n wyneb, wynepryd ▶ vb wynebu
Facebook vt: **I'll Facebook her** Mi wna i gysylltu â hi ar Facebook ▶ n Facebook
face cloth n clwtyn ymolchi
face value n arwynebwerth
facilitate vt hwyluso, hyrwyddo
facilities npl cyfleusterau
fact n ffaith, gwirionedd; **as a matter of fact** mewn gwirionedd
factor n ffactor; **prime factor** ffactor cysefin
factory n ffatri
factual adj ffeithiol
faculty n cynneddf; cyfadran
fad n mympwy, chwilen
fade vb diflannu, gwywo; colli ei liw
fag n caledwaith, lludded; gwas bach

fail vi ffaelu, methu, pallu, diffygio; **without fail** yn ddi-ffael
failure n methiant
faint adj llesmeiriol, gwan, llesg ▶ vi llewygu ▶ n llesmair, llewyg
fair¹ n ffair
fair² adj teg, glân; gweddol; golau
fairground n cae ffair
fairly adv yn deg/lân, yn weddol
fair trade n masnach deg
fairy n un o'r tylwyth teg
fairy-tale n stori hud, chwedl werin
faith n ffydd
faithful adj ffyddlon, cywir
faithfully adv yn fyddlon, yn gywir; **yours faithfully** yr eiddoch yn gywir
fake n ffug ▶ vb ffugio
falcon n hebog, cudyll
fall (pt **fell**, pp **fallen**) vi cwympo, syrthio ▶ n cwymp; **fall out** cweryla; **fall through** methu; **fall down** vi syrthio i lawr; **fall for** vt (person) syrthio mewn cariad â; (trick) llyncu; **fall out** vi (quarrel) anghytuno
false adj gau, ffug, ffals, twyllodrus; **false teeth** dannedd gosod/dodi
fame n enwogrwydd, clod, bri
familiar adj cynefin, cyfarwydd
family n teulu, tylwyth
famine n newyn
famous adj enwog
fan n gwyntyll; ffan ▶ vt gwyntyllio, chwythu
fanatic n penboethyn, ffanatig

fancy n dychymyg, ffansi, serch ► vt dychmygu, ffansïo, serchu; **fancy dress** gwisg ffansi

fantastic adj ffantastig, rhyfeddol

fantasy n ffantasi

far adj pell(ennig) ► adv ymhell; **as far as** hyd at

farce n ffars

fare n cost, pris; ymborth ► vi bod, dod ymlaen, byw

Far East n: **the Far East** y Dwyrain Pell

farewell excl yn iach, ffarwel ► n ffarwel; **to bid farewell** canu'n iach

farm n fferm ► vt amaethu, ffarmio

farmer n ffarmwr, ffermwr, amaethwr; **Young Farmers' Club** Clwb y Ffermwyr Ifainc

farmhouse n ffermdy

farming n ffermio; **intensive farming** ffermio dwys

farmyard n buarth, clos

fascinate vt hudo, swyno

fascinating adj hudol, swynol

fashion n ffasiwn, arfer, dull ► vt llunio, gwneud

fashionable adj ffasiynol

fast¹ vi ymprydio ► n ympryd

fast² adj tyn, sownd; buan, cyflym, clau

fasten vb sicrhau, cau, clymu

fast food n bwyd sydyn

fat adj tew, bras ► n braster, bloneg

fatal adj angheuol, marwol

fatality n trychineb, marwolaeth

fate n tynged, ffawd ► vt tynghedu

father n tad ► vt tadogi

Father Christmas n Siôn Corn

father-in-law n tad-yng-nghyfraith

fatigue n lludded, blinder ► vt lluddedu, blino

fatty adj seimlyd, brasterog

fault n bai, diffyg, nam; **at fault** ar fai

faulty adj gwallus, diffygiol

favour n ffafr, cymwynas ► vt ffafrio; **in favour of** o blaid

favourable adj ffafriol

favourite adj, n ffefryn ► adj hoff

fawn¹ n elain ► adj llwyd

fawn² vi cynffonna, gwenieithio

fax n ffacs ► vt ffacsio

fear n ofn, braw, arswyd ► vb ofni, arswydo

fearful adj ofnus, brawychus, arswydus

feasible adj dichonadwy

feast n gwledd, gŵyl ► vb gwledda

feat n camp, gorchest

feather n pluen, plufyn ► vt pluo, plufio

feature n arwedd, nodwedd

February n Chwefror, Mis Bach

federal adj cynghreiriol, ffederal

fed up adj wedi cael llond bol

fee n ffi

feeble adj gwan, eiddil

feed (pt, pp **fed**) vb porthi, ymborthi, bwydo ► n porthiant, ffîd, ymborth; gwledd

feedback n adborth, ymateb ► vb adborthi

feel (pt, pp **felt**) vb teimlo

feeling n teimlad, synhwyriad

fell vb cwympo, cymynu ► n ffridd, rhos

fellow

fellow n cymar; cymrawd ▸ *prefix* cyd-
fellowship n cymdeithas, cyfeillach; cymrodoriaeth
felt n ffelt ▸ vb ffeltio
female adj, n benyw
feminine adj benywaidd, benywol
feminist n ffeminist
fence n clawdd, ffens ▸ vb cau, amgáu
fencing n ffensio, cleddyfaeth
fend vb cadw draw; ymdopi
ferment n eples, cynnwrf ▸ vb eplesu, cynhyrfu
fern n rhedynen, rhedyn
ferocious adj ffyrnig, milain
ferret n ffured ▸ vt ffuredu, chwilota
ferry n fferi ▸ vb cludo dros
fertile adj ffrwythlon, toreithiog
fertilize vb ffrwythloni; gwrteithio
fertilizer n gwrtaith
festival n gŵyl, dydd gŵyl; **singing festival** cymanfa ganu
festive adj llawen, llon
fetch vt cyrchu, hôl, ymofyn, nôl
fête n gŵyl, miri ▸ vi gwledda
feud n cynnen, ffiwd
fever n twymyn
feverish adj â thwymyn
few adj ychydig, prin, anaml
fiancé n darpar-ŵr
fiancée n darpar-wraig
fib n anwiredd, celwydd
fibre n edefyn, ffibr
fibreglass n ffibr gwydrog
fickle adj anwadal, oriog, gwamal
fiction n ffuglen
fiddle n ffidil ▸ vi canu'r ffidl; ffidlan

fidelity n ffyddlondeb, cywirdeb
fidget vt ffwdanu, aflonyddu ▸ n un ffwdanus, un aflonydd
field n cae, maes ▸ vb maesu
field marshal n maeslywydd
fierce adj ffyrnig, milain; tanbaid
fifteen adj, n pymtheg
fifteenth adj pymthegfed
fifth adj, n pumed
fifty adj, n hanner cant, deg a deugain
fig n ffigysen
fight (*pt, pp* fought) vb ymladd, cwffio, brwydro, rhyfela ▸ n ymladdfa, brwydr
fighting n ymladd
figure n ffigur; llun, ffurf ▸ vb cyfrif; llunio; ymddangos; **figure of speech** troad ymadrodd; **figure out** vt deall
file n ffeil, rhathell; rhes ▸ vb ffeilio, rhathu
filing cabinet n cwpwrdd ffeilio
fill vb llenwi ▸ n llenwad, llonaid, gwala; **fill in** vt (*hole*) llenwi
fillet n llain, ffiled
fillet steak n stêc ffiled
filling n llenwad, mewnyn
film n pilen, caenen; ffilm ▸ vb ffilmio
film star n seren ffilmiau
filter n hidl, hidlydd ▸ vb hidlo, ffiltro
filter tip n hidl difaco
filth n brynti, budreddi, baw
filthy adj brwnt, budr, aflan
fin n adain, asgell, ffin
final adj terfynol, olaf; **semi-final** cynderfynol
finale n ffinale, diweddglo

finally adv o'r diwedd, yn olaf

finance n cyllid ▸ vb cyllido, codi arian

financial adj cyllidol, ariannol

find (pt, pp **found**) vt darganfod ▸ n darganfyddiad; **find out** vb darganfod

fine¹ adj main; mân; gwych; braf

fine² n dirwy ▸ vt dirwyo

finger n bys ▸ vt bysio, bodio; **little finger** bys bach; **third finger** bys y fodrwy; **middle finger** y bys canol

fingernail n ewin

fingerprint n bysbrint, ôl bys

finish vb diweddu, gorffen, cwblhau ▸ n diwedd; gorffeniad

finished adj gorffenedig

Finland n y Ffindir

Finn n Ffiniad

Finnish n (language) Ffinneg ▸ adj Ffinnaidd; (in language) Ffinneg

fir n ffynidwydden

fire n tân ▸ vb tanio, ennyn; **wild fire** tân gwyllt; **fire precautions** rhagofalon tân

firearm n arf-tân

fire brigade n brigâd dân

fire engine n peiriant tân

fire escape n grisiau tân

fire-extinguisher n diffoddydd tân

firefighter n diffoddwr tân

fireman n taniwr, diffoddwr tân

fireplace n lle tân

fire station n gorsaf dân

firewood n coed tân, cynnud

fireworks npl tân gwyllt

firm n cwmni, ffyrm ▸ adj cadarn, diysgog

firmly adv yn gadarn, yn ddiysgog

first adj cyntaf, blaenaf, prif ▸ adv yn gyntaf

first aid n cymorth cyntaf

first class adj dosbarth cyntaf

first floor n llawr cyntaf

first-hand adj o lygad y ffynnon

firstly adv yn gyntaf

first-rate adj campus, ardderchog, rhagorol

fir tree n ffynidwydden

fish n pysgodyn, pysgod ▸ vb pysgota; **fish and chips** pysgodyn a sglodion

fisherman n pysgotwr

fish fingers npl sglodion pysgod

fishing n pysgota

fishing boat n cwch pysgota

fishing tackle n offer pysgota

fishmonger n gwerthwr pysgod

fishy adj (inf) amheus; pysgodol

fist n dwrn

fit¹ n llewyg, ffit; mesur

fit² adj addas, cymwys, gweddus; heini ▸ vb ffitio ▸ **fit in** vi (person) ffitio i mewn

fitness n ffitrwydd, addasrwydd

fitting n ffitiad ▸ vb ffitio ▸ adj priodol, gweddus, addas; **fittings** npl mân daclau, ffitiadau

five adj pum ▸ n pump

fix vb sicrhau, sefydlu, gosod ▸ n cyfyngder, cyfyng-gyngor

fixed n sefydlog

fixture n gosodyn, peniant (byd chwarae)

fizzy adj byrlymog

flag n baner, lluman; fflagen ▸ vb llumanu; llaesu

flake n fflaw, caenen; (snow) pluen (eira)

flamboyant

flamboyant *adj* coegwych

flame *n* fflam ▸ *vi* fflamio, ffaglu

flan *n* fflan

flank *n* ystlys, ochr ▸ *vb* ymylu, ystlysu

flannel *n* gwlanen

flap *n* llabed, fflap ▸ *vb* fflapio

flare *vb* fflêr, fflach; fflerio, fflachio

flash *vb* fflachio ▸ *n* fflach

flashback *n* ôl-fflach

flashlight *n* fflachlamp

flask *n* costrel, fflasg

flat *n* fflat, gwastad; meddalnod ▸ *adj* fflat, gwastad, lleddf ▸ *vb* fflatio

flatten *vb* gwastatáu

flatter *vt* gwenieithio

flaunt *vb* fflawntio, rhodresa

flavour *n* blas, cyflas ▸ *vt* blasu, cyflasu

flavouring *n* cyflasyn

flaw *n* bai, diffyg, nam

flea *n* chwannen

flee *(pt, pp* **fled***) vb* ffoi, cilio

fleece *n* cnu ▸ *vt* cneifio; *(inf)* ysbeilio

fleet *n* llynges, fflyd ▸ *adj* cyflym, buan

fleeting *adj* diflanedig

flesh *n* cig, cnawd; **flesh and blood** cig a gwaed; **flesh and bones** cnawd ac esgyrn

flex *n* fflecs

flexible *adj* hyblyg, ystwyth

flexitime *n* oriau hyblyg

flick *vt* cyffwrdd â blaen chwip, cnithio

flight *n* hediad, ffo; rhes

flight attendant *n* gweinydd awyren

flimsy *adj* tenau, simsan, bregus

flinch *vi* cilio yn ôl, gwingo, llwfrhau

fling *(pt, pp* **flung***) vt* taflu, bwrw, lluchio ▸ *n* tafliad

flint *n* callestr, carreg dân, fflint

flip *vb* cnithio ▸ *n* cnith

flipper *n* asgell

flirt *vb* cellwair caru, fflyrtan ▸ *n* fflyrten, fflyrtyn

float *n* arnofyn, fflôt ▸ *vb* arnofio

flock *n* diadell, praidd ▸ *vi* heidio

flood *n* llif, dilyw, cenllif ▸ *vt* llifo, gorlifo

flooding *n* llifogydd

floodlight *n* llifolau ▸ *vb* llifoleuo

floor *n* llawr ▸ *vt* llorio; **ground floor** daearlawr; **first floor** llawr cyntaf

flop *n* methiant ▸ *vb* ymollwng

flora *n* fflora, planhigion

floral *adj* fflurol

florist *n* tyfwr neu werthwr blodau

flour *n* blawd, can

flourish *vb* blodeuo; ffynnu; ysgwyd ▸ *n* rhwysg; cân cyrn

flow *vi* llifo, llifeirio ▸ *n* llif, llanw

flower *n* blodeuyn, blodyn ▸ *vi* blodeuo; **flowerpot** pot blodau

flu *n* ffliw, anwydwst

fluctuate *vi* amrywio, anwadalu

fluency *n* huodledd, llithrigrwydd

fluent *adj* llithrig, rhugl

fluff *n* fflwcs, fflwff ▸ *vb* bwnglera, methu

fluid *adj* hylif, llifol ▸ *n* hylif, llifydd

fluke *n* pry'r afu; ffliwc, lwc

fluoride *n* fflworid

flurry *n* cyffro, ffwdan

flush n gwrid; rhuthr dŵr ▸ adj cyfwyneb, gorlawn ▸ vb gwrido, cochi; gorlifo

flute n ffliwt

flutter vb dychlamu, siffrwd ▸ n dychlamiad, siffrwd

fly¹ n gwybedyn, cleren, pryf

fly² (pt **flew**, pp **flown**) vb ehedeg, ehedfan
▸ **fly away** vi hedfan i ffwrdd

flying adj hedegog, cyflym

flyover n pontffordd, trosffordd

foal n ebol, eboles ▸ vb bwrw ebol; **in foal** cyfebol

foam n ewyn ▸ vi ewynnu, glafoerio

focus n canolbwynt, ffocws ▸ vb canolbwyntio

fog n niwl

foggy adj niwlog

foil vt rhwystro, trechu ▸ n ffoil, ffwyl, dalen

fold n plyg; corlan ▸ vb plygu; corlannu

folder n plygell

folding n plygiant

foliage n dail, deiliant

folk npl pobl, gwerin

folklore n llên gwerin

folk song n cân werin

follow vb canlyn, dilyn

follower n dilynwr, canlynwr

following adj dilynol, canlynol ▸ n dilyniad, canlynwyr

fond adj hoff, annwyl

food n bwyd, ymborth; **tinned food** bwyd tun

food poisoning n gwenwyn bwyd

fool n ffŵl, ynfytyn ▸ vb ynfydu, twyllo

foolish adj ffôl, ynfyd

foot n troed; troedfedd ▸ vb troedio

foot and mouth disease n clwyf y traed a'r genau

football n pêl-droed

footballer n peldroediwr

footbridge n pont gerdded, pompren

foothold n gafael troed, troedle

footie n ffwtbol

footing n sylfaen, safle

footnote n troednodiad

footpath n llwybr troed

footprint n ôl troed

footstep n cam, ôl troed

footwear n troedwisg

KEYWORD

for prep 1 (indicating destination, intention, purpose) i; **the train for London** y trên i Lundain; **he left for Rome** ymadawodd i fynd i Rufain; **he went for the paper** aeth i gasglu'r papur; **is this for me?** i mi y mae hwn?; **it's time for lunch** mae'n amser cinio; **what's it for?** i beth y mae'n dda?; **what for?** (why?) pam? (to what end?) i ba ddiben?; **for sale** ar werth; **to pray for peace** gweddïo dros heddwch 2 (on behalf of, representing) dros, ar ran; **the MP for Anglesey** yr Aelod dros Fôn; **to work for sb/sth** gweithio dros rhn/rhth; **I'll ask him for you** gofynnaf iddo ar eich rhan; **A for Apple** A am Afal 3 (because of) o achos, oherwydd, oblegid; **for this reason** am y rheswm hwn; **for fear of being**

forbid

criticized rhag ofn ichi gael eich beirniadu
4 *(with regard to)* o, o ran; **he is big for his age** mae'n fawr o'i oed; **a gift for languages** dawn o ran ieithoedd
5 *(in exchange for)*: **I sold it for £5** fe'i gwerthais am £5; **to pay 50 pence for a ticket** talu 50 ceiniog am docyn
6 *(in favour of)* dros, o blaid; **are you for or against us?** a ydych o'n plaid ynteu yn ein herbyn?; **I'm all for it** rwy'n gadarn o blaid y peth; **vote for X** pleidleisiwch dros X
7 *(referring to distance)* am; **there are roadworks for 5 km** mae yna waith ar y ffordd am 5 km; **we walked for miles** cerddasom filltiroedd
8 *(referring to time)* am; ers; erbyn; **he was away for 2 years** bu i ffwrdd am 2 flynedd; **she will be away for a month** bydd i ffwrdd am fis; **it hasn't rained for 3 weeks** mae hi heb fwrw glaw ers 3 wythnos; **I have known her for years** rwy'n ei hadnabod ers blynyddoedd; **can you do it for tomorrow?** alli di ei wneud erbyn yfory?
9 *(with infinitive clauses)*: **it would be best for you to leave** byddai'n well ichi ymadael; **there is still time for you to do it** mae amser ar gael o hyd ichi wneud y peth; **for this to be possible ...** er mwyn i hyn fod yn bosibl ...; **10** *(in spite of)*: **for all that** er gwaethaf hynny, serch hynny; **for all his work/**

efforts er gwaethaf/serch ei holl waith/ymdrechion; **for all his complaints, he's very fond of her** er/serch ei gwynion, mae'n hoff iawn ohoni
▶ *conj (since, as)* *(form)* achos, canys, oblegid, oherwydd

forbid *(pt* **forbad, forbade,** *pp* **forbidden)** *vt* gwahardd, gwarafun, gomedd
forbidden *adj* gwaharddedig
force *n* grym; trais ▶ *vt* gorfodi; **centrifugal force** grym allgyrchol; **centripetal force** grym mewngyrchol; **the forces** y lluoedd arfog
forceful *adj* grymus, egnïol
ford *n* rhyd ▶ *vt* rhydio
fore *adj* blaen, blaenaf ▶ *adv* ymlaen ▶ *prefix* cyn-, rhag-, blaen-; **to the fore** amlwg, blaenllaw
forearm *n* elin ▶ *vb* rhagarfogi
forecast *n* rhagolygon, rhagolwg ▶ *vb* rhagddweud, darogan
forefinger *n* mynegfys
forefront *n* lle blaen ▶ *adj* blaen
foreground *n* blaendir
forehead *n* talcen
foreign *adj* estron, tramor; **foreign affairs** materion tramor
foreigner *n* estron, tramorwr
foreman *n* fforman
foremost *adj* blaenaf ▶ *adv* ym mlaenaf
forensic *adj* fforensig
forerunner *n* rhagredegydd
foresee *vt* rhagweld, rhagwybod
foreseeable *adj* rhagweladwy

forest n coedwig, fforest ▸ vt coedwigo, fforestu
forestry n coedwigaeth; **forestry commission** Comisiwn Coedwigaeth
forever adv am byth
foreword n rhagair, rhagymadrodd
forfeit n fforffed ▸ vt fforffedu, colli
forge n gefail ▸ vb gofannu; ffugio
forget (pt **forgot**, pp **forgotten**) vt anghofio
forgetful adj anghofus
forgive vt maddau
fork n fforch, fforc ▸ vb fforchio
forlorn adj amddifad, truan, anobeithiol
form n ffurf; mainc; ffurflen ▸ vb ffurfio; **application form** ffurflen gais
formal adj ffurfiol, defodol
former adj blaenaf, blaenorol
formerly adv gynt, yn flaenorol
formidable adj arswydus, ofnadwy, grymus
formula n rheol, fformwla
fort n caer
forthcoming adj ar ddod, gerllaw
fortify vt cadarnhau, cryfhau
fortnight n pythefnos
fortnightly adj, adv bob pythefnos
fortress n amddiffynfa, caer
fortunate adj ffodus, ffortunus
fortunately adv yn ffodus, yn lwcus
fortune n ffawd; ffortun
fortune teller n un sy'n dweud ffortun
forty adj, n deugain
forum n fforwm

forward n blaenwr ▸ adj eofn, hy; blaen ▸ adv ymlaen ▸ vb anfon ymlaen; hwyluso, hyrwyddo; **inside forward** mewnwr; **wing forward** blaenasgellwr
forward slash n blaenslaes
fossil n ffosil ▸ adj ffosilaidd
foster vt magu, meithrin, coleddu
foster-child n plentyn maeth
foul adj aflan; annheg; afiach ▸ n ffowl(en) ▸ vb ffowlio, llychwino; **foul play** anfadwaith
found vt dechrau, sylfaenu, sefydlu
foundation n sail, sylfaen
founder vb ymddryllio, suddo ▸ n sylfaenydd
fountain n ffynnon, ffynhonnell
fountain pen n pin llenwi
four adj, n pedwar; pedair
fourteen adj, n pedwar (pedair) ar ddeg
fourteenth adj pedwerydd (pedwaredd) ar ddeg
fourth adj pedwerydd; pedwaredd
four-wheel drive n (car) gyriant pedair-olwyn
fowl n dofedn, ffowlyn, ffowl
fox n cadno, llwynog
foyer n cyntedd
fraction n ffracsiwn; **improper fraction** ffracsiwn pendrwm; **vulgar fraction** ffracsiwn cyffredin; **proper fraction** ffracsiwn bondrwm
fracture n toriad, drylliad ▸ vt torri, dryllio
fragile adj brau, bregus
fragment n dryll, darn
fragrance n perarogl, persawr
frail adj brau, bregus, gwan, eiddil

frame

frame *n* ffrâm; agwedd ▸ *vt* fframio, llunio; **frame of mind** agwedd meddwl

framework *n* fframwaith

France *n* Ffrainc

franchise *n* etholfraint ▸ *vb* etholfreinio

frank *adj* didwyll, agored

frantic *adj* cyffrous, gwallgof

fraud *n* twyll, hoced

fraught *adj* llwythog, llawn

fray *n* ymryson, ymgiprys, ffrae ▸ *vb* treulio

freak *n* mympwy, peth od

freckle *n* brych, brychni

free *adj* rhydd; hael; di-dâl, rhad ▸ *vb* rhyddhau

freedom *n* rhyddid, rhyddfraint

free kick *n* cic rydd

freelance *adj* llawrydd ▸ *adv* yn llawrydd; **a freelance translator** cyfieithydd llawrydd

freely *adv* yn rhydd, yn hael

free-range *adj* maes

free trade *n* masnach rydd

freeway *n* traffordd

free will *n* ewyllys rydd, o'i fodd

freeze (*pt* **froze**, *pp* **frozen**) *vb* rhewi, fferru

freezer *n* rhewgist, rhewgell

freezing *adj* rhewllyd

freezing point *n* rhewbwynt

freight *n* llwyth llong ▸ *vt* llwytho llong

French *n* (*language*) Ffrangeg ▸ *adj* Ffrengig; (*in language*) Ffrangeg

French beans *npl* ffa Ffrengig

Frenchman *n* Ffrancwr

Frenchwoman *n* Ffrances

frenzy *n* gorffwylltra, cynddaredd

frequency *n* amlder, mynychder

frequent *adj* mynych, aml ▸ *vt* mynychu

frequently *adv* yn fynych, yn aml

fresh *adj* ffres, crai, cri, croyw, newydd

freshen *vb* ffresáu, ireiddio

fret *vb* sorri, poeni ▸ *n* soriant, trallod; ffret

friction *n* ffrithiant, ymrafael

Friday *n* dydd Gwener

fridge *n* oergell, rhewadur

fried *adj* ffriedig

friend *n* cyfaill, ffrind

friendly *adj* cyfeillgar

friendship *n* cyfeillgarwch

fright *n* dychryn, ofn, braw

frighten *vb* dychrynu, brawychu, codi ofn ar

frightened *adj* ofnus

frightening *adj* dychrynllyd

frightful *adj* dychrynllyd, brawychus

frill *n* ffril

fringe *n* ymyl, rhidens ▸ *vb* ymylu; **fringe benefits** cilfanteision

fritter *vt* afradu, ofera, gwastraffu

frivolous *adj* gwamal; disylwedd

fro *adv*: **to and fro** yn ôl ac ymlaen

frock *n* ffrog

frog *n* llyffant (melyn), broga

[KEYWORD]

from *prep* **1** (*indicating starting place, origin etc*) o; **where do you come from? where are you from?** un o ble ydych chi?, o ble rydych chi'n dod?; **where has he come from?** o ble y daeth ef?; **from London to Cardiff** o Lundain i Gaerdydd; **to**

escape from sb/sth dianc rhag rhn/rhth; **a letter/telephone call from my sister** llythyr/galwad ffôn gan fy chwaer; **to drink from the bottle** yfed o'r botel; **tell him from me that ...** dywed wrtho fy mod i'n dweud ...

2 (indicating time) o; **from one o'clock to** or **until** or **till two** o un o'r gloch tan ddau o'r gloch; **from January (on)** o fis Ionawr (ymlaen)

3 (indicating distance) o; **the hotel is one kilometre from the beach** mae'r gwesty un cilometr o'r traeth

4 (indicating price, number etc) o; **prices range from £10 to £50** mae'r prisiau'n amrywio o £10 i £50; **the interest rate was increased from 9% to 10%** codwyd y gyfradd log o 9% i 10%

5 (indicating difference): **he can't tell red from green** ni all wahaniaethu rhwng coch a gwyrdd; **to be different from sb/sth** bod yn wahanol i rn/rhth

6 (because of, on the basis of): **from what he says** o'r hyn y mae'n ei ddweud, ar sail yr hyn y mae'n ei ddweud; **weak from hunger** gwan oherwydd eisiau bwyd

front n wyneb, blaen, ffrynt, talcen ▸ vb wynebu ▸ adj blaen; **front door** drws ffrynt; **front page** tudalen flaen
frontier n ffin, terfyn, goror
frost n rhew
frostbite n ewinrhew
frosty adj rhewllyd

froth n ewyn ▸ vi ewynnu
frown vi cuchio, gwgu ▸ n cuwch, gwg
frozen adj wedi rhewi
fruit n ffrwyth, ffrwythau; **fruit juice** sudd ffrwyth; **fruit salad** salad ffrwythau
fruit machine n peiriant ffrwythau
frustrate vt rhwystro, llesteirio
frustrated adj rhwystredig
fry (pt, pp **fried**) vb ffrio ▸ n sil, silod; **small fry** (inf) pobl ddibwys
frying-pan n ffrimpan, padell ffrio
fudge n cyffug
fuel n tanwydd; cynnud; **fuel cell** cynudydd
fulfil vt cyflawni
full adj llawn, cyflawn ▸ n llonaid
full stop n atalnod llawn
full-time adj amser llawn
fully adv yn gyfan gwbl, yn gyflawn, yn hollol
fumble vb palfalu, bwnglera
fume n tarth, mwg; llid ▸ vb mygu; llidio, sorri
fumes n mwg
fun n difyrrwch, digrifwch, hwyl
function n swydd, swyddogaeth; (mathematics) ffwythiant
fund n cronfa, trysorfa
fundamental adj sylfaenol
funds npl arian
funeral n angladd, cynhebrwng, claddedigaeth
funfair n ffair bleser
fungus n ffwng
funnel n twmffat, twndis
funny adj digrif, ysmala; rhyfedd, hynod
fur n blew, ffwr

fur coat n cot ffwr
furious adj cynddeiriog, ffyrnig
furnish vt dodrefnu, rhoddi
furnishings npl dodrefn
furniture n dodrefn, celfi
furry adj blewog
further adj pellach ▸ adv
  ymhellach ▸ vt hyrwyddo;
  further education addysg bellach
fury n cynddaredd, ffyrnigrwydd
fuse n ffiws ▸ vb ffiwsio
fuss n ffwdan, helynt, stŵr ▸ vb
  ffwdanu
fussy adj ffwdanus
future adj, n dyfodol
fuzzy adj blewog, aneglur

gadget n dyfais
Gaelic n (language) Gaeleg ▸ adj
  Gaelaidd
gag n smaldod; safnglo ▸ vb
  smalio; safngloi, cau ceg
gain vb ennill, elwa ▸ n ennill,
  elw, budd
gale n gwynt cryf; tymestl
gallery n oriel, llofft
gallon n galwyn
gallop n carlam ▸ vb carlamu
gamble vb hapchwarae, gamblo
  ▸ n gambl
gambling n gamblo
game n gêm, chwarae, camp;
  helwriaeth ▸ adj dewr, glew
gamer n person sy'n chwarae
  gêmau cyfrifiadurol
games console n consol gêmau
game show n sioe gêm, sioe
  gêmau
gammon n gamwn
gang n mintai, haid, gang

gangster n troseddwr
gap n bwlch, adwy
gape vi rhythu, syllu ▸ n rhythiad
gap year n blwyddyn bwlch
garage n modurdy, garej
garbage n ysbwriel, sothach
garden n gardd ▸ vi garddio
gardener n garddwr
gardening n garddwriaeth
garlic n garlleg
garment n dilledyn, gwisg
garnish vt addurno, harddu
gas n nwy ▸ vb gwenwyno â nwy;
gas cooker ffwrn nwy; **gas fire** tân
nwy; **gas ring** cylch nwy
gasket n gasged
gasp vb ebychu, anadlu'n drwm
gate n porth, llidiart, clwyd, gât, iet
gateway n mynedfa
gather vb casglu, cynnull, crynhoi,
hel
gathering n casgliad, cynulliad
gauge n mesur; lled ▸ vt mesur
gay adj hoyw
gaze vi syllu, tremio ▸ n golwg,
trem
GCSE n abbr TGAU = Tystysgrif
Gyffredin Addysg Uwchradd
gear n gêr, offer, taclau ▸ vb taclu,
harneisio
gearbox n gerbocs
gear lever n lifer gêr
gel n gel
gem n glain, gem, tlws
Gemini n yr Efeilliaid
gender n cenedl
gene n genyn
general adj cyffredin, cyffredinol
▸ n cadfridog

general election n etholiad
cyffredinol
generalize vb cyffredinoli
general knowledge n
gwybodaeth gyffredinol
generally adv yn gyffredinol
general practitioner n meddyg
teulu
generate vt cenhedlu, cynhyrchu,
generadu
generation n cenhedliad;
cenhedlaeth, to
generator n cynhyrchydd;
generadur
generosity n haelioni
generous adj hael, haelionus,
haelfrydig
genetic adj genetig
genetically modified adj:
genetically modified food bwyd a
addaswyd yn enynnol
genetics n geneteg
Geneva n Genefa
genitals npl organau cenhedlu
genius n athrylith
gentle adj bonheddig; mwyn, tyner
gentleman n gŵr bonheddig
gently adv yn dyner, addfwyn;
gan bwyll
gents npl toiledau dynion
genuine adj dilys, diffuant
geography n daearyddiaeth
geology n daeareg
geometry n geometreg
gerbil n gerbil
germ n hedyn, eginyn, germ
German adj Almaenaidd ▸ n
Almaenwr; (language) Almaeneg;
German measles y frech
Almeinig

Germany

Germany *n* yr Almaen
gesture *n* ystum, arwydd, mosiwn

KEYWORD

get (*pt, pp* **got**, (*US*) *pp* **gotten**) *vi*
1 (*become, be*) dod, mynd; **to get
old/tired** mynd yn hen/flinedig,
heneiddio/blino; **to get drunk**
meddwi; **to get dirty** mynd yn
frwnt, baeddu; **to get married**
priodi; **when do I get paid?** pa bryd
y caf fy nhalu?; **it's getting late**
mae'n mynd yn hwyr
2 (*go*): **to get to/from** mynd i/o; **to
get home** cyrraedd adref/mynd
adref; **how did you get here?** sut
cyrhaeddaist ti yma?, sut dest
ti yma?
3 (*begin*) dechrau; **to get to know
sb** dod i adnabod rhn; **I'm getting
to like him** rwy'n dechrau dod i'w
hoffi; **let's get going** *or* **started**
gadewch inni ddechrau
4 (*modal aux vb*): **you've got to do it**
rhaid ichi ei wneud; **I've got to tell
the police** rhaid imi ddweud wrth
yr heddlu
▸ *vt* **1**: **to get sth done** (*do*) cyflawni
rhth, gwneud rhth; **to get sth/
sb ready** paratoi rhth/rhn; **to get
one's hair cut** cael torri'ch gwallt;
to get the car going *or* **to go**
cychwyn y car; **to get sb to do sth**
gofyn i rn wneud rhth, cael gan rn
wneud rhth
2 (*obtain: money, permission, results*)
cael, sicrhau; (*buy*) prynu; (*find:
job, flat*) dod o hyd i; (*fetch: person,
doctor, object*) nôl; **to get sth**

for sb cael rhth i rn; **get me Mr
Jones, please** (*on phone*) rhowch
fi drwodd i Mr Jones, os gwelwch
yn dda; **can I get you a drink?** ga i
gynnig diod ichi?
3 (*receive: present, letter*) cael,
derbyn; **what did you get for your
birthday?** beth gest ti ar dy ben-
blwydd?; **how much did you get
for the painting?** faint gawsoch
chi am y darlun?
4 (*catch*) dal; (*hit: target etc*) taro;
to get sb by the arm/throat dal
rhn gerfydd y fraich/y gwddf; **get
him!** daliwch ef!; **the bullet got
him in the leg** trawodd y bwled ef
yn y goes
5 (*take, move*): **to get sth to sb**
cael rhth i rn, mynd â rhth i rn; **do
you think we'll get it through the
door?** ydych chi'n credu y cawn ni
ef trwy'r drws?
6 (*catch, take: plane, bus etc*) dal;
**where do I get the train for
Birmingham?** ble mae dyn yn dal y
trên i Birmingham?
7 (*understand*) deall; (*hear*) clywed;
I've got it! rwy'n deall!, mi wn i!; **I
don't get your meaning** dwy ddim
yn eich deall; **I didn't get your
name** chlywes i mo'ch enw
8 (*have, possess*): **to have got** bod
gennych rth; **how many have you
got?** faint sydd gennych?
9 (*illness*) bod arnoch rth; **I've got
a cold** mae arnaf i annwyd; **she
got pneumonia and died** cafodd
niwmonia a bu farw
▸ **get away** *vi* mynd i ffwrdd;
(*escape*) dianc

▸ **get away with** vt fus (crime etc) cael maddau rhth

▸ **get back** vi (return) dychwelyd; vt adennill, adfer; **when do we get back?** pryd byddwn yn cyrraedd yn ôl?

▸ **get in** vi dod i mewn, mynd i mewn; (arrive home) cyrraedd adref; (train) cyrraedd

▸ **get into** vt fus mynd i mewn i; (car, train etc) mynd i mewn i; (clothes) gwisgo, gwisgo amdanoch; **to get into bed** mynd i'r gwely; **to get into a rage** cynddeiriogi, gwylltio

▸ **get off** vi (from train etc) disgyn; (depart: person, car) ymadael

▸ vt (remove: clothes, stain) tynnu, codi

▸ vt fus (train, bus) disgyn, dod i lawr [oddi ar rth]; **where do I get off?** ble dylwn i ddisgyn?

▸ **get on** vi (at exam etc) mynd ati; (agree) **to get on (with)** dod ymlaen (gyda); **how are you getting on?** sut mae'n mynd?

▸ vt fus dringo, esgyn; (horse) mynd ar gefn

▸ **get out** vi ymadael; (of vehicle) dod allan

▸ vt tynnu

▸ **get out of** vt fus dod allan [o rth], dianc; (duty etc) osgoi

▸ **get over** vt fus (illness) gwella [ar ôl rhth]

▸ **get through** vi (Tel) mynd trwodd; **to get through to sb** egluro/esbonio rhth i rn

▸ **get together** vi: **you must get together** (meet) rhaid ichi ddod at

eich gilydd

▸ **get up** vi (rise) codi

▸ vt fus codi

Ghana n Ghana

ghastly adj erchyll, gwelw

ghost n ysbryd, drychiolaeth, bwgan

giant n cawr ▸ adj cawraidd

gift n rhodd, dawn, anrheg, gwobr

gifted adj dawnus, talentog

gig n (inf, concert) gig

gigantic adj cawraidd, dirfawr, anferth

giggle vb lledchwerthin, giglan

gimmick n gimig

gin n jin; hoenyn

ginger n sinsir

gipsy n sipsi

giraffe n siráff

girl n merch, geneth, hogen

girlfriend n cariadferch, anwylyd

gist n ergyd, sylwedd

give (pt **gave**, pp **given**) vb rhoddi, rhoi; **give back** vt rhoi nôl; **give in** vi ildio; **give out** vt dosbarthu; **give up** vb rhoi'r gorau i

glacier n rhewlif, glasier

glad adj llawen, llon, balch

gladly adv yn llawen, â phleser

glamorous adj swynol, cyfareddol, hudol

glamour n swyn, cyfaredd, hud

glance vb ciledrych, tremio ▸ n cipolwg, trem, cip

gland n chwarren, gland

glare vb disgleirio; rhythu ▸ n disgleirdeb, tanbeidrwydd

glass n gwydr; gwydraid

▸ **glasses** npl gwydrau, sbectol

g

glaze vt gwydro; sgleinio ▸ n sglein, gwydredd

gleam n pelydryn, llewyrch ▸ vi pelydru, llewyrchu

glen n glyn, cwm, dyffryn

glide vi llithro, llifo ▸ n llithr, llithrad

glimmer vi llewyrchu'n wan ▸ n llewyrchyn, llygedyn

glimpse n trem, cipolwg

glint vb fflachio ▸ n fflach, llewyrch

glisten vi disgleirio

glitter vi tywynnu, pelydru ▸ n pelydriad

gloat vb llawenhau

global adj hollfydol, cyffredinol

globalization n globaleiddio

global warming n cynhesu byd-eang

globe n pêl, pelen

gloom n caddug, prudd-der, tywyllwch

gloomy adj prudd, digalon, tywyll

glorious adj gogoneddus

glory n gogoniant ▸ vi ymffrostio, gorfoleddu

gloss n sglein; glòs

glossary n geirfa

glossy adj llathraidd

glove n maneg

glow vi twymo, gwrido ▸ n gwres, gwrid

glue n glud ▸ vt gludio, asio

GM abbr: **GM food** bwyd a addaswyd yn enynnol

gnaw vb cnoi, cnewian

go (pt **went**, pp **gone**) vi mynd ▸ n tro; **go after** vt dilyn; **go ahead** vi mynd ymlaen; **go away** vi mynd i ffwrdd; **go back** vi mynd yn ôl; **go by** vi mynd heibio; **go down** vi mynd i lawr; (decrease) disgyn; **go for** vt mynd am; **go in** vi mynd i mewn; **go off** vi (depart) mynd i ffwrdd; **go on** vi (happen) digwydd; **to go on doing sth** dal i wneud rhth; **go out** vi mynd allan; **go past** vi mynd heibio ▸ vt mynd heibio i; **go round** vi mynd o gwmpas; **go through** vi mynd trwodd ▸ vt mynd trwy; **go up** vi (ascend) mynd i fyny; (increase) codi; **go with** vt (match) cyd-fynd â

goal n gôl, nod

goalkeeper n gôl-geidwad, golwr

goat n gafr

god n duw; **God** Duw

godchild n mab bedydd, merch fedydd

goddaughter n merch fedydd

goddess n duwies

godfather n tad bedydd

godmother adj mam fedydd

godson n mab bedydd

goggles npl gwydrau

gold n aur ▸ adj aur, euraid

golden adj euraid

goldfish npl eurbysg, pysgod aur

golf n golff; **golf links** maes golff

golf course n maes golffio

golfer n golffwr

gong n gong, cloch fwyd

good adj da, daionus; cryn ▸ n da, daioni, lles; **good morning** bore da; **good afternoon** prynhawn da; **good evening** noswaith dda; **good night** nos da; **good enough** digon da; **no good** dim gwerth, da i

ddim; **Good Friday** Dydd Gwener y Groglith; **good humour** natur dda
good-bye *excl*, *n* da boch chi, yn iach!, ffarwel
Good Friday *n* Dydd Gwener y Groglith
good-looking *adj* golygus
good-natured *adj* hynaws, rhadlon
goodness *n* daioni
goods *npl* nwyddau, eiddo
goodwill *n* ewyllys da; braint (masnachol)
google *vb* gwglo
goose *n* gŵydd
gooseberry *n* eirinen Fair, gwsbersen
gorge *n* hafn, ceunant ▸ *vb* safnio, traflyncu
gorgeous *adj* ysblennydd, gwych
gorilla *n* gorila
gospel *n* efengyl
gossip *n* clec, clonc, clebryn, clebran ▸ *vb* clebran, clecian, hel straeon
govern *vb* llywodraethu
government *n* llywodraeth
governor *n* llywodraethwr
gown *n* gŵn
GP *n abbr* meddyg teulu
grab *vb* crafangu, cipio ▸ *n* gwanc, crap
grace *n* gras, rhad; gosgeiddrwydd ▸ *vt* harddu, prydferthu
graceful *adj* graslon, rhadlon; gosgeiddig, lluniaidd
gracious *adj* graslon, grasol, rhadlon, hynaws
grade *n* gradd, safon ▸ *vb* graddio
gradient *n* graddiant

gradual *adj* graddol
gradually *adv* yn raddol
graduate *vb* graddio, graddoli ▸ *n* gŵr gradd, graddedig
graduation *n* graddedigaeth, graddnod
graffiti *n* graffiti
graft *n* impyn, hunan-les ▸ *vt* impio, grafftio
grain *n* grawn, gronyn; mymryn; graen
gram *n* gram
grammar *n* gramadeg
grammar school *n* ysgol ramadeg
grammatical *adj* gramadegol
gramme *n* gram
grand *adj* mawreddog, crand; prif, uchel
grandchild *n* ŵyr, wyres
granddad *(inf)* *n* taid, tad-cu
granddaughter *n* wyres
grandfather *n* taid, tad-cu
grandma *(inf)* *n* nain, mam-gu
grandmother *n* nain, mam-gu
grandpa *(inf)* *n* taid, tad-cu
grandparents *n* taid a nain, tad-cu a mam-gu
grandson *n* ŵyr
granite *n* gwenithfaen, ithfaen
granny *(inf)* *n* nain, mam-gu
grant *vt* rhoddi, caniatáu ▸ *n* rhodd, grant; **to take for granted** cymryd yn ganiataol
grapefruit *n* grawnffrwyth
graph *n* graff
graphic *adj* graffig; byw
graphics *npl* graffigwaith, graffeg
grasp *vb* gafael; amgyffred ▸ *n* gafael; amgyffrediad
grass *n* glaswellt, porfa

g

grasshopper n ceiliog y rhedyn, sioncyn y gwair
grate n grat ▸ vb rhygnu, crafellu; merwino
grateful adj diolchgar; dymunol
grater n grater, crafellydd
gratitude n diolchgarwch
grave¹ adj difrifol, dwys
grave² n bedd, beddrod
gravel n graean, gro, grafel
gravestone n beddfaen, carreg fedd
graveyard n mynwent
gravity n disgyrchiant; pwysigrwydd; **centre of gravity** craidd disgyrchiant
gravy n grefi
graze vb pori; crafu, rhwbio
grease n saim, iraid ▸ vt iro, seimio
greasy adj seimllyd, ireidlyd
great adj mawr; **a great many** llawer iawn
Great Britain n Prydain Fawr
great grandfather n hen daid, hen-dad-cu
greatly adv yn fawr
Greece n Groeg
greed n trachwant, gwanc
greedy adj barus, trachwantus, gwancus
Greek n (language) Groeg; Groegwr ▸ adj Groegaidd
green adj gwyrdd, glas, ir ▸ vb glasu
greengrocer n grîngroser, gwerthwr llysiau
greengrocer's n siop ffrwythau a lysiau
greenhouse n tŷ gwydr
greenhouse gas n nwy tŷ gwydr

Greenland n Yr Ynys Las
greet vt annerch, cyfarch
greeting n cyfarchiad
greetings card n cerdyn cyfarch
grey adj llwyd
greyhound n milgi
grid n grid, alch; **grid reference** cyfeirnod grid
grief n galar
grievance n cwyn
grieve vb galaru
grill n gril, gridyll ▸ vb grilio, gridyllu; **mixed grill** gril cymysg
grille n gril, dellt
grim adj sarrug, milain, difrifol
grin vb lledwenu ▸ n gwên
grind (pt, pp **ground**) vb (corn etc) malu
grip vb gafael, gwasgu ▸ n gafael, crap
grit n grit; pybyrwch
groan vi, n griddfan
grocer n groser
groceries npl nwyddau
grocer's n siop groser
groin n cesail morddwyd, gwerddyr
groom n priodfab; gwastrawd ▸ vb trwsio
groove n rhigol, rhych ▸ vt rhigoli, rhychu
grope vi ymbalfalu
gross n gros; crynswth ▸ adj bras, aflednais; **gross profit** elw gros
ground n llawr, daear, tir; sail; gwaelod ▸ vt daearu, llorio
ground floor n daearlawr
groundwork n sylfaen, sail
group n grŵp ▸ vt grwpio; **discussion group** cylch trafod
grouse n grugiar ▸ vb grwgnach

grovel *vi* ymgreinio

grow (*pt* **grew**, *pp* **grown**) *vb* tyfu, prifio, cynyddu, codi; **grow up** *vi* tyfu i fyny, tyfu lan

growl *vi* chwyrnu

grown-up *n* rhywun mewn oed, oedolyn

growth *n* twf, tyfiant, cynnydd

grub *n* pryf, cynrhonyn; (*inf*) bwyd

grubby *adj* budr, brwnt

grudge *vt* gwarafun, grwgnach ▸ *n* dig

gruesome *adj* erchyll, ffiaidd

grumble *vi* grwgnach, tuchan

grumpy *adj* sarrug, diserch

grunt *vi* rhochian ▸ *n* rhoch

guarantee *n* gwarant, ernes ▸ *vt* gwarantu, mechnïo

guard *n* gard, gwarchodydd; sgrin ▸ *vb* gwarchod

guardian *n* gwarcheidwad

guess *vb* dyfalu, dyfeisio ▸ *n* amcan

guest *n* gwestai, gŵr/gwraig (g)wadd

guesthouse *n* gwesty

guidance *n* cyfarwyddyd

guide *n* arweinydd ▸ *vt* arwain, cyfarwyddo

guide book *n* teithlyfr

guide-dog *n* arweingi

guide-lines *npl* canllawiau

guild *n* urdd

guilt *n* euogrwydd, bai

guilty *adj* euog

guinea pig *n* mochyn cwta

guitar *n* gitâr

guitarist *n* gitarydd

gulf *n* gwlff, geneufor; gagendor

gull *n* gwylan

gulp *vt* llawcian, traflyncu ▸ *n* llawc, traflwnc

gum *n* gwm, glud ▸ *vt* gymio, gludio

gun *n* gwn, dryll

gunpoint *n*: **at gunpoint** o flaen gwn

gunpowder *n* powdr gwn

gunshot *n* ergyd gwn

gush *vb* ffrydio, llifeirio ▸ *n* ffrwd, hyrddwynt

gust *n* chwythwm

gut *n* perfeddyn, coluddyn ▸ *vt* diberfeddu; difrodi, ysbeilio

gutter *n* ffos, cwter, cafn

guy *n* (*inf*, *man*) boi

gym *n* campfa

gymnasium *n* gymnasiwm, campfa

gymnast *n* mabolgampwr

gymnastics *n* gymnasteg

gynaecologist *n* gynaecolegydd

gypsy *n* sipsi

g

h

haberdashery n dilladach, siop ddillad
habit n arferiad; anian; gwisg ▶ vt gwisgo, dilladu
habitat n cartref, cynefin
habitual adj arferol, cyson
hack vb hacio, torri ▶ n hac
hacker n (Comput) haciwr
haddock n corbenfras, hadog
haemorrhage n gwaedlif
haemorrhoids npl clwyf y marchogion
haggle vi bargeinio'n daer
hail¹ n cenllysg, cesair ▶ vb bwrw cesair
hail² vb cyfarch, galw
hair n gwallt, blew, rhawn; **hair's breadth** trwch y blewyn; **hair splitting** hollti blew
hairbrush n brws gwallt
haircut n triniaeth gwallt, toriad, crop
hairdo n steil gwallt

hairdresser n triniwr gwallt
hairdresser's n siop trin gwallt
hair dryer n sychwr gwallt
hair gel n jel gwallt
hair spray n chwistrelliad gwallt
hairstyle n steil gwallt
hairy adj blewog
hake n cegddu
half n hanner
half-brother n hanner brawd
half fare n hanner pris
half-hearted adj diawydd, llugoer
half-hour n hanner awr
half-price adj hanner pris
half-sister n hanner chwaer
half term n (school) hanner tymor
half-time n hanner amser
halfway adv: **halfway (to)** hanner ffordd (i)
hall n llys, neuadd, plas; cyntedd
hallmark n dilysnod
hallo excl helô
Halloween n nos Galangaeaf
Hallowe'en n Calan Gaeaf
hallucination n geuddrych, rhithwelediad
halo n corongylch, halo, lleugylch
halt vb sefyll ▶ n safiad; gorsaf, arosfa
halve vt haneru
ham n morddwyd, ham
hamburger n hambyrgyr
hamlet n pentref
hammer n morthwyl ▶ vb morthwylio
hammock n hamog, gwely crog
hamper vt rhwystro, llesteirio
hamster n bochdew
hamstring n llinyn y gar

hand *n* llaw; *(of clock)* bys ▸ *vt*
estyn, trosglwyddo; **to be on hand**
bod with law
handbag *n* bag llaw
handbook *n* llawlyfr
handbrake *n* brec llaw
handcuffs *n* gefynnau
handful *n* dyrnaid, llond llaw
handicap *n* rhwystr, llestair,
anfantais
handkerchief *n* cadach poced,
hances, macyn, neisied
handle *n* carn, coes, troed, dolen,
clust, dwrn ▸ *vt* trin, trafod; **to fly
off the handle** colli tymer
handlebars *npl* cyrn
handmade *adj* wedi ei wneud
â llaw
hands-free *adj* heb afael; **hands-
free kit** teclyn heb afael
handsome *adj* golygus, hardd
handwriting *n* llawysgrifen
handy *adj* hylaw, deheuig, cyfleus
hang *(pt, pp* **hung)** *vb* crogi,
hongian; **hang around** *vi* loetran;
hang on *vi* dal; **hang up** *vt* rhoi
ar y hoel
hanger *n* cambren
hang-gliding *vb* barcuta
hangover *n* blinder ddoe, pen
mawr
happen *vi* digwydd
happily *adv* yn hapus
happiness *n* dedwyddwch,
hapusrwydd
happy *adj* dedwydd, hapus
harass *vt* poeni, blino
harassment *n* poen, blinder

harbour *n* porthladd, harbwr ▸ *vb*
llochesu
hard *adj* caled, anodd; **hard of
hearing** trwm ei glyw; **to be hard
done by** cael cam; **hard headed**
hirben
hardboard *n* caledfwrdd
hard disk *n (Comput)* disgen galed,
disg caled
harden *vb* caledu
hardly *adv*: **she hardly speaks
English** prin ei bod hi'n siarad
Saesneg; **hardly anyone came** ni
ddaeth braidd neb
hardship *n* caledi
hard shoulder *n* llain galed
hard-up *adj (inf)* prin o arian
hardware *n* nwyddau metel
hard-working *adj* gweithgar,
diwyd
hardy *adj* caled, gwydn
hare *n* ysgyfarnog, ceinach
harm *n* niwed, drwg ▸ *vt* niweidio
harmful *adj* niweidiol
harmless *adj* diniwed, diddrwg
harmony *n* harmoni, cynghanedd
harness *n* harnais, gêr ▸ *vt*
harneisio
harp *n* telyn ▸ *vi* canu'r delyn
harsh *adj* garw, gerwin, aflafar
harvest *n* cynhaeaf ▸ *vt* cynaeafu
hassle *n (inf)* helynt, trafferth
haste *n* brys, hast ▸ *vi* brysio,
prysuro
hasten *vb* brysio, prysuro, hastu
hastily *adv* yn frysiog
hasty *adj* brysiog, byrbwyll
hat *n* het
hatch¹ *vb* deor, gori ▸ *n* deoriad
hatch² *n* gorddrws, rhagddor, dôr

hatchback

hatchback *n* car cefn codi
hate *vt* casáu ▸ *n* cas, casineb
hatred *n* cas, casineb
haul *vb* tynnu, llusgo ▸ *n* dalfa
haunt *vt* mynychu; trwblu,
  aflonyddu ▸ *n* cynefin, cyrchfa
haunted *adj*: **a haunted house**
  tŷ â bwgan

have (*pt, pp* **had**) *aux vb* **1** bod wedi
  gwneud rhth; **to have eaten/slept**
  bod wedi bwyta/cysgu; **to have
  arrived/gone** bod wedi cyrraedd/
  mynd; **having finished** *or* **when
  he had finished, he left** ar ôl iddo
  orffen, ymadawodd; **we'd already
  eaten** roedden ni wedi bwyta
  eisoes
  2 (*in tag questions*): **you've done
  it, haven't you?** rydych chi wedi'i
  wneud, on'd ydych?
  ▸ *modal aux vb* (*be obliged*): **to have
  (got) to do sth** gorfod gwneud
  rhth; **she has (got) to do it** rhaid
  iddi ei wneud; **you haven't to
  tell her** rhaid ichi beidio â dweud
  wrthi; **do you have to book?** oes
  rhaid archebu lle?
  ▸ *vt* **1** (*possess*) bod gennych rth; **he
  has (got) blue eyes/dark hair** mae
  ganddo lygaid glas/wallt brown
  2 (*referring to meals etc*): **to have
  breakfast** bwyta brecwast;
  to have dinner/lunch bwyta
  cinio, ciniawa; **to have a drink**
  cymryd diod, yfed diod; **to have a
  cigarette** cymryd sigarét, ysmygu
  sigarét
  3 (*receive*): cael, derbyn; (*obtain*)
  sicrhau; **may I have your address?**
  a ga i'ch cyfeiriad?; **you can have
  it for £5** fe'i cewch am £5; **I must
  have it for tomorrow** rhaid imi
  ei gael at yfory; **to have a baby**
  esgor ar blentyn, cael plentyn,
  geni plentyn
  4 (*maintain, allow*) **I won't have it!**
  wnaiff hyn mo'r tro!; **we can't have
  that** allwn ni ddim caniatáu hyn
  5 (*by sb else*): **to have sth done** cael
  gwneud rhth; **to have one's hair
  cut** cael torri'ch gwallt; **to have sb
  do sth** cael gan rn wneud rhth
  6 (*experience, suffer*) bod â rhth
  arnoch; **to have a cold/flu** bod
  ag annwyd/ffliw arnoch; **to have
  an operation** cael llawdriniaeth;
  she had her bag stolen cafodd
  ddwyn ei bag
  7 (*+noun*): **to have a swim/walk**
  nofio/mynd am dro; **to have a
  bath/shower** cael bath/cawod;
  let's have a look gadewch inni
  weld; **to have a meeting** cyfarfod,
  cynnal cyfarfod; **to have a party**
  cynnal parti; **let me have a try**
  gadewch i mi roi cynnig arni

haven *n* hafan, porthladd
havoc *n* hafog, difrod
hawk *n* hebog, cudyll, curyll ▸ *vb*
  heboca
hawthorn *n* draenen wen
hay *n* gwair
hay fever *n* y dwymyn wair, clefyd
  y gwair
hazard *n* perygl ▸ *vt* peryglu
hazardous *adj* peryglus, enbydus
haze *n* niwl, tarth, tawch

hazel n collen ▸ adj gwinau golau
hazelnut n cneuen gyll
hazy adj aneglur, niwlog
he pron ef, efe; efo, fo, o
head n pen ▸ vb blaenori, penio
headache n dolur (cur) yn y pen, pen tost
heading n pennawd
headlamp n lamp fawr
headlight n prif olau
headline n pennawd
headmaster n prifathro
headmistress n prifathrawes
headphones npl ffonau clust
headquarters npl pencadlys
headteacher n (man) prifathro; (woman) prifathrawes
heal vb iacháu, meddyginiaethu
health n iechyd
health centre n canolfan iechyd
health food shop n siop bwyd iach
Health Service n y Gwasanaeth Iechyd
healthy adj iach, iachus
heap n crug, pentwr ▸ vt crugio, pentyrru
hear (pt, pp **heard**) vb clywed
hearing n clyw
hearing aid n cymorth clywed
hearse n hers
heart n calon
heart attack n trawiad y galon
heartbroken adj calonddrylliog
heartburn n dŵr poeth
heart disease n clefyd y galon
hearth n aelwyd
hearty adj calonnog, cynnes
heat n gwres, poethder ▸ vb twymo, poethi; **heat up** vb twymo

heater n gwresogydd
heather n grug
heating n gwres
heaven n nef, nefoedd
heavenly adj nefol, nefolaidd
heavily adv yn drwm, yn drymaidd
heavy adj trwm, trymaidd, trymllyd
Hebrew n Hebrëwr; (language) Hebraeg ▸ adj Hebraeg; Hebreig
hectare n hectar
hectic adj prysur
hedge n clawdd, gwrych, perth
hedgehog n draenog
heed vt ystyried, talu sylw ▸ n ystyriaeth
heel n sawdl ▸ vb sodli
height n uchder, taldra
heir n etifedd, aer
heiress n etifeddes, aeres
helicopter n hofrennydd
hell n uffern
hello excl helô!, hylô!
helmet n helm
help vt helpu, cynorthwyo ▸ n help, cymorth, cynhorthwy
helper n cynorthwywr, helpwr
helpful adj defnyddiol, cymwynasgar, buddiol
helping n dogn, cyfran (o fwyd)
helpless adj diymadferth
helpline n llinell gymorth
hem n hem, ymyl ▸ vt hemio
hemisphere n hemisffer
hen n iâr
hence adv oddi yma ▸ excl ymaith!
henceforth adv rhag llaw, mwyach, o hyn ymlaen
hen night, hen party n noson merched (cyn priodas)

hepatitis n hepatitis
her pron ei, hi, hithau
herb n llysieuyn, sawr-lysieuyn
herbal adj llysieuol
herbal tea n te llysieuol
herd n gyr, cenfaint, gre ▸ vb heidio
here adv yma
hereditary adj etifeddol
heritage n etifeddiaeth, treftadaeth
hernia n hernia, torllengig
hero n arwr, gwron
heroic adj arwrol
heroin n heroin
heroine n arwres
heron n crëyr, crychydd
herring n pennog, ysgadenyn
hers pron (her one) un hi; **the house is hers** hi sy biau'r tŷ
herself pron ei hun
hesitant adj petrusgar
hesitate vi petruso
hesitation n petruster
heterosexual n heterorywiol
heyday n anterth
hi excl heia
hibernate vi gaeafu
hiccup n yr ig ▸ vi igian
hiccups n: **I've got hiccups** mae'r ig arnaf i
hide¹ (pt hid, pp hidden) vb cuddio, celu, ymguddio
hide² n croen
hideous adj hyll, erchyll
hi-fi n hei-ffei
high adj uchel; mawr; cryf; llawn
high chair n cadair ar gyfer plentyn
higher education n addysg uwch
high jump n naid uchel

highlight vt pwysleisio ▸ n uchelbwynt; **highlights** npl (hair) aroleuadau
highlighter n (pen) aroleuydd
highly adv yn fawr, yn uchel
highness n uchelder
high-rise n: **high-rise flats** twr fflatiau
high street n stryd fawr
highway n priffordd, ffordd fawr
hijack vb cipio
hijacker n herwgipiwr
hike vb crwydro ▸ n taith gerdded
hiking n heicio
hilarious adj llawen, llon, siriol, hoenus
hill n bryn, allt
hill-walking n dringo bryniau
hilly adj bryniog, mynyddig
him pron ef, efe; efo, fo; yntau
himself pron ei hun
hind¹ adj ôl
hind² n ewig
hinder vt rhwystro, atal, llesteirio
Hindu n Hindw ▸ adj Hindwaidd
hinge n colyn drws ▸ vb troi, dibynnu
hint n awgrym ▸ vt awgrymu
hip n clun, pen uchaf y glun
hippie n hipi
hippo n hipo
hire vt cyflogi, hurio, llogi ▸ n cyflog, hur
hire car n car llog
hire purchase n hurbwrcas
his adj ei ▸ pron (his one) un fe; **the car is his** fe sy biau'r car; **his car** ei gar e
hiss vb hisian
historian n hanesydd

historic *adj* hanesyddol
historical *adj* hanesyddol
history *n* hanes
hit *(pt, pp* **hit)** *vb* taro ► *n* ergyd, trawiad
hitch *vb* bachu ► *n* cwlwm; atalfa, rhwystr
hitchhike *vb* bodio
hitchhiker *n* bodiwr
hitchhiking *n* bodio
HIV *n abbr* HIV; **HIV-negative/positive** HIV negyddol/positif
hive *n* cwch gwenyn; **hive off** *vb (inf)* rhannu, trosglwyddo, newid
HIV-negative *adj* HIV-negyddol
HIV-positive *adj* HIV-positif
hoard *n* cronfa, cuddfa ► *vt* cronni
hoarse *adj* cryg, cryglyd
hoax *vt* twyllo ► *n* cast, tric, twyll
hob *n* pentan
hobble *vb* hercian
hobby *n* difyrwaith, hobi
hockey *n* hoci
hog *n* mochyn
hoist *vt* codi, dyrchafu
hold¹ *(pt, pp* **held)** *vb* dal, credu; atal; cadw ► *n* gafael, dalfa ► **hold on** *vt (grip)* gafael; *(wait)* aros; **to hold onto sth** gafael yn rhth
hold² *n* ceudod llong, howld
holdall *n* celsach
hole *n* twll, ffau
holiday *n* gŵyl, dygwyl
Holland *npl* Yr Iseldiroedd
hollow *adj* cau, gwag ► *n* ceudod, pant ► *vt* tyllu, cafnio
holly *n* celyn, celynnen
holocaust *n* lladdfa
holy *adj* sanctaidd, glân

home *n, adj* cartref ► *adv* adref; **at home** gartref
homeland *n* mamwlad
homeless *adj* digartref
homely *adj* cartrefol
home-made *adj* cartref
homeopathy *n* homeopatheg
home page *(Internet)* tudalen gartref, tudalen hafan
homesick *adj* hiraethus
homework *n* gwaith cartref
homicide *n* dynleiddiad, llofruddiaeth
homosexual *n* rhn cyfunrhywiol
homosexuality *n* cyfunrhywioldeb
honest *adj* (g)onest, didwyll
honestly *adv* yn onest
honesty *n* (g)onestrwydd
honey *n* mêl
honeymoon *n* mis mêl
honeysuckle *n* gwyddfid
honorary *adj* mygedol
honour *n* anrhydedd ► *vt* anrhydeddu
honourable *adj* anrhydeddus
hood *n* cwfl, cwcwll
hoodie *n (hooded top)* hwdi
hoof *n* carn
hook *n* bach ► *vb* bachu
hooligan *n* adyn, dihiryn
hoop *n* cylch, cant ► *vt* cylchu, cantio
hooray *excl* hwrê
hoot *vb* hwtian, hwtio ► *n* hŵt
Hoover *n* hwfer
hoover *vt* hwfro
hop *vb* hercian ► *n* llam, herc
hope *n* gobaith ► *vb* gobeithio
hopefully *adv (let's hope)* gobeithio
hopeless *adj* anobeithiol; diobaith

h

horizon n gorwel
horizontal adj llorwedd
hormone n hormon
horn n corn ▸ vt cornio, twlcio
horoscope n horosgôp
horrible adj erchyll, ofnadwy
horrid adj erchyll, echrydus
horrifying adj brawychus
horror n arswyd, erchylltod
horse n march, ceffyl
horse-racing n rasio ceffylau
hose n pibell ddŵr
hospital n ysbyty
hospitality n lletygarwch, croeso
host n lletywr, gwesteiwr
hostage n gwystl
hostel n llety efrydwyr, neuadd breswyl
hostess n croesawferch
hostile adj gelyniaethus
hot adj poeth, twym
hot dog n ci poeth
hotel n gwesty
hot-water bottle n potel dŵr twym
hound n bytheiad, helgi ▸ vt hela, erlid
hour n awr
hourly adj, adv bob awr
house n tŷ, annedd ▸ vb lletya
household n teulu, tylwyth
householder n deiliad tŷ
housekeeper n gofalyddes
housewife n gwraig tŷ
housework n gwaith tŷ
housing n tai
hover vi hofran
hovercraft n hofrenfad
how adv pa mor, pa fodd, pa sut, sut

however adv pa fodd bynnag, sut bynnag
howl vi udo, oernadu ▸ n udiad, oernad
huddle vb tyrru, gwthio
huff vb sorri, tramgwyddo ▸ n soriant
hug vt cofleidio, gwasgu
huge adj anferth, enfawr, dirfawr
hull n corff llong; cibyn, plisgyn
hum vb mwmian ▸ n si, sibrwd
human adj dynol
human being n bod dynol
humane adj tirion, tosturiol, trugarog
humanist n dyneiddiwr
humanitarian n dyngarwr
humanity n dynoliaeth, dynolryw
humble adj gostyngedig, ufudd ▸ vt darostwng
humid adj llaith
humiliate vt bychanu, gwaradwyddo, darostwng
humiliation n darostyngiad
humour n hwyl, donioldeb ▸ vt boddio
hump n crwmach, crwmp, crwb
hunch n syniad, tybiaeth
hundred adj cant, can ▸ n cant; cantref
Hungarian n (person) Hwngariad; (language) Hwngareg ▸ adj Hwngaraidd; (in language) Hwngareg
Hungary n Hwngari
hunger n newyn, chwant bwyd ▸ vi newynu
hungry adj newynog
hunt vb hela, erlid ▸ n helwriaeth, hela

hunter *n* heliwr; ceffyl hela
hunting *n* hela
hurdle *n* clwyd
hurl *vt* hyrddio
hurricane *n* corwynt
hurry *vb* brysio ▸ *n* brys
hurt (*pt, pp* **hurt**) *vb* niweidio, dolurio, brifo ▸ *n* niwed, dolur
husband *n* gŵr, priod ▸ *vt* cynilo
hush *excl* ust ▸ *vb* distewi ▸ *n* distawrwydd
husky *adj* sych, cryglyd
hut *n* caban, cwt
hyacinth *n* croeso haf
hygiene *n* iechydaeth, hylendid
hymn *n* emyn ▸ *vb* emynu
hypermarket *n* archfarchnad
hyphen *n* cyplysnod, cysylltnod
hypnotize *vt* swyno, rheibio
hypocrite *n* rhagrithiwr
hypothesis *n* damcaniaeth
hysterical *adj* hysterig

I *pron* mi, myfi; fi, i; minnau, innau
ice *n* iâ, rhew ▸ *vt* taenu (megis) â rhew
iceberg *n* mynydd rhew
ice cream *n* hufen iâ
ice cube *n* ciwb iâ
ice hockey *n* hoci iâ
Iceland *n* Gwlad yr Iâ
ice lolly *n* loli iâ
ice rink *n* llain iâ
ice-skating *n* sglefrio iâ
icing *n* eising
icon *n* eicon
ICT *n* TGCh
icy *adj* rhewllyd
ID card *n* cerdyn adnabod
idea *n* drychfeddwl, syniad
ideal *adj* delfrydol, ideal ▸ *n* delfryd
identical *adj* yr un (yn union)
identification *n* (*recognition*) adnabyddiaeth

identify

identify vt adnabod; uniaethu;
  identify with uniaethu â
identity n unfathiant, hunaniaeth
identity card n cerdyn adnabod
idiom n priod-ddull, idiom
idiot n gwirionyn, hurtyn
idiotic adj gwirion
idle adj segur, ofer ▸ vb segura,
  ofera
idol n eilun
i.e. abbr (= id est) h.y.
if conj os, pe
ignite vb ennyn, tanio, cynnau
ignition n taniad
ignorance n anwybodaeth
ignorant adj anwybodus
ignore vt anwybyddu, diystyru
ill adj drwg; gwael, claf ▸ adv yn
  ddrwg ▸ n drwg, niwed
illegal adj anghyfreithlon
illegible adj annarllenadwy,
  aneglur
illegitimate adj anghyfreithlon
illiterate adj anllythrennog
illness n afiechyd, salwch
illuminate vt goleuo, addurno
illusion n rhith, lledrith
illustrate vt darlunio
illustration n darlun
image n delw, llun, delwedd
imaginary adj dychmygol
imagination n dychymyg,
  darfelydd
imaginative adj dychmygus
imagine vt dychmygu, tybio
imbalance n anghydbwysedd
imitate vt dynwared, efelychu
imitation n dynwarediad ▸ adj
  ffug
immaculate adj difrycheulyd, pur

immature adj anaeddfed
immediate adj agos, presennol
immediately adv ar unwaith
immense adj anferth, eang
immerse vt trochi, suddo
immigrant n mewnfudwr
immigration n mewnfudiad
imminent adj gerllaw, agos
immoral adj anfoesol
immortal adj anfarwol
immune adj rhydd rhag
immunize vb gwrtheintio
impact n ardrawiad,
  gwrthdrawiad
impair vt amharu
impartial adj diduedd, amhleidiol
impatience n diffyg amynedd
impatient adj diamynedd
impatiently adv yn ddiamynedd
impeccable adj di-fai
impending adj agos, gerllaw
imperative n gorchymyn ▸ adj
  gorchmynnol, gorfodol
imperfect adj amherffaith
imperial adj ymerodrol
impersonal adj amhersonol
impersonate vt personoli
impetus n cymhelliad, symbyliad
implant vt plannu, gwreiddio
implement n offeryn, arf ▸ vb
  gweithredu
implication n ymhlygiad,
  goblygiad
implicit adj dealledig, ymhlyg,
  goblygedig
imply vt arwyddo, awgrymu
impolite adj anfoesgar
import vt mewnforio ▸ n
  mewnforyn; arwyddocâd, pwys
importance n pwys, pwysigrwydd

important *adj* pwysig

importer *n* mewnforiwr

impose *vb* gosod

imposing *adj* llethol, mawreddog

impossible *adj* amhosibl

impotent *adj* di-rym, analluog

impress *vt* argraffu, pwyso, dylanwadu ► *n* argraffiad

impressed *adj* edmygus

impression *n* argraff

impressive *adj* trawiadol

imprison *vt* carcharu

improbable *adj* annhebygol

improper *adj* anweddus

improve *vb* gwella, diwygio

improvement *n* gwelliant

improvise *vb* addasu ar y pryd

impulse *n* cymhelliad, ysgogiad

impulsive *adj* byrbwyll

[KEYWORD]

in *prep* **1** *(followed by a definite object or a proper noun)* yn; **in the house/ the fridge** yn y tŷ/yr oergell; **in the garden** yn yr ardd; **in town** yn y dref; **in the country** yn y wlad; **in school** yn yr ysgol; **in here/there** yma/acw

2 *(followed by an indefinite object)* mewn; **in a house** mewn tŷ; **in a garden** mewn gardd; **in a town** mewn tref; **in a school** mewn ysgol

3 *(with place names: of town, region, country)*: **in Cardiff** yng Nghaerdydd; **in Wales** yng Nghymru; **in Japan** yn Japan; **in the United States** yn yr Unol Daleithiau

4 *(indicating time: during)*: **in**

spring yn y gwanwyn; **in summer** yn yr haf; **in May/2017** ym mis Mai/yn 2017; **in the afternoon** yn y prynhawn; **at 4 o'clock in the afternoon** am 4 o'r gloch y prynhawn

5 *(indicating time: in the space of)* mewn; *(: future)* ymhen; **I did it in 3 hours/days** fe'i gwnes mewn 3 awr/diwrnod; **I'll see you in 2 weeks** *or* **in 2 weeks' time** fe wela i ti ymhen pythefnos

6 *(indicating manner etc)* mewn/ yn; **in a loud/soft voice** mewn llais cryf/tawel; **in pencil** mewn pensel; **in writing** mewn ysgrifen; **in Welsh** yn Gymraeg; **the boy in the blue shirt** y bachgen yn y crys glas

7 *(indicating circumstances)*: **in the sun** yn yr haul; **in the shade** yn y cysgod; **in the rain** yn y glaw; **a change in policy** newid polisi

8 *(indicating mood, state)*: **in tears** mewn dagrau, yn ei ddagrau; **in anger** mewn dicter; **in despair** mewn anobaith; **in good condition** mewn cyflwr da; **to live in luxury** byw yn fras

9 *(with ratios, numbers)*: **1 in 10 households, 1 household in 10** 1 aelwyd mewn 10; **20 pence in the pound** 20 ceiniog yn y bunt; **they lined up in twos** safasant mewn rhes fesul dau/mewn deuoedd; **in hundreds** fesul cant; **10** *(referring to people, works)* mewn, ymysg; **the disease is common in children** mae'r clefyd yn gyffredin ymysg plant; **in (the works of) Owen** yng ngwaith Owen; **11** (*with present participle*): **in saying this** wedi dweud hynny

▸ *adv*: **to be in** (*person: at home, work*) bod yno (*train, ship, plane*) bod wedi cyraedd (*in fashion*) bod mewn ffasiwn; **to ask sb in** gwahodd rhywun [i ddod] i mewn; **to run/limp in** dod i mewn gan redeg/hercian

▸ *n*: **the ins and outs (of)** (*of proposal, situation etc*) manylion

inability *n* anallu
inaccurate *adj* anghywir, anfanwl
inadequate *adj* annigonol
inadvertent *adj* anfwriadol, amryfus
inappropriate *adj* amhriodol
inaugurate *vt* urddo, agor, dechrau
inbox *n* blwch derbyn
incapable *adj* analluog
incense¹ *n* arogldarth
incense² *vt* llidio, cythruddo
incentive *adj* cymelliadol ▸ *n* cymhelliad
inch *n* modfedd
incident *n* digwyddiad
incidentally *adv* gyda llaw
inclination *n* tuedd, gogwydd
incline *vb* tueddu, gogwyddo ▸ *n* llethr
include *vt* cynnwys
including *prep* gan gynnwys
inclusive *adj* cynwysedig, gan gynnwys
income *n* incwm; **income tax** treth incwm
income tax *n* treth incwm

incompatible *adj* anghytûn
incompetent *n* anghymwys
incomplete *adj* anghyflawn
inconsistent *adj* anghyson
inconspicuous *adj* anamlwg
inconvenience *n* anghyfleustra
inconvenient *adj* anghyfleus
incorporate *vb* corffori, ymgorffori
incorporated *adj* corfforedig
incorrect *adj* anghywir
increase *vb* cynyddu ▸ *n* cynnydd
incredible *adj* anhygoel, anghredadwy
incur *vt* ysgwyddo; achosi
indecent *adj* anweddus
indeed *adv* yn wir; iawn, dros ben
independence *n* annibyniaeth
independent *adj* annibynnol ▸ *n* annibynnwr
index *n* mynegai; **index finger** mynegfys
India *n* India
Indian *adj* Indiaidd ▸ *n* Indiad
indicate *vt* dangos, arwyddo
indicative *adj* arwyddol, mynegol
indicator *n* dangosydd
indict *vt* cyhuddo
indifference *n* difaterwch, difrawder
indifferent *adj* difater; dibwys
indigenous *adj* cynhenid
indigestion *n* diffyg traul, camdreuliad
indignant *adj* dig, dicllon
indirect *adj* anuniongyrchol
indispensable *adj* anhepgorol
individual *adj* unigol ▸ *n* un, unigolyn
Indonesia *n* Indonesia
indoor *adj*, *adv* dan do

indoors *adv* dan do
induce *vt* denu, cymell
indulge *vb* boddio; maldodi
indulgence *n* ymfoddhad; maldod
indulgent *adj* ffafriol, maldodus
industrial *adj* diwydiannol,
gweithfaol
industrial estate *n* stad
ddiwydiannol
industry *n* diwydrwydd; diwydiant
inefficient *adj* aneffeithlon
inequality *n* anghysondeb
inevitable *adj* anochel, anesgorol
inexpensive *adj* rhad
inexperienced *adj* amhrofiadol,
dibrofiad
infamous *adj* gwaradwyddus,
gwarthus
infant *n* baban; un dan oed
infantry *n* gwŷr traed, milwyr
traed
infant school *n* ysgol fach
infect *vt* heintio, llygru
infection *n* haint
infectious *adj* heintus
infer *vt* casglu
inferior *adj* is, israddol ▸ *n* isradd
infertile *adj* anffrwythlon
infertility *n* anffrwythlondeb
infinite *adj* anfeidrol
infirmary *n* ysbyty, clafdy
inflamed *adj* llidus
inflammation *n* enyniad, llid
inflatable *adj* y gellir ei chwyddo
neu ei chwythu
inflate *vt* chwyddo
inflation *n* chwyddiant
inflexible *adj* anhyblyg
inflict *vt* peri, gweinyddu (cosb,
poen *etc*)

influence *n* dylanwad ▸ *vt*
dylanwadu
influenza *n* ffliw
influx *n* dylifiad
inform *vb* hysbysu
informal *adj* anffurfiol
information *n* gwybodaeth,
hysbysrwydd
information technology *n*
technoleg gwybodaeth
infra-red *adj* is-goch
infrastructure *n* seilwaith
infrequent *adj* anaml
infuriate *vt* ffyrnigo, cynddeiriogi
infuriating *adj*: he's infuriating
mae o'n ddigon i'ch gwylltio
ingenious *adj* medrus, celfydd
ingredients *npl* cynhwysion
inhabit *vt* cyfaneddu, preswylio
inhabitable *adj* cyfannedd,
trigadwy
inhabitant *n* preswyliwr
inhale *vt* anadlu
inhaler *n* anadlydd
inherent *adj* cynhenid, greddfol
inherit *vt* etifeddu
inheritance *n* etifeddiaeth
inhibit *vt* gwahardd, atal
inhibition *n* ataliad, atalnwyd
initial *adj* dechreuol ▸ *n* llythyren
gyntaf
initiate *vt* derbyn; dechrau
initiative *n* cynhoredd, menter
inject *vt* chwistrellu
injection *n* chwistrelliad, pigiad
injure *vt* niweidio, anafu
injury *n* niwed, cam, anaf
injustice *n* anghyfiawnder, cam
ink *n* inc ▸ *vt* incio
inland *adj* canoldirol ▸ *n* canoldir

Inland Revenue

Inland Revenue n Cyllid y Wlad
in-laws npl teulu-yng-nghyfraith
inmate n trigiannydd, preswylydd
inn n tafarn, tafarndy
inner adj mewnol
innocence n diniweidrwydd
innocent adj diniwed, gwirion, dieuog
innovation n newyddbeth
input n mewnbwn, cyfraniad
inquest n cwest; trengholiad
inquire vb ymofyn, ymholi, gofyn
inquiry n ymholiad
insane adj gwallgof, gorffwyll, ynfyd
insect n pryf, trychfil
insect repellent n eli ymlid pryfed
insert vb mewnosod
inside n tu mewn ▸ adj mewnol
  ▸ prep y tu mewn i ▸ adv i mewn, o fewn
inside-out adv o chwith
insight n mewnwelediad
insignificant adj di-nod, distadl, dibwys
insincere adj annidwyll, ffuantus
insist vi mynnu
insomnia n anhunedd
inspect vt arolygu, archwilio
inspection n archwiliad, arolygiad
inspector n arolygwr
inspiration n ysbrydoliaeth
inspire vb ysbrydoli
instability n ansadrwydd
install vt sefydlu, gorseddu
instalment n cyfran, rhandal
instance n enghraifft ▸ vt enwi, nodi
instant adj taer, ebrwydd ▸ n eiliad, moment

instant coffee n coffi powdr
instantly adv ar drawiad
instead adv yn lle
instinct n greddf
institute n athrofa
institution n sefydliad
instruct vt hyfforddi
instruction n hyfforddiant
instructor n hyfforddwr
instrument n offeryn
insufficient adj annigonol
insulate vt ynysu, inswleiddio
insulin n inswlin
insult vt sarhau ▸ n sarhad
insurance n yswiriant
insurance policy n polisi yswiriant
insure vb yswirio
intact adj cyfan, dianaf
integral adj cyfan, cyflawn
integrate vb cyfannu
integrity n cywirdeb, gonestrwydd
intellect n deall
intellectual n deallusyn ▸ adj deallus, deallgar
intelligence n deallusrwydd; hysbysrwydd
intelligent adj deallus
intend vt bwriadu
intense adj angerddol, dwys
intensive adj dwys
intensive care unit n uned gofal arbennig
intent n bwriad, amcan; ystyr; diben
intention n bwriad
intentional adj bwriadol
interaction n rhyngweithiad
interactive adj rhyngweithiol
intercept vt rhyng-gipio

interchange vt cyfnewid, ymgyfnewid

intercourse n cyfathrach

interest n budd, buddiant; diddordeb; llog ▸ vt diddori

interested adj â chanddo ddidordeb

interesting adj diddorol

interest rate n cyfradd llog

interface n cydwyneb

interfere vt ymyrryd, ymhél

interference n ymyrraeth

interim adj dros dro ▸ n cyfamser

interior adj mewnol ▸ n tu mewn, canol, perfeddwlad

interior designer n cynllunydd tai

intermediate adj canol, cano(radd

intern vt carcharu

internal adj mewnol

international adj cydwladol, rhyngwladol

internet n rhyngrwyd; internet café caffi rhyngrwyd, caffe rhyngrwyd

internet café n caffi/caffe rhyngrwyd

internet user n defnyddiwr rhyngrwyd

interpret vt dehongli; cyfieithu

interpretation n dehongliad; cyfieithiad

interpreter n lladmerydd, cyfieithydd

interrogate vt holi

interrogative adj gofynnol

interrupt vt torri ar, torri ar draws, ymyrryd

interruption n toriad

intersection n croesdoriad

interval n egwyl, saib

intervene vi ymyrryd

interview n cyfweliad ▸ vb cyfweld

interviewer n cyfwelydd

intimate¹ adj cyfarwydd, agos ▸ n cydnabod

intimate² vt arwyddo, hysbysu

intimidate vt dychrynu, brawychu

into prep i, i mewn i

intranet n intranet, mewnrwyd

intransitive adj (grammar) cyflawn

intricate adj dyrys, cymhleth, astrus

intrigue vi, n cynllwyn

introduce vt cyflwyno

introduction n cyflwyniad, rhagarweiniad

introductory adj dechreuol, agoriadol, rhagarweiniol

introvert adj mewnblyg

intrude vb ymyrryd

intruder n ymyrrwr, ymwthiwr

intuition n sythwelediad

inundate vt gorlifo, boddi

invade vt goresgyn

invalid¹ adj di-rym, annilys

invalid² n un afiach, un methedig

invaluable adj amhrisiadwy

invariably adv yn ddieithriad

invasion n goresgyniad

invent vt dyfeisio, dychmygu

invention n dyfais

inventory n rhestr, stocrestr

inverted commas npl dyfynodau

invest vt buddsoddi; arwisgo

investigate vt chwilio, archwilio, ymchwilio

investigation n ymchwiliad

investigator n ymchwiliwr

investment n buddsoddiad

investor n buddsoddwr
invisible adj anweledig, anweladwy
invitation n gwahoddiad
invite vt gwahodd
invoice n anfoneb
involve vt drysu; cynnwys, ymwneud
involvement n ymwneud, ymglymiad
inward adj mewnol
iPad n iPad
iPhone n iPhone
iPod n iPod
IQ n abbr IQ, CD, cyniferydd deallusrwydd
Iran n Iran
Iraq n Irac
Iraqi n Iraciad ▸ adj Iracaidd
Ireland n Iwerddon
iris n iris; gellesgen
Irish adj Gwyddelig ▸ n (language) Gwyddeleg
Irishman n Gwyddel
Irishwoman n Gwyddeles
iron n, adj haearn ▸ vt smwddio
ironic adj eironig
ironing n smwddio
ironing board n bwrdd smwddio
irony n eironi
irrational adj direswm, afresymol
irregular adj afreolaidd
irrelevant adj amherthnasol
irresistible adj anorchfygol
irresponsible adj anghyfrifol
irritable n croendenau, anniddig, llidiog
irritate vt blino, poeni, cythruddo
irritating adj pryfoclyd
is vi mae, sydd, yw, ydy(w), oes

Islam n Islam
Islamic adj Islamaidd
island, isle n ynys
isolated adj wedi ei neilltuo, wedi ei wahanu
isolation n neilltuaeth, arwahanrwydd
ISP n abbr (= Internet Service Provider) ISP, Darparydd Gwasanaeth Rhyngrwyd
Israel n Israel
Israeli n Israeliad ▸ adj Israelaidd
issue n llif; agorfa, arllwysfa; hiliogaeth, plant; canlyniad, pwnc ▸ vb tarddu, deillio; cyhoeddi
IT n abbr (= information technology) TG, technoleg gwybodaeth

[KEYWORD]

it pron 1 (in a single word answer to a question, it is conveyed by the 3rd sing. ending of the appropriate verb): **it is** ydyw; **it may** caiff; **it can** gall; **it did** gwnaeth
2 (after prep): **about/from/of it** y peth; **I spoke to him about it** siaradais ag ef am y peth; **what did you learn from it?** beth ddysgest ti o'r peth?; **I'm proud of it** rwy'n falch o'r peth
3 (impersonal, usually) hi; **it's Friday tomorrow** dydd Gwener yw hi yfory; **it's 6 o'clock** mae hi'n 6 o'r gloch; **how far is it? — it's 10 miles** pa mor bell yw hi? — mae'n 10 milltir; **who is it? — it's me** pwy sy yna? — fi sy yma; **it's raining** mae hi'n bwrw [glaw]
4: **it was a book he lost** llyfr a

gollodd ef; **it was Wales who won the match** Cymru a enillodd y gêm

Italian *adj* Eidalaidd ▶ *n* Eidalwr; *(language)* Eidaleg
italics *npl* llythrennau italaidd
Italy *n* Yr Eidal
itch *vi* ysu, cosi ▶ *n* y crafu, ysfa
itchy *adj* coslyd
item *n* eitem
itinerary *n* taith, teithlyfr
its *adj* ei
itself *pron* ei hun, ei hunan
ivory *n* ifori
ivy *n* eiddew, iorwg

jab *n (inf)* jab, pigiad ▶ *vb* procio, gwanu
jack *n* jac
jacket *n* siaced
jagged *adj* danheddog, ysgithrog
jail *n* carchar
jam¹ *n* jam; tagfa
jam² *vt* jamio, tagu
Jamaica *n* Jamaica
janitor *n* porthor
January *n* Ionawr
Japan *n* Japan, Siapan
Japanese *adj* Japaneiadd, Siapaneaidd ▶ *n* Japanead, Siapanead; *(language)* Japaneg, Siapaneg
jar *n* jar
jargon *n* jargon
javelin *n* picell, gwaywffon
jaw *n* gên, cern; **jaws** safn
jazz *n* jas
jealous *adj* eiddigus, cenfigennus
jealousy *n* cenfigen, eiddigedd

jeans

jeans *n* jîns
jelly *n* jeli
jellyfish *n* slefren fôr
jerk *n* plwc, ysgytiad ▸ *vb* plycio, ysgytio
jersey *n* siersi
Jesus *n* Iesu
jet *n* ffrwd, jet; muchudd
jetlag *n* jetludded
jet-ski *n* jet-sgi ▸ *vi* jet-sgïo
jetty *n* jeti, glanfa
Jew *n* Iddew
jewel *n* gem, tlws
jeweller *n* gemydd
jeweller's shop *n* siop gemydd
jewellery *n* gemwaith, gemau
Jewish *adj* Iddewig
jib *n* hwyl flaen llong, jib
jig-saw *n* jig-so
job *n* gorchwyl, gwaith
Job Centre *n* Canolfan Gwaith
jobless *adj* diwaith
jockey *n* joci
jog *vb* loncian
jogging *n* loncian
join *vb* cydio, cysylltu, uno
joiner *n* asiedydd, saer coed
joint *n* cyswllt, cymal ▸ *adj* cyd; **joint of meat** darn o gig
joke *n* cellwair, maldod ▸ *vb* cellwair, ysmalio
jolly *adj* braf, difyr, llawen
jolt *n* ysgytiad ▸ *vb* ysgytio
Jordan *n* Iorddonen
jotter *n* nodlyfr
journal *n* newyddiadur
journalism *n* newyddiaduraeth
journalist *n* newyddiadurwr
journey *n* taith, siwrnai ▸ *vt* teithio

joy *n* llawenydd, gorfoledd
judge *n* barnwr, beirniad ▸ *vb* barnu, beirniadu
judo *n* jwdo
jug *n* jwg
juggle *vb* siwglo
juggler *n* siwglwr
juice *n* sudd
juicy *adj* llawn sudd
July *n* Gorffennaf
jumble *vb* cymysgu, cyboli ▸ *n* cymysgfa, cybolfa
jumble sale *n* ffair sborion
jump *vb* neidio, llamu ▸ *n* naid, llam
jumper *n* neidiwr; siwmper
junction *n* cydiad; uniad; cyffordd
June *n* Mehefin
jungle *n* jyngl, coedwig; drysi
junior *adj* iau, ieuengach; ieuaf
junior school *n* ysgol iau
junk *n* sothach
junk food *n* bwyd sothach
junk mail *n* post sothach
jurisdiction *n* awdurdod
juror *n* rheithiwr
jury *n* rheithgor
just *adj* cyfiawn, uniawn, teg ▸ *adv* yn union; prin, braidd; newydd; **just now** gynnau (fach)
justice *n* cyfiawnder; ynad, ustus
justice of the peace *n* ynad heddwch
justify *vt* cyfiawnhau
jut *vi* taflu allan, ymwthio
juvenile *adj* ieuanc

k

kangaroo *n* cangarŵ
karaoke *n* karaoke
karate *n* karate
kebab *n* cebab
keel *n* cêl, trumbren, cilbren
keen *adj* craff, llym, awchus
keep (*pt*, *pp* **kept**) *vb* cadw, cynnal
  ▶ *n* cadw; amddiffynfa; **keep
  on** *vi*: **to keep on doing sth** dal
  i wneud rhywbeth; **keep up** *vi*
  dal i fyny
keeper *n* ceidwad
keep-fit *n* cadw'n heini
kennel *n* cenel, cwb ci
Kenya *n* Cenia
kerb *n* cwrbyn
kettle *n* tegell
key *n* agoriad, allwedd; cywair
keyboard *n* allweddell
keyhole *n* twll clo
key ring *n* cylch allweddi
khaki *adj*, *n* caci
kick *vb* cicio, gwingo ▶ *n* cic

kick-off *n* cic gychwyn
kid *n* myn; (*inf*) plentyn
kidnap *vt* herwgipio
kidney *n* aren
kidney beans *npl* ffa dringo,
  cidnebêns
kill *vt* lladd
killer *n* lladdwr
killing *n* lladd
kiln *n* odyn
kilo *n* cilo
kilogram *n* cilogram
kilometre *n* cilomedr
kilowatt *n* cilowat
kilt *n* cilt
kin *n* perthynas, tras, carennydd
kind¹ *n* rhyw, rhywogaeth, math
kind² *adj* caredig
kindergarten *n* ysgol feithrin
kindle *vb* ennyn, cynnau
kindly *adj* caredig, hynaws
kindness *n* caredigrwydd
king *n* brenin
kingdom *n* teyrnas
kingfisher *n* glas y dorlan
kiosk *n* ciosg, bwth
kipper *n* ciper, ysgadenyn hallt
  (neu sych)
kiss *vt* cusanu ▶ *n* cusan
kit *n* cit, pac
kitchen *n* cegin
kite *n* barcut
kitten *n* cath fach ▶ *vb* bwrw
  cathod
knack *n* cnac, medr
knee *n* pen-lin, pen-glin
kneel (*pt*, *pp* **knelt**) *vi* penlinio;
  kneel down *vi* penlinio
knickers *npl* nicers
knife *n* cyllell

knight *n* marchog ▸ *vt* urddo yn
   farchog
knit *vb* gwau; clymu
knitting *n* gwaith gwau; **I like
   knitting** Dw i'n hoffi gwau
knitting needle *n* gwaell
knob *n* cnap, cnwc; dwrn
knock *vb* cnocio, taro, curo ▸ *n*
   cnoc, ergyd; **knock down** *vt* taro i
   lawr; **knock out** *vt* llorio
knot *n* cwlwm ▸ *vt* clymu
know (*pt* **knew**, *pp* **known**) *vb*
   gwybod, adnabod
knowing *adj* gwybodus
knowingly *adv* yn fwriadol
knowledge *n* gwybodaeth
knowledgeable *adj* gwybodus
knuckle *n* cymal, migwrn, cwgn
Koran *n* Coran
Korea *n* Corea
kosher *adj* kosher
Kosovo *n* Cosofo
Kuwait *n* Kuwait, Coweit

label *n* llabed, label ▸ *vt* llabedu,
   enwi
laboratory *n* labordy
labour *n* llafur; gwewyr esgor
   ▸ *vb* llafurio; **the Labour Party** y
   Blaid Lafur
labourer *n* gweithiwr, labrwr
lace *n* las, les; carrai ▸ *vb* cau
   (esgidiau)
lack *n* eisiau, diffyg ▸ *vb* bod
   mewn eisiau
lacquer *n* lacer ▸ *vb* lacro
lad *n* bachgen, hogyn, llanc
ladder *n* ysgol; rhwyg (mewn
   hosan)
ladies *npl* toiledau merched
ladle *n* lletwad, llwy
lady *n* arglwyddes; boneddiges,
   bonesig
ladybird *n* buwch goch gota
lag *vi* llusgo ar ôl, ymdroi, llercian
lagoon *n* morlyn, lagŵn
laid-back *adj* didaro

lake *n* llyn
lamb *n* oen ▸ *vb* bwrw ŵyn, wyna
lame *n* cloff ▸ *vt* cloffi
lament *vb* galaru, cwynfan
lamp *n* lamp, llusern
lamppost *n* polyn lamp
lampshade *n* lamplen
land *n* tir, gwlad ▸ *vb* tirio, glanio
landing *n* glaniad, glanio; glanfa; pen y grisiau
landlady *n* perchennog llety, gwraig llety
landlord *n* meistr tir; lletywr, tafarnwr
landscape *n* tirlun
lane *n* lôn
language *n* iaith
language laboratory *n* labordy iaith
lantern *n* llusern
lap¹ *n (knee)* arffed, glin
lap² *vb* llepian, lleibio
lapel *n* llabed
lapse *n* methiant, gwall ▸ *vi* llithro, methu
laptop, laptop computer *n* gliniadur
lard *n* bloneg ▸ *vt* blonegu
larder *n* bwtri, pantri
large *adj* mawr, helaeth, eang
largely *adv* gan mwyaf
lark¹ *n (bird)* ehedydd
lark² *n* sbort, miri ▸ *vi* cellwair, prancio
laryngitis *n* gwddf tost, laringitis
lasagne *n* lasagne
laser *n* laser
lash *n* llach, fflangell ▸ *vb* llachio, fflangellu; rhwymo
lass *n* llances

last¹ *adj* olaf, diwethaf ▸ *adv* yn olaf, yn ddiwethaf; **at last** o'r diwedd; **last night** neithiwr; **last week** yr wythnos ddiwethaf
last² *vi* parhau, para
lastly *adv* yn olaf
latch *n* clicied ▸ *vt* clicedu
late *adj* hwyr, diweddar; **late developers** plant hwyrgynnydd
lately *adv* yn ddiweddar
later *adv* wedyn, eto, yn ddiweddarach
latest *adj* diweddaraf
lather *n* trochion ▸ *vb* seboni, trochioni; golchi
Latin *adj, n* Lladin
Latin America *n* America Ladin
Latin American *adj* Lladin-Americanaidd
latitude *n* lledred; penrhyddid
latter *adj* diwethaf
laugh *vb* chwerthin ▸ *n* chwerthiniad; **laugh at** *vt (joke, situation)* chwerthin am; *(person)* chwerthin am ben
laughter *n* chwerthin
launch *vb* lansio
laundry *n* golchdy; dillad golch
lavatory *n* tŷ bach
lavender *n* lafant
lavish *adj* hael, afradlon, gwastraffus ▸ *vb* afradu, gwastraffu
law *n* cyfraith, deddf; **law and order** cyfraith a threfn; **law of the land** cyfraith gwlad
lawful *adj* cyfreithlon
lawless *adj* digyfraith
lawn *n* lawnt, llannerch
lawnmower *n* peiriant torri porfa

337

lawsuit n cyngaws, cyfraith
lawyer n cyfreithiwr, twrnai
lax adj llac, esgeulus
laxative n carthlyn
lay¹ (pt, pp **laid**) vt gosod, dodi;
dodwy
  ▸ **lay off** vt (dismiss) danfon adref
lay² adj lleyg
lay-by n gorffwysfan
layer n haen
layout n cynllun
lazy adj diog, dioglyd
lead¹ n plwm
lead² (pt, pp **led**) vb arwain, tywys
  ▸ n blaenoriaeth
leader n arweinydd; erthygl flaen
leadership n arweinyddiaeth
lead-free adj di-blwm
lead singer n prif ganwr
leaf n deilen, dalen
leaflet n taflen
league n cynghrair ▸ vi
cynghreirio
leak n agen, coll ▸ vi gollwng,
diferu, colli
lean¹ adj main, tenau, cul
lean² (pt, pp **leaned**, **leant**) vb
pwyso, gogwyddo
  ▸ **lean forward** vi pwyso ymlaen
  ▸ **lean on** vi pwyso ar
  ▸ **lean over** vi pwyso
leap (pt, pp **leaped**, **leapt**) vb
neidio, llamu ▸ n naid, llam
leap year n blwyddyn naid
learn (pt, pp **learned**, **learnt**) vb
dysgu
learner n dysgwr
learner driver n dysgwr gyrru
learning n dysg, dysgeidiaeth
lease n prydles ▸ vt prydlesu

leash n cynllyfan, tennyn ▸ vt
cynllyfanu
least adj lleiaf; **at least** o leiaf
leather n lledr
leave¹ n cennad, caniatâd
leave² (pt, pp **left**) vb gadael,
ymadael
  ▸ **leave out** vi gadael allan
Lebanon n Libanus
lecture n darlith ▸ vb darlithio
lecturer n darlithydd
lecture theatre n darlithfa
ledge n silff, ysgafell; crib
leek n cenhinen
left adj aswy, chwith
left-hand adj chwith
left-handed adj llawchwith
left luggage n lle cadw bagiau
left-luggage office n storfa baciau
leg n coes
legacy n etifeddiaeth, cymynrodd
legal adj cyfreithiol, cyfreithlon
legalize vb cyfreithloni
legend n chwedl
leggings n legins
legible adj darllenadwy, eglur
legislation n deddfwriaeth
legislative adj deddfwriaethol
legitimate adj cyfreithlon
leisure n hamdden
leisure centre n canolfan
hamdden
leisurely adj hamddenol
lemon n lemwn
lemonade n diod lemwn, lemonêd
lend (pt, pp **lent**) vt benthyca, rhoi
benthyg
length n hyd, meithder
lengthen vb estyn, hwyhau
lengthy adj hir, maith

lens *n* lens; **concave lens** lens ceugrwm; **convex lens** lens amgrwm

Lent *n* y Grawys

lentil *n* corbysen, lentil

Leo *n* y Llew

leopard *n* llewpart

leprosy *n* gwahanglwyf

lesbian *n* lesbiad ▸ *adj* lesbiaidd

less *adj, adv* llai

lessen *vb* lleihau

lesson *n* gwers; llith

let (*pt, pp* **let**) *vt* gadael, goddef; gollwng; gosod, rhentu; **let down** *vt* gollwng; siomi; **let in** *vt*: **to let sb in** gadael rhywun i mewn

lethal *adj* marwol, angheuol

letter *n* llythyren; llythyr

letterbox *n* bocs llythyrau

lettuce *n* letysen

level *n, adj* lefel, gwastad ▸ *vt* lefelu, gwastatáu; **spirit level** lefelydd

level crossing *n* croesfan

lever *n* trosol

levy *vt* codi, trethu ▸ *n* treth

liability *n* cyfrifoldeb, rhwymedigaeth

liable *adj* atebol

liar *n* gŵr celwyddog, celwyddgi

libel *n* athrod, enllib ▸ *vt* athrodi, enllibio

liberal *adj* hael, rhyddfrydig, rhyddfrydol ▸ *n* rhyddfrydwr

liberate *vt* rhyddhau

liberation *n* rhyddhad

liberty *n* rhyddid

Libra *n* y Fantol

librarian *n* llyfrgellydd

library *n* llyfrgell

Libya *n* Libya

licence *n* trwydded; penrhyddid; **driving licence** trwydded yrru

license *vt* trwyddedu

licensed *adj* trwyddedig

lick *vt* llyfu, llyo; (*inf*) curo

lid *n* caead, clawr

lie¹ (*pt, pp* **lied**) *vi* (*tell lies*) dweud celwydd ▸ *n* celwydd, anwiredd

lie² (*pt* **lay**, *pp* **lain**) *vi* gorwedd ▸ **lie down** *vi* gorwedd i lawr

lie-in *n*: **to have a lie-in** cysgu'n hwyr

lieutenant *n* is-gapten; rhaglaw

life *n* bywyd, einioes, oes

lifeboat *n* bad achub

lifeguard *n* achubwr

life insurance *n* yswiriant bywyd

life jacket *n* siaced achub

lifestyle *n* ffordd o fyw

lifetime *n* oes, einioes, hoedl

lift *vt* codi, dyrchafu ▸ *n* llifft

light¹ (*pt, pp* **lighted**, **lit**) *n* golau, goleuni ▸ *adj* golau ▸ *vb* goleuo, cynnau

light² *adj* ysgafn

light bulb *n* bwlb golau

lighter *n* goleuydd, taniwr

light-hearted *adj* ysgafnfryd

lighthouse *n* goleudy

lightning *n* mellt, lluched

like¹ *adj* tebyg, cyffelyb

like² *vb* caru, hoffi

likeable *adj* hoffus; dymunol

likelihood *n* tebygolrwydd

likely *adj, adv* tebygol, tebyg

likewise *adv* yn gyffelyb, yn yr un modd

lilac *n* lelog

lily *n* lili, alaw

limb *n* aelod, cainc
lime *n* calch
limelight *n* amlygrwydd
limestone *n* carreg galch
limit *n* terfyn, ffin ▸ *vt* cyfyngu
limited *adj* cyfyngedig
limousine *n* limwsîn
limp¹ *adj* llipa
limp² *vi* hercian, cloffi
line *n* llinell, lein, rhes; llinach ▸ *vt* llinellu, rhesu
linear *adj* llinellog, llinellaidd, llinol
linen *n* lliain
liner *n* leiner
linger *vb* ymdroi, aros
lingo *(inf)* *n* iaith ddieithr, cleber
linguist *n* ieithydd
lining *n* leinin
link *n* dolen, cyswllt ▸ *vb* cydio, cysylltu
lion *n* llew
lip *n* gwefus, min, gwefl
lip-read *vi* darllen gwefusau
lipstick *n* minlliw
liquid *n* hylif ▸ *adj* gwlyb, hylif
liquidizer *n* hylifydd
liquor *n* diod, gwirod
lisp *n* bloesgni ▸ *vb* siarad yn floesg
list¹ *n* rhestr ▸ *vt* rhestru
list² *n (incline)* gogwydd, goledd ▸ *vi* pwyso, gwyro, gogwyddo
listen *vi* gwrando
listener *n* gwrandawr
literacy *n* llythrennedd
literal *adj* llythrennol
literary *adj* llenyddol
literature *n* llenyddiaeth
lithe *adj* ystwyth, hyblyg
litre *n* litr

litter *n* elorwely; ysbwriel, gwasarn; torllwyth, tor
litter bin *n* bin sbwriel
little *adj* bach, bychan; mân, ychydig ▸ *n* ychydig, tipyn
live¹ *adj* byw, bywiol, bywiog
live² *vi* byw
  ▸ **live on** *vt* byw ar
  ▸ **live together** *vi* cyd-fyw
livelihood *n* bywoliaeth
lively *adj* bywiog, heini, sionc
liver *n* iau, afu
living *n* bywoliaeth
living room *n* ystafell fyw
lizard *n* madfall, modrchwilen
load *n* llwyth ▸ *vb* llwytho
loaf *n* torth
loan *n* benthyg, benthyciad
loathe *vt* ffieiddio, casáu
lobby *n* cyntedd, lobi
lobster *n* cimwch
local *adj* lleol
local government *n* llywodraeth leol
locate *vt* lleoli, sefydlu, gosod
location *n* lleoliad
loch *n* llyn
lock *n* clo; llifddor ▸ *vb* cloi, cau; **lock out** *vt*: **to lock sb out** cloi rhn allan
locker *n* cwpwrdd clo
locomotive *adj* ymsymudol ▸ *n* peiriant rheilffordd
lodge *n* lluest, llety; cyfrinfa ▸ *vb* lletya
lodger *n* lletywr
lodging *n*, **lodgings** *npl* llety
loft *n* taflod, llofft
log *n* cyff, boncyff, pren; **log in, log on** *vi (Comput)* mewngofnodi,

logio i mewn; **log off, log out** *vi*
(Comput) allgofnodi, logio allan
logic *n* rhesymeg
logical *adj* rhesymegol
lollipop *n* lolipop
London *n* Llundain
Londoner *n* Llundeiniwr
loneliness *n* unigrwydd
lonely *adj* unig
long¹ *adj, adv* hir, maith, llaes
long² *vi* hiraethu, dyheu
longing *n* hiraeth, dyhead
longitude *n* hydred
long jump *n* naid hir
long-term *adj* yn y tymor hir
loo *n* (inf) tŷ bach
look *vb* edrych, syllu ► *n*
edrychiad, golwg; **look after** *vt*
gwarchod, gofalu (am); **look at** *vt*
edrych ar; **look for** *vt* chwilio am;
look round *vi* (turn head) edrych
yn ôl; **look up** *vi* edrych i fyny ► *vt*
(in dictionary etc) edrych; **things
are looking up** mae pethau'n
gwella
lookout *n* gwyliwr
loom¹ *n* gwŷdd
loom² *vi* ymrithio, ymddangos
loop *n* dolen ► *vb* dolennu
loophole *n* dihangdwll
loose *adj* rhydd, llac ► *vt* gollwng
loosen *vb* rhyddhau, llacio
loot *n* anrhaith, ysbail ► *vb*
ysbeilio, anrheithio
lopsided *adj* unochrog,
anghymesur, anghyfartal
lord *n* arglwydd ► *vb*
arglwyddiaethu
lorry *n* lori
lorry driver *n* gyrrwr lori

lose (pt, pp **lost**) *vb* colli
loser *n*: **we are the losers** ni sy'n
colli
loss *n* colled
lost *adj* ar goll
lost-and-found *n* swyddfa eiddo
colledig
lot *n* coelbren; rhan, tynged; **a lot**
llawer
lotion *n* golchdrwyth, eli
lottery *n* hapchwarae, raffl
loud *adj* uchel, croch
loudly *adv* yn uchel
loud speaker *n* corn siarad
lounge *n* lolfa ► *vi* segura,
gorweddian
louse *n* lleuen
lousy *adj* (inf) lleuog, brwnt
love *n* cariad, serch ► *vt* caru
lovely *adj* hawddgar, teg, hyfryd
lover *n* cariad, carwr
loving *adj* cariadus, serchog
low¹ *adj* isel
low² *vi* brefu ► *n* bref (buwch)
lower *vb* gostwng, darostwng,
iselu
loyal *adj* teyrngar
loyalty *n* teyrngarwch,
ffyddlondeb
loyalty card *n* cerdyn teyrngarwch
luck *n* lwc
luckily *adv* yn ffodus
lucky *adj* ffodus, lwcus
ludicrous *adj* chwerthinllyd,
gwrthun
luggage *n* bagiau
luggage rack *n* silff eiddo
lukewarm *adj* claear, llugoer
lull *vt* suo, gostegu ► *n* gosteg
lullaby *n* hwiangerdd

lumber *vb* pentyrru; llusgo
luminous *adj* golau, disglair, llachar
lump *n* lwmp, clamp, clap, talp; **lump sum** cyfandaliad
lunatic *n (offensive)* lloerigyn, gwallgofddyn
lunch *n* byrbryd, cinio canol dydd ▸ *vi* ciniawa (ganol dydd)
lung *n* ysgyfaint
lure *n* hud ▸ *vt* hudo, denu
lurk *vi* llercian, llechu
lush *adj* toreithiog, ffrwythlon
lust *n* chwant, trachwant ▸ *vi* trachwantu
Luxembourg *n* Lwcsembwrg
luxurious *adj* moethus
luxury *n* moeth, moethusrwydd
lying *adj* celwyddog
lyrics *n* geiriau

macaroni *n* macaroni
machine *n* peiriant
machine gun *n* gwn peiriant
machinery *n* peiriannau
mackerel *n* macrell
mackintosh *n* cot law
mad *adj* cynddeiriog, gwallgof, ynfyd
madam *n* madam
made-to-measure *adj* wedi ei dorri gan deiliwr
madman *n* ynfytyn, gwallgofddyn
madness *n* ynfydrwydd, gwallgofrwydd
magazine *n* ystorfa, arfdy; cylchgrawn
maggot *n* cynrhonyn
magic *adj* cyfareddol ▸ *n* hud, swyngyfaredd
magician *n* swynwr, dewin
magistrate *n* ynad
magnet *n* magned
magnetic *n* magnetig

magnificent *adj* gwych, ysblennydd
magnify *vt* mawrhau, mwyhau, chwyddo
magnifying-glass *n* chwyddwydr
magpie *n* pioden
maid *n* merch, morwyn
maiden name *n* enw morwynol
mail *n* y post
mailbox *n* blwch postio
main¹ *n* prif bibell; prif gebl; cefnfor; **in the main** yn bennaf, gan mwyaf
main² *adj* pennaf, prif, mwyaf
main course *n* prif gwrs
mainland *n* y tir mawr
mainly *adv* yn bennaf
main road *n* priffordd, ffordd fawr
maintain *vt* dal, cynnal, maentumio
maintenance *n* cynhaliaeth, gofalaeth
maize *n* indrawn, india corn
majesty *n* mawrhydi, mawredd
major *adj* mwy, mwyaf, pennaf ▸ *n* uwchgapten
Majorca *n* Maiorca, Mallorca
majority *n* mwyafrif; oedran llawn
make *(pt, pp* **made)** *vt* gwneud, gwneuthur, peri ▸ *n* gwneuthuriad; **make out** *vt* *(understand, decipher)* deall; **make up** *vt* *(invent)* dyfeisio; *(constitute)* gwneud; **to be made up of** cynnwys
maker *n* gwneuthurwr, creawdwr
make-up *n* colur
making *n* gwneuthuriad, ffurfiad
Malaysia *n* Maleisia
male *n, adj* gwryw
malicious *adj* maleisus

malignant *adj* malaen; maleisus
mall *n* canolfan siopa
mallet *n* gordd
malnutrition *n* gwallfaethiad, camluniaeth
malt *n* brag ▸ *vb* bragu
Malta *n* Malta
mammal *n* mamal
mammoth *n* mamoth ▸ *adj* anferth
man *n* dyn, gŵr
manage *vb* rheoli; ymdopi, llwyddo
manageable *adj* hydrin
management *n* rheolaeth, goruchwyliaeth
manager *n* goruchwyliwr, rheolwr
manageress *n* rheolwraig
mandarin *n (fruit)* mandarin; *(language)* Mandarin
mandate *n* gorchymyn, arch
mane *n* mwng
mango *n* mango
manhood *n* dyndod
mania *n* gwallgofrwydd, gorawydd
maniac *n* gwallgofddyn
manifest *adj* amlwg ▸ *vt* amlygu, dangos
manifesto *n* datganiad, maniffesto
manipulate *vt* trin, trafod
mankind *n* dynolryw
manly *adj* dynol, gwrol
manner *n* modd; moes
mansion *n* plas
manslaughter *n* dynladdiad
mantelpiece *n* silff ben tân
manual *adj* perthynol i'r llaw ▸ *n* llawlyfr
manufacture *n* gwaith, nwydd ▸ *vt* gwneuthur, gwneud

343

manufacturer

manufacturer n cynhyrchwr
manure n tail, gwrtaith
manuscript n llawysgrif
many adj aml, sawl, llawer; **as
    many** cymaint, cynifer; **how
    many** sawl
map n map
maple n masarnen
mar vt difetha, andwyo, hagru
marathon n marathon
marble n marmor; marblen
March n (mis) Mawrth
march¹ vb ymdeithio ► n ymdaith
march² n mers, goror
mare n caseg
margarine n margarîn
margin n ymyl, cwr, goror
marigold n gold Mair
marijuana n mariwana
marine adj morol ► n môr-filwr;
    llynges
marital n priodasol
maritime adj morol, arforol
mark n nod, marc ► vt nodi,
    marcio, sylwi
market n marchnad ► vb
    marchnata
marketing n marchnata
marmalade n marmalêd
maroon vb rhoi a gadael ar ynys
    anial ► adj coch tywyll
marriage n priodas
married adj priod
marrow n mêr; (vegetable) pwmpen
marry vb priodi
Mars n Mawrth
marsh n morfa, cors, mignen
marshal n cadlywydd, marsialydd
    ► vt byddino, trefnu
martyr n merthyr ► vt merthyru

marvel n rhyfeddod ► vi rhyfeddu,
    synnu
marvellous adj rhyfeddol, gwych
Marxism n marcsiaeth
Marxist adj marcsaidd
mascara n masgara, colur llygaid
masculine adj gwryw, gwrywaidd
mash n cymysg, stwnsh ► vt
    stwnsio
mashed potatoes n tatws stwnsh
mask n mwgwd ► vt mygydu,
    cuddio
mason n saer maen
mass¹ n pentwr, talp, crynswth,
    màs; **the masses** y werin
mass² n offeren
massacre n cyflafan ► vt cyflafanu
massage n, vb tylino
massive adj anferth
mast n hwylbren
master n meistr, athro, capten
    (llong) ► vt meistroli
masterpiece n campwaith,
    gorchest
mat n mat ► vt matio, plethu
match¹ n (for fire) matsien
match² n cymar; priodas;
    ymrysonfa, gêm ► vb cystadlu;
    cyfateb
mate n cymar, cydymaith; (inf)
    mêt ► vt cymharu
material adj materol; perthnasol,
    o bwys ► n defnydd
maternal adj mamol; o du'r fam
maternity n mamolaeth
mathematics npl mathemateg
maths n mathemateg
matron n metron
matter n mater; crawn ► vi bod
    o bwys

memory card

mattress *n* matras
mature *adj* aeddfed; mewn oed ▸ *vb* aeddfedu
mature student *n* myfyriwr hŷn
maturity *n* aeddfedrwydd
maul *vt* baeddu, pwyo ▸ *n* sgarmes
mauve *n* lliw porffor, piws
maximum *n* uchafswm
May *n* Mai
may *n* blodau drain gwynion
maybe *adv* efallai, hwyrach, dichon
May Day *n* Calan Mai
mayonnaise *n* mayonnaise
mayor *n* maer
mayoress *n* maeres
me *pron* myfi, mi, fi, i; minnau
meadow *n* dôl, gwaun, gweirglodd
meagre *adj* prin, tlodaidd, llwm
meal¹ *n (flour)* blawd
meal² *n* pryd o fwyd
mean¹ *n* cyfrwng, modd; cymedr
mean² *(pt, pp* **meant)** *vt* meddwl, golygu, bwriadu
mean³ *adj* gwael, isel, crintach
meaning *n* ystyr, meddwl
meantime, meanwhile *adv* yn y cyfamser
measles *npl* y frech goch
measure *vt, n* mesur
meat *n* cig
Mecca *n* Mecca
mechanic *n* peiriannydd
mechanical *adj* mecanyddol
mechanism *n* peirianwaith
medal *n* bathodyn, medal
meddle *vi* ymyrryd, busnesa, ymhél
media *npl* cyfryngau
mediaeval *adj* canoloesol

mediate *vi* canoli, cyfryngu
medical *adj* meddygol
medication *n* meddyginiaeth
medicine *n* meddyginiaeth; ffisig, moddion
mediocre *adj* canolig, cyffredin
meditate *vb* myfyrio
meditation *n* myfyrdod
Mediterranean *n*: the Mediterranean Môr y Canoldir
medium *n* canol; cyfrwng ▸ *adj* canol, canolig
medium-sized *adj* o faint canolig
meek *adj* llariaidd, addfwyn
meet *(pt, pp* **met)** *vb* cyfarfod, cwrdd ▸ *adj* addas; **meet up** *vb* cwrdd
meeting *n* cyfarfod, cyfarfyddiad
mega *adv (inf)* mega rich cyfoethog dros ben
melancholy *adj* prudd, pruddglwyfus ▸ *n* pruddglwyf, y felan
melody *n* peroriaeth, melodi
melon *n* melon
melt *vb* toddi, ymdoddi
member *n* aelod
Member of Parliament *n* Aelod Seneddol
membership *n* aelodaeth
memento *n* cofarwydd
memorable *adj* cofiadwy, bythgofiadwy
memorandum *n* cofnod, cofnodiad
memorial *adj* coffadwriaethol ▸ *n* coffadwriaeth; cofeb
memory *n* cof; coffadwriaeth
memory card *n* cerdyn cof, cofgerdyn

m

memory stick n cof bach
menace n bygythiad ▸ vt bygwth
mend vb gwella, cyweirio, trwsio
meningitis n llid yr ymennydd
menstruation n y misglwyf
mental adj meddyliol
mental hospital n ysbyty'r meddwl
mention vt crybwyll, sôn ▸ n crybwylliad
menu n bwydlen, arlwy
mercenary adj ariangar, chwannog i elw ▸ n huriwr, milwr cyflog
merchandise n marsiandïaeth
merchant n masnachwr, marsiandwr
merciless adj didrugaredd
mercury n arian byw, mercwri
mercy n trugaredd
mere adj unig, pur, hollol
merge vb soddi, colli, ymgolli
merger n ymsoddiad, cyfuniad, ymdoddiad
merit n haeddiant, teilyngdod ▸ vt haeddu, teilyngu
mermaid n môr-forwyn
merry adj llawen, llon
merry-go-round n ceffylau bach
mesh n masgl, magl, rhwydwaith
mess n llanastr, annibendod ▸ vb ymhél; maeddu; **mess about** vb (inf) stwna; **mess up** vt (inf) gwneud cawl o
message n cenadwri, neges
messenger n cennad, negesydd
messy adj (dirty) brwnt; (untidy) anniben
metabolism n metaboleg, metabolaeth

metal n metel ▸ adj metelaidd
metaphor n trosiad
meteor n seren wib
meter n mesurydd; metr
method n trefn, method, dull
Methodist n Methodist ▸ adj Methodistaidd
meticulous adj gorfanwl
metre n mesur, mydr
metric adj metrig
Mexico n Mecsico
micro-chip n meicro-sglodyn
microphone n meicroffon, meic
microscope n chwyddwydr, meicrosgop
microwave n meicrodon; **microwave oven** ffwrn meicrodon, popty ping
mid adj canol
midday n canol dydd, hanner dydd
middle n, adj canol
middle-aged adj canol oed
middle-class adj dosbarth canol
Middle East n Dwyrain Canol
middle name n enw canol
middle school n ysgol ganolraddol
midge n gwybedyn
midget n (inf!) corrach
midnight n canol nos, hanner nos
midst n canol, plith
midsummer n canol haf
Midsummer Day n gŵyl Ifan
midwife n (pl **midwives**) n bydwraig
might n nerth, cadernid, gallu
mighty adj cadarn, galluog, nerthol
migraine n meigryn
migrant n mudwr, ymfudwr, crwydrwr ▸ adj mudol, crwydrol
migrate vi symud, mudo

migration n mudiad, ymfudiad
mike n meic
mild adj tyner, tirion, mwyn; gwan, ysgafn
mile n milltir
mileage n milltiredd
milestone n carreg filltir
military adj milwrol
milk n llaeth, llefrith ▸ vt godro
milk chocolate n siocled llaeth
milkman n dyn llaeth
mill n melin ▸ vt melino, malu
millennium n mil blynyddoedd
millimetre n milimedr
million n miliwn
millionaire n miliynydd
mime n meim
mimic vt dynwared, gwatwar
mince vt malu ▸ n briwgig, briwfwyd
mind n meddwl, bryd, cof ▸ vb gofalu, cofio
mine n mwynglawdd, pwll
miner n mwynwr, glöwr
mineral adj mwynol ▸ n mwyn
mineral water n dŵr pistyll
mingle vb cymysgu, britho
miniature n mân ddarlun ▸ adj bychan
minibus n bws mini, minibws
minimize vt lleihau, bychanu
minimum n lleiafswm, isafrif
mining n mwyngloddiaeth; **opencast mining** mwyngloddio brig
miniskirt n scyrt fini
minister n gweinidog ▸ vb gwasanaethu, gweinidogaethu
ministry n gweinidogaeth; gweinyddiaeth

minor adj llai, lleiaf; lleddf ▸ n un dan oed
minority n minoriaeth; lleiafrif
mint¹ n bathdy ▸ vt bathu
mint² n (plant) mintys
minus adj, pron llai, heb ▸ n minws
minute¹ adj bach, bychan, mân; manwl
minute² n munud; cofnod
miracle n gwyrth
miraculous adj gwyrthiol
mirage n rhithlun, lleurith
mirror n drych ▸ vt adlewyrchu
misbehave vi camymddwyn
miscarriage n erthyliad
miscarriage of justice n aflwyddo cyfiawnder
miscellaneous adj amrywiol
mischief n drwg, drygioni, direidi
mischievous adj drygionus, direidus
misconception n camsyniad, cam-dyb
misconduct n camymddygiad ▸ vb camymddwyn
miser n cybydd
miserable adj truenus, gresynus, anhapus
misery n trueni, gresyni, adfyd
misfortune n anffawd, aflwydd
mishap n anap, anffawd, aflwydd
misinterpret vb camddehongli
misjudge vb camfarnu, camddeall
mislead vb camarwain, twyllo
misprint n cambrint ▸ vb camargraffu
misrepresent vt camddarlunio, camliwio
miss vt methu, ffaelu, colli ▸ n meth

missile *n* saethyn, taflegryn
missing *adj* yn eisiau, yngholl, ar goll
mission *n* cenhadaeth
missionary *n* cenhadwr ▸ *adj* cenhadol
misspell *vb* camsillafu
mist *n* niwl, nudden, tarth, caddug
mistake *vt* camgymryd, methu ▸ *n* camgymeriad, gwall
mistletoe *n* uchelwydd
mistress *n* meistres; athrawes; Mrs
mistrust *vt* drwgdybio, amau
misty *adj* niwlog
misunderstand *vt* camddeall
misunderstanding *n* camddealltwriaeth
mix *vb* cymysgu; **mix up** *vt* cymysgu
mixed *adj* cymysg
mixer *n*: he's a good mixer mae e'n gymdeithaswr da
mixture *n* cymysgedd, cymysgfa
mix-up *n* dryswch
moan *n, vb* ochain, griddfan, udo
moat *n* ffos (castell)
mob *n* torf, tyrfa, haid ▸ *vt* ymosod ar
mobile *adj* symudol, symudadwy; mudol (cemeg)
mobile home *n* cartref symudol
mobile phone *n* ffôn symudol
mobilize *vt* dygyfor, byddino
mock *vb* gwatwar ▸ *adj* gau, ffug
mockery *n* gwatwar
mode *n* modd, dull
model *n* cynllun, patrwm ▸ *vt* llunio
modem *n* modem

moderate *adj* cymedrol ▸ *vt* cymedroli
moderation *n* cymedroldeb
modern *adj* modern, diweddar
modernize *vb* moderneiddio
modest *adj* gwylaidd, diymhongar
modesty *n* gwylder, gwyleidd-dra
modify *vt* newid, lleddfu
module *n* modiwl
moist *adj* llaith, gwlyb
moisture *n* lleithder, gwlybaniaeth
moisturizer *n* lleithydd
mole[1] *n* (birthmark) man geni
mole[2] *n* (mammal) gwadd, twrch daear
molecule *n* molecwl ▸ *adj* molecylig
molest *vt* molestu, aflonyddu
molten *adj* tawdd
moment *n* moment; pwys, pwysigrwydd
momentum *n* momentwm
monarch *n* brenin, brenhines, teyrn
monarchy *n* brenhiniaeth
monastery *n* mynachlog, mynachdy
Monday *n* dydd Llun
monetary *adj* ariannol
money *n* arian, pres
mongrel *adj* cymysgryw ▸ *n* mwngrel
monitor *n* monitor
monk *n* mynach
monkey *n* mwnci
monologue *n* ymson
monopoly *n* monopoli
monotonous *adj* undonog
monsoon *n* monsŵn

monster n anghenfil; clamp ▸ adj anferth
month n mis
monthly adj misol ▸ n misolyn
monument n cofadail, cofgolofn
mood n hwyl, tymer; modd
moody adj oriog, cyfnewidiol
moon n lleuad, lloer; **harvest moon** lleuad fedi
moonlight n golau leuad
moor[1] n morfa, rhos
moor[2] vt angori, bachu, sicrhau
mop n mop ▸ vt mopio, sychu
mope vi pendrymu, delwi
moped n moped
moral adj moesol ▸ n moeswers, addysg
morality n moesoldeb
morbid adj afiach

KEYWORD

more adj 1 (greater in number etc) mwy (na), rhagor (na); **more people/work (than)** mwy o bobl/ waith (na)
2 (additional) rhagor, ychwaneg (o); **do you want (some) more tea?** gymerwch chi ychwaneg o de?; **is there any more wine?** a oes rhagor o win?; **I have no** or **I don't have any more money** nid oes gennyf ragor o arian; **it'll take a few more weeks** bydd yn cymryd ychydig wythnosau'n rhagor
▸ pron rhagor, ychwaneg, mwy; **more than 10** mwy na 10; **it cost more than we expected** costiodd fwy na'r disgwyl; **I want more** mae arnaf eisiau ychwaneg; **is there any more?** a oes ychwaneg?;

there's no more nid oes ychwaneg; **a little more** ychydig yn rhagor; **many/much more** llawer mwy
▸ adv 1 for most adjectives of one or two syllables in Welsh the comparative degree is formed by the ending -ach; **more ready (than)** parotach (na)
2 (for most adjectives of more than two syllables the comparative is formed by using the word mwy): **more pleasant (than)** mwy dymunol (na); **more and more expensive** mwy a mwy drud; **more or less** mwy neu lai; **more than ever** mwy nag erioed; **once more** unwaith eto, unwaith yn rhagor

moreover adv heblaw hynny, hefyd
morning n bore ▸ adj bore, boreol
Morocco n Moroco
mortal adj marwol, angheuol ▸ n dyn marwol
mortar n morter
mortgage n morgais, arwystl ▸ vt morgeisio, arwystlo
mortuary n marwdy
mosaic adj brith, amryliw ▸ n brithwaith, mosaig
Moscow n Moscow
Moslem n, adj = Muslim
mosque n mosg
mosquito n mosgito
moss n mwswgl, mwsogl
most adj mwyaf, amlaf
mostly adv gan mwyaf, fynychaf
moth n gwyfyn
mother n mam

mother-in-law n mam yng nghyfraith, chwegr
Mother's Day n dydd Sul y Mamau
motion n symudiad; cynigiad
motivate vt ysgogi, cymell
motivated adj brwdfrydig
motivation n ysgogiad
motive adj symudol, ysgogol ▸ n cymhelliad, motif
motor n modur
motorbike n beic modur
motorboat n cwch modur
motor cycle n beic modur
motorcyclist n beicwr (modur)
motorist n modurwr
motor racing n rasio modur
motorway n trafordd
motto n arwyddair
mould¹ n mold; delw ▸ vt moldio, llunio, delweddu
mould² n (mildew) llwydni, llwydi
mouldy adj wedi llwydo
mound n twmpath, crug
mount¹ n mynydd, bryn
mount² vb esgyn, mynd ar gefn; gosod
mountain n mynydd
mountain bike n beic mynydd
mountaineer n mynyddwr
mountaineering n mynydda
mountainous adj mynyddig
mourn vb galaru
mourning n galar; galarwisg
mouse (pl **mice**) n llygoden ▸ vb llygota
mouse mat n mat llygoden
mousse n mousse
moustache n trawswch, mwstas
mouth n ceg ▸ vb cegu, safnu
mouthful n cegaid

move vb symud; cymell; cynnig; cyffroi; **move forward** vb symud ymlaen; **move in** vi symud i mewn; **move over** vb symud
movement n symudiad; mudiad
movie n ffilm
moving adj (in motion) yn symud
mow (pt **mowed**, pp **mowed**, **mown**) vt lladd (gwair) ▸ n mwdwl, medel
MP n abbr AS (aelod seneddol)
MP3 n MP3
MP3 player n peiriant MP3
mph abbr (= miles per hour) mya
Mr n Mr
Mrs n Mrs
MS n (= multiple sclerosis) sglerosis ymledol
Ms n Ms
much adj llawer ▸ adv yn fawr
muck n tail, tom, baw ▸ vt tomi, baeddu
mucus n llys, llysnafedd
mud n mwd, llaid
muddle vi drysu ▸ n dryswch; **muddle up** vt drysu
muddy adj mwdlyd
muesli n mwsli
mug n cwpan, godart ▸ vt mygio
mugging n ysbeiliad
mule n mul, bastard mul
multiple adj amryfal ▸ n cynhwysrif, lluosrif
multiple choice n amlddewis, dewis lluosog
multiplication n amlhad, lluosogiad
multiply vb amlhau, lluosogi, lluosi
multi-storey adj aml-lawr
mum n mam

mumble *vb* grymial, myngial
mummy *n* mwmi
mumps *n* clwy'r pennau, y dwymyn doben
munch *vt* cnoi
municipal *adj* dinesig, bwrdeisiol
mural *adj* murol ▸ *n* murlun
murder *vt* llofruddio ▸ *n* llofruddiaeth
murderer *n* llofrudd
murky *adj* tywyll, cymylog, dudew
murmur *vb, n* murmur, grwgnach
muscle *n* cyhyr, cyhyryn
muscular *adj* cyhyrog
muse *vi* myfyrio, synfyfyrio
museum *n* amgueddfa
mushroom *n* madarch
music *n* miwsig, cerdd, cerddoriaeth
musical *adj* cerddorol
musical instrument *n* offeryn cerdd
musician *n* cerddor
Muslim *adj* Moslemaidd, Mwslimaidd ▸ *n* Moslem, Mwslim
mussel *n* misglen; **mussels** *npl* cregyn gleision
must *vb def* rhaid
mustard *n* mwstart
mute *adj* mud
mutilate *vt* anafu, hagru, llurgunio
mutiny *n* terfysg, gwrthryfel
mutter *vb* mwmian
mutton *n* cig dafad, cig mollt
mutual *adj* cyd, o boptu, y naill a'r llall
muzzle *n* genau, ffroen ▸ *vt* cau safn, rhoi taw ar
my *pron* fy

myself *pron* myfi fy hun
mysterious *adj* dirgel, rhyfedd, dirgelaidd
mystery *n* dirgelwch
mystify *vt* synnu, syfrdanu
myth *n* chwedl, myth
mythology *n* chwedloniaeth

m

n

nag vb cadw sŵn ▸ n ceffyl

nail n hoel, hoelen; ewin ▸ vt hoelio

nailbrush n brws ewinedd

nail file n ffeil/rhathell ewinedd

nail scissors n siswrn ewinedd

nail varnish n farnis ewinedd

naïve adj diniwed

naked adj noeth

name n enw ▸ vt enwi, galw

namely adv sef, nid amgen

nanny n nani

nap vi cysgu, pendwmpian ▸ n cyntun

napkin n napcyn, cewyn

nappy n cewyn, clwt

narrative n naratif

narrow adj cul, cyfyng ▸ vb culhau, cyfyngu

nasal adj trwynol

nasty adj cas

nation n cenedl

national adj cenedlaethol

national anthem n anthem genedlaethol

nationalism n cenedlaetholdeb

nationalist n cenedlaetholwr

nationality n cenedl, cenedligrwydd

nationalize vb gwladoli, cenedlaetholi

National Lottery n Loteri Genedlaethol

national park n parc cenedlaethol

native n brodor ▸ adj brodorol; cynhenid

natural adj anianol, naturiol

naturally adv yn naturiol

nature n anian, natur

nature reserve n gwarchodfa natur

naughty adj drwg, drygionus

nausea n cyfog

naval adj llyngesol, morol

nave n corff eglwys

navel n bogail

navigate vt mordwyo, llywio

navy n llynges

navy blue n, adj nefi-blw

near adj, adv, prep agos, ger, gerllaw ▸ vb agosáu, nesu

nearby adv gerllaw, yn ymyl

nearly adv bron

neat adj destlus, twt; pur

neatly adv yn daclus

necessarily adv o angenrheidrwydd

necessary adj angenrheidiol

necessity n anghenraid

neck n gwddf

necklace n mwclis

need n, vb (bod mewn) angen, eisiau

needle n nodwydd; gwaell
needless adj afreidiol, dianghenraid
needlework n gwniadwaith
negative adj nacaol, negyddol
neglect vt esgeuluso ▶ n esgeulustra
neglected adj esgeulusedig
negotiate vb negodi
negotiation n trafodaeth, cyd-drafodaeth
neighbour n cymydog
neighbourhood n cymdogaeth
neither conj na, nac, ychwaith ▶ adj, pron na'r naill na'r llall, nid yr un o'r ddau
nephew n nai
nerve n nerf
nervous adj nerfus
nest n nyth ▶ vb nythu
Net n: the Net (Internet) y Rhyngrwyd
net¹ n rhwyd, rhwyden
net² adj union, net ▶ vt rhwydo
netball n pêl rwyd
Netherlands npl: the Netherlands yr Iseldiroedd
nettle n danadl
network n rhwydwaith
networking n rhwydweithio; **social networking** rhwydweithio cymdeithasol
neuter adj diryw
neutral adj amhleidiol ▶ n amhleidydd
never adv ni ... erioed, ni ... byth
nevertheless adv, conj eto, er hynny
new adj newydd
newcomer n newydd-ddyfodiad

news n newydd, newyddion
newsagent n gwerthwr papurau newyddion
newspaper n papur newydd, newyddiadur
newsreader n darllenydd newyddion
newt n madfall
New Year n Y Calan, Y Flwyddyn Newydd
New Year's Eve n Nos Galan
New York n Efrog Newydd
New Zealand n Seland Newydd
New Zealander n Selandwr Newydd
next adj nesaf ▶ adv yn nesaf
NHS n GIG
nibble vb deintio, cnoi
nice adj neis, hardd; cynnil
niche n cloer, cilfach
nickname n llysenw ▶ vt llysenwi
niece n nith
Nigeria n Nigeria
night n nos; noson, noswaith; **by night** liw nos
night club n clwb nos
nightdress n gŵn nos, coban
nightie n coban
nightmare n hunllef
nil n dim
nine adj, n naw
nineteen adj, n pedwar (pedair) ar bymtheg, un deg naw
nineteenth adj pedwerydd (pedwaredd) ar bymtheg
ninety adj, n deg a phedwar ugain, naw deg
ninth adj nawfed
nip vb brathu, cnoi; deifio
nipple n teth
nitrogen n nitrogen

353

no

KEYWORD

no adv (answer to unemphatic question: na/nac + verb) **are you coming? — no (I'm not)** a ydych yn dod? — nac ydw; **would you like some more? — no thank you** a hoffech gael rhagor? — na hoffwn; (question in past tense): **did you see the programme? — no (I did not)** a welsoch y rhaglen? — naddo; (emphatic question: na, nage): **are you the owner of this dog? — no** ai chi yw perchennog y ci hwn? — nage
▸ adj (not any) dim, yr un, unrhyw; **I have no money/books** nid oes gennyf unrhyw arian/nid oes gennyf yr un llyfr; **no student would have done it** ni fyddai'r un myfyriwr wedi gwneud y peth; **"no smoking"** "dim ysmygu"; **"no dogs"** "dim cŵn"
▸ n y na m

nobility n bonedd
noble adj pendefigaidd ▸ n pendefig
nobody n neb
nod vb amneidio; pendrymu ▸ n amnaid
noise n sŵn
noisy adj swnllyd
nominal adj enwol, mewn enw
nominate vt enwi, enwebu
nomination n enwebiad
none pron neb, dim, dim un
nonsense n lol
non-smoking adj dim ysmygu
non-stop adv yn ddi-baid ▸ adj di-baid

noodles n nwdls
noon n hanner dydd, canol dydd
no-one pron neb
nor conj na, nac
normal adj cyffredin, safonol
normally adv fel arfer
Normandy n Normandi
north n gogledd ▸ adj gogleddol
North America n Gogledd America
northeast n gogledd-ddwyrain ▸ adj gogledd-ddwyreiniol
northern adj gogleddol
Northern Ireland n Gogledd Iwerddon
North Pole n Pegwn y Gogledd
North Sea n Môr y Gogledd
northwest n gogledd-orllewin
Norway n Norwy
Norwegian n (person) Norwyad; (language) Norwyeg ▸ adj Norwyaidd
nose n trwyn ▸ vb trwyno
nosebleed n gwaedlif o'r trwyn
nostalgia n hiraeth
nostril n ffroen
nosy adj (inf) busneslyd
not adv na, nac, nad, ni, nid
notable adj nodedig, enwog
notch n rhic
note n nod, nodyn ▸ vt nodi, sylwi; **note down** vt nodi
notebook n llyfr nodiadau, nodlyfr
noted adj nodedig
note pad n pad ysgrifennu
notepaper n papur ysgrifennu
nothing n dim; **nothing at all** dim byd, dim byd o gwbl
notice n sylw, rhybudd ▸ vt sylwi

noticeboard n hysbysfwrdd
notify vt hysbysu, rhoi rhybudd
notion n amcan, syniad
notorious adj hynod, rhemp
notwithstanding conj er ▸ prep er, er gwaethaf
nought n dim; gwagnod (o)
noun n enw
nourish vt maethu, meithrin
nourishment n maeth
novel adj newydd ▸ n nofel
novelist n nofelydd
November n Tachwedd
novice n newyddian, nofis
now adv, conj, n yn awr, rŵan, bellach; **just now** gynnau; **now and then** yn awr ac yn y man
nowadays adv yn y dyddiau hyn
nowhere adv dim yn unlle
nozzle n ffroenell
nuclear adj niwclear
nucleus n cnewyllyn, bywyn
nude adj noeth, noethlymun
nudge vt pwnio, penelino
nuisance n pla, poendod
numb adj diffrwyth, cwsg ▸ vt fferru, merwino
number n nifer, rhif; rhifyn ▸ vt rhifo, cyfrif
number plate n plât rhif
numerical adj rhifiadol
numerous adj niferus
nun n lleian, mynaches
nurse n gweinyddes, nyrs ▸ vt magu, meithrin, nyrsio
nursery n magwrfa, meithrinfa
nursery school n ysgol feithrin
nurture n maeth, magwraeth ▸ vt maethu, meithrin

nut n cneuen
nutrition n maeth, maethiad
nutritious adj maethlon
nuts adj (inf, mad) gwirion
nylon n neilon

n

O

oak *n* derwen; derw
oar *n* rhwyf
oatcake *n* bara ceirch, teisen geirch
oath *n* llw
oatmeal *n* blawd ceirch
oats *npl* ceirchen, ceirch
obedience *n* ufudd-dod
obedient *adj* ufudd
obese *adj* tew, corffol
obesity *n* gor-dewdra
obey *vb* ufuddhau
obituary *n* marwgoffa
object *n* gwrthrych; amcan ► *vb* gwrthwynebu
objection *n* gwrthwynebiad
objective *adj* gwrthrychol ► *n* amcan, nod
obligation *n* dyled, rhwymau
oblige *vt* rhwymo; boddio; gorfodi
oblique *adj* lleddf, ar osgo
obliterate *vt* dileu
oblong *adj* hirgul ► *n* oblong

obnoxious *adj* atgas, ffiaidd
oboe *n* obo
obscene *adj* anllad, anniwair
obscure *adj* tywyll; anhysbys ► *vt* tywyllu
observation *n* sylw; sylwadaeth
observatory *n* arsyllfa
observe *vb* sylwi, arsyllu; cadw
observer *n* sylwedydd, arsyllwr
obsessed *adj* obsesedig
obsession *n* obsesiwn
obsolete *adj* anarferedig, ansathredig
obstacle *n* rhwystr, atalfa
obstinate *adj* cyndyn, ystyfnig
obstruct *vt* cau, tagu; rhwystro, lluddio
obtain *vt* cael, ennill
obvious *adj* eglur, amlwg
obviously *adv* yn amlwg; *(of course)* wrth gwrs; **he's obviously happy** mae'n amlwg ei fod yn hapus
occasion *n* achlysur ► *vt* achlysuro
occasional *adj* achlysurol, anaml
occasionally *adv* ambell waith
occult *adj* cudd, dirgel
occupation *n* galwedigaeth; meddiant
occupy *vt* meddu, meddiannu; llenwi; dal
occur *vi* digwydd; taro i'r meddwl
occurrence *n* digwyddiad
ocean *n* cefnfor, eigion
o'clock *adv* o'r gloch
October *n* Hydref
octopus *n* octopws
odd *adj* od, hynod; **odd number** odrif
odds *npl* ots, gwahaniaeth
odour *n* aroglau

of prep 1 (gen): **a friend of ours** ffrind
i ni; **a boy of 10** bachgen 10 oed;
that was kind of you buoch yn
garedig iawn
2 (expressing quantity, amount, dates
etc) o; **a kilo of flour** cilogram o
flawd; **how much of this do you
need?** faint ohono y mae arnoch ei
angen?; **there were three of them**
roedd 3 ohonynt; **three of us went**
aeth 3 ohonom; **the 5th of July** y
5ed o Orffennaf
3 (from, out of) o; **a statue of
marble** ceflun o farmor; **made of
wood** (wedi'i wneud) o goed

off adv ymaith, i ffwrdd ▸ prep
oddi, oddi wrth, oddi ar; **off and
on** yn awr ac yn y man
offence n tramgwydd, trosedd
offend vb tramgwyddo, troseddu;
digio
offender n troseddwr
offensive adj atgas, ffiaidd;
ymosodol
offer vb cynnig, cyflwyno; offrymu
▸ n cynnig
office n swydd; swyddfa
office block n bloc swyddfeydd
officer n swyddog, swyddwr
official adj swyddogol ▸ n
swyddog
off-licence n siop diodydd
offside n camochr, camsefyll ▸ vb
camochri, camsefyll
offspring n epil
often adv yn amlwg
oh excl O!
oil n olew, oel ▸ vt iro, oelio

oil rig n llwyfan olew
ointment n ennaint, eli
okay excl popeth yn iawn
old adj hen, oedrannus; **of old** gynt;
old age henaint, henoed; **old and
infirm** hen a methedig
old-fashioned adj henffasiwn, od
old people's home n cartref
henoed
old stager n hen law
olive n olewydden
olive oil n olew olewydd
Olympic adj Olympaidd; **the
Olympic Games, the Olympics** y
Chwaraeon Olympaidd
omelette n crempog wyau
omen n argoel, arwydd
ominous adj argoelus, bygythiol
omit vt gadael allan, esgeuluso

on prep 1 (indicating position) ar; **on
the table** ar y bwrdd; **on the wall**
ar y wal; **on the left** ar y chwith
2 (indicating means, method,
condition etc): **on foot** ar
ddeudroed; **on the train/plane**
(be) ar y trên/awyren; **on the
telephone/radio/television** ar y
ffôn/radio/teledu; **to be on drugs**
bod ar gyffuriau; **on holiday** ar
eich gwyliau
3 (referring to time): **on Friday**
ddydd Gwener; **on Fridays** ar
ddydd Gwener; **on June 20th** ar yr
20fed o Fehefin; **a week on Friday**
wythnos i ddydd Gwener; **on
arrival** ar ôl cyrraedd; **on seeing
this** o weld hyn
4 (about, concerning): **a book on**

Dylan Thomas/physics llyfr am Dylan Thomas/ffiseg
▸ *adv* **1** (*referring to dress*): **to have one's coat on** bod â'ch cot amdanoch; **to put one's coat on** gwisgo'ch cot; **what's she got on?** beth mae'n ei wisgo?
2 (*further*): (*continuously*): **to walk on** cerdded ymlaen; **from that day on** o'r diwrnod hwnnw ymlaen
▸ *adj* **1** (*in operation*): (*machine*) ymlaen; (*radio, TV, light*) ymlaen; (*tap*) yn agored; (*brakes*) wedi'u cau [yn dynn]; **is the meeting still on?** (*not cancelled*) a yw'r cyfarfod yn dal ymlaen?; **when is this film on?** pryd mae'r ffilm hon ymlaen?
2 (*inf*): **that's not on!** (*not acceptable*) wnaiff hyn mo'r tro! (*not possible*) amhosibl!

once *adv* unwaith; gynt
one *num* un; **one hundred and fifty** cant a hanner; **one by one** fesul un, o un i un, bob yn un; **one day** un diwrnod ▸ *adj* (*sole*) unig; **the one book which** yr unig lyfr a; **the one man who** yr unig ddyn a; (*same*) yr un; **they came in the one car** daethant yn yr un car ▸ *pron*: **this one** hwn (hon); **that one** hwnnw (honno); **I've already got one/a red one** mae un/un coch gennyf eisoes; **which one do you want?** pa un a hoffech ei gael?; **one another** y naill a'r llall; **to look at one another** edrych ar eich gilydd; (*impersonal*) rhywun, chi, dyn; **one never knows** wyddoch chi byth,

ŵyr neb byth, does wybod; **to cut one's finger** torri'ch bys; **one needs to eat** rhaid i ddyn fwyta
oneself *pron* ei hun
onion *n* wynwynyn, nionyn
online *adj adv* ar-lein
only *adj* unig ▸ *adv* yn unig; ond
onset *n* ymosodiad, cyrch; cychwyn
onward, onwards *adj, adv* ymlaen
onwards *adv* ymlaen
ooze *n* llaid, llysnafedd ▸ *vi* chwysu
opaque *adj* afloyw, tywyll
open *adj* agored ▸ *vb* agor, ymagor
open-air *n, adj* awyr agored
opening *n* agoriad, agorfa
opening hours *n* oriau agor
opera *n* opera
operate *vb* gweithredu, gweithio
operation *n* gweithrediad; gweithred, triniaeth lawfeddygol
operator *n* gweithredydd, trafodwr
opinion *n* barn, opiniwn
opinion poll *n* arolwg barn
opponent *n* gwrthwynebydd
opportunity *n* cyfle, egwyl
oppose *vt* gwrthwynebu, cyferbynnu
opposed *n*: **to be opposed to sth** gwrthwynebu rhywbeth; **as opposed to** yn hytrach na
opposite *adj, adv, prep* gwrthwyneb, cyferbyn
opposition *n* gwrthwynebiad, gwrthblaid
oppress *vt* gorthrymu, llethu
optician *n* optegydd

optimism n optimistiaeth
optimist n optimist
optimistic adj optimistaidd
option n dewisiad, dewis
optional adj dewisol
or conj neu, ai, ynteu, naill ai
oral adj geneuol; llafar
orange n oren, oraens ▸ adj melyngoch
orbit n rhod, tro, cylchdro
orchard n perllan
orchestra n cerddorfa
ordeal n prawf llym
order n trefn; gorchymyn, archeb; urdd ▸ vb trefnu, gorchymyn; archebu; urddo; **in order to** er mwyn
orderly adj trefnus ▸ n gwas milwr
ordinary adj cyffredin, arferol
ore n mwyn
organ n organ, offeryn
organic adj organaidd
organization n trefn, cyfundrefn, trefniadaeth; sefydliad
organize vb trefnu
organized adj trefnus
organizer n trefnydd
orgy n gloddest, cyfeddach
oriental adj dwyreiniol ▸ n dwyreiniwr
orientate vb cyfeirio
origin n dechreuad, tarddiad
original adj, n gwreiddiol
originally adv yn wreiddiol
originate vb dechrau, tarddu
ornament n addurn ▸ vt addurno
ornate adj addurnedig, mawrwych
orphan adj, n amddifad
orthodox adj uniongred

osteopath n osteopath
ostrich n estrys
other adj, pron arall, llall
otherwise adv amgen, fel arall
otter n dyfrgi, dwrgi
ought vb: **I ought to do it** dylwn i ei wneud; **she ought to win** dylai hi ennill
ounce n owns
our pron ein, ein … ni
ours pron un ni; **the garden is ours** ni sy biau'r ardd
ourselves pron ein hun
oust vt disodli
out adv allan, i maes; **out of date** (passport; ticket) â'r dyddiad wedi mynd heibio
outcast n alltud, gwrthodedig
outcome n canlyniad, ffrwyth
outcry n gwaedd; dadwrdd
outdoor adj yn yr awyr agored
outdoors adv yn yr awyr agored
outer adj allanol
outfit n dillad
outing n pleserdaith, gwibdaith
outlaw n herwr
outlay n traul, cost
outlet n allfa
outline n amlinelliad, amlinell ▸ vb amlinellu
outlook n rhagolwg, argoel; golygfa
outrageous adj gwarthus; beiddgar, cywilyddus
outset n dechrau, dechreuad
outside n tu allan, tu faes ▸ adj, adv allan(ol), oddi allan ▸ prep tu allan i, tu faes i
outskirts npl cyrrau, maestrefi

outstanding

outstanding *adj* amlwg; dyledus
outward *adj* allanol
outwards *adv* tuag allan
outweigh *vt* gorbwyso
oval *adj* hirgrwn
ovary *n* ofari
oven *n* ffwrn, popty
over *prep* uwch, tros ▸ *adv* gor,
rhy, tra
overall *adj* o ben i ben ▸ *n* troswisg
overcast *adj* cymylog
overcharge *vt* gorbrisio, codi
gormod
overcoat *n* cot fawr/uchaf
overcome *vt* gorchfygu, trechu
overdo *vb* gorwneud
overdose *n* gor-ddogn
overdraft *n* gorddrafft
overflow *n* gorlif(iad) ▸ *vb* gorlifo
overhead *adj, adv* uwchben
overheat *vi* gorboethi
overload *vb* gorlwytho
overlook *vb* edrych dros; esgeuluso
overnight *adv* dros nos
overpower *vb* trechu
overrun *vb* goresgyn
overseas *adv* tramor, dros y môr
overtake *vt* goddiweddyd
overthrow *n* dymchweliad ▸ *vt*
dymchwelyd
overtime *n* goramser, oriau
ychwanegol
overturn *vt* troi, dymchwelyd
overweight *adj* dros bwysau
overwhelm *vt* llethu, gorlethu
owe *vb* bod mewn dyled
owing to *prep* oherwydd
owl *n* tylluan, gwdihŵ

own *adj* eiddo dyn ei hun, priod
▸ *vt* meddu; arddel; **own up**
vi cyfaddef
owner *n* perchen, perchennog
ox *n* ych, eidion
oxygen *n* ocsigen
oyster *n* llymarch, wystrysen
ozone layer *n* haen osôn

p

pace *n* cam; cyflymdra ▸ *vb* camu, cerdded
pacemaker *n (device)* rheoliadur y galon, rheoliadur calon
Pacific *n*: the Pacific (Ocean) Môr Tawel
pack *n* pac, swp ▸ *vb* pacio
package *n* pecyn
packaging *n* deunydd lapio
packed *adj (crowded)* gorlawn
packed lunch *n* tocyn, pryd wedi ei bacio
packet *n* sypyn, paced
pact *n* cyfamod, cynghrair
pad *n* pad ▸ *vt* padio
paddle *n* padl ▸ *vb* padlo
paddling pool *n* pwll padlo
paddock *n* marchgae, cae bach
padlock *n* clo clap
paedophile *n* pedoffeil, pedoffilydd
page *n* tudalen
pain *n* poen, dolur ▸ *vt* poeni
painful *adj* poenus

painkiller *n* lladdwr poen
painstaking *adj* gofalus, trylwyr
paint *n* paent, lliw ▸ *vt* peintio, lliwio
paintbrush *n* brwsh paent
painter *n* peintiwr; arlunydd
painting *n* llun, darlun
pair *n* pâr, dau, cwpl ▸ *vb* paru
Pakistan *n* Pacistan
Pakistani *adj* Pacistanaidd ▸ *n* Pacistaniad
palace *n* palas
pale *adj* gwelw ▸ *vb* gwelwi
Palestine *n* Palestina
Palestinian *adj* Palestiniaid ▸ *n* Palestiniad
palm¹ *n (of hand)* palf, cledr llaw
palm² *n (tree)* palmwydden; **Palm Sunday** Sul y Blodau
pamper *vt* mwytho, maldodi
pamphlet *n* pamffled, llyfryn
pan *n* padell
pancake *n* crempog, cramwythen, ffroisen
pane *n* cwarel, paen
panel *n* panel
panic *n* dychryn, panig
pansy *n* trilliw, llysiau'r Drindod
pant *vi* dyheu
panther *n* panther
panties *npl* pantos
pantomime *n* pantomeim
pants *npl* pants
paper *n* papur ▸ *vb* papuro; **blotting paper** papur sugno; **brown paper** papur llwyd; **tissue paper** papur sidan
paperback *n* llyfr clawr meddal
paperclip *n* clip papur
paper round *n* rownd bapurau

par n cyfartaledd, llawn werth
parachute n parasiwt
parade n rhodfa; rhodres, rhwysg
paradise n paradwys, gwynfyd
paradox n gwrthddywediad, paradocs
paraffin n paraffîn
paragraph n paragraff
parallel adj cyfochrog, paralel
paralysed adj parlysedig
paralysis n parlys
paramedic n parafeddyg
parasite n un yn byw ar gefn un arall, cynffonnwr
parcel n parsel
pardon n maddeuant, pardwn ▸ vt maddau, pardynu
parent n rhiant; **parents** npl rhieni
Paris n Paris
parish n plwyf ▸ adj plwyf, plwyfol
park n parc ▸ vb parcio
parking n: **no parking** dim parcio
parking meter n amserydd parcio, rheolydd parcio
parking ticket n tocyn parcio
parliament n senedd
parliamentary adj seneddol
parole n gair, addewid, parôl
parrot n parot, perot
parsley n persli
parsnip n panasen
parson n person, offeiriad
part n rhan; parth ▸ vb rhannu, parthu; gwahanu; ymadael
partial adj rhannol; tueddol
participate vb cyfranogi
particle n mymryn, gronyn; geiryn
particular adj neilltuol, penodol ▸ n pwnc; **particulars** npl manylion

particularly adv yn arbennig
parting n ymadael
partition n gwahanfur, palis
partly adv mewn rhan, yn rhannol
partner n partner; cymar
partridge n petrisen
part-time adj rhan amser
party n plaid; parti, mintai
pass vb mynd heibio, llwyddo, pasio; treulio ▸ n bwlch; trwydded; pas; **pass away** vi marw; **pass out** vi llewygu
passable adj y gellir mynd heibio iddo; purion
passage n tramwyfa; mordaith; cyfran
passenger n teithiwr
passion n dioddefaint; gwŷn, nwyd
passionate adj angerddol, nwydwyllt
passive adj goddefol
passport n trwydded deithio, pasbort
password n cyfrinair
past adj, n gorffennol ▸ prep wedi ▸ adv heibio
pasta n pasta
paste n past ▸ vt pastio, gludio
pasteurized adj wedi ei basteureiddio
pastime n difyrrwch, adloniant
pastor n bugail (eglwys), gweinidog
pastry n crwst
pasture n porfa
pasty n pastai
pat vt patio
patch n clwt, darn ▸ vt clytio
patent adj agored, amlwg; breintiedig ▸ n breintlythyr

paternal adj tadol
path n llwybr
pathetic adj gresynus, pathetig
patience n amynedd
patient adj amyneddgar, dioddefus
  ▸ n dioddefydd, claf
patio n patio
patriotic adj gwladgarol
patrol n patrôl
patrol car n car patrôl
patron n noddwr
patronizing adj nawddogol
patter vb curo (fel glaw ar ffenestr)
pattern n patrwm, cynllun
pause n saib, seibiant ▸ vi aros
pave vt palmantu
pavement n palmant, pafin
pavilion n pabell, pafiliwn
paw n palf, pawen ▸ vb palfu, pawennu
pawn n gwystl; (chess) gwerinwr
  ▸ vt gwystlo
pay (pt, pp **paid**) vb talu ▸ n tâl, pae; **back pay** ôl-dâl
pay-as-you-go adj talu-wrth-ddefnyddio
payment n taliad, tâl
payphone n ffôn talu
PC n abbr (= personal computer) PC, cyfrifiadur personol; (= police constable) cwnstabl (heddlu)
  ▸ adj abbr (= politically correct) PC, gwleidyddol-gywir
PE n abbr (= physical education) AG, addysg gorfforol
pea n pysen
peace n heddwch, tangnefedd
  ▸ excl gosteg!, ust!
peaceful adj heddychol, tangnefeddus, llonydd

peach n eirinen wlanog
peacock n paun
peak n pig; copa; uchafbwynt
peanut n cneuen ddaear
peanut butter n menyn pysgnau
pear n gellygen
pearl n perl
peasant n gwladwr, gwerinwr
peat n mawn
pebble n carreg lefn, cerrigyn
peck vb pigo, cnocellu ▸ n cnoc, pigiad
peculiar adj priod, priodol; hynod
pedal n pedal ▸ vb pedalu
pedestal n troed, gwaelod
pedestrian adj ar draed, pedestrig
  ▸ n gŵr traed, cerddwr
pedestrian crossing n croesfan cerddwyr
pedigree n achau, bonedd
pee (inf) n pisiad ▸ vb pisio
peel n pil, croen, rhisgl ▸ vb pilio, plicio, crafu
peep vi cipedrych, sbïo ▸ n cipolwg, cip
peer[1] vi ciledrych, syllu
peer[2] n cydradd; pendefig
peg n hoel bren, peg ▸ vt pegio
pelt vt lluchio, taflu, peledu
pelvis n pelfis
pen[1] n pin, ysgrifbin
pen[2] n (enclosure) lloc, ffald ▸ vt ffaldio, llocio
penalty n cosb, cosbedigaeth
penalty (kick) n cic gosb
pence npl ceiniogau, pres
pencil n pensel, pensil
pencil case n cas pensiliau
pencil sharpener n naddwr pensiliau

p

363

pendant n tlws
pending prep hyd, nes, yn ystod
penetrate vb treiddio; dirnad
penfriend n cyfaill llythyru
penguin n pengwin
penicillin n penisilin
peninsula n gorynys
penis n cala, pidyn
penitentiary n carchar
penknife n cyllell boced
penniless adj heb geiniog
penny (pennies) n ceiniog
pension n blwydd-dal, pensiwn
pensioner n pensiynwr
people npl pobl, gwerin
pepper n pupur
peppermill n melin bupur
peppermint n mintys poethion
per prep trwy, wrth, yn ôl
perceive vt canfod, dirnad, deall
per cent adv y cant
percentage n canran
perception n canfyddiad, canfod
perch n perc; clwyd ▶ vb clwydo
percussion n trawiad,
gwrthdrawiad; **percussion band**
seindorf daro
perennial adj bythol, lluosflwydd
perfect adj perffaith ▶ vt
perffeithio
perfection n perffeithrwydd
perfectly adv yn berffaith
perform vb cyflawni; perfformio
performance n perfformiad
performer n perfformiwr
perfume n perarogl, persawr ▶ vt
perarogli
perhaps adv efallai, hwyrach
perimeter n amfesur, perimedr

period n cyfnod; cyfadran
(miwsig); diweddnod; misglwyf
periodical n cyfnodolyn
perish vi trengi, marw, darfod;
llygru
perjury n anudon, anudoniaeth
perk (inf) n mantais; **perk up** vb
bywhau, adfywio
permanent adj parhaol
permission n caniatâd, cennad
permit vb caniatáu ▶ n trwydded
perplex vt drysu
persecute vt erlid
persevere vi dyfalbarhau
persist vi dal ati; mynnu, taeru
persistent adj dyfal, taer, cyndyn,
parhaus
person n person
personal adj personol
personal assistant n
cynorthwyydd personol
personality n personoliaeth
personally adv yn bersonol
perspective n persbectif, safbwynt
perspiration n chwys
persuade vt darbwyllo, perswadio
perverse adj gwrthnysig
pervert vt gwyrdoi, llygru ▶ n
cyfeiliornwr
pessimism n pesimistiaeth
pessimist n pesimist
pessimistic adj pesimistaidd
pest n pla, poendod
pester vt blino, aflonyddu, poeni
pet n anwylyn, ffafryn ▶ adj
llywaeth, swci ▶ vt anwesu,
canmol
petal n petal
petite adj bychan
petition n deisyfiad; deiseb

petrified adj stond
petrol n petrol
petroleum n petroliwm
petrol pump n pwmp petrol
petrol station n gorsaf betrol
petticoat n pais
petty adj bach, bychan, mân
pew n eisteddle, côr, sedd
pewter n piwter
phantom n rhith, drychiolaeth
pharmacy n fferylliaeth; fferyllfa
phase n gwedd; tro
pheasant n ffesant
phenomenon n ffenomen
Philippines n Pilipinas
philosopher n athronydd
philosophical adj athronyddol
philosophy n athroniaeth
phlegm n llysnafedd, fflem
phobia n ffobia
phone n ffôn, teleffon ▸ vb ffonio
phone bill n bil ffôn
phone book n cyfeiriadur ffôn
phone box n caban ffôn
phone call n galwad ffôn
phone number n rhif ffôn
phonetics n seineg
phoney adj ffug
photo n ffoto
photocopier n llungopïydd
photocopy n llungopi ▸ vb
  llungopio
photograph n llun, ffotograff
photographer n ffotograffydd
photography n ffotograffiaeth
phrase n ymadrodd; cymal ▸ vt
  geirio
phrase book n llyfr ymadroddion
physical adj corfforol; ffisegol

physical education n addysg
  gorfforol
physician n meddyg, ffisigwr
physicist n ffisegydd
physics n ffiseg
physiotherapist n ffisiotherapydd
physiotherapy n ffisiotherapi
physique n corffolaeth,
  cyfansoddiad
pianist n pianydd
piano n piano
pick¹ n (tool) caib
pick² vb dewis, dethol ▸ n dewis
  ▸ **pick on** vt pigo ar
  ▸ **pick out** vt (choose) dewis
  ▸ **pick up** vt (person, object) codi;
  (information, language) dysgu
pickle n picl, heli ▸ vt piclo, halltu
pickpocket n pigwr poced,
  codleidr
picnic n picnic
picture n llun, darlun; **picture book**
  llyfr lluniau
picture messaging n negeseuon
  llun
picturesque adj darluniaidd,
  gwych
pie n pastai
piece n darn, dryll
pie chart n siart olwyn
pier n pier
pierce vb brathu, gwanu
pig n mochyn
pigeon n colomen
piggy bank n cadw-mi-gei, blwch
  cynilo
pigsty n twlc mochyn
pigtail n pleth
pike n gwaywffon; penhwyad

P

365

pile¹ n (heap) crug, pentwr ▸ vt
pentyrru

pile² n (of carpet) blew, ceden

piles npl clwyf y marchogion

pilgrim n pererin

pilgrimage n pererindod

pill n pelen, pilsen

pillar n colofn, piler

pillar box n bocs postio

pillow n gobennydd, clustog

pillow case n cas gobennydd

pilot n cyfarwyddwr llongau, peilot

pimple n ploryn, tosyn

PIN n abbr (= personal identification
number) PIN, Rhif Adnabod
Personol

pin n pin ▸ vt pinio, hoelio

pinafore n brat, piner

pinch vb pinsio, gwasgu ▸ n pins,
pinsiad; cyfyngder

pine¹ n pinwydden

pine² vi dihoeni, nychu

pineapple n afal pîn

pink adj, n pinc

pinpoint vb pinbwyntio

pint n peint

pioneer n arloeswr, arloesydd

pious adj duwiol, duwiolfrydig

pip n hedyn afal etc

pipe n pib, pibell ▸ vb canu pibell

pirate n môr-leidr

Pisces n y Pysgod

piss vi (pej) pisio

pissed adj (pej) meddw

pistol n llawddryll, pistol

pit n pwll, pydew ▸ vt pyllu; **coal
pit** pwll glo

pitch¹ n (tar) pyg ▸ vt pygu

pitch² vb bwrw; gosod; taro (tôn)
▸ n gradd, mesur, traw

pitfall n magl, perygl

pith n bywyn; mwydion; mêr; grym

pitiful adj truenus, tosturiol

pity n tosturi, trueni, gresyn ▸ vt
tosturio, pitio

pizza n pitsa

placard n murlen, hysbyslen

place n lle, man ▸ vt gosod; **to
take place** digwydd; **in the first
place** yn y lle cyntaf

placement n (during studies)
lleoliad

placid adj tawel, llonydd

plague n pla, haint ▸ vt poeni,
blino

plaice n lleden

plain adj plaen, eglur ▸ n
gwastadedd

plain chocolate n siocled tywyll

plaintiff n achwynwr, hawlydd

plait n pleth ▸ vt plethu

plan n cynllun, plan ▸ vt cynllunio,
planio

plane¹ adj, n (even) gwastad, lefel

plane² n plaen; awyren ▸ vt
plaenio

planet n planed

plank n astell, planc

planning n cynllunio; **planning
permission** caniatâd cynllunio

plant n planhigyn; offer; ffatri ▸ vt
plannu

plaster n plaster ▸ vt plastro

plastic n, adj plastig; **plastic bag**
cwdyn plastig

plate n plât; llestri aur etc ▸ vt
platio

plateau n gwastatir uchel

platform n llwyfan, esgynlawr

platoon n platŵn

platter n plât

plausible adj teg neu resymol yr olwg, ffals

play vb chwarae; canu (offeryn) ▸ n chwarae; **play down** vt bychanu

player n chwaraewr

playful adj chwareus

playground n chwaraele

playgroup n grŵp chwarae

playing card n cerdyn chwarae

playing field n maes chwarae

playtime n amser chwarae

playwright n dramodydd

plea n ple; esgus

plead vb pledio, ymbil

pleasant adj hyfryd, pleserus

please vb boddhau, boddio; **if you please** os gwelwch yn dda

pleased adj boddhaus, bodlon; **pleased to meet you** mae'n dda gen i gwrdd â chi

pleasure n pleser, hyfrydwch

pleat n plet, pleten ▸ vt pletio

pledge n gwystl, ernes ▸ vt gwystlo

plenty n digon, helaethrwydd

pliers npl gefel fechan

plight n cyflwr

plod vb troedio, ymlafnio

plot n darn o dir; cynllwyn; cynllun, plot ▸ vb cynllwynio; cynllunio

plough n aradr, gwŷdd ▸ vb aredig, troi

ploy n cynllun, strategaeth

pluck vt tynnu; pluo ▸ n glewder

plug n topyn, plwg ▸ vt topio, plygio; **plug in** vt plygio i mewn

plum n eirinen

plumber n plymwr

plumbing n gwaith plymwr

plump adj tew ▸ vb pleidleisio i un (yn unig)

plunge n plymiad ▸ vb plymio, trochi

pluperfect adj gorberffaith

plural adj lluosog

plus n plws, ychwaneg ▸ prep, adj ychwanegol

ply vb arfer, defnyddio

plywood n pren haenog (tair-haen, pum-haen)

p.m. abbr (= post meridiem) y.h.

pneumonia n llid yr ysgyfaint, niwmonia

poach¹ vb herwhela, potsio

poach² vt (egg) berwi (wy) heb ei blisg

poached adj: **poached egg** wŷ wedi ei botsio

pocket n poced, llogell ▸ vt pocedu; **pocket knife** cyllell boced; **pocket money** arian poced

pod n coden, cibyn

podcast n podlediad

poem n cerdd, cân

poet n bardd, prydydd

poetry n barddoniaeth, prydyddiaeth

poignant adj ingol, aethus

point n pwynt; man; blaen ▸ vb pwyntio; dangos; **to be on the point of doing sth** bod ar fin gwneud rhywbeth; **to get the point** deall; **there's no point (in doing)** does dim diben (gwneud); **point out** vt nodi

pointer n cyfeirydd; mynegfys

367

pointless

pointless *adj* dibwynt, diystyr
point of view *n* safbwynt
poison *n* gwenwyn ▸ *vt* gwenwyno
poisonous *adj* gwenwynig
poke *vb* pwnio, procio
poker *n* pocer
Poland *n* Gwlad Pwyl
polar *adj* pegynol
polar bear *n* arth wen
pole *n* pawl, polyn; pegwn
police *n* heddlu
police car *n* car heddlu
policeman *n* heddwas, plismon
police officer *n* swyddog heddlu
police station *n* gorsaf heddlu
policewoman *n* heddferch, plismones
policy *n* polisi
Polish *adj* Pwylaidd; *(in language)* Pwyleg ▸ *n (language)* Pwyleg
polish *vb* cwyro, caboli, gloywi, llathru ▸ *n* cwyr
polite *adj* moesgar, boneddigaidd
politely *adv* yn gwrtais
political *adj* gwleidyddol
politician *n* gwleidydd, gwleidyddwr
politics *n* gwleidyddiaeth
poll *n* pen, copa; pôl ▸ *vb* cneifio; pleidleisio, polio
pollen *n* paill
polling station *n* gorsaf bleidleisio
pollute *vt* difwyno, llygru
polluted *adj* llygredig
pollution *n* llygredd
polo neck *n* jersi polo
polythene bag *n* bag polythen
pomegranate *n* pomgranad
pompous *adj* rhwysgfawr, balch

pond *n* llyn, pwll
ponder *vb* ystyried, myfyrio
pony *n* merlyn, poni, merlen; **pony trekking** merlota
ponytail *n* cynffon merlen
poodle *n* pwdl
pool[1] *n* pwll, llyn
pool[2] *n (fund)* cronfa; pwll ▸ *vt* cydgyfrannu
poor *adj* tlawd, truan, gwael, sâl
poorly *adj* sâl, gwael
pop *vb* ffrwydro; picio; **pop in** *vi* picio i mewn; **pop out** *vi* picio allan; **pop round** *vi* picio heibio
popcorn *n* popgorn
pope *n* pab
poplar *n* poplysen
poppy *n* pabi (coch), llygad y bwgan
popular *adj* poblogaidd
population *n* poblogaeth
porcelain *n* porslen
porch *n* porth, cyntedd
pore[1] *n* mandwll
pore[2] *vi* myfyrio
pork *n* cig moch, porc
pornography *n* pornograffi
porridge *n* uwd
port[1] *n* porth, porthladd
port[2] *n (on ship)* ochr chwith llong
port[3] *n (drink)* port
portable *adj* cludadwy
porter *n* porthor
portfolio *n* cas papurau, portffolio
portion *n* rhan, cyfran
portrait *n* llun, darlun
portray *vt* portreadu, darlunio
Portugal *n* Portiwgal**

Portuguese adj Portiwgalaidd; (in language) Portiwgaleg ▸ n (language) Portiwgaleg
pose vb sefyll, cymryd ar ▸ n ystum, rhodres
posh adj (inf) hardd, coeth
position n safle, sefyllfa; swydd
positive adj cadarnhaol, pendant
possess vt meddu, meddiannu
possession n meddiant
possibility n posibilrwydd
possible adj posibl, dichonadwy
possibly adv dichon, efallai
post¹ n (stake) post, cledr ▸ vt gosod, cyhoeddi
post² n post, llythyrfa; safle, swydd ▸ vb postio
postage n cludiad (llythyr, etc.)
postal adj post
postal order n archeb bost
postbox n bocs postio
postcard n cerdyn post
postcode n cod post
poster n hysbyslen, poster
postgraduate adj graddedig
postman n postmon
postmark n postfarc
post office n llythyrdy, swyddfa'r post
postpone vt gohirio, oedi
posture n ystum, osgo
postwoman n merch post
pot n pot, potyn; crochan ▸ vb potio
potato n taten, pytaten
potent adj grymus, nerthol
potential adj dichonadwy, dichonol ▸ n potensial
pothole n ceubwll
potter vb diogi, swmera

pottery n llestri pridd; crochendy
potty n pot
pouch n cod
poultry n dofednod, ffowls
pounce vb disgyn ar, dod ar warthaf
pound¹ n pwys; punt
pound² vb pwnio
pour vb tywallt, arllwys
pout vi pwdu, sorri
poverty n tlodi
powder n powdr ▸ vt powdro
powdered milk n llaeth powdr
power n grym; pŵer
power cut n toriad yn y cyflenwad
power failure n pall ar y cyflenwad
powerful adj nerthol, grymus
powerless adj dirym
power station n pwerdy
PR n abbr (= public relations) PR, cysylltiadau cyhoeddus
practical adj ymarferol
practically adv (almost) bron; **practically certain** bron yn sicr
practice n arfer, arferiad
practise vb arfer, ymarfer
practising adj ymarferol; yn dilyn ei swydd
practitioner n meddyg; cyfreithiwr
prairie n paith
praise vt canmol, moli ▸ n canmoliaeth, mawl
pram n coets, pram
prank n cast, pranc
prawn n corgimwch
pray vb gweddïo
prayer n gweddi
preach vb pregethu
preacher n pregethwr
precarious adj ansicr, peryglus

precaution n rhagofal, gofal
precede vb blaenori, rhagflaenu
precedent n cynsail
precinct n cyffin, rhodfa
precious adj gwerthfawr
precise adj penodol, manwl
precisely adv yn union
predecessor n rhagflaenydd
predicament n helynt
predict vt rhagfynegi
preface n rhagymadrodd, rhaglith
prefect n rhaglaw; swyddog
prefer vt dewis yn hytrach, bod yn well gan
preferable adj gwell
preference n dewis, hoffter
prefix n rhagddodiad
pregnancy n beichiogrwydd
pregnant adj beichiog, llawn
prehistoric adj cynhanesiol
prejudice n rhagfarn; niwed ▸ vt rhagfarnu, niweidio
prejudiced adj rhagfarnllyd
preliminary adj arweiniol, rhagarweiniol
prelude n rhagarweiniad; preliwd
premature adj anaeddfed, cynamserol
premier adj blaenaf, pennaf, prif ▸ n prif weinidog
premises npl (building) adeilad; (site) safle
premium n premiwm
preoccupied adj wedi ymgolli
prep n gwaith paratoi
prepaid adj wedi ei dalu ymlaen llaw, rhagdalwyd
preparation n paratoad, darpariaeth
prepare vb paratoi

prepared adj parod; effro
preposition n arddodiad
prep school n ysgol baratoi
prerequisite n rhaganghenraid
prescribe vb gorchymyn, cyfarwyddo
prescription n presgripsiwn
presence n gŵydd, presenoldeb
present¹ adj, n presennol
present² n (gift) anrheg ▸ vt anrhegu; cyflwyno; dangos
presentation n cyflwyniad
presenter n cyflwynydd
presently adv yn fuan
preserve vt cadw, diogelu ▸ n jam
preside vi llywyddu
president n llywydd, arlywydd
press vb gwasgu ▸ n gwasg; cwpwrdd
pressing adj taer, dwys
press-up n ymwythiad
pressure n pwysau; gwasgedd, pwysedd
prestige n bri, braint
presumably adv yn ôl pob tebyg, gellid tybio
presume vb tybio; beiddio, rhyfygu
pretence n rhith, esgus
pretend vb ffugio, cymryd ar, cogio; honni hawl
pretext n esgus, cochl
pretty adj pert ▸ adv cryn, go
prevail vi tycio, ffynnu; gorfod, trechu
prevalent adj cyffredin; nerthol
prevent vt atal, rhwystro
preview n rhagolwg
previous adj blaenorol, cynt
previously adv gynt

prey *n* ysglyfaeth, aberth ► *vi* ysglyfaethu
price *n* pris ► *vt* prisio
price list *n* rhestr prisiau
prick *n* pigyn, swmbwl ► *vb* pigo; picio, codi
pride *n* balchder ► *vt* balchïo, ymfalchïo
priest *n* offeiriad
primarily *adv* yn bennaf
primary *adj* prif, cyntaf, cysefin; cynradd
primary school *n* ysgol gynradd
prime¹ *adj* prif, cyntaf; gorau ► *n* anterth
prime² *vt* llwytho, llenwi
prime minister *n* prif weinidog
primitive *adj* cyntefig; garw, amrwd
primrose *n* briallen
prince *n* tywysog
princess *n* tywysoges; Princess Charlotte y Dywysoges Charlotte
principal *adj* prif ► *n* pen; prifathro; corff
principle *n* egwyddor, elfen
print *n* argraff, print, ôl ► *vb* argraffu, printio
printer *n* argraffydd
printout *n* allbrint
prior *adj* cynt, blaenorol ► *n* prior, priol
priority *n* blaenoriaeth
prison *n* carchar, carchardy
prisoner *n* carcharor
pristine *adj* cyntefig, cysefin
private *adj* preifat
private enterprise *n* menter breifat
privilege *n* braint, rhagorfraint

prize *n* (*reward*) gwobr ► *vt* prisio, gwerthfawrogi
prize-giving *n* cyfarfod gwobrwyo
prizewinner *n* enillydd gwobr
probability *n* tebygolrwydd
probable *adj* tebygol, tebyg
probably *adv* mae'n debyg, yn ôl pob tebyg; **it will probably be all right** bydd hi'n iawn, mae'n debyg *or* yn ôl pob tebyg
probation *n* prawf
probe *n* profiedydd ► *vt* profi, chwilio
problem *n* problem
procedure *n* trefn, gweithdrefn
proceed *vi* myned, deillio; erlyn
proceeds *npl* enillion, elw
process *n* proses
procession *n* gorymdaith
proclaim *vt* cyhoeddi, datgan
prod *vt* procio
produce *vt* cynhyrchu, epilio; dwyn ► *n* cynnyrch, ffrwyth
producer *n* cynhyrchydd
product *n* cynnyrch, ffrwyth
production *n* cynhyrchiad
profession *n* proffes, galwedigaeth
professional *adj* proffesiynol
professor *n* proffeswr; athro
profile *n* ystlyslun, cernlun
profit *n* elw, proffid ► *vb* llesáu, proffidio
profitable *adj* (*financially*) proffidiol, yn dwyn elw; (*advantageous*) proffidiol, manteisiol
profound *adj* dwfn, dwys
program *n* rhaglen ► *vb* rhaglennu
programme *n* rhaglen
programmer *n* rhaglennydd

progress n cynnydd; taith ► vi cynyddu
progressive adj cynyddgar, blaengar
prohibit vt gwahardd
project[1] n project
project[2] vb bwrw; bwriadu; ymestyn; taflunio
projector n taflunydd
prolific adj ffrwythlon, toreithiog
prolong vt hwyhau, estyn
promenade n rhodfa ► vb rhodianna
prominent adj yn sefyll allan, amlwg
promise n addewid ► vb addo, argoeli
promote vt hyrwyddo, dyrchafu
promotion n (at work) dyrchafiad; (of event) hyrwyddiad
prompt adj parod, buan ► vt cofweini; cymell
prone adj â'i wyneb i waered; tueddol
prong n fforch, pig fforch
pronoun n rhagenw
pronounce vb cynanu, yngan; cyhoeddi, datgan
pronunciation n cynaniad
proof n prawf; proflen
prop n ateg, prop ► vt ategu
propaganda n propaganda
proper adj priod, priodol
properly adv yn iawn
property n priodoledd; eiddo; priodwedd (cemeg)
prophecy n proffwydoliaeth
prophet n proffwyd
proportion n cyfartaledd, cyfrannedd

proportional adj cyfrannol
proportionate adj cymesur
proposal n cynnig
propose vb cynnig, bwriadu
proposition n cynigiad; gosodiad
proprietor n perchen, perchennog
prose n rhyddiaith
prosecute vt erlyn
prosecutor n erlynydd
prospect n rhagolwg
prospectus n prosbectws
prosper vb llwyddo, ffynnu
prosperity n llwyddiant, ffyniant
prostitute n putain
protect vt amddiffyn, noddi
protection n amddiffyn, diogelwch
protective adj amddiffynnol
protein n protein
protest vb gwrthdystio ► n gwrthdystiad
Protestant n Protestant ► adj Protestannaidd
protester n protestiwr
proud adj balch
prove vb profi
proverb n dihareb
provide vt darparu; **provide for** vt darparu ar gyfer
province n talaith; cylch, maes
provision n darpariaeth; **provisions** npl darbodion; ymborth
provoke vt cythruddo, profocio
prowl vi ysglyfaetha, prowlan
proximity n agosrwydd
proxy n dirprwy
prudent adj pwyllog, doeth
prune n eirinen sych
pry vi chwilota, chwilenna
pseudonym n ffugenw

psychiatrist n seiciatrydd
psychological adj seicolegol, meddyliol
psychologist n seicolegydd
psychology n seicoleg
PTO abbr (= please turn over) trosodd
pub n tafarn
puberty n blaenaeddfedrwydd
public adj cyhoeddus ▸ n y cyhoedd
public house n tŷ tafarn
publicity n cyhoeddusrwydd
public relations npl cysylltiadau cyhoeddus
public school n ysgol fonedd
public transport n cludiant cyhoeddus
publish vt cyhoeddi
publisher n cyhoeddwr
pudding n pwdin
puddle n pwll, pwllyn
puff n pwff, chwa, chwyth ▸ vb pwffio, chwythu
puff pastry n crwst pwff
pull vt tynnu ▸ n tynfa, tyniad; **pull down** vt tynnu i lawr; **pull out** vb tynnu allan; **pull through** vi dod trwyddi; **pull up** vi (stop) stopio
pulley n troell, pwli
pullover n gwasgod wlân
pulp n bywyn, mwydion
pulpit n pulpud
pulse¹ n (of heart) curiad y galon, curiad y gwaed
pulse² n (vegetables) pys, ffa etc
pump n sugnedydd, pwmp ▸ vb pwmpio; **pump up** vt pwmpio gwynt i
pumpkin n pwmpen

pun n gair mwys, mwysair
punch n pwns; dyrnod ▸ vt pwnsio, dyrnodio
punch-up n (inf) ysgarmes
punctual adj prydlon
punctuation n atalnodiad
puncture n twll ▸ vt tyllu
punish vt cosbi; poeni
punishment n cosb, cosbedigaeth
pupil n disgybl; cannwyll llygad
puppet n pyped; gwas
puppy n ci bach
purchase vt prynu, pwrcasu ▸ n pryniant, pwrcas
pure adj pur, noeth
purify vt puro
purity n purdeb
purple adj, n porffor
purpose n pwrpas, bwriad, arfaeth
purr vb canu crwth, grwnan
purse n pwrs, cod ▸ vt crychu
pursue vb dilyn, erlyn, erlid, ymlid
pursuit n ymlidiad; ymchwil, gorchwyl
pus n crawn, gôr
push vb gwthio ▸ n gwth, ysgŵd; ymdrech; **push around** vt gwthio o gwmpas; **push through** vt gwthio trwodd
pushchair n coets
push-up n ymwythiad
put (pt, pp put) vb gosod, dodi, rhoddi, rhoi; **put aside** vt rhoi o'r neilltu; **put away** vt rhoi i gadw; **put back** vt (replace) rhoi yn ôl; (postpone) gohirio; **put down** vt (object) rhoi i lawr; (animal) difa; **put in** vt (install) gosod; **put off** vt (postpone) gohirio; (discourage)

digalonni; *(switch off)* diffodd; **put on** *vt* gwisgo; troi ymlaen; **to put on weight** ennill pwysau; **put out** *vt (fire; light)* diffodd; **put through** *vt (on phone)* rhoi drwodd; **put up** *vt (tent)* gosod; *(price)* codi

puzzle *n* pos ▸ *vb* drysu, pyslo

puzzled *adj* dryslyd

pyjamas *npl* pyjamas, gwisg nos

pyramid *n* pyramid, bera

Pyrenees *pl*: **the Pyrenees** y Pyreneau

quack¹ *n* crachfeddyg, cwac

quack² *vi* cwacian

quadruple *adj* pedwarplyg

quail *n* sofliar

quaint *adj* od, henffasiwn

quake *vi* crynu

qualification *n* cymhwyster; cymhwysiad

qualified *adj* cymwys

qualify *vt* cymhwyso, cyfaddasu

quality *n* ansawdd, rhinwedd

qualm *n* petruster, amheuaeth

quantity *n* swm, maint, mesur

quarantine *n* cwarant, neilltuaeth

quarrel *n* ymrafael, ffrae, cweryl ▸ *vi* ffraeo

quarry *n* chwarel, cwar

quart *n* chwart, cwart

quarter *n* chwarter; man; trugaredd; **quarters** *npl* llety; **a quarter of an hour** chwarter awr; **quarter final** rownd gogynderfynol

quarter final *n*: the quarter-finals y rownd gogynderfynol
quartet, quartette *n* pedwarawd
quartz *n* creigrisial, cwarts
quay *n* cei
queen *n* brenhines
queer *adj* od, hynod
quench *vt* diffodd, dofi, torri
query *n* holiad, gofyniad ▸ *vb* holi, amau
quest *n* ymchwiliad, cwest
question *n* gofyniad, cwestiwn ▸ *vt* holi, amau
questionable *adj* amheus
question mark *n* gofynnod
questionnaire *n* holiadur
queue *n* ciw
quick *adj* byw; buan, cyflym; **to the quick** i'r byw
quickly *adv (rapidly)* yn gyflym; *(promptly)* yn ddi-oed
quid *n (inf)* punt
quiet *adj* llonydd, tawel, distaw ▸ *n* llonyddwch, tawelwch ▸ *vt* llonyddu, tawelu
quietly *adv* yn dawel
quilt *n* cwilt, cwrlid ▸ *vt* cwiltio
quirky *adj* od, hynod
quit *(pt, pp* **quit**, **quitted)** *vt* gadael, symud ▸ *adj* rhydd
quite *adv* eithaf; cwbl, llwyr, hollol
quits *adj* yn gyfartal
quiver[1] *n* cawell saethau
quiver[2] *vi* crynu, dirgrynu
quiz *vt* holi
quota *n* cwota
quotation *n* dyfyniad; prisiant
quote *vt* dyfynnu; nodi (prisiau)

rabbi *n* rabi
rabbit *n* cwningen
rabies *n* y gynddaredd
race[1] *n* ras ▸ *vi* rasio
race[2] *n (ancestry)* hil
racecourse *n* cae rasys
racetrack *n* trac rasio
racial *adj* hiliol
racing car *n* car rasio
racing driver *n* gyrrwr rasio
racism *n* hiliaeth
racist *adj* hiliol ▸ *n* hilydd, hiliwr
rack *n* rac; arteithglwyd ▸ *vt* arteithio, dirdynnu
racket *n* twrf, mwstwr; *(for tennis etc)* raced
racquet *n* raced
radar *n* radar
radiation *n* ymbelydredd
radiator *n* rheiddiadur
radical *adj* gwreiddiol, cynhenid; trylwyr ▸ *n* radical
radio *n* radio

radioactive adj ymbelydrol
radio station n gorsaf radio
radish n rhuddygl, radis
RAF n RAF
raffle n raffl
raft n rafft
rag n carp, clwt
rage n cynddaredd ▸ vi terfysgu, cynddeiriogi
ragged adj carpiog, bratiog
raid n rhuthr, cyrch ▸ vb anrheithio, ysbeilio
rail n canllaw, cledren, rheilen
railcard n cerdyn rheilffordd
railway n rheilffordd
railway station n gorsaf reilffordd
rain n glaw ▸ vb glawio, bwrw glaw
rainbow n enfys
raincoat n cot law
rainforest n fforest law
rainy adj glawog
raise vt codi, dyrchafu
raisin n rhesinen
rake n cribin, rhaca ▸ vb cribinio, rhacanu
rally vb atgynnull; adgyfnerthu, gwella ▸ n cynulliad
ram n hwrdd, maharen ▸ vt hyrddio, pwnio
ramble vi gwibio, crwydro ▸ n gwib
rambler n crwydrwr
ramp n ramp
random n siawns, damwain ▸ adj damweiniol
range n amrediad; ystod; lle tân â ffwrn ▸ vb rhestru, cyfleu; crwydro
ranger n coedwigwr, ceidwad parc

rank¹ n rheng, gradd ▸ vb rhestru; **the rank and file** y bobl gyffredin
rank² adj mws; gwyllt; rhonc
ransom n pridwerth ▸ vt prynu, gwaredu
rant vi bragaldian, brygawthan
rap n cnoc ▸ vt cnocio, curo
rape vt treisio ▸ n trais
rapid adj cyflym, buan
rapids n dyfroedd gwyllt
rapist n treisiwr
rare adj prin; godidog; tenau
rash¹ adj byrbwyll
rash² n brech, tarddiant
rasher n tafell
raspberry n afanen, mafonen
rat n llygoden fawr, llygoden ffrengig ▸ vi llygota
rate¹ vt dwrdio, dweud y drefn
rate² n cyflymder; treth; (of interest) cyfradd
rather adv braidd, hytrach, go, lled
ratio n cymhareb
ration n dogn, saig ▸ vt dogni
rational adj rhesymol
rattle vb rhuglo, trystio ▸ n rhugl, rhwnc
rave vi gwallgofi, ynfydu
raven n cigfran
ravine n hafn, ceunant
raw adj amrwd; crai; cri; noeth; dolurus, garw; dibrofiad ▸ n cig noeth, dolur
ray¹ n paladr, pelydryn
ray² n (fish) cath fôr
razor n ellyn, rasal ▸ vt eillio
razor blade n llafn ellyn
re prep ym mater, mewn perthynas â

reach vb cyrraedd, estyn ▸ n cyrraedd
react vi adweithio
reaction n adwaith
reactor n adweithydd
read (pt, pp **read**) vb darllen; **read out** vt darllen yn uchel
reader n darllenydd
readily adv yn barod, yn ddiffwdan
reading n darllen
ready adj parod, rhwydd
real adj gwir, real, go-iawn
realistic adj realistig, realaidd
reality n gwirionedd, sylwedd; dirwedd, realiti
realize vt sylweddoli; gwireddu
really adv gwir, hollol, mewn difrif
realm n teyrnas, gwlad
reappear vb ailymddangos
rear¹ n cefn, pen ôl
rear² vb codi, magu; codi ar ei draed ôl
reason n rheswm ▸ vb rhesymu
reasonable adj rhesymol
reasonably adv: **reasonably good/quick** eitha da/cyflym
reassurance n calondid
reassure vt calonogi, cysuro
reassuring adj: **to be reassuring** twaleu'r meddwl
rebate n ad-daliad
rebel vi gwrthryfela ▸ n gwrthryfelwr
rebellion n gwrthryfel
rebellious adj gwrthryfelgar
recall vt galw yn ôl; galw i gof, cofio
receipt n derbyniad; derbynneb
receive vt derbyn
receiver n derbynnydd
recent adj diweddar

recently adv yn ddiweddar
reception n derbyniad, croeso
reception desk n man croeso, man derbyn
receptionist n croesawferch, croesawydd
recharge vt aildrydanu
recipe n rysáit
recipient n derbyniwr, derbynnydd
recital n adroddiad, datganiad
recite vb adrodd
reckless adj anystyriol, rhyfygus, dibris
reckon vb cyfrif, barnu, bwrw
reclaim vt adennill, diwygio
recline vb lledorwedd, gorwedd, gorffwys
recognition n adnabyddiaeth, cydnabyddiaeth
recognize vt adnabod, cydnabod
recommend vt cymeradwyo, argymell
recommendation n cymeradwyaeth
reconcile vt cymodi, cysoni
reconsider vb ailfeddwl
record vt cofnodi, recordio ▸ n cofnod, record
recorded delivery n dosbarthiad cofnodedig
recorder n (musical instrument) recordydd
recording n recordiad
record player n chwaraewr recordiau
recount vt adrodd
re-count vb ailgyfrif
recover vb adennill; ymadfer; adferiad
recovery n gwellhad

r

recreation

recreation *n* difyrrwch, adloniant
recruit *n* recriwt; newyddian ▸ *vt* recriwtio
rectangle *n* petryal
rectangular *adj* petryalog
rectify *vt* unioni, cywiro; puro, coethi
rector *n* rheithor
recur *vi* ailddigwydd, dychwelyd
recurring *adj* cylchol
recycle *vb* ailgylchu
recycling *n* ailgylchu
red *adj, n* coch, rhudd
Red Cross *n*: the Red Cross y Groes Goch
redcurrants *npl* cyrans coch
redecorate *vb* ailaddurno
redeem *vt* prynu (yn ôl), gwaredu
reduce *vt* lleihau, gostwng; rhydwytho
reduced *adj* gostyngol
reduction *n* lleihad, gostyngiad
redundancy *n* anghyflogaeth
redundant *adj* gormodol; anghyflog, digyflog
reed *n* cawnen, corsen
reef *n* creigle (yn y môr), creigfa, rîff
reel¹ *n* ril ▸ *vb* dirwyn
reel² *vi* troi, chwyldroi ▸ *n (dance)* dawns
refectory *n* ffreutur
refer *vb* cyfeirio, cyfarwyddo
referee *n* dyfarnwr; canolwr ▸ *vt* dyfarnu
reference *n* cyfeiriad; geirda
refill *n* adlenwad ▸ *vt* adlenwi
refine *vb* puro, coethi
reflect *vb* adlewyrchu; myfyrio
reflection *n* adlewyrchiad, myfyrdod

reflex *n* adweithred, atgyrch
reform *vb* diwygio, gwella ▸ *n* diwygiad
refrain¹ *vb* ymatal
refrain² *n* byrdwn
refresh *vt* adfywio
refreshing *adj* adfywiol
refreshments *npl* ymborth, lluniaeth
refrigerator *n* rhewgell, oergell
refuge *n* noddfa, lloches
refugee *n* ffoadur
refund *n* ad-daliad ▸ *vb* ad-dalu
refurbish *vb* adnewyddu
refusal *n* gwrthodiad, nacâd
refuse¹ *vb* gwrthod
refuse² *n* ysbwriel
regain *vt* adennill
regard *vt* edrych ar, ystyried ▸ *n* sylw, parch, hoffter
regarding *prep* ynglŷn â, ynghylch
regardless *adj* heb ofal, diofal
regenerate *vt* aileni
regiment *n* catrawd
region *n* ardal, bro, rhanbarth
regional *adj* rhanbarthol
register *n* cofrestr ▸ *vt* cofrestru
registered *adj* cofrestredig
registrar *n* cofrestrydd
registration *n* cofrestriad
registration number *n* rhif cofrestru, rhif trethiant
regret *vt* gofidio, edifaru ▸ *n* gofid
regular *adj* rheolaidd, cyson
regularly *adv* yn rheolaidd
regulate *vt* rheoleiddio
regulation *n* rheol, trefniant
rehabilitation *n* adferiad
rehearsal *n* rihyrsal, practis

rehearse vt adrodd; ymarfer ymlaen llaw
reign vi teyrnasu ▸ n teyrnasiad
reimburse vt talu yn ôl, ad-dalu
rein n afwyn, awen ▸ vt ffrwyno
reindeer n carw
reinforce vt atgyfnerthu
reinstate vt adfer i safle/braint
reject vt gwrthod, bwrw ymaith
rejection n gwrthodiad
rejoice vb llawenhau, gorfoleddu
relate vb adrodd, mynegi; perthyn
related adj yn perthyn; wedi ei ddweud
relating to prep yn ymwneud â
relation n adroddiad; perthynas
relationship n perthynas
relative adj perthnasol ▸ n perthynas; **relative pronoun** rhagenw perthynol
relatively adv yn gymharol
relax vb llacio, llaesu, ymlacio
relaxation n ymlacio
relaxed adj ymlaciedig
relaxing adj ymlaciol
relay n cyflenwad newydd, cyfnewid; darlledu ▸ vb ailosod
relay race n ras gyfnewid
release vt rhyddhau, gollwng ▸ n rhyddhad
relegate vt darostwng
relent vi tyneru, tirioni
relevant adj perthnasol
reliable adj y gellir dibynnu arno, dibynadwy
relic n crair; gweddillion
relief n cynhorthwy; gollyngdod; ymwared; tirwedd
relieve vt cynorthwyo; esmwytho, ysgafnhau; rhyddhau, gollwng

relieved adj: **to feel relieved** teimlo rhyddhad
religion n crefydd
religious adj crefyddol
relish n blas; enllyn, mwyniant ▸ vb blasio, hoffi
reluctance n amharodrwydd, anfodlonrwydd
reluctant adj anfodlon, anewyllysgar
reluctantly adv yn amharod
rely vi hyderu, ymddiried, dibynnu; **rely on** vt dibynnu ar
remain vi aros, parhau
remainder n gweddill, rhelyw
remaining adj ar ôl
remains npl olion, gweddillion
remand vt aildraddodi
remand home n cartref i droseddwyr ifanc
remark vb sylwi ▸ n sylw
remarkable adj nodedig, hynod
remarkably adv: **remarkably good** hynod o dda
remarry vi ailbriodi
remedy n meddyginiaeth ▸ vt meddyginiaethu, gwella
remember vt cofio
remind vt atgoffa
remnant n gweddill, gwarged
remorse n edifeirwch
remote adj pell, pellennig, anghysbell
remote control n rheolaeth bell
remotely adv o bell
removal n symudiad, diswyddiad
remove vb symud, dileu; mudo
renaissance n dadeni
render vb talu; datgan; gwneud; troi, cyfieithu

379

rendezvous *n* cyrchfa, man
 cyfarfod
renew *vt* adnewyddu
renewable *adj* adnewyddadwy
renovate *vt* adnewyddu
rent *n* rhent ▸ *vt* rhentu
rental *n* rent
reorganize *vt* ad-drefnu
rep *n* cynrychiolydd; **sales rep**
 gwerthwr/gwerthwraig
repair *vi* atgyweirio, trwsio ▸ *n*
 cywair
repay *vt* ad-dalu
repeat *vb* ailadrodd, ailgyflawni
repeatedly *adv* dro ar ôl tro
repetition *n* ailadroddiad
repetitive *adj* ailadroddus
replace *vb* ailosod, dodi'n ôl;
 cymryd lle (arall)
replacement *n* un sy'n cymryd
 lle arall
replay *vb* ailchwarae
replica *n* copi cywir, cyflun
reply *vi* ateb ▸ *n* ateb, atebiad
report *vt* adrodd, hysbysu ▸ *n*
 adroddiad; sŵn ergyd
reporter *n* gohebydd
represent *vt* portreadu; cynrychioli
representative *adj* yn cynrychioli
 ▸ *n* cynrychiolydd
repress *vt* atal, gostegu, llethu
repression *n* ataliad, darostyngiad
reprimand *n* cerydd ▸ *vt* ceryddu
reproduce *vt* atgynhyrchu, epilio
reproduction *n* atgynhyrchiad,
 copi; epiliad
reptile *n* ymlusgiad
republic *n* gweriniaeth,
 gwerinlywodraeth
repulsive *adj* atgas, ffiaidd

reputable *adj* parchus, cyfrifol
reputation *n* gair, cymeriad,
 enw da
request *n* cais ▸ *vt* ceisio, gofyn
require *vt* gofyn, mynnu
rescue *vt* achub ▸ *n* achubiad
research *n* ymchwil, ymchwiliad
 ▸ *vb* ymchwilio
resemblance *n* tebygrwydd
resemble *vt* tebygu i
resent *vt* tramgwyddo, digio
resentful *adj* digofus, llidiog
resentment *n* dig, dicter
reservation *n* cadw, cadfa
reserve *vt* cadw yn ôl, cadw wrth
 gefn ▸ *n* yr hyn a gedwir, cronfa;
 swildod
reserved *adj* swil; wedi ei gadw;
 reserved seat sedd gadw
reservoir *n* cronfa, llyn
reshuffle *vb* aildrefnu
resident *adj* preswylydd
residential *adj* preswyl
residue *n* gweddill
resign *vb* ymddiswyddo
resignation *n* ymddiswyddiad
resilient *adj* hydwyth, ystwyth
resin *n* ystor, rhwsin
resist *vb* gwrthsefyll,
 gwrthwynebu
resistance *n* gwrthwynebiad,
 gwrthsafiad
resit *vt (exam)* ailsefyll ▸ *n*
 ailarholiad, ailgynnig
resolution *n* penderfyniad
resolve *vb* penderfynu ▸ *n*
 penderfyniad
resort *vi* cyrchu ▸ *n* cyrchfa;
 ymwared

resource *n* sgil, dyfais; **resources** *npl* adnoddau
respect *vt* parch ▸ *n* golwg; parch
respectable *adj* parchus
respectful *adj* boneddigaidd, yn dangos parch
respective *adj* priodol, ar wahân
respite *n* saib, seibiant
respond *vi* ateb, ymateb; porthi
response *n* ateb, atebiad
responsibility *n* cyfrifoldeb
responsible *adj* atebol, cyfrifol
responsive *adj* ymatebol
rest¹ *n, vb* gorffwys ▸ *n* (*in music*) tawnod
rest² *n* (*remainder*) gweddill
restaurant *n* tŷ bwyta, bwyty
restless *adj* aflonydd, rhwyfus
restore *vt* adfer; atgyweirio
restrain *vt* atal, ffrwyno
restraint *n* atalfa, ffrwyn
restrict *vt* cyfyngu, caethiwo
restriction *n* cyfyngiad
result *vi* deillio, canlyn ▸ *n* canlyniad
resume *vt* ailddechrau
résumé *n* crynodeb
resuscitate *vb* adfywhau, dadebru
retail *vt* manwerthu, adwerthu ▸ *n* adwerth
retailer *n* manwerthwr
retain *vb* cadw, dal; llogi
retaliation *n* dial
retire *vi* ymneillltuo, encilio, cilio, ymddeol
retired *adj* wedi ymddeol
retirement *n* ymddeoliad
retort *vb* gwrthateb ▸ *n* ateb parod; ritort (cemeg)

retreat *vi* cilio, encilio, ffoi ▸ *n* encil, ffo
retrieve *vt* olrhain; adennill, adfer
retrospect *n* ad-drem, adolwg
return *vb* dychwelyd ▸ *n* dychweliad; enillion
return (ticket) *n* tocyn dwyffordd
reunion *n* aduniad
reveal *vt* datguddio
revel *vi* gloddesta; ymhyfrydu ▸ *n* gloddest
revenge *vb, n* dial
revenue *n* refeniw
reverend *adj* parchedig
reversal *n* dymchweliad, cwymp
reverse *adj* gwrthwyneb, chwith ▸ *vb* troi, gwrthdroi ▸ *n* gwrthdro, aflwydd
reverse (gear) *n* gêr ôl
reverse charge call *n* galwad y telir amdani'r pen arall
revert *vb* troi yn ôl, dychwelyd
review *vt* adolygu ▸ *n* adolygiad
revise *vt* cywiro, diwygio
revision *n* cywiriad; adolygiad
revival *n* adfywiad, diwygiad
revive *vb* adfywio, adnewyddu
revolt *vb* gwrthryfela ▸ *n* gwrthryfel
revolting *adj* atgas, ffiaidd
revolution *n* chwyldro, chwyldroad
revolutionary *adj* chwildroadol ▸ *n* chwildrowr
revolve *vb* troi, cylchdroi
revolver *n* llawddryll
reward *n* gwobr ▸ *vt* gwobrwyo
rewarding *adj* buddiol
rewind *vt* ailweindio

r

rheumatism n cryd cymalau, gwynegon
Rhine n Rhein
rhinoceros n rhinoseros
Rhone n Rhôn
rhubarb n rhiwbob
rhyme n odl, rhigwm ▸ vb odli, rhigymu
rhythm n rhythm, rhediad
rib n asen, eisen
ribbon n rhuban, ysnoden
rice n reis
rich adj cyfoethog, goludog, bras
rid (pt, pp **rid**) vt gwared
riddle n dychymyg, pos
ride (pt **rode**, pp **ridden**) vb marchogaeth, marchocáu
rider n marchogwr; atodiad
ridge n trum, cefn, crib
ridicule n gwawd ▸ vt gwawdio, chwerthin am ben
ridiculous adj chwerthinllyd
riding n marchogaeth
riding school n ysgol farchogaeth
rife adj cyffredin, rhemp
rifle n dryll, reiffl
rift n agen, hollt
rig vb rigio, taclu ▸ n rig
right adj iawn, uniawn; deau ▸ adv yn iawn ▸ vt unioni, cywiro ▸ n iawnder, hawl; **right wing** (politics) asgell dde
right angle n ongl sgwâr
rightful adj cyfreithlon, iawn
right-hand adj llaw dde
right-handed adj llawdde
rightly adv yn gywir
rigid adj anhyblyg
rim n ymyl, cylch, cant
rind n croen, crawen, rhisgl

ring¹ n (jewellery) modrwy; (circle) cylch ▸ vb modrwyo
ring² (pt **rang**, pp **rung**) vb (sound) canu cloch, atseinio; (person; by phone) ffonio ▸ n sŵn cloch, tinc
▸ **ring back** vt, vi ffonio'n ôl
▸ **ring up** vt, vi ffonio
ring binder n ffeil fodrwy
ring road n cylchffordd
ring tone n tôn ffôn
rinse vt golchi, trochi
riot n terfysg, gloddest ▸ vi terfysgu
rip vb rhwygo ▸ n rhwyg; **rip up** vt rhwygo
ripe adj aeddfed
rip-off n (inf) lladrad amlwg
ripple n crych ▸ vb crychu
rise (pt **rose**, pp **risen**) vi codi, cyfodi ▸ n codiad
risk n perygl, risg ▸ vt peryglu, mentro
rite n defod
ritual adj defodol ▸ n defod
rival n cydymgeisydd ▸ vb cystadlu
river n afon
rivet n rhybed, rifet ▸ vb rhybedu, rifetio
road n ffordd, heol; angorfa
road map n map ffyrdd, map moduro
road rage n cythraul gyrru
road sign n arwydd ffordd
road tax n treth ffordd
road works npl gwaith cynnal y ffordd
roam vi crwydro, gwibio
roar vi rhuo ▸ n rhu, rhuad
roast vb rhostio

rob *vt* lladrata, ysbeilio
robber *n* lleidr, ysbeiliwr
robbery *n* lladrad
robe *n* gwisg, gŵn
robin *n* brongoch
robot *n* robot
robust *adj* cadarn, cryf
rock¹ *vb* siglo
rock² *n* craig
rocket *n* roced
rocky *adj* creigiog; sigledig
rod *n* gwialen, llath
rodent *n* cnofil
roe¹ *n (deer)* iyrches, ewig
roe² *n (of fish)* grawn pysgod, gronell
rogue *n* gwalch, cnaf
role *n* rhan, rôl
roll *vb* rholio, treiglo ▸ *n* rhòl
roll call *n* galw enwau (ar restr)
Rollerblading *n* llafnrolio
roller skates *npl* esgidiau sglefrolio
roller-skating *n* sglefrolio
rolling pin *n* rholbren
Roman *n* Rhufeiniwr ▸ *adj* Rhufeinaidd, Rhufeinig
Roman Catholic *n* Pabydd
romance *n* rhamant ▸ *vi* rhamantu
Romania *n* Rwmania
Romanian *n (person)* Rwmaniad; *(language)* Rwmaneg ▸ *adj* Rwmanaidd; *(in language)* Rwmaneg
romantic *adj* rhamantus
Rome *n* Rhufain
roof *n* to, nen ▸ *vt* toi
rook *n* ydfran, brân
room *n* lle; ystafell
roommate *n* cydletywr

room service *n* gwasanaeth ystafell
roomy *adj* helaeth, eang
rooster *n* ceiliog
root *n* gwraidd, gwreiddyn ▸ *vb* gwreiddio; diwreiddio; **root around** *vi* chwilota; **root out** *vt* gwaredu
rope *n* rhaff ▸ *vt* rhaffu, rhwymo; **rope in** *vt* rhwydo
rose *n* rhosyn
rose hips *npl* egroes
rosy *adj* rhosynnaidd, gwritgoch
rot *vb* pydru, braenu ▸ *n* pydredd; *(inf)* lol
rota *n* rhod, trefn
rotate *vi* troi, cylchdroi
rotten *adj* pwdr, pydredig
rough *adj* garw, gerwin, bras
roughly *adv (not gently)* yn arw; *(approximately)* yn fras
round *adj* crwn ▸ *n* crwn, tro, rownd ▸ *adv, prep* o glych, o amgylch ▸ *vb* crynio, rowndio; **round off** *vt* terfynu; **round up** *vt* talgrynnu
roundabout *n* cylchfan; ceffylau bach ▸ *adj* cwmpasog
rounders *n* rownders
round trip *n* taith mynd a dod
rouse *vb* dihuno, deffroi
route *n* llwybr, hynt
routine *n* defod, arfer
row¹ *n* rhes, rhestr
row² *vb* rhwyfo
row³ *n* cythrwfl, ffrae
rowing *n* rhwyfo
rowing boat *n* cwch rhwyfo
royal *adj* brenhinol
royalty *n* brenhiniaeth; breindal

r

rub

rub *vb* rhwbio; **rub out** *vt* rhwbio allan, dileu

rubber *n* rwber

rubbish *n* ysbwriel, sothach; lol

rubbish bin *n* bin ysbwriel
 ▸ **rubbish dump** *n* tomen ysbwriel

rubbish dump *n* tomen ysbwriel

rubble *n* rhwbel

ruby *n* rhuddem ▸ *adj* coch, rhudd

rucksack *n* rhychsach

rudder *n* llyw

rude *adj* anfoesgar; anghelfydd, garw

ruffle *vb* crychu, cyffroi, aflonyddu

rug *n* ryg

rugby *n* rygbi

rugged *adj* garw, gerwin, clogyrnog

ruin *n* distryw, dinistr; adfail ▸ *vb* difetha, andwyo

rule *n* rheol ▸ *vb* rheoli; llinellu; **rule out** *vt* diystyru

ruler *n* llywodraethwr; pren mesur, rhiwl

ruling *n* dyfarniad, barn ▸ *adj* llywodraethol, mewn grym

rum *n* rym ▸ *adj* od, rhyfedd

Rumania *n* Rwmania

rumble *vi* trystio, tyrfu

rumour *n* si, sôn

run (*pt* **ran,** *pp* **run**) *vb* rhedeg, llifo ▸ *n* rhediad, rhedfa; **in the long run** yn y pen draw; **run away** *vi* ffoi, rhedeg i ffwrdd; **run out** *vi* dod i ben; **run out of** *vt* rhedeg allan o; **run over** *vt*: **she was run over by a car** cafodd ei tharo i lawr gan gar

rung *n* ffon ysgol

runner *n* rhedwr

runner-up *n*: **the runner-up** yr ail

running *n* rhedeg

runway *n* rhedfa

rupture *n* rhwyg; torllengig ▸ *vb* rhwygo

rural *adj* gwledig, gwladaidd

rush¹ *n* brwynen, pabwyryn

rush² *vb* rhuthro ▸ *n* rhuthr

rush hour *n* awr brysur

Russia *n* Rwsia

Russian *n* (*person*) Rwsiad; (*language*) Rwseg ▸ *adj* Rwsiaidd; (*in language*) Rwseg

rust *n* rhwd ▸ *vb* rhydu

rusty *adj* rhydlyd

ruthless *adj* didostur, diarbed, creulon

rye *n* rhyg

S

Sabbath n Sabath, Saboth
sabotage n difrod bwriadol ▸ vb difrodi
sack n sach, ffetan ▸ vt sachu; difrodi; diswyddo
sacred adj cysegredig, glân, sanctaidd
sacrifice n aberth, offrwm ▸ vb aberthu
sad adj trist
saddle n cyfrwy ▸ vt cyfrwyo; beichio
sadness n tristwch, prudd-der
safe adj diogel, saff ▸ n sêff
safety n diogelwch; **safety belt** gwregys diogelwch; **safety pin** pin cau
saffron n saffrwm ▸ adj melyn
sag vb sagio, ymollwng
sage n saets
Sagittarius n y Saethydd
Sahara n Sahara
sail n hwyl ▸ vb hwylio

sailing n hwylio
sailing boat n llong hwylio
sailor n morwr, llongwr
saint n sant
sake n mwyn; **for the sake of** er mwyn
salad n salad
salami n salami
salary n cyflog
sale n gwerth, gwerthiant
sales assistant n (man) dyn siop; (woman) merch siop
salesman n gwerthwr
saleswoman n gwerthwraig
saline adj helïaidd, hallt ▸ n heli
saliva n poer
salmon n eog, samwn
saloon n neuadd, salŵn
salt n halen; (Chem) halwyn ▸ adj hallt ▸ vt halltu
salt cellar n llestr halen
salt water n dŵr hallt, dŵr y môr
salty adj hallt
salute vt cyfarch; saliwtio ▸ n cyfarchiad; saliwt
Salvation Army n: **the Salvation Army** Byddin yr Iachawdwriaeth
same adj yr un, yr un fath
sample n sampl, enghraifft ▸ vt samplu, samplo
sanction n caniatâd; cosb; sancsiwn (moeseg) ▸ vt caniatáu; cosbi
sanctuary n cysegr; noddfa, nawdd
sand n tywod ▸ vt tywodi
sandal n sandal
sand castle n castell tywod
sandpaper n papur gwydrog
sandpit n pwll tywod

sandwich *n* brechdan
sandy *adj* tywodlyd; melyngoch
sane *adj* iach, call
sanity *n* iechyd meddwl, iawn bwyll
Santa Claus *n* Siôn Corn
sap¹ *n* nodd, sugn
sap² *vb* tangloddio, diseilio
sapphire *n* saffir ▸ *adj* glas
sarcasm *n* gwawdiaith, coegni
sarcastic *adj* gwawdlyd, coeglyd
sardine *n* sardîn
satchel *n* sachell, cod lyfrau
satellite *n* canlynwr, cynffonnwr; lleuad; lloeren
satellite dish *n* dysgl loeren, soser lloeren
satin *n* satin, pali
satire *n* dychan, gogan
satisfaction *n* bodlonrwydd; iawn
satisfactory *adj* boddhaol; iawnol
satisfied *adj* bodlon
satisfy *vt* bodloni, diwallu, digoni
sat nav *n* offer llywio lloeren
Saturday *n* dydd Sadwrn
sauce *n* saws; haerllugrwydd
saucepan *n* sosban
saucer *n* soser
Saudi Arabia *n* Saudi Arabia, Sawdi Arabia
sausage *n* selsig, selsigen
savage *adj* milain, anwar ▸ *n* anwariad
save *vb* achub, arbed, gwaredu; cynilo ▸ *prep* ond; **save up** *vi* cynilo
saving *adj* achubol, darbodus
savoury *n* blasusfwyd ▸ *adj* sawrus

saw *(pt* **sawed**, *pp* **sawed, sawn)** *n* llif ▸ *vb* llifio
sawdust *n* blawd llif
saxophone *n* sacsoffon
say *(pt, pp* **said)** *vb* dweud
saying *n* dywediad, ymadrodd, gair
scab *n* crachen, cramen; clafr
scald *vt* ysgaldio, sgaldan(u)
scale¹ *n (balance)* clorian, tafol, mantol
scale² *n* graddfa ▸ *vb* dringo
scales *npl* clorian
scallop *n* cylfgragen; gwlf ▸ *vt* gylfu, minfylchu
scalp *n* copa, croen y pen ▸ *vt* penflingo
scam *n (inf)* sgam
scampi *n* sgampi
scan *vb* corfannu; sganio
scandal *n* tramgwydd, gwarth
Scandinavia *n* Llychlyn
Scandinavian *n* Sgandinafiad ▸ *adj* Sgandinafaidd
scanner *n* sganydd; sganiwr; **virus scanner** sganiwr feirws
scapegoat *n* bwch dihangol
scar *n* craith ▸ *vt* creithio
scarce *adj, adv* prin
scarcely *adv* prin, braidd
scare *vt* brawychu, tarfu ▸ *n* dychryn
scarecrow *n* bwgan brain
scared *adj* wedi cael ofn, wedi brawychu
scarf *n* crafat, sgarff
scarlet *adj* ysgarlad
scary *adj (inf)* sgêri
scatter *vb* gwasgaru, chwalu, taenu
scene *n* lle; golwg, golygfa

scenery n golygfa
scenic adj hardd, golygfaol
scent n aroglau, perarogl; trywydd
  ▶ vt arogli
sceptical adj amheugar
schedule n atodlen, cofrestr
scheduled flight n ehediad
  rhestredig
scheme n cynllun ▶ vb cynllunio
scholar n ysgolhaig, ysgolor
scholarship n ysgolheictod;
  ysgoloriaeth
school n ysgol, ysgoldy ▶ vt
  addysgu
schoolbag n bag ysgol
schoolbook n llyfr ysgol
schoolboy n bachgen ysgol
schoolchildren npl plant ysgol
schoolgirl n merch ysgol
school uniform n gwisg ysgol
science n gwyddor, gwyddoniaeth
science fiction n ffuglen wyddonol
scientific adj gwyddonol
scientist n gwyddonydd
scissors npl siswrn
scold vb dwrdio, tafodi, cerydu,
  cymhennu ▶ n cecren
scone n sgon
scoop n lletwad ▶ vt cafnu, cafnio
scooter n sgwter
scope n ergyd, bwriad; cwmpas
score¹ n rhic; cyfrif; sgôr; ugain
score² vb rhicio, cyfrif, sgori(o)
scorn n dirmyg ▶ vb dirmygu,
  gwatwar
Scorpio n y Sgorpion
scorpion n ysgorpion
Scot n Ysgotyn, Albanwr
Scotch adj Ysgotaidd, Albanaidd
scotch vt hacio, darnio, trychu

Scotland n Yr Alban
Scots adj Albanaidd; (in language)
  Scoteg
Scotsman n Albanwr
Scotswoman n Albanes
Scottish adj Albanaidd
scour¹ vt (scrub) carthu, ysgwrio
scour² vb rhedeg; chwilio
scout n sgowt, ysbïwr ▶ vt
  sgowta, ysbïo
scowl vb cuchio, gwgu ▶ n cilwg,
  gwg
scramble vi, n ciprys, ymgiprys
scrambled egg n cymysgwy
scrap n tamaid, dernyn
scrapbook n llyfr lloffion
scrape vb crafu ▶ n helynt, helbul,
  crafiad
scratch vb crafu, cripio
scratch card n cerdyn crafu
scream vi ysgrechian ▶ n ysgrech,
  gwawch
screen n llen, cysgod; sgrin ▶ vt
  cysgodi
screen saver n arbedwr sgrin
screw n sgriw, hoel dro ▶ vb
  ysgriwio
screwdriver n tyrnsgriw
scribble n ysgribl ▶ vb ysgriblo,
  ysgriblan
script n sgript
scroll n rhôl, plyg llyfr
scrub n prysgwydd; ysgwrfa ▶ vt
  ysgwrio
scrum, scrummage n sgrym,
  ysgarmes
scrutiny n archwiliad
sculptor n cerflunydd
sculpture n cerfluniaeth; cerflun
  ▶ vb cerflunio, torri

S

scum *n* sgum; *(inf)* gwehilion, sorod
scurry *vi* ffrystio ▸ *n* ffrwst, ffwdan
scuttle *vi* heglu ffoi, dianc
sea *n* môr
seafood *n* bwyd môr
seagull *n* gwylan
seal¹ *n (animal)* morlo
seal² *n* sêl, insel ▸ *vt* selio
sea level *n* lefel y môr
seam *n* gwnïad, gwrym; haen, gwythïen; craith
search *vb* chwilio, profi ▸ *n* ymchwil
search engine *n* peiriant chwilio, chwiliadur
search party *n* criw chwilio
seashore *n* glan y môr
seasick *adj* sâl môr; **to be seasick** dioddef o salwch môr
seaside *n* glan y môr
season *n* tymor ▸ *vb* tymheru; halltu; **high/low season** tymor prysur/llac
seasonal *adj* tymhorol
season ticket *n* tocyn tymor
seat *n* sedd, sêt ▸ *vi* eistedd
seat belt *n* gwregys diogelwch
sea water *n* dŵr y môr
seaweed *n* gwymon, gwmon
second *adj* ail ▸ *n* ail; eiliad ▸ *vt* eilio
secondary *adj* eilradd, uwchradd
secondary school *n* ysgol uwchradd
second class *adj* ail ddosbarth; isradd
second-hand *adj* ail-law
secondly *adv* yn ail

secret *adj* dirgel, cyfrinachol ▸ *n* cyfrinach
secretary *n* ysgrifennydd
Secretary of State *n* Ysgrifennydd Gwladol
secretive *adj* yn celu, tawedog
secretly *adv* yn gyfrinachol
sect *n* sect, enwad
section *n* toriad, trychiad; rhan, adran
sector *n* sector
secular *adj* seciwlar
secure *adj* sicr, diogel ▸ *vt* sicrhau, diogelu
security *n* diogelwch, sicrwydd, gwystl
security guard *n* gwarchodwr
sedate *adj* tawel, digyffro ▸ *vb* rhoi i gysgu, tawelu
sedative *adj* lleddfol, lliniarol
seduce *vt* llithio, hudo, twyllo
seductive *adj* llithiol, deniadol
see *(pt* **saw**, *pp* **seen)** *vb* gweld, canfod
seed *n* had, hedyn ▸ *vb* hadu, hedeg
seek *(pt, pp* **sought)** *vb* ceisio, ymofyn, chwilio
seem *vi* ymddangos
seesaw *n* siglenydd
segment *n* segment
segregate *vt* didoli, neilltuo, gwahanu
seize *vb* gafael mewn, atafaelu
seizure *n* daliad; ymosodiad, strôc
seldom *adv* anfynych, anaml
select *vt* dewis, dethol
selection *n* detholiad
self *n* hun, hunan
self- *prefix* hunan-, ym-

self-catering *adj* hunan arlwy
self-confidence *n* hunanhyder
self-confident *adj* hunanhyderus
self-conscious *adj* hunanymwybodol, swil
self-contained *adj* annibynnol, ar wahân
self-control *n* hunanlywodraeth
self-defence *n* hunanamddiffyniad
self-employed *adj* hunangyflogedig
self-interest *n* hunan-les
selfish *adj* hunanol
self-respect *n* hunan-barch
self-service *n* hunanwasanaeth
sell (*pt, pp* **sold**) *vb* gwerthu; siomi
▸ *n* siom; **sell off** *vt* gwerthu; **sell out** *vi*: they've sold out maen nhw wedi gwerthu'r cwbl
sell-by date *n* dyddiad olaf gwerthu
seller *n* gwerthwr
semicircle *n* hanner cylch
semidetached (house) *n* tŷ pâr
semi-final *n*: the semi-finals y rownd cynderfynol
seminar *n* seminar
semi-skimmed *adj* hanner-sgim
semi-skimmed milk *n* llaeth hanner sgim
senate *n* senedd
send (*pt, pp* **sent**) *vt* anfon, danfon, gyrru; **send back** *vt* anfon yn ôl; **send off** *vt*: he was sent off cafodd ei anfon o'r cae; **send out** *vt* anfon allan
senile *adj* hen a methedig, heneiddiol
senior *adj* hŷn ▸ *n* hynaf
senior citizen *n* henwr

sensation *n* ymdeimlad, teimlad; cyffro, ias, syndod
sensational *adj* iasol, cyffrous
sense *n* synnwyr, pwyll, ystyr; **sense of humour** synnwyr digrifwch
senseless *adj* dienaid, disynnwyr, hurt
sensible *adj* synhwyrol; teimladwy
sensitive *adj* teimladwy; hydeiml
sensual *adj* cnawdol; trythyll, chwantus
sensuous *adj* teimladol, synhwyrus
sentence *n* brawddeg; dedfryd
▸ *vt* dedfrydu
sentiment *n* syniad, teimlad
sentimental *adj* sentimental
separate *adj* ar wahân ▸ *vb* gwahanu, neilltuo, ysgar; ymwahanu
separately *adv* ar wahân
separation *n* gwahaniad
September *n* Medi
septic *adj* braenol, pydrol, madreddol
sequel *n* canlyniad
sequence *n* trefn, dilyniad
Serbia *n* Serbia
sergeant *n* rhingyll, sarsiant
serial *adj* cyfresol, bob yn rhifyn
▸ *n* stori gyfres
serial killer *n* llofrudd cyfresol
series *n* rhes, cyfres
serious *adj* difrifol
seriously *adv* yn ddifrifol
sermon *n* pregeth
servant *n* gwas; morwyn
serve *vb* gwasanaethu, gweini
server *n* gweinydd

S

389

service

service n gwasanaeth, oedfa; llestri
service charge n tâl am wasanaeth
service station n gorsaf gwasanaethau
serviette n napcyn
session n eisteddiad; sesiwn; tymor
set (pt, pp set) vb gosod, dodi; plannu; sadio; sefydlu; machlud ▸ n set; impyn, planhigyn; **set off** vi cychwyn; **set out** vi cychwyn
settee n sgiw, setl
setting n lleoliad, safle; machludiad
settle vb sefydlu; penderfynu; cytuno, setlo; plwyfo; talu; **settle down** vi (calm down) tawelu; **settle down!** byddwch yn llonydd!; **settle in** vi setlo
settlement n cytundeb; gwladfa, anheddiad
seven adj, n saith
seventeen adj, n dau (dwy) ar bymtheg, un deg saith
seventeenth adj ail ar bymtheg
seventh adj seithfed
seventy adj, n deg a thrigain, saith deg
sever vb gwahanu, datod, torri
several adj amryw; gwahanol
severe adj caled, tost, llym, gerwin
sew (pt sewed, pp sewn) vb gwnïo, pwytho; **sew up** vt gwnïo
sewage n carthffosiaeth, carthion
sewer n ceuffos, carthffos
sewing n gwnïo
sewing machine n peiriant gwnïo
sex n rhyw

sex education n addysg ryw
sexism n rhywiaeth
sexist adj rhywiaethol, secsist
sexual adj rhywiol
sexuality n rhywioldeb
sexy adj rhywiol
shabby adj carpiog, gwael, aflêr
shack n caban
shade n cysgod; ysbryd ▸ vt cysgodi
shadow n cysgod ▸ vt cysgodi
shady adj cysgodol; amheus
shaft n paladr; braich; siafft; gwerthyd
shake (pt shook, pp shaken) vb ysgwyd, siglo, crynu
shaky adj ansad, crynedig
shallow adj bas ▸ n basle, beisle
sham vb ffugio ▸ adj ffug, gau, coeg ▸ n ffug, ffugbeth
shambles npl galanastra
shame n cywilydd, gwaradwydd, gwarth ▸ vb cywilyddio, gwaradwyddo
shameful adj cywilyddus, gwarthus
shampoo vt golchi pen ▸ n siampŵ
shandy n siandi
shape n siâp, llun ▸ vt siapio, llunio
share n rhan, cyfran ▸ vb rhannu; cyfranogi; **share out** vt rhannu
shareholder n cyfranddaliwr
shark n siarc, morgi, twyllwr
sharp adj siarp, llym, miniog ▸ n llonnod (cerdd)
sharpen vb hogi, minio
sharpener n naddwr
sharply adv yn sydyn

shatter vb dryllio, chwilfriwio; ysigo

shattered adj drylliedig; (inf) wedi blino'n lân

shave vb eillio; rhasglio

shaver n: (electric) shaver eilliwr (trydan)

shaving cream n sebon eillio

shaving foam n ewyn eillio

shavings npl naddion

shawl n siôl

she pron hi ▸ adj prefix benyw

sheath n gwain; (contraceptive) maneg atal cenhedlu

shed¹ n penty, sied

shed² (pt, pp shed) vt tywallt; gollwng; colli; dihidlo, bwrw

sheep n dafad

sheepdog n ci defaid

sheer¹ vi gwyro o'r ffordd, cilio

sheer² adj pur, glân, noeth, syth, serth

sheet n llen; cynfas; hwylraff; dalen

shelf n silff, astell

shell n cragen; plisgyn, masgl; tân-belen

shellfish npl cregynbysg

shelter n cysgod, lloches ▸ vb cysgodi, llochesu; ymochel; llechu

shelve vi llechweddu, llethru

shepherd n bugail ▸ vt bugeilio

sheriff n sirydd, siryf

sherry n sieri

Shetland n Shetland

shield n tarian ▸ vt cysgodi, amddiffyn

shift vb newid, symud; ymdaro ▸ n newid; tro, stem, shifft

shin n crimog, crimp coes

shine (pt, pp shone) vb disgleirio, llewyrchu, tywynnu ▸ n disgleirdeb, sglein, llewyrch

shingle n graean, gro

shingles npl yr eryr, yr eryrod

shiny adj gloyw, disglair

ship n llong ▸ vt trosglwyddo

shipping n llongau (gwlad)

shipwreck n llongddrylliad

shirt n crys

shiver vi crynu

shoal n haig ▸ vi heigio

shock n sioc, ergyd, ysgytiad ▸ vt ysgytio

shocking adj arswydus, ysgytiol

shoe (pt, pp shod) n esgid; pedol ▸ vt pedoli

shoelace n carrai/lasen esgid

shoe polish n cwyr esgidiau

shoe shop n siop esgidiau

shoot (pt, pp shot) vb tarddu, blaguro; saethu ▸ n ysbrigyn, blaguryn

shooting n saethu

shop n siop ▸ vb siopa

shop assistant n (man) dyn siop; (woman) merch siop

shopkeeper n siopwr

shoplifting n siopladrad

shopping n siopa

shop window n ffenestr siop

shore n glan, traeth

short adj byr, cwta, prin

shortage n prinder, diffyg

shortcoming n diffyg, bai

short cut n llwybr tarw, llwybr llygad, ffordd fer

shorthand n llaw-fer

shortly adv ymhen ychydig

shorts npl trowsus cwta

S

short-sighted *adj (person)* â golwg byr; *(action, attitude)* byrweledol
shot *n* ergyd; saethwr
shotgun *n* gwn haels
shoulder *n* ysgwydd, palfais ▸ *vt* ysgwyddo
shoulder blade *n* sgapwla, pont yr ysgwydd
shout *vb* bloeddio, gweiddi ▸ *n* bloedd, gwaedd
shove *vb* gwthio
shovel *n* llwyarn ▸ *vt* rhofio
show *(pt* showed, *pp* shown*)* *vb* dangos, arddangos ▸ *n* arddangosfa, sioe, siew; **show off** *vt* dangos eich hun ▸ *vt (display)* arddangos; **show up** *vi (inf)* ymddangos
shower *n* cawod, cawad ▸ *vb* cawodi, bwrw
shower gel *n* gel cawod
shred *n* llarp, cerpyn ▸ *vb* rhwygo, torri'n fân
shrewd *adj* craff
shriek *vb* ysgrechian ▸ *n* ysgrech
shrimp *n* berdysen ▸ *vi* berdysa
shrine *n* creirfa; cysegr, seintwar
shrink *(pt* shrank, *pp* shrunk*)* *vb* crebachu, cilio
shrivel *vb* crychu, crebachu
shroud *n* amdo ▸ *vt* amdoi, cuddio, celu
Shrove Tuesday *n* Mawrth Ynyd
shrub *n* prysgwydden, llwyn
shrug *vb* codi'r ysgwyddau
shudder *n* crynfa, arswyd ▸ *vi* crynu, arswydo
shuffle *vb* siffrwd; llusgo
shun *vt* gochelyd, osgoi

shut *(pt, pp* shut*)* *vb* cau ▸ *adj* caeëdig; **shut down** *vt* cau; **shut up** *vt (inf)* cau
shutter *n* caead, clawr
shuttle *n* gwennol (gwëydd)
shuttlecock *n* gwennol
shy *adj* swil ▸ *vi* osgoi, rhusio
siblings *npl* brodyr/chwiorydd
sick *adj* claf; yn chwydu, â chyfog arno; wedi diflasu
sickening *adj* atgas, diflas, cyfoglyd
sick leave *n* seibiant salwch
sickly *adj* afiach, nychlyd
sickness *n* afiechyd
side *n* ochr, ystlys; tu, plaid ▸ *vi* ochri
sideboard *n* seld
side effect *n* sgil-effaith
sidetrack *vb* troi o'r neilltu
sideways *adv* tua'r ochr, yn wysg ei ochr
siege *n* gwarchae
sieve *n* gogr, gwagr, rhidyll
sift *vt* gogrwn, nithio, hidlo, rhidyllio
sigh *vb* ochneidio ▸ *n* ochenaid
sight *n* golwg, golygfa ▸ *vt* gweld
sightseeing *n* taith i weld y wlad
sign *n* arwydd, argoel ▸ *vb* arwyddo, llofnodi; **sign on** *vi* cofrestru
signal *adj* hynod ▸ *n* arwydd
signature *n* llofnod
significance *n* arwyddocâd, ystyr
significant *adj* arwyddocaol; o bwys
signify *vb* arwyddo, arwyddocáu
sign language *n* iaith arwyddion

signpost n mynegbost, arwyddbost

silence n taw, distawrwydd ▸ vt rhoi taw ar

silent adj distaw, tawedog

silhouette n cysgodlun, silŵet

silk n sidan

silly adj gwirion, ffôl

silver n arian ▸ vt ariannu

silver paper n papur arian

similar adj tebyg, cyffelyb

simmer vi lledferwi, goferwi

simple adj syml; gwirion, diniwed

simplicity n symlrwydd, unplygrwydd

simplify vt symleiddio

simply adv yn syml; yn ddi-lol; yn wirioneddol

simulate vt ffugio, dynwared

simultaneous adj cyfamserol, ar y pryd

sin n pechod ▸ vb pechu

since conj gan, yn gymaint ▸ prep er, er pan

sincere adj diffuant, didwyll

sincerely adv yn ddiffuant; **Yours sincerely** yr eiddoch yn gywir

sing (pt **sang**, pp **sung**) vb canu

singer n canwr, cantwr, cantores

singing n canu

single adj sengl, dibriod

single bed n gwely sengl

single-minded adj unplyg, cywir

single parent n rhiant sengl

single room n ystafell sengl

singular adj unigol; hynod

sinister adj ysgeler; chwithig

sink (pt **sank**, pp **sunk**) vb soddi, suddo ▸ n sinc

sip vt llymeitian ▸ n llymaid, llymeidyn

sir n syr

siren n corn, seiren

sirloin n llwyn eidion

sister n chwaer

sister-in-law n chwaer yng nghyfraith

sit (pt, pp **sat**) vb eistedd; **sit down** vi eistedd

site n safle, lle ▸ vb lleoli

sitting n eisteddiad

sitting room n parlwr, lolfa, ystafell fyw

situated adj yn sefyll, wedi ei leoli

situation n lle, safle; sefyllfa

six adj, n chwech

sixteen adj, n un ar bymtheg, un deg chwech

sixteenth adj unfed ar bymtheg

sixth adj chweched

sixth form n chweched dosbarth

sixth-form college n coleg chweched dosbarth

sixty adj, n trigain, chwe deg

size n maint, maintioli

sizzle vb ffrio

skate¹ n (fish) cath fôr

skate² n sgêt ▸ vb ysglefrio

skateboard n bwrdd sglefrio

skateboarding n sgrialfyrddio

skates n esgidiau sglefrio

skating n sglefrio

skeleton n ysgerbwd; amlinelliad

sketch n llun, braslun ▸ vb braslunio, tynnu

skewer n gwaell, gwachell

ski n sgi ▸ vb sgïo

skid vb llithro (naill ochr)

skier n sgiwr

skiing n sgïo
skilful adj medrus
skill n medr, medrusrwydd
skilled adj medrus, crefftus
skim vb tynnu, codi (hufen)
skimmed milk n llaeth glas, llaeth sgim
skin n croen ▸ vb blingo
skinhead n pencroen
skinny adj tenau; prin, crintach
skip vi llamu, sgipio
skipper n capten llong
skipping rope n rhaff sgipio
skirt n godre, sgyrt ▸ vt dilyn gyda godre
skive (inf) vi sgelcian; **skive off** vi sgelcian
skull n penglog
skunk n drewgi
sky n wybren, awyr
skyscraper n nendwr
slab n llech
slack adj llac, diofal, esgeulus
slam vb cau yn glats, clepian
slander n enllib ▸ vt enllibio
slang n iaith sathredig, slang ▸ vt difrïo
slant vb gwyro, gogwyddo ▸ n gogwydd
slap vt clewtian ▸ n clewt(en), palfod
slash n slaes, hac ▸ vt slasio, chwipio
slate[1] n llech, llechen
slate[2] vt sennu, difrïo
slaughter n lladdedigaeth, lladdfa ▸ vt lladd
slaughterhouse n lladd-dy
slave n slaf, caethwas ▸ vi slafio

slavery n caethiwed, caethwasanaeth
slay (pt **slew**, pp **slain**) vt lladd
sled, sledge, sleigh n car llusg, sled
sledge n sled
sledging n sledio
sleek adj llyfn, graenus
sleep (pt, pp **slept**) vb cysgu, huno ▸ n cwsg, hun; **sleep around** vi neidio o wely i wely; **sleep in** vi cysgu'n hwyr; **sleep together** vi: they're sleeping together maen nhw'n cysgu gyda'i gilydd
sleeper n (person) cysgwr; sliper
sleeping bag n sach gysgu
sleeping pill n pilsen gysgu
sleepy adj cysglyd
sleet n eirlaw
sleeve n llawes
slender adj main
slice n tafell, ysglisen ▸ vt tafellu, ysglisio
slick adj llyfn, tafodrydd, slic
slide (pt, pp **slid**) vb llithro, sglefrio ▸ n llithren, sleid
slight adj ysgafn, eiddil, prin ▸ vt diystyru ▸ n diystyrwch, sarhad
slightly adj ychydig
slim adj main, eiddil
sling (pt, pp **slung**) vt taflu, lluchio ▸ n ffon dafl
slip vb llithro; gollwng ▸ n slip; **slip up** vi llithro
slipper n llopan, sliper
slippery adj llithrig, diafael, di-ddal
slip-up n llithriad
slit (pt, pp **slit**) vb hollti, agennu ▸ n hollt
slog vb gweithio'n galed

slope n llethr, gogwydd ▸ vb gogwyddo
sloppy adj lleidiog; meddal; anniben
slot n agen, twll
Slovakia n Slofacia
Slovenia n Slofenia
slow adj araf ▸ vb arafu; **slow down** vi arafu
slowly adj yn araf (deg)
slug n gwlithen, malwoden
sluggish adj dioglyd
slum n slym
slump n cwymp, gostyngiad; dirwasgiad
slur vb difrio ▸ n llithriad, cyflusg (cerdd.); anfri
slush n llaid, llaca, eira gwlyb
sly adj cyfrwys, dichellgar
smack n (slap) smac ▸ vb smacio, chwipio
small adj bach, bychan, mân
smart vi gwynio, dolurio ▸ n gwŷn, dolur ▸ adj llym, bywiog; ffraeth; crand
smartphone n ffôn clyfar
smash vb torri, malu, chwilfriwio
smear vt iro, dwbio
smell (pt, pp **smelt**, **smelled**) n arogl, aroglau ▸ vb arogli
smelly adj drewllyd
smile vb gwenu ▸ n gwên
smirk vi cilwenu, glaswenu ▸ n cilwen
smog n smog, mwgwl
smoke n mwg ▸ vb mygu; ysmygu, smocio
smoke alarm n larwm mwg, larwm fwg
smoked adj wedi ei fygu

smoker n ysmygwr
smoking n ysmygu
smoky adj myglyd
smooth adj llyfn, esmwyth ▸ vt llyfnhau
smother vb mygu, llethu
SMS n SMS
SMS message n neges SMS
smudge n baw, smotyn ▸ vb difwyno, trochi
smug adj hunanol, cysetlyd
smuggle vt smyglo
smuggler n smyglwr
smuggling n smyglo
snack n tamaid, byrbryd
snack bar n lle am damaid
snag n rhwystr, maen tramgwydd
snail n malwoden, malwen
snake n neidr
snap vb clecian; tynnu llun ▸ n clec
snarl vi ysgyrnygu, chwyrnu
snatch vb cipio ▸ n cip; tamaid
sneak (US, pt, pp **snuck**) vi llechian ▸ n (inf) llechgi
sneer vb gwawdio, glaswenu ▸ n gwawd, glaswen
sneeze vi tisian
sniff vb ffroeni, gwyntio
snigger vb glaschwerthin
snip vb torri, cynhinio ▸ n demyn, toriad
snob n crechyn, snob
snooker n snwcer
snooze vb hepian ▸ n cyntun
snore vi chwyrnu
snort vi ffroeni, ffroenochi
snow n eira, ôd ▸ vb bwrw eira, odi
snowball n pelen eira
snowdrift n lluwch
snowman n dyn eira**S**

snow plough n aradr eira
snub¹ vt sennu ▸ n sen
snub² adj pwt, smwt
snug adj clyd, diddos

[KEYWORD]

so adv 1 (thus, likewise) felly, fel hyn, yn yr un modd; **if so** os felly; **so do** or **have I** minnau hefyd; **it's 5 o'clock — so it is!** mae'n 5 o'r gloch — ydy wir! or yn hollol!; **I hope so** gobeithio ['n wir, felly, hynny]; **so far** hyd yn hyn

2 (in comparisons etc, to such a degree) mor, cyn; **so big** mor fawr or cymaint; **she's not so clever as her brother** nid yw hi mor ddeallus â'i brawd

3: **so much** (adj, adv) cymaint; **I've got so much work** mae gennyf gymaint o waith; **I love you so much** rwy'n dy garu di gymaint; **so many** cynifer

4 (phrases): **10 or so** rhyw, tua, oddeutu, o gwmpas 10; **so long!** (inf, goodbye) da bo ti! (da boch chi!), hwyl fawr!; **so (what)?** (inf) beth am hynny?, be' wedyn?

▸ conj **1** (expressing purpose): **so as to do** er mwyn gwneud; **so (that)** i or er mwyn i; **she opened the door, so that I might go in** agorodd y drws [er mwyn] i mi gael mynd i mewn

2 (expressing result) fel; **he held me so that I could not move** fe'm daliodd fel na allwn symud; **so that's the reason!** felly dyna'r rheswm!; **so you see, I could have**

gone felly rwyt ti'n gweld, fe allwn i fod wedi mynd

soak vb mwydo; slotian
soaking adj gwlyb socian
soap n sebon ▸ vb seboni
soap opera n opera sebon
soap powder n powdr golchi
soar vi ehedeg, esgyn
sob vi igian, beichio ▸ n ig, ebwch
sober adj sobr, sad ▸ vb sobri;
sober up vi sobri
so-called adj dywededig
soccer n pêl-droed, y bêl gron
sociable adj cymdeithasgar
social adj cymdeithasol
social club n clwb cymdeithasol
socialism n sosialaeth
socialist n sosialydd
socialize vi cymdeithasu
social network n rhwydwaith cymdeithasol
social networking n rhwydweithio cymdeithasol
social security n nawdd cymdeithasol
social work n gwaith cymdeithasol
social worker n gweithiwr cymdeithasol
society n cymdeithas, cyfeillach
sociology n cymdeithaseg
sock n hosan
socket n twll, crau, soced
sofa n soffa
soft adj meddal, tyner; distaw; gwirion
soft drink n diod ysgafn
software n meddalwedd
soggy adj gwlyb, lleidiog
soil¹ n pridd, daear, gweryd

soil² *vt* difwyno, baeddu
solar *adj* heulog, solar
solar power *n* ynni'r haul, ynni haul
soldier *n* milwr
sole¹ *adj* unig, unigol, un
sole² *n* (of foot) gwadn
sole³ *n* (fish) lleden chwithig
solemn *adj* difrifol, dwys
solicitor *n* cyfreithiwr
solid¹ *adj* solet, cadarn
solid² *n* solid
solitary *adj* unig; anghyfannedd
solitude *n* unigedd
solo *n* unawd
soloist *n* unawdydd
soluble *adj* toddadwy, hydawdd
solution *n* dehongliad, esboniad; toddiant
solve *vt* datrys, dehongli
solvent *adj* yn gallu talu, di-ddyled
  ► *n* toddfa
sombre *adj* tywyll, prudd

(KEYWORD)

some *adj* **1** (a certain amount or number of) rhyw, peth, rhywfaint o (sometimes not translated); **some tea/water/ice cream** te/dŵr/hufen iâ; **some children/apples** plant/afalau; **I've got some money but not much** mae gennyf rywfaint o arian ond dim llawer
2 (certain: in contrasts): **some people say that ...** mae rhai/rhywrai yn dweud ...; **some films were excellent, but most were mediocre** roedd rhai ffilmiau'n rhagorol, ond gweddol oedd y mwyafrif
3 (unspecified): **some woman was asking for you** roedd rhyw fenyw yn gofyn amdanat; **he was asking for some book (or other)** roedd yn gofyn am ryw lyfr (neu ei gilydd); **some day** ryw ddiwrnod; **some day next week** ryw ddiwrnod yr wythnos nesaf
  ► *pron* **1** (a certain number) rhyw, peth, rhywfaint o; **I've got some** (books etc) mae gennyf rywfaint (o lyfrau etc); **some (of them) have been sold** mae rhai (ohonynt) wedi'u gwerthu
2 (a certain amount) rhywfaint, peth; **I've got some** (money, milk) mae gennyf rywfaint (o arian/laeth); **would you like some?** hoffech chi gael peth?, hoffech chi gael rhywfaint?; **could I have some of that cheese?** ga i rywfaint/beth o'r caws yna?; **I've read some of the book** rwyf wedi darllen rhywfaint/peth o'r llyfr
  ► *adv*: **some 10 people** rhyw 10 o bobl, tua 10 o bobl

somebody *pron* = someone
somehow *adv* rywfodd, rhywsut
someone *pron* rhywun
something *n* rhywbeth
sometime *adv* rywbryd, gynt
sometimes *adv* weithiau
somewhat *adv* go, lled, braidd
somewhere *adv* (yn) rhywle
son *n* mab
song *n* cân
son-in-law *n* mab yng nghyfraith
soon *adv* buan
sooner *adv* (time) ynghynt, yn gynt; **I would sooner do** (preference)

byddai'n well gennyf wneud;
sooner or later yn hwyr neu'n
hwyrach
soothe *vt* lliniaru, lleddfu, dofi,
tawelu
sophisticated *adj* soffistigedig
soprano *n* soprano
sordid *adj* brwnt
sore *adj* tost, blin, dolurus ▸ *n*
dolur
sorrow *n* tristwch, gofid, galar ▸ *vi*
tristáu, gofidio
sorry *adj* drwg gan, edifar; salw
sort *n* modd; math, bath ▸ *vt*
trefnu, dosbarthu; **sort out** *vt*
(problem) datrys; *(objects)* trefnu
so-so *adv* gweddol
soul *n* enaid
sound¹ *n* sain ▸ *vb* seinio
sound² *n (strait)* culfor, swnt
sound³ *adj* dianaf, cyfan, dilys
soundboard *n* seinfwrdd
sound effects *npl* effeithiau sain
soundtrack *n* trac sain
soup *n* potes, cawl
sour *adj* sur ▸ *vb* suro
source *n* ffynhonnell, tarddiad
south *n* deau, de
South Africa *n* De Affrica
southeast *n* de-ddwyrain ▸ *adj*
de-ddwyreiniol
southern *adj* deheuol
South Pole *n*: the South Pole
Pegwn y De
southwest *n* de-orllewin ▸ *adj*
de-orllewinol
souvenir *n* cofrodd
sovereign *adj* pen ▸ *n* penadur;
sofren
sow¹ *n* hwch

sow² *(pt* **sowed,** *pp* **sown)** *vt* hau
soya *n* soya
soya beans *npl* ffa soya
soy sauce *n* saws soi
space *n* lle, gwagle, gofod
spacecraft *n* llong ofod
spaceship *n* llong ofod
spacious *adj* eang, helaeth
spade *n* rhaw, pâl
Spain *n* Sbaen
spam *n* sbam ▸ *vt* sbamio
span *n* rhychwant ▸ *vt*
rhychwantu
Spaniard *n* Sbaenwr
Spanish *adj* Sbaenaidd ▸ *n*
(language) Sbaeneg
spank *vt* slapio, smacio, chwipio
tin
spanner *n* sbaner
spare *adj* prin; tenau; sbâr ▸ *vt*
arbed; hepgor
spare time *n* oriau hamdden,
amser sbâr
spark *n* gwreichionen
sparkle *vi* gwreichioni, pefrio
sparkling *adj* gloyw, llachar;
byrlymog
sparrow *n* aderyn y to
sparse *adj* tenau, prin, gwasgarog
spasm *n* pwl, gwayw
spate *n* llifeiriant sydyn
speak *(pt* **spoke,** *pp* **spoken)** *vb*
llefaru, siarad; **speak up** *vi (raise
voice)* siarad yn uwch
speaker *n* llefarydd, siaradwr
spear *n* gwaywffon, picell ▸ *vt*
trywanu
special *adj* neilltuol, arbennig
special effects *npl* effeithiau
arbennig

specialist n arbenigwr
speciality n arbenigrwydd
specialize vi arbenigo
specially adv yn arbennig
special needs npl anghenion arbennig
species n rhywogaeth
specific adj penodol
specify vt enwi, penodi
specimen n enghraifft, cynllun
speck n brycheuyn, ysmotyn
specs n (inf) sbectol
spectacle n drych, golygfa
spectacular adj ysblennydd, trawiadol
spectator n edrychwr, gwyliwr
spectrum n spectrwm
speculate vi dyfalu; anturio, mentro
speech n llafar, lleferydd; araith
speechless adj mud
speed (pt, pp **sped**) n cyflymder, buander ▸ vb prysuro, cyflymu; **speed up** (pt, pp **speeded up**) vi cyflymu
speedboat n cwch cyflym
speeding n goryrru, gyrru'n rhy gyflym
speed limit n terfyn cyflymder
speedometer n mesurydd cyflymdra
spell¹ n (enchantment) cyfaredd, swyn
spell² n sbel, hoe, ysbaid
spell³ (pt, pp **spelt**, **spelled**) vt sillafu
spellchecker n gwiriwr sillafu
spelling n sillafiad
spend (pt, pp **spent**) vb treulio; gwario

sperm n had
sphere n sffêr; cylch, maes
spice n perlysiau, peraroglau, sbeis
spicy adj blasus; ffraeth, diddorol; coch
spider n corryn, pryf copyn
spike n pig
spill (pt, pp **spilt**, **spilled**) vb colli, tywallt
spin (pt, pp **spun**) vb nyddu; troi, troelli
spinach n pigoglys, sbinais
spin-dryer n trowasgwr
spine n asgwrn cefn; draen, pigyn
spiral adj fel cogwrn tro, troellog
spire n meindwr, pigdwr
spirit n ysbryd; gwirod
spirits n gwirodydd
spiritual adj ysbrydol
spit¹ n bêr
spit² (pt, pp **spat**) vb poeri
spite n sbeit, malais ▸ vt sbeitio
spiteful adj maleisus, sbeitlyd
splash vb sblasio, tasgu
splendid adj ysblennydd, gwych, campus
splinter vb ysgyrioni ▸ n ysgyren, fflaw
split (pt, pp **split**) vb hollti, rhannu, gwahanu; **split up** vi hollti
spoil (pt, pp **spoiled**, **spoilt**) n ysbail ▸ vb ysbeilio, difetha
spoiled adj maldodi
spoilsport n surbwch
spoilt adj: a spoilt child plentyn sydd wedi cael ei faldodi
spoke n adain olwyn, sbogen, braich
spokesman n llefarwr, llefarydd
spokeswoman n llefaryddes

399

sponge n sbwng ▸ vb ysbyngu
sponsor n noddwr
spontaneous adj gwirfoddol,
digymell
spooky adj (inf) bwganllyd
spoon n llwy ▸ vb llwyo; caru
spoonful n llwyaid
sport n sbort, chwarae, hwyl
sports centre n canolfan
chwaraeon
sportsman n mabolgampwr
sportswear n dillad chwarae
sportswoman n mabolgampwraig
sporty adj: she's very sporty mae
hi'n hoff iawn o chwaraeon
spot n llecyn; brycheuyn, ysmotyn
▸ vt mannu, brychu, ysmotio
▸ adj ar y pryd
spotless adj difrycheulyd, glân
spotlight n sbotolau
spotty adj smotiog
spouse n priod
sprain vt ysigo
sprawl vi ymdaenu
spray¹ n gwlith, tawch, trochion
▸ vt taenellu; chwistrellu
spray² n (bouquet) ysbrigyn, cainc;
chwistrellydd
spread (pt, pp **spread**) vb lledu,
taenu, lledaenu, gwasgaru;
spread out vt (blanket, net) taenu
▸ vi (get broader) ymledu
spreadsheet n taenlen
spree n sbri
spring (pt **sprang**, pp **sprung**)
vb tarddu, deillio; llamu, neidio
▸ n ffynnon; llam; sbring;
gwanwyn
spring-clean n glanhau'r
gwanwyn

springtime n gwanwyn
sprinkle vb taenellu, ysgeintio
sprint vb gwibio
sprinter n gwibiwr
spur n ysbardun, swmbwl ▸ vb
ysbarduno, symbylu
spurt n ysbonc
spy n ysbïwr ▸ vb ysbïo
spying n (espionage) ysbïaeth
squabble vi cweryla, ffraeo ▸ n
ffrwgwd, ffrae
squad n carfan, mintai
squadron n sgwadron
squander vt gwastraffu, afradu
square adj, n sgwâr, petryal
squash vt gwasgu, llethu ▸ n
sboncen; **orange squash** sudd
oren
squat vi swatio, cyrcydu
squeak vi gwichian ▸ n gwich
squeal vi gwichian
squeeze vb gwasgu; **squeeze in**
vb gwasgu i mewn
squint vb ciledrych, cibedrych ▸ n
llygaid croes
squirm vb gwingo
squirrel n gwiwer
squirt vb chwistrellu, tasgu ▸ n
chwistrell, gwn dŵr
stab vb gwanu, trywanu
stable¹ n ystabl
stable² adj sefydlog, safadwy, sad
stack n tas, bera; corn simnai, stac
stadium n stadiwm
staff n ffon; staff
staffroom n ystafell staff
stag n carw, hydd
stage n pwynt; gradd, lefel; llwyfan
stagger vb gwegian; syfrdanu
stagnant adj llonydd, marw

stag night, stag party n noson stag

stain vb ystaenio, llychwino ▸ n staen

stainless steel n dur gloyw

staircase n grisiau

stairs n grisiau

stake n polyn, ystanc

stale adj hen; diflas

stalemate n sefyllfa ddiddatrys

stalk¹ vb torsythu, stelcian, mynd ar drywydd

stalk² n gwelltyn, coes

stall n côr; stondin; talcen glo ▸ vb stolio

stamina n saf, ynni

stammer vb bloesgi, siarad ag atal arno

stamp n stamp, argraff ▸ vb stampio; curo traed

stampede n chwalfa, rhuth

stand (pt, pp **stood**) vb sefyll ▸ n safiad; eistedde; stondin; **stand for** vi (represent) golygu; (tolerate) goddef; **stand out** vi sefyll allan; **stand up** vi sefyll

standard n lluman, baner; post; safon

standard of living n safon byw

staple¹ n (basic item) prif nwydd; edefyn (gwlân etc)

staple² n ystwffwl, stapal

star n seren ▸ vb serennu

starch n starts

stare vb llygadrythu, synnu

stark adj syth, moel, rhonc ▸ adv hollol

start vb dechrau, cychwyn; **start off** vi cychwyn

starter n (first course) cwrs cyntaf

startle vt brawychu, dychrynu, rhusio

starvation n newyn

starve vb newynu; fferru, rhynnu

state¹ n ystad, cyflwr, ansawdd; gwladwriaeth; talaith

state² vt mynegi, datgan

statement n mynegiad, datganiad

statesman n gwladweinydd

station n gorsaf, stesion; safle, sefyllfa

stationary adj sefydlog

stationer's n (shop) siop bapurau

statistics npl ystadegau

statue n cerflun

stature n uchder, taldra, corffolaeth

status n safle, statws

staunch adj pybyr, cywir

stay vb aros; ategu; atal ▸ n arhosiad; ateg; **stay behind** vi aros ar ôl; **stay in** vi (at home) aros gartref; **stay up** vi: don't stay up tonight peidiwch ag aros ar eich traed heno

steadily adv yn bwyllog, yn gyson

steady adj sad, diysgog; cyson, gwastad

steak n golwyth, stec

steal (pt **stole**, pp **stolen**) vb dwyn, lladrata

steam n ager, stêm ▸ vb ageru

steel n dur ▸ vt caledu

steep¹ adj serth ▸ n dibyn, clogwyn, llethr

steep² vt mwydo

steeple n clochdy

steer vb llywio; cyfeirio

steering n llywio

steering wheel n llyw

S

401

stem n corsen, coes, bôn; ach
step vi camu; cerdded ▶ n cam; gris
step- prefix llys-
stepbrother n llysfrawd
stepdaughter n llysferch
stepfather n llystad
stepladder n ysgol risiau
stepmother n llysfam, mam wen
stepsister n llyschwaer
stepson n llysfab
stereo n stereo
stereotype n ystrydeb ▶ vt ystrydebu
sterile adj diffrwyth, sych
sterilize vb diffrwythloni; diheintio
sterling adj ysterling; diledryw, diffuant
stern¹ adj llym, penderfynol
stern² n starn, pen ôl llong
stew vb araf ferwi, stiwio ▶ n stiw
steward n stiward, goruchwyliwr, distain
stewardess n stiwardes
stick¹ n ffon, pric, gwialen
stick² (pt, pp **stuck**) vb glynu; gwanu
▶ **stick out** vi sticio allan
sticker n sticer
sticky adj gludiog, glynol; anodd
stiff adj syth, anhyblyg
stigma n gwarthnod, stigma
still¹ adj llonydd; marw ▶ vb llonyddu
still² adv eto, er hynny; byth
stimulate vt symbylu
stimulus n symbyliad, swmbwl
sting (pt, pp **stung**) vb pigo, brathu, colynnu ▶ n colyn

stink (pt **stank**, pp **stunk**) vi, n drewi
stir vb cyffroi, cynhyrfu, symud ▶ n stŵr, cynnwrf
stitch n pwyth; gwayw, pigyn ▶ vt pwytho, gwnio
stock n cyff; stoc, ystôr; **stocks** npl cyffion; **stock up** vt: to stock up on sth cael stôr o rywbeth
stock cube n ciwb stoc
stock exchange n cyfnewidfa stoc
stocking n hosan
stole n ystola
stomach n cylla, stumog
stomach-ache n poen stumog
stone n carreg, maen ▶ vt llabyddio
stool n ystôl
stoop vb plygu, gwargrymu
stop vb atal, rhwystro; stopio, cau; aros, sefyll ▶ n atalfa; atalnod
stoppage n (pay) ataliad; (strike) streic
stopwatch n stopwatsh
storage n stôr, storfa
store n ystôr, ystorfa ▶ vt ystorio
storey, story n llawr
storm n (y)storm, tymestl
stormy adj stormus, tymhestlog
story n hanes, stori; celwydd
stout adj tew, ffyrf, pybyr, gwrol, glew
stove n stof, ffwrn
straight adj union, syth
straighten vb unioni
straightforward adj syml; didwyll, gonest
strain vb straenio, ysigo; tynhau; hidlo ▶ n straen
strainer n hidl(en)

strait adj cyfyng, cul, caeth ▸ n cyfyngder; culfor

strand n cainc (rhaff), edau

strange adj dieithr, estronol, rhyfedd

stranger n dyn dieithr, estron

strangle vt tagu, llindagu

strap n strap, cengl

strategic adj strategol

strategy n strategaeth

straw n gwellt; gwelltyn, blewyn

strawberry n mefysen, syfien

stray vi crwydro, cyfeiliorni

streak n llinell, rhes, rhesen; stremp ▸ vb gwibio

stream n ffrwd ▸ vb ffrydio, llifo

street n heol, stryd

strength n cryfder

strengthen vb cryfhau, nerthu

strenuous adj egniol, ymdrechgar

stress n pwysau, straen

stretch vb estyn, tynhau ▸ n estyniad

stretcher n trestl, stretsier

stretchy adj elastig

strict adj cyfyng, caeth, llym

stride (pt **strode**, pp **stridden**) vb camu, brasgamu ▸ n cam

strike (pt, pp **struck**) vb taro; gostwng ▸ n trawiad, streic

striker n streiciwr

striking adj trawiadol, hynod

string n llinyn, tant, cortyn

strip¹ n llain; **film strip** striplun, stribed ffilm

strip² vb diosg, ymddiosg, ymddihatru

stripe n rhes, rhesen; gwialennod

striped adj rhesog, streipiog

strive (pt **strive**, pp **striven**) vi ymdrechu; ymryson

stroke¹ n dyrnod, ergyd, trawiad; llinell

stroke² vt llochi, dylofi, pratio

stroll vi crwydro, rhodianna

strong adj cryf, cadarn

stronghold n amddiffynfa, cadarnle

strongly adv yn gryf

structure n adeilad, adeiledd, strwythur

struggle vi gwingo; ymdrechu ▸ n ymdrech

stub n bonyn

stubble n sofl

stubborn adj cyndyn, ystyfnig

student n myfyriwr, efrydydd

studio n stiwdio

study n astudiaeth, efrydiaeth ▸ vb myfyrio, efrydu, astudio

stuff n defnydd, stwff ▸ vb stwffio, gwthio

stuffing n stwffin

stuffy adj myglyd, trymllyd, trymaidd

stumble vb baglu, syrthio

stump n bonyn, boncyff

stun vt syfrdanu, hurtio

stunned adj: **to be stunned** (amazed) syfrdan

stunning adj syfrdanol

stunt vt crabio

stuntman n styntiwr

stuntwoman n styntwraig

stupid adj hurt, dwl, twp

sturdy adj cadarn, cryf

stutter vi siarad ag atal arno, bloesgi

style n dull, arddull; cyfenw, teitl
▸ vt cyfenwi
stylish adj dillyn, trwsiadus
subconscious n isymwybod ▸ adj
isymwybodol
subject¹ n deiliad; pwnc, testun;
goddrych
subject² vt darostwng, dwyn dan
subjective adj goddrychol
subjunctive adj dibynnol
submarine adj tanforol ▸ n llong
danfor
submission n ymostyngiad; ufudd-
dod; cyflwyniad
submit vb ymostwng,
ymddarostwng; datgan barn;
cyflwyno
subordinate adj israddol ▸ vt
darostwng
subscribe vb tanysgrifio, cyfrannu
subscription n tanysgrifiad,
cyfraniad
subsequent adj canlynol, dilynol
subsequently adv wedyn, ar ôl
hynny
subside vi soddi, ymollwng; darfod
subsidiary adj israddol;
ychwanegol, atodol
subsidy n arian cymorth,
cymhorthdal
substance n sylwedd, defnydd; da
substantial adj sylweddol
substitute n eilydd ▸ vt rhoi yn lle
subtitled adj gydag isdeitlau
subtitles npl is-deitlau
subtle adj cyfrwys, craff
subtract vt tynnu ymaith
suburb n maestref
subway n isffordd
succeed vb dilyn, canlyn; llwyddo

success n llwyddiant
successful adj llwyddiannus
successfully adv yn llwyddiannus
succession n dilyniad, olyniaeth
successive adj dilynol, olynol
succumb vi ildio, marw
such adj cyfryw, y fath, cyffelyb
such-and-such adj : such-and-such
a place y lle a'r lle
suck vb sugno, dyfnu
sudden adj sydyn, disymwth,
disyfyd
suddenly adv yn sydyn
sue vb erlyn; erfyn, deisyf
suede n swêd
suffer vb dioddef; goddef, caniatáu
suffering n dioddef
suffice vb bod yn ddigon, digoni
sufficient adj digon, digonol
suffocate vb mygu, tagu
sugar n siwgr ▸ vt siwgro
suggest vt awgrymu
suggestion n awgrym, awgrymiad
suicide n hunanladdiad
suicide bomber n bomiwr
hunanleiddiol
suit n cyngaws; siwt ▸ vb siwtio,
gweddu
suitable adj addas
suitcase n bag dillad
suite n cyfres; gosgordd, nifer
sulk vi sorri, pwdu
sullen adj sarrug
sulphur n sylffwr
sultanas npl swltanas
sum n swm ▸ vt crynhoi, symio;
sum up vt, vi crynhoi
summarize vb crynhoi
summary adj byr, cryno ▸ n
crynodeb

summer *n* haf
summertime *n* haf
summit *n* pen, copa
summon *vt* gwysio, dyfynnu
sun *n* haul ► *vt* heulo
sunbathe *vb* torheulo, bolaheulo
sunbed *n* gwely haul
sunblock *n* eli atal haul
sunburn *n* llosg haul
sunburnt *adj* wedi cael llosg haul
Sunday *n* dydd Sul
Sunday school *n* ysgol Sul
sunflower *n* blodyn yr haul
sunglasses *npl* sbectol haul
sunlight *n* golau'r haul
sunny *adj* heulog
sunrise *n* codiad haul
sunroof *n* to haul
sunscreen *n* eli atal haul
sunset *n* machlud haul
sunshine *n* heulwen
sunstroke *n* ergyd (yr) haul
suntan *n* lliw haul
superb *adj* ysblennydd, godidog
superficial *adj* arwynebol, bas
superintendent *n* arolygwr,
  arolygydd
superior *adj* uwch, gwell;
  uwchraddol ► *n* uchafiad,
  uwchradd
superlative *adj* uchaf; eithaf
supermarket *n* archfarchnad
supernatural *adj* goruwchnaturiol
superstition *n* coelgrefydd,
  ofergoeliaeth
superstitious *adj* coelgrefyddol,
  ofergoelus
supervise *vt* arolygu
supervision *n* arolygiaeth

supervisor *n* goruchwyliwr,
  arolygydd
supper *n* swper
supple *adj* ystwyth, hyblyg
supplement *n* atodiad ► *vt* atodi
supplier *n* cyflenwr, cyflenwydd
supplies *n* cyflenwadau
supply *vt* cyflenwi, cyflawni ► *n*
  cyflenwad
supply teacher *n* athro llanw
support *vt* cynnal ► *n* cynhaliaeth
supporter *n* cefnogwr, cefnogydd
suppose *vt* tybio, tybied, bwrw
suppress *vt* llethu, gostegu;
  atal; celu
supreme *adj* goruchaf, prif, pennaf
surcharge *n* gordal, gordoll ► *vb*
  codi gormod
sure *adj, adv* siŵr, sicr; diamau, diau
surely *adv* yn sicr, yn ddiau
surf *n* traethfor, beiston; gorewyn
  ► *vb* brigo, brigdonni
surface *n* wyneb, arwynebedd
surfboard *n* astell feiston
surfing *n* syrffio
surge *vi* ymchwyddo ► *n*
  ymchwydd
surgeon *n* llawfeddyg
surgery *n* llawfeddygaeth;
  meddygfa
surname *n* cyfenw ► *vt* cyfenwi
surpass *vt* rhagori ar, trechu
surplus *n* gormod, gwarged
surprise *n* syndod ► *vt* synnu
surprised *adj* syn, wedi synnu
surprising *adj* syn, rhyfedd
surrender *vb* traddodi, ildio
surrogate mother *n* mam fenthyg
surround *vt* amgylchu,
  amgylchynu

S

surroundings *npl* amgylchoedd
surveillance *n* arolygiaeth, gwyliadwriaeth
survey *vt* edrych, arolygu; mesur ▸ *n* arolwg
survival *n* goroesiad
survive *vb* goroesi
survivor *n* goroeswr
suspect *vt* drwgdybio, amau ▸ *n* un a ddrwgdybir
suspend *vt* crogi; gohirio, atal
suspended sentence *n* dedfryd wedi'i gohirio
suspense *n* pryder, petruster, oediad
suspension *n* ataliad
suspension bridge *n* pont grog
suspicion *n* drwgdybiaeth, amheuaeth
suspicious *adj* drwgdybus, amheus
sustain *vt* cynnal; dioddef
swallow¹ *n* gwennol
swallow² *vt* llyncu ▸ *n* llwnc
swamp *n* cors ▸ *vt* gorlifo, boddi
swan *n* alarch
swap *vb* ffeirio
swarm *n* haid ▸ *vi* heidio, heigio
sway *vb* siglo, gwegian; llywio ▸ *n* llywodraeth, swae
swear (*pt* **swore**, *pp* **sworn**) *vb* tyngu, rhegi
swearword *n* rheg
sweat *n* chwys ▸ *vb* chwysu
sweater *n* cot wlan, sweter
sweatshirt *n* crys chwys
sweaty *adj* chwyslyd
Swede *n* Swediad
swede *n* rwden, sweden
Sweden *n* Sweden

Swedish *adj* Swedaidd; *(language)* Swedeg
sweep (*pt*, *pp* **swept**) *vb* ysgubo ▸ *n* ysgubiad; ysgubwr
sweet *adj* melys, pêr, peraidd ▸ *n* pwdin
sweetcorn *n* corn melys
sweetheart *n* cariad
swell (*pt* **swelled**, *pp* **swollen**, **swelled**) *vb* chwyddo ▸ *n* chwydd, ymchwydd; gŵr mawr
swelling *n* chwydd(i)
swerve *vi* gwyro, osgoi
swift *adj* cyflym, clau
swim (*pt* **swam**, *pp* **swum**) *vb* nofio ▸ *n* nawf
swimmer *n* nofiwr
swimming *n* nofio
swimming pool *n* pwll nofio
swimming trunks *npl* trowsus nofio
swimsuit *n* dillad nofio, gwisg nofio
swing (*pt*, *pp* **swung**) *vb* siglo ▸ *n* sigl, siglen, swing
swipe card *n* cerdyn sweip
swirl *vb* troi, chwyldroi, chwyrndroi
Swiss *n* Swisiad ▸ *adj* Swisaidd
switch *n* swits, botwm ▸ *vb* troi, newid; **switch off** *vt* diffodd; **switch on** *vt* dodi, troi ymlaen; cychwyn
switchboard *n* switsfwrdd
Switzerland *n* y Swistir
swivel *n* bwylltid ▸ *vb* troi
swollen *adj* chwyddedig, wedi chwyddo
swoop *vb* dod ar warthaf, disgyn
swop *vt* cyfnewid, ffeirio
sword *n* cleddyf

swot n swot ► vi swotio
syllable n sillaf
syllabus n rhaglen, maes llafur
symbol n symbol
symmetrical adj cymesur
symmetry n cymesuredd
sympathetic adj cydymdeimladol
sympathize vi cydymdeimlo
sympathy n cydymdeimlad
symphony n symffoni
symptom n arwydd
synagogue n synagog
syndicate n cwmni
synonym n (gair) cyfystyr
Syria n Syria
syringe n chwistrell ► vt
  chwistrellu
syrup n surop; triagl (melyn)
system n system
systematic adj cyfundrefnol

tab n tafod, llabed
table n bwrdd, bord; tabl
table-cloth n lliain bord (bwrdd)
tablespoon n llwy fwrdd
tablet n llechen, llech; tabled
table tennis n tennis bwrdd, ping
  pong
taboo n ysgymunbeth;
  gwaharddiad, tabŵ
tack n tac, pwyth, brasbwyth
  ► vb tacio
tackle n taclau, offer; (in rugby)
  tacl, taclad ► vb ymosod ar,
  taclo
tact n tact, doethineb
tactful adj doeth, pwyllog
tactics npl cynlluniau, tactegau
tactile adj cyffyrddol
tactless adj di-dact, annoeth
tadpole n penbwl, penbwla
tag n clust, dolen
tail n cynffon, cwt
tailor n teiliwr

take (*pt* **took**, *pp* **taken**) *vb*
cymryd; **take after** *vt*: **to take**
after sb bod yn debyg i rywun;
take apart *vt* datgymalu; **take**
away *vt* mynd â; **take back** *vt*
mynd yn ôl â; **take down** *vt*
(*dismantle, remove*) tynnu i lawr;
(*make a note of*) nodi; **take in** *vi*
(*grasp*) deall; **take off** *vi* (*plane*)
esgyn, mynd i'r awyr ► *vt* (*remove*)
tynnu; **take out** *vt* (*produce,*
remove) tynnu; **take over** *vi*
cymryd drosodd; **to take over**
from someone cymryd lle rhywun

takeaway *n* (*food*) bwyd parod;
(*shop*) siop bwyd parod

tale *n* chwedl, clec, clep

talent *n* talent

talented *adj* talentog

talk *vb, n* siarad

talkative *adj* siaradus

tall *adj* tal, uchel

tambourine *n* tambwrîn

tame *adj* dof, gwâr ► *vt* dofi

tamper *vi* ymhél(â), ymyrryd(â)

tampon *n* tampwn

tan *vb* trin lledr; llosgi, melynu

tangerine *n* tanjerîn

tangle *vb* drysu, cymysgu ► *n*
dryswch, cymhlethdod

tank *n* dyfrgist, tanc

tanker *n* tancer, llong olew

Tanzania *n* Tansanïa

tap¹ *vb* taro yn ysgafn

tap² *n* tap, feis

tape *n* tâp, incil

tape measure *n* tâp mesur

tape recorder *n* recordydd tâp,
peiriant recordio

tapestry *n* tapestri

tar *n* tar; llongwr, morwr

target *n* nod, targed

tariff *n* toll; rhestr taliadau, rhestr
prisiau

tarmac *n* tarmac

tarpaulin *n* tarpolin

tart¹ *n* tarten, pastai

tart² *adj* sur, surllyd

tartan *n* brithwe, plod

task *n* gorchwyl, tasg ► *vt* rhoi
tasg

taste *vb* blasu, profi ► *n* blas;
chwaeth

tasty *adj* blasus

tattoo *n* tatŵ ► *vb* torri llun (yn
y croen)

taunt *vt* edliw, dannod, gwatwar
► *n* gwaradwydd, sen

Taurus *n* y Tarw

taut *adj* tyn

tax *n* treth ► *vt* trethu

taxi *n* tacsi

taxi driver *n* gyrrwr tacsi

taxi rank *n* lloc dacsi

tea *n* te

tea bag *n* bag te, cwdyn te

teach (*pt, pp* **taught**) *vt* dysgu,
addysgu

teacher *n* athro

teaching *n* dysgeidiaeth; dysgu

teaching assistant *n*
cynorthwydd dysgu

teacup *n* disgl de, cwpan te

tea leaves *n* dail te

team *n* gwedd, pâr, tîm

teapot *n* tebot

tear¹ *n* deigryn, deigr

tear² (*pt* **tore**, *pp* **torn**) *vb* rhwygo,
llarpio ► *n* rhwyg
► **tear up** *vt* rhwygo

tearful *adj* dagreuol
tease *vt* pryfocio, plagio, poeni
teaspoon *n* llwy de
teatime *n* amser te
tea towel *n* lliain sychu llestri
technical *adj* technegol
technician *n* technegydd
technique *n* techneg
technology *n* technoleg
teddy, teddy bear *n* tedi, tedi bêr
tedious *adj* blin, poenus
teenage *adj*: **a teenage boy** bachgen yn ei arddegau
teenager *n* un yn yr arddegau
teens *n* arddegau
telegram *n* teligram
telephone *n* teliffon, ffôn
telephone box *n* bocs ffonio
telephone call *n* galwad ffôn
telephone directory *n* cyfeirlyfr ffôn
telescope *n* ysbienddrych, telisgob
televise *vb* teledu
television *n* teledu
tell (*pt, pp* **told**) *vb* dweud, adrodd; cyfrif, rhifo; **tell off** *vt* dweud y drefn wrth, cystwyo
telly *n* (*inf*) teledu
temper *n* tymer, naws ▸ *vt* tymheru
temperament *n* anianawd
temperamental *adj* gwamal, oriog, di-ddal
temperature *n* tymheredd
temple¹ *n* (*building*) teml
temple² *n* (*Anat*) arlais
temporary *adj* dros dro, tymhorol
tempt *vt* temtio, profi
temptation *n* temtiad, temtasiwn
tempting *adj* deniadol

ten *adj, n* deg
tenant *n* deiliad, tenant
tend *vi* tueddu
tendency *n* tuedd, gogwydd
tender *adj* tyner, tirion, mwyn; meddal
tendon *n* gewyn
tennis *n* tennis
tennis ball *n* pêl dennis
tennis court *n* cwrt tennis
tennis player *n* chwaraewr tennis
tennis racket *n* raced tennis
tenor *n* cyfeiriad, tuedd, rhediad; tenor
tenpin bowling *n* bowlio decbinnau
tense¹ *adj* tyn
tense² *n* amser (berf)
tension *n* tyndra, pwysau
tent *n* pabell
tentative *adj* arbrofiadol, dros dro; ansicr
tenth *adj* degfed
tepid *adj* claear
term *n* terfyn; term; teler; tymor ▸ *vt* galw, enwi
terminal *adj* terfynol, termol
terminally *adv*: **terminally ill** gydag afiechyd terfynol
terminate *vb* terfynu
terminology *n* terminoleg
terminus *n* terfynfa
terrace *n* rhes dai, teras
terraced *adj*: **terraced house** tŷ rhes
terrain *n* tir
terrestrial *adj* daearol
terrible *adj* dychrynllyd, ofnadwy, arswydus
terribly *adv* yn ofnadwy

t

terrier n daeargi
terrific adj dychrynllyd, arswydus
terrified adj mewn arswyd; **to be terrified of sth** arswydo rhag rhywbeth
terrify vt brawychu, dychrynu
terrifying adj brawychus, dychrynllyd
territorial adj tiriogaethol
territory n tir, tiriogaeth
terror n dychryn, braw, arswyd
terrorism n terfysgaeth
terrorist n terfysgwr, brawychwr
test n prawf ▶ vt profi
testicle n caill, carreg
testify vb tystio
testimony n tystiolaeth
test tube n tiwb prawf
tetanus n gên glo, tetanws
text[1] n testun, adnod
text[2] vt tecstio
textbook n gwerslyfr
textile adj gweol
text message n neges destun
texture n gwead, cyfansoddiad
Thailand n Gwlad Thai
Thames n Tafwys
than conj na, nag
thank vt, n diolch
thankful adj diolchgar
thanks npl diolch, diolchiadau
thanksgiving n diolchgarwch

[KEYWORD]

that adj (pl **those**) (demonstrative, after masc. n.) hwnnw (hynny), pl, yna, acw; (after fem. n.) honno (hynny), yna, acw; **that book** y llyfr hwnnw, y llyfr yna (within sight) y llyfr acw; **those books** y llyfrau hynny, y llyfrau yna (within sight)

y llyfrau acw; **that one** hwnyna (honyna), hwnna (honna)
▶ pron 1 (pl **those**) (demonstrative) hwnyna (honyna), hwnna (honna); **who's that?** pwy yw hwnna?, pwy yw honna?; **what's that?** beth yw hynny?; **is that you?** [ai] ti sydd yna?; **I prefer this to that** mae'n well gen i hwn/hon na hwnna/honna; **that's what he said** dyna a ddywedodd; **will you eat all that?** a wnei di fwyta hynny i gyd?; **that is (to say)** hynny yw 2 (relative: subject) a (plus inflected form of verb: all tenses,) or (in present tense) yr hwn, yr hon, y rhai sydd yn + vn; **the book that I read** y llyfr a ddarllenais; **the books that are in the library** y llyfrau sydd yn y llyfrgell; **all that I have** y cyfan sydd gennyf; **the box that I put it in** y blwch y rhoddais y peth ynddo; **the people that I spoke to** y bobl y siaredais â nhw 3 (relative: of time): **the day that he came** y diwrnod y daeth e
▶ conj bod; **he thought that I was ill** roedd yn credu fy mod yn sâl
▶ adv (demonstrative): **I don't like it that much** dwy ddim yn ei hoffi gymaint â hynny; **I didn't know it was that bad** wyddwn i ddim ei bod hi gynddrwg â hynny; **it's about that high** mae tua mor uchel â hynny

thaw vb dadlaith, dadmer, meirioli

[KEYWORD]

the def art 1 (gen) y, yr, 'r; **the boy** y bachgen; **the apple** yr afal; **the**

history of the world hanes y byd;
give it to the postman rhowch e
i'r postmon
2 *(+ adj to form n)*: **the rich and the
poor** y cyfoethogion a'r tlodion; **to
attempt the impossible** mentro'r
amhosibl
3 *(in titles)*: **Elizabeth the First**
Elisabeth y gyntaf; **Peter the Great**
Pedr Fawr
4 *(in comparisons)*: **the more he
works, the more he earns** mwya'n
y byd y mae'n gweithio, mwya'n y
byd y mae'n ei ennill

theatre *n* theatr; maes, golygfa
theft *n* lladrad
their *pron* eu
theirs *pron* yr eiddynt, eiddynt
hwy
them *pron* hwy, hwynt, hwythau
theme *n* thema
theme park *n* parc thema
themselves *pron* eu hunain
then *adv* y pryd hwnnw, yna
▸ *conj* yna
theology *n* diwinyddiaeth
theory *n* damcaniaeth, tyb
therapy *n* therapi

(KEYWORD)

there *adv* **1**: **there is, there are** mae
yna; **there are 3 of them** *(people,
things)* mae yna 3 ohonynt; **there
is no-one here/no bread left** nid
oes neb yma/bara ar ôl; **there has
been an accident** mae damwain
wedi digwydd
2 *(referring to place)* acw, yna, yno;

it's there mae e acw; **in/on/up/
down there** yn/ar/i fyny/i lawr
[yn y] fanna; **he went there on
Friday** aeth yno ddydd Gwener; **I
want that book there** y llyfr yna yr
hoffwn ei gael; **there he is!** dyna fe!
3: **there, there!** *(esp to child)*
dyna ni!

thereafter *adv* wedyn
thereby *adv* trwy hynny
therefore *conj* gan hynny, am
hynny
thermal *adj* thermol
thermometer *n* thermomedr,
mesurydd gwres
these *adj pl* y rhai hyn, y rhai yma
thesis *n* gosodiad; traethawd,
thesis
they *pron* hwy, hwynt, hwynt-hwy
thick *adj* tew, praff, trwchus
thicken *vb* tewhau, tewychu
thickness *n* trwch, tewder
thief *n* lleidr
thigh *n* clun, morddwyd
thin *adj* tenau, cul, main; anaml,
prin ▸ *vb* teneuo
thing *n* peth, dim
think *(pt, pp* **thought***) vb*
meddwl
third *adj* trydydd, trydedd
thirdly *adv* yn drydydd
Third World *n* Trydydd Byd
thirst *n* syched ▸ *vi* sychedu
thirsty *adj* sychedig; **I am thirsty**
mae syched arna i
thirteen *adj, n* tri (tair) ar ddeg, un
deg tri (tair)

411

thirteenth adj trydydd (trydedd) ar ddeg

thirty adj, n deg ar hugain, tri deg

[KEYWORD]

this adj (pl **these**) (demonstrative) hwn m, hon f, hyn pl or indeter; **this man/woman** y dyn hwn/y fenyw hon; **this one** hwn, hon, hyn
▶ pron (pl **these**) (demonstrative) hwn, hon, hyn (not that one) hwn yma, hon yma, hyn yma; **who's this?** pwy yw hwn?; **what's this?** beth yw hwn?; **I prefer this to that** mae'n well gennyf hwn yma na hwn yna; **this is where I live** dyma ble rwy'n byw; **this is what he said** dyma'r hyn a ddywedodd; **this is Mr Brown** (in introductions) dyma Mr Brown (in photo) dyma Mr Brown (on telephone) Mr Brown yn siarad
▶ adv (demonstrative): **it was about this big** roedd tua'r maint yma; **I didn't know it was this bad** wyddwn i ddim ei bod hi gynddrwg â hyn

thistle n ysgallen
thorn n draen, draenen; pigyn
thorough adj trwyadl, trylwyr
those adj pl y rhai hynny, y rhai yna
though conj er
thought n meddwl
thoughtful adj meddylgar, ystyriol
thoughtless adj difeddwl, anystyriol
thousand adj, n mil
thousandth adj milfed
thrash vt dyrnu, ffusto, curo

thread n edau, edefyn
threat n bygwth, bygythiad
threaten vt bygwth
threatening adj bygythiol
three adj, n tri, tair
threshold n trothwy, rhiniog
thrill vb gwefreiddio ▶ n ias, gwefr
thrilled adj: **I'm thrilled** dw i wrth fy modd; **she was thrilled to hear that** roedd hi wrth ei bodd o glywed hynny
thriller n stori iasoer
thrilling adj cyffrous, gwefreiddiol
throat n gwddf
throb vi dychlamu, curo
throne n gorsedd, gorseddfainc
through prep trwy ▶ adv trwodd
throughout prep trwy, trwy gydol
▶ adv trwodd
throw (pt **threw**, pp **thrown**) n tafliad ▶ vb taflu, lluchio; **throw away** vt taflu, lluchio; **throw out** vt taflu; **throw up** vi taflu i fyny
thrush n bronfraith
thrust (pt, pp **thrust**) vb gwthio
▶ n gwth
thud n twrf, sŵn trwm
thug n llindagwr, dihiryn
thumb n bawd ▶ vt bodio
thump vb dyrnodio, pwnio
thunder n taran(au), tyrfau, trystau ▶ vb taranu
thunderstorm n storm dyrfau
Thursday n dydd Iau
thus adv fel hyn, felly
thwart vb rhwystro
thyme n teim
tick¹ n tipian, tic
tick² vt (mark) ticio ▶ n tic
ticket n tocyn, ticed

to

ticket collector n tocynnwr
ticket inspector n arolygwr tocynnau
ticket office n swyddfa docynnau
tickle vb goglais, gogleisio ▸ n goglais
ticklish n gogleisiol; anodd, dyrys
tide n llanw, teid; **high tide** penllanw; **low tide** trai
tidy adj taclus, twt, destlus; **tidy up** vt tacluso
tie vt clymu, rhwymo ▸ n cwlwm, cadach; **tie up** vt clymu
tier n rhes, rheng
tiger n teigr
tight adj tyn, cryno, twt; cyfyng
tighten vb tynhau
tightly adv yn dyn
tights npl teits
tile n priddlech, teilsen
till prep, conj hyd
tilt vb gogwyddo
timber n coed, pren
time n amser ▸ vt amseru
timely adj amserol, prydlon
timetable n amserlen
timid adj ofnus, llwfr
timing n amseriad
tin n alcam, tun
tinfoil n ffoel alcam
tingle vi ysu
tinker n (inf) tincer ▸ vb tincera
tinned adj mewn tun, tun
tin opener n agorwr tuniau
tint n lliw, arlliw, gwawr ▸ vt lliwio
tinted adj wedi ei liwio
tiny adj bychan, bach, pitw
tip¹ n (point) blaen, pen

tip² vb troi, dymchwelyd; gwobrwyo ▸ n tip, tomen; cyngor; gwobr, cil-dwrn
tiptoe n: **on tiptoe** ar flaenau ei draed
tire¹ vb blino, lluddedu, diffygio
tire², tyre n teiar
tired adj blinedig
tiring adj blinedig
tissue n meinwe
tissue paper n papur sidan
title n teitl

KEYWORD

to prep (with noun/pronoun) **1** (direction) i; (towards) tua; at; **to go to France/London/school** mynd i Ffrainc/i Lundain/i'r ysgol; **to go to John's** mynd i dŷ John, mynd i weld John; **to go to the doctor's** mynd at y meddyg; **the road to Edinburgh** y ffordd i Gaeredin **2** (as far as) i, hyd at; **to count to 10** cyfrif i 10, cyfrif hyd at 10; **from 40 to 50 people** o 40 i 50 o bobl **3** (with expressions of time): **a quarter to 5** chwarter i 5; **it's twenty to 3** mae'n ugain munud i 3 **4** (for, of): **the key to the front door** allwedd y drws blaen; **a letter to his wife** llythyr at ei wraig **5** (expressing indirect object) i; **to give sth to sb** rhoi rhth i rn; **to talk to sb** siarad â rhn; **to be a danger to sb** bod yn berygl i rn **6** (in relation to) i; **3 goals to 2** 3 gôl i 2; **30 miles to the gallon** 30 milltir i'r galwyn **7** (purpose, result): **to come to sb's aid** cynorthwyo/helpu rhn, dod i

413

gynorthwyo/helpu rhn, dod i roi
cymorth i rn; **to sentence sb to
death** dedfrydu rhn i farwolaeth;
to my surprise er syndod i mi
▶ *prep (with vb):* **1** *(simple infinitive):*
to go/eat bwyta/mynd
2 *(following another vb):* **to want/
try/start to do** dymuno/ceisio/
dechrau gwneud
3 *(with vb omitted):* **I don't want to**
nid oes arnaf eisiau [gwneud]
4 *(purpose, result)* i; **I did it to help
you** fe'i gwneuthum i'ch helpu
5 *(equivalent to relative clause):* **I
have things to do** mae gennyf
bethau i'w gwneud; **the main
thing is to try** y peth pwysig yw
rhoi cynnig arni
6 *(after adjective etc):* **ready to go**
parod i fynd; **too old/young to ...**
rhy hen/ifanc i ...
▶ *adv:* **push/pull the door to**
gwthio/tynnu'r drws

toad *n* llyffant du dafadennog
toadstool *n* caws llyffant, bwyd
y boda
toast *n* tost; llwncdestun ▶ *vb*
tostio
toaster *n* tostiwr
toastie *n* (*inf*) brechdan grasu
tobacco *n* tybaco, baco
toboggan *n* tybogan, car llusg
today *adv* heddiw
toddler *n* plentyn bach
toe *n* bys troed; blaen carn ceffyl
toffee *n* taffi, cyflaith
together *adv* ynghyd, gyda'i gilydd
toilet *n* trwsiad, gwisgiad; ystafell
ymolchi, tŷ bach

toilet paper *n* papur tŷ bach
toiletries *n* pethau ymolchi
toilet roll *n* rholyn toiled, rholyn
tŷ bach
toilet water *n* dŵr Groeg
token *n* arwydd, argoel; tocyn
tolerant *adj* goddefgar
tolerate *vt* goddef
toll¹ *n* toll, treth
toll² *vb* canu (cloch, cnul)
tomato *n* tomato
tomb *n* bedd, beddrod
tomboy *n* hoeden, rhampen
tomorrow *adv* yfory
ton *n* tunnell
tone *n* tôn, oslef ▶ *vb* tyneru,
lleddfu
tongs *npl* gefel
tongue *n* tafod; iaith
tonic *n* meddyginiaeth gryfhaol,
tonic
tonic water *n* dŵr tonig
tonight *adv* heno
tonsil *n* tonsil
tonsillitis *n* llid y tonsil
tonsils *n* tonsiliau
too *adv* rhy; hefyd; **too much**
gormod
tool *n* arf, erfyn
tooth *n* dant
toothache *n* dannoedd
toothbrush *n* brws dannedd
toothpaste *n* sebon dannedd, past
dannedd
toothpick *n* pic dannedd
top *n* pen, brig, copa ▶ *vt* tocio;
rhagori ar; **top up** *vt* ail-lenwi; **to
top up one's mobile (phone)** rhoi
credyd ar eich ffôn symudol
topic *n* pwnc

topical *adj* amserol
topple *vb* syrthio, cwympo, dymchwel
torch *n* torts, ffagl
torment *n* poen, poenedigaeth ▸ *vt* poeni, poenydio
torn *adj* wedi ei rwygo, rhwygedig
tornado *n* hyrddwynt, corwynt
torpedo *n* torpedo
torrent *n* cenllif, llifeiriant, rhyferthwy
torrential *adj* llifeiriol, trwm
tortoise *n* crwban
torture *n* dirboen, artaith ▸ *vt* arteithio
Tory *n* Tori, ceidwadwr ▸ *adj* toriaidd
toss *vb* taflu, lluchio
total *adj* hollol, cyflawn ▸ *n* cyfan, cyfanswm
totalitarian *adj* totalitaraidd
totally *adv* yn llwyr, yn gyfan, yn ei grynswth
touch *vb* teimlo, cyffwrdd ▸ *n* teimlad
touched *adj* dan deimlad
touching *adj* teimladwy
touch-line *n* yr ystlys
touchpad *n* pad cyffwrdd
tough *adj* gwydn, caled, cyndyn
tour *n* tro, taith
tourism *n* twristiaeth
tourist *n* teithiwr, ymwelydd, twrist
tourist office *n* swyddfa twristiaid
tournament *n* twrnamaint
tow¹ *n* carth
tow² *vt* llusgo, tynnu
toward, towards *prep* tua, tuag at
towel *n* lliain sychu, tywel

tower *n* tŵr ▸ *vi* esgyn, ymgodi, sefyll yn uchel
town *n* tref
town centre *n* canol(y) dref
town clerk *n* clerc y dref
town council *n* cyngor y dref
town hall *n* neuadd y dref
toxic *adj* gwenwynig
toy *n* tegan ▸ *vi* chwarae, maldodi
trace *vt* olrhain, dilyn
track *n* ôl, brisg; llwybr ▸ *vt* olrhain; **track down** *vt* dod o hyd i
tracksuit *n* tracwisg
tract *n* (*of land*) ardal, rhandir
tractor *n* tractor
trade *n* masnach; crefft ▸ *vb* masnachu
trade-mark *n* nod masnach
trader *n* masnachwr
trade-union *n* undeb llafur
tradition *n* traddodiad
traditional *adj* traddodiadol
traffic *vb* masnachu, trafnidio ▸ *n* masnach, trafnidiaeth
traffic jam *n* tagfa
traffic lights *npl* goleuadau traffig
traffic warden *n* warden traffig
tragedy *n* trasiedi, trychineb
tragic *adj* trychinebus, alaethus
trail *n* ôl ▸ *vb* llusgo
trailer *n* ôl-gerbyd, cart; rhaglun (ffilm)
train *vb* hyfforddi, ymarfer ▸ *n* gosgordd; godre; trên, cerbydres
trainee *adj, n* hyfforddedig
trainer *n* hyfforddwr
trainers *npl* esgidiau ymarfer, treners, trenars
training *n* hyfforddiant, disgyblaeth

t

training course n cwrs hyfforddiant

training shoes npl esgidiau ymarfer

trait n nodwedd

traitor n bradwr, teyrnfradwr

tram n tram

tramp vb crwydro, trampio ► n crwydryn

trample vb sathru, sangu

trampoline n trampolîn

tranquil adj tawel, llonydd, digyffro

tranquillizer n tawelyn, tawelydd

transaction n trafodaeth

transcript n copi, adysgrifiad

transfer vt trosglwyddo ► n trosglwyddiad

transform vt trawsffurfio

transformation n trawsffurfiad

transfusion n trosglwyddiad (gwaed), trallwysiad (gwaed)

transit n mynediad dros, trosiad

transition n trosiad, trawsgyweiriad

transitive adj anghyflawn

translate vt cyfieithu

translation n cyfieithiad

translator n cyfieithydd

transmission n trosglwyddiad

transmit vt anfon, trosglwyddo

transmitter n trosglwyddydd

transparent adj tryloyw

transplant vt trawsblannu

transport vt trosglwyddo; alltudio ► n trosglwyddiad; cludiant; perlewyg, gorawen

trap n trap, magl; car bach ► vt dal, maglu

trash n (inf) sothach, gwehilion, ysbwriel

travel vb teithio, trafaelio ► n teithio

travel agency n swyddfa deithio

travel agent n asiant teithio

traveller n teithiwr, trafaeliwr

traveller's cheque n siec deithio

travelling adj teithiol

travel sickness n salwch teithio

tray n hambwrdd

treacherous adj twyllodrus

treacle n triagl

tread (pt **trod**, pp **trodden**) vb sathru, sengi, troedio ► n sang

treasure n trysor ► vt trysori

treasurer n trysorydd

treasury n trysorfa, trysordy, y Trysorlys

treat vb trin; tretio; traethu ► n gwledd, amheuthun

treatment n triniaeth, ymdriniaeth

treaty n cyfamod, cytundeb

treble adj triphlyg ► n trebl ► vb treblu

tree n pren, coeden

trek vi mudo ► n mud, mudo

tremble vi crynu

tremendous adj dychrynllyd, ofnadwy, anferth

trench n ffos, rhych ► vb ffosi

trend vi tueddu ► n tuedd, gogwydd

trendy adj trendi

trespass vi tresmasu ► n tresmasiad

trial n prawf, profedigaeth, treial

trial period n cyfnod prawf

triangle n triongl

triangular adj trionglog

tribe n llwyth, tylwyth, gwehelyth

tribunal n tribiwnlys

tribute n teyrnged, treth

trick n tric, cast, ystryw ▸ vt castio

trickle vi diferu, diferynnu

tricky adj ystrywgar; anodd

tricycle n treisigl

trifle n gronyn, mymryn; treiffl ▸ vt ofera, cellwair

trigger n cliced, triger

trim adj taclus, twt ▸ vb taclu, trwsio ▸ n diwyg, trefn

trio n triawd

trip vb tripio, maglu; disodli ▸ n trip, tro

triple adj triphlyg

triplets n tripledi

tripod n trybedd

triumph n gorfoledd, buddugoliaeth ▸ vi gorfoleddu; buddugoliaethu

triumphant adj buddugoliaethus

trivial adj dibwys, diwerth

trolley, trolly n troli

trombone n trombôn

troop n torf, mintai ▸ vb tyrru; **troops** npl lluoedd, minteioedd

trophy n gwobr, tlws

tropical adj trofannol

trot vb tuthio, trotian ▸ n tuth, trot

trouble vt blino, trafferthu ▸ n blinder, helbul, trafferth

troubled adj anesmwyth, pryderus

troublemaker n codwr twrw

troublesome adj blinderus, trafferthus

trough n cafn

trousers npl trowsus, trwser

trout n brithyll

truant n triawnt, mitsiwr

truce n cadoediad

truck n trwc, gwagen

true adj gwir, cywir

truly adv yn wir, yn ddiau, yn gywir

trumpet n trwmped

trunk n cyff, cist; corff; duryn, trwnc

trust n ymddiriedaeth; ymddiriedolaeth ▸ vb hyderu, ymddiried

trustworthy adj y gellir dibynnu arno

truth n gwir, gwirionedd

truthful adj geirwir

try vb ceisio, treio; **try on** vt: **to try sth on** trio rhywbeth amdanoch chi; **try out** vt: **to try sth out** rhoi rhywbeth ar brawf

trying adj poenus, anodd, blin

T-shirt n crys-T

tub n twba, twb

tube n tiwb

tuberculosis n darfodedigaeth, dicáu, dicléin

tuck vt cwtogi, plygu ▸ n plyg, twc

Tuesday n dydd Mawrth

tug vb llusgo, tynnu

tuition n addysg, hyfforddiant

tulip n tiwlip

tumble vb cwympo ▸ n codwm, cwymp

tumble dryer n peiriant sychu dillad

tumbler n gwydryn

tummy n (inf) bola

tumour n tiwmor

tuna n tiwna

tune n tôn, tiwn, cywair ▸ vb cyweirio

tunic n crysbais, siaced

417

Tunisia n Tunisia
tunnel n ceuffordd, twnnel
turbulence n terfysg, cynnwrf
turf n tywarchen
Turk n Twrc
Turkey n Twrci
turkey n twrci
Turkish adj Twrcaidd
turmoil n trafferth, ffwdan, berw
turn vb troi ▸ n tro, trofa; **turn
  back** vi troi yn ôl; **turn down**
  vt (lower) troi i lawr; (refuse)
  gwrthod; **turn off** vt difodd; **turn
  on** vt troi ymlaen; **turn round**
  vi troi o gwmpas; **turn up** vb
  troi i fyny
turning n tro; tröedigaeth
turning point n trobwynt
turnip n erfinen, meipen
turnout n cynulliad
turnover n trosiant
turquoise n maen glas
  (gwerthfawr)
turtle n crwban môr
tusk n ysgithrddant, ysgithr
tutor n athro, hyfforddwr ▸ vt
  hyfforddi
tutorial adj tiwtorial
TV n abbr teledu
tweed n brethyn gwlân, twid
tweezers n gefel fach
twelfth adj deuddegfed
twelve adj, n deuddeg, un deg dau
twentieth adj ugeinfed
twenty adj, n ugain
twice adv dwywaith
twig n brigyn, ysbrigyn, impyn
twilight n cyfnos, cyfddydd
twin n gefell
twinkle vi serennu, pefrio

twinned adj gefeilliedig
twin town n gefeilldref
twist vb nyddu, cyfrodeddu; troi
  ▸ n tro; edau gyfrodedd
twit (inf) n dannod, edliw; un ffôl
twitch vb tymhigo, brathgnoi ▸ n
  tymig
two adj, n dau, dwy
type n math, teip
typewriter n teipiadur, peiriant
  teipio
typhoid n twymyn yr ymysgaroedd
typhoon n corwynt
typical adj arwyddol,
  nodweddiadol
typist n teipydd
tyre n teiar

u

UFO *n* UFO
Uganda *n* Uganda, Iwganda
ugly *adj* hagr, hyll
UK *n abbr* (= *United Kingdom*) Deyrnas Unedig, DU
ulcer *n* wlser
ultimate *adj* diwethaf, olaf, eithaf
ultimately *adv* o'r diwedd
ultimatum *n* y gair olaf, y rhybudd olaf
umbrella *n* ambarél, ymbarél
umpire *n* dyfarnwr, canolwr
unable *adj* analluog
unacceptable *adj* anghymeradwy, annerbyniol
unanimous *adj* unfrydol
unarmed *adj* diamddiffyn, heb arfau
unavoidable *adj* anorfod
unaware *adj* anymwybodol
unawares *adv* yn ddiarwybod
unbearable *adj* annioddefol
unbelievable *adj* anhygoel

unbutton *vb* datod, datfotymu
uncalled-for *adj* di-alw-amdano
uncanny *adj* rhyfedd
uncertain *adj* ansicr
uncle *n* ewythr
uncomfortable *adj* anghysurus
uncommon *adj* anghyffredin
unconditional *adj* diamod
unconscious *adj* anymwybodol
uncontrollable *adj* aflywodraethus
unconventional *adj* anghonfensiynol
uncover *vb* datguddio
undecided *adj* petrus, mewn penbleth
undeniable *adj* anwadadwy
under *prep* tan ▸ *adv* tanodd, oddi tanodd
underage *adj* dan oed
underestimate *vb* prisio'n rhy isel
undergraduate *n* myfyriwr israddedig
underground *adj* tanddaearol
underline *vb* tanlinellu, pwysleisio
undermine *vb* tanseilio
underneath *adv* oddi tanodd ▸ *prep* tan
underpants *n* trôns
underpass *n* ffordd danddaearol, tanffordd
understand *vt* deall, dirnad
understanding *n* amgyffred, dealltwriaeth
understatement *n* tanosodiad
undertake *vb* ymgymryd
undertaker *n* ymgymerydd; saer (coffinau)
undertaking *adj* ymrwymiad
underwater *adj* tanddwr

underwear n dillad isaf
underworld n annwn
undesirable adj annymunol
undisputed adj diamheuol
undo vt dadwneud; datod; andwyo, difetha
undress vb dadwisgo
uneasy adj anesmwyth
unemployed adj di-waith, segur
unemployment n diweithdra, anghyflogaeth
unequal adj anghyfartal
uneven adj anwastad
uneventful adj diddigwyddiad
unexpected adj annisgwyliadwy
unexpectedly adv yn annisgwyl
unfair adj annheg
unfaithful adj anffyddlon
unfamiliar adj anghyfarwydd
unfashionable adj anffasiynol
unfasten vb datod
unfavourable adj anffafriol
unfinished adj anorffenedig
unfit adj anghymwys; afiach
unfold vb datblygu
unforgettable adj bythgofiadwy
unfortunate adj anffodus
unfortunately adj yn anffodus
unfriendly adj anghyfeillgar
unfurnished adj diddodrefn
ungrateful adj anniolchgar
unhappiness n anhapusrwydd
unhappy adj anhapus
unhealthy adj afiach
uni n abbr (= university) prifysgol
uniform adj unffurf ▸ n gwisg swyddogol
unify vt unoli, uno
unimportant adj dibwys
uninhabited adj anghyfannedd

unintentional adj anfwriadol
union n undeb; uniad
Union Jack n: the Union Jack Jac yr Undeb
unique adj dihafal, digymar
unit n un, rhif un; uned; undod
unite vb uno
united adj, n unol, unedig; the United Kingdom y Deyrnas Unedig; the United States yr Unol Daleithiau
United Kingdom n: the United Kingdom y Deyrnas Unedig
United Nations n: the United Nations y Cenhedloedd Unedig
United States n: the United States yr Unol Daleithiau
unity n undod
universal adj cyffredinol
universe n bydysawd
university n prifysgol
unjust adj anghyfiawn, annheg
unkind adj angharedig
unknown adj anadnabyddus, anenwog
unlawful adj anghyfreithlon
unleaded petrol n petrol di-blwm
unless conj oni, onid
unlike adj annhebyg
unlikely adj annhebygol
unlimited adj diderfyn
unload vb dadlwytho
unlock vb datgloi
unlucky adj anlwcus
unmarried adj dibriod
unmistakable adj digamsyniol
unnatural adj annaturiol
unnecessary adj dianghenraid
unpack vb dadbacio
unpaid adj di-dâl, didal

unpleasant *adj* annymunol
unplug *vt*: **to unplug sth** tynnu plwg rhywbeth
unpopular *adj* amhoblogaidd
unprotected *adj* diamddiffyn
unqualified *adj* heb gymhwyster
unrealistic *adj* afrealaidd, afrealistig
unreasonable *adj* afresymol
unrelated *adj* amherthnasol; heb berthyn
unreliable *adj* annibynadwy
unroll *vt* dadrolio
unruly *adj* afreolus
unsafe *adj* anniogel
unsatisfactory *adj* anfoddhaol
unscrew *vt* agor; llacio; datroi
unsettled *adj* ansefydlog
unsightly *adj* diolwg, blêr
unskilled *adj* anghelfydd
unstable *adj* ansefydlog
unsteady *adj* ansefydlog
unsuccessful *adj* aflwyddiannus
unsuitable *adj* anaddas
untidy *adj* anniben
untie *vb* datod
until *prep, conj* hyd, hyd oni, nes, tan
untrue *adj* celwyddog
unusual *adj* anarferol
unveil *vb* dadorchuddio
unwell *adj* anhwylus
unwilling *adj* anfodlon, amharod
unwise *adj* annoeth
unwittingly *adv* yn ddiarwybod
unwrap *vt* dadlapio

[KEYWORD]

up *prep*: **he went up the stairs/the hill** aeth i fyny'r grisiau/bryn; **the cat was up a tree** roedd y gath ar ben coeden; **they live further up the street** maent yn byw ymhellach ar hyd y stryd; **go up that road and turn left** ewch ar hyd y ffordd honno a throwch i'r chwith

▸ *adv* **1** i fyny; *(upwards, higher)* **up in the sky/the mountains** i fyny yn yr awyr/y mynyddoedd **put it a bit higher up** rhowch y peth ychydig yn uwch; **to stand up** *(get up)* sefyll, codi *(be standing)* sefyll; **up there** i fyny [yn y] fanna; **up above** uchod, uwchben, uwchlaw
2: **to be up** *(out of bed)* bod wedi codi *(prices)* bod wedi codi *(finished)* **when the year was up** pan oedd y flwyddyn ar ben
3: **up to** *(as far as)* hyd at; **up to now** hyd yn hyn
4: **to be up to** *(depending on)* **it's up to you** mater i chi yw e *(equal to)* **he's not up to it** *(job, task etc)* nid yw'n gallu ei wneud, nid yw'n abl i'w wneud, nid yw'n ddigon o ddyn i'w wneud *(inf, be doing)* **what is he up to?** beth mae e'n ei wneud, beth sydd ganddo ar y gweill?
▸ *n*: **the ups and downs of life** troeon yr yrfa

upbringing *n* magwraeth
upheaval *n* cyffro, terfysg
uphill *adj* i fyny
upload *vt* llwytho i fyny
upon *prep* ar
upper *adj* uwch, uchaf
upper sixth *n*: **the upper sixth** y chweched uchaf

421

upright

upright *adj* syth, unionsyth
uprising *n* terfysg, gwrthryfel
uproar *n* terfysg, cythrwfl, dadwrdd
upset *vb* troi, dymchwelyd; cyffroi, gofidio
upside-down *adj, adv* (â'i) wyneb i waered
upstairs *n* llofft
up-to-date *adj* cyfoes
upward, upwards *adj, adv* i fyny
uranium *n* wranium
urban *adj* dinasol, dinesig
urge *vt* cymell, annog
urgency *n* brys
urgent *adj* taer, pwysig, yn gofyn brys
urine *n* troeth, iwrin
US *n abbr* (= *United States*) UD, Unol Daleithiau
us *pron* ni, nyni, ninnau; 'n
USA *n abbr* (= *United States of America*) Unol Daleithiau America, UDA
use *n* iws, defnydd ▸ *vb* iwsio, defnyddio; **use up** *vt* defnyddio'r cyfan o, defnyddio'r cwbl o
used *adj* arferedig, mewn arfer; (*car*) ail-law
useful *adj* defnyddiol
useless *adj* diwerth
user *n* defnyddiwr
user-friendly *adj* hawdd ei drin
username *n* enw defnyddiwr
usual *adj* arferol, cynefin
usually *adv* fel arfer, fel rheol
utensil *n* offeryn, llestr
utility *n* defnyddioldeb, budd, lles; cyfleustod
utilize *vt* defnyddio

utmost *adj* eithaf, pellaf
utter¹ *adj* eithaf, pellaf; hollol, llwyr
utter² *vt* yngan, dywedyd
U-turn *n* tro pedol

V

vacancy *n* lle gwag, swydd wag, gwacter
vacant *adj* gwag
vacate *vt* ymadael â, gadael yn wag
vacation *n* seibiant, gwyliau
vaccination *n* y frech, brechiad
vaccine *n* brech
vacuum *n* gwagle, gwactod
vacuum cleaner *n* sugnydd llwch
vagina *n* fagina
vague *adj* amwys, amhenodol
vain *adj* balch, coegfalch; ofer
Valentine card *n* cerdyn Ffolant
Valentine's Day *n* Dydd Sant Ffolant
valid *adj* dilys
valley *n* dyffryn, cwm, glyn
valuable *adj* gwerthfawr
value *n* gwerth ▸ *vt* gwerthfawrogi, prisio
valve *n* falf
vampire *n* sugnwr gwaed

van *n* men, fan
vandal *n* fandal
vandalism *n* fandaliaeth
vandalize *vt* fandaleiddio
vanilla *n* fanila
vanish *vi* diflannu, darfod
vanity *n* gwagedd, gwegi, coegfalchder
vapour *n* tawch, tarth
variable¹ *adj* cyfnewidiol, anwadal, oriog
variable² *n* newidyn (rhifyddiaeth)
variant *n* amrywiad
variation *n* amrywiad
varied *adj* amrywiol
variety *n* amrywiaeth
various *adj* gwahanol, amrywiol
varnish *n* barnais, farnais ▸ *vt* barneisio, farneisio
vary *vb* amrywio; newid
vase *n* cwpan, cawg
Vaseline® *n* faselin, eli
vast *adj* dirfawr, anferth
vat *n* cerwyn
vault *n* daeargell, claddgell; cromen ▸ *vb* neidio, llamu
veal *n* cig llo
veer *vb* troi, cylchdroi; trawshwylio
vegan *adj* feganaidd, figanaidd ▸ *n* fegan, figan
vegetable *adj* llysieuol ▸ *n* llysieuyn ymborth
vegetarian *n* llysieuwr
vegetation *n* tyfiant llysiau, llystyfiant
vehicle *n* cerbyd; cyfrwng
veil *n* gorchudd, llen ▸ *vt* gorchuddio
vein *n* gwythïen
velvet *n* melfed

vending machine

vending machine n peiriant gwerthu
vendor n gwerthwr
Venetian blind n llen Fenis
vengeance n dial, dialedd
venison n cig carw, fenswn
venom n gwenwyn
vent n agorfa, twll, arllwysfa ▸ vt arllwys, gollwng
ventilation n awyriad, gwyntylliad
venture n anturiaeth, mentr ▸ vb anturio, mentro
venue n man cyfarfod
Venus n Gwener, duwies serch
verb n berf
verbal adj berfol; geiriol
verdict n dyfarniad, rheithfarn
verge n min, ymyl ▸ vi ymylu
verify vt gwiro, gwireddu
versatile adj amryddawn
verse n adnod, pennill; prydyddiaeth
version n fersiwn; esboniad
versus prep yn erbyn
vertical adj fertigol
very adj, adv iawn, pur, tra
vessel n llestr
vest n gwasgod, crys isaf ▸ vb arwisgo, cynysgaeddu
vet vb arholi, archwilio ▸ n milfeddyg
veteran n un hen a chyfarwydd
veto n gwaharddiad ▸ vt gwahardd
via prep trwy, ar hyd
viable adj abl i fodoli, dichonadwy
vibrate vb crynu, dirgrynu
vibration n dirgryniad
vicar n ficer
vice¹ n drygioni

vice² n (tool) gwasg, feis
vice- prefix rhag-, is-
vice-chairman n is-gadeirydd
vice-versa adv i'r gwrthwyneb
vicinity n cymdogaeth
vicious adj drygionus, gwydus
victim n aberth, ysglyfaeth
victor n gorchfygwr
victorious adj buddugol, buddugoliaethus
victory n buddugoliaeth
video n fideo
video camera n camera fideo
video game n gêm fideo
vie vi cystadlu, cydymgeisio
Vienna n Fienna
Vietnam n Fietnam
Vietnamese n (person) Fietnamiad; (language) Fietnameg ▸ adj Fietnamaidd; (in language) Fietnameg
view n golygfa, barn ▸ vt edrych
viewer n gwyliwr (teledu)
viewpoint n safbwynt
vigilant adj gwyliadwrus
vigorous adj grymus, egnïol
vile adj gwael, brwnt
villa n fila
village n pentref
villager n pentrefwr
villain n cnaf, adyn, dihiryn
vine n gwinwydden
vinegar n finegr
vineyard n gwinllan
vintage n cynhaeaf gwin
viola n fiola
violate vt torri, troseddu, treisio
violation n treisiad, trosedd
violence n ffyrnigrwydd, trais
violent adj treisgar

violet n fioled, crinllys
violin n ffidil
virgin n gwyryf, morwyn
Virgo n y Forwyn, y Wyryf
virtual adj rhinweddol
virtually adv i bob pwrpas
virtual reality n rhith-wirionedd, rhithrealiti
virtue n rhinwedd
virus n firws
visa n fisa
visible adj gweladwy, gweledig
vision n gweledigaeth; golwg, gweled
visit vt ymweld, gofwyo ▸ n ymweliad
visitor n ymwelwr, ymwelydd
visitor centre n canolfan ymwelwyr
visual adj gweledol, golygol; **visual aids** cyfarpar gweld
vital adj bywiol, hanfodol
vitality n bywyd, bywiogrwydd
vitamin n fitamin
vivid adj byw, clir, llachar
viz. adv sef (talfyriad o videlicet)
vocabulary n geirfa
vocal adj lleisiol, llafar
vocational adj galwedigaethol, gyrfaol
vodka n fodca
vogue n arfer, ffasiwn, bri
voice n llais, lleferydd; (grammar) stad
voicemail n (message) neges lais
void adj gwag; ofer, di-rym ▸ n gwagle ▸ vt gwagu, gollwng; gwacáu
volatile adj anwadal, gwamal; anweddol

volcano n llosgfynydd, mynydd tân
volleyball n pêl-foli
volt n uned grym trydan, folt
voltage n foltedd
volume n cyfrol; swm, crynswth, cyfaint (mathemateg)
voluntary adj gwirfoddol
volunteer n gwirfoddolwr ▸ vb gwirfoddoli
vomit vb chwydu, cyfogi
vote n pleidlais ▸ vb pleidleisio
voter n pleidleisiwr
voucher n tocyn
vow n adduned, diofryd ▸ vb addunedu
vowel n llafariad; **vowel affection** affeithiad; **vowel mutation** gwyriad
voyage n mordaith ▸ vb mordeithio, mordwyo
vulgar adj cyffredin; isel, di-foes, aflednais
vulnerable adj archolladwy, hyglwyf, hawdd ei niweidio
vulture n fwltur

V

425

waddle *vi* siglo, honcian
wade *vb* beisio, rhydio
wafer *n* afrlladen
wag *vb* ysgwyd, siglo
wage *n* cyflog, hur
wagon *n* men, gwagen
wail *vb* cwynfan, wylofain, udo
waist *n* gwasg, canol
waistcoat *n* gwasgod
wait *vb* aros; gweini ▸ *n* arhosiad;
  wait up *vi*: **don't wait up**
  peidiwch ag aros ar eich traed
waiter *n* gweinydd
waiting list *n* rhestr aros
waiting room *n* ystafell aros
waitress *n* gweinyddes
wake (*pt* **woke**, **waked**, *pp*
  woken, waked) *vb* deffro ▸ *n*
  gwylmabsant; gwylnos; **wake**
  up *vb* deffro
Wales *n* Cymru

walk *vb* cerdded, rhodio ▸ *n*
  rhodfa; tro
walker *n* cerddwr
walkie-talkie *n* set radio symud
  a siarad
walking *n* cerddediad; cerdded;
  walking stick ffon gerdded
walking stick *n* ffon gerdded
wall *n* mur, wal ▸ *vt* murio
wallet *n* ysgrepan, gwaled
wallpaper *n* papur wal
walnut *n* cneuen Ffrengig
walrus *n* morfarch
waltz *n* wols
wand *n* hudlath
wander *vb* crwydro, cyfeiliorni
want *n* angen, eisiau, diffyg ▸ *vb*
  bod mewn angen
war *n* rhyfel ▸ *vb* rhyfela
ward *n* gward; gwarchodaeth ▸ *vt*
  gwarchod, amddiffyn
warden *n* gwarden, gwarcheidwad
wardrobe *n* cwpwrdd dillad,
  gwardrob
warehouse *n* warws
warfare *n* milwriaeth, rhyfel
warm *adj* cynnes ▸ *vb* cynhesu;
  warm up *vb* cynhesu
warmth *n* cynhesrwydd
warn *vt* rhybuddio
warning *n* rhybudd
warrant *n* gwarant, awdurdod
  ▸ *vt* gwarantu, cyfreithloni
warrior *n* rhyfelwr
warship *n* llong rhyfel
wart *n* dafad, dafaden
wary *adj* gwyliadwrus, gochelgar
was *vi* oedd, bu
wash *vb* golchi ▸ *n* golchiad,
  golchfa; golchion; **wash up** *vt*

golchi ► *vi (do dishes)* golchi'r llestri

washbasin *n* basn ymolchi

washcloth *n* lliain ymolchi

washing *n* golch

washing machine *n* peiriant golchi

washing powder *n* powdr golchi

washing-up *n*: **to do the washing-up** golchi'r llestri

washing-up liquid *n* sebon golchi llestri

wasp *n* cacynen, gwenynen feirch

waste *vb* gwastraffu ► *n* gwastraff

wastepaper basket *n* basged sbwriel

watch *vb* gwylio, gwylied, gwarchod ► *n* gwyliadwriaeth; oriawr, wats; **watch out** *vi* bod yn ofalus

water *n* dwfr, dŵr ► *vb* dyfrhau

watercolour *n* dyfrlliw

watercress *n* berwr dŵr

waterfall *n* rhaeadr, pistyll

watering can *n* can dŵr

watermelon *n* melon dŵr

waterproof *adj* diddos

water skiing *n* sglefrio ar ddŵr

watt *n* wat, uned pŵer trydan

wave *vb* chwifio; tonni ► *n* ton

waver *vi* anwadalu, gwamalu

wax *n* cwyr ► *vt* cwyro

way *n* ffordd, modd

we *pron* ni, nyni, ninnau

weak *adj* gwan, egwan

weaken *vb* gwanhau, gwanychu

weakness *n* gwendid

wealth *n* golud, cyfoeth

wealthy *adj* cyfoethog

weapon *n* arf

wear *(pt* **wore***, pp* **worn***) vb* gwisgo, treulio ► *n* traul; gwisg

weary *adj* blin, blinedig ► *vb* blino

weasel *n* gwenci, bronwen

weather *n* tywydd, hin ► *vt* dal, dioddef

weather forecast *n* rhagolygon y tywydd

weave *(pt* **wove***, pp* **woven***) vb* gwehyddu; plethu

web *n* gwe; **the (World-Wide) Web** y We (Fyd-Eang)

web address *n* cyfeiriad gwe

web browser *n* porwr gwe

webcam *n* gwe-gamera

web page *n* tudalen we

website *n* gwefan, safle gwe

wed *(pt, pp* **wedded***) vb* priodi, ymbriodi

wedding *n* priodas

wedge *n* cŷn, gaing, lletem ► *vt* cynio; gwthio i mewn

Wednesday *n* dydd Mercher

wee *adj* bach, bychan, pitw

weed *n* chwynnyn, chwyn ► *vb* chwynnu

week *n* wythnos

weekday *n* diwrnod gwaith

weekend *n* dros y Sul, penwythnos

weekly *n (publication)* wythnosolyn ► *adj* wythnosol ► *adv* yn wythnosol

weep *(pt, pp* **wept***) vb* wylo, wylofain, llefain

weigh *vb* pwyso; codi (angor)

weight *n* pwys, pwysau

weir *n* cored

weird *adj* annaearol, iasol

W

welcome *excl, n* croeso ▸ *vt*
croesawu ▸ *adj* derbyniol,
dymunol
weld *vt* asio
welfare *n* llwydd, lles
welfare state *n* gwladwriaeth les
well¹ *adv* yn dda ▸ *adj* da, iach
▸ *excl* wel
well² *n* ffynnon, pydew
well-balanced *adj* cytbwys
well-behaved *adj* ufudd
wellingtons *npl* esgidiau glaw
well-known *adj (person)*
adnabyddus; *(fact)* hysbys
well-off *adj* cefnog, da ei fyd
well-paid *adj* â chyflog da
Welsh *adj* Cymreig; Cymraeg ▸ *n*
Cymraeg
Welshman *n* Cymro
Welshwoman *n* Cymraes
west *n* gorllewin ▸ *adj*
gorllewinol
westbound *adj (line, lane)* am y
gorllewin; *(vehicle)* yn mynd i'r
gorllewin
western *adj* gorllewinol
West Indian *n* Caribïad ▸ *adj*
Caribïaidd
West Indies *npl*: **the West Indies**
India'r Gorllewin
wet *adj* gwlyb ▸ *vt* gwlychu ▸ *n*
gwlybaniaeth
whack *vb* llachio, ffonodio
whale *n* morfil
wharf *n* porthfa, llwythfa

KEYWORD

what *adj* 1 *(in questions)* pa; **what
size is he?** pa faint yw e?; **what**

colour is it? pa liw yw e?; **what
books do you need?** pa lyfrau sydd
arnoch eu hangen?
2 *(in exclamations)*: **what a mess!**
am lanast!; **what a fool I am!** dyna
ffŵl ydw i!, am ffŵl ydw i!
▸ *pron* 1 *(interrogative)* beth; **what
are you doing?** beth rydych chi'n
ei wneud?; **what is happening?**
beth sy'n digwydd?; **what are
you talking about?** am beth
rydych chi'n siarad?; **what are you
thinking about?** am beth rydych
chi'n meddwl?; **what is it called?**
beth yw ei enw e?, beth mae dyn
yn ei alw e; **what about me?** beth
amdana i?; **what about doing …?**
beth am wneud …?
2 *(relative, subject)* yr hyn, y
peth; *(direct object)* yr hyn, y
peth; *(indirect object)* yr hyn, pa
beth; **I saw what you did/was
on the table** gwelais yr hyn a
wnaethoch/a oedd ar y bwrdd;
tell me what you remember
dywedwch yr hyn yr ydych yn ei
gofio; **what I want is a cup of tea**
cwpanaid fyddai'n dda
▸ *excl (disbelieving)* sut!, beth!

whatever *pron* beth bynnag
whatsoever *pron* pa beth bynnag
wheat *n* gwenith
wheel *n* olwyn, rhod, troell ▸ *vt*
olwyno, powlio
wheelbarrow *n* berfa (drol),
whilber
wheelchair *n* cadair olwyn
wheeze *vi* gwichian ▸ *n* gwich

when adv pryd, pa bryd; **when did he go?** pa bryd yr aeth e?
▶ conj **1** (at, during, after the time that) pan; **she was reading when I came in** roedd hi'n darllen pan ddeuthum i mewn
2 (on): (at which) **on the day when I met him** y diwrnod y cyfarfûm ag ef
3 (whereas) tra; **I thought I was wrong when in fact I was right** roeddwn yn meddwl fy mod yn anghywir tra oeddwn yn gywir mewn gwirionedd

whenever adv pa bryd bynnag
where adv ym mha le; yn y lle, lle
whereabouts adv ymhle
whereas conj gan, yn gymaint â
whereby adv trwy yr hyn
whether conj ai, pa un ai

which adj **1** (interrogative; direct, indirect) pa; **which picture do you want?** pa ddarlun hoffech chi ei gael?; **which one?** pa un?
2: **in which case** ac os felly; **we got there at 8pm, by which time the cinema was full** fe gyrhaeddon ni erbyn 8pm, ac erbyn hynny roedd y sinema'n llawn
▶ pron **1** (interrogative) pa un, pa rai pl; **I don't mind which** nid oes gwahaniaeth gennyf ba un; **which (of these) are yours?** pa un (o'r rhain) sy'n perthyn i chi?; **tell me which you want** dywedwch ba un

yr hoffech ei gael
2 (relative, subject) a plus conjugated verb form; (in present tense) sydd + yn + vn (often contracted to sy'n + vn); (object) a; (indirect object) y; **the apple which you ate/which is on the table** yr afal a fwyteaist/sydd ar y bwrdd; **the chair on which you are sitting** y gadair yr ydych yn eistedd arni; **the book of which you spoke** y llyfr y buoch yn siarad amdano; **he said he knew, which is true** dywedodd ei fod yn gwybod, sy'n wir; **after which** ac ar ôl hynny

whichever pron, adj pa un bynnag
while n ennyd, talm, amser ▶ vt treulio ▶ adv tra
whilst adv cyhyd, tra
whim n mympwy, chwim
whine vb swnian crio, cwynfan
whip vb chwipio, fflangellu ▶ n chwip, fflangell
whipped cream n hufen chwip
whirl vb chwyrlïo, chwyrnellu, chwyrndroi
whisk n tusw ▶ vb ysgubo; chwyrlïo
whiskers npl blew, barf
whisky n chwisgi
whisper vb, n sibrwd, sisial
whistle vb chwibanu ▶ n chwiban, chwibanogl
white adj gwyn
whiteboard n bwrdd gwyn
whitewash n gwyngalch ▶ vb gwyngalchu
whiting n gwyniad

W

Whitsun, Whitsunday *n*
Sulgwyn

whittle *vt* naddu, lleihau

who *pron* a, pwy

whoever *pron* pwy bynnag

whole *adj* cyfan, holl; iach, holliach
▸ *n* cyfan

wholemeal *adj* â'r grawn cyfan,
cyflawn

wholesale *n* cyfanwerth ▸ *adj* yn
y crynswth

wholly *adv* yn hollol, yn gyfan
gwbl, yn llwyr

KEYWORD

whom *pron* **1** (*interrogative*) pwy;
whom did you see? pwy welsoch
chi?; **to whom did you give it?** i
bwy y'i rhoesoch?
2 (*relative*) a..., yr hwn *m* a..., yr hon
f; y rhai *pl* a ...; **the man whom I
saw** y dyn a welais
3 (*indirect obj. and after prep.,
positive*) y ... iddo/iddi/iddynt, y ...
ohono/ohoni/ohonynt; (*negative*)
na/nad ... iddo/iddi/iddynt, na/
nad ... ohono/ohoni/ohonynt;
the man to whom I gave the book
y dyn y rhoddais y llyfr iddo

whore *n* (*inf!*) putain, hŵr

KEYWORD

whose *adj* **1** (*possessive;
interrogative*): **whose book is this?
whose is this book?** llyfr pwy
yw hwn?, pwy biau'r llyfr hwn?;
whose pencil have you taken?
pensel pwy gymerest ti?; **whose**
daughter are you? merch pwy
wyt ti?
2 (*possessive; relative*): **the man
whose son you rescued** y dyn yr
achubaist ei fab; **the girl whose
sister you were speaking to** y
ferch y buoch yn siarad â'i chwaer;
the woman whose car was stolen
y fenyw y cafodd ei char ei ddwyn
▸ *pron*: **whose is this?** pwy biau
hwn?; **I know whose it is** rwy'n
gwybod pwy a'i piau

KEYWORD

why *adv* pam; **why not?** pam lai?
▸ *conj*: **I wonder why he said that**
pam dywedodd e hynny, tybed?;
that's not why I'm here nid dyna
pam rwyf i yma; **the reason why** y
rheswm pam
▸ *excl* dew!, duwcs!, jiw jiw!; **why,
it's you!** dew, chi sy yna!; **why,
that's impossible!** mae hynny'n
amhosibl, debyg iawn!

wicked *adj* drwg, drygionus,
ysgeler

wicket *n* wiced, clwyd

wide *adj* llydan, eang, helaeth

widely *adj* yn eang

widen *vb* lledu, llydanu

widespread *adj* cyffredinol

widow *n* gweddw ▸ *n* gwraig
weddw, gwidw

widower *n* gwidman

width *n* lled, ehangder

wield *vt* llywio, rheoli; trin

wife *n* gwraig, gwraig briod, priod

Wi-Fi *n* Wi-Fi
wig *n* gwallt gosod, wig
wild *adj* gwyllt ▸ *n* diffeithle
wilderness *n* anialwch
wildlife *n* bywyd gwyllt

KEYWORD

will *aux vb* **1** (*forming future tense*): I
will finish it tomorrow byddaf yn
ei orffen yfory; I will have finished
it by tomorrow byddaf wedi'i
orffen erbyn yfory; will you do it?
— yes I will/no I won't a wnewch
chi ef? — gwnaf/na wnaf
2 (*in conjectures, predictions*): he
will *or* he'll be there by now fe fydd
yno erbyn hyn; that will be the
postman y postman fydd yno
3 (*in commands, requests, offers*):
will you be quiet! wnewch chi fod
yn ddistaw!, tewch!, byddwch
ddistaw!; will you help me?
wnewch chi fy helpu?; will you
have a cup of tea? gymerwch chi
gwpanaid o de?; I won't put up
with it! wna i ddim goddef y peth!
▸ *vt* (*pt, pp* **willed**) to will sb to
do mynnu bod rhn yn gwneud
rhth; he willed himself to go on
mynnodd fynd yn ei flaen
▸ *n* **1** ewyllys *f*; against one's will yn
erbyn eich ewyllys
2 (*document*) ewyllys *f*

willing *adj* ewyllysgar, bodlon
willingly *adj* o wirfodd
willow *n* helygen, pren helyg
willpower *n* grym ewyllys
win (*pt, pp* **won**) *vb* ennill

wince *vi* gwingo
wind¹ *n* gwynt
wind² (*pt, pp* **wound**) *vb* dirwyn,
troi
windfall *n* lwc, ffawd dda
windmill *n* melin wynt
window *n* ffenestr
windowpane *n* cwarel
windscreen *n* ffenestr flaen
windscreen wiper *n* braich law
windsurfing *n* bordhwylio
windy *adj* gwyntog
wine *n* gwin
wineglass *n* gwydr gwin
wing *n* adain, asgell; (*rugby*)
asgellwr
wink *vb* wincio, cau llygad ▸ *n*
winc
winner *n* enillydd
winning *adj* enillgar, deniadol
winter *n* gaeaf ▸ *vb* gaeafu
winter sports *npl* chwaraeon
y gaeaf
wintertime *n* tymor y gaeaf
wipe *vt* sychu; **wipe up** *vt* glanhau
wire *n* gwifr, gwifren
wireless *n* radio ▸ *adj* di-wifr;
wireless network rhwydwaith
di-wifr
wiring *n* weiro
wisdom *n* doethineb
wise *adj* doeth
wish *vb* dymuno, chwennych ▸ *n*
dymuniad
wistful *adj* awyddus, hiraethus
wit *n* synnwyr; arabedd; rhywun
ffraeth
witch *n* dewines, gwrach

W

431

with

with *prep* **1** *(in the company of)*: gyda, efo; *(at the home of)* **we stayed with friends** buom yn aros gyda ffrindiau; **I'll be with you in a minute** byddaf gyda chi mewn munud, dof atoch mewn munud
2 *(descriptive)*: **a room with a view** ystafell â golygfa; **the man with the grey hat/blue eyes** y dyn â'r het lwyd/llygaid glas
3 *(indicating manner, means, cause)*: **with tears in her eyes** â dagrau yn ei llygaid; **to walk with a stick** cerdded â ffon; **red with anger** yn goch gan ddicter; **to shake with fear** crynu gan ofn; **to fill sth with water** llenwi rhth â dŵr
4 *(in phrases)*: **I'm with you** *(I understand)* rwy'n deall, rwy'n gweld; **to be with it** *(inf)* *(up-to-date)* bod yn ffasiynol

withdraw *vb* tynnu yn ôl, encilio; codi arian
withdrawal *n* enciliad
wither *vb* gwywo, crino
withhold *vt* atal, cadw yn ôl
within *adv, n, prep* i mewn, o fewn
without *prep* heb, di- ▸ *adv, n* tu allan
withstand *vt* gwrthsefyll
witness *n* tyst; tystiolaeth ▸ *vb* tystio
witty *adj* arab, arabus, ffraeth
wizard *n* swynwr, dewin
wobble *vi* siglo, honcian, anwadalu
woe *n* gwae
wolf *n* blaidd

woman *n* gwraig, merch
womb *n* croth, bru
wonder *n* rhyfeddod, syndod ▸ *vi* rhyfeddu, synnu
wonderful *adj* rhyfeddol
wood *n* coed, coedwig; pren
wooden *adj* o goed, o bren; trwsgl, trwstan
woodwind *npl* chwythoffer pren
woodwork *n* gwaith coed, gwaith saer
wool *n* gwlân
woollen *adj* gwlanog, gwlân
woolly *adj* gwlanog
word *n* gair ▸ *vt* geirio
wording *n* geiriad
word processing *n* prosesu geiriau, geirbrosesu
word processor *n* prosesydd geiriau
work *n* gwaith ▸ *vb* gweithio
worker *n* gweithiwr
work experience *n* profiad gwaith
working-class *adj* dosbarth gweithiol
workman *n* gweithiwr
workout *n* sesiwn ymarfer
worksheet *n* taflen waith
workshop *n* gweithdy
workspace *n* gweithle
workstation *n* gweithfan
world *n* byd
worldwide *adj* byd-eang
worm *n* pryf, abwydyn; llyngyren ▸ *vb* ymnyddu
worn *adj* treuliedig
worn-out *adj* wedi blino; wedi treulio
worried *adj* pryderus, gofidus

worry *vb* poeni ► *n* pryder
worse *adj* gwaeth
worsen *vb* gwaethygu
worship *n* addoliad ► *vb* addoli
worst *vt* gorchfygu, trechu
worth *n* gwerth, teilyngdod
worthless *adj* diwerth
worthy *adj* teilwng ► *n* gŵr o fri
wound *n* archoll, clwyf ► *vt*
archolli, clwyfo
wrap *vt* plygu, lapio; **wrap up** *vt*
lapio
wrapping paper *n* papur lapio
wreath *n* torch
wreck *n* llongddrylliad ► *vb*
llongddryllio
wren *n* dryw, dryw bach
wrench *vt* rhwygo ymaith, tyndroi
► *n* tyndro
wrestle *vi* ymgodymu, ymaflyd
codwm
wrestler *n* ymgodymwr, taflwr
codwm
wrestling *n* ymgodymu
wretched *adj* truan, truenus
wriggle *vb* gwingo, ymnyddu
wring (*pt, pp* **wrung**) *vt* troi,
gwasgu
wrinkle *n* crych, crychni ► *vb*
crychu
wrist *n* arddwrn
write (*pt* **wrote**, *pp* **written**) *vb*
ysgrifennu; **write down** *vt* nodi
writer *n* ysgrifennwr, awdur
writing *n* ysgrifen; ysgrifennu
writing paper *n* papur ysgrifennu
wrong *adj* anghywir, o'i le ► *n* cam
► *vt* gwneud cam â, niweidio

Xmas *n* Dolig
X-ray *n* pelydr X ► *vt* tynnu llun
pelydr X
xylophone *n* seiloffon

y

you *pron* **1** *(subject)* ti; *(polite form)* chi; *(plural)* chi; **you are very kind** rydych yn garedig iawn; **you enjoy your food** rydych yn mwynhau'ch bwyd; **you and I will go** fe ei di a minnau; **there you are!** dyna chi! **2** *(object, direct, indirect)* di, chi; **I know you** rwy'n d'adnabod di *or* rwy'n eich adnabod chi; **I gave it to you** fe'i rhoddais i ti **3** *(stressed)* tydi; chwychwi; **I told you to do it** wrthyt ti *or* wrthych chi y dywedais am wneud y peth **4** *(after prep, in comparisons)* ti; chi; **it's for you** i ti *or* i chi y mae e; **she's younger than you** mae hi'n iau na thi *or* chi **5** *(impersonal; one)* chi; **fresh air does you good** mae awyr iach yn gwneud lles i chi; **you never know** dydych chi byth yn gwybod; **you can't do that!** allwch chi ddim gwneud hynny!

yacht *n* llong bleser, iot
yard¹ *n* llath, llathen; hwyl-lath
yard² *n (enclosure)* iard, buarth, clos
yarn *n* edau, edafedd; stori, chwedl
yawn *vi* dylyfu gên, agor ceg
year *n* blwyddyn, blwydd
yearly *adv* blynyddol
yearn *vi* hiraethu, dyheu
yeast *n* burum
yell *vb* ysgrechian ▸ *n* ysgrech, nâd
yellow *adj, n* melyn
yes *adv* ie, do, oes *etc*
yesterday *n, adv* doe
yet *conj, adv* er hynny, eto
yew *n* yw, ywen
Yiddish *n* Almaeneg Iddewaidd
yield *vb* ildio ▸ *n* cynnyrch
yoga *n* ioga
yoghurt *n* iogwrt
yolk *n* melyn wy, melynwy

young *adj* ifanc, ieuanc
youngster *n* bachgennyn, plentyn
your *pron* eich, 'ch
yours *pron* eiddoch, yr eiddoch
yourself *pron* eich hun(an)
yourselves *pron* eich hunain
youth *n* ieuenctid; llanc
youth club *n* clwb ieuenctid
youthful *adj* ieuanc, ieuengaidd
youth hostel *n* hostel ieuenctid
Yugoslavia *n* Iwgoslafia

Z

zany *adj* gwirion
zeal *n* sêl, brwdfrydedd
zebra *n* sebra
zebra crossing *n* croesfan sebra
zero *n* dim, sero; gwagnod
zest *n* awch, blas, afiaith
zigzag *adj, n* igam-ogam
Zimbabwe *n* Zimbabwe
zinc *n* sinc
zip[1] *n* sip
zip[2] *vt (file)* sipio
zip file *n* ffeil sip
zipper *n* sip
zodiac *n* sidydd
zone *n* cylch, parth
zoo *n* sw
zoology *n* milofyddiaeth, swoleg